HAMMOND'S

FAMILY REFERENCE

WORLD ATLAS

New Revised Edition

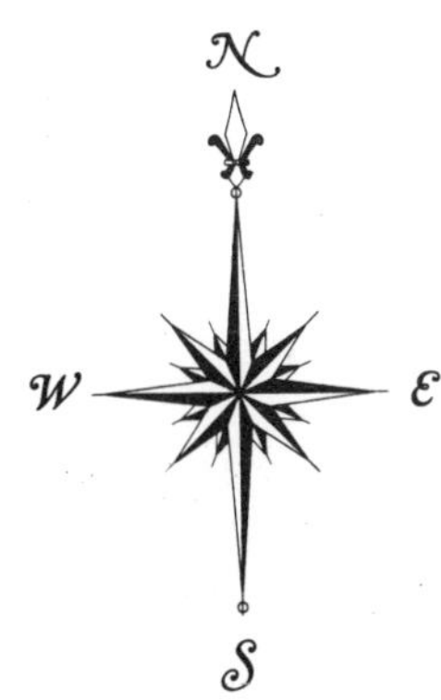

HANOVER HOUSE
GARDEN CITY NEW YORK

PRINTED IN THE UNITED STATES OF AMERICA

Contents

GAZETTEER-INDEX OF THE WORLD

This alphabetical list of grand divisions, countries, states, colonial possessions, etc., gives area, population and index references and numbers of plates on which they are shown on the largest scale. The mother country of colonial possessions is indicated by abbreviations enclosed in parentheses. The index reference shows the square on the respective map in which the name of the country, state or colonial possession is located.

ABBREVIATIONS

Aust. —Australian
Belg. —Belgian or Belgium
Br. —British Commonwealth of Nations
Dan. —Danish or Denmark
E. —East
Fr. —France or French
Gr. —Greece or Greek
Indon. —Indonesia
I. —Island
Is. —Islands
It. —Italian or Italy
N. —North
Neth. —Netherlands
N.Z. —New Zealand
Pak. —Pakistan
pen. —peninsula
Port. —Portugal or Portuguese
Rep. —Republic
S. —South
Sp. —Spain or Spanish
sq. mi. —Square miles
S.S.R. —Soviet Socialist Republic
Trust. —Trust Territory
U.A.R. —United Arab Republic
U.S.A. —United States of America
U.S.Adm.—U.S. Administration
U.S.S.R. —Union of Soviet Socialist Republics
U. of So. Africa —Union of South Africa
W. —West

Country	Area (Square Miles)	Population	Index Ref.	Plate No.
Aden (incl. Protectorate) (Br.)	112,000	650,000	E 7	56
Aden Colony	75	80,516	E 7	56
Admiralty Is. (Aust. Tr.)	820	13,000	E 6	68
Afghanistan	250,000	12,000,000	H 3	57
Africa	11,850,000	190,000,000	......	62,65
Alabama, U.S.A.	51,078	3,061,743	......	82
Alaska, U.S.A.	571,065	128,643	......	80
Albania	11,096	1,112,355	E 5	50
Alberta, Canada	248,800	1,123,116	......	186
Aleutian Islands (U.S.A.)	6,800	5,600	D 4	80
Algeria (Fr.)	851,284	8,681,785	G 5	62
Andaman Is. (India)	2,508	21,316	E 3	59
Andorra	191	5,265	G 1	46
Angola (Port.)	481,351	4,111,796	K14	64
Antarctica	5,500,000	....	......	35
Antigua (Br.) (incl. Barbuda and Redonda)	171	41,757	G 3	75
Antilles, Greater and Lesser	....	....	D 3	75
Arabia	1,000,000	10,700,000	D 5	56
Arctic Ocean	....	....	......	36
Argentina	1,078,266	21,000,000	......	70,72
Arizona, U.S.A.	113,580	759,587	......	84
Arkansas, U.S.A.	52,725	1,909,511	......	86
Armenian S.S.R. (U.S.S.R.)	11,500	1,345,000	F 6	53
Ascension Island (Br.)	34	159	D13	64
Asia	16,500,000	1,301,000,000	......	54
Australia, Commonwealth of (Br.)	2,974,581	7,579,358	......	66
Australian Capital Territory	939	16,905	J 7	67
Austria	32,369	6,918,959	B 3	48
Azerbaidzhan S.S.R. (U.S.S.R.)	33,100	3,100,000	G 6	53
Azores Islands (Port.)	890	318,558	H 4	34
Bahama Islands (Br.)	4,404	79,000	C 1	75
Bahrein Islands (Br.)	213	109,650	F 4	57
Balearic Islands (Sp.)	1,936	422,127	H 3	46
Barbados	166	192,800	G 4	75
Barbuda and Redonda Is. (Br.)	63	979	G 3	75
Basutoland (Br.)	11,716	563,854	M17	65
Bechuanaland Prot. (Br.)	275,000	294,232	L16	65
Belgian Congo	902,274	11,121,463	L12	65
Belgium	11,775	8,512,195	C 6	44
Bermuda (Br.)	21	37,000	G 2	75
Bhutan	18,000	300,000	E 2	59
Bismarck Archipelago (Aust. Trust.)	19,660	145,000	E 6	68
Bolivia	412,777	3,019,031	G 7	70
Bonin Is. (U.S. Adm.)	76	....	E 3	68
Borneo	208,286	....	E 5	61
Brazil	3,286,170	52,645,479	......	71,73
British Columbia, Canada	359,279	1,398,464	......	188
British Honduras	8,867	59,220	B 1	76
Brunei (Br.)	2,226	40,657	E 5	61
Bulgaria	42,796	7,022,206	G 4	50
Burma	261,610	18,489,000	E 2	59
Byelorussian S.S.R. (White Russian S.S.R.) (U.S.S.R.)	80,100	7,220,000	C 4	53
California, U.S.A.	156,803	10,586,223	......	88
Cambodia	69,884	3.748.000	C 3	61

Country	Area (Square Miles)	Population	Index Ref.	Plate No.
Cameroons (Br. Trust.)	34,081	1,027,100	J10	62
Cameroun (Fr. Trust.)	161,787	3,065,800	J10	62
Canada	3,621,616	16,081,791	......	174
Canal Zone (U.S.A.)	362	52,822	E 3	76
Canary Islands (Sp.)	2,894	776,912	B 4	46
Cape of Good Hope, U. of So. Africa	277,169	4,053,848	L18	65
Cape Verde Islands (Port.)	1,557	147,328	H 5	34
Caroline Islands (U.S. Trust.)	525	36,980	E 5	68
Cayman Is., Jamaica (Br.)	104	6,670	B 3	75
Celebes	72,986	5,500,000	G 6	61
Central America	217,813	8,918,547	......	76
Ceylon	25,332	6,657,339	D 4	59
Chad (Fr.)	455,598	2,052,469	K 8	63
Channel Islands (Br.)	75	102,776	B 3	40
Chatham Islands (N.Z.)	372	505	J10	68
Chile	286,396	5,809,000	G 8	70,72
China	3,724,273	464,743,549	E 1	59,60
Christmas Island	60	866	O11	55
Colombia	439,828	11,260,000	F 3	70
Colorado, U.S.A.	103,967	1,325,089	......	90
Comoro Is. (Is. Comores) (Fr.)	849	156,150	P14	65
Connecticut, U.S.A.	4,899	2,007,280	......	92
Cook Islands (N.Z.)	99	14,088	K 7	69
Corsica (Corse) (Fr.)	3,367	267,873	G 6	41
Costa Rica	19,238	800,875	C 3	76
Cuba	42,857	5,3[illegible],000	B 2	75
Curaçao (Neth. Antilles)	173	95,195	E 4	75
Cyprus	3,572	450,114	B 2	56
Czechoslovakia	49,356	12,090,164	D 2	48
Dahomey (Fr.)	42,471	1,476,000	G10	62
Daito Is. (U.S. Adm.)	18	2,691	M 6	60
Damão (Port.)	213	63,521	C 2	59
Delaware, U.S.A.	1,978	318,085	......	115
Denmark	16,556	4,279,151	B 3	43
District of Columbia, U.S.A.	61	802,178	B 5	114
Diu (Port.)	12	19,731	C 2	59
Dominica (Br.)	305	53,900	G 4	75
Dominican Republic	19,129	2,121,083	D 3	75
Ecuador approx.	115,000	3,076,933	E 4	70
Egypt, U.A.R.	386,000	19,087,304	M 6	63
England and Wales	58,340	43,744,924	......	39
Eritrea	15,754	1,086,000	O 8	63
Estonia (Estonian S.S.R.) (U.S.S.R.)	17,400	1,000,000	C 3	52
Ethiopia (excl. Eritrea)	350,000	10,000,000	O 9	63
Europe	4,129,908	551,000,000	......	37
Faeröe Islands (Dan.)	540	29,178	D 2	37
Falkland Islands (Br.) (incl. S. Georgia)	5,618	2,239	J14	73
Federation of Malaya	50,690	4,908,086	C 4	61
Fernando Póo (island) (Sp. Guinea)	800	17,249	H11	62
Fiji (Br.)	7,036	259,638	H 8	68
Finland	130,500	4,029,803	E 2	43
Florida, U.S.A.	54,262	2,771,305	......	94
Formosa (Taiwan) (China)	13,885	9,863,264	K 7	60
France	212,736	40,502,513	......	40
Franz Josef Land (Zemlya Frantsa Iosifa)	....	....	A 7	36

Country	Area (Square Miles)	Population	Index Ref.	Plate No.
French Equatorial Africa.	961,392	4,168,910	K10 & J12	63 64
French Sudan	584,942	3,137,000	F 8	62
French West Africa	1,814,852	16,377,000	F 8	62
Gabon (Fr.)	90,733	423,904	J12	64
Galápagos Islands, Ecuador	3,042	1,346	F 6	34
Gambia (Br.)	4,033	278,858	C 9	62
Georgia, U.S.A.	58,518	3,444,578	......	96
Georgian S.S.R.(U.S.S.R.)	29,400	3,555,000	F 6	53
Germany, East (German Democratic Rep.)	41,535	18,488,316	......	42
Germany, West (Federal Republic of).	95,914	50,579,878	......	42
Ghana	99,536	4,118,450	F10	62
Gibraltar (Br.)	2	23,232	D 4	46
Gilbert, Ellice and Phoenix Islands	196	32,311	J 6	69
Gôa (Port.)	1,313	540,925	C 3	59
Great Britain and Northern Ireland	94,279	50,210,472	......	38
Greece	51,182	7,856,000	......	51
Greenland (Dan.)	839,999	21,412	B12	36
Grenada (Br.)	133	72,387	F 4	75
Guadeloupe and Dependencies (Fr.)	688	278,864	F 3	75
Guam (U.S.A.)	203	59,498	E 4	68
Guatemala	45,452	2,787,030	B 2	76
Guiana, British	89,480	375,701	J 2	70
Guiana, French	35,135	25,499	K 3	71
Guiana, Netherlands (Surinam)	54,300	219,000	J 3	71
Guinea	96,525	2,130,000	D 9	62
Guinea, Portuguese	13,948	510,736	C 9	62
Guinea, Spanish	10,830	161,032	H11	64
Haiti	10,714	3,111,973	D 3	75
Hawaii (U.S.A.)	6,420	499,794	......	81
Holland (Netherlands).land	12,883	9,625,499	E 4	44
Honduras	45,000	1,505,465	C 2	76
Honduras, British	8,867	59,220	B 1	76
Hong Kong (Br.)	391	1,857,000	J 7	60
Hungary	35,875	9,204,799	E 3	48
Iceland	39,709	144,263	C 2	37
Idaho, U.S.A.	82,808	588,637	......	98
Ifni (Sp.)	676	45,852	D 5	62
Illinois, U.S.A.	55,947	8,712,176	......	100
India	1,059,342	356,755,978	C 2	59
Indiana, U.S.A.	36,205	3,934,224	......	102
Indochina	285,927	26,876,510	C 2	61
Indonesia	735,286	79,260,000	C 6	61
Iowa, U.S.A.	55,986	2,621,073	......	104
Iran (Persia)	628,000	19,000,000	F 3	57
Iraq	116,600	4,799,500	D 3	56
Ireland	26,601	2,898,264	B 4	39
Ireland, Northern	5,238	1,369,579	C 3	38
Isle of Man (Br.)	221	55,213	D 3	39
Israel	7,978	1,813,000	B 3	58
Italy	116,000	47,020,536	......	47
Ivory Coast (Fr.)	183,397	2,066,000	E10	62
Jamaica (Br.)	4,411	1,237,391	C 3	75
Japan	142,272	83,199,637	N 4	60
Java and Madura	51,032	52,000,000	K 2	61
Jordan	34,750	1,329,174	D 4	58
Kansas, U.S.A.	82,113	1,905,299	......	106
Kentucky, U.S.A.	40,109	2,944,806	......	108
Kenya (Br.)	219,730	5,377,393	O11	65
Kerguelen Arch. (Fr.)	....	....	M 8	34
Korea, North	49,096	6,474,000	L 4	60
Korea, South	36,152	21,526,374	L 4	60
Krētē (Crete), Greece	3,232	441,687	E 6	51
Kuria Muria Is. (Br.)	....	70	G 6	57
Kuril Is. (Chishima), (U.S.S.R.)	5,700	15,000	T 5	54
Kuwait	8,000	170,000	E 4	56
Laccadive Islands(India)	746	21,035	C 3	59
Laos	89,343	1,200,000	C 2	61
Latvia (Latvian S.S.R.) (U.S.S.R.)	24,600	1,800,000	B 3	52
Lebanon	3,475	1,165,208	C 3	56
Leeward Islands	423	108,838	F 3	75
Liberia	43,000	1,600,000	E10	62
Libya	679,358	1,100,000	J 6	62
Liechtenstein	65	13,757	E 1	45
Lithuania (Lithuanian S.S.R.) (U.S.S.R.)	31,200	2,700,000	B 3	52
Louisiana, U.S.A.	45,177	2,683,516	......	110
Loyalty Islands (Fr.)	800	11,854	G 8	68

* Member of Federation of Rhodesia and Nyasaland.

Country	Area (Square Miles)	Population	Index Ref.	Plate No.
Luxembourg	999	290,992	H 8	44
Macao (Port.)	6	389,000	P 7	55
Madagascar (Fr.)	241,094	4,294,985	R16	65
Madeira Islands (Port.)	308	269,179	A 2	46
Madura I.	1,752	2,444,000	K 2	61
Maine, U.S.A.	31,040	913,777	......	112
Malaya, Fed. of	50,690	4,908,086	C 4	61
Maldive Islands	115	82,068	L 9	55
Malta (Br.)	122	305,991	E 7	47
Manchuria (China)	412,801	36,903,000	K 2	60
Manitoba, Canada	219,723	850,040	......	182
Mariana Islands (U.S. Trust.)	142	6,286	E 4	68
Marquesas Is. (Fr.)	480	2,976	N 6	69
Marshall Islands (U.S. Trust.)	61	11,033	G 4	68
Martinique (Fr.)	425	261,595	G 4	75
Maryland, U.S.A.	9,887	2,343,001	......	114
Massachusetts, U.S.A.	7,907	4,690,514	......	116
Mauritania (Fr.)	328,185	523,900	D 8	62
Mauritius (Br.)	720	432,468	S19	65
Mexico	760,373	25,581,250	......	77
Michigan, U.S.A.	57,022	6,371,766	......	118
Middle Congo (Fr.)	175,676	675,400	J 2	64
Midway Islands (U.S.A.).	2	437	J 3	69
Minnesota, U.S.A.	80,009	2,982,483	......	120
Mississippi, U.S.A.	47,420	2,178,914	......	122
Missouri, U.S.A.	69,270	3,954,653	......	124
Moldavian S.S.R. (U.S.S.R.)	13,100	2,660,000	C 5	53
Molucca Islands	30,168	544,302	C 5	68
Monaco	370 Acres	19,242	G 6	41
Mongolian Republic	625,946	2,000,000	O 5	54
Montana, U.S.A.	146,316	591,024	......	126
Montserrat	32	14,333	G 3	75
Morocco	171,583	9,809,387	E 5	62
Mozambique (Port.)	297,731	5,730,930	N16	65
Natal, U. of So. Africa..	35,284	2,202,392	N17	65
Nauru (Aust.-N.Z.—Br. Tr. Terr.)	8	2,855	G 6	68
Nebraska, U.S.A.	76,653	1,325,510	......	128
Nepal	54,000	6,910,000	D 2	59
Netherlands(Holland).land	12,883	9,625,499	E 4	44
Netherlands Antilles	383	154,914	E 4	75
Nevada, U.S.A.	109,802	160,083	......	130
New Britain (island) (Aust. Trust.)	14,600	105,000	F 6	68
New Brunswick, Canada..	27,473	554,616	C 3	176
New Caledonia (Fr.)	7,201	61,250	G 8	68
Newfoundland, Canada...	42,734	415,074	J 4	177
New Guinea, Netherlands.	161,514	1,000,000	K 6	61
New Guinea, Territory of (Aust. Trust.)	93,000	1,100,023	B 7	61
New Hampshire, U.S.A.	9,024	533,242	......	132
New Hebrides Islands (Br. and Fr.)	5,700	48,538	G 7	68
New Ireland (island) (Aust. Trust.)	3,800	33,960	F 6	68
New Jersey, U.S.A.	7,522	4,835,329	......	134
New Mexico, U.S.A.	121,511	681,187	......	136
New South Wales, Australia	309,432	2,984,838	H 6	67
New York, U.S.A.	47,929	14,830,192	......	138
New Zealand, Dominion of (Br.)	103,934	1,702,298	K 6	67
Nicaragua	57,143	1,053,189	C 2	76
Nicobar Islands (India)...	635	12,452	E 4	59
Nigeria (Br.)	338,593	24,300,000	H10	62
Niger Colony (Fr.)	501,930	2,168,000	H 8	62
Niue I. (Br.)	100	4,253	K 7	69
North America	9,124,000	216,400,000	......	74
North Borneo (Br.)	29,387	331,361	F 4	61
North Carolina, U.S.A.	49,142	4,061,929	......	140
North Dakota, U.S.A.	70,054	619,636	......	142
Northern Ireland (Br.)	5,238	1,369,579	C 3	38
Northern Rhodesia (Br.*)	290,320	1,849,000	L15	65
Northern Territory, Algeria	80,117	7,864,792	G 4	62
Northern Territory, Aust.	523,620	10,868	E 3	66
Northwest Territories, Canada	1,258,217	19,313	......	191
Norway	124,560	3,278,546	B 2	43
Nova Scotia, Canada	20,743	694,717	D 5	176
Nyasaland Prot. (Br.*)	36,829	2,178,013	N14	65
Ohio, U.S.A.	41,122	7,946,627	......	144
Oklahoma, U.S.A.	69,283	2,233,351	......	146
Oman, Sultanate of	82,000	830,000	G 6	57
Ontario, Canada	363,282	5,404,933	......	180
Orange Free State, U. of South Africa	49,647	879,071	M17	65

Country	Area (Square Miles)	Population	Index Ref.	Plate No.
Oregon, U.S.A.	96,350	1,521,341	......	148
Orkney Islands, Scotland.	376	21,258	E 1	38
Oubangui-Chari (Fr.)	239,382	1,068,400	K10	63
Pacific Islands (excl. Australia)	262,718	4,313,654	......	68,69
Pakistan	364,218	75,843,000	B2,D2	59
Palau Islands (U.S. Trust)	189	6,596	D 5	68
Panamá (excl. Canal Zone)	28,575	801,290	D 3	76
Papua Territory (Aust.)	90,540	282,072	B 7	61
Paraguay	150,518	1,251,517	H 8	70
Pennsylvania, U.S.A.	45,045	10,498,012	......	150
Persia (Iran)	628,000	19,000,000	F 3	57
Peru approx.	513,000	9,651,000	E 5	70
Philippines, Republic of the	115,600	19,234,182	H 3	61
Phoenix Is. (U.S. and Br.)	16	984	J 6	69
Pitcairn Island (Br.)	2	138	O 8	69
Poland	119,734	24,976,926	......	49
Portugal	35,413	8,490,455	B 3	46
Prince Edward Island, Canada	2,184	99,285	F 3	177
Principe and S. Tomé (Port.)	372	62,000	H11	64
Puerto Rico (U.S.A.)	3,423	2,210,703	G 2	75
Qatar	5,000	31,000	F 4	57
Québec, Canada	523,860	4,628,378	......	178
Queensland, Australia	670,500	1,106,269	G 4	67
Réunion (Fr.)	970	242,067	R20	65
Rhode Island, U.S.A.	1,058	791,896	H 5	117
Rio de Oro (Sp.)	71,583	24,000	D 7	62
Rio Muni (continental Sp. Guinea)	10,040	142,237	H11	64
Ruanda-Urundi (Belg. Tr.)	20,309	3,889,051	N12	65
Rumania	91,671	15,872,624	G 3	50
Russian S.F.S.R. (U.S.S.R.)	6,501,500	113,200,000	F 3	52
Ryukyu Islands (U.S. Adm.)	921	914,462	L 6	60
Saguia el Hamra (Sp.)	31,660	14,298	D 6	62
St. Croix, Virgin Is. (U.S.A.)	80	12,103	H 2	75
St. Helena I. (Br.)	47	4,748	E15	64
St. John, Virgin Is. (U.S.A.)	20	749	H 1	75
St. Lucia	233	70,113	G 4	75
St. Pierre and Miquelon Is. (Fr.)	93	4,354	H 6	177
St. Thomas, Virgin Is. (U.S.A.)	32	13,813	G 1	75
St. Vincent	150	61,647	G 4	75
Sakhalin (U.S.S.R.)	35,400	300,000	T 4	54
Salvador, El	13,176	1,858,656	B 2	76
Samoa, Western (N.Z. Tr.)	1,133	78,155	J 7	69
Samoa (U.S.A.)	76	18,937	J 7	69
San Marino	38	12,100	D 3	47
Sarawak (Br.)	47,071	546,385	E 5	61
Sardinia (Sardegna) (It.)	9,301	1,273,714	B 4	47
Saskatchewan, Canada	237,975	880,665	......	184
Saudi Arabia, Kingdom of	350,000	5,500,000	D 4	56
Scotland	30,405	5,095,969	......	38
Senegal	77,401	1,720,000	D 9	62
Seychelles	157	34,637	M 6	34
Shetland Islands, Scotland	550	19,343	G 1	38
Siam (Thailand)	200,148	17,324,581	C 2	61
Sicily (It.)	9,926	4,452,773	D 6	47
Sierra Leone (Br.)	27,925	1,858,275	D10	62
Sikkim	2,745	129,000	D 2	59
Singapore	220	940,824	C 5	61
Sinkiang, China	660,977	4,012,330	D 1	59
Society Islands (Fr.)	650	41,798	L 7	69
Socotra	1,400	12,000	J 8	55
Solomon Islands (Aust. Tr.)	4,070	49,067	F 6	68
Solomon Islands Prot. (Br.)	14,600	94,965	G 6	68
Somaliland, French	8,492	44,800	P 9	63
Somaliland, (Italian Tr.)	194,000	916,300	P11	63,65
Somaliland Prot. (Br.)	68,000	700,000	P11	63,65
South America	6,894,000	109,500,000	......	70,73
South Australia, Australia	280,070	646,073	E 5	66
South Carolina, U.S.A.	30,594	2,117,027	......	152
South Dakota, U.S.A.	76,536	652,740	......	154
Southern Rhodesia (Br.*)	150,333	1,794,000	M15	65
Southern Territories, Algeria	767,435	816,993	G 6	62
South West Africa (U. of South Africa Mand.)	317,725	350,037	K16	64
Spain	195,258	27,909,009	......	46
Spanish Sahara	103,243	38,298	C 7	62
Spanish West Africa	113,958	96,150	D 7	62
Sudan	967,500	8,309,663	M 9	63
Sumatra	164,148	12,000,000	C 6	61
Surinam (Netherlands Guiana)	54,300	219,000	J 3	71
Svalbard, Norway (Spitsbergen)	24,294	1,539	A 1	43
Swaziland (Br.)	6,704	185,215	N17	65
Sweden	173,394	7,046,920	C 2	43
Switzerland	15,944	4,714,992	......	45
Syria, U.A.R.	72,587	3,135,000	C 2	56
Tahiti (island), (Fr.)	600	29,684	L 7	69
Tanganyika Territory (Br. Trust.)	342,706	7,408,096	N13	65
Tasmania, Australia	26,215	257,078	H 8	67
Tchad (Chad) (Fr.)	455,598	2,052,469	K 8	63
Tennessee, U.S.A.	41,961	3,291,718	......	156
Texas, U.S.A.	263,644	7,711,194	......	158
Thailand (Siam)	200,148	17,324,581	C 2	61
Tibet, China	469,413	2,000,000	D 1	59
Timor (Port.)	7,332	424,132	H 7	61
Timor Archipelago (Indon.)	24,450	1,657,376	H 7	61
Togo (Fr. Trust.)	20,733	923,000	G10	62
Tokelau (Union Group) (N.Z. and U.S.)	4	1,388	J 6	69
Tonga (Friendly) Is. (Br.)	269	46,870	J 8	69
Transvaal, Union of South Africa	110,450	4,283,038	M17	65
Trinidad and Tobago	1,980	557,970	G 5	75
Tristan da Cunha (Br.)	38	230	J 7	34
Trucial Oman	12,000	95,000	F 5	57
Tuamotu (Low) Arch. (Fr.)	332	5,127	M 7	69
Tunisia	48,300	2,230,952	H 5	62
Turkey	296,185	24,121,778	B 2	56
Turks and Caicos Is., Jamaica	202	6,138	D 2	75
Ubangi-Shari (Fr.)	239,382	1,068,400	K10	63
Uganda Protectorate (Br.)	80,301	4,959,196	N11	65
Ukrainian S.S.R. (U.S.S.R.)	220,600	40,500,000	C 5	53
Union of South Africa	472,494	11,418,349	L18	65
Union of Soviet Socialist Republics	8,570,600	191,595,000	......	52
United Arab Republic	458,587	22,222,304	B 4 & C 2	56 56
United Kingdom	94,279	50,210,472	......	38,39
United States of America (incl. Alaska) land; land and water	3,548,193; 3,608,787	150,826,004	......	78
Upper (Haute) Volta (Fr.)	....	3,070,000	F 9	62
Uruguay	72,172	2,353,000	J10	73
Utah, U.S.A.	82,346	688,862	......	160
Vatican City	109 Acres	1,010	C 4	47
Venezuela	352,143	4,985,716	G 2	70
Vermont, U.S.A.	9,278	377,747	......	162
Victoria, Australia	87,884	2,054,701	G 7	67
Vietnam, North	63,370	12,000,000	D 2	61
Vietnam, South	65,726	12,963,900	D 2	61
Virgin Islands (Br.)	58	6,508	H 1	75
Virgin Islands (U.S.A.)	132	26,665	H 1	75
Virginia, U.S.A.	39,899	3,318,680	......	164
Volcano Is. (U.S. Adm.)	29	....	E 3	68
Wake Island (U.S.A.)	3	....	G 4	68
Wales (excluding Monmouthshire)	7,466	2,172,339	E 4	39
Walvis Bay (Br.)	430	2,263	J16	64
Washington, U.S.A.	66,977	2,378,963	......	166
Western Australia, Australia	975,920	502,480	C 4	66
West Indies (Br. Fed.)	8,000	3,000,000	......	75
West Indies (Islands)	90,000	17,000,000	......	75
West Virginia, U.S.A.	24,090	2,005,552	......	168
White Russian S.S.R. (Byelorussian S.S.R.) (U.S.S.R.)	80,100	7,220,000	C 4	53
Windward Islands	821	251,771	G 4	75
Wisconsin, U.S.A.	54,715	3,434,575	......	170
World land area	57,500,000	2,200,000,000	......	34
Wyoming, U.S.A.	97,506	290,529	......	172
Yap (U.S. Trust.)	87	2,560	D 5	68
Yemen	75,000	3,500,000	D 7	56
Yugoslavia	99,079	15,751,935	C 3	50
Yukon Territory, Canada.	205,346	12,190	......	190
Zanzibar Prot. (Br.)	1,020	264,162	P13	65

* Member of Federation of Rhodesia and Nyasaland.

TABLES OF

SOCIAL AND ECONOMIC DATA

OF THE WORLD

THE HEADLINE EVENTS of the last half-century have made the average person acutely curious of the vast world beyond his country's borders. This new national concern for the external world and its problems is one of the hopeful signs pointing to a better future for mankind. However, no matter how well-intentioned our concern for international relations may be, it is of no value unless it is grounded on an intelligent appreciation of the great diversity of social, economic and political forms extant throughout the globe.

On the following pages the editors have presented information on the world's nations, products, peoples and governments arranged in easily-found tabular form. This arrangement by tables makes comparison between political units a simpler task. These data, used with the maps in this atlas, complete the story of the nations of the world.

POLITICAL DIVISION	GOVERNMENT	MONETARY UNIT	LANGUAGE	MAJOR PRODUCTS
ADEN	British colony administered by a governor and an executive and legislative council.	East African shilling	Arabic Hindu	Salt, cigarettes, dhow building, fish, cloth, dyeing, sesame oil, soap, sorghum, ship-bunkering.
ADEN PROTECTORATE	Ruled by native sultans and sheiks advised by a British agent responsible to the governor of Aden.	East African shilling	Arabic	Dates, gums, tobacco, fish oil, butter, wheat, barley, sesame, millet, sorghum, aloes, ghee; goats, sheep, camels, cattle.
AFGHANISTAN	A constitutional monarchy ruled by a king, a cabinet and a bicameral legislative assembly.	Afghani rupee	Afghan (Pushtu) Persian	Wheat, barley, millet, corn, sorghum, lentils, vegetables, fruits, nuts, castor beans, madder, asafetida, cotton, tobacco, fat-tailed sheep (karakul), camels, zebus; wool, skins; sheepskin, textiles, leather, carpets, rugs; gold, iron, lapis lazuli, coal, copper. lead. silver.
ALBANIA	A Soviet-type republic with president, cabinet and one-house legislature. Actually ruled by the communist party politburo.	lek	Albanian	Corn, tobacco, wheat, flax, oats, barley, rye, rice, olives, fruit; cattle, sheep; fish; wool, hides; dairy products, furs; bitumen, salt, lignite, aluminum, petroleum, copper, chromite; flour, olive oil, cheese, cement, leather.
ALGERIA	Consists of overseas territories of France headed by a resident minister assisted by a federative elective assembly and council.	franc	Arabic French Berber	Wheat, barley, oats, corn, grapes, olives, tobacco, dates, figs, flax, pomegranates, prunes, apricots, legumes, potatoes; sheep, goats, cattle, mules, horses, pigs, camels; sardines, anchovies, tuna; forestry products; iron phosphates, zinc, petroleum; wine, olive oil, distilling, flour, carpet weaving, alcohol, cotton weaving, tobacco products, wool, cork.
ANDORRA	A republic under the joint suzerainty of the French State and the Bishop of Urgel, with a council general of 24 elective members. Executive authority is vested in the First Syndic.	franc and peseta	Catalan	Tobacco, potatoes, barley; sheep, cattle; lumber.
ANGOLA	Portuguese overseas province with a governor general.	angolar	Bantu languages Portuguese	Coffee, corn, sugar, palm oil and kernels, cotton, sisal, wax, tobacco; diamonds; whale oil, fish oil, sugar, palm oil,
ARGENTINA	A republic with a president, vice-president, appointive cabinet, elective senate and house of deputies.	peso	Spanish	Wheat, corn, oats, barley, linseed, rye, grapes and other fruit, tobacco, vegetables; yerba maté; cattle, sheep; quebracho, lumber; petroleum, natural gas, gold, lead, silver, tungsten; vegetable oils, wines, hides, wool, meats, textiles, metal products, vehicles and machinery, chemicals, wood and paper products, leather, clothing and shoes.
ASCENSION ISLAND	Possession of Gr. Britain, administered through the government of St. Helena by a resident magistrate and a Justice of the Peace.	pound	English	
AUSTRALIA	Member of the British Commonwealth of Nations with a governor-general, prime minister and cabinet. Parliament consists of a senate and house of commons.	Australian pound	English,	Wheat, oats, rice and other grains, fruits, vegetables, honey; sheep, cattle; gold, coal, copper, iron, lead, silver, tin, zinc; iron and steel, wool, textiles, electrical and radio equipment and appliances, drugs and chemicals, paints, optical instruments, agricultural implements and machinery, metal work and machinery, clothing, leather, furniture, airplanes, engines, ships, processed fruit and vegetables, building materials, confectionery, automobiles.
AUSTRIA	Republic with a president, chancellor and vice-chancellor, cabinet of ministers, and two-house assembly.	schilling	German	Rye, wheat, oats, barley, corn, potatoes, sugar beets, hops, grapes, rapeseed, flax, hemp, tobacco; iron, copper, lead, magnesite, graphite, coal, aluminum, petroleum, lignite, salt; timber, pulp, poultry and livestock; steel, machinery, machine tools, chemicals, textiles, paper, building materials, processed foods, leather.
BAHAMAS	British colony with governor, executive and legislative council and house of assembly.	pound	English	Tomatoes, pineapples, okra, vegetables, citrus fruits, bananas, sisal; crawfish, shells; lumber; salt; handcraft products.
BAHREIN	Arab Sheikhdom protected by Great Britain and advised by British political agent.	rupee	Arabic	Pearl fishing, petroleum, boat building, fishing; reed mats, dates, lucerne; donkeys; textiles.
BARBADOS •	British colony with governor, executive and legislative council and house of assembly.	B.W.I dollar	English	Sugar cane, cotton; flying fish; manjak (asphalt); sugar, molasses, rum, edible oil, margarine.

• Member of The West Indies (British Caribbean Federation)

POLITICAL DIVISION	GOVERNMENT	MONETARY UNIT	LANGUAGE	MAJOR PRODUCTS
BASUTOLAND	British colony. Governed by a resident commissioner under High Commissioner for Basutoland, Bechuanaland and Swaziland.	pound	Bantu languages Afrikaans English	Corn, wheat, sorghum, barley, oats, beans, peas; cattle, sheep, goats, horses, donkeys, pigs, mules; wool, mohair.
BECHUANALAND	British protectorate. Governed by a resident commissioner under High Commissioner for Basutoland, Bechuanaland and Swaziland.	pound	Bantu languages Bushman English	Kaffir, wheat and wheatmeal; cattle, sheep, goats, pigs; hides, gold.
BELGIAN CONGO	Belgian colony administered by a governor-general.	franc	Bantu languages French Flemish	Palm oil and kernels, cotton, coffee, oil cakes, copal, rice, groundnuts; rubber, manioc, fibers; copper, cement, coal, silver, cassiterite (tin), diamonds, gold, cobalt, radium, uranium, tantulum, zinc.
BELGIUM	Constitutional, hereditary monarchy. King appoints a cabinet of ministers. Parliament consists of a senate and chamber of deputies.	franc	French and Flemish	Wheat, rye, oats, barley, potatoes, sugar beets, flax, tobacco, vegetables, fruit, hops, hemp, bulbs, livestock, fish; coal, iron, zinc, lead, copper, tin, silver; coke, steel, machinery, textiles, lace, glass, chemicals, uranium refining, sugar, margarine, cheese, vinegar, alcohol, beer, matches, paper, foods, beverages, wool, cut diamonds, dairy products.
BERMUDA	British colony with governor, executive and legislative council and house of assembly.	pound	English	Lily bulbs, onions, bananas, cabbage, tomatoes, beans; coral; fish; perfume.
BHUTAN	Ruled by a Maharaja and advised by India in foreign relations.	rupee	Bhutanese (Tibetan dialect)	Rice, corn, millet, lac, wax, musk; elephants, ponies, chowries; cloth, baskets, mats, metalwork, guns, swords.
BISMARCK ARCHIPELAGO	A part of the territory of New Guinea administered by Australia as a U.N. trust territory.	Australian pound	Papuan English Chinese	Coconuts, cocoa, coffee, kapok, rubber, grains; cattle, goats, pigs; fish.
BOLIVIA	A republic with a president, vice-president, appointive ministers of state, and an elective senate and chamber of deputies.	boliviano	Spanish, Indian	Potatoes, corn, barley, quinoa, nuts, coca, vanilla, rubber, quinine; tin, zinc, lead, copper, silver, antimony, tungsten, sulphur, petroleum; cattle; textiles, flour, cement, tobacco products, hides, beer, earthenware.
BONIN ISLANDS	Administered by the United States.	dollar yen	Japanese	Vegetables, sugar, coca; poultry, pigs, cattle; fish.
BRAZIL	Federal republic with a president, vice-president, appointive secretaries of state and a bicameral legislature.	cruzeiro	Portuguese	Coffee, corn, rice, cotton, cacao, sugar cane, cassava, beans, carnauba wax, medicinal plants, oranges, balata, tobacco, fibers, castor oil; livestock; timbo, brazil nuts; iron, manganese, gold, rutile, zirconium, diamonds, mica, bauxite, quartz, beryllium, chrome, tungsten, silver; foods, textiles, chemicals, pharmaceuticals, metallurgical products, paper and wood products, hides, vegetable oils, machinery.
BRITISH HONDURAS	British colony with governor, executive council, legislative assembly.	Br. Honduras dollar	English and Spanish	Rice, maize, beans, bananas, coconuts, citrus fruits, sugar cane; mahogany, chicle, pine, cedar; fish; rum, food products.
BRUNEI	A sultanate under British protection administered by a British resident.	Malayan dollar	Malay English	Rice, sago, rubber, jelutong, cutch, sugar cane, tapioca, bananas, pineapples; timber; domestic birds, buffalo, pigs, cattle; petroleum, natural gas; boat building, cloth, brass and silverware.
BULGARIA	Soviet-type republic with a one-house legislature, which elects a presidium whose president is the nominal chief of state. Actual power is communist politburo.	lev	Bulgarian	Wheat, corn, barley, oats, rye, tobacco, fruit, cotton, sugar beets, potatoes; livestock, silkworm cocoons; fish; coal, salt, bauxite, copper, iron, lead, manganese, silver, kaolin; tobacco products, attar of roses, sugar, flour, textiles, leather goods, shoes, lead concentrates, wines and spirits.
BURMA, UNION OF	A republic with a president elected by a bicameral legislature.	kyat	Burmese Karen Shan Kachin	Rice, sesame, peanuts, corn, cotton, millet, tobacco, sugar, beans, fruit, vegetables, pulses, rubber; teak wood, lumber; cattle, buffalo, pigs, goats, sheep; petroleum, silver, lead, zinc, tin, copper, tungsten, rubies, sapphires, amber, jade, nickel, gold, antimony, cobalt, salt; textiles, hides, matches, lacquer ware.
CAMBODIA	Constitutional monarchy with a national assembly.	riel	Khmer Tao	Rice, tobacco, kapok, cotton, pepper, coin, sugar, rubber; timber; cattle; fish; silk, cotton, textiles, pottery, rush mats, precious stones, phosphates.
CAMEROONS	Under United Nations trusteeship, administered by Great Britain.	pound	Bantu and Sudanese languages	Cocoa, coffee, rubber, bananas, palm oil and kernels; cattle, goats, sheep, horses.
CAMEROUN	Under United Nations trusteeship, administered by France.	franc	Sudanese and Bantu languages Arabic French	Cocoa, palm kernels, bananas, caoutchouc, coffee, cacao, palm oil; timber; cattle, sheep, pigs, horses, asses; rubber, tobacco.
CANADA	Member of the British Commonwealth with a governor-general, prime minister and cabinet. Parliament consists of a senate and house of commons.	dollar	English French	Wheat, oats, barley, flax, rye, potatoes, turnips, vegetables, sugar beets, tobacco, fruits, dairy products, livestock; fish; forestry products; furs; gold, copper, nickel, zinc, lead, silver, platinum, iron ore, titanium, cobalt, radium, uranium, petroleum, natural gas, coal, asbestos, salt, gypsum, quartz, sulphur, cement, clay; hydro-electric power; foods, beverages, transportation equipment, iron and steel products, aluminum, metal products, pulp, paper and wood products, textiles, electrical apparatus, chemicals.
CANARY ISLANDS	Islands forming two provinces of Spain, governed by a Cabildo Insular.	peseta	Spanish	Bananas, cochineal, potatoes, sugar cane, onions, fruits; fish; wine, sugar.
CAPE VERDE ISLANDS	Portuguese overseas province, ruled by a governor.	escudo	Portuguese	Coffee, castor beans, corn, fruit, grains, tobacco; goats, oxen, pigs, asses; hides, skins; preserved fish, salt, lime, sugar.
CAROLINE ISLANDS	A group in the United States trust territory of the Pacific Islands and administered by a high commissioner.	dollar	Micronesian dialects Malayo-Polynesian languages	Copra, breadfruit, cassava, taro, sweet potatoes; pigs, cattle, poultry, fish; phosphates.
CEYLON	Dominion of the British Commonwealth ruled by a governor-general, a prime minister, a cabinet and a bicameral legislature.	rupee	Singhalese Tamil	Tea, coconuts, rubber, rice, millet, tobacco, cacao, cinnamon, citronella, cloves, fruits, palmyra, fish; cattle, buffalo, goats, swine, sheep; graphite, plumbago, mica, ilmenite, monazite, iron ore; salt, pearls, zircon, glass sands, copra, plywood, leather, shoes, glass, steel, acetic acid, ceramics, quinine, strychine, shark-liver oil, coconut oil, textiles.
CHILE	A republic with a president, vice-president, appointive cabinet of ministers of state, elective senate and chamber of deputies.	peso	Spanish	Wheat, potatoes, oats, rice, barley, corn, kidney beans, lentils, fruits; fish; livestock; copper, silver, nitrates, iodine, iron, sulphur, gold, manganese, coal; foods, textiles, leather, wood products, cement, chemicals and pharmaceuticals, wines and beer, wool.
CHINA: MAINLAND (COMMUNIST)	In theory, government power resides in the National People's Congress and the State Council. In practice, power resides in the Communist Party's Central Committee.	Chinese dollar	Chinese Mongol Turki	Rice, wheat, sweet potatoes, corn, barley, millet, kaoliang, soybeans, cotton, tea, sugar cane, tobacco, peanuts, peas, beans, opium, tung, silk; pigs, oxen, sheep, goats, buffalo, donkeys, horses, mules, poultry; timber; fish; iron, coal, tungsten, tin, antimony, mercury, copper, lead, zinc, silver, salt, soda, gold, petroleum, bismuth, molybdenum; foodstuffs, textiles, chemicals, machinery, metal work, metallurgical products, bristles, cement, clothing, embroideries, ceramics.

POLITICAL DIVISION	GOVERNMENT	MONETARY UNIT	LANGUAGE	MAJOR PRODUCTS
CHINA: FORMOSA (NATIONALIST)	A republic whose supreme organ of government is the popularly elected National Assembly. The Assembly elects the president and vice-president. Legislative powers reside with the Legislative Yuan.	dollar	Chinese (Amoy dialect) Formosan	Rice, tea, sugar, sweet potatoes, ramie, jute, tumeric, pineapples, bananas, camphor; pigs, buffalo, cattle, goats, horses.
CHRISTMAS ISLAND	A part of Australia.	Malayan dollar	Chinese Malay English	Phosphate of lime.
COLOMBIA	A centralized federal republic with a president, vice-president, appointive cabinet, elective senate and house of representatives.	peso	Spanish	Coffee, sugar cane, corn, rice, root crops, cotton, bananas, cacao, wheat, tobacco, cinchona; cattle; rubber, fibers; petroleum, gold, silver, platinum, emeralds, salt; textiles, beer, sugar, cement, flour, tobacco products.
COMORO ISLANDS	An overseas territory of France with an administrator, privy council and an elective general council.	franc	Arabic French	Sugar cane, vanilla, rice, sweet potatoes, yams, copra, sisal, cacao, perfume plants; rum distilling.
COOK ISLANDS	Territory of New Zealand administered by a resident commissioner.	New Zealand pound	Polynesian dialects English	Citrus fruits, coconuts, copra, tomatoes, arrowroot, pineapples, breadfruit, taro, kumaras, plantains, yams; mother-of-pearl.
COSTA RICA	Republic with president, cabinet and one-house legislature.	colon	Spanish	Coffee, bananas, cocoa, abaca, sugar cane, maize, rice, tobacco; cattle; tuna; gold, silver; cigars and cigarettes, textiles, furniture and woodwork, sugar.
CUBA	Republic with president, vice-president, cabinet and a two-house legislature.	peso	Spanish	Sugar cane, tobacco, coffee, pineapples, citrus fruits, bananas, henequen; cattle; cedar, mahogany and other woods; fish; chromite, iron, manganese, copper, nickel, asphalt; sugar, textiles, alcohol, molasses, chemicals, tobacco products, electrical goods, clothing.
CURAÇAO (NETH. ANTILLES)	Self-governing part of Netherlands Union with governor, executive council and one-house legislature.	guilder	Dutch and Papiamento	Fish; dividivi (tannin), crude salt, phosphates; refined petroleum.
CYPRUS	British colony ruled by a governor with the assistance of an executive council.	pound	Greek Turkish	Wheat, barley, oats, grapes, raisins, olives, fodder crops, potatoes, carobs, cotton, tobacco, linseed, hemp, flax, citrus fruits, bread beans, corn, sesame, melons; sponges, fish; sheep, goats, donkeys, cattle, pigs, horses, mules; copper pyrites, asbestos, chromite, gypsum, amber, copper concentrates; tobacco products, buttons, wines, spirits, false teeth, lace, gum, boots and shoes, dried fruits, cheese.
CZECHOSLOVAKIA	Soviet-type republic with a president and a one-house elective parliament. Actual power resides in politburo, highest body of communist party.	koruna	Czech and Slovak	Wheat, rye, barley, oats, corn, hops, sugar beets, grapes, potatoes; poultry, livestock; timber; coal, lignite, iron, graphite, garnets, silver, copper, lead, salt, manganese, zinc; beer, spirits, malt, metals, munitions, machinery, iron and steel, porcelain, shoes, textiles, wood products, pulp and paper, sugar, leather, foods, chemicals, rubber products.
DAHOMEY	Territory of Fr. West Africa with a governor and an elective representative assembly.	franc	Sudanese languages French	Palm oil, shea nuts, groundnuts, cotton fiber, copra, castor oil, kapok, millet; gold, diamonds, bauxite, iron ore.
DAMÃO	Portuguese overseas province subject to government at Gôa and ruled by lieutenant-governor.	rupia	Portuguese Marathi	Salt, fish, rice, wheat, tobacco; palm-mat weaving.
DENMARK	Constitutional, hereditary monarchy with a two-house, elective legislature and an appointive council of ministers.	krone	Danish	Barley, mixed grains, oats, rye, wheat, potatoes, sugar beets; livestock, fish; clay; ships and transportation equipment, butter, bacon, eggs, cheese, milk, footwear, clothing, machines, chemicals, tobacco products, metal goods, leather goods, beverages; stone, earthenware and glassware, electrical goods.
DIU	Portuguese overseas province subject to government at Gôa and ruled by lieutenant-governor.	rupia	Portuguese Marathi	Salt; fish.
DOMINICAN REPUBLIC	Republic with president, cabinet and two house legislature.	peso	Spanish	Sugar cane, cacao, coffee, tobacco, bananas, rice, corn; cattle; lumber; gold; starch, alcohol, molasses, sugar, chocolate, meats, cigars, cigarettes, leather.
EASTER ISLAND (RAPA NUI)	Administered as part of Valparaíso province in Chile.	peso	Polynesian dialect Spanish	Plantains, sweet potatoes; fish; cattle, sheep; wool.
ECUADOR	A centralized republic with a president, a cabinet and an elective bicameral legislature, the senate including representatives of various social, economic and governmental groups.	sucré	Spanish, Indian	Rice, cacao, coffee, bananas, rubber, kapok, cotton, tagua (ivory) nuts, cinchona; livestock; gold, petroleum, salt, balsa wood; textiles, toquilla (panama) hats, buttons, sugar, flour, shoes, beer and liquors, chemicals, pharmaceuticals, cement, soap, candles.
EGYPT (See United Arab Republic)	Province of United Arab Republic.	Egyptian pound	Arabic	Cotton, barley, wheat, rice, sugar cane, onions, corn, millet, fruits, vegetables; sheep, goats, cattle, buffalo, donkeys, pigs, horses, mules; fish; petroleum, cement, phosphates, asbestos, chromite, cotton ginning, milling, pottery, perfume, soap.
ENGLAND AND WALES	England is governed directly by the government of Great Britain and Northern Ireland. Executive power resides nominally in the Crown but actually in the prime minister and cabinet. Parliament consists of two houses.	pound	English and Welsh (Celtic)	Potatoes, turnips, beets, oats, wheat, barley, rye, hay, beans, peas, cabbage, vetches, hops, fruits; sheep, cattle, pigs, horses, poultry; fish; coal, coke, gas, iron, copper, lead, nickel, tin, clay; dairy products, wool, cotton and linen textiles; electrical goods, vehicles, steel, scientific instruments, cutlery, foods and beverages, tobacco products, clothing and shoes, chemicals, pottery, china, machinery, locomotives, carpets, knitwear, lace, pharmaceuticals.
ERITREA	Autonomous state federated with Ethiopia. Administered locally by a representative legislature.	Ethiopian dollar	Hamitic languages Arabic	Coffee, barley, sisal, bananas, legumes, gum arabic, wheat, tobacco, dates, dom nuts, senna; goats, sheep, camels, horses, mules, donkeys, cattle; hides, skins; fish-meal; pearls, mother-of-pearl; gold, salt, potassium salts, matting.
ETHIOPIA	Constitutional monarchy with an emperor assisted by a council of ministers and a bicameral legislature. (See Eritrea).	Ethiopian dollar	Amharic Hamitic languages Arabic	Coffee, teff, barley, durra, wheat, cotton, sugar cane; cattle, sheep, goats, horses, mules; hides, skins; wax, gold, rocksalt.
FALKLAND ISLANDS	British colony with a governor and an executive and a legislative council.	pound	English	Forage crops, sheep; wool, skins, tallow, whale oil, whale-meat meal.
FIJI	British colony ruled by a governor with an executive and legislative council.	Fiji pound	English Fijian Hindustani Chinese	Sugar cane, coconuts, bananas, pineapples, rice, root vegetables, citrus fruits, cotton, rubber, castor oil seeds, taro, yams, cassava, sweet potatoes, groundnuts, pulses, corn, fodder crops, tobacco; cattle, pigs; tuna, bêche-de-mer, trochus shell; gold, silver; sugar, copra, coconut oil, soap, biscuits, molasses, paint, butter, ghee, candlenut oil.

POLITICAL DIVISION	GOVERNMENT	MONETARY UNIT	LANGUAGE	MAJOR PRODUCTS
FINLAND	A republic with a president, a one-house elective diet and appointive council of state.	markka	Finnish and Swedish	Hay, potatoes, wheat, oats, barley, rye, sugar beets, flax, hemp, vegetables; cattle, horses, sheep, pigs, poultry, reindeer; wood and timber; fish; copper; lumber, plywood, furniture, pulp and paper, cardboard, textiles, butter, eggs, cheese, flour, leather, chemicals, china and glass, foodstuffs.
FRANCE	A republic with a president, a two-house elective parliament and an appointive council of ministers.	franc	French	Sugar beets, potatoes, wheat, oats, barley, rye; corn, turnips, fruits, nuts, wine grapes, buckwheat; cattle, sheep, pigs, horses; fish; coal, iron ore, lignite, salt, bauxite, pyrites, potash salts, leeks, kaolin, natural gas, iron and steel, chemicals; silk, cotton, rayon, wool and linen, textiles; clothing, lace, perfumes and cosmetics, automobiles, machinery, dairy products, beet sugar, wines, porcelain, aluminum, foods, leather, spirits.
FRENCH EQUATORIAL AFRICA	Federated overseas territory of France with a governor-general and an elective grand assembly representing the 4 constituent territories.	franc	Bantu and Sudanese languages Arabic French	Palm oil and kernels, coconuts, cotton, coffee, cocoa, groundnuts, kapok, butter; hides; timber, rubber, copal gum, wax; ivory, gold, copper, lead, zinc, diamonds.
FRENCH SUDAN	Territory of Fr. West Africa with a governor and an elective representative assembly.	franc	Sudanese languages Hamitic languages Arabic French	Millet, rice, groundnuts, corn, sweet potatoes, cotton, manioc, tobacco, karite, shea nuts, yams, kapok, sisal; cattle, goats, sheep, horses, asses, camels; hides and skins; pottery, bricks, jewelry, weaving, leather, rice mills, soap.
FRENCH WEST AFRICA	Overseas territory of France with a governor-general and an elective grand assembly representing the 8 constituent territories.	franc	Sudanese and Hamitic languages Arabic French	Millet, rice, corn, cotton and fibers, nuts, oilseeds and oil, manioc, coffee, bananas, cocoa; cattle; gold, diamonds, iron ore, bauxite.
GAMBIA	Crown colony and protectorate of Great Britain administered by a governor, executive and legislative councils.	pound	Sudanese languages English	Groundnuts, palm kernels; hides and skins; beeswax.
GAMBIER ISLANDS	A group of islands in French Polynesia governed from Tahiti.	franc	Polynesian dialects	Coconuts, copra, oranges, breadfruit; pearls, pearl shell, fish.
GERMANY	Country is divided between two governments—a democratic **Federal Republic of Germany** in the west and a Soviet-dominated **German "Democratic" Republic** in the east. **Federal Republic** has an elected federal diet and council who jointly elect the president. **German "Democratic" Republic** has a communist-controlled legislative branch which selects the president, cabinet and prime minister.	East German and West German Deutsche Mark	German	Wheat, rye, barley, oats, potatoes, sugar beets, fruits, hops; pigs, cattle, poultry, horses; fish; forest products; coal, lignite, iron, copper, potash, sulphur, salt, uranium, lead, zinc, fluor spar, gypsum, vanadium, aluminum; automobiles, steel, cement, diesel oil, gasoline, cotton yarn, woolen yarn, rayon fiber, beet sugar, beer, wines, optical instruments, sulphuric acid, sodium bicarbonate, chemicals.
GHANA	Member of the British Commonwealth with an appointed governor-general and an elective parliament.	pound	Sudanese languages English	Cocoa, palm oil and kernels, sorghum, millet, corn, yams, cassava, groundnuts, cotton.
GIBRALTAR	British Crown Colony administered by a governor, executive council, and a legislative council.	pound	English and Spanish	Fish for export and processing of commodities for local consumption.
GILBERT AND ELLICE ISLS.	British colony administered by a resident commissioner.	Australian pound	English Gilbertese Samoan	Coconuts, copra, phosphate of lime; pearl shell, fish; hats, mats.
GÕA	Portuguese overseas province ruled by a governor assisted by executive and legislative councils.	rupia	Portuguese Marathi	Rice, cashew nuts, betel nuts, grains, vegetables, coconuts, mangoes; teak, bamboo, blackwood; fish; salt, manganese, asbestos, asphalt, guano, silica, coal, petroleum; sugar, textiles, distilling, dessicated coconut, tobacco products, rice milling, cocoa, coconut oil, embroideries.
GREAT BRITAIN: (see England, N. Ireland and Scotland).				
GREECE	A constitutional hereditary monarchy with a prime minister, cabinet of ministers and an elective assembly.	drachma	Greek	Wheat, barley, corn, oats, rye, tobacco, currants, sultana raisins, olives, figs, grapes, cottonseed, sesame seed; sheep, goats, cattle, pigs, horses, mules; fish; iron ore, sulphur, emery, magnesite, zinc, lead, lignite, marble, bauxite; textiles, olive oil, foods, wines, chemicals, leather, wood and paper, metal products, machinery.
GREENLAND	An integral part of the Danish kingdom, with representation in Parliament.	krone	Danish and Greenlandic	Grass for fodder; cod and other fish; sheep, furs; cryolite; processed fish, hides.
GUADELOUPE	Overseas department of France with a prefect and elective general council.	franc	French, French Patois	Sugar cane, bananas, coffee, cocoa, vanilla, cassava; fish; alcohol, rum.
GUAM	Territory of the United States administered by a governor and advisory and legislative bodies.	dollar	English Chamorro Spanish	Copra, coconut oil, corn, taro, bananas, citrus fruits, mangoes, papayas, breadfruit, sweet potatoes, cocoa, cassava, sugar cane, pineapples; cattle, pigs, poultry, buffalo.
GUATEMALA	Republic with a president, cabinet and one-house legislature.	quetzal	Spanish	Coffee, bananas, sugar cane, rubber, chicle, cacao, abaca, cattle; mahogany and dye woods; essential oils; gold; textiles.
GUIANA, BRITISH	A British colony with a governor and partly nominated, partly elected legislative and executive councils.	B.W.I. dollar	English	Sugar cane, rice, coconuts, coffee, citrus fruits, cacao; balata, rubber, green heart and other timber; livestock; bauxite, diamonds, gold; textiles, milled rice, beer and rum, lime rum and oil, sugar, woods, molasses, charcoal, matches.
GUIANA	Independent republic.	franc	French	Rice, cacao, bananas, sugar cane, corn, cassava, woods; gold; hides, rosewood essence, shoes, rum, fish glue.
GUIANA, NETH. (SURINAM)	Self-governing part of the Netherlands Union with an appointed governor, an appointive council of ministers, an advisory council and an elective legislative body.	guilder	Dutch	Rice, citrus fruits, coconuts, coffee, bananas, sugar cane, cacao, balata, corn, tobacco; lumber; gold, bauxite; sugar, rum, plywood, molasses.
GUINEA	Independent republic.	franc	Sudanese languages French	Rice, groundnuts, palm oil and nuts, wax, honey, bananas, indigo, kola, orange products, coffee; cattle, sheep, goats, pigs; hides and skins; bauxite, iron ore, gold.
GUINEA, PORTUGUESE	Portuguese overseas province ruled by a governor.	escudo	Sudanese languages Portuguese	Rice, palm kernels and oil, wax, groundnuts; hides.

POLITICAL DIVISION	GOVERNMENT	MONETARY UNIT	LANGUAGE	MAJOR PRODUCTS
GUINEA, SPANISH	Spanish colony ruled by a governor.	peseta	Bantu languages Spanish	Cocoa, coffee, vegetables and fruit; wood.
HAITI	Republic with a president, cabinet and a two-house legislature.	gourde	Creole, French	Coffee, sugar, fig bananas, sisal, cotton, rice, cocoa; logwood; molasses, sisal products.
HAWAII	Territory of the United States administered by a governor, a senate and a house of representatives.	dollar	English Japanese Hawaiian	Sugar, pineapples, coffee, molasses, bananas, rice, flowers, cotton, tobacco; beef cattle, swine, sheep, poultry; hides, wood, stone, fish, printing, foodstuffs, ironworks, fertilizers, chemicals, clothing, fiber insulating board, handicrafts.
HONDURAS	Republic with a president, council of ministers and a one-house legislature.	lempira	Spanish	Bananas, coffee, coconuts, tobacco, grapefruit, rice, henequen; mahogany; cattle; gold, silver.
HONG KONG	A British colony ruled by governor assisted by executive and legislative council.	Hong Kong dollar	Chinese English	Rice, sugar cane, peanuts, sweet potatoes; fish; poultry, pigs; kaolin, lead, iron, wolfram, granite, silver, cement; shipbuilding and repair; rape, rubber shoes, enameled hollow-ware, textiles, electric flashlights and batteries, preserved ginger.
HUNGARY	Soviet-type republic with a president and a presidential council selected by the national assembly. Actual power in hands of politburo, highest organ of communist party.	forint	Hungarian	Wheat, corn, rye, barley, oats, potatoes, sugar beets, tobacco, grapes and other fruits, peppers, hemp, flax; pigs, cattle, sheep, horses, poultry; fish; coal, lignite, petroleum, natural gas, iron ore, bauxite, manganese; flour, sugar, distilling, brewing, iron and steel, wines, textiles, paprika, chemicals, leather, metal products, wood and paper products.
ICELAND	A republic with a president, an elective, two-house legislature and an appointive cabinet of ministers.	krona	Icelandic	Hay, potatoes, turnips, hothouse fruits and vegetables; sheep, poultry, horses, cattle; fish; dairy products, meats, animal and vegetable oils, hides, skins, leather, clothing, textiles, frozen fish, herring oil, herring meal.
IFNI	Spanish territory ruled by a subgovernor.	peseta	Berber Arabic Spanish	Barley, alfalfa, corn, tomatoes, argan oil, wheat; fish.
INDIA	An independent republic within the British Commonwealth with a president, cabinet and a bicameral legislature.	rupee	Indo-Aryan (Hindi, Bengali, Gujarati, Punjabi, Urdu) and Dravidian (Tamil, Kanarese, Telugan) English	Rice, wheat, legumes, groundnuts, oilseeds, tea, tobacco, jute, cotton, rubber, coffee, sugar cane, barley, millet, corn; cattle, goats, buffalo, sheep, pigs; fish; coal, manganese, gold, petroleum, salt, mica, iron, copper, chromite, ilmenite, diamonds, silver, bauxite; textiles, shawls, carpets, jute manufacturers, wood-carving and metal work, leather, chemicals, shipbuilding, petroleum refining, sugar refining, cotton ginning, iron and steel mills, glass, soap, matches.
INDONESIA	Republic with president, cabinet and unicameral legislature.	rupiah	Indonesian (Malay, Javanese, etc.)	Rice, sugar cane, rubber, palm oil, tobacco, corn, coconuts, copra, cassava, sweet potatoes, groundnuts, soya beans, cotton, kapok, coffee, cinchona, cocoa, pepper, fruits, vegetables; cattle, buffalo; tin, coal, petroleum, bauxite, manganese; rubber goods, chemicals, shipyards, textiles, paper, breweries, glass, handicrafts.
IRAN	Constitutional monarchy governed by a shah, prime minister, cabinet and a bicameral legislature.	rial	Persian Arabic Kurdish	Wheat, cotton, gums, opium, fruit, rice, barley, sugar beets, tobacco, tea, corn, millet, legumes, vegetables, nuts; sheep, goats, cattle, asses, horses, mules; fish; petroleum oil, red oxide, copper, sulphur, arsenic, coal, salt, marble, nickel, manganese, lead, cobalt, turquoise, iron ore; carpets, rugs, textiles, leather, glass, matches, chemicals, jute, tobacco products, oil refining, casings, wood, oils.
IRAQ	Independent republic	dinar	Arabic Turkish Kurdish	Dates, other fruits, barley, wheat, rice, tobacco, cotton, beans, corn, sorghum, sesame; sheep, goats, asses, camels, horses, buffalo; oil, salt, wool, textiles, cigarettes, distilling.
IRELAND	A republic with a president, premier and an elective, two-house parliament.	pound	English and Gaelic	Hay, potatoes, turnips, fodder, beets, sugar beets, oats, wheat, barley, cabbage, rye, flax; cattle, sheep, pigs, horses, poultry; fish; coal, peat, gypsum; tobacco, dairy products, foodstuffs, beer, malt, clothing, meats, textiles, boots and shoes, wood and paper products.
ISRAEL	Republic with president, prime minister, cabinet and elective unicameral legislature.	Israeli pound	Hebrew Arabic	Dairy products, vegetables, eggs, fruits, green fodder, wheat, hay, barley, corn, durra; goats, sheep, cattle, camels, poultry; fish; textiles, clothing, foods, beverages, tobacco, diamond polishing, shoes, metal and woodwork, furniture, building materials, leather, dairy products, electrical products, paper, printing, false teeth, pharmaceuticals, chemicals, dyes, soap, radios, oil refining, wines.
ITALY	A republic with a president, a two-house, elective legislature and an appointive cabinet.	lira	Italian	Wheat, corn, oats, sugar beets, potatoes, tomatoes, rice, olives, grapes, lemons and other fruits, hemp, tobacco, nuts; fish; sheep and goats, cattle, pigs, horses, donkeys; iron ore, sulphur, zinc, bauxite, lead, mercury, barite, copper, marble, manganese, lignite; textiles, chemicals, wines, automobiles and machinery, electrical goods, beet sugar, olive oil, cheese, clothing, processed foods.
IVORY COAST	Territory of Fr. West Africa with a governor and an elective representative assembly.	franc	Sudanese languages French	Coffee, cocoa, bananas, manioc, corn, rice, yams, kola, coconuts, palm oil, groundnuts, cotton, millet, tobacco; mahogany, caoutchouc; sheep, cattle, goats, pigs; gold, diamonds, manganese, iron ore, ilmenite.
JAMAICA*	British colony with a governor, executive and legislative councils and house of representatives.	pound	English	Sugar cane, bananas, tobacco, coconuts, cacao, pimentoes, coffee, ginger; bauxite; honey; logwood; rum, textiles, cigars.
JAPAN	Constitutional monarchy with the executive power vested in prime minister and cabinet, the legislative power residing in a two-house parliament. The duties of the emperor are merely ceremonial.	yen	Japanese	Rice, wheat, barley, mulberry trees, potatoes, sweet potatoes, fruits, rape, vegetables, oats, tobacco, soy beans, tea, flax, hemp, camphor; timber, bamboo; horses, cattle, sheep, goats, pigs, rabbits; fish, agar, pearl oysters; silk worms; coal, pyrites, gold, copper, pyrethrum, manganese, silver, sulphur, chromite, zinc, salt, tin, lead, iron, petroleum; textiles, steel, paper, porcelain, earthenware, lacquer ware, vegetable oil, toys, slippers, shoes, machinery.
JORDAN	Constitutional monarchy with cabinet and bicameral legislature.	Jordan dinar	Arabic	Wheat, barley, legumes, vegetables, fruits, olives; sheep, goats, camels; salt, phosphate, potash; wool, tobacco products, flour milling, building materials, olive oil.
KENYA	Colony and protectorate of Great Britain with a governor, a council of ministers, an appointive executive and a partly elective legislative council.	East African shilling	Swahili English Sudanese Hamitic Bantu	Sisal, wheat, tea, coffee, pyrethrum, cotton, corn, sugar cane, sesame, groundnuts, wattle; hides and skins; sodium carbonate, gold, kyanite, salt, silver, lime, bags, butter, sugar, sisal products.
KOREA	Divided into two parts by Armistice Line of August, 1953, pending final decisions of peace treaty. Communist "People's Republic" in North Korea; South Korea headed by a president, a prime minister, a cabinet and a bicameral legislature.	hwan	Korean	Rice, barley, millet, wheat, soya beans, red beans, cotton, tobacco, hemp, ginseng, fruit, radishes; timber; draft cattle, pigs, horses, mules, donkeys, sheep, goats, rabbits; fish; gold, iron ore, coal, tungsten, copper, silver, graphite, salt, kaolin, talc, bismuth, flourite, minerals (N. Korea), textiles, fertilizer, chemicals, cement, heavy industries (N. Korea); textiles, cement, tobacco, silkworms, chemicals, machinery, metal, rubber, wood and paper and tobacco products (S. Korea).
KUWAIT	Arab sheikhdom protected by Great Britain and advised by British political agent.	Indian rupee	Arabic	Petroleum, shipbuilding (dhows), pearls, skins, wool.

* Member of The West Indies (British Caribbean Federation)

POLITICAL DIVISION	GOVERNMENT	MONETARY UNIT	LANGUAGE	MAJOR PRODUCTS
LAOS	Constitutional monarchy with a cabinet and a national assembly.	kip	Khmer (Annamese) Lao	Rice, coffee, tea, citrus fruits, corn, cinchona, gum, benzoin, cardamon; stick-lac; teak; tin.
LEBANON	Independent republic governed by a president, cabinet and an elective legislature.	Lebanese pound	Arabic French	Wheat, barley, corn, potatoes, citrus and other fruits, onions, olives, tobacco (Latakia); goats, asses, cattle, buffalo, sheep, horses, mules; iron, lignite; textiles, cement, olive oil, tobacco products, soap, matches, petroleum refining, gasoline, leather.
LIBERIA	Republic with president, cabinet, senate and house of representatives.	dollar	English Sudanese languages	Rubber, rice, coffee, cassava, sugar cane, cacao, palm oil and kernels, piassava, groundnuts; rum; iron ore.
LIBYA	A federal kingdom with a bicameral legislature, constituted under U.N. auspices and comprising the three provinces of Cyrenaica, Tripolitania and the Fezzan.	Libyan pound	Arabic	Barley, wheat, olives, grapes, dates, almonds, figs, tobacco, esparto; goats, sheep, camels, cattle, donkeys, mules and horses; sponge and tuna fishing; matting, carpets, leather articles, embroidered fabrics.
LIECHTENSTEIN	A principality headed by a prince and an elective, one-house legislature.	Swiss franc	German	Grain, fruit, grapes, wood; cattle, pigs, chickens; cotton textiles, wine, leather, false teeth, pottery, wood-carving.
LUXEMBOURG	A grand duchy and hereditary, constitutional monarchy with an elective chamber of deputies and appointive minister of state and cabinet.	franc	Mosel-frankisch (German dialect)	Oats, potatoes, wheat, rye, grapes; livestock; iron ore, slate, gypsum, sand and gravel; iron, steel and metal working; chemicals, non-metallic minerals, beverages, tobacco, leather, wines, dairy products, quarrying.
MACAO	Portuguese overseas province ruled by a governor.	pataca	Chinese Portuguese	Fish; preserves, firecrackers, vegetable oil, cement, metal work, lumber, tobacco (processed), matches, wine.
MADAGASCAR	Autonomous republic within the French Community of Nations.	franc	French Malagasy and Bantu languages	Cassava, rice, corn, potatoes, coffee, sugar cane, haricot beans, groundnuts, sisal, castor oil, tobacco, raffia; cattle, pigs, goats, sheep; graphite, mica, gold, rock crystal, corundum, phosphates, agate; textiles, sugar and rice factories, tapioca.
MALAYA, FEDERATION OF	Fed. of 9 sultanates and 2 settlements within Br. Commonwealth. It is a constitutional monarchy with cabinet and two-house legislature.	Malayan dollar	Malay Chinese English	Rubber, rice, coconuts, pineapples, tapioca, pepper, spices, tobacco, fibers, gambier, vegetables, tea; buffalo, swine, oxen, goats, sheep; fish; guano, tin, coal, iron ore, bauxite, manganese, copra, palm oil, timber, gold, rubber products, gutta percha, wood products, canned pineapples, textiles.
MALDIVE ISLANDS	An independent sultanate, under British protection, with a bicameral legislature.	rupee	Singhalese Arabic Dravidian	Coconuts, copra, coir, fruit, nuts; fish, cowries; cloth, mats, boats.
MALTA	A self-governing colony of Great Britain with a governor, lt. governor and an elective legislative assembly.	pound	Maltese and English	Wheat, barley, potatoes, onions, grapes and other fruits, cumin seed, cotton; goats, sheep, pigs, cattle; fish; lace, filigree, wine, footwear, beer, cigarettes, buttons, pipes, gloves.
MARIANA ISLANDS	A group of islands in the United States trust territory of the Pacific administered by a high commissioner.	dollar	Micronesian dialects Spanish	Fruits, corn, sweet potatoes, vegetables, breadfruit, cacao; fish; phosphates.
MARQUESAS ISLANDS	A group of islands in French Polynesia administered from Tahiti	franc	Marquesan French	Bananas, breadfruit, yams, bamboo, coconuts, sugar cane.
MARSHALL ISLANDS	A group of islands in the United States trust territory of the Pacific administered by a high commissioner.	dollar	Micronesian dialects	Arrowroot, breadfruit, coconuts, pandanus, taro, vegetables, copra, bananas; poultry, pigs; fish.
MARTINIQUE	Overseas department of France with a prefect and elective general council.	franc	Creole, French	Sugar cane, cocoa, pineapples, bananas, coffee; rum, sugar.
MAURITANIA	Territory of Fr. West Africa with a governor and an elective representative assembly.	franc	Arabic Hamitic and Sudanese languages French	Millet, gum, dates, corn, watermelons, wheat, henna; sheep and goats, cattle, camels, asses, horses; hides and skins; salt.
MAURITIUS	British colony ruled by a governor, an executive council and a legislative council.	rupee	English Hindustani French	Sugar, aloe fiber, rice, vanilla beans, hemp, sisal, groundnuts, tea, yams, manioc, pineapples, tobacco, coconuts; alcohol, molasses, rum, copra.
MEXICO	Federative republic with a president, council of ministers and a two-house legislature.	peso	Spanish	Corn, wheat, beans, chick peas, sugar, bananas, barley, cotton, coffee, vegetables; cattle; henequen; fish; silver, petroleum, lead, gold, zinc, copper; textiles, sugar, alcohol, foundry products.
MONACO	A principality. The prince's authority exercised through a state ministry and 3 government counsellors. The one-house legislative body is elective.	franc	French	Principal revenue derived from Monte Carlo gambling casino. Tobacco, postage stamps, perfume, liqueurs, olive oil, oranges.
MONGOLIAN REPUBLIC	Communist republic, whose prime minister is also head of communist party politburo, which is the actual ruler.	Tugrik	Mongolian Russian	Stock raising (sheep, goats, cattle, horses, camels); milk, butter, cheese; wool, hides, skins, horns, bricks, machinery; coal, lead, gold.
MOROCCO	Constitutional monarchy with a cabinet and a consultative national assembly.	Moroccan franc	Arabic Berber French	Wheat, barley, olives, almonds, citrus fruits, dates, beans, grapes, vegetables, linseed; cork, cedar; sheep, goats, cattle, asses, camels, horses, mules, pigs; fish; phosphate, iron ore, anthracite, manganese, lead, zinc, cobalt, copper, antimony; leather, carpets.
MOZAMBIQUE	Portuguese overseas province ruled by a governor and a government council.	escudo	Bantu languages Portuguese	Sugar, corn, cotton, copra, sisal, cashew nuts, bananas, coffee, kapok, sorghum, manioc, beeswax, tea, tobacco, vegetable oils; mangrove bark, timber; oxen, goats, pigs, sheep, cattle; gold, silver, asbestos, uranium, bauxite, samerskite.
NAURU	Trust territory of Great Britain, Australia and New Zealand. Administered by Australia.	Australian pound	English Micronesian Chinese	Phosphates; fishing; mats.
NEPAL	An independent kingdom governed by a maharaja, prime minister and a bicameral legislature.	Nepalese rupee	Indo-Aryan languages Tibetan	Rice, grains, jute, sugar cane, tea, vegetables, tobacco, cotton, potatoes, medicinal herbs; timber; cattle, hides, skins, ghee; iron, coal, copper, lead, zinc; cotton cloth, pottery, paper.

POLITICAL DIVISION	GOVERNMENT	MONETARY UNIT	LANGUAGE	MAJOR PRODUCTS
NETHERLANDS	A constitutional, hereditary monarchy governed by the queen, her ministers and a two-house legislature, partly elective and partly chosen by provincial councils.	guilder	Dutch	Potatoes, sugar beets, rye, wheat, oats, barley, flax, legumes, flower bulbs, seeds, vegetables, fruit; cattle, pigs, sheep, horses, poultry; fish; coal, petroleum, salt; leather, rubber, footwear; metal products, textiles, paper, building materials, chemicals, foods and beverages, clothing, shipbuilding, cheese and other dairy products, fertilizers, ceramics, cement, tobacco products.
NEW CALEDONIA	French overseas territory administered by high commissioner assisted by an appointive executive council and an elective general council.	franc	Melanesian dialects French	Coconuts, copra, coffee, cotton, manioc, corn, tobacco, bananas, pineapples, wheat, rice, kauri logs; cattle, pigs, horses, goats, sheep, hides; guano, trochus shell; nickel, chrome, manganese, iron, cobalt, copper, lead, platinum; canned meat.
NEW GUINEA, NETHERLANDS	A Dutch colony, its status undetermined pending negotiations with Indonesian government.	guilder	Papuan Dutch Negrito	Sago, coconuts, sweet potatoes, wild nutmeg, mace, copra; bird of paradise plumes; petroleum.
NEW HEBRIDES	British and French condominium administered by British and French resident commissioners.	Australian currency Bank of Indochina Notes	Melanesian dialects Pidgin English English French	Coconuts, copra, cocoa, coffee, yams, taro, manioc, fruits; kauri pine; cattle, pigs; trochus shells.
NEW ZEALAND	A member of the British Commonwealth with dominion status governed by a governor-general, cabinet and unicameral assembly.	New Zealand pound	English Maori	Wheat, oats, barley, seeds, kauri, gum; sheep, cattle, pigs, horses; hides, skins; fish; gold, silver, coal, copper, limestone, manganese, iron, tungsten; dairy products, meats, wool, clothing, lumber, woodwork, furniture, electrical and radio goods, motor assembly, printing, publishing, biscuits, confections, footwear, rubber products, chemical fertilizers, tobacco products, brewing.
NICARAGUA	Republic with a president, cabinet and a two-house legislature.	córdoba	Spanish	Coffee, sugar cane, sesame, corn, bananas, rice, cacao, cotton, beans; cattle; hardwoods; gold, silver; sugar, wood products.
NIGER	Territory of Fr. West Africa with a governor and an elective representative assembly.	franc	Sudanese Hamitic Arabic French	Millet, manioc, groundnuts, rice, wheat, cotton, gum arabic, kapoc, kidney beans, corn, onions, sorghum, dates, sugar cane; goats, sheep, cattle, asses, camels, horses; hides and skins, leather; natron, sodium sulphate, salt.
NIGERIA	A federated colony and protectorate of Great Britain with a governor-general, a council of ministers and a federal house of representatives.	pound	Sudanese languages Arabic English	Palm oil and kernels, cacao, groundnuts, cotton, rubber, bananas, benni seeds, shea nuts, yams, cassava, corn, rice, fruits, millet, coffee; cattle, sheep, goats; hides and skins; timber; tin, coal, columbite, lead, gold, silver, zinc; cigarettes, soap, sugar.
NIUE	Dependency of New Zealand administered by a resident commissioner.	New Zealand pound	Mixed Melanesian and Polynesian dialects English	Copra, sweet potatoes, bananas; hats, baskets.
NORFOLK ISLAND	Administered by Australia.	Australian pound	English	Citrus, passion fruits, bananas, cherry guavas; hides; fish.
NORTH BORNEO	British colony ruled by a governor and assisted by executive and legislative councils.	Malayan dollar	Malay Indonesian languages English Chinese	Rubber, coconuts, copra, tobacco, manila hemp, sago, rice, cutch, sugar, pepper, kapok, groundnuts, derris root, vegetables; timber; fish.
NORTHEAST (TERR. OF) NEW GUINEA	Trust territory of Australia governed by administrator of Papua.	Australian pound	Papuan Pidgin English English	Coconuts, copra, cocoa, dairying; timber; gold, silver, platinum; boat making.
NORTHERN IRELAND	Executive power vested in appointed governor and cabinet responsible to legislative two-house parliament.	pound	English and Gaelic	Potatoes, oats, flax, turnips, hay; cattle, sheep, pigs, poultry; basalt and igneous rocks, sand and gravel, grit and conglomerate, chalk, clays; linen, rayon, woolen goods, carpets, hosiery, cotton goods, shirts, collars, underwear, shipbuilding, aircraft, marine machinery, rope, tobacco, whiskey.
NORTHERN RHODESIA*	British protectorate administered by a governor and executive and legislative council.	pound	Bantu languages English	Corn, wheat, potatoes, tobacco, sorghum, millet, groundnuts, cassava, rice, beans, cow-peas, cotton; lumber; cattle and other livestock.
NORWAY	A constitutional, hereditary monarchy headed by the king, his council of state and a two-house, elective legislature.	krone	Norwegian	Hay, potatoes, oats, barley, wheat, rye, fruits, vegetables; dairy products, livestock; herring, cod and other fish; sulphur, iron, copper, zinc, silver, nickel, molybdenum; timber, pulp, cellulose, paper, canned foods, electro-chemical products, transportation equipment, salted, dried and canned fish, leather, basic metals, textiles, fertilizers, shipbuilding.
NYASALAND*	British protectorate administered by a governor and executive and legislative council.	pound	Bantu languages English	Tobacco, tea, cotton, pulses, tung-oil, sisal, corn, cassava, wheat, rice, millet, groundnuts, rubber, beeswax; timber; goats, cattle, pigs, sheep; hides, skins, meat, ghee, soap; gold, mica, corundum.
OMAN AND MUSCAT	An independent sultanate.	rupee (official) Maria Theresa dollar	Arabic	Dates, pomegranates, limes and other fruits, sugar cane; dried fish.
PAKISTAN	Self-governing republic of the British Commonwealth ruled by a president, cabinet and unicameral legislature.	Pakistani rupee	Indo-Aryan languages (Bengali, Urdu, Punjabi, etc.)	Rice, wheat, corn, jute, cotton, sugar cane, fruit, oilseeds, tobacco, tea, fibers; timber; cattle, goats, sheep, horses, camels, poultry; hides, skins, wool; fish; salt, copper, petroleum, chromite, gypsum, magnisite, sulphur, antimony; textiles, flour milling, cement, iron and steel foundries, sugar, leather, chemicals, glass, sportsgoods, handicrafts, surgical instruments.
PALAU ISLANDS	A civil administrative district in the Western Carolines and part of the United States Pacific trust territory.	dollar	Micronesian dialects	Coconuts, manioc, taro, pineapples, sweet potatoes, papayas; poultry, pigs, goats; fish; phosphate; handicrafts.
PANAMA	Republic with a president, two vice-presidents, and a one-house legislature.	balboa	Spanish	Bananas cacao, abaca, coconuts, rice, sugar cane, coffee, pineapples; cattle; hardwoods; gold; hides, sugar, wood products.
PAPUA TERRITORY	Australian colony governed by an administrator.	Australian pound	Papuan Pidgin English English	Coconuts, rubber, sweet potatoes, yams, taro, sago, rice, bananas, coffee, kapok, bamboo, sisal hemp, copra; shells, sponges; cattle, goats, poultry; gold, copper, manganese.
PARAGUAY	A centralized republic with a president, an appointed cabinet and a one-house legislature.	guarani	Spanish, Indian	Cotton, tobacco, sugar cane, rice, cassava, yerba maté, corn, citrus fruits; cattle, hides; lumber, quebracho; iron, manganese, copper; canned meats, vegetable oils, petit-grain oil, tobacco products.
PERU	A republic with a president, two vice-presidents, appointive cabinet and a two-house legislature.	sol	Spanish, Indian	Cotton, sugar, potatoes, barley, corn, rice, wheat, coca, quinoa, cacao, tobacco, coffee, quinine, flax, rubber, balata, guano; fish; livestock; petroleum, lead, zinc, copper, silver, gold, vanadium; textiles, foodstuffs, cement, leather, wool, hides, pharmaceuticals, paper products, clothing, metal products.

*Member of Federation of Rhodesia and Nyasaland.

POLITICAL DIVISION	GOVERNMENT	MONETARY UNIT	LANGUAGE	MAJOR PRODUCTS
PHILIPPINES	Republic governed by a president, cabinet and a bicameral legislature.	peso	Malayan languages (Tagalog, Visayan, etc.) English Spanish	Rice, sugar cane, copra, manila hemp (abacá), corn, tobacco, maguey, rubber, bananas, pineapples, mangoes, papaya, citrus fruits, other fruits; hogs, carabaos, cattle, horses, goats, sheep; fish; timber, gum resins, tan and dye barks, dye woods; gold, iron, copper, chromite, silver, manganese, asbestos, asphalt, guano, silica, coal, petroleum; sugar, textiles, distilling, dessicated coconuts, tobacco products, rice milling, cocoa, coconut oil, embroideries.
PITCAIRN ISLAND	British colony administered by a chief magistrate responsible to the governor of Fiji.	Fiji pound	English Tahitian	Fruits, vegetables, goats, poultry; handicraft.
POLAND	A Soviet-type "People's Republic" headed by a one-party legislative Sejm which elects an executive Council of Ministers. Acutal power in the hands of politburo, highest organ of communist party.	zloty	Polish	Potatoes, straw and hay, rye, sugar beets, mangolds, oats, barley, wheat, peas, beans, flax, hemp, rapeseed; livestock; fish; zinc, lead, coal, salt, iron ore, petroleum, natural gas, phosphates, lignite; iron and steel products, coke, foods and beverages, textiles, cement, lime, bricks, electrical goods, chemicals, wood, timber, paper, cellulose, leather and leather products, glass.
PORTUGAL	A "unitary corporative republic" with a president, premier, and a one-house, elective legislature.	escudo	Portuguese	Wheat, corn, oats, barley, rye, rice, French beans, potatoes, grapes, olives; livestock; cork, lumber, resin; sardines, tuna and other fish; copper pyrites, coal, copper, tin, kaolin, cement, wolfram, sulphur, tungsten, iron; wines, olive oil, canned sardines, textiles, porcelain, tiles, embroideries, lace.
PRINCIPE AND SÃO TOMÉ	Portuguese overseas province administered by a governor.	escudo	Bantu languages Portuguese	Cacao, coffee, coconuts, copra, palm oil, cinchona, bananas.
PUERTO RICO	A self-governing commonwealth associated with the U.S., with a governor, an executive council and a bicameral legislature.	dollar	Spanish, English	Sugar cane, tobacco, fruits, pineapples, grapefruit, coconuts, coffee, cotton, livestock, vegetables; molasses, embroideries, rum, canned fruit and juice, alcohol, cordials, tobacco products.
QATAR	Sheikdom under British protection.	rupee riyal	Arabic	Dates; pearl fishing, dried fish; camels; petroleum.
RÉUNION	French overseas department administered by a prefect and a council-general.	franc	French	Sugar, rum, vanilla, tapioca, essences, fruit and vegetable preserves.
RUANDA—URUNDI	Under United Nations trusteeship, administered by Belgium and governed by a vice-governor general.	franc	Bantu languages Flemish French	Foods; cattle; hides.
RUMANIA	A Soviet-type "People's Republic" with a 17-member presidium, cabinet of ministers and a one-house legislature. Supreme power resides in communist party politburo.	leu	Rumanian	Wheat, barley, rye, corn, oats, potatoes, sugar beets, hemp, flax, grapes, fruits, tobacco; lumber; sheep, cattle, pigs, horses; petroleum, natural gas, salt, coal, lignite, iron and copper ores, gold, silver, bauxite, lead, manganese, zinc; flour, brewing and distilling, iron and steel, metal products, textiles, wood and paper products.
RYUKYU IS.	Administered by the United States.	yen	Luchuan Japanese English	Sweet potatoes, sugar cane, rice, fruits, mulberries; swine, cattle, goats, horses, poultry; silkworms; fish; Panama hats, textiles, lacquer, pottery, china, glassware, tiles.
ST. HELENA	British colony with a governor, an executive and an advisory council.	pound	English	Hemp, lily bulbs, potatoes, tow, rope and twine, lace; sheep, goats, cattle, donkeys, poultry.
ST. PIERRE AND MIQUELON	French territory with a governor, privy council and elective general council.	franc	French	Fish, silver fox; dried cod and cod liver oil; sienna earth, yellow ocher.
SALVADOR	Republic with a president and a one-house legislature.	colón	Spanish	Coffee, cotton, corn, tobacco, henequen, sugar cane, rice; balsam and other woods; gold, silver; cotton textiles, henequen bags, sugar.
SAMOA, EASTERN	Possession of the United States with a governor and a bicameral legislature.	dollar	English Samoan	Copra, taro, breadfruit, yams, bananas, arrowroot, pineapples, oranges; mats.
SAMOA, WESTERN	Under United Nations trusteeship administered by New Zealand.	New Zealand pound	Samoan English	Copra, cocoa beans, bananas, taro; fish; pigs, poultry.
SAN MARINO	Republic with two regents, council of state, one-house legislature.	lira	Italian	Cattle, hides, wines, quarrying.
SARAWAK	British colony administered by a governor and an executive and legislative council.	Malayan dollar	Malay Indonesian languages Chinese English	Rice, rubber, sago, pepper, coconuts, pineapples, tobacco, coffee, fruits, vegetables; timber, rattan cane, guttas; buffalo, cattle, pigs, goats; fish; petroleum, gold, antimony, phosphate, cutch.
SAUDI ARABIA	Absolute monarchy, with premier and cabinet responsible to the king, and advisory councils.	riyal	Arabic	Dates, sorghums, wheat, rice, henna, coffee, fruits, nuts, vegetables, honey, gum, sesame oil; fish; camels, sheep, goats, cattle, donkeys, poultry, horses; hides, wool, clarified butter, charcoal, pottery, tile, salt, soap, weaving; petroleum, gold, pearls.
SCOTLAND	A secretary of state for Scotland in the British cabinet has in his charge four departments for Scotland (agriculture, education, health and home.) Authority in other matters is exercised by other members of the British cabinet.	pound	English and Gaelic	Turnips, potatoes, wheat, barley, sugar beets, flax, vegetables, forage crops, fruits; sheep, cattle, pigs, horses; coal, iron ore, granite, sandstone, limestone, slate, lead, clay; steel, machinery, tools, locomotives, electronic equipment, linoleum, shipbuilding and repair, watches, clocks, jute, bagging, burlap, textiles, hosiery, thread, lace, carpet, yarn, chemicals, whiskey, ale, paper, bricks and other clay products, preserves, boots and shoes, furniture.
SENEGAL	Territory of Fr. West Africa with a governor and an elective representative assembly.	franc	Sudanese languages Arabic French	Millet, groundnuts, manioc, rice, corn, gum arabic, palm nuts, honey, sweet potatoes, sisal, indigo; sheep, goats, cattle, asses, horses; fish; titanium, zircon; brick, pottery, weaving, jewelry, oil cakes.
SEYCHELLES	A British colony ruled by a governor and legislative and executive councils.	rupee	English French	Coconuts, cinnamon, patchouli, copra, vanilla, corn; guano; salted fish, tortoise shell, calipee.
SIERRA LEONE	A British colony and protectorate ruled by a governor and legislative and executive councils.	pound	Sudanese languages English	Palm oil and kernels, kola nuts, ginger, piassava, groundnuts, cocoa; diamonds, iron ore, chrome ore.
SIKKIM	A protectorate of India ruled by a maharaja and a council.	rupee	Nepali Tepcha Bhutia	Millet, corn, pulse, rice, fruits; cattle; woolen cloth.
SINGAPORE	British Crown colony administered by a governor, council of ministers and legislative assembly.	Malayan dollar	Chinese Malay Hindi English	Rubber, coconuts, fruits, vegetables, rice, coffee, tapioca, tobacco, sweet potatoes, pepper, pineapples; pigs, poultry, cattle; fish; tin, tin smelting, rubber milling, coconut milling, soap, beer, pineapple canning, biscuits, brick making, shipping, textiles, palm oil, cigarettes, gasoline, kerosene.

POLITICAL DIVISION	GOVERNMENT	MONETARY UNIT	LANGUAGE	MAJOR PRODUCTS
SOCIETY ISLANDS	Part of Fr. Polynesia governed from Tahiti.	franc	Polynesian	Copra, vanilla, pearls, mother-of-pearl, vanilla, phosphates, sugar, rum.
SOLOMON ISLANDS	A protectorate administered by the British high commissioner of the Western Pacific.	Australian pound	Melanesian Pidgin English English	Copra, pigs, poultry; trochus shell, turtle shell, bêche-de-mer.
SOLOMON ISLANDS (NORTHERN)	Part of the territory of New Guinea and governed as an Australian trust territory.	Australian pound	Melanesian Pidgin English English	Coconuts, copra, bananas, yams, taro, fruits; trochus shell, green snail shell, rubber.
SOMALILAND	Under United Nations trusteeship and administered by Italy with U. N. and local advisory councils.	Somalo	Somali Arabic Italian	Sugar, cotton, tobacco, bananas, aromatic gums, resin, kapok, grains, beans; camels, goats, sheep, cattle; skins, hides; tunny, mother-of-pearl.
SOMALILAND, BRITISH	British protectorate ruled solely by governor, assisted by advisory councils.	Indian rupee East African shilling	Somali Arabic	Millet, sorghum, corn; sheep, goats, camels, cattle; skins, hides; gums, salt.
SOMALILAND, FRENCH	Overseas territory of France with a governor and an elective representative assembly.	Djibouti franc	Hamitic languages Arabic French	Boats, sheep; salt.
SOUTHERN RHODESIA†	A self-governing colony and member of British Commonwealth with governor and elective executive and legislative councils.	pound	Bantu languages English	Corn, tobacco, groundnuts, wheat, potatoes, citrus and other fruits; cattle, sheep, pigs, goats; meats, hides; gold, asbestos, chromite, coal; footwear, apparel, cigarettes, flour, groundnut oil, wood products.
SPAIN	A nominal monarchy governed by a chief of state. The legislative Cortés prepares laws subject to the veto of the chief of state. A king is to be chosen by a regency council upon the death or incapacitation of the chief of state.	peseta	Spanish Catalan	Wheat, barley, potatoes, oranges, olives, oats, rye, rice, corn, peas, beans, grapes, onions, sugar beets, esparto, flax, hemp, pulse, cork, nuts; pigs, sheep, goats, donkeys, mules, horses, poultry; sardines, tuna, cod and other fish; coal, lignite, iron ore, lead, iron pyrites, potash, zinc, mercury, sulphur, copper; textiles, wines, olive oil, paper, cement, hides, preserved and canned fish and shellfish, paper products.
SPANISH SAHARA	Spanish territory, consisting of Saguia el Hamra and Rio de Oro, ruled by sub-governors.	peseta	Arabic Spanish	Barley, corn; goats, sheep, camels; fish.
SUDAN	A republic with a bicameral parliament and council of ministers. Executive power resides temporarily in a council of state.	Egyptian pound	Arabic Sudanese Hamitic languages English	Cotton, cotton seed, gum arabic, Senna leaves and pods, groundnuts, sesame, millet, dates, dom nuts (vegetable ivory), wheat, shea nuts; sheep, goats, cattle, camels, asses; mahogany; hides and skins, ivory, gold, salt, trochus shell, mother-of-pearl.
SURINAM (see Guiana, Neth.)				
SWAZILAND	British protectorate governed by a resident commissioner under the High Commissioner for Basutoland, Bechuanaland and Swaziland.	pound	Bantu languages English	Tobacco, corn, groundnuts, kaffir-corn, wheat, oats, rye, barley, fruits; cattle, goats, sheep, pigs; butter; hides, skins; asbestos, gold, tin.
SWEDEN	A constitutional hereditary monarchy with a prime minister, council of state and a two-house, elective legislature.	krona	Swedish	Hay, sugar beets, potatoes, fodder crops, oats, wheat, rye, barley; forest products, cattle, pigs, sheep, horses, poultry; fish; iron ore, sulphur, arsenic, zinc, copper, silver, gold, lead, manganese; lumber and wood products, machinery, textiles, iron and steel and metal goods, chemicals, dairy products, electric power, tobacco products, brick, porcelain and glass, shipbuilding, matches.
SWITZERLAND	A republic with a president, vice-president, an executive federal council and a two-house, elective legislature.	franc	German, French, Italian, Romansch	Wheat, potatoes, sugar beets, rye, oats barley, fruits, tobacco; livestock; salt, iron, manganese; dairy products, textiles, watches and clocks, chemicals, foods, wines, dyes, instruments.
SYRIA (See United Arab Republic)	Province of United Arab Republic.	Syrian pound	Arabic Turkish Kurdish	Wheat, barley, sorghum, corn, cotton, lentils, chickpeas, sesame, vegetables, olives, grapes, tobacco (Latikia); sheep, goats, cattle, donkeys, camels, horses, poultry; wool, hides, skins; gypsum; leather, textiles, food, tobacco, wine, flour.
TANGANYIKA TERRITORY	Under United Nations trusteeship and administered by Great Britain. Ruled by a governor and a legislative and executive council.	East African shilling	Bantu languages Swahili English	Sisal, cotton, coffee, bananas, tobacco, papain, beeswax, grains, sugar; cattle, goats, sheep; hides, skins; wood, timber, wax, gum arabic; diamonds, gold, tin, mica, salt, camphor, tungsten.
TANGIER	International zone of Tangier was dissolved in 1956 and joined to independent Morocco.	franc peseta	Arabic French Spanish English	Wheat, barley, chickpeas; soap, canned fish, essential oils.
THAILAND (SIAM)	Constitutional monarchy ruled by a king, prime minister and a legislative assembly.	baht	Thai Khmer	Rice, rubber, coconuts, tobacco, cotton, corn, beans; teak and other woods; bullocks, buffalo, horses, elephants; fish; tin, wolfram.
TIBET	Theocracy. Nominally independent but under effective Chinese Communist control. Religious affairs are directed by the Dalai Lama.	sang	Tibetan	Barley, wheat, pulse, corn, vegetables, rice; yaks, asses, sheep, goats, donkeys; hides, wool, furs, musk; borax, salt, gold; cult objects.
TIMOR, PORTUGUESE	Portuguese overseas province ruled by a governor.	escudo	Malay Portuguese	Coffee, copra, sandalwood, wax, cocoa; hides, shells.
TOGO	Under United Nations trusteeship administered by France as an autonomous republic.	franc	Sudanese languages French	Palm oil and kernels, tapioca, cocoa, yams, coffee, plantains, corn, groundnuts, cotton, copra, kola, cassava, rubber; sheep, goats, pigs, cattle, asses, horses.
TOKELAU ISLANDS	An island territory of New Zealand administered by a high commissioner.	New Zealand pound	Samoan	Coconuts, fiber, taro, copra; pigs, chickens; fish; hats, mats.
TONGA	Constitutional monarchy under Br. protection ruled by queen with cabinet and legislative assembly.	Tongan pound	Tongan English	Copra, bananas, fungus, candlenuts; pigs, cattle, goats.
TRIESTE	Former free territory was dissolved in 1954 and joined to Italy and Yugoslavia respectively.	lira	Italian and Slovene	Vineyards, shipyards, oil refineries, steel, vegetable oils, fishing.
TRINIDAD AND TOBAGO *	British colony with a governor and executive and legislative councils.	B.W.I. dollar	English	Coffee, cocoa, sugar cane, citrus fruits; cattle; petroleum, asphalt; rum, canned grapefruit juice, sugar.
TRISTAN DA CUNHA	Possession of Great Britain governed by an administrator and an island council responsible to St. Helena.	pound	English	Potatoes, fruit; cattle, sheep; fish.

* Member of The West Indies (British Caribbean Federation)

† Member of Federation of Rhodesia and Nyasaland.

POLITICAL DIVISION	GOVERNMENT	MONETARY UNIT	LANGUAGE	MAJOR PRODUCTS
TRUCIAL OMAN	Seven sheikhdoms under British protection with a British agent.	rupee riyal	Arabic	Dates, grains, vegetables; fishing, pearl fishing.
TUAMOTU ARCHIPELAGO	Part of Fr. Polynesia governed from Tahiti.	franc	Polynesian dialects French	Copra, pearls, pearl shell.
TUBUAI ARCHIPELAGO	Part of Fr. Polynesia governed from Tahiti.	franc	Roman Catholic Tribal religions	Copra, arrowroot.
TUNISIA	A republic with a president, a cabinet of secretaries of state, and an assembly.	franc	Arabic French Berber	Wheat, barley, oats, corn, sorghum, beans, grapes, olives, citrus fruits, dates, alfa grass, almonds, oranges, shaddocks, pistachios, cork; sheep, goats, cattle, horses, asses, mules, camels, pigs; fish, sponges; flour milling, oil refining, wool spinning, pottery, leather, silk weaving; phosphates, iron ore, lignite, lead, zinc.
TURKEY	A republic with a president and a one-house, elective legislature.	pound	Turkish	Tobacco, cereals, olives, cotton, figs, nuts, fruits; cattle, livestock; fish; chromium, iron ore, copper, coal, lignite, meerschaum, manganese; textiles, iron and steel, paper, rugs, olive oil.
UGANDA	British protectorate controlled by a governor with executive and legislative councils. Native kings and their assemblies rule locally.	East African shilling	Bantu and Sudanese languages English	Cotton, coffee, plantains, millet, cotton seed, tobacco, chilies, sugar cane, rubber; cattle, sheep, goats; hides, skins; tin; cigarettes.
UNION OF SOUTH AFRICA	Member of British Commonwealth with a governor general, cabinet, elective senate and house of assembly.	pound	Afrikaans English Bantu languages Bushman	Corn, wheat, potatoes, oats, kaffir-corn, barley, tobacco, sugar cane, tea, citrus fruits, rye, groundnuts, grapes, pineapples; cattle, sheep, goats, pigs, horses, donkeys, mules; gold, coal, diamonds, copper, asbestos, manganese, lime, limestone, platinum, chrome, iron, silver, tungsten, mercury, vanadium, tin, antimony, silver, scheelite, talc; hides, chemicals, wool, footwear, rubber, machinery, clothing, textiles, food, vehicles, printing, furniture, building materials.
U.S.S.R.	A federation of 15 socialist republics with a two-chamber legislative assembly (Supreme Soviet) which elects the executive presidium and council of ministers. The policy of the state is largely defined by the Central Committee of the communist party, the only legal party.	ruble	Russian, Ukrainian, White Russian, Uzbek, Tatar, Azerbaizhani, Georgian, Lithuanian, Armenian, Yiddish, Latvian, Mordvinian, Chuvash, Tadzhik, Esthonian, Kazakh.	Wheat, rye, oats, barley, corn, sugar beets, sunflower seeds, cotton, forage crops, flax, hemp, potatoes, tobacco; cattle, sheep, goats, pigs, horses; lumber, furs; fish; coal, peat, petroleum, iron, lignite, copper, lead, zinc, nickel, aluminum, phosphates, manganese, gold, sulphur, potash, asbestos, platinum, salt, chromite; steel, machinery, textiles, sugar, flour, meats, automobiles, paper, synthetic rubber, foods, wines, chemicals.
UNITED ARAB REPUBLIC	The union of Egypt and Syria as the United Arab Republic was proclaimed on February 1, 1958 in Cairo. The new state possesses a president, cabinet and unicameral legislature with its capital located at Cairo.	Egyptian and Syrian pound	See Egypt and Syria	See Egypt and Syria.
UNITED STATES	Federal republic with a president, vice-president and two-house legislature.	dollar	English	Corn, hay, tobacco, wheat, cotton, oats, soy beans, potatoes, barley, sorghums, peanuts, rye, rice, citrus fruits, fruits, sugar beets, sugar cane, vegetables, tree nuts, feed grains and hay; livestock; fish; lumber; petroleum, coal, cement, iron, natural gas, copper, sand and gravel, zinc, lead, stone, gold, silver, molybdenum, bauxite, phosphates, mica, sulphur; foods, transportation equipment, machinery, primary metal products, electrical machinery, textiles, chemicals, paper and wood products, beverages, dairy products.
UPPER VOLTA	Territory of Fr. West Africa with a governor and an elective representative assembly.	franc	Sudanese languages French	Millet, groundnuts, corn, karite nuts and butter (shea nut), vegetables, rice, tapes, cotton, kapok, sesame, sorghum, tea; sheep, goats, cattle, asses, pigs; gold, manganese, copper, silver, chrome, lignite, iron.
URUGUAY	A republic governed (as of March, 1955) by a National Council, an appointed cabinet and a two-house elective legislature.	peso	Spanish	Wheat, corn, linseed, oats, sunflower seeds, peanuts, barley, rice, citrus fruits, peaches, grapes, vegetables, tobacco; sheep, cattle; gold; meat, hides, wool, textiles, leather, boots and shoes, wines.
VATICAN CITY	The Pope, who is elected for life by the cardinals of the Roman Catholic Church, exercises absolute legislative, executive and judicial power. He appoints a governor of the state and delegates diplomatic and judicial power.	lira	Italian Latin	
VENEZUELA	A republic with a president, appointive cabinet, and elective two-house legislature.	bolivar	Spanish	Coffee, cacao, sugar cane, cotton, tobacco, coconuts, tonka beans; balata, dividivi, rubber; livestock; fish and pearls; petroleum, iron, gold, coal, copper, phosphates, magnesite, asphalt, salt, diamonds; textiles, leather, sugar, cement, wood products, foodstuffs, beverages, soap, tobacco products, meats, milk; refined petroleum.
VIETNAM	Divided in two parts by Armistice Line Sept. 1954. North of 17th parallel is Communist controlled "republic". South is a republic with a president and an assembly.	piaster	Khmer (Annamese) Lao	Rice, corn, sugar, tobacco, coffee, fruits, manioc, betel nuts, arrowroot, tea, cotton, areca nut, medicinal plants, cardamom, soya, rubber, copra, groundnuts, haricots, sweet potatoes, cinnamon; mulberries, bamboo, silk; cattle, buffalo, pigs; lumber; gold, tin, copper, coal, zinc, iron, cement, limestone, calamine, tungsten, manganese, phosphate, lead, bauxite.
VIRGIN ISLANDS (U. S.)	Territory of the U. S. with an appointed governor.	dollar	English, Creole	Sugar cane, vegetables, citrus fruits, coconuts; cattle; fish; rum, bay rum, bay oil, molasses, handicrafts, sugar, lime juice, hides, bitters.
VOLCANO ISLANDS	Administered by the United States.	dollar yen	Japanese	Sugar cane; fish; sulphur.
WEST INDIES	A federation of colonies within the Br. Commonwealth with a governor-general, council of state and bicameral legislature.	B.W.I. dollar	English	Sugar cane, cocoa, coffee; citrus fruit, bananas, coconuts, pimentos, ginger; edible oil, margarine, honey, nutmeg; sugar, molasses, rum, bitters; petroleum, asphalt, charcoal.
YAP	Administered by a civil administrator of the Palau district as a part of the United States Pacific trust territory.	dollar	Micronesian dialects	Coconuts, breadfruit, sweet potatoes, taro, manioc, vegetables; poultry, pigs; fish.
YEMEN†	Independent kingdom.	riyal	Arabic	Coffee, barley, wheat, millet, sesame; cattle, hides; fish.
YUGOSLAVIA	A Soviet-type republic combining 6 republics under a central government with a president, fed. executive council and two-house elective legislature. Actually ruled by Communist League.	dinar	Serbian-Croatian, Slovenian Macedonian	Wheat, barley, rye, oats, corn, sugar beets, hemp, hops, opium, tobacco, flax, alfalfa, vegetables, fruits; sheep, cattle, pigs, goats, horses, poultry; coal, lignite, iron, copper, lead, salt, zinc, mercury, antimony, petroleum, bauxite, chrome, cement; lumber, textiles, foods, beverages, sugar, wood-distillates, wines.
ZANZIBAR	British protectorate nominally ruled by a sultan but under the effective control of a governor and a legislative and executive council.	East African shilling	Bantu languages Swahili English	Sisal, cotton, coffee, bananas, tobacco, papain, beeswax, grains, sugar; cattle, goats, sheep; hides, skins; wood, gum arabic; diamonds, gold, tin, mica, salt, camphor, tungsten.

† Allied member of the United Arab Republic.

WHAT A MAP IS . . .

A *map* is like a picture of the earth taken from high in the air.

A *globe* is the only true map of the earth because it shows us the roundness of the earth. A globe shows us all the lands and seas in their true shapes and positions. A globe is really a *model* or small copy of our earth.

A doll is a model of a person.

A toy airplane is a model of a real airplane.

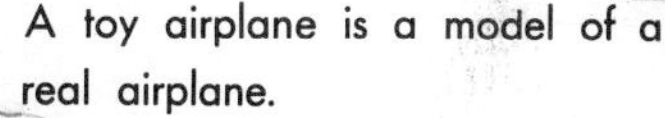

ROUTES

MAN-MADE FEATURES

NATURAL FEATURES

A map can show us many things that are located upon the earth. A few of them are shown here.

WHAT A MAP DOES . . .

1. A map tells you in which *direction* one object or place is from another.

You can find direction on the ground in the following ways.....

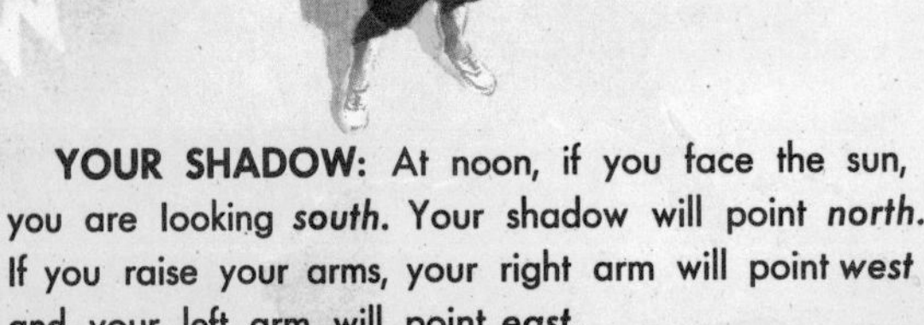

YOUR SHADOW: At noon, if you face the sun, you are looking *south*. Your shadow will point *north*. If you raise your arms, your right arm will point *west* and your left arm will point *east*.

THE NORTH STAR: If you face the North Star, you are facing *north*.

NORTH STAR

BIG DIPPER

The two pointer stars of the Big Dipper point to the North Star.

HOW T

A MAGNETIC COMPASS

The needle compass poin ward *north*.

The compass-rose tells you where *north* is located on your map.

USE A MAP...

TO FIND YOUR WAY: You should turn the map so that N on the compass rose will point *north*. When this is done the position of the features on the map will be the same as on the earth.

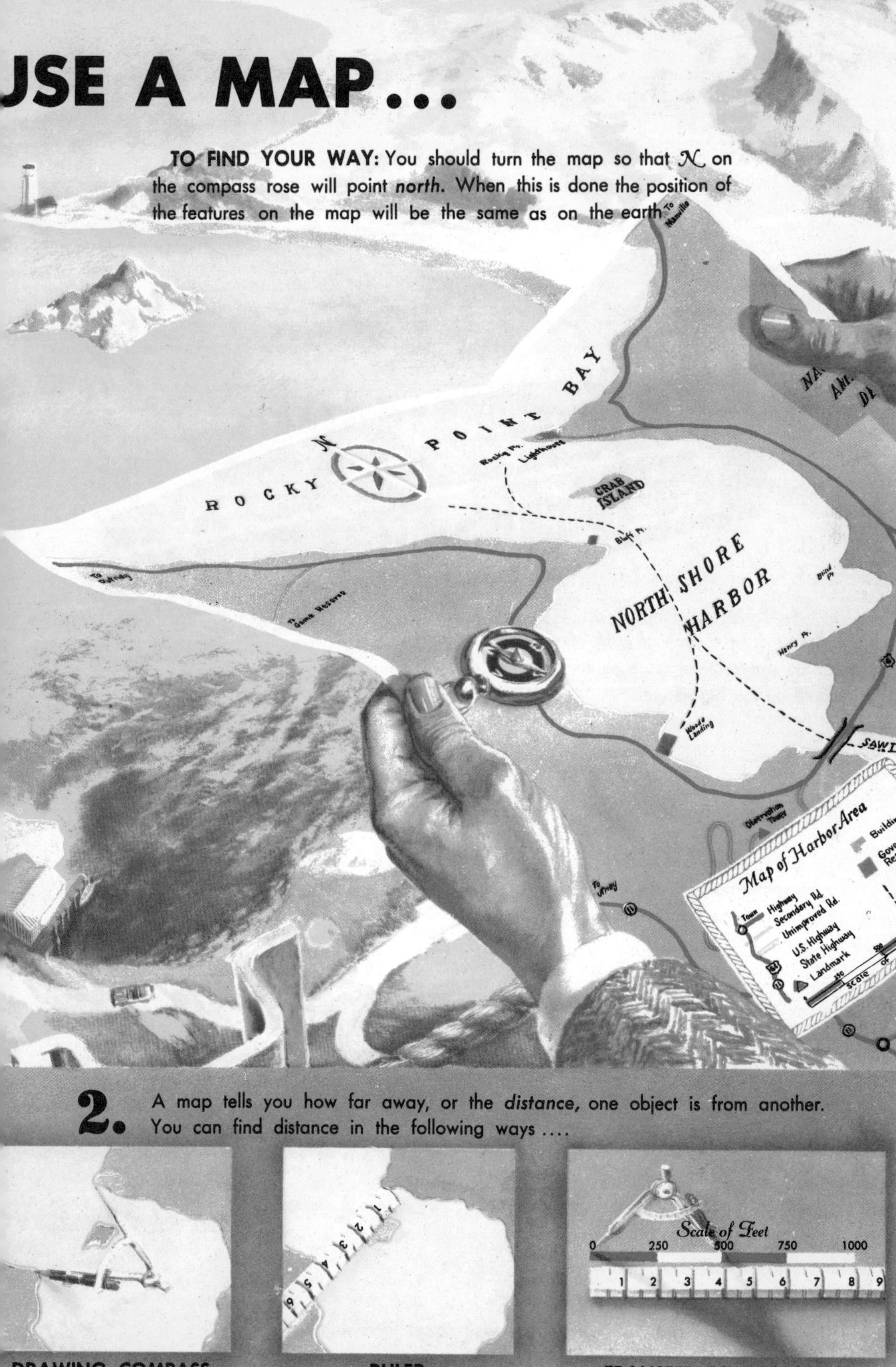

2. A map tells you how far away, or the *distance,* one object is from another. You can find distance in the following ways ....

DRAWING COMPASS

RULER

TRANSFER TO BAR SCALE

WHAT SCALE MEANS...

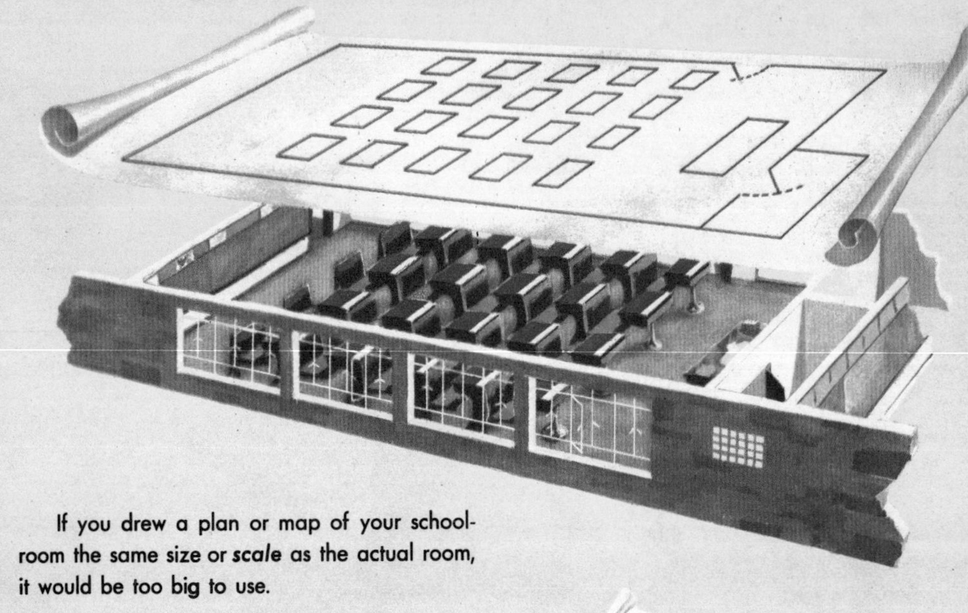

If you drew a plan or map of your schoolroom the same size or *scale* as the actual room, it would be too big to use.

If you drew the plan or map somewhat smaller, it still would be too large to use easily.

A still smaller plan or map could be drawn to a convenient size or scale.

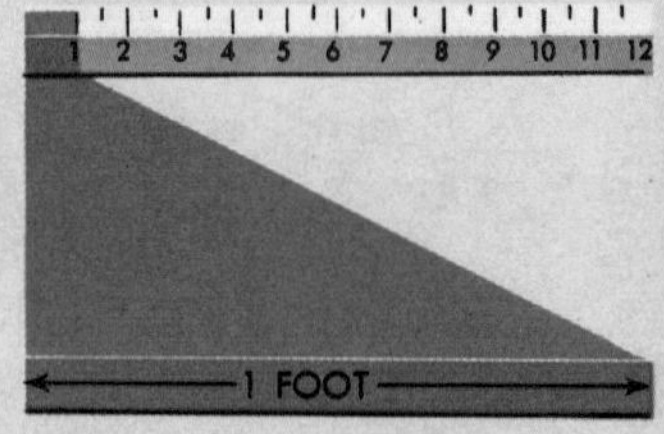

We do this by making a small length, such as an inch, stand for a large one, such as a foot or a mile. This diagram shows one inch equaling a foot.

The maps on this page will show you how *bar scales,* all of the same length, can stand for different distances.

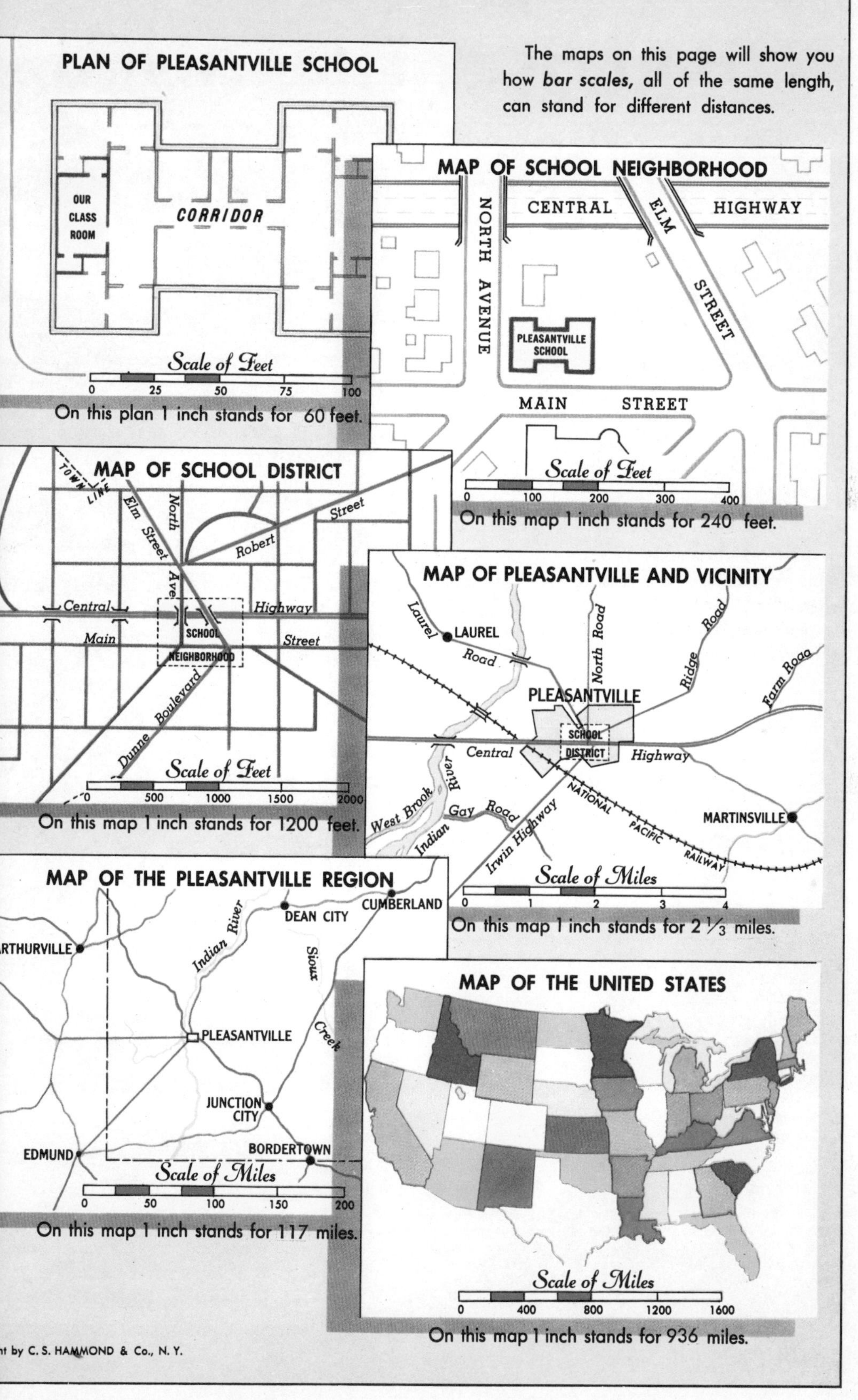

On this plan 1 inch stands for 60 feet.

On this map 1 inch stands for 240 feet.

On this map 1 inch stands for 1200 feet.

On this map 1 inch stands for 2 1/3 miles.

On this map 1 inch stands for 117 miles.

On this map 1 inch stands for 936 miles.

PROJECTION: CHANGIN

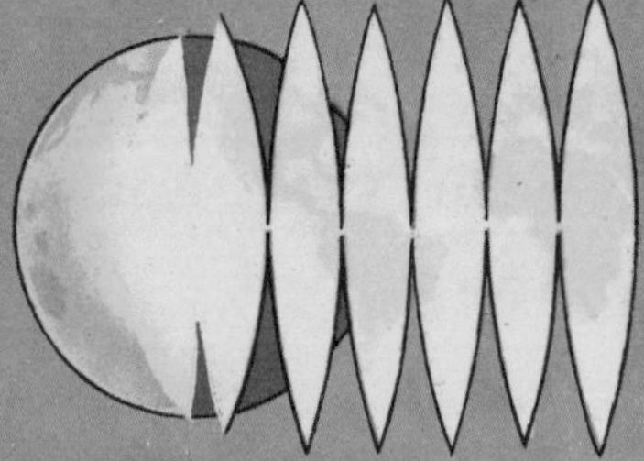

We can peel a globe as we can peel an orange. However, a map separated in this manner is difficult to use.

A better way to make a world map is to *proje*
features of the round globe onto a flat surface. W
something like this when we make shadow pictures o
wall with our hands.

Greenland as it appears on the world map shown at the right.

Greenland as it appears on a globe.

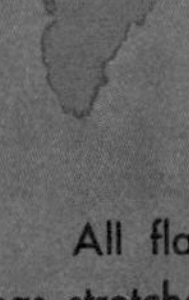

All flat maps show some areas stretched out of size or shape. Here is an example of a *distorted* area on a flat map.

A GLOBE INTO A FLAT MAP

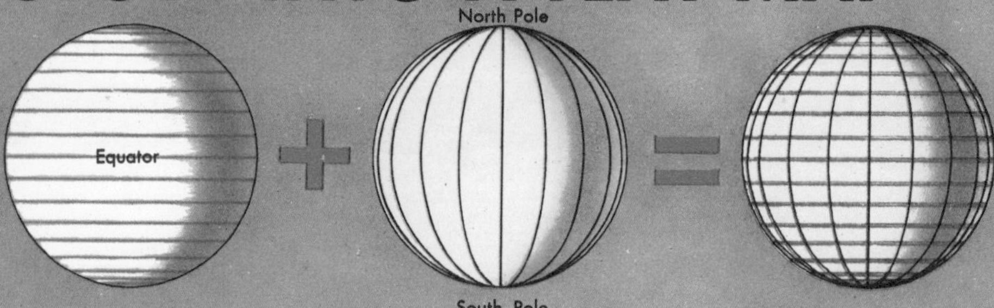

Latitude – imaginary lines that extend around the globe in the same direction as the equator.

Longitude – imaginary half-circles that extend from the North Pole to the South Pole.

When placed together they form a *grid* which helps to find the location of any place on earth.

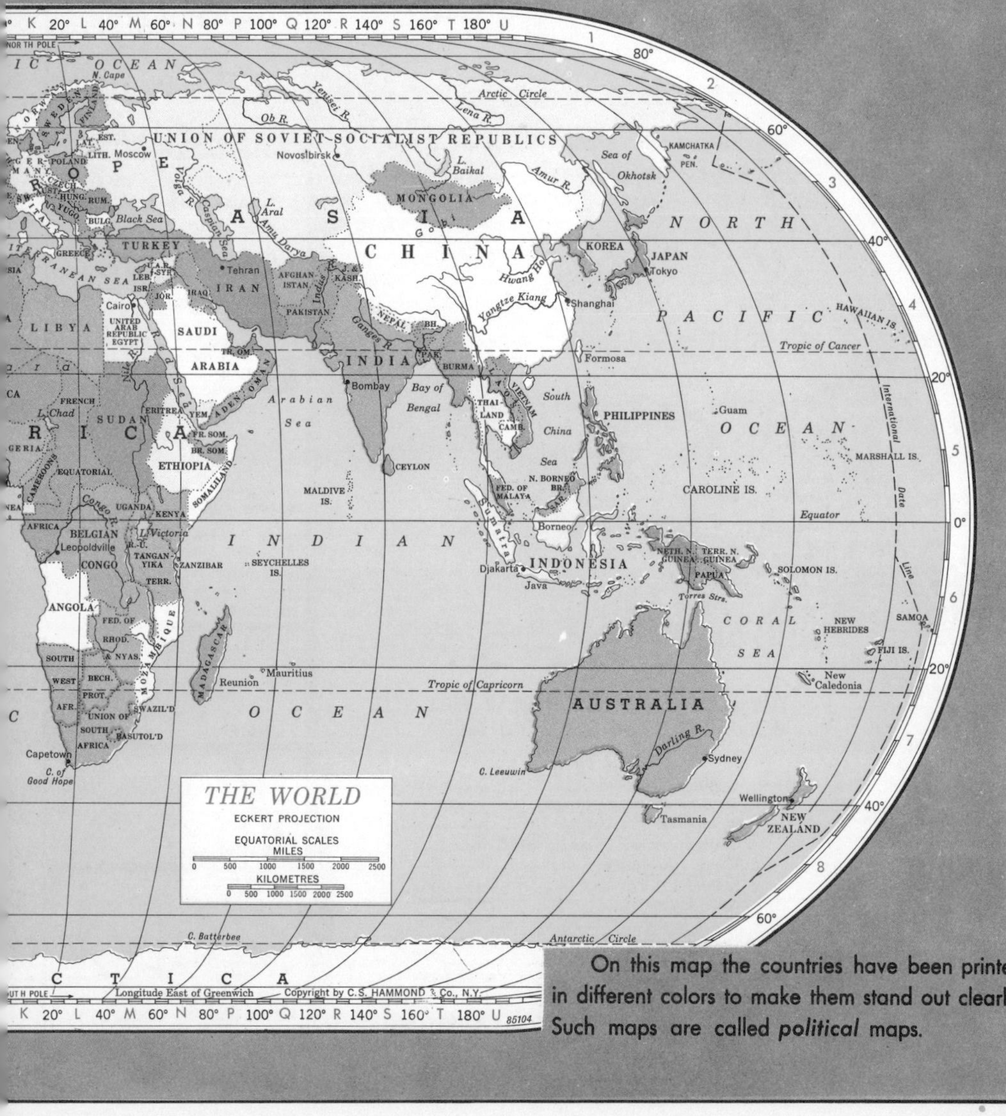

THE WORLD
ECKERT PROJECTION
EQUATORIAL SCALES
MILES
0 500 1000 1500 2000 2500
KILOMETRES
0 500 1000 1500 2000 2500

Longitude East of Greenwich — Copyright by C.S. HAMMOND & Co., N.Y.

On this map the countries have been printed in different colors to make them stand out clearly. Such maps are called *political* maps.

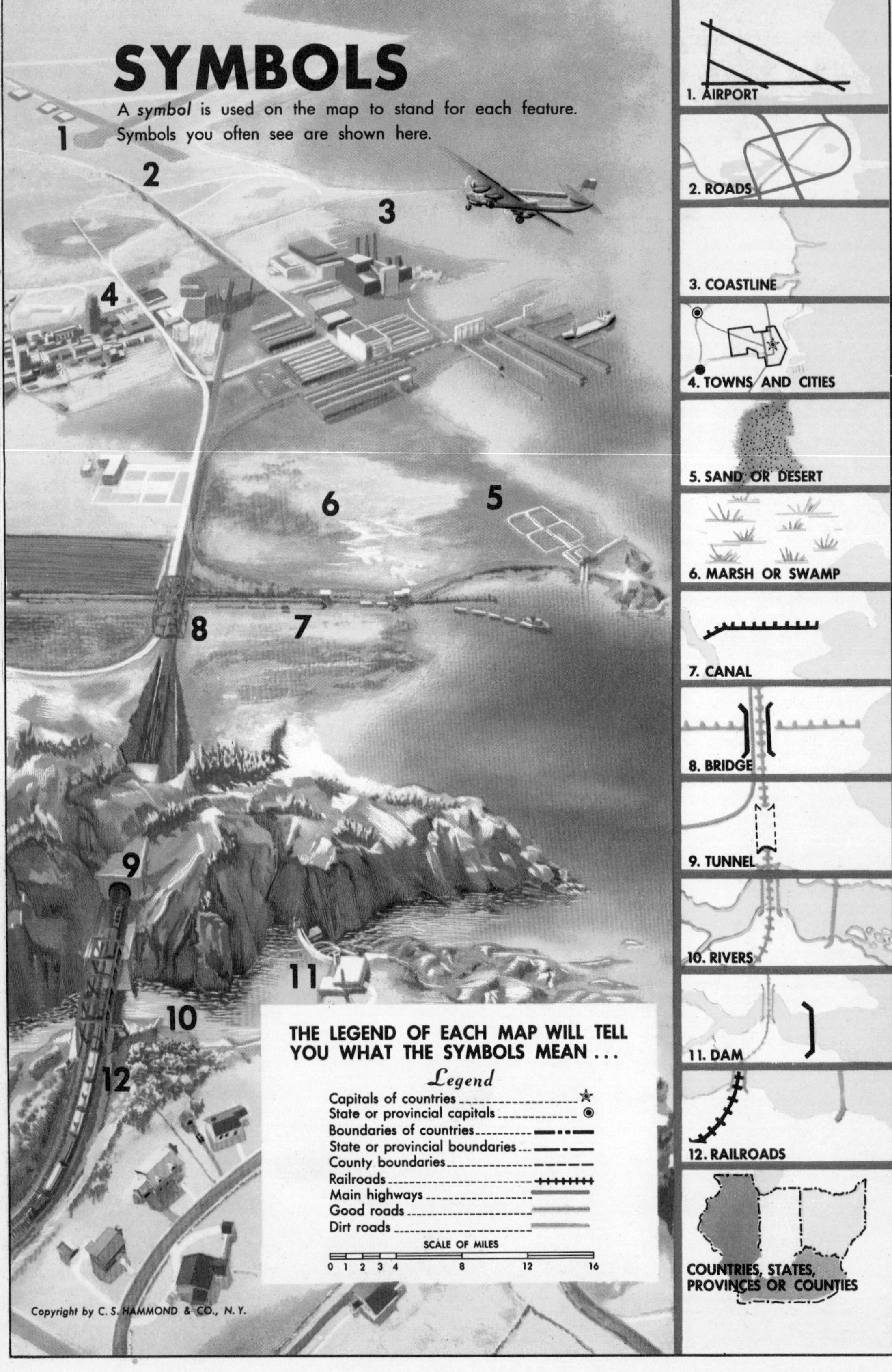

SYMBOLS
A *symbol* is used on the map to stand for each feature.
Symbols you often see are shown here.
1
2
3
4
5
6
7
8
9
10
11
12
1. AIRPORT
2. ROADS
3. COASTLINE
4. TOWNS AND CITIES
5. SAND OR DESERT
6. MARSH OR SWAMP
7. CANAL
8. BRIDGE
9. TUNNEL
10. RIVERS
11. DAM
12. RAILROADS
COUNTRIES, STATES, PROVINCES OR COUNTIES
THE LEGEND OF EACH MAP WILL TELL YOU WHAT THE SYMBOLS MEAN . . .
Legend
Capitals of countries
State or provincial capitals
Boundaries of countries
State or provincial boundaries
County boundaries
Railroads
Main highways
Good roads
Dirt roads
SCALE OF MILES
0 1 2 3 4 8 12 16

CONTOURS: WHAT THEY ARE... HOW TO USE THEM...

Some maps show highlands and lowlands. There are many ways of doing this on a map. One important way of showing the height and shape of land on a map is by means of ***contour lines.*** A contour is a line drawn on a map to connect all points that are the same height or ***altitude*** above the sea.

Sea-level means the level of the ocean. We start measuring from sea-level because it is the same all over the world.

If you made a clay model of the mountain shown above and sliced it into layers of the same thickness, the cuts would show on the surface as lines or ***contour lines.***

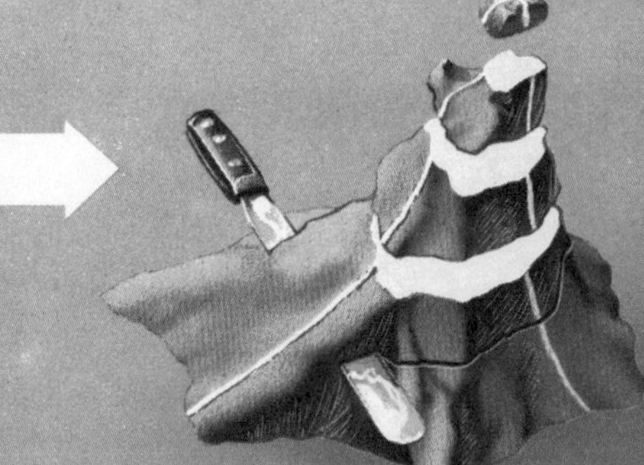

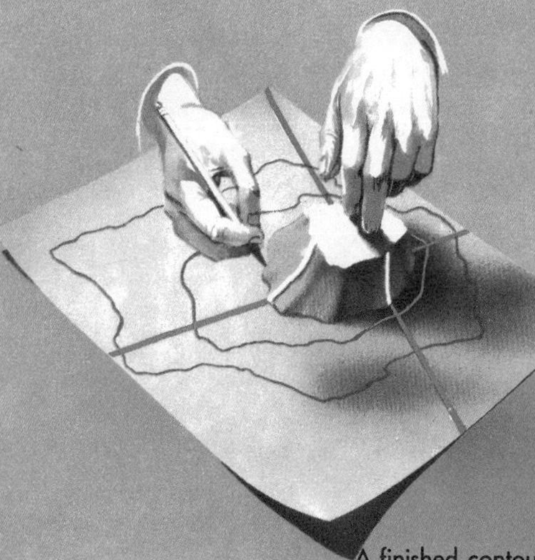

If you traced the outline of each layer on a piece of paper, your drawing would look something like this. Contour lines spaced closely together indicate a steep slope. Lines spaced far apart indicate a gentle slope.

A finished contour map may appear as...

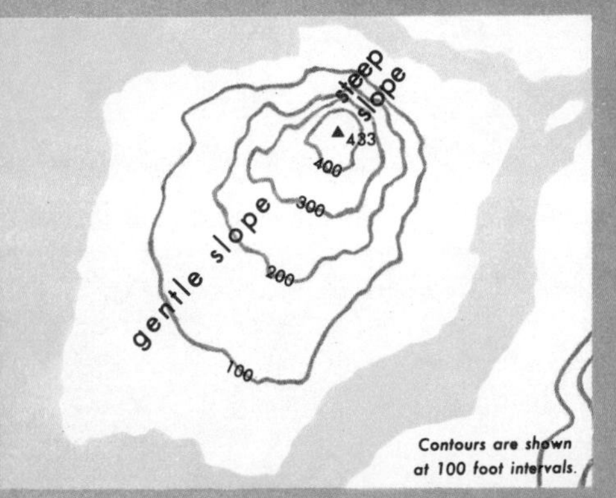

Lines with altitudes given in feet.

OR

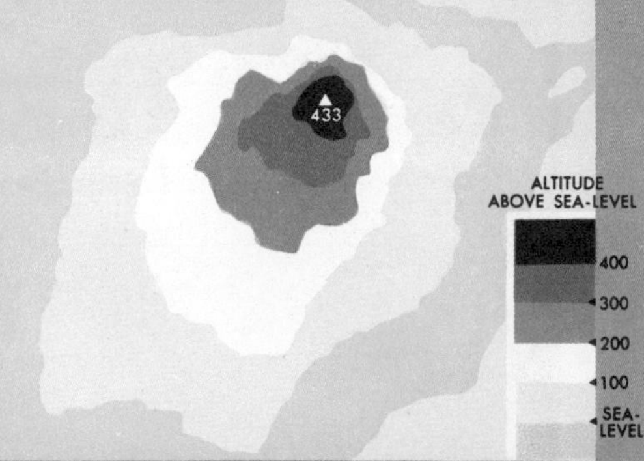

Colored areas with an altitude scale

FACTS ABOUT OUR

This picture shows the trip our earth takes around the sun every year. The circular path that it follows in ***revolving*** around the sun is known as its ***orbit.***

HOW WE KNOW THE EARTH IS ROUND...

We know that our earth is round because we can see a ship go out of sight as it sails below the horizon.

NIGHT AND DAY

Our earth turns or ***rotates*** on its ***axis*** once every 24 hours. We are carried by the spinning earth from daylight into darkness and, about 12 hours later, into daylight again.

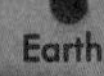

The sun is much larger than the earth. This is how our earth would look if it were placed next to the sun.

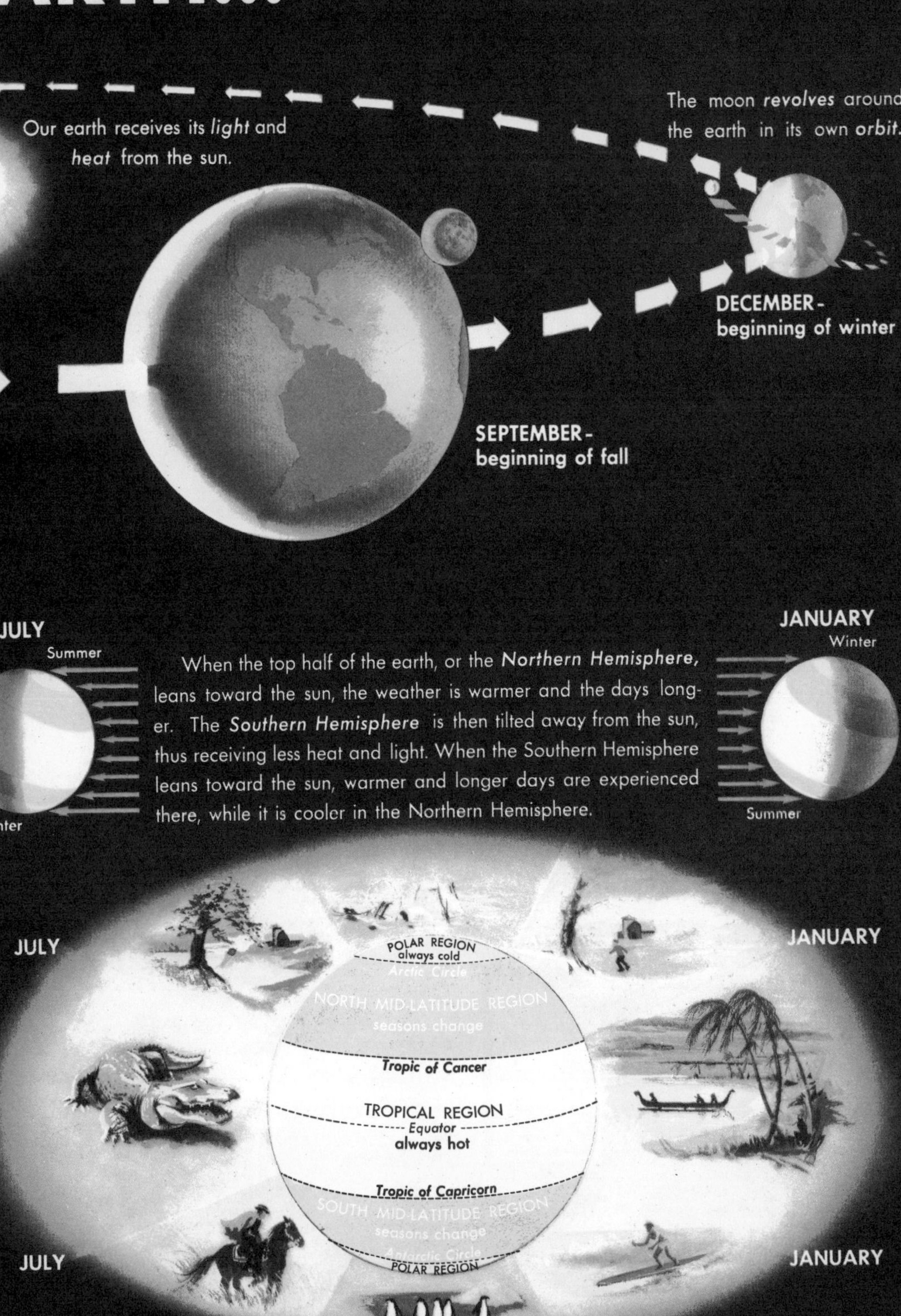
ARTH...
Our earth receives its *light* and *heat* from the sun.
The moon *revolves* around the earth in its own *orbit*.
DECEMBER - beginning of winter
SEPTEMBER - beginning of fall
JULY
Summer
inter
JANUARY
Winter
Summer
When the top half of the earth, or the *Northern Hemisphere,* leans toward the sun, the weather is warmer and the days longer. The *Southern Hemisphere* is then tilted away from the sun, thus receiving less heat and light. When the Southern Hemisphere leans toward the sun, warmer and longer days are experienced there, while it is cooler in the Northern Hemisphere.
JULY
JANUARY
POLAR REGION
always cold
Arctic Circle
NORTH MID-LATITUDE REGION
seasons change
Tropic of Cancer
TROPICAL REGION
Equator
always hot
Tropic of Capricorn
SOUTH MID-LATITUDE REGION
seasons change
Antarctic Circle
POLAR REGION
JULY
JANUARY

MAN'S STORY IN MAPS..
FOREST
DWELLERS
80°
ASIA
BERING
STRAIT
AMERICAN INDIANS
NORTH
AMERICA
ATLANTIC OCEAN
EUROPE
FERTILE
CRESCENT
EGYPT
Desert
EGYPTIAN
CIVILIZATION
after 3000 B. C.
AFRICA
INDIAN
CIVILIZATION
after 1000 B. C.
CHINESE
CIVILIZATION
after 2200 B. C.
40°
PACIFIC OCEAN
20°
Pacific Islanders
AZTEC
CIVILIZATION
after 1300 A. D.
MAYAN
CIVILIZATION
after 400 A. D.
0°
Equator
INCA
CIVILIZATION
after 1100 A. D.
INDIAN
OCEAN
N
W
E
S
PEOPLES OF
THE EQUATORIAL
FOREST
AUSTRALIA
20°
Islanders
Easter
Island
SOUTH
AMERICA
New
Zealand
40°
Pacific
ATLANTIC OCEAN
ATLANTIC OCEAN
20° 0° 20° 40° 60° 80° 100° 120° 140° 160° 180° 160° 140° 120° 100° 80° 60° 40°
60°
THE WORLD AT THE
DAWN OF HISTORY
Copyright by C. S. HAMMOND & CO., N. Y.

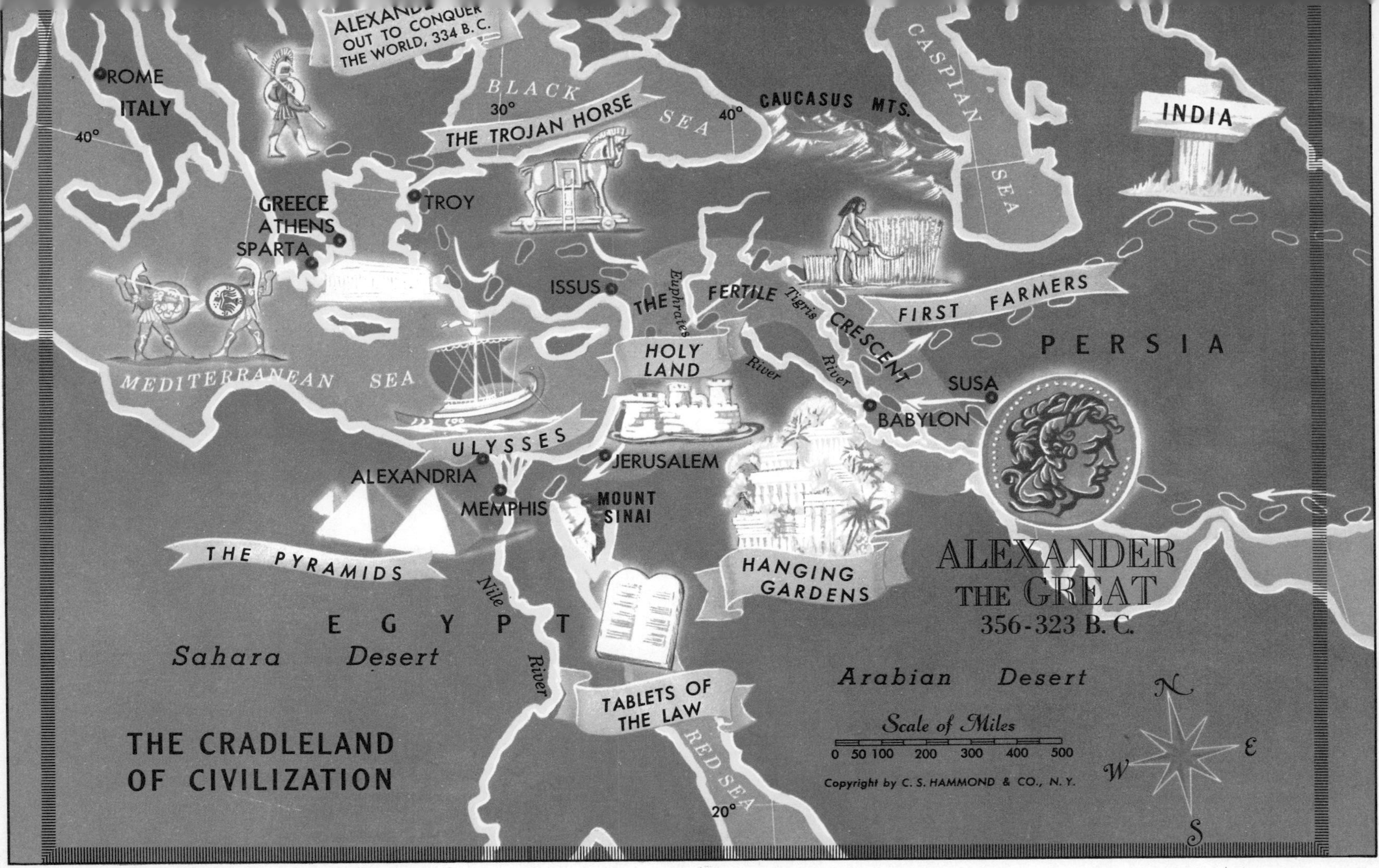
ALEXANDER OUT TO CONQUER THE WORLD, 334 B.C.
ROME
ITALY
40°
BLACK SEA
30°
THE TROJAN HORSE
40°
CAUCASUS MTS.
CASPIAN SEA
INDIA
GREECE
ATHENS
SPARTA
TROY
ISSUS
THE FERTILE CRESCENT
Euphrates River
Tigris River
FIRST FARMERS
PERSIA
HOLY LAND
MEDITERRANEAN SEA
SUSA
BABYLON
ULYSSES
JERUSALEM
ALEXANDRIA
MEMPHIS
MOUNT SINAI
THE PYRAMIDS
HANGING GARDENS
ALEXANDER
THE GREAT
356-323 B.C.
Nile River
EGYPT
Sahara Desert
TABLETS OF THE LAW
Arabian Desert
Scale of Miles
0 50 100 200 300 400 500
Copyright by C. S. HAMMOND & CO., N. Y.
N
E
W
S
RED SEA
20°
THE CRADLELAND
OF CIVILIZATION

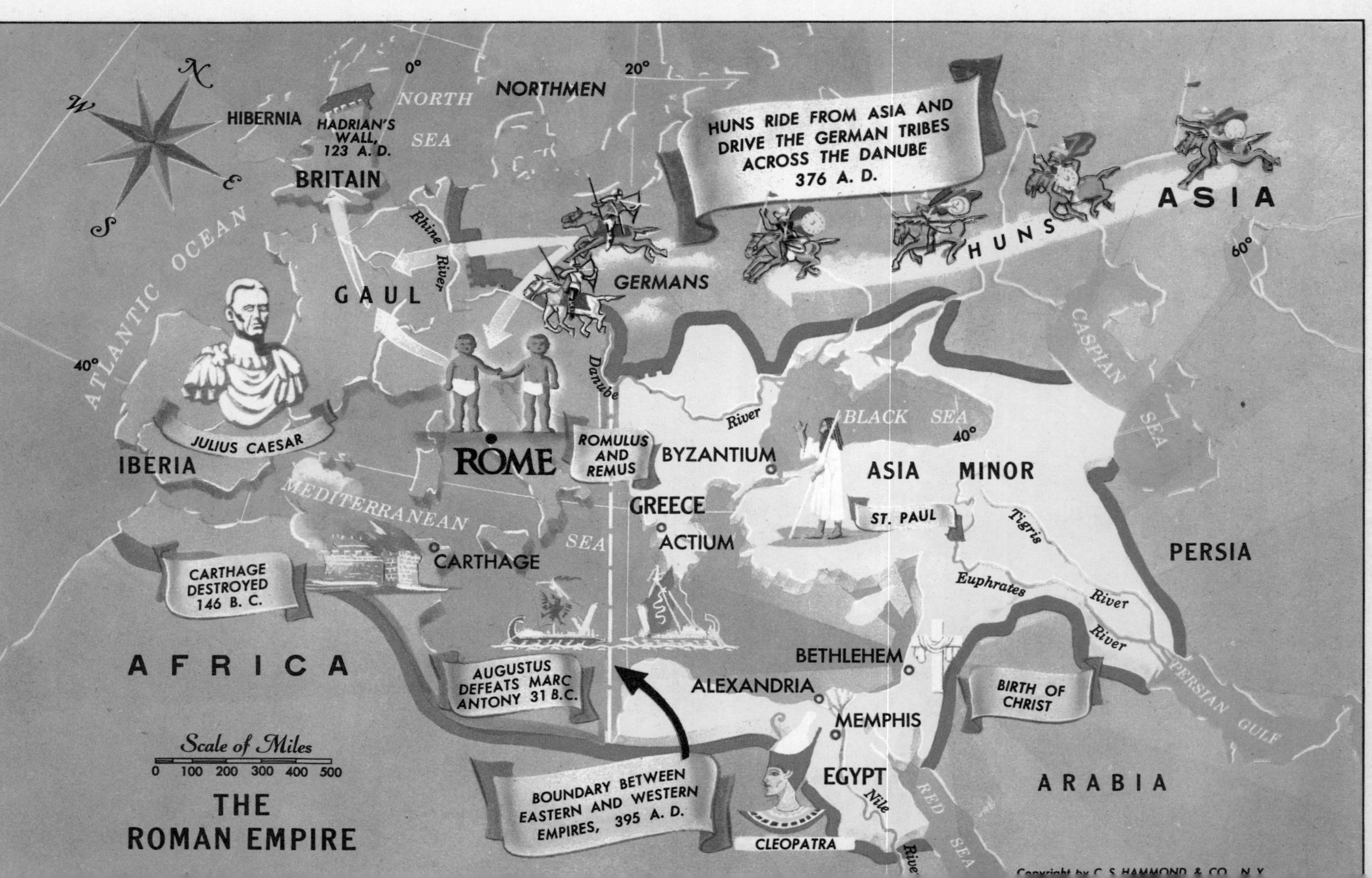
HIBERNIA
HADRIAN'S WALL, 123 A. D.
BRITAIN
NORTH SEA
NORTHMEN
HUNS RIDE FROM ASIA AND DRIVE THE GERMAN TRIBES ACROSS THE DANUBE 376 A. D.
HUNS
ASIA
GAUL
Rhine River
GERMANS
ATLANTIC OCEAN
CASPIAN SEA
JULIUS CAESAR
IBERIA
ROME
ROMULUS AND REMUS
Danube River
BYZANTIUM
BLACK SEA
ASIA MINOR
GREECE
ACTIUM
ST. PAUL
Tigris River
Euphrates River
PERSIA
MEDITERRANEAN SEA
CARTHAGE
CARTHAGE DESTROYED 146 B. C.
AFRICA
AUGUSTUS DEFEATS MARC ANTONY 31 B.C.
BETHLEHEM
ALEXANDRIA
MEMPHIS
BIRTH OF CHRIST
PERSIAN GULF
EGYPT
Nile River
RED SEA
ARABIA
CLEOPATRA
BOUNDARY BETWEEN EASTERN AND WESTERN EMPIRES, 395 A. D.
Scale of Miles
0 100 200 300 400 500
THE ROMAN EMPIRE
N W E S
0° 20° 40° 60°
Copyright by C. S. HAMMOND & CO., N. Y.

THE OLD WORLD IN THE MIDDLE AGES 570 to 1400 A. D.

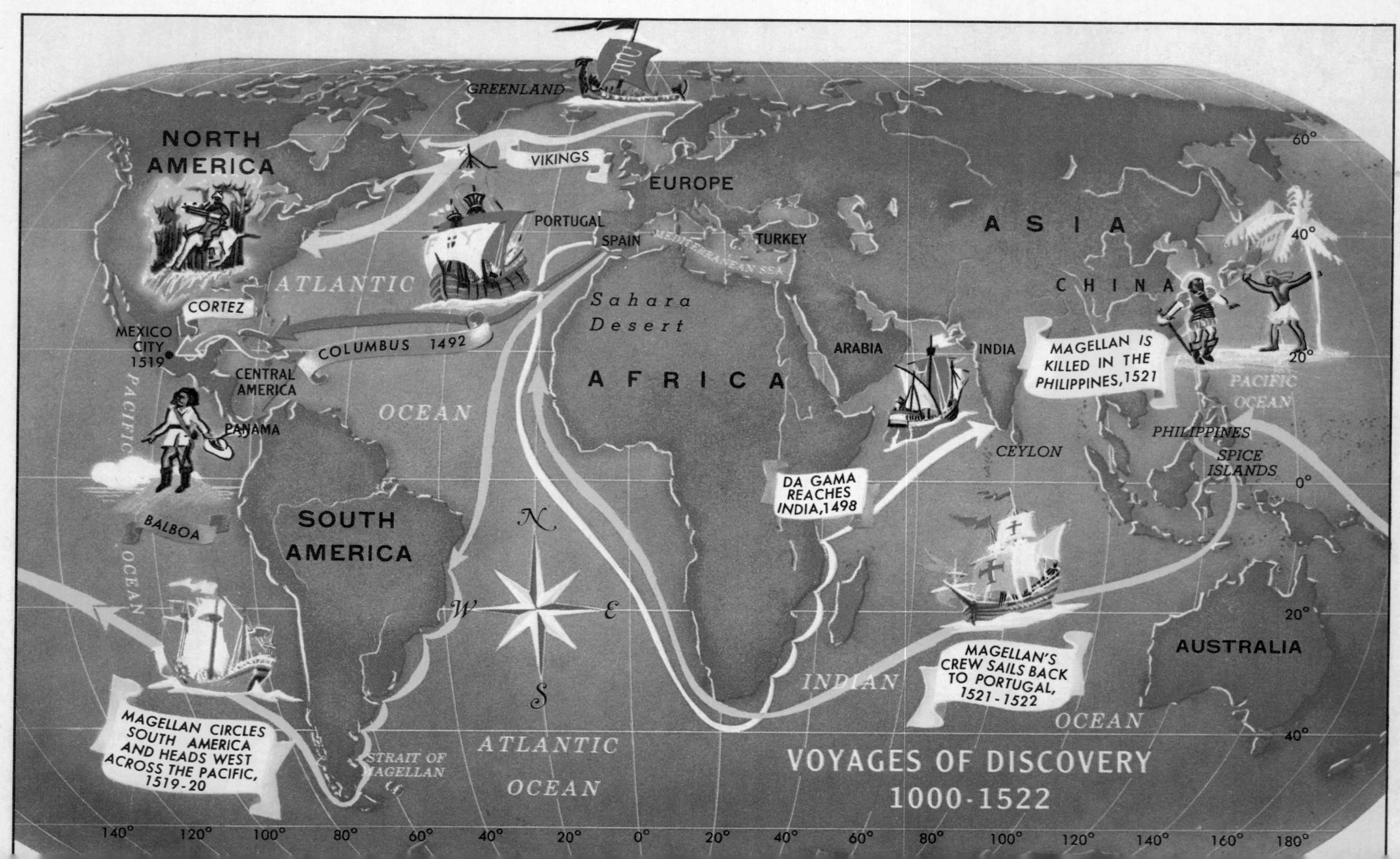
VOYAGES OF DISCOVERY
1000-1522
NORTH AMERICA
SOUTH AMERICA
EUROPE
ASIA
AFRICA
AUSTRALIA
GREENLAND
VIKINGS
PORTUGAL
SPAIN
TURKEY
MEDITERRANEAN SEA
Sahara Desert
ARABIA
INDIA
CEYLON
CHINA
PHILIPPINES
SPICE ISLANDS
PACIFIC OCEAN
ATLANTIC OCEAN
INDIAN OCEAN
CORTEZ
MEXICO CITY 1519
CENTRAL AMERICA
PANAMA
BALBOA
STRAIT OF MAGELLAN
COLUMBUS 1492
DA GAMA REACHES INDIA, 1498
MAGELLAN IS KILLED IN THE PHILIPPINES, 1521
MAGELLAN'S CREW SAILS BACK TO PORTUGAL, 1521-1522
MAGELLAN CIRCLES SOUTH AMERICA AND HEADS WEST ACROSS THE PACIFIC, 1519-20
N
W
E
S
60°
40°
20°
0°
20°
40°
140°
120°
100°
80°
60°
40°
20°
0°
20°
40°
60°
80°
100°
120°
140°
160°
180°

UNITED
NATIONS 1945
CANADA CONFEDERATION
1867
THE WORLD WARS
1914-1918 &
1939-1945
MEDICAL &
SCIENTIFIC
RESEARCH
NORTH
AMERICA
EUROPE
ASIA
RUSSIAN
REVOLUTION
1917
JAPAN
SUEZ
CANAL
1869
THE INDUSTRIAL
REVOLUTION
ABOUT 1800
CHINA
ARABIA
INDIA
CONSTITUTION
OF THE UNITED
STATES, 1789
AFRICA
ATOMIC
BOMB 1945
PACIFIC
OCEAN
CENTRAL
AMERICA
PANAMA
CANAL,
1914
ATLANTIC
OCEAN
STANLEY AND
LIVINGSTONE 1871
INDIAN OCEAN
SOUTH
AMERICA
LATIN AMERICAN
INDEPENDENCE
AFTER 1800
ATOMIC
ENERGY
N
W
E
S
AUSTRALIA
20°
0°
40°
THE MODERN AGE
1700 TO THE PRESENT
ELECTRIC POWER,
COMMUNICATION
AND ELECTRONICS
SUPERSONIC
TRAVEL
140°
120°
100°
80°
60°
40°
20°
0°
20°
40°
60°
80°
100°
120°
Copyright by C. S. HAMMOND & CO., N. Y.

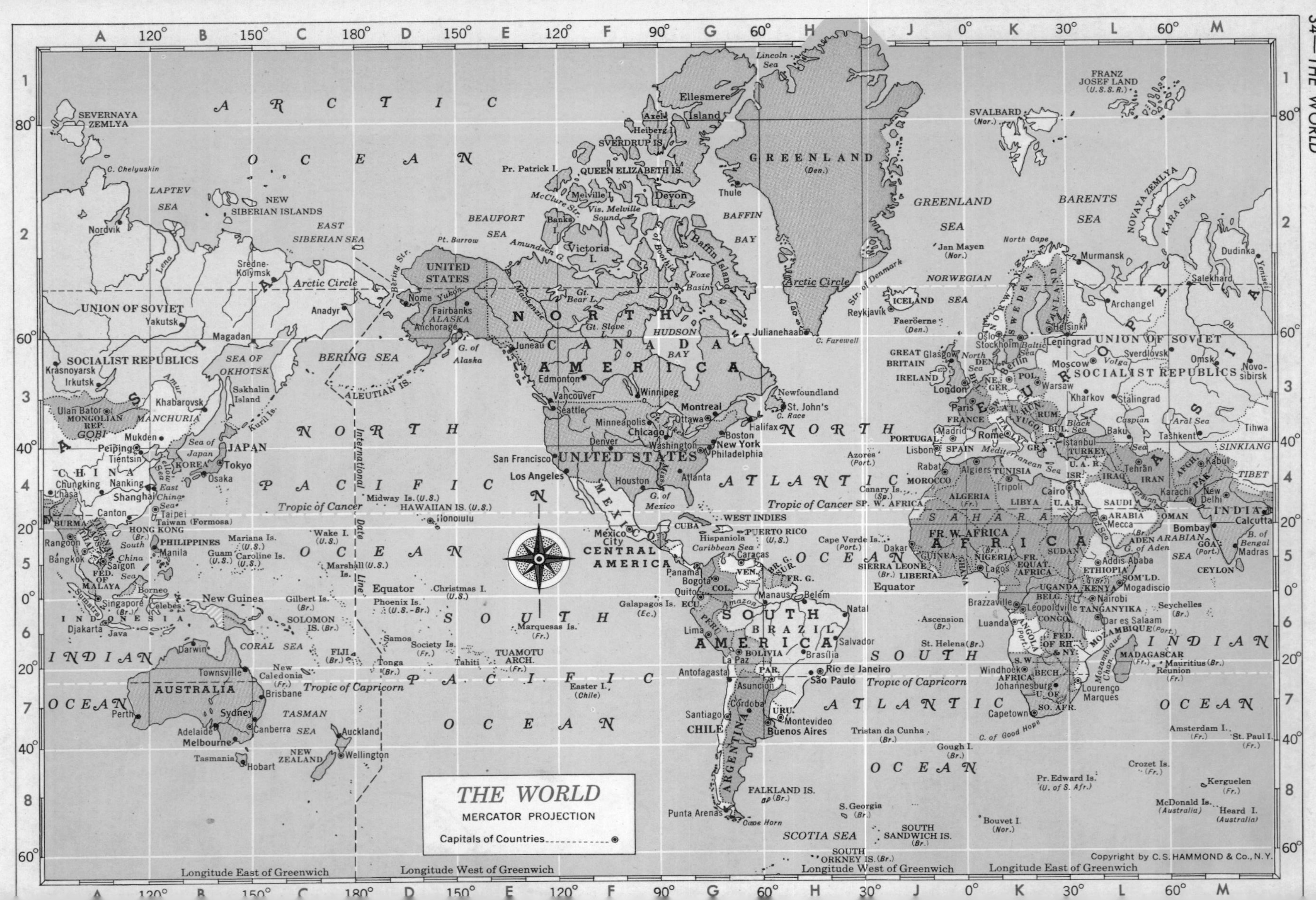
THE WORLD
MERCATOR PROJECTION
Capitals of Countries
Copyright by C.S. HAMMOND & Co., N.Y.
Longitude East of Greenwich
Longitude West of Greenwich
ARCTIC OCEAN
NORTH PACIFIC OCEAN
SOUTH PACIFIC OCEAN
NORTH ATLANTIC OCEAN
SOUTH ATLANTIC OCEAN
INDIAN OCEAN
NORTH AMERICA
SOUTH AMERICA
EUROPE
AFRICA
ASIA
AUSTRALIA
UNION OF SOVIET SOCIALIST REPUBLICS
UNITED STATES
CANADA
GREENLAND
International Date Line
Tropic of Cancer
Tropic of Capricorn
Arctic Circle
Equator

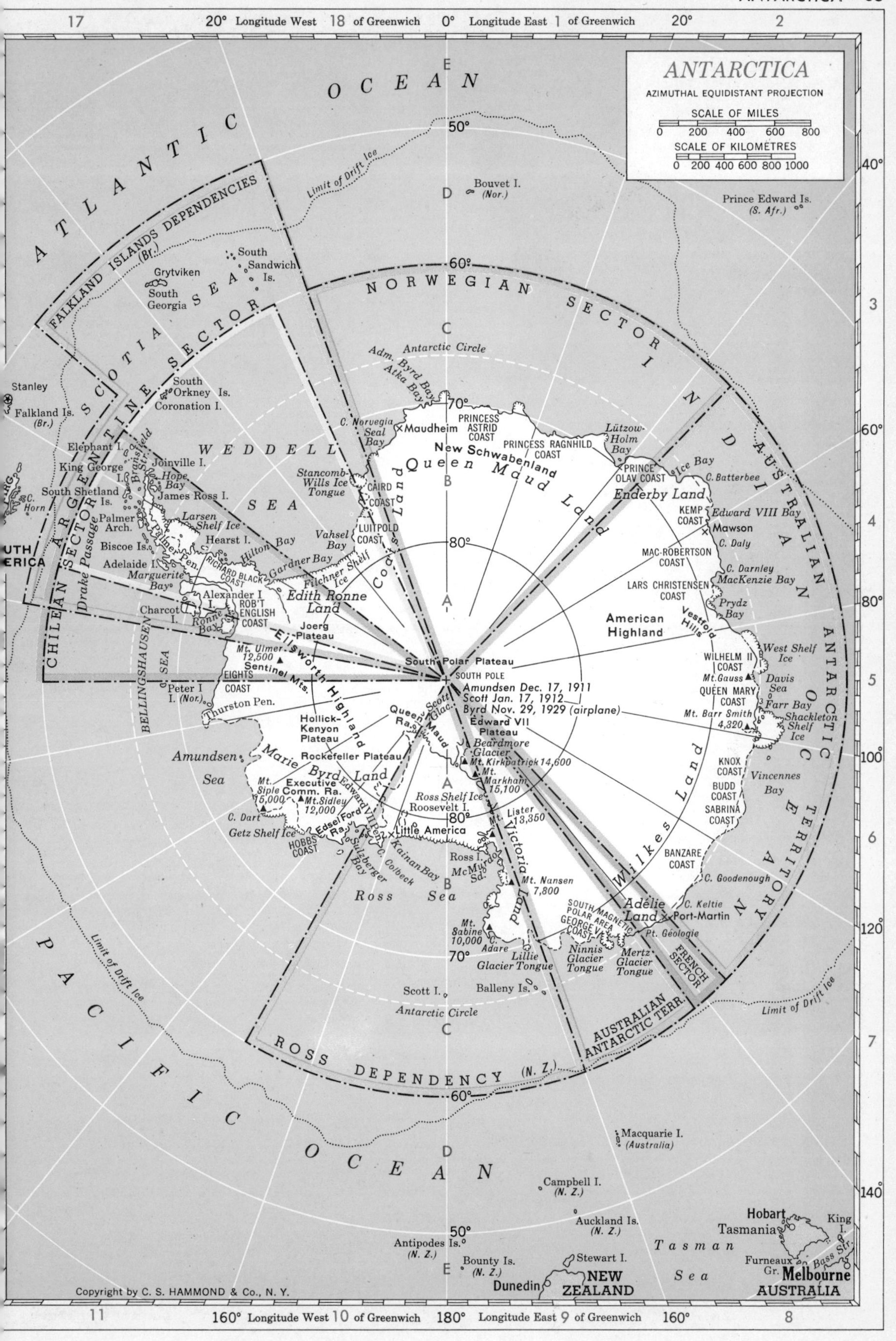
ANTARCTICA
AZIMUTHAL EQUIDISTANT PROJECTION
SCALE OF MILES
0 200 400 600 800
SCALE OF KILOMETRES
0 200 400 600 800 1000
20° Longitude West 18 of Greenwich 0° Longitude East 1 of Greenwich 20°
160° Longitude West 10 of Greenwich 180° Longitude East 9 of Greenwich 160°
ATLANTIC OCEAN
PACIFIC OCEAN
FALKLAND ISLANDS DEPENDENCIES (Br.)
SCOTIA SEA
ARGENTINE SECTOR
CHILEAN SECTOR
NORWEGIAN SECTOR
INDIAN
AUSTRALIAN ANTARCTIC TERRITORY
FRENCH SECTOR
AUSTRALIAN ANTARCTIC TERR.
ROSS DEPENDENCY (N. Z.)
Limit of Drift Ice
Antarctic Circle
Bouvet I. (Nor.)
Prince Edward Is. (S. Afr.)
Grytviken
South Georgia
South Sandwich Is.
South Orkney Is.
Coronation I.
Stanley
Falkland Is. (Br.)
Elephant I.
King George I.
South Shetland Is.
C. Horn
Drake Passage
Bransfield Str.
Joinville I.
Hope Bay
James Ross I.
Palmer Arch.
Biscoe Is.
Adelaide I.
Marguerite Bay
Alexander I I.
Charcot I.
Palmer Pen.
Larsen Shelf Ice
Hearst I.
Hilton Bay
Gardner Bay
RICHARD BLACK COAST
ROB'T ENGLISH COAST
Ronne Bay
WEDDELL SEA
Stancomb-Wills Ice Tongue
Vahsel Bay
CAIRD COAST
LUITPOLD COAST
Coats Land
Filchner Shelf Ice
Edith Ronne Land
Joerg Plateau
Adm. Byrd Bay
Atka Bay
C. Norvegia
Seal Bay
Maudheim
PRINCESS ASTRID COAST
PRINCESS RAGNHILD COAST
New Schwabenland
Queen Maud Land
Lützow-Holm Bay
PRINCE OLAV COAST
Ice Bay
C. Batterbee
Enderby Land
KEMP COAST
Edward VIII Bay
Mawson
C. Daly
MAC-ROBERTSON COAST
C. Darnley
MacKenzie Bay
LARS CHRISTENSEN COAST
Prydz Bay
American Highland
Vestfold Hills
West Shelf Ice
WILHELM II COAST
Mt. Gauss
Davis Sea
QUEEN MARY COAST
Farr Bay
Mt. Barr Smith 4,320
Shackleton Shelf Ice
KNOX COAST
Vincennes Bay
BUDD COAST
SABRINA COAST
Wilkes Land
BANZARE COAST
C. Goodenough
C. Keltie
Adélie Land
Port-Martin
Pt. Géologie
SOUTH MAGNETIC POLAR AREA
GEORGE V COAST
Ninnis Glacier Tongue
Mertz Glacier Tongue
South Polar Plateau
SOUTH POLE
Amundsen Dec. 17, 1911
Scott Jan. 17, 1912
Byrd Nov. 29, 1929 (airplane)
Edward VII Plateau
Beardmore Glacier
Mt. Kirkpatrick 14,600
Mt. Markham 15,100
Mt. Lister 13,350
Victoria Land
Mt. Nansen 7,800
Mt. Sabine 10,000
C. Adare
Lillie Glacier Tongue
Scott I.
Balleny Is.
Ellsworth Highland
Mt. Ulmer 12,500
Sentinel Mts.
EIGHTS COAST
BELLINGSHAUSEN SEA
Peter I I. (Nor.)
Thurston Pen.
Hollick-Kenyon Plateau
Queen Maud Ra.
Scott Glac.
Rockefeller Plateau
Marie Byrd Land
Amundsen Sea
Mt. Siple 15,000
Executive Comm. Ra.
Mt. Sidley 12,000
C. Dart
Getz Shelf Ice
HOBBS COAST
Edsel Ford Ra.
Edward VII Pen.
Sulzberger Bay
C. Colbeck
Ross Shelf Ice
Roosevelt I.
Little America
Kainan Bay
Ross I.
McMurdo Sd.
Ross Sea
Macquarie I. (Australia)
Campbell I. (N. Z.)
Auckland Is. (N. Z.)
Antipodes Is. (N. Z.)
Bounty Is. (N. Z.)
Stewart I.
Dunedin
NEW ZEALAND
Tasman Sea
Hobart
Tasmania
King I.
Furneaux Gr.
Bass Str.
Melbourne
AUSTRALIA

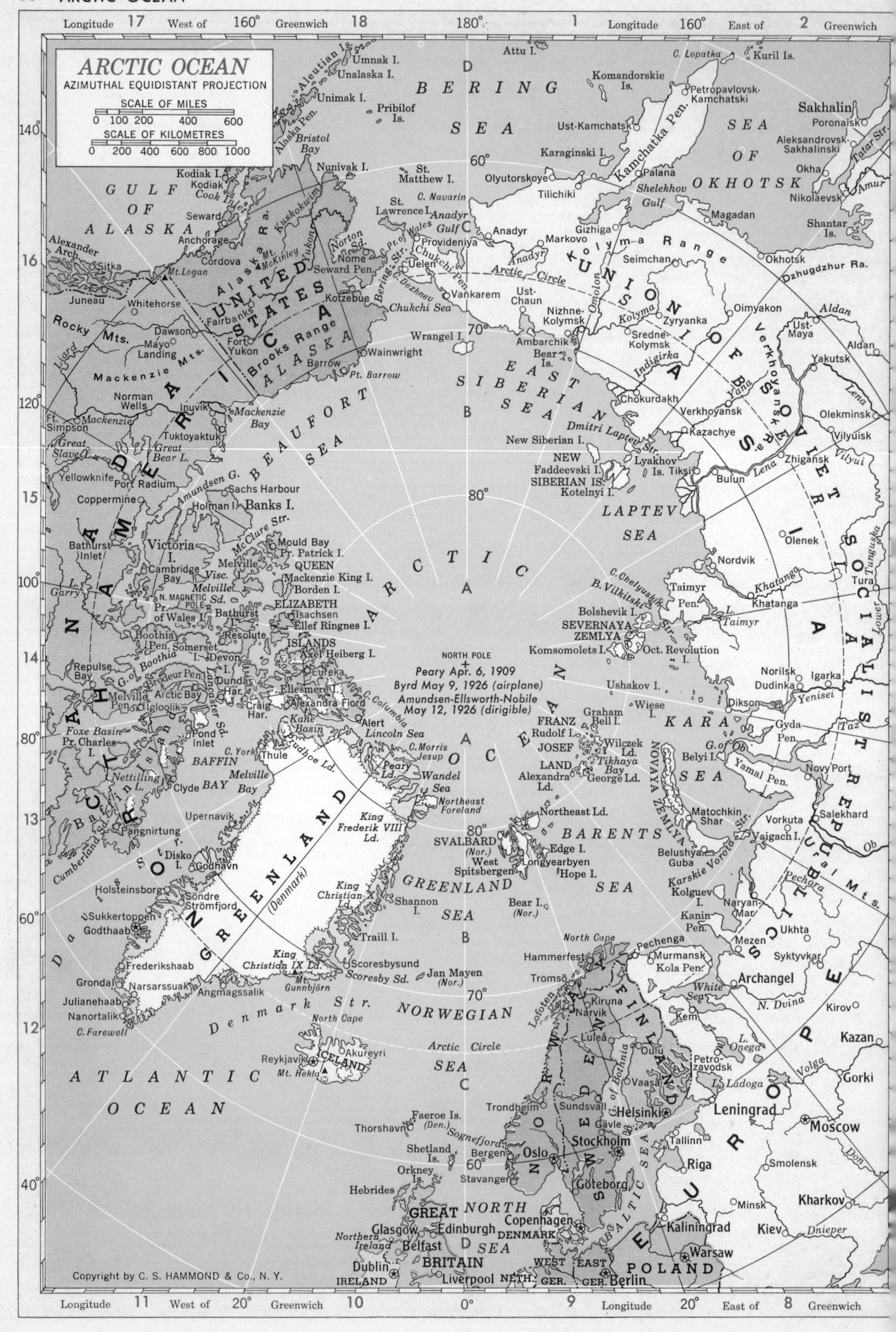
ARCTIC OCEAN
AZIMUTHAL EQUIDISTANT PROJECTION
SCALE OF MILES
0 100 200 400 600
SCALE OF KILOMETRES
0 200 400 600 800 1000
Longitude 17 West of 160° Greenwich 18 180° 1 Longitude 160° East of 2 Greenwich
Longitude 11 West of 20° Greenwich 10 0° 9 Longitude 20° East of 8 Greenwich
140° 16 120° 15 100° 14 80° 13 60° 12 40°
BERING SEA
SEA OF OKHOTSK
GULF OF ALASKA
BEAUFORT SEA
ARCTIC OCEAN
EAST SIBERIAN SEA
LAPTEV SEA
KARA SEA
BARENTS SEA
GREENLAND SEA
NORWEGIAN SEA
NORTH SEA
ATLANTIC OCEAN
BAFFIN BAY
Chukchi Sea
Lincoln Sea
Wandel Sea
Denmark Str.
Davis Str.
Arctic Circle
NORTH POLE
Peary Apr. 6, 1909
Byrd May 9, 1926 (airplane)
Amundsen-Ellsworth-Nobile
May 12, 1926 (dirigible)
UNITED STATES
ALASKA
NORTH AMERICA
UNION OF SOVIET SOCIALIST REPUBLICS
GREENLAND
(Denmark)
EUROPE
NORWAY
SWEDEN
FINLAND
POLAND
GREAT BRITAIN
IRELAND
DENMARK
WEST GER.
EAST GER.
NETH.
ICELAND
QUEEN ELIZABETH ISLANDS
NEW SIBERIAN IS.
SEVERNAYA ZEMLYA
FRANZ JOSEF LAND
NOVAYA ZEMLYA
SVALBARD (Nor.)
Aleutian Is.
Umnak I.
Unalaska I.
Unimak I.
Pribilof Is.
Alaska Pen.
Bristol Bay
Kodiak I.
Kodiak
Cook Inlet
Nunivak I.
St. Matthew I.
St. Lawrence I.
Seward
Anchorage
Cordova
Alaska Ra.
Mt. McKinley
Kuskokwim
Yukon
Norton Sd.
Nome
Seward Pen.
Kotzebue
Brooks Range
Fairbanks
Fort Yukon
Wainwright
Barrow
Pt. Barrow
Alexander Arch.
Sitka
Juneau
Mt. Logan
Whitehorse
Dawson
Mayo Landing
Rocky Mts.
Mackenzie Mts.
Liard
Norman Wells
Inuvik
Mackenzie Bay
Ft. Simpson
Mackenzie
Great Slave L.
Great Bear L.
Tuktoyaktuk
Yellowknife
Port Radium
Coppermine
Amundsen G.
Sachs Harbour
Holman I.
Banks I.
McClure Str.
Victoria I.
Bathurst Inlet
Cambridge Bay
Mould Bay
Pr. Patrick I.
Melville I.
Melville Visc.
Mackenzie King I.
Borden I.
Melville Sd.
N. MAGNETIC POLE
Pr. of Wales I.
Bathurst I.
Isachsen
Ellef Ringnes I.
Resolute
Axel Heiberg I.
Eureka
Boothia Pen.
Somerset I.
Devon I.
G. of Boothia
Repulse Bay
Brodeur Pen.
Lancaster Sd.
Dundas Har.
Arctic Bay
Ellesmere I.
Craig Har.
Alexandra Fiord
C. Columbia
Alert
Kane Basin
Melville Pen.
Igloolik
Foxe Basin
Pr. Charles I.
Pond Inlet
Baffin I.
C. York
Thule
Prudhoe Ld.
Melville Bay
Peary Ld.
C. Morris Jesup
Nettilling L.
Clyde
Upernavik
Pangnirtung
Cumberland Sd.
Disko I.
Godhavn
Holsteinsborg
Söndre Strömfjord
Sukkertoppen
Godthaab
Frederikshaab
Grondal
Narsarssuak
Julianehaab
Nanortalik
C. Farewell
Angmagssalik
King Frederik VIII Ld.
Northeast Foreland
King Christian X Ld.
Shannon I.
Traill I.
Scoresbysund
Scoresby Sd.
King Christian IX Ld.
Mt. Gunnbjörn
Jan Mayen (Nor.)
North Cape
Reykjavik
Akureyri
Mt. Hekla
Faeroe Is. (Den.)
Thorshavn
Shetland Is.
Orkney Is.
Hebrides
Glasgow
Edinburgh
Northern Ireland
Belfast
Dublin
Liverpool
Sognefjord
Bergen
Stavanger
Oslo
Trondheim
Stockholm
Göteborg
Copenhagen
Berlin
Warsaw
Kaliningrad
Lofoten Is.
Narvik
Kiruna
Tromsö
Hammerfest
Luleå
Oulu
G. of Bothnia
Vaasa
Sundsvall
Gävle
Helsinki
Tallinn
Riga
Minsk
Kiev
Dnieper
Kharkov
Smolensk
Moscow
Don
Leningrad
L. Ladoga
Petrozavodsk
L. Onega
Gorki
Volga
Kazan
Kirov
Kem
White Sea
N. Dvina
Archangel
Kola Pen.
Murmansk
Pechenga
Mezen
Syktyvkar
Ukhta
Kanin Pen.
Kolguev I.
Naryan-Mar
Pechora
Ural Mts.
Vorkuta
Salekhard
Ob
Vaigach I.
Karskie Vorota Str.
Belushya Guba
Matochkin Shar
Yamal Pen.
Novy Port
Belyi I.
G. of Ob
Gyda Pen.
Taz
Dikson
Yenisei
Dudinka
Igarka
Norilsk
Northeast Ld.
West Spitsbergen
Longyearbyen
Edge I.
Hope I.
Bear I. (Nor.)
Alexandra Ld.
George Ld.
Tikhaya Bay
Rudolf I.
Wilczek Ld.
Graham Bell I.
Wiese I.
Ushakov I.
Komsomolets I.
Oct. Revolution I.
Bolshevik I.
B. Vilkitski Str.
C. Chelyuskin
Taimyr Pen.
L. Taimyr
Khatanga
Tura
Lower Tunguska
Nordvik
Olenek
Vilyuisk
Vilyui
Zhigansk
Lena
Bulun
Tiksi
Olekminsk
Yakutsk
Aldan
Ust-Maya
Kotelnyi I.
Faddeevski I.
New Siberian I.
Lyakhov Is.
Dmitri Laptev Str.
Kazachye
Verkhoyansk
Verkhoyansk Ra.
Yana
Chokurdakh
Indigirka
Sredne-Kolymsk
Zyryanka
Kolyma
Oimyakon
Kolyma Range
Seimchan
Nizhne-Kolymsk
Ambarchik
Bear Is.
Omolon
Ust-Chaun
Wrangel I.
Vankarem
Chukchi Pen.
C. Dezhnev
Uelen
Bering Str.
G. Pr. of Wales
Provideniya
Anadyr Gulf
C. Navarin
Anadyr
Markovo
Olyutorskoye
Tilichiki
Karaginski I.
Ust-Kamchatsk
Kamchatka Pen.
Palana
Shelekhov Gulf
Gizhiga
Magadan
Okhotsk
Dzhugdzhur Ra.
Komandorskie Is.
Attu I.
C. Lopatka
Kuril Is.
Petropavlovsk-Kamchatski
Sakhalin
Poronaisk
Aleksandrovsk-Sakhalinski
Tatar Str.
Okha
Amur
Nikolaevsk
Shantar Is.
Copyright by C. S. HAMMOND & Co., N. Y.

EUROPE
LAMBERT AZIMUTHAL EQUAL-AREA PROJECTION
SCALE OF MILES
0 100 200 300 400 500 600
SCALE OF KILOMETRES
0 100 200 300 400 500 600
Capitals of Countries
International Boundaries
Internal Boundaries
Copyright by C. S. HAMMOND & CO., N.Y.
Longitude West
of Greenwich
0° Longitude East
of Greenwich
ATLANTIC OCEAN
BRITISH ISLES
NORTH SEA
BALTIC SEA
BARENTS SEA
BLACK SEA
CASPIAN SEA
MEDITERRANEAN SEA
ADRIATIC SEA
IONIAN SEA
TYRRHENIAN SEA
AEGEAN SEA
SEA OF AZOV
White Sea
Bay of Biscay
English Channel
St. George's Channel
IRISH SEA
Skagerrak
Kattegat
Gulf of Bothnia
G. of Finland
Str. of Gibraltar
Arctic Circle
ICELAND
Reykjavik
Akureyri
Faeroe Is. (Dan.)
Shetland Is.
Orkney Is.
HEBRIDES
SCOTLAND
GREAT BRITAIN
ENGLAND
WALES
NO. IRELAND
IRELAND
Glasgow
Edinburgh
Belfast
Dublin
Cork
Manchester
Liverpool
Birmingham
Bristol
London
Lands End
NORWAY
SWEDEN
FINLAND
DENMARK
Tromsö
Narvik
Lofoten
North Cape
Trondheim
Bergen
Stavanger
Oslo
Göteborg
Stockholm
Gävle
Umeå
Luleå
Norrköping
Hälsingborg
Malmö
Gotland
Copenhagen
Vaasa
Tampere
Turku
Helsinki
NETH.
BELG.
LUX.
Amsterdam
The Hague
Antwerp
Brussels
FRANCE
Paris
Lille
Rouen
Le Havre
Brest
Rennes
Nantes
Tours
Limoges
Bordeaux
Toulouse
Marseille
Nice
Lyon
St. Etienne
Dijon
Nancy
Strasbourg
Seine
Loire
Rhone
Pyrenees
ANDORRA
SPAIN
PORTUGAL
Madrid
Barcelona
Valencia
Murcia
Bilbao
Gijon
Valladolid
Saragossa
Ebro
Tagus
Córdoba
Seville
Málaga
Cádiz
GIBRALTAR (Br.)
Lisbon
Oporto
Vigo
C. Finisterre
C. St. Vincent
BALEARIC IS.
Majorca
Minorca
Corsica
Ajaccio
Sardinia
Cagliari
SWITZ.
Bern
Geneva
LIECHT.
AUSTRIA
Vienna
Graz
ITALY
Milan
Turin
Genoa
Venice
Trieste
Florence
Rome
Naples
Bari
Palermo
Catania
Sicily
Malta (Br.)
GERMANY
Hamburg
Bremen
Berlin
Essen
Cologne
Bonn
Frankfurt
Leipzig
Dresden
Nuremberg
Munich
Elbe
Rhine
Danube
CZECHOSLOVAKIA
Prague
Brno
POLAND
Warsaw
Lódź
Cracow
Poznań
Wrocław (Breslau)
Szczecin (Stettin)
Gdańsk (Danzig)
Kaliningrad
R.S.F.S.R.
Vistula
HUNGARY
Budapest
Szeged
YUGOSLAVIA
Zagreb
Rijeka (Fiume)
Split
Sarajevo
Belgrade
Skopje
ALBANIA
Tirane
GREECE
Salonika
Larisa
Athens
Patras
Corfu
Crete
Candia
RUMANIA
Bucharest
Cluj
Ploeşti
Galaţi
BULGARIA
Sofia
Plovdiv
Varna
TURKEY
Istanbul
Izmir
Cyprus
AFRICA
Tangier
Rabat
Algiers
Tunis
UNION OF SOVIET SOCIALIST REPUBLICS
RUSSIAN SOVIET FEDERATED SOCIALIST REPUBLIC
EST. S.S.R.
LATVIAN S.S.R.
LITHUANIAN S.S.R.
WHITE RUSSIAN S.S.R.
UKRAINIAN S.S.R.
MOLD. S.S.R.
GEORGIAN S.S.R.
AZERBAIDZHAN S.S.R.
ARMENIAN S.S.R.
Tallinn
Riga
Vilna
Minsk
Vitebsk
Gomel
Brest
Lvov
Chernovtsy
Kishinev
Odessa
Kiev
Kharkov
Dnepropetrovsk
Krivoi Rog
Stalino
Rostov
Krasnodar
Sevastopol
Crimean Pen.
Dnieper
Don
Leningrad
L. Ladoga
Pskov
Kalinin
Moscow
Smolensk
Tula
Kursk
Voronezh
Yaroslavl
Rybinsk Res.
Gorki
Kazan
Kuibyshev
Saratov
Penza
Stalingrad
Astrakhan
Volga
Ural
Kama
Kirov
Izhevsk
Perm
Ufa
Orenburg
Sverdlovsk
Chelyabinsk
Magnitogorsk
Tobolsk
Tobol
Irtish
Ob
Ural Mts.
Grozny
Tbilisi
Erivan
Baku
Caucasus
Murmansk
Kola Pen.
Archangel
Petrozavodsk
L. Onega
Northern Dvina
Syktyvkar
Naryan Mar
Pechora
Kolguev I.

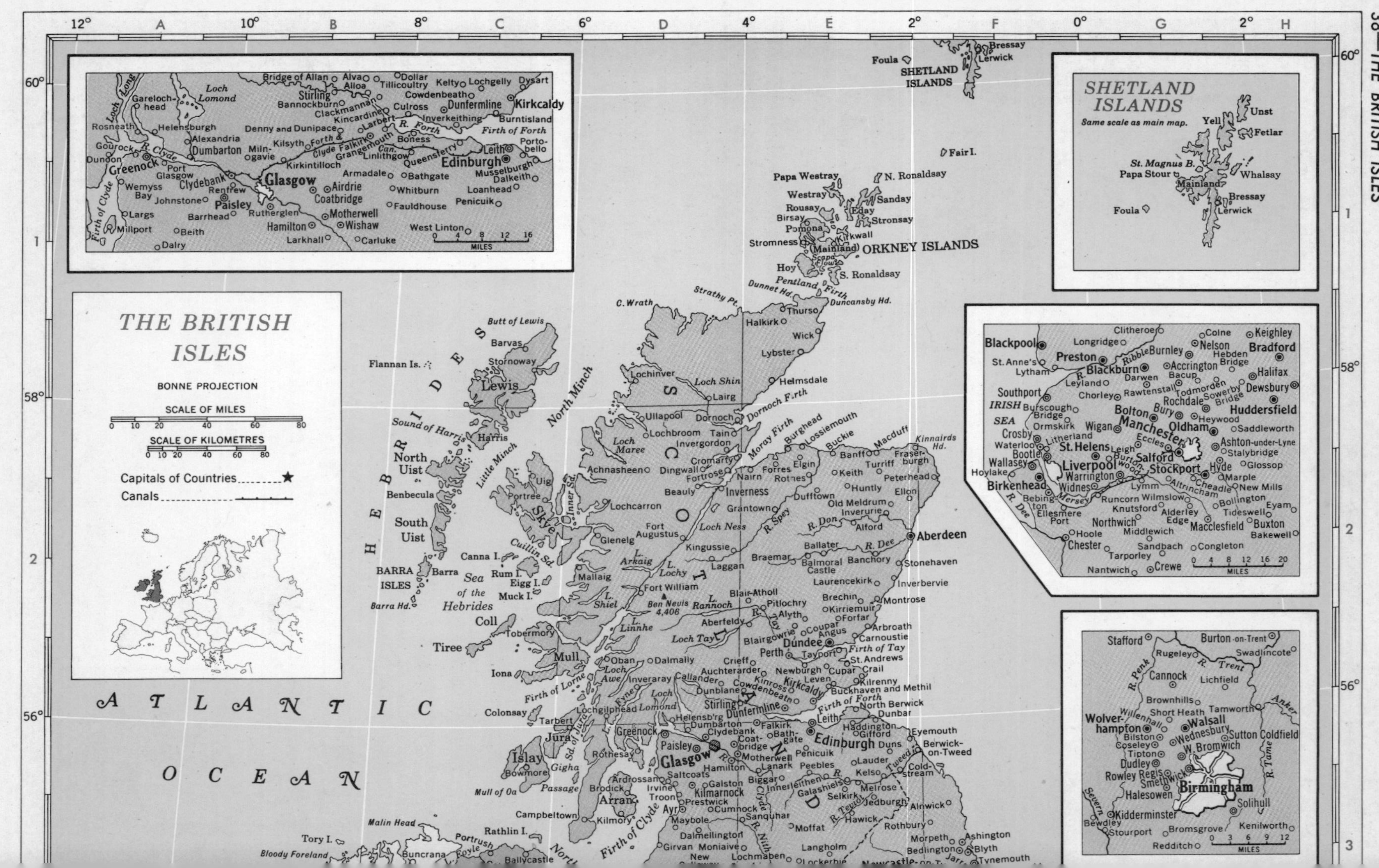
THE BRITISH
ISLES
BONNE PROJECTION
SCALE OF MILES
0 10 20 40 60 80
SCALE OF KILOMETRES
0 10 20 40 60 80
Capitals of Countries
Canals
SHETLAND
ISLANDS
Same scale as main map.
Unst
Fetlar
Yell
Whalsay
Bressay
Lerwick
Mainland
St. Magnus B.
Papa Stour
Foula
SHETLAND
ISLANDS
Fair I.
ORKNEY ISLANDS
Papa Westray
Westray
N. Ronaldsay
Sanday
Stronsay
Rousay
Birsay
Pomona
Kirkwall
(Mainland)
Stromness
Hoy
S. Ronaldsay
Pentland Firth
Dunnet Hd.
Duncansby Hd.
ATLANTIC
OCEAN
SCOTLAND
HEBRIDES
Butt of Lewis
Barvas
Stornoway
Lewis
Harris
Flannan Is.
Sound of Harris
North Minch
Little Minch
North Uist
Benbecula
South Uist
BARRA ISLES
Barra
Barra Hd.
Canna I.
Rum I.
Eigg I.
Muck I.
Sea of the Hebrides
Skye
Uig
Portree
Inner Sd.
Cuillin Sd.
Coll
Tiree
Tobermory
Mull
Iona
Firth of Lorne
Colonsay
Tarbert
Jura
Islay
Bowmore
Gigha
Mull of Oa
Campbeltown
Rathlin I.
Malin Head
Tory I.
Bloody Foreland
Buncrana
Portrush
Ballycastle
C. Wrath
Strathy Pt.
Thurso
Halkirk
Wick
Lybster
Helmsdale
Lochinver
Loch Shin
Lairg
Dornoch Firth
Ullapool
Dornoch
Tain
Lochbroom
Invergordon
Loch Maree
Achnasheen
Cromarty
Dingwall
Fortrose
Moray Firth
Nairn
Forres
Elgin
Rothes
Burghead
Lossiemouth
Buckie
Banff
Macduff
Kinnairds Hd.
Fraserburgh
Turriff
Peterhead
Keith
Huntly
Ellon
Inverness
Beauly
Lochcarron
Grantown
Dufftown
Old Meldrum
Inverurie
Alford
R. Don
R. Spey
Loch Ness
Fort Augustus
Glenelg
Kingussie
Aberdeen
Ballater
R. Dee
Braemar
Balmoral Castle
Banchory
Stonehaven
Laurencekirk
Inverbervie
Mallaig
L. Arkaig
L. Lochy
Laggan
Fort William
Ben Nevis 4,406
L. Shiel
L. Rannoch
Blair-Atholl
Pitlochry
Brechin
Kirriemuir
Montrose
Forfar
Arbroath
Alyth
L. Linnhe
Aberfeldy
Coupar Angus
Carnoustie
Loch Tay
Blairgowrie
Dundee
Tayport
Firth of Tay
St. Andrews
Perth
Cupar
Crail
Oban
Dalmally
Crieff
Newburgh
Kilrenny
Loch Awe
Inveraray
Auchterarder
Kinross
Leven
Callander
Cowdenbeath
Kirkcaldy
Buckhaven and Methil
Dunblane
Firth of Forth
North Berwick
Lochgilphead
Loch Lomond
Stirling
Dunfermline
Dunbar
Helensb'rg
Dumbarton
Falkirk
Leith
Haddington
Gifford
Eyemouth
Greenock
Clydebank
Bathgate
Edinburgh
Duns
Berwick-on-Tweed
Paisley
Glasgow
Coatbridge
Motherwell
Penicuik
Lauder
Cold-stream
Rothesay
Hamilton
Lanark
Peebles
Kelso
Ardrossan
Saltcoats
Biggar
Innerleithen
Galashiels
Melrose
Brodick
Irvine
Galston
Kilmarnock
Selkirk
Jedburgh
Alnwick
Arran
Troon
Prestwick
R. Clyde
R. Teviot
Hawick
Ayr
Cumnock
Sanquhar
Kilmory
Firth of Clyde
Maybole
Moffat
Rothbury
Dalmellington
Morpeth
Ashington
Girvan
Moniaive
Langholm
Bedlington
Blyth
New
Lochmaben
Tynemouth
Inset: Forth–Clyde
Loch Long
Gareloch-head
Loch Lomond
Rosneath
Helensburgh
Alexandria
Gourock
R. Clyde
Dumbarton
Dunoon
Greenock
Port Glasgow
Wemyss Bay
Clydebank
Renfrew
Johnstone
Paisley
Largs
Barrhead
Millport
Beith
Dalry
Firth of Clyde
Bridge of Allan
Alva
Dollar
Tillicoultry
Kelty
Lochgelly
Dysart
Stirling
Alloa
Cowdenbeath
Bannockburn
Clackmannan
Culross
Dunfermline
Kirkcaldy
Kincardine
Inverkeithing
Burntisland
Denny and Dunipace
Larbert
R. Forth
Firth of Forth
Milngavie
Kilsyth
Forth & Clyde Can.
Falkirk
Grangemouth
Bo'ness
Leith
Portobello
Linlithgow
Queensferry
Edinburgh
Kirkintilloch
Musselburgh
Glasgow
Armadale
Bathgate
Dalkeith
Airdrie
Whitburn
Loanhead
Coatbridge
Penicuik
Rutherglen
Fauldhouse
Motherwell
Hamilton
Wishaw
West Linton
Larkhall
Carluke
0 4 8 12 16
MILES
Blackpool
Longridge
Clitheroe
Colne
Keighley
St. Anne's
Lytham
Preston
Ribble
Burnley
Nelson
Bradford
Blackburn
Accrington
Hebden Bridge
Halifax
R.
Leyland
Darwen
Bacup
Southport
Chorley
Rawtenstall
Todmorden
Sowerby Bridge
Dewsbury
IRISH SEA
Burscough Bridge
Rochdale
Huddersfield
Ormskirk
Bolton
Bury
Heywood
Crosby
Wigan
Manchester
Oldham
Saddleworth
Waterloo
Litherland
Eccles
Ashton-under-Lyne
Bootle
St. Helens
Leigh
Stalybridge
Wallasey
Liverpool
Salford
Hyde
Glossop
Hoylake
Warrington
Stockport
Marple
Birkenhead
Widnes
Lymm
Altrincham
Cheadle
New Mills
R. Dee
Bebington
Mersey
Runcorn
Wilmslow
Bollington
Ellesmere Port
Knutsford
Alderley Edge
Tideswell
Eyam
Northwich
Macclesfield
Buxton
Hoole
Middlewich
Bakewell
Chester
Sandbach
Congleton
Tarporley
Nantwich
Crewe
0 4 8 12 16 20
MILES
Stafford
Burton-on-Trent
Swadlincote
Rugeley
R. Trent
R. Penk
Cannock
Lichfield
Anker
Brownhills
Short Heath
Tamworth
Willenhall
Walsall
Wolverhampton
Wednesbury
Sutton Coldfield
Bilston
W. Bromwich
R. Tame
Coseley
Tipton
Dudley
Rowley Regis
Smethwick
Birmingham
Halesowen
Solihull
Severn
Kidderminster
Bewdley
Stourport
Bromsgrove
Kenilworth
Redditch
0 3 6 9 12
MILES

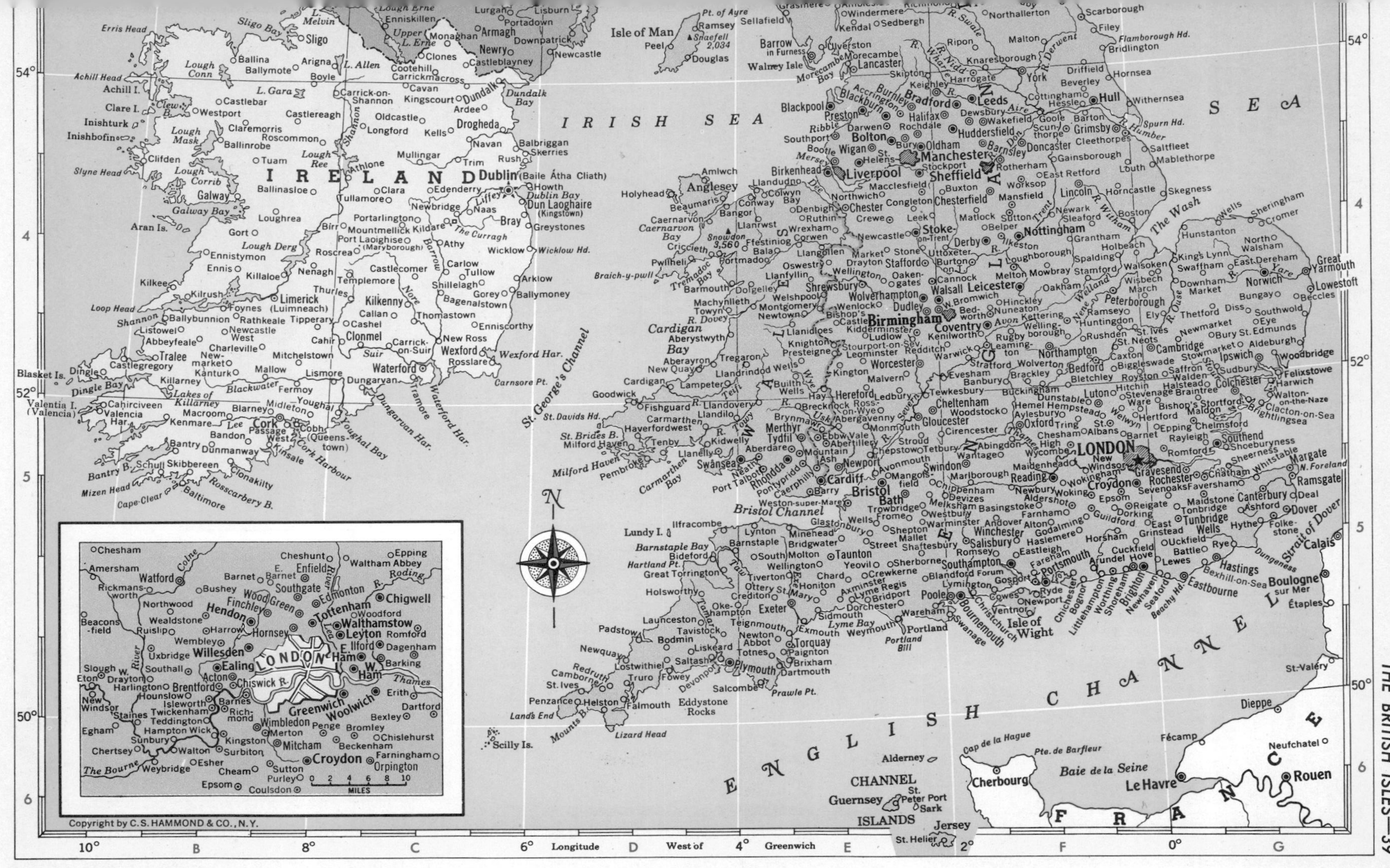
IRISH SEA
NORTH SEA
ENGLISH CHANNEL
IRELAND
FRANCE
Isle of Man
CHANNEL ISLANDS
Isle of Wight
Bristol Channel
St. George's Channel
Cardigan Bay
The Wash
Strait of Dover
Baie de la Seine
LONDON
Dublin (Baile Átha Cliath)
Liverpool
Manchester
Sheffield
Leeds
Birmingham
Bristol
Cardiff
Cork
Limerick
Galway
Waterford
Plymouth
Southampton
Le Havre
Rouen
Cherbourg
Boulogne
Calais
Jersey
Guernsey
Alderney
Sark
Scilly Is.
Land's End
Lizard Head
Lundy I.
Anglesey
Longitude West of Greenwich
Copyright by C.S. HAMMOND & CO., N.Y.
Chesham
Watford
Hendon
Willesden
Ealing
Tottenham
Walthamstow
Leyton
Chigwell
Greenwich
Woolwich
Croydon
Wimbledon
Mitcham
Epsom
Dartford
MILES

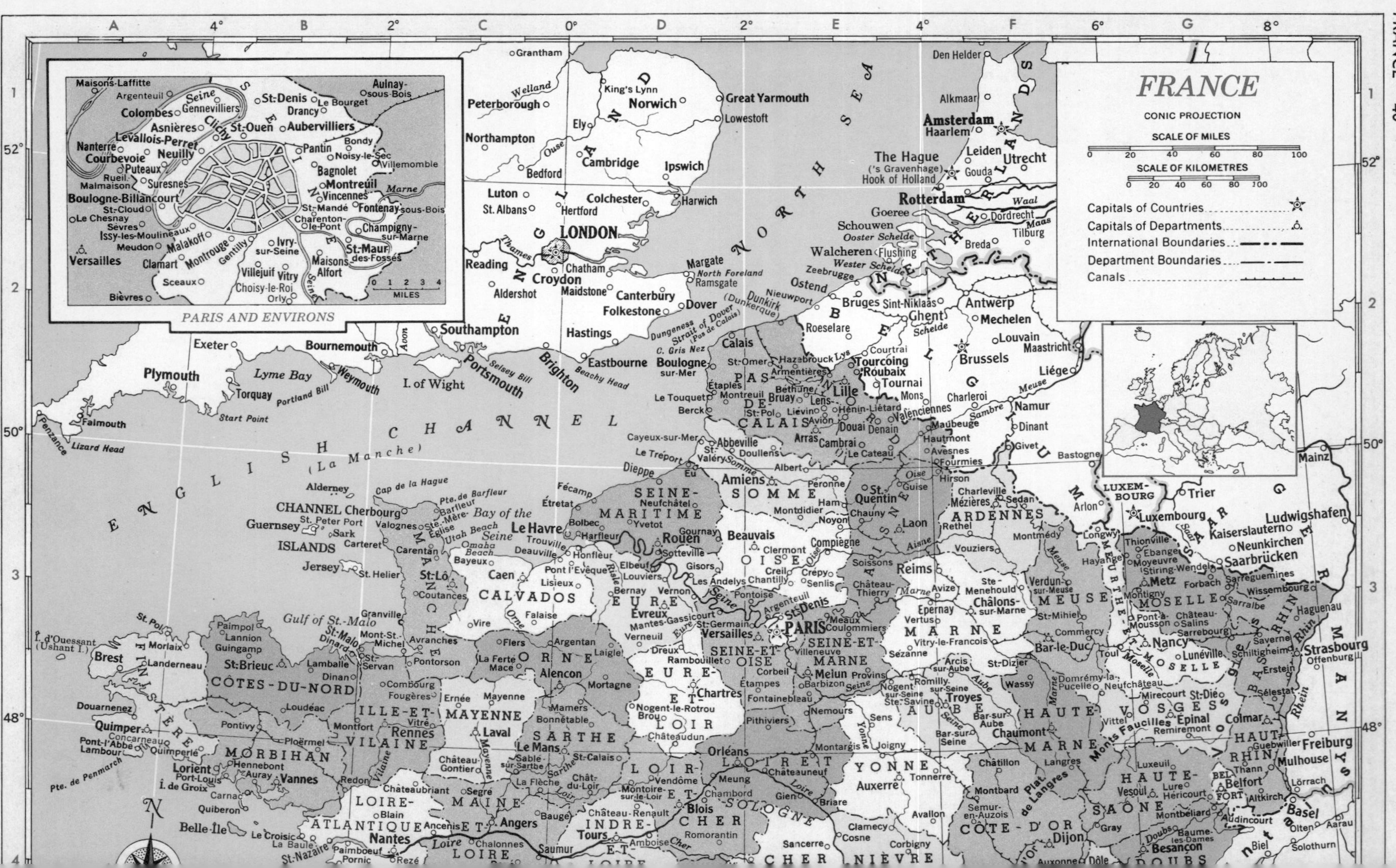
FRANCE
CONIC PROJECTION
SCALE OF MILES
0 20 40 60 80 100
SCALE OF KILOMETRES
0 20 40 60 80 100
Capitals of Countries
Capitals of Departments
International Boundaries
Department Boundaries
Canals
PARIS AND ENVIRONS
MILES
NORTH SEA
ENGLISH CHANNEL (La Manche)
ENGLAND
NETHERLANDS
BELGIUM
GERMANY
LUXEMBOURG
CHANNEL ISLANDS
LONDON
PARIS
Amsterdam
The Hague ('s Gravenhage)
Rotterdam
Brussels
Antwerp
Luxembourg
Strasbourg
Saarbrücken
Basel
Freiburg
Mulhouse
Nancy
Metz
Reims
Lille
Calais
Dunkirk (Dunkerque)
Boulogne sur-Mer
Amiens
Rouen
Le Havre
Caen
Cherbourg
Rennes
Nantes
Brest
Lorient
Vannes
St-Brieuc
Le Mans
Orléans
Tours
Angers
Chartres
Versailles
Troyes
Dijon
Besançon
Portsmouth
Southampton
Plymouth
Brighton
Dover
Canterbury
Norwich
Cambridge
Ipswich
Great Yarmouth
SEINE-MARITIME
CALVADOS
SOMME
OISE
MARNE
MEUSE
MOSELLE
VOSGES
ARDENNES
AISNE
NORD
PAS-DE-CALAIS
SEINE-ET-MARNE
SEINE-ET-OISE
EURE
EURE-ET-LOIR
LOIRET
LOIR-ET-CHER
INDRE-ET-LOIRE
SARTHE
MAYENNE
ORNE
MANCHE
ILLE-ET-VILAINE
CÔTES-DU-NORD
MORBIHAN
FINISTÈRE
LOIRE-ATLANTIQUE
MAINE-ET-LOIRE
AUBE
YONNE
HAUTE-MARNE
HAUTE-SAÔNE
CÔTE-D'OR
HAUT-RHIN
BAS-RHIN

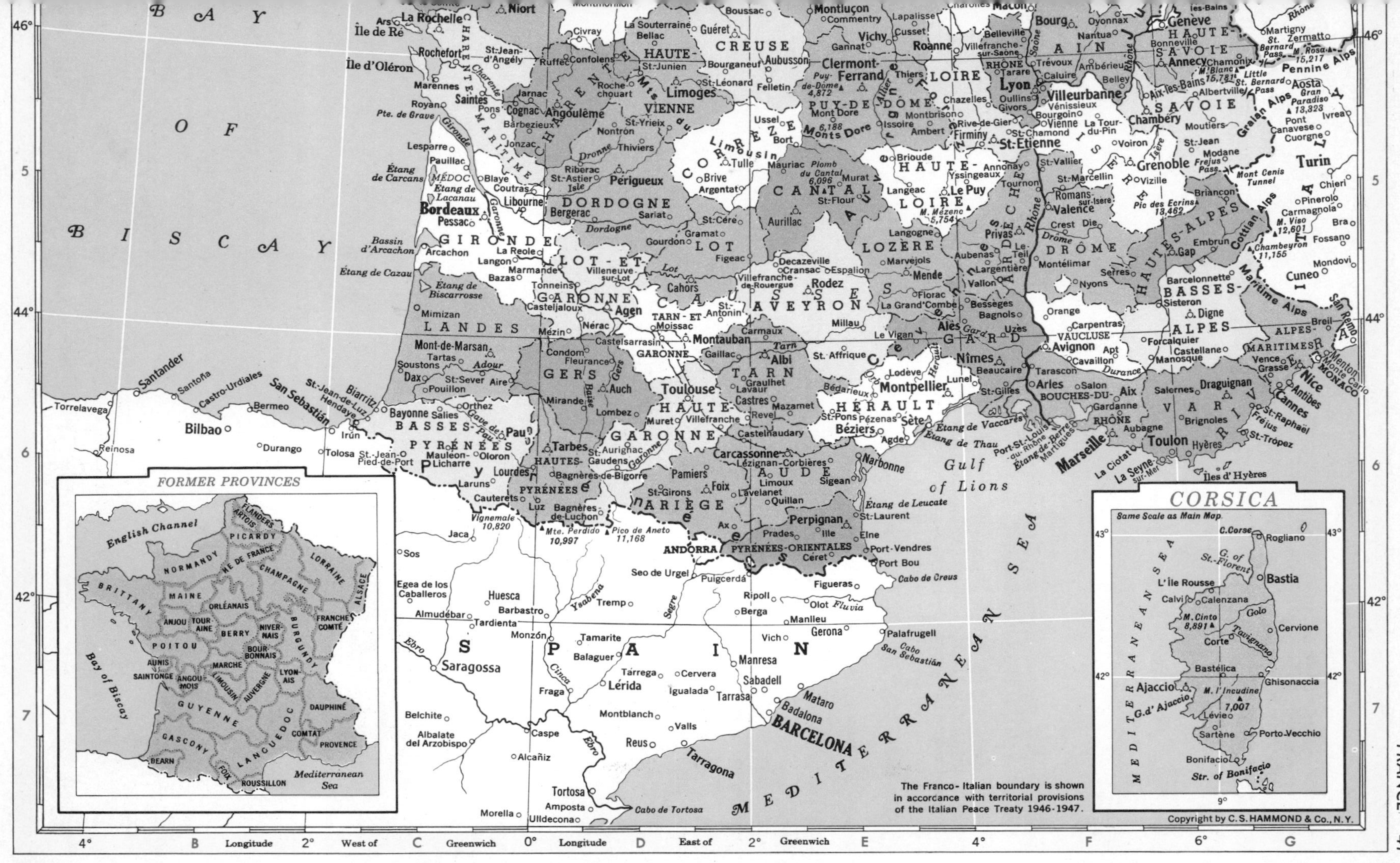
BAY OF BISCAY
Gulf of Lions
MEDITERRANEAN SEA
SPAIN
ANDORRA
MONACO
BARCELONA
CORSICA
Same Scale as Main Map
FORMER PROVINCES
English Channel
Bay of Biscay
Mediterranean Sea
The Franco-Italian boundary is shown in accordance with territorial provisions of the Italian Peace Treaty 1946-1947.
Copyright by C.S. HAMMOND & Co., N.Y.
Longitude West of Greenwich
Longitude East of Greenwich

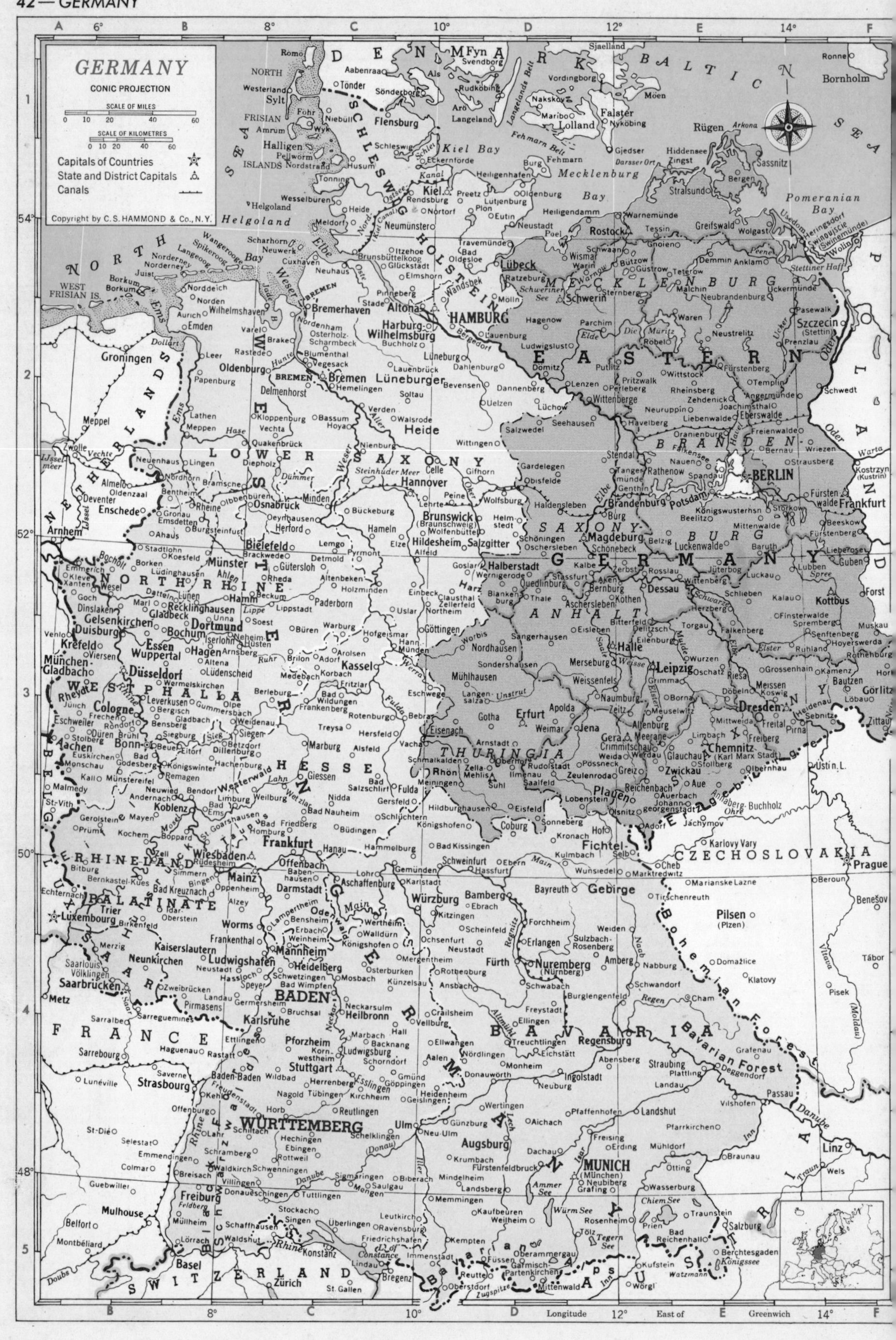

GERMANY
CONIC PROJECTION
SCALE OF MILES
0 10 20 40 60
SCALE OF KILOMETRES
0 10 20 40 60
Capitals of Countries
State and District Capitals
Canals
Copyright by C. S. HAMMOND & Co., N.Y.
A B C D E F
6° 8° 10° 12° 14°
1 2 3 4 5
54° 52° 50° 48°
Longitude East of Greenwich
DENMARK
BALTIC SEA
NORTH SEA
NETHERLANDS
BELGIUM
LUXEMBOURG
FRANCE
SWITZERLAND
AUSTRIA
CZECHOSLOVAKIA
POLAND
SCHLESWIG-HOLSTEIN
LOWER SAXONY
MECKLENBURG
EASTERN GERMANY
BRANDENBURG
SAXONY-ANHALT
SAXONY
THURINGIA
NORTH RHINE-WESTPHALIA
RHINELAND-PALATINATE
SAAR
HESSE
BADEN
WÜRTTEMBERG
BAVARIA
NORTH FRISIAN ISLANDS
WEST FRISIAN IS.
Helgoland
Kiel Bay
Mecklenburg Bay
Pomeranian Bay
Bornholm
Rügen
Fehmarn
Lolland
Falster
Sjaelland
Fyn
Sylt
Flensburg
Kiel
Lübeck
HAMBURG
Bremerhaven
BREMEN
Bremen
Oldenburg
Emden
Wilhelmshaven
Groningen
Rostock
Wismar
Schwerin
Stralsund
Greifswald
Szczecin (Stettin)
Hannover
Brunswick (Braunschweig)
Hildesheim
Salzgitter
Osnabrück
Münster
Bielefeld
Magdeburg
Halberstadt
BERLIN
Potsdam
Frankfurt
Dessau
Halle
Leipzig
Dresden
Chemnitz (Karl Marx Stadt)
Zwickau
Plauen
Gera
Jena
Weimar
Erfurt
Gotha
Eisenach
Kassel
Göttingen
Dortmund
Essen
Bochum
Duisburg
Gelsenkirchen
Düsseldorf
Wuppertal
Krefeld
Cologne
Bonn
Aachen
Koblenz
Wiesbaden
Mainz
Frankfurt
Darmstadt
Offenbach
Trier
Luxembourg
Saarbrücken
Kaiserslautern
Ludwigshafen
Mannheim
Heidelberg
Karlsruhe
Pforzheim
Stuttgart
Heilbronn
Würzburg
Bamberg
Bayreuth
Nuremberg (Nürnberg)
Fürth
Erlangen
Regensburg
Ingolstadt
Augsburg
MUNICH (München)
Ulm
Freiburg
Strasbourg
Mulhouse
Basel
Zürich
Konstanz
Lake of Constance
Salzburg
Linz
Passau
Prague
Pilsen (Plzen)
Karlovy Vary
Bavarian Forest
Bohemian Forest
Bavarian Alps
Black Forest
Odenwald
Harz
Rhön
Fichtel-Gebirge
Erzgebirge
Westerwald
Taunus
Rhine
Elbe
Weser
Ems
Oder
Danube
Main
Neckar
Moselle
Saale
Spree
Havel
Isar
Inn
Lech
Zugspitze

NORWAY, SWEDEN, FINLAND and DENMARK
CONIC PROJECTION
Copyright by C. S. HAMMOND & Co., N. Y.
SCALE OF MILES
0 50 100 150 200
KILOMETRES
0 50 100 150 200
Capitals of Countries
International Boundaries
Canals
Longitude 18° East of Greenwich
SVALBARD (SPITSBERGEN)
NORWEGIAN SEA
West Spitsbergen
Northeast Land
Barents I.
Edge I.
Hope I.
Longyearbyen
North Cape
South Cape
Stockholm
Södertälje
Solna
Sundbyberg
Lidingö
Enköping
Mälaren
Strängnäs
Ornö
Oslo
Hönefoss
Lilleström
Drammen
Ski
Dröbak
Son
Moss
Horten
Tönsberg
Sandefjord
Sarpsborg
Larvik
ARCTIC OCEAN
ATLANTIC OCEAN
NORWEGIAN SEA
NORTH SEA
SKAGERRAK
KATTEGAT
BALTIC SEA
GULF OF BOTHNIA
Gulf of Finland
Gulf of Riga
NORWAY
SWEDEN
FINLAND
LAPLAND
DENMARK
U.S.S.R.
ESTONIA
LATVIA
LITH.
POLAND
GERMANY
NETHERLANDS
Arctic Circle
Hammerfest
Tromsö
Narvik
Bodö
Trondheim
Bergen
OSLO
Stavanger
Kristiansand
Ålesund
Kiruna
Luleå
Umeå
Sundsvall
Gävle
Uppsala
STOCKHOLM
Västerås
Örebro
Norrköping
Linköping
Jönköping
Göteborg
Malmö
Helsingborg
Kalmar
Karlskrona
Gotland
Öland
Bornholm
COPENHAGEN
Aalborg
Aarhus
Odense
Esbjerg
Flensburg
Kiel
Lübeck
HAMBURG
Bremen
Rostock
Gdańsk
Gdynia
Szczecin (Stettin)
Kaliningrad (Königsberg)
Klaipėda
Liepāja
Riga
Tallinn
LENINGRAD
Vyborg (Viipuri)
HELSINKI
Turku
Tampere
Pori
Vaasa
Oulu
Kemi
Tornio
Rovaniemi
Kuopio
Jyväskylä
Lahti
Murmansk
Monchegorsk
Kirovsk
Kandalaksha
Lake Ladoga
Lake Peipus
Ahvenanmaa (Åland Is.)
Mariehamn
Lofoten Is.
Vesterålen Is.
Jotunheimen
Dovrefjell
Kebnekaise 6,965
Sulitjelma 6,279
Galdhöpiggen 8,097
Mt. Haltia 4,343

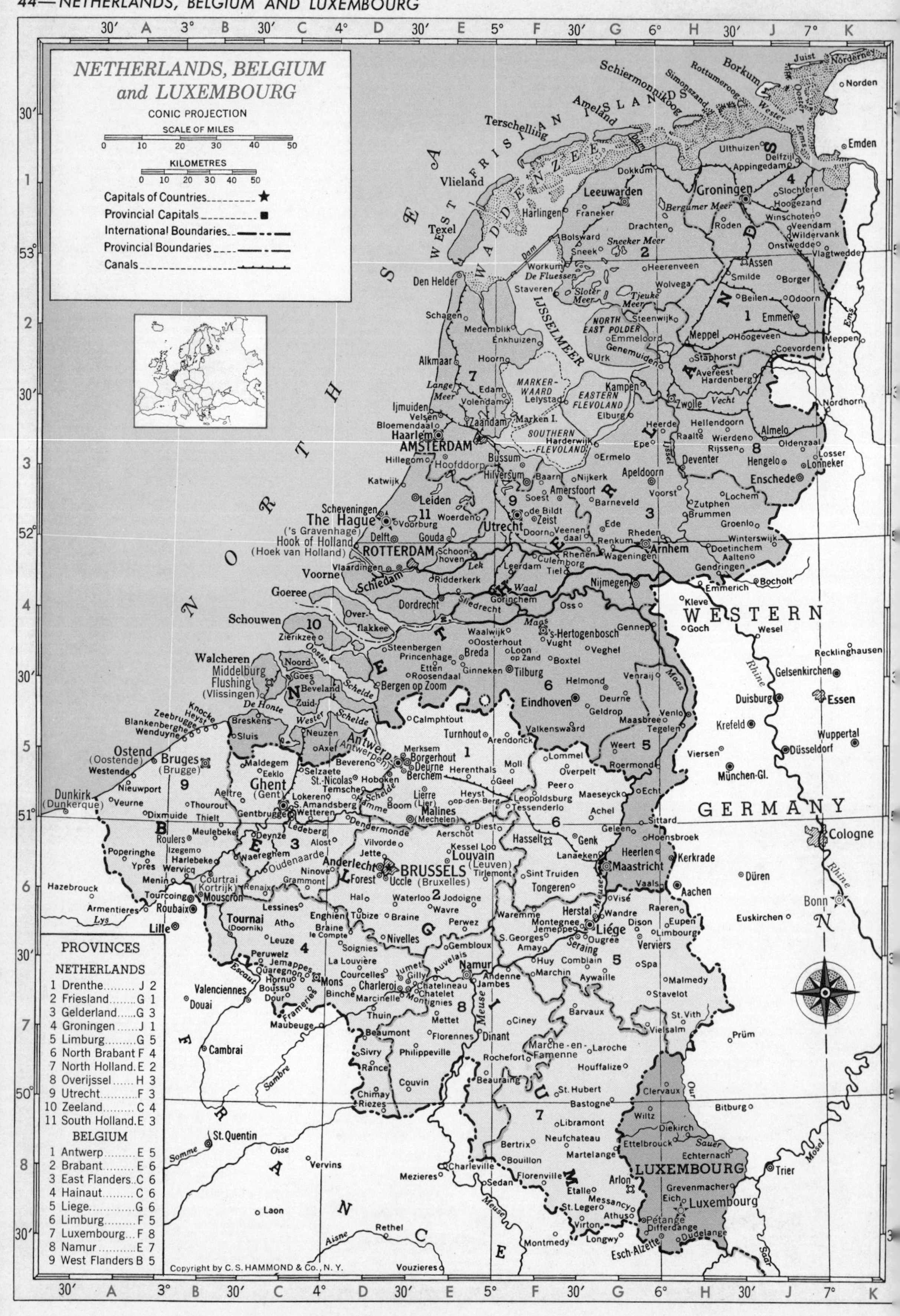
NETHERLANDS, BELGIUM
and LUXEMBOURG
CONIC PROJECTION
SCALE OF MILES
0 10 20 30 40 50
KILOMETRES
0 10 20 30 40 50
Capitals of Countries
Provincial Capitals
International Boundaries
Provincial Boundaries
Canals
PROVINCES
NETHERLANDS
1 Drenthe......... J 2
2 Friesland........G 1
3 Gelderland......G 3
4 Groningen ......J 1
5 Limburg.........G 5
6 North Brabant F 4
7 North Holland. E 2
8 Overijssel...... H 3
9 Utrecht...........F 3
10 Zeeland.........C 4
11 South Holland.E 3
BELGIUM
1 Antwerp......... E 5
2 Brabant.......... E 6
3 East Flanders..C 6
4 Hainaut......... C 6
5 Liege..............G 6
6 Limburg......... F 5
7 Luxembourg... F 8
8 Namur ....E 7
9 West Flanders B 5
Copyright by C. S. HAMMOND & Co., N. Y.
NORTH SEA
WEST FRISIAN ISLANDS
WADDENZEE
IJSSELMEER
NETHERLANDS
BELGIUM
LUXEMBOURG
FRANCE
WESTERN GERMANY
AMSTERDAM
ROTTERDAM
The Hague
('s Gravenhage)
Hook of Holland
(Hoek van Holland)
Utrecht
Haarlem
Leiden
Groningen
Leeuwarden
Arnhem
Nijmegen
Eindhoven
's-Hertogenbosch
Maastricht
BRUSSELS
(Bruxelles)
Antwerp
(Antwerpen)
Ghent
(Gent)
Bruges
(Brugge)
Ostend
(Oostende)
Liége
Namur
Charleroi
Mons
Louvain
(Leuven)
Luxembourg
Lille
Cologne
Aachen
Düsseldorf
Essen
Duisburg
Bonn
Trier
Rhine
Maas
Meuse
Schelde
Mosel

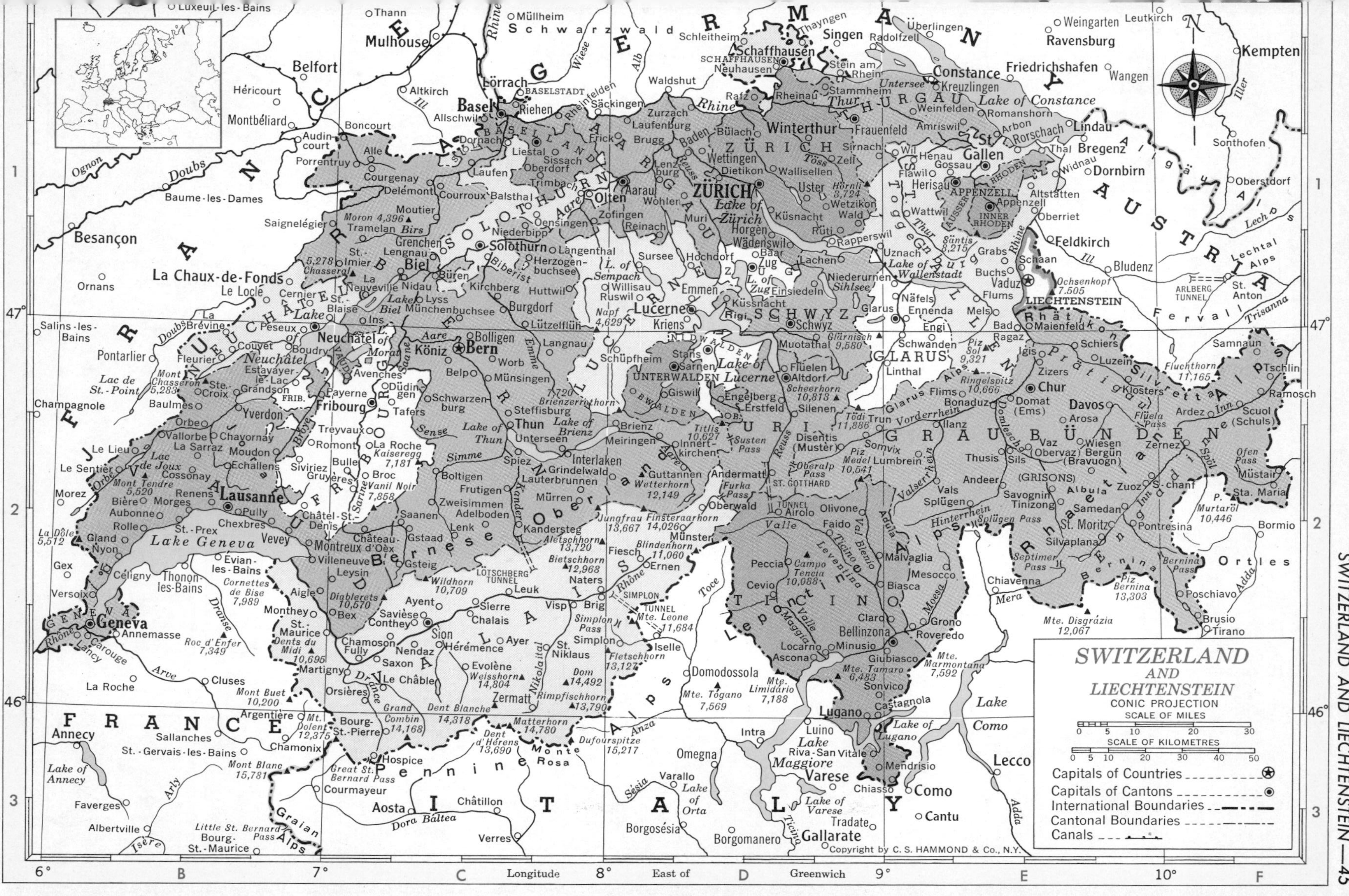
SWITZERLAND
AND
LIECHTENSTEIN
CONIC PROJECTION
SCALE OF MILES
0 5 10 20 30
SCALE OF KILOMETRES
0 5 10 20 30 40 50
Capitals of Countries
Capitals of Cantons
International Boundaries
Cantonal Boundaries
Canals
GERMANY
AUSTRIA
ITALY
FRANCE
LIECHTENSTEIN
Bern
Vaduz
Zürich
Basel
Geneva
Lausanne
Lucerne
Lake Geneva
Lake of Constance
Lake of Neuchâtel
Lake of Lucerne
Lake Maggiore
Lake Como
Longitude 8° East of Greenwich
Copyright by C. S. HAMMOND & Co., N.Y.

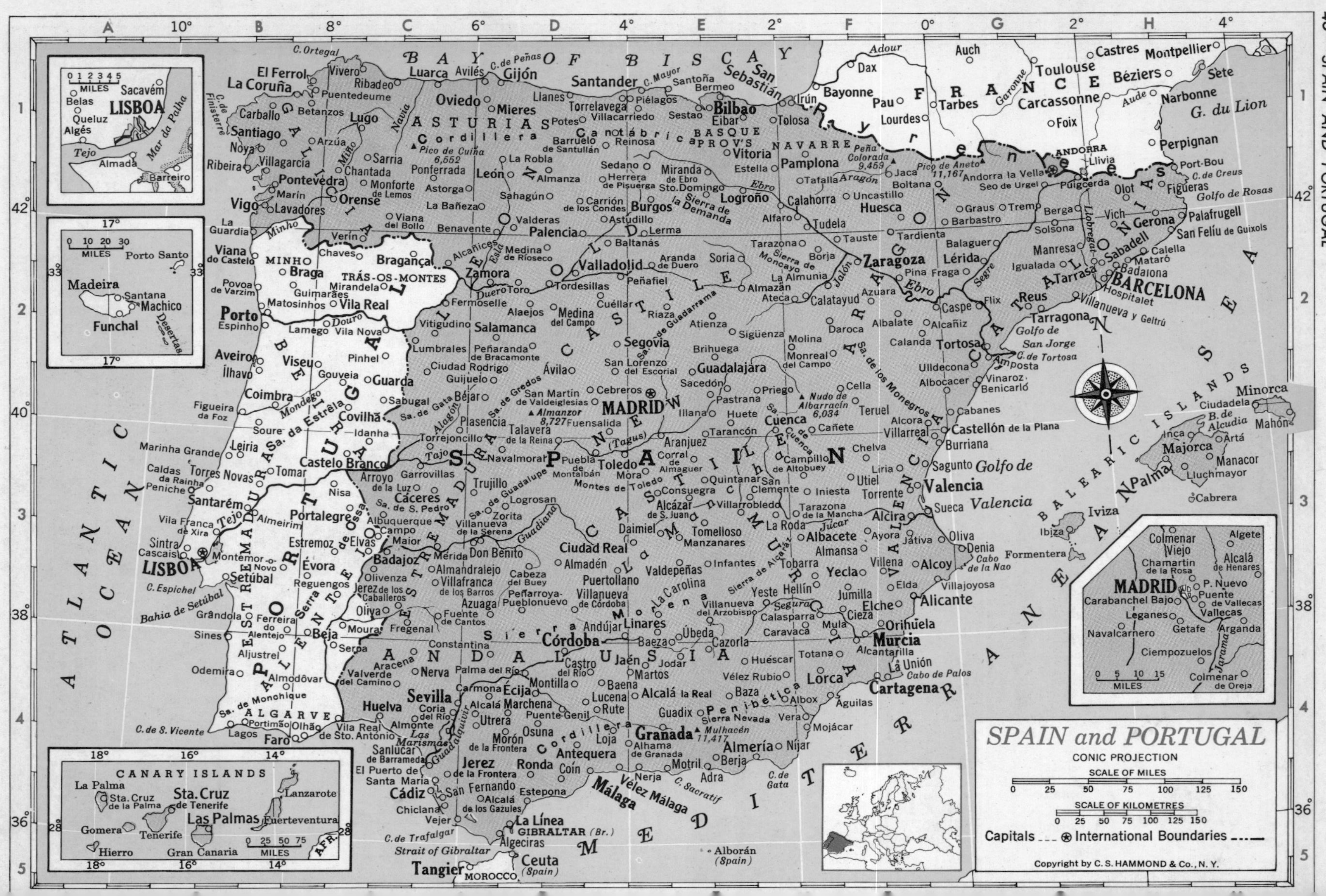
SPAIN and PORTUGAL
CONIC PROJECTION
SCALE OF MILES
0 25 50 75 100 125 150
SCALE OF KILOMETRES
0 25 50 75 100 125 150
Capitals ⊛ International Boundaries
Copyright by C. S. HAMMOND & Co., N. Y.
MADRID
LISBOA
CANARY ISLANDS
Madeira
Funchal
Porto Santo
Desertas
ATLANTIC OCEAN
BAY OF BISCAY
MEDITERRANEAN SEA
BALEARIC ISLANDS
FRANCE
PYRENEES
G. du Lion
Golfo de Valencia
Strait of Gibraltar
GIBRALTAR (Br.)
Ceuta (Spain)
Tangier
MOROCCO
Alborán (Spain)
Minorca
Majorca
Iviza
Formentera
Cabrera
BARCELONA
Valencia
Sevilla
Málaga
Zaragoza
Bilbao
Porto
Coimbra
Granada
Córdoba
Murcia
Cartagena
Alicante

ITALY
CONIC PROJECTION
SCALE OF MILES
0 20 40 60 80 100 120
SCALE OF KILOMETRES
0 20 40 60 80 100 120
Capitals of Countries
Regional Capitals
Copyright by C. S. HAMMOND & CO., N. Y.
A 8° B 10° C 12° D 14° E 16° F 18° G
46° 44° 42° 40° 38° 36°
C Longitude 12° East of D Greenwich 14°
GERMANY
AUSTRIA
SWITZERLAND
LIECHTENSTEIN
FRANCE
MONACO
YUGOSLAVIA
TUNISIA
ALGERIA
SAN MARINO
VATICAN CITY
CORSICA
LIGURIAN SEA
TYRRHENIAN SEA
ADRIATIC SEA
IONIAN SEA
MEDITERRANEAN SEA
Malta Channel
Basel
Rhine
Winterthur
L. of Constance
Bregenz
Zürich
St. Gallen
Kufstein
Inn
Bruck
Biel
Luzern
Innsbruck
Hohe Tauern
Niedere Tauern
Lac de Neuchatel
Bern
Landeck
Brenner Pass
Gr. Glockner 12,460
Mur
Graz
Davos
Lienz
Drau
Klagenfurt
Carnic Alps
Drava
Villach
L. Geneva
Brig
Rhône
Lepontine Alps
St. Moritz
Locarno
Merano
Brunico
Bolzano
ALTO ADIGE
TRENTINO
Alpi Dolomiti
Cortina d'Ampezzo
FRIULI-VENEZIA GIULIA
Julian Alps
Sava
Ljubljana
St. Bernard Pass
Lake Maggiore
Intra
Sondrio
Tirano
Lago di Como
Trento
Belluno
Udine
M. Rosa 15,217
M. Blanc 15,781
VALLE D'AOSTA
Aosta
Varese
Como
Lecco
Clusone
Rovereto
Feltre
Pordenone
Bassano
Piave
Gorizia
Portogruaro
Monfalcone
Trieste
Biella
Monza
LOMBARDIA
Bergamo
Lago di Garda
Treviso
Novara
MILANO
Brescia
Vicenza
VENETO
Golfo di Venezia
Karlovac
Rijeka (Fiume)
Frejus Pass
PIEMONTE
Vercelli
Pavia
Cremona
Verona
Padova
Mira
Venezia
Torino
Voghera
Mantova
Rovigo
Este
Chioggia
Adige
Rovinj (Rovigno)
Cottian Alps
Pinerolo
Asti
Piacenza
Suzzara
Po
Porto Tolle
Krk
Alessandria
Parma
Carpi
Panaro
Ferrara
Pula (Pola)
Cres
Alba
Novi Ligure
Reggio
Modena
Comacchio
Saluzzo
EMILIA ROMAGNA
Bologna
Ravenna
Losinj
Pag
Cuneo
Mondovi
LIGURIA
Genova
Golfo di Genova
Imola
Forli
Cesena
Savona
La Spezia
Carrara
Pistoia
Rimini
Dugiotok
Zadar (Zara)
Finale Lig.
Massa
Lucca
Prato
Pesaro
Fano
Nice
Imperia
Viareggio
Firenze
Arno
Senigallia
Sibenik
Sarajevo
San Remo
Ventimiglia
Pisa
Empoli
Monte-varchi
Cagli
MARCHE
Ancona
Split
Livorno
Volterra
Arezzo
Fabriano
Iesi
Pto. Civitanova
Rosignano
Umbertide
TOSCANA
Siena
Macerata
Brač
Mostar
Capraia
C. Corse
Massa Marittima
Trasimeno
Perugia
UMBRIA
Fermo
Vis
Hvar
Piombino
Assisi
Foligno
San Benedetto
Korčula
Portoferraio
Elba
Grosseto
Orvieto
Ascoli Piceno
Giulianova
Dubrovnik
Bastia
Lastovo
Mljet
Calvi
Pianosa
L. di Bolsena
Terni
Spoleto
Teramo
M. Cinto 8,891
Orbetello
Narni
M. Corno 9,560
Pescara
Chieti
Pelagruž (Pelagosa)
Ercegnovi
Cetinje
Giglio
Viterbo
Rieti
Corte
Ronciglione
L'Aquila
LAZIO
Lanciano
Civitavecchia
Avezzano
ABRUZZI E MOLISE
Vasto
Termoli
Ajaccio
Tevere
Sulmona
Tivoli
ROMA
Larino
Testa del Gargano
San Marco
S. Severo
Manfredonia
Lido
Porto Vecchio
Velletri
Frosinone
Sora
Campobasso
Bonifacio
Str. of Bonifacio
Anzio
Latina
Cassino
Minturno
Lucera
Foggia
Barletta
Andria
Molfetta
La Maddalena
Terracina
Volturno
Cerignola
Bari
Asinara
Gaeta
Golfo di Gaeta
Caserta
Benevento
PUGLIA
Corato
Mola di Bari
Olbia
ISOLE PONTINE
Napoli
Aversa
Avellino
Altamura
Monopoli
Porto Torres
CAMPANIA
Lavello
Ostuni
Sassari
Ozieri
Ischia
Vesuvio 3,858
Eboli
Potenza
Gioia del Colle
Brindisi
Alghero
Tre. Annunziata
Capri
Sorrento
Amalfi
Salerno
Sala Consilina
Matera
Taranto
Str. of Otranto
Bosa
Nuoro
Tirso
SARDEGNA
BASILICATA
Pisticci
Golfo di Taranto
Nardo
Lecce
Dorgali
Lauria
Gallipoli
6,017
Monti del Gennargentu
G. di Policastro
C. S. Maria di Leuca
Oristano
Terralba
Castrovillari
Corigliano
CALABRIA
Paola
S. Giovanni
Carbonia
Cagliari
Cosenza
S. Pietro
Quartu Sant' Elena
Crotone
C. Carbonara
Nicastro
C. d. Colonne
C. Spartivento
G. di S. Eufemia
Catanzaro
Stromboli
ISOLE LIPARI
Salina
Ustica
Vibo Valentia
Lipari
Palmi
Gioiosa Ionica
Messina
Siderno
C. S. Vito
Palermo
Reggio di Calabria
Trapani
Bagheria
Barcellona
C. Spartivento
ISOLE EGADI
Alcamo
Termini
Mistretta
Taormina
Stretto di Messina
Corleone
SICILIA
Nicosia
Etna 10,741
Marsala
Castelvetrano
Caltanissetta
Paterno
Acireale
La Galite
Mazara del Vallo
Enna
Catania
Sciacca
Canicatti
Lentini
Augusta
Bizerte
C. Blanc
Agrigento
Niscemi
Caltagirone
Siracusa
Menzel Bourguiba (Ferryville)
G. de Tunis
C. Bon
Licata
Gela
Ragusa
Bône
Béja
Vittoria
Modica
Noto
Tunis
Medjerda
Pantelleria
C. Passero
Golfo de Hammamet
Gozo
Malta (Br.)
Valletta
Sousse
Linosa
Kairouan
Sebkha Sidi-el-Hani
Tébessa
Mehedia
Lampedusa

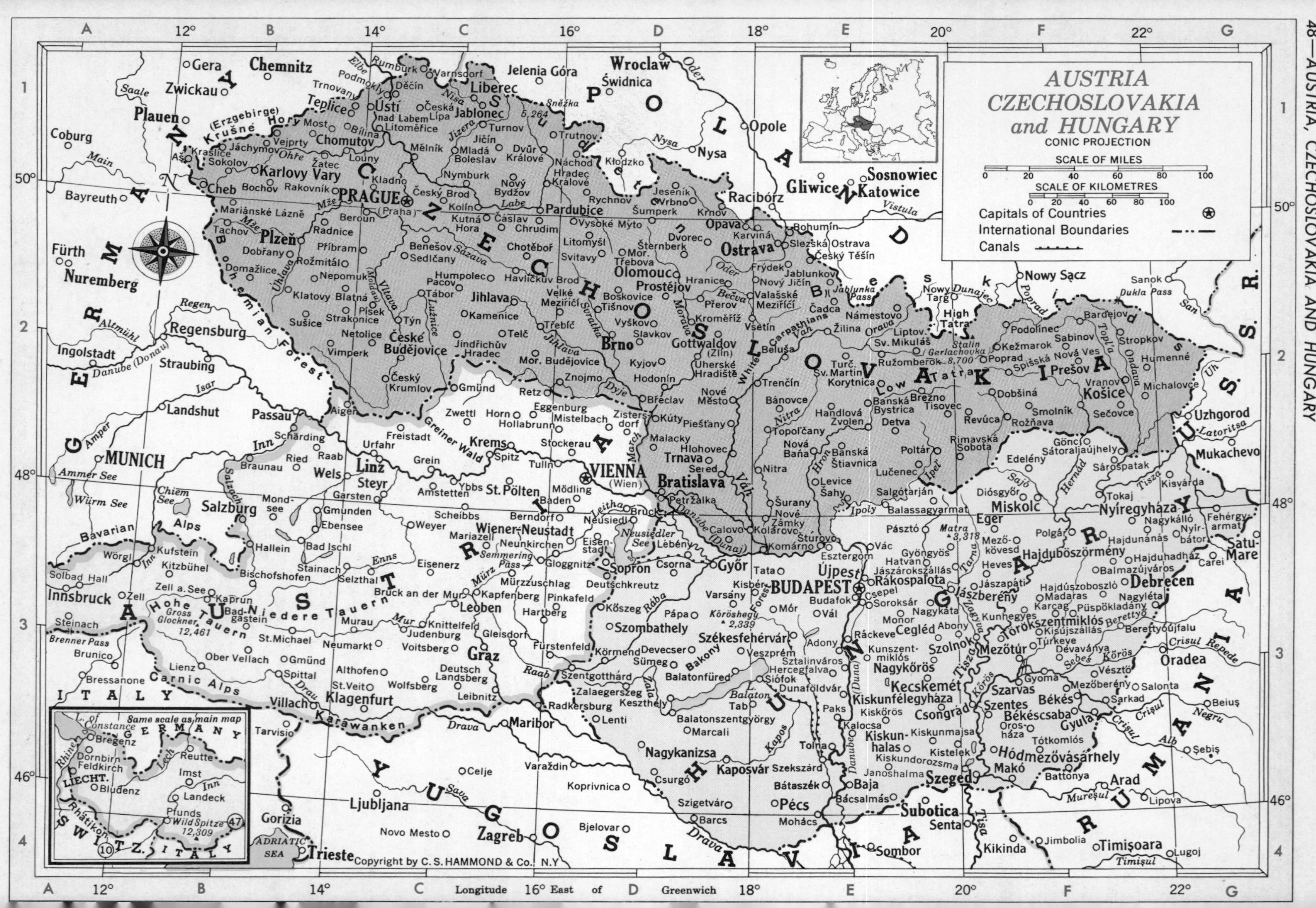
AUSTRIA
CZECHOSLOVAKIA
and HUNGARY
CONIC PROJECTION
SCALE OF MILES
SCALE OF KILOMETRES
Capitals of Countries
International Boundaries
Canals
Same scale as main map
Copyright by C. S. HAMMOND & Co. N.Y
Longitude 16° East of Greenwich

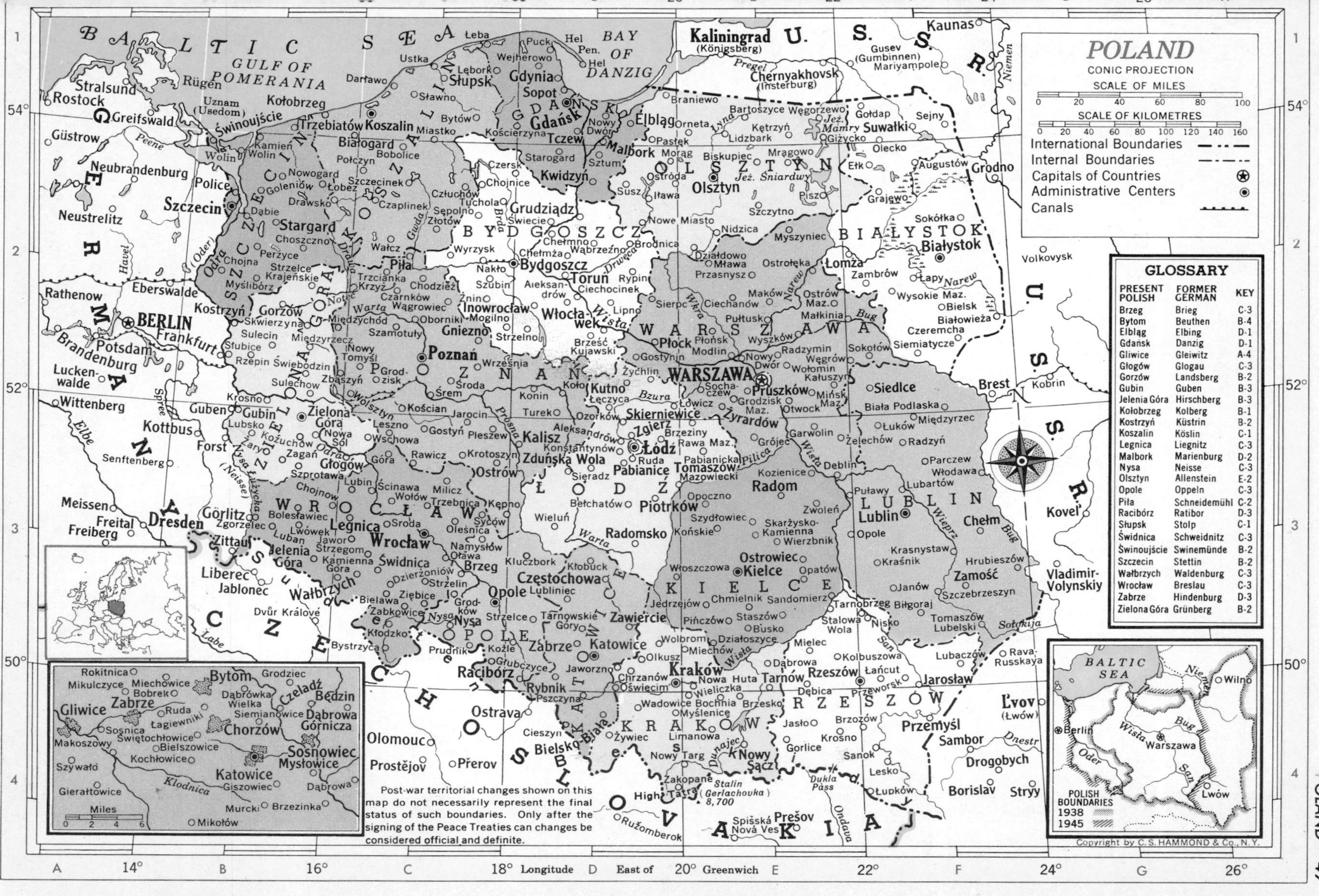

PRESENT POLISH	FORMER GERMAN	KEY
Brzeg	Brieg	C-3
Bytom	Beuthen	B-4
Elbląg	Elbing	D-1
Gdańsk	Danzig	D-1
Gliwice	Gleiwitz	A-4
Głogów	Glogau	C-3
Gorzów	Landsberg	B-2
Gubin	Guben	B-3
Jelenia Góra	Hirschberg	B-3
Kołobrzeg	Kolberg	B-1
Kostrzyń	Küstrin	B-2
Koszalin	Köslin	C-1
Legnica	Liegnitz	C-3
Malbork	Marienburg	D-2
Nysa	Neisse	C-3
Olsztyn	Allenstein	E-2
Opole	Oppeln	C-3
Piła	Schneidemühl	C-2
Racibórz	Ratibor	D-3
Słupsk	Stolp	C-1
Świdnica	Schweidnitz	C-3
Świnoujście	Swinemünde	B-2
Szczecin	Stettin	B-2
Wałbrzych	Waldenburg	C-3
Wrocław	Breslau	C-3
Zabrze	Hindenburg	D-3
Zielona Góra	Grünberg	B-2

POLAND
CZECHOSLOVAKIA
U. S. S. R.
HUNGARY
AUSTRIA
RUMANIA
YUGOSLAVIA
BULGARIA
GERMANY
ADRIATIC SEA
BLACK SEA
Carpathian Mountains
Transylvanian Alps
Dinaric Alps
Balkan Mts.
VIENNA (Wien)
BUDAPEST
BUCHAREST (București)
Belgrade (Beograd)
Sofia
SLOVENIA
CROATIA
BOSNIA
HERCEGOVINA
MONTENEGRO
VOYVODINA
SERBIA
MACEDONIA
KOSOVO-METOHIYAN
ALBANIA
ITALY
Bratislava
Zagreb
Sarajevo
Ljubljana
Trieste
Cluj
Iași
Kishinev
Chernovtsy
Constanța
Varna
Plovdiv
Szeged
Debrecen
Timișoara
Brăila
Galați
Ploești
Craiova
Split
Dubrovnik (Ragusa)
Skopje
L. Balaton
Danube

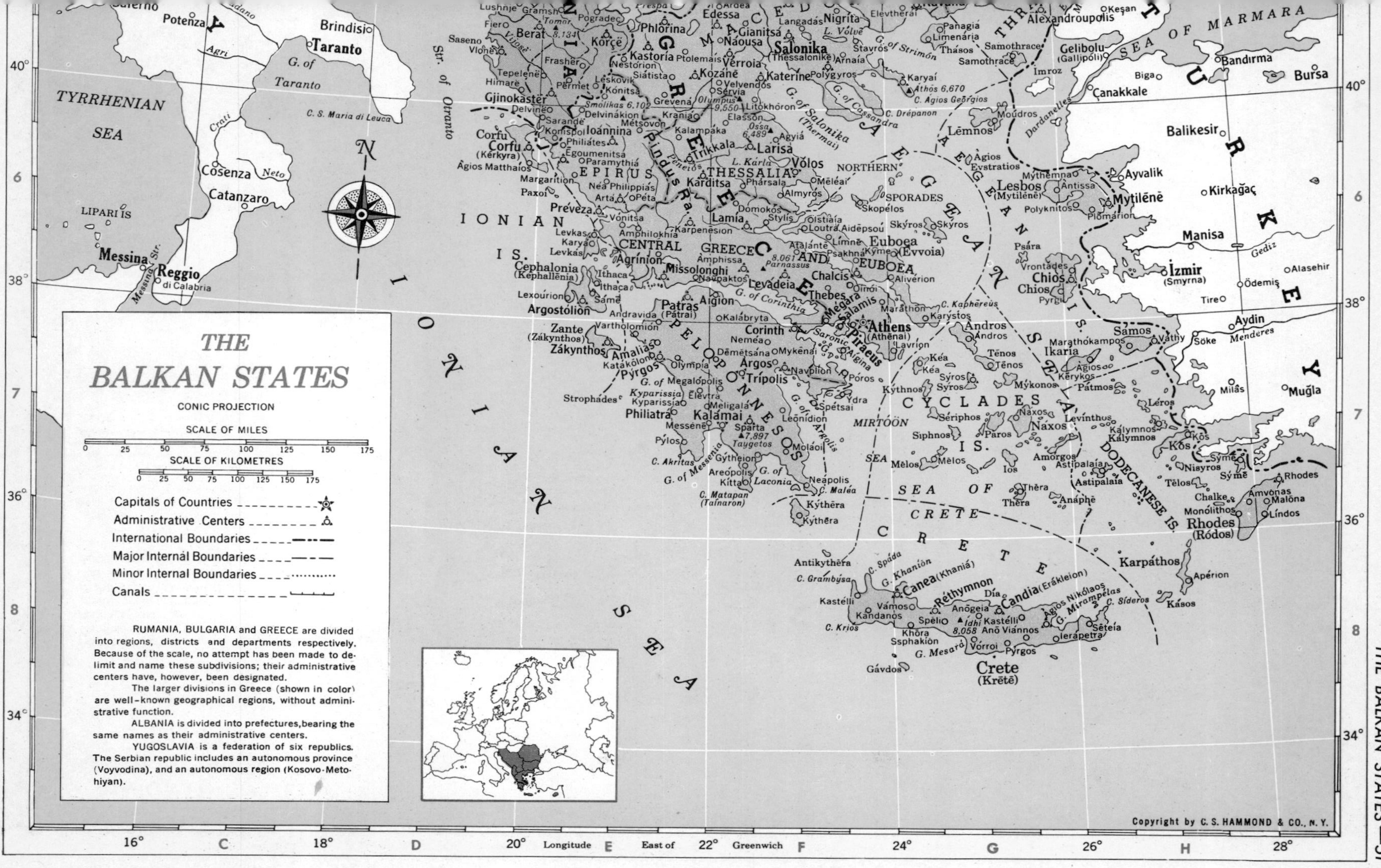
THE BALKAN STATES
CONIC PROJECTION
SCALE OF MILES
0 25 50 75 100 125 150 175
SCALE OF KILOMETRES
0 25 50 75 100 125 150 175
Capitals of Countries
Administrative Centers
International Boundaries
Major Internal Boundaries
Minor Internal Boundaries
Canals
RUMANIA, BULGARIA and GREECE are divided into regions, districts and departments respectively. Because of the scale, no attempt has been made to delimit and name these subdivisions; their administrative centers have, however, been designated.
The larger divisions in Greece (shown in color) are well-known geographical regions, without administrative function.
ALBANIA is divided into prefectures, bearing the same names as their administrative centers.
YUGOSLAVIA is a federation of six republics. The Serbian republic includes an autonomous province (Voyvodina), and an autonomous region (Kosovo-Metohiyan).
Copyright by C. S. HAMMOND & CO., N. Y.
TURKEY
SEA OF MARMARA
AEGEAN SEA
IONIAN SEA
TYRRHENIAN SEA
SEA OF CRETE
MIRTOON SEA
Str. of Otranto
G. of Taranto
G. of Salonika (Thermai)
G. of Corinth
CYCLADES IS.
DODECANESE IS.
IONIAN IS.
NORTHERN SPORADES
PELOPONNESUS
CENTRAL GREECE AND EUBOEA
THESSALIA
EPIRUS
Pindus Ra.
Athens (Athenai)
Piraeus
Salonika (Thessaloníke)
Crete (Krētē)
Rhodes (Ródos)
Corfu (Kérkyra)
Taranto
Brindisi
Messina
Reggio di Calabria
İzmir (Smyrna)
Longitude East of Greenwich

UNION OF SOVIET
SOCIALIST REPUBLICS
European Part
CONIC PROJECTION
SCALE OF MILES
0 50 100 200 300
SCALE OF KILOMETRES
0 50 100 200 300
National Capitals
Capitals of Union Republics
Administrative Centers
International boundaries
Union Republic boundaries
A.S.S.R., Oblast, Kray boundaries
Autonomous Oblast boundaries
Canals
The government of the United States does not recognize the incorporation of Estonia, Latvia and Lithuania into the Soviet Union.
Post-war territorial changes shown on this map do not necessarily represent the final status of such boundaries. Only after the signing of peace treaties can changes be considered official and definite.
ARCTIC OCEAN
KARA SEA
WHITE SEA
GULF OF BOTHNIA
GULF OF OB
NORWAY
FINLAND
SWEDEN
ESTONIAN S.S.R.
LATVIAN S.S.R.
SOCIALIST FEDERATED SOCIALIST REPUBLIC
LENINGRAD
Archangel
Murmansk
Helsinki
Stockholm
Tallinn
Riga
Vologda
Kirov
Perm
Sverdlovsk
Yaroslavl

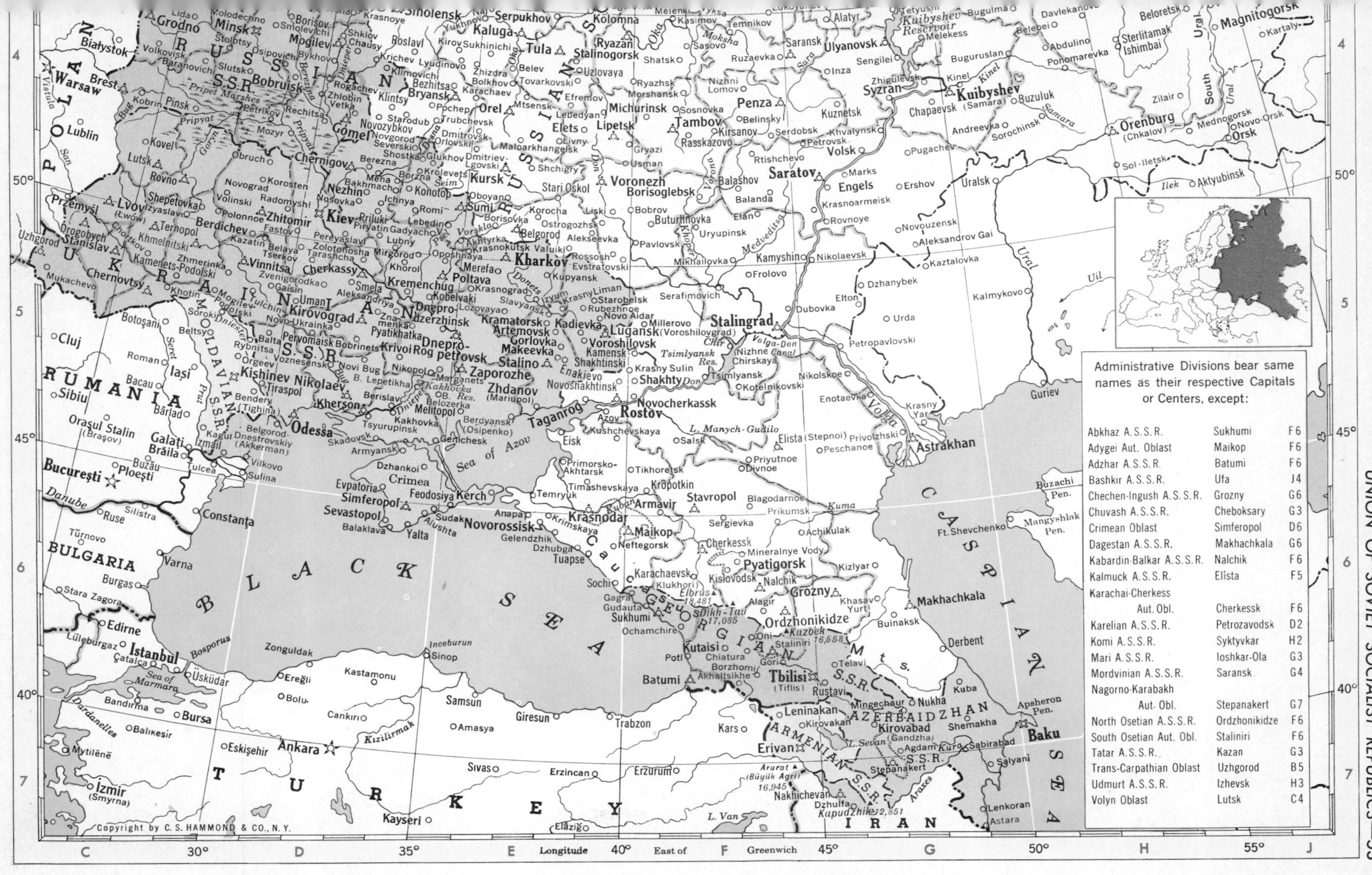

Administrative Divisions bear same names as their respective Capitals or Centers, except:

Division	Capital	Key
Abkhaz A.S.S.R.	Sukhumi	F6
Adygei Aut. Oblast	Maikop	F6
Adzhar A.S.S.R.	Batumi	F6
Bashkir A.S.S.R.	Ufa	J4
Chechen-Ingush A.S.S.R.	Grozny	G6
Chuvash A.S.S.R.	Cheboksary	G3
Crimean Oblast	Simferopol	D6
Dagestan A.S.S.R.	Makhachkala	G6
Kabardin-Balkar A.S.S.R.	Nalchik	F6
Kalmuck A.S.S.R.	Elista	F5
Karachai-Cherkess Aut. Obl.	Cherkessk	F6
Karelian A.S.S.R.	Petrozavodsk	D2
Komi A.S.S.R.	Syktyvkar	H2
Mari A.S.S.R.	Ioshkar-Ola	G3
Mordvinian A.S.S.R.	Saransk	G4
Nagorno-Karabakh Aut. Obl.	Stepanakert	G7
North Osetian A.S.S.R.	Ordzhonikidze	F6
South Osetian Aut. Obl.	Staliniri	F6
Tatar A.S.S.R.	Kazan	G3
Trans-Carpathian Oblast	Uzhgorod	B5
Udmurt A.S.S.R.	Izhevsk	H3
Volyn Oblast	Lutsk	C4

ATLANTIC OCEAN
ARCTIC OCEAN
PACIFIC OCEAN
BERING SEA
SEA OF OKHOTSK
BARENTS SEA
KARA SEA
LAPTEV SEA
NORTH SEA
BALTIC SEA
BLACK SEA
CASPIAN SEA
ADRIATIC SEA
AEGEAN SEA
MEDITERRANEAN SEA
SEA OF JAPAN
YELLOW SEA
RED
GREENLAND
UNITED STATES
ALASKA
Aleutian Is.
North Pole
Iceland
Arctic Circle
UNION OF SOVIET SOCIALIST REPUBLICS
RUSSIAN SOVIET FEDERATED SOCIALIST REPUBLIC
KAZAKH S.S.R.
UZBEK S.S.R.
TURKMEN S.S.R.
MONGOLIAN PEOPLE'S REPUBLIC
MANCHURIA
KOREA
JAPAN
Honshu
CHINA
SINKIANG
INNER MONGOLIA
TURKEY
IRAQ
IRAN (PERSIA)
AFGHANISTAN
SAUDI
Moscow
Leningrad
London
Paris
Berlin
Warsaw
Kiev
Stalingrad
Ankara
Tehran
TOKYO
PEIPING
NANKING
SHANGHAI
SEOUL
Vladivostok
Irkutsk
Novosibirsk
Omsk
Tashkent
Alma Ata
Ulan Bator
Kolyma Range
Sikhote-Alin
Kamchatka
Sakhalin I.
Kurile Is.
New Siberian Is.
Novaya Zemlya
Franz Josef Ld.
Svalbard (Spitsbergen)
Severnaya Zemlya
Caucasus
Ural Mountains
Altai
Tien Shan
Kunlun Mountains
The Gobi
Takla Makan
L. Baikal
L. Balkhash
Lena
Yenisei
Ob
Amur
Volga

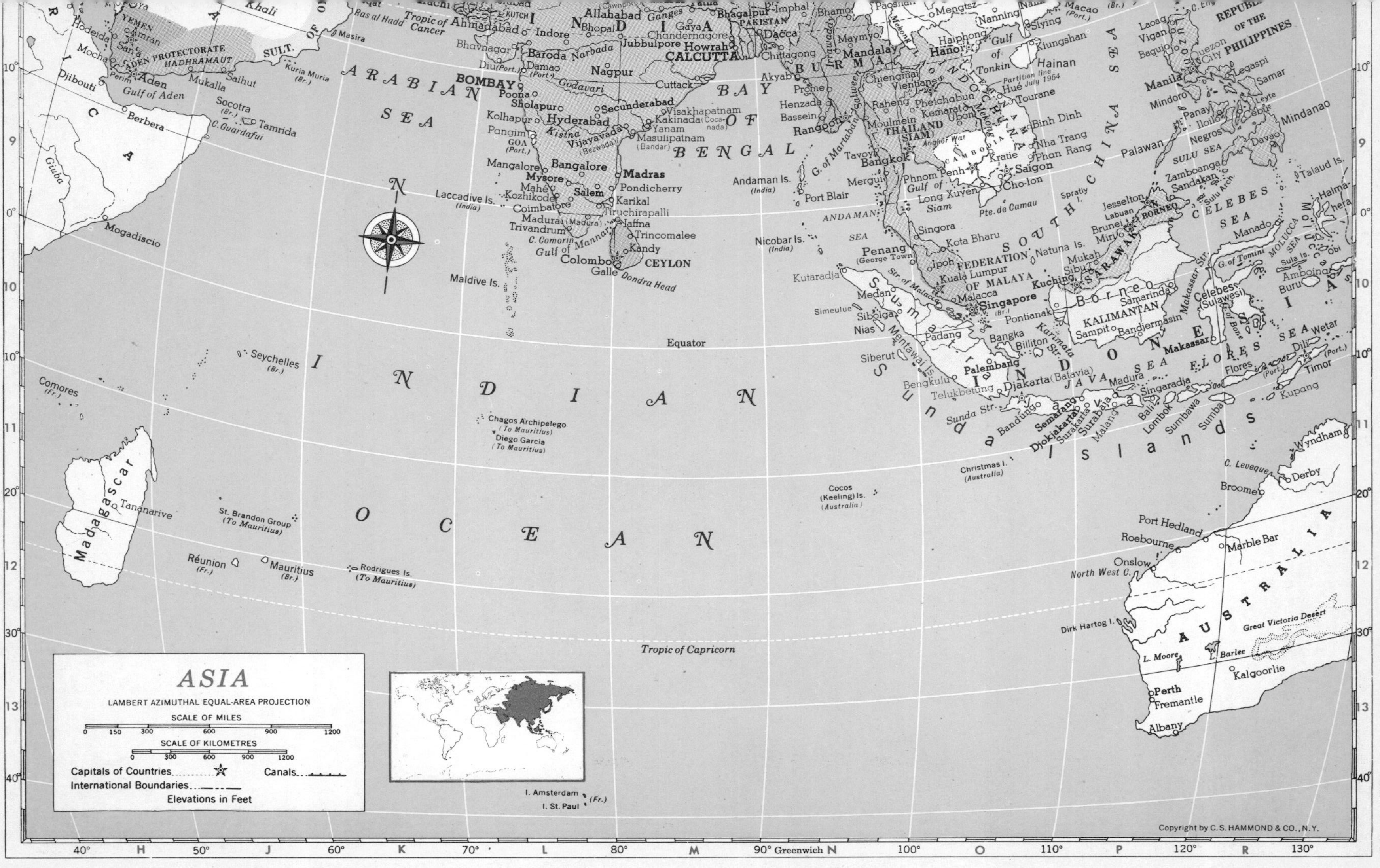

ASIA
LAMBERT AZIMUTHAL EQUAL-AREA PROJECTION
SCALE OF MILES
0 150 300 600 900 1200
SCALE OF KILOMETRES
0 300 600 900 1200
Capitals of Countries
International Boundaries
Canals
Elevations in Feet
Copyright by C. S. HAMMOND & CO., N. Y.
I N D I A N O C E A N
ARABIAN SEA
BAY OF BENGAL
SOUTH CHINA SEA
SULU SEA
CELEBES SEA
JAVA SEA
FLORES SEA
ANDAMAN SEA
Equator
Tropic of Capricorn
Tropic of Cancer
90° Greenwich
REPUBLIC OF THE PHILIPPINES
INDONESIA
AUSTRALIA
FEDERATION OF MALAYA
THAILAND (SIAM)
BURMA
PAKISTAN
INDIA
CEYLON
ADEN PROTECTORATE
YEMEN
Madagascar
BOMBAY
CALCUTTA
Madras
Colombo
Bangkok
Saigon
Hanoi
Singapore
Djakarta (Batavia)
Manila
Perth
Fremantle
Albany
Kalgoorlie
Port Hedland
Broome
Derby
Wyndham
Great Victoria Desert
Maldive Is.
Laccadive Is. (India)
Andaman Is. (India)
Nicobar Is. (India)
Chagos Archipelego (To Mauritius)
Diego Garcia (To Mauritius)
Seychelles (Br.)
Mauritius (Br.)
Réunion (Fr.)
Rodrigues Is. (To Mauritius)
St. Brandon Group (To Mauritius)
Comores (Fr.)
Cocos (Keeling) Is. (Australia)
Christmas I. (Australia)
I. Amsterdam (Fr.)
I. St. Paul
Socotra (Br.)
Mogadiscio
Djibouti
Berbera
Aden
Gulf of Aden
Tananarive

BLACK SEA
MEDITERRANEAN SEA
AEGEAN SEA
TURKEY
UNITED ARAB REPUBLIC
SYRIA
LEBANON
ISRAEL
JORDAN
IRAQ
SAUDI ARABIA
UNITED ARAB REPUBLIC EGYPT
SUDAN
ETHIOPIA
ERITREA
YEMEN
ADEN PROT.
KUWAIT
CYPRUS (Br.)
RED SEA
İSTANBUL
Ankara
İzmir (Smyrna)
Bursa
Konya
Adana
Trabzon
Erzurum
Tbilisi
Erivan
Tabriz
Aleppo (Haleb)
Homs
Hama
Beirut
Damascus (Dimishq)
Haifa
Tel Aviv
Jerusalem
Amman
Nicosia
Alexandria
Port Said
CAIRO (El Qahira)
Suez
Asyut
Aswan
Wadi Halfa
Khartoum
Omdurman
Khartoum North
Atbara
Port Sudan
Kassala
Asmara
Massawa
Mosul
Kirkuk
Baghdad
Basra
Hamadan
Kermanshah
Medina
Mecca
Jidda
Riyadh
Taif
Hodeida
San'a
Aden
Mocha
Nubian Desert
Arabian Desert
Libyan Desert
Nefud
Red Desert
Syrian Desert
Tropic of Cancer
Nile
Euphrates
Tigris
Taurus Mts.
Caucasus
L. Van
L. Urmia
L. Sevan
Dead Sea
Sea of Galilee
Gulf of Suez
Gulf of Aqaba
Suez Canal
Sinai Pen.
Qattara Depression
Bahr es Safi (Al Ahqaf)
Jebel Shammar
Arma Plateau
DAHLAK ARCHIPELAGO
JEZ. FARASAN
Bab el Mandeb
Kazbek 16,558
Ararat (Büyük Ağrı) 16,945
Mt. Sinai
1st Cataract
2nd Cataract
3rd Cataract
4th Cataract
5th Cataract
6th Cataract
ASWAN DAM
SENNAR DAM

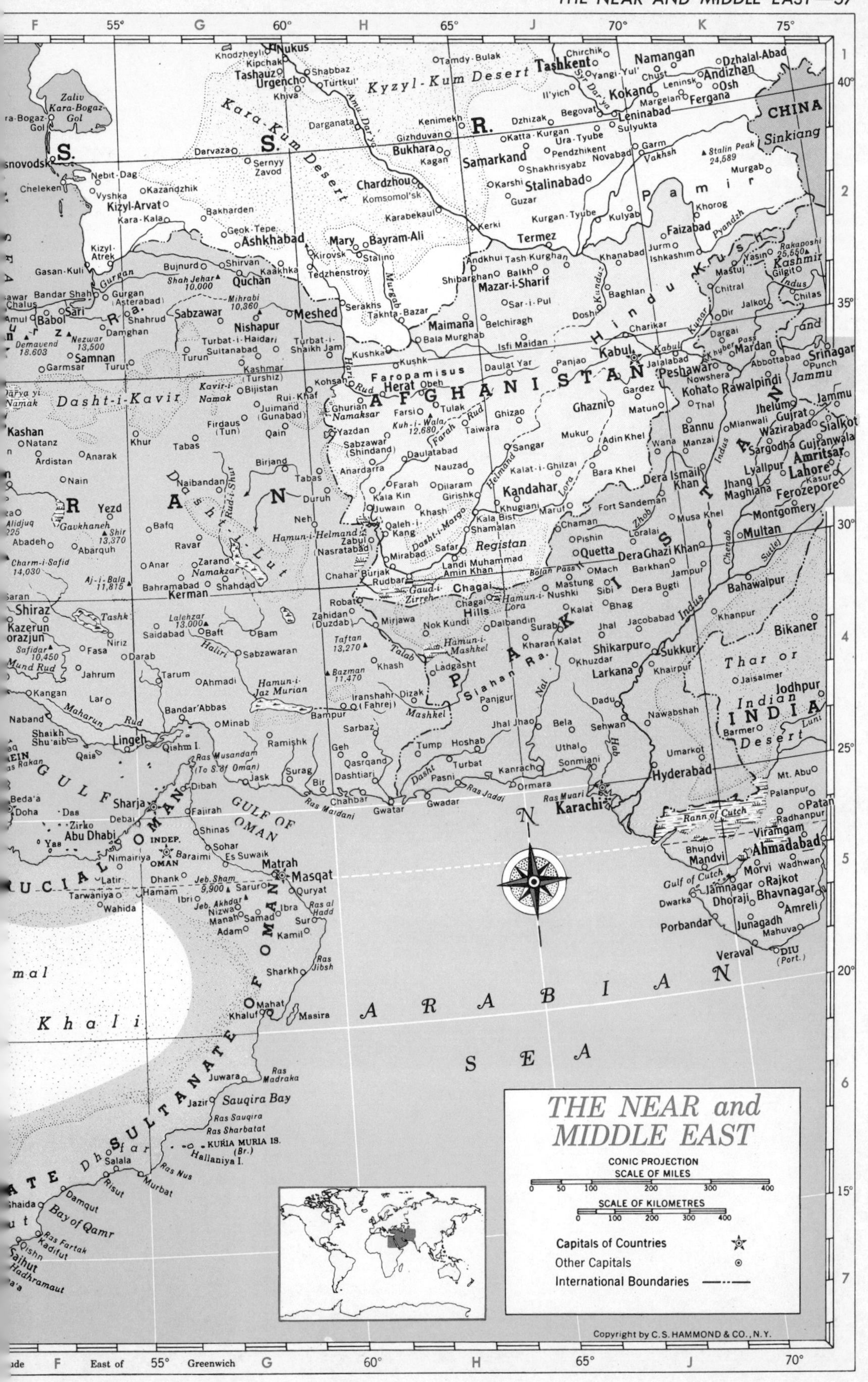
THE NEAR and MIDDLE EAST
CONIC PROJECTION
SCALE OF MILES
0 50 100 200 300 400
SCALE OF KILOMETRES
0 100 200 300 400
Capitals of Countries
Other Capitals
International Boundaries
Copyright by C. S. HAMMOND & CO., N.Y.
F 55° G 60° H 65° J 70° K 75°
ude F East of 55° Greenwich G 60° H 65° J 70°
1 2 3 4 5 6 7
40° 35° 30° 25° 20° 15°
Kyzyl-Kum Desert
Kara-Kum Desert
Zaliv Kara-Bogaz-Gol
Kara-Bogaz-Gol
CHINA
Sinkiang
Pamir
Hindu Kush
Stalin Peak 24,589
Rakaposhi 25,550
Kashmir
AFGHANISTAN
PAKISTAN
INDIA
Thar or Indian Desert
Rann of Cutch
Gulf of Cutch
Dasht-i-Kavir
Dasht-i-Lut
Faropamisus
Registan
Chagai Hills
Siahan Ra.
GULF OF OMAN
ARABIAN SEA
SULTANATE OF OMAN
INDEP. OMAN
Khali
Tashkent
Namangan
Dzhalal-Abad
Andizhan
Osh
Fergana
Kokand
Leninabad
Chirchik
Yangi-Yul'
Chust
Margelan
Nukus
Khodzheyli
Kipchak
Tashauz
Urgench
Khiva
Shabbaz
Turtkul'
Tamdy-Bulak
Darganata
Kenimekh
Gizhduvan
Bukhara
Kagan
Samarkand
Katta-Kurgan
Ura-Tyube
Pendzhikent
Shakhrisyabz
Novabad
Garm
Dzhizak
Begovat
Sulyukta
Il'yich
Chardzhou
Komsomol'sk
Karshi
Guzar
Stalinabad
Murgab
Khorog
Kurgan-Tyube
Kulyab
Faizabad
Karabekaul
Kerki
Termez
Darvaza
Sernyy Zavod
Krasnovodsk
Nebit-Dag
Cheleken
Vyshka
Kazandzhik
Kizyl-Arvat
Kara-Kala
Bakharden
Geok-Tepe
Ashkhabad
Mary
Bayram-Ali
Kirovsk
Stalino
Tedzhenstroy
Kizyl-Atrek
Gasan-Kuli
Bujnurd
Shirvan
Kaakhka
Quchan
Shah Jehar 10,000
Mihrabi 10,360
Gurgan (Asterabad)
Bandar Shah
Chalus
Amul
Babol
Sari
Shahrud
Damghan
Demavend 18,603
Nezwar 13,500
Semnan
Garmsar
Sabzawar
Nishapur
Meshed
Serakhs
Takhta-Bazar
Turbat-i-Haidari
Sultanabad
Turun
Turbat-i-Shaikh Jam
Kashmar (Turshiz)
Kavir-i-Namak
Bijistan
Juimand (Gunabad)
Firdaus (Tun)
Qain
Tabas
Khur
Kashan
Natanz
Ardistan
Anarak
Nain
Yezd
Gavkhaneh
Shir 13,370
Abarquh
Abadeh
Bafq
Ravar
Anar
Zarand
Namakzar
Kerman
Bahramabad
Shahdad
Birjand
Naibandan
Rud-i-Shur
Duruh
Neh
Hamun-i-Helmand
Zabul (Nasratabad)
Mirabad
Chahar Burjak
Rudbar
Gaud-i-Zirreh
Charm-i-Safid 14,030
Aj-i-Bala 11,815
Shiraz
Tashk
Kazerun
Niriz
Safidar 10,450
Fasa
Darab
Mund Rud
Jahrum
Lar
Kangan
Maharun
Naband
Shaikh Shu'aib
Qais
Lingeh
Qishm I.
Bandar'Abbas
Minab
Rud
Tarum
Ahmadi
Hamun-i-Jaz Murian
Lalehzar 13,000
Baft
Bam
Saidabad
Haliri
Sabzawaran
Zahidan (Duzdab)
Robat
Mirjawa
Taftan 13,270
Talab
Khash
Bazman 11,470
Iranshahr (Fahrej)
Dizak
Bampur
Mashkel
Sarbaz
Ramishk
Geh
Qasrqand
Dashtiari
Surag
Bir
Jask
Ras Musandam (To S. of Oman)
Chahbar
Ras Maidani
Gwatar
Gwadar
Pasni
Ras Jaddi
Turbat
Tump
Hoshab
Dasht
Kanrach
Ormara
Ras Muari
Karachi
Panjgur
Jhal Jhao
Bela
Uthal
Sonmiani
Sehwan
Hab
Dadu
Nawabshah
Umarkot
Hyderabad
Larkana
Shikarpur
Sukkur
Khairpur
Jhal
Jacobabad
Khuzdar
Kalat
Kharan Kalat
Nushki
Mastung
Sibi
Bhag
Dera Bugti
Mach
Bolan Pass
Quetta
Pishin
Chaman
Loralai
Fort Sandeman
Zhob
Barkhan
Dera Ghazi Khan
Jampur
Musa Khel
Dera Ismail Khan
Chenab
Sutlej
Indus
Multan
Bahawalpur
Khanpur
Bikaner
Jaisalmer
Jodhpur
Barmer
Luni
Mt. Abu
Palanpur
Patan
Radhanpur
Viramgam
Ahmadabad
Bhuj
Mandvi
Morvi
Wadhwan
Jamnagar
Rajkot
Dwarka
Dhoraji
Bhavnagar
Amreli
Porbandar
Junagadh
Mahuva
Veraval
DIU (Port.)
Montgomery
Lyallpur
Jhang Maghiana
Ferozepore
Kasur
Lahore
Amritsar
Gujranwala
Sialkot
Sargodha
Wazirabad
Gujrat
Jhelum
Jammu
Mianwali
Bannu
Thal
Kohat
Rawalpindi
Nowshera
Peshawar
Mardan
Abbottabad
Punch
Srinagar
Khyber Pass
Jalalabad
Kabul
Charikar
Kunar
Dargai
Dir
Chitral
Mastuj
Yasin
Gilgit
Chilas
Jalkot
Khanabad
Jurm
Ishkashim
Pyandzh
Kunduz
Baghlan
Doshi
Andkhui
Tash Kurghan
Shibarghan
Balkh
Mazar-i-Sharif
Sar-i-Pul
Belchiragh
Maimana
Bala Murghab
Murgab
Kushka
Kushk
Isfi Maidan
Daulat Yar
Panjao
Kohsan
Herat
Obeh
Hari Rud
Ghurian
Namaksar
Farsi
Tulak
Kuh-i-Wala 12,680
Farah Rud
Ghizao
Taiwara
Yazdan
Sabzawar (Shindand)
Daulatabad
Anardarra
Nauzad
Farah
Kala Kin
Dilaram
Girishk
Juwain
Khash
Qaleh-i-Kang
Dasht-i-Margo
Kala Bist
Shamalan
Khugiani
Safar
Landi Muhammad Amin Khan
Chagai
Hamun-i-Lora
Dalbandin
Nok Kundi
Hamun-i-Mashkel
Ladgasht
Surab
Helmand
Kandahar
Kalat-i-Ghilzai
Marui
Lora
Bara Khel
Sangar
Mukur
Adin Khel
Ghazni
Gardez
Matun
Wana
Manzai
Sharja
Dibah
Fajirah
Debai
Das
Zirko
Abu Dhabi
Yas
Doha
Beda'a
Shinas
Sohar
Es Suwaik
Baraimi
Nimairiya
Latir
Dhank
Jeb. Sham 9,900
Saruq
Matrah
Masqat
Quryat
Tarwaniya
Hamam
Ibri
Wahida
Jeb. Akhdar
Nizwa
Manah
Samad
Ibra
Ras al Hadd
Sur
Adam
Kamil
Ras Jibsh
Sharkh
Mahat
Khaluf
Masira
Ras Madraka
Juwara
Jazir
Sauqira Bay
Ras Sauqira
Ras Sharbatat
KURIA MURIA IS. (Br.)
Hallaniya I.
Salala
Dhofar
Ras Nus
Murbat
Risut
Damqut
Bay of Qamr
Ras Fartak
Kadifut
Qishn
Saihut
Hadhramaut
Shaida

ISRAEL
and
JORDAN
CYLINDRICAL PROJECTION
SCALE OF MILES
SCALE OF KILOMETRES
Capitals of Countries
District Capitals
International Boundaries
District Boundaries
Sub-District Boundaries
Israel is shown according to the terms of the Israeli-Jordanian and Israeli-Egyptian armistice agreements. The districts and sub-districts of the former Palestinian Mandate are shown for reference only and are not the present-day administrative divisions.
MEDITERRANEAN SEA
LEBANON
UNITED ARAB REPUBLIC
SYRIA
JORDAN
UNITED ARAB REPUBLIC
EGYPT
JORDANIAN ADMINISTRATION
EGYPTIAN ADMINISTRATION
GALILEE
ACRE
HAIFA
SAMARIA
LYDDA
JERUSALEM
GAZA
BEERSHEBA
HAIFA
TEL AVIV
Jaffa
JERUSALEM
Amman
Bay of Acre
Bahret Tabariye (Sea of Galilee)
Bahret Lut (Dead Sea)
Jordan
Beersheba
Hebron
Bethlehem
Nablus
Jericho
Ramallah
Tiberias
Nazareth
Acre
Gaza
Irbid
Salt
Madaba
Gulf of 'Aqaba
Elath
'Aqaba
Negeb
Longitude
East of Greenwich
Copyright by C. S. HAMMOND & CO., N.Y.

THE INDIAN AND INDOCHINESE PENINSULAS
LAMBERT AZIMUTHAL EQUAL-AREA PROJECTION
SCALE OF MILES
0 100 200 300 400 500
SCALE OF KILOMETRES
0 100 200 300 400 500
Capitals of Countries
International Boundaries
Copyright by C. S. HAMMOND & Co., N. Y.
Longitude D East of Greenwich 90°

EASTERN CHINA, JAPAN & KOREA
CONIC PROJECTION
SCALE OF MILES
0 50 100 200 300 400
SCALE OF KILOMETRES
0 50 100 200 300 400
Capitals of Countries
Provincial Capitals
Trade Routes
Canals
Copyright by C. S. HAMMOND & Co., N. Y.
Longitude 125° East of Greenwich 130°
U. S. S. R.
MONGOLIAN REP.
SAKHALIN ISLAND (U.S.S.R.)
HOKKAIDO
HONSHU
SHIKOKU
KYUSHU
JAPAN
KOREA
SEA OF JAPAN
YELLOW SEA
EAST CHINA SEA
SOUTH CHINA SEA
PACIFIC OCEAN
PHILIPPINES
LUZON
TAIWAN (Formosa)
HONG KONG (Br.)
PEIPING (Peking)
TIENTSIN
NANKING
SHANGHAI
TOKYO
SEOUL
Vladivostok
Khabarovsk
Blagoveshchensk
Mukden
Shenyang
Harbin
Canton
Foochow
Hangchow
Hankow
Taipei
Naha
P'yŏngyang
Pusan
Osaka
Kyoto
Kobe
Nagoya
Yokohama
Sapporo
Hakodate
Hiroshima
Nagasaki
Kagoshima
Sendai
Niigata
Kanazawa
HEILUNGKIANG
SUNGKIANG
KIRIN
LIAOPEH
NUNKIANG
HINGAN
JEHOL
CHAHAR
SUIYUAN
SHANSI
HOPEH
SHANTUNG
HONAN
ANHWEI
KIANGSU
CHEKIANG
KIANGSI
FUKIEN
KWANGTUNG
HUPEH
HUNAN
Korea Strait
La Perouse Str.
Tatarski Strait
Tsugaru Str.
Formosa Strait
Bashi Channel
Balintang Channel
Batan Is.
Babuyan Is.
RYUKYU IS.
DAITO ISLANDS (U.S. Administration)
BONIN ISLANDS
VOLCANO IS.
Iwo Jima
Tropic of Cancer

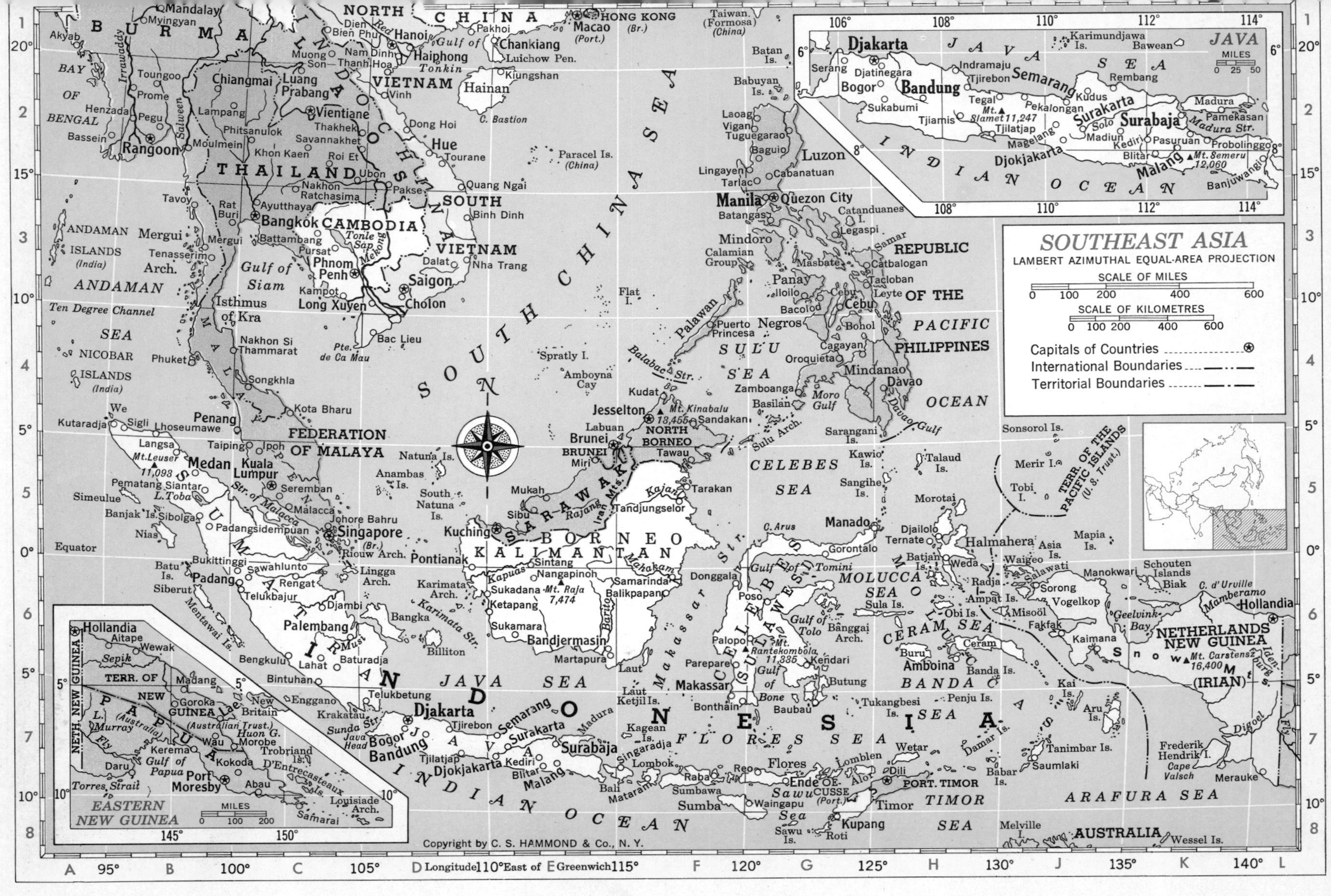
SOUTHEAST ASIA
LAMBERT AZIMUTHAL EQUAL-AREA PROJECTION
SCALE OF MILES
0 100 200 400 600
SCALE OF KILOMETRES
0 100 200 400 600
Capitals of Countries
International Boundaries
Territorial Boundaries
JAVA
EASTERN NEW GUINEA
SOUTH CHINA SEA
INDIAN OCEAN
JAVA SEA
BURMA
THAILAND
CAMBODIA
SOUTH VIETNAM
NORTH VIETNAM
FEDERATION OF MALAYA
REPUBLIC OF THE PHILIPPINES
INDONESIA
NORTH BORNEO
SARAWAK
BRUNEI
NETHERLANDS NEW GUINEA (IRIAN)
AUSTRALIA
Copyright by C. S. HAMMOND & Co., N. Y.
Longitude 110° East of Greenwich 115°

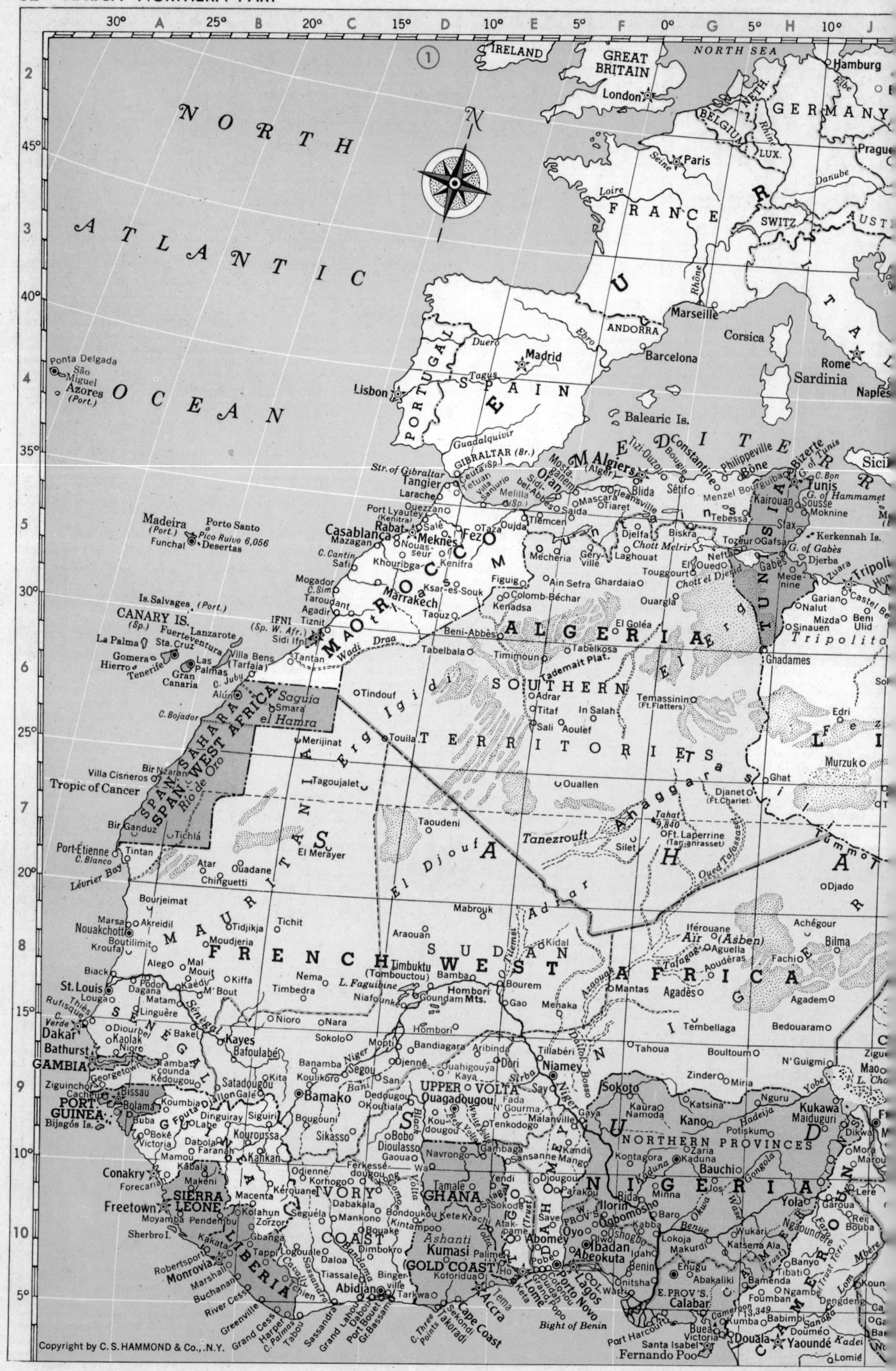

Map continued

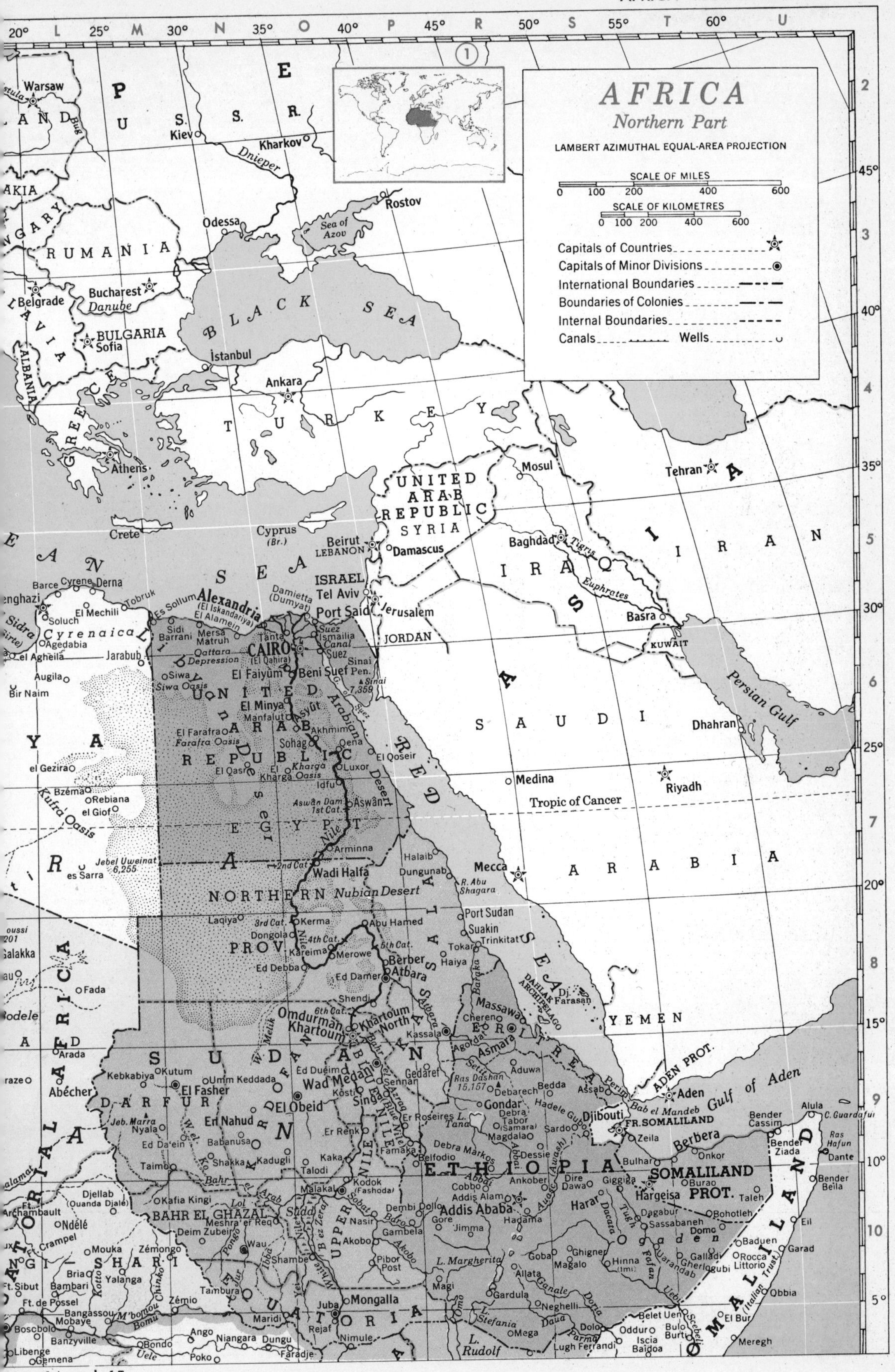
AFRICA
Northern Part
LAMBERT AZIMUTHAL EQUAL-AREA PROJECTION
SCALE OF MILES
0 100 200 400 600
SCALE OF KILOMETRES
0 100 200 400 600
Capitals of Countries
Capitals of Minor Divisions
International Boundaries
Boundaries of Colonies
Internal Boundaries
Canals
Wells
20° L 25° M 30° N 35° O 40° P 45° R 50° S 55° T 60° U
2
45°
3
40°
4
35°
5
30°
6
25°
7
20°
8
15°
9
10°
10
5°
U. S. S. R.
Warsaw
Kiev
Kharkov
Dnieper
Rostov
Sea of Azov
Odessa
RUMANIA
Bucharest
Danube
Belgrade
BULGARIA
Sofia
ALBANIA
GREECE
Athens
BLACK SEA
İstanbul
Ankara
TURKEY
Crete
Cyprus (Br.)
Beirut
LEBANON
Damascus
UNITED ARAB REPUBLIC
SYRIA
Mosul
Tehran
IRAN
Baghdad
Tigris
Euphrates
IRAQ
Basra
KUWAIT
Persian Gulf
Dhahran
ISRAEL
Tel Aviv
Jerusalem
JORDAN
Port Said
Suez
Ismailia
Suez Canal
Sinai Pen.
Damietta (Dumyat)
Alexandria (El Iskandariya)
El Alamein
Es Sollum
Tobruk
Derna
Cyrene
Barce
Soluch
El Mechili
Cyrenaica
Agedabia
el Agheila
Jarabub
Augila
Bir Naim
Sidi Barrani
Mersa Matruh
Qattara Depression
Tanta
CAIRO (El Qahira)
El Faiyum
Beni Suef
Siwa
Siwa Oasis
El Minya
Manfalut
Asyût
Akhmim
Sohag
Qena
El Farafra
Farafra Oasis
El Qasr
El Kharga
Kharga Oasis
Luxor
Idfu
Aswân Dam
1st Cat.
Aswân
El Qoseir
UNITED ARAB REPUBLIC
EGYPT
Libyan Desert
Arabian Desert
RED SEA
el Gezira
Bzéma
Rebiana
el Giof
Kufra Oasis
Jebel Uweinat 6,255
es Sarra
Arminna
2nd Cat.
Wadi Halfa
Halaib
Dungunab
R. Abu Shagara
NORTHERN
Nubian Desert
PROV.
Laqiya
3rd Cat.
Kerma
Abu Hamed
Dongola
4th Cat.
5th Cat.
Kareima
Merowe
Berber
Atbara
Ed Debba
Ed Damer
Shendi
6th Cat.
Omdurman
Khartoum
Khartoum North
Port Sudan
Suakin
Trinkitat
Tokar
Haiya
Kassala
Massawa
Chereno
Asmara
ERITREA
DAHLAK ARCHIPELAGO
Dj. Farasan
Medina
Tropic of Cancer
Riyadh
Mecca
SAUDI ARABIA
YEMEN
ADEN PROT.
Aden
Gulf of Aden
Perim
Bab el Mandeb
Assab
Djibouti
FR. SOMALILAND
Zeila
Berbera
Bulhar
Onkor
SOMALILAND PROT.
Hargeisa
Burao
Taleh
Alula
C. Guardafui
Bender Cassim
Bender Ziada
Ras Hafun
Dante
Bender Beila
Eil
Garad
Obbia
SOMALIA
(Italian Trust.)
El Bur
Meregh
ETHIOPIA
Addis Ababa
Gondar
Debra Tabor
Magdala
Dessie
Dire Dawa
Harar
Jimma
Gore
Ras Dashan 15,157
L. Tana
Aduwa
Debarech
Bedda
Debra Markos
Ankober
L. Margherita
Gardula
Neghelli
Lugh Ferrandi
Dolo
Oddur
Iscia Baidoa
Bulo Burti
Belet Uen
L. Stefania
L. Rudolf
Mega
Juba
Mongalla
Rejaf
Nimule
SUDAN
DARFUR
KORDOFAN
BLUE NILE
UPPER NILE
BAHR EL GHAZAL
EQUATORIA
El Fasher
El Obeid
En Nahud
Kutum
Kebkabiya
Umm Keddada
Jeb. Marra
Nyala
Ed Da'ein
Babanusa
Shakka
Kadugli
Talodi
Kaka
Malakal
Kodok (Fashoda)
Wad Medani
Ed Dueim
Kosti
Sennar
Singa
Gedaref
Er Roseires
Er Renk
Famaka
Belfodio
Nasir
Akobo
Gambela
Pibor Post
Wau
Meshra' er Req
Deim Zubeir
Shambe
Tambura
Maridi
Sudd
Abécher
Fada
Arada
Kafia Kingi
Djellab (Ouanda Djalé)
Ft. Archambault
Ndélé
Ft. Crampel
Mouka
Zémongo
Bria
Yalanga
Ft. Sibut
Bambari
Ft. de Possel
Bangassou
Mobaye
Zémio
Boscbolo
Banzyville
Libenge
Gemena
Bondo
Ango
Niangara
Dungu
Poko
Faradje
Uele
Bomu
Mbomou

ges 64 and 65

Map continued

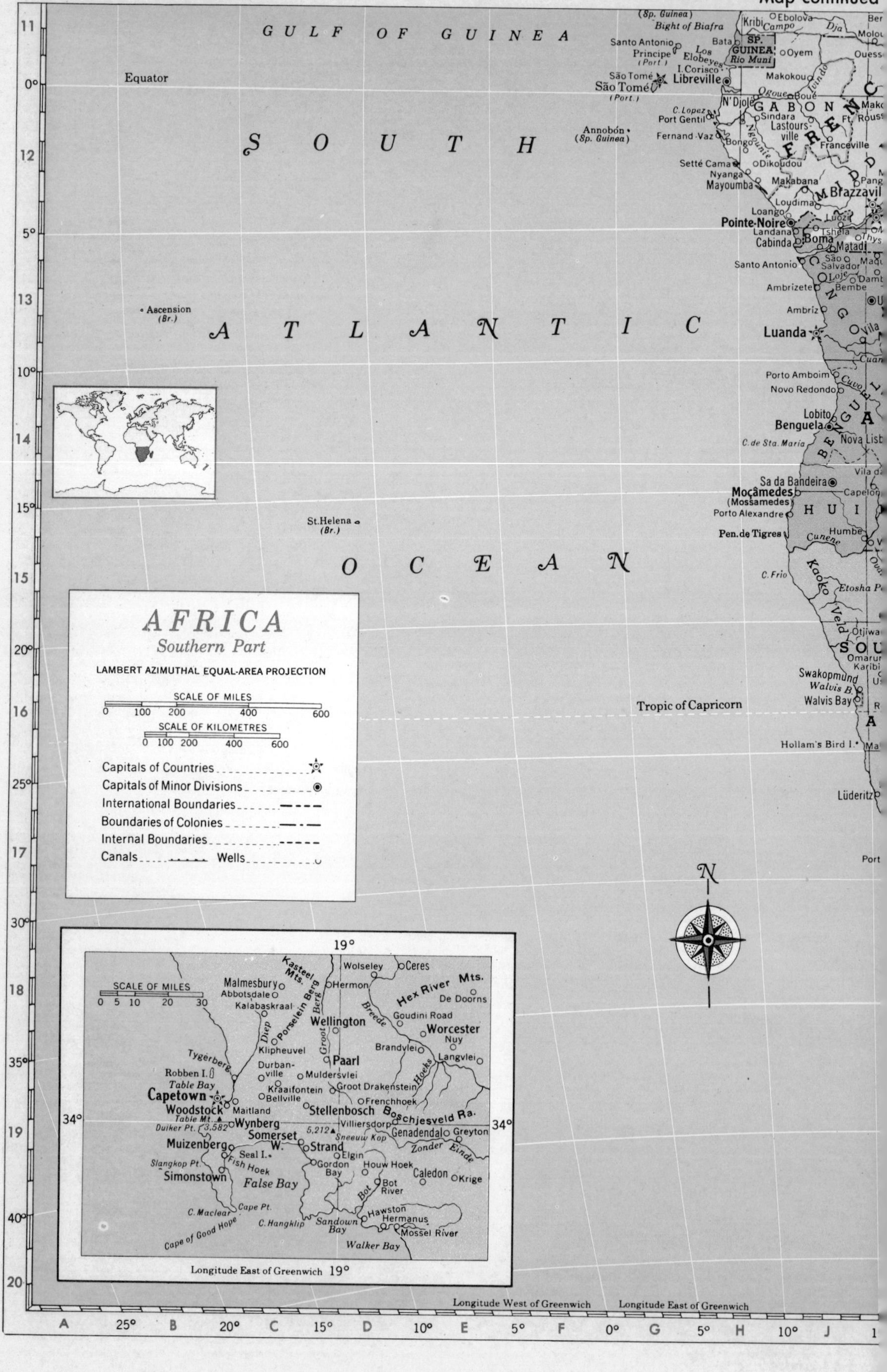

AFRICA
Southern Part

LAMBERT AZIMUTHAL EQUAL-AREA PROJECTION

SCALE OF MILES
0 100 200 400 600

SCALE OF KILOMETRES
0 100 200 400 600

Capitals of Countries
Capitals of Minor Divisions
International Boundaries
Boundaries of Colonies
Internal Boundaries
Canals
Wells

GULF OF GUINEA
SOUTH ATLANTIC OCEAN
Equator
Tropic of Capricorn
Ascension (Br.)
St.Helena (Br.)
Annobón (Sp. Guinea)
São Tomé (Port.)
Santo Antonio
Principe (Port.)
Bight of Biafra
Libreville
Port Gentil
Pointe-Noire
Cabinda
Luanda
Lobito
Benguela
Moçâmedes (Mossamedes)
Porto Alexandre
Pen.de Tigres
C. Frio
Swakopmund
Walvis Bay
Hollam's Bird I.
Lüderitz

19°
Wolseley
Ceres
Malmesbury
Abbotsdale
Kalabaskraal
Hermon
Hex River Mts.
De Doorns
Goudini Road
Wellington
Worcester
Nuy
Klipheuvel
Paarl
Brandvlei
Langvlei
Tygerberg
Robben I.
Table Bay
Durbanville
Muldersvlei
Kraaifontein
Bellville
Groot Drakenstein
Capetown
Woodstock
Maitland
Stellenbosch
Frenchhoek
Boschjesveld Ra.
34°
Table Mt. 3,582
Duiker Pt.
Wynberg
Somerset W.
5,212
Villiersdorp
Genadendal
Greyton
Sneeuw Kop
Zonder Einde
Muizenberg
Seal I.
Strand
Elgin
Slangkop Pt.
Fish Hoek
Gordon Bay
Houw Hoek
Caledon
Krige
Simonstown
False Bay
Bot River
C. Maclear
Cape Pt.
Cape of Good Hope
C. Hangklip
Sandown Bay
Hawston
Hermanus
Mossel River
Walker Bay

SCALE OF MILES
0 5 10 20 30

Longitude East of Greenwich 19°

Longitude West of Greenwich
Longitude East of Greenwich

A 25° B 20° C 15° D 10° E 5° F 0° G 5° H 10° J

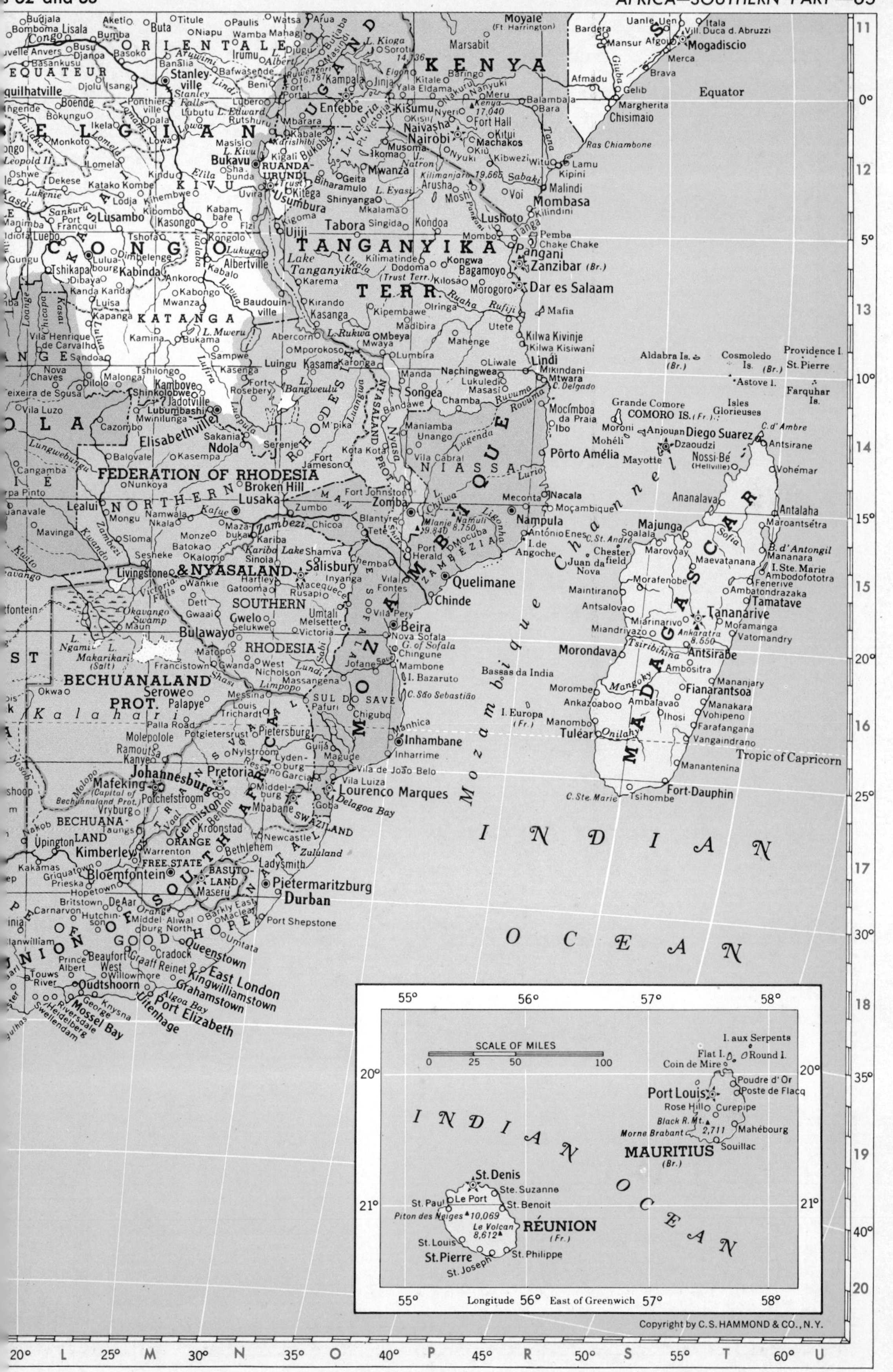
KENYA
UGANDA
TANGANYIKA TERR.
BELGIAN CONGO
ORIENTALE
EQUATEUR
KIVU
KATANGA
KASAI
RUANDA-URUNDI (Trust)
FEDERATION OF RHODESIA & NYASALAND
NORTHERN RHODESIA
SOUTHERN RHODESIA
NYASALAND PROT.
MOZAMBIQUE
NIASSA
ZAMBEZIA
MANICA E SOFALA
SUL DO SAVE
BECHUANALAND PROT.
BECHUANA-LAND
UNION OF SOUTH AFRICA
TRANSVAAL
ORANGE FREE STATE
NATAL
CAPE OF GOOD HOPE
BASUTO-LAND
SWAZILAND
Zululand
Kalahari
MADAGASCAR
COMORO IS. (Fr.)
Mozambique Channel
INDIAN OCEAN
Equator
Tropic of Capricorn
Moyale (Ft. Harrington)
Marsabit
Bardera
Uanle Uen
Itala
Vill. Duca d. Abruzzi
Mogadiscio
Merca
Brava
Mansur
Afgoi
Afmadu
Gelib
Margherita
Chisimaio
Ras Chiambone
Baringo
Nanyuki
Meru
Kenya 17,040
Fort Hall
Nairobi
Naivasha
Machakos
Kitui
Kiu
Nyuki
Kibwezi
Witu
Lamu
Kipini
Malindi
Mombasa
Kilindini
Voi
Sabaki
Tana
Balambala
Bara
Kisumu
Kisii
L. Victoria
Entebbe
Kampala
Jinja
Elgon
Kitale
Eldama
Nakuru
Nyeri
L. Kioga
Soroti
14,136
Bukoba
Masindi
Butiaba
Mbarara
Fort Portal
Ruwenzori 16,787
L. Albert
L. Edward
Rutshuru
Lubero
Beni
Djugu
Mahagi
Arua
Aketi
Buta
Titule
Niapu
Paulis
Watsa
Wamba
Irumu
Bafwasende
Stanleyville
Stanley Falls
Ponthierville
Lubutu
Opala
Lowa
Aruwimi
Lindi
Bumba
Lisala
Bomboma
Budjala
Congo
Busu Djanoa
Basoko
Basankusu
Coquilhatville
Djolu
Isangi
Boende
Bokunguo
Ikela
Monkoto
Lomela
Lomami
Leopold II
Dekese
Katako Kombe
Lodja
Kindu
Kibombo
Kongolo
Kabalo
Kasongo
Kabambare
Fizi
Uvira
Bukavu
L. Kivu
Masisi
Kigali
Kabale
Karisimbi
Shabunda
Elila
Sankuru
Port Francqui
Lusambo
Luebo
Tshofa
Lulua
Dimbelenge
Tshikapa
Luluabourg
Kabinda
Dibaya
Kanda Kanda
Luisa
Kapanga
Kamina
Bukama
Ankoro
Albertville
Lukuga
Lualaba
Kabongo
Mwanza
Baudouinville
Kirando
L. Mweru
Kasenga
Sampwe
Tshilongo
Kambove
Jadotville
Shinkolobwe
Lubumbashi
Elisabethville
Sakania
Ndola
Mwinilunga
Cazombo
Malonga
Dilolo
Nova Chaves
Teixeira de Sousa
Vila Luzo
Vila Henrique de Carvalho
Sandoa
Lunda
Kasai
Kwango
Loange
Chicapa
Lulua
Gungu
Ngozi
Kitega
Usumbura
Kigoma
Ujiji
Uvinza
Lake Tanganyika
Karema
Geita
Biharamulo
Mwanza
Ikoma
Musoma
Shinyanga
Mkalama
Natron
L. Eyasi
Arusha
Moshi
Kilimanjaro 19,565
Pangani
Lushoto
Tanga
Mombo
Pemba
Chake Chake
Zanzibar (Br.)
Bagamoyo
Dar es Salaam
Morogoro
Kilosa
Dodoma
Kongwa
Kilimatinde
Tabora
Singida
Kondoa
Ugalla
Mafia
Rufiji
Ruaha
Iringa
Utete
Kilwa Kivinje
Kilwa Kisiwani
Lindi
Mikindani
Mtwara
C. Delgado
Kipembawe
Madibira
Mahenge
Kasanga
Abercorn
L. Rukwa
Mbeya
Mwaya
Mporokoso
Lumbira
Luingu
Kasama
Kafonga
Tunduru
Liwale
Nachingwea
Lukuledi
Masasi
Manda
Songea
Chamba
Bandawe
Ruvuma
Mocímboa da Praia
Ibo
Pôrto Amélia
Maniamba
Unango
Lugenda
Vila Cabral
Kota Kota
Fort Jameson
Serenje
L. Bangweulu
Fort Rosebery
Luapula
Mpika
Luangwa
Kasempa
Balovale
Cangamba
Lungwebungu
Nunkoya
Broken Hill
Lusaka
Mongu
Lealui
Namwala
Nkala
Kafue
Mazabuka
Monze
Batoka
Kalomo
Sesheke
Livingstone
Victoria Falls
Wankie
Kariba
Lake Kariba
Zambezi
Chicoa
Zumbo
Fort Johnston
Zomba
Blantyre
Tete
Mlanje 9,840
Namuli 8,750
Mocuba
Port Herald
Shire
Nyasa
Chiuta
Lurio
Meconta
Nampula
Nacala
Moçambique
António Enes
Angoche
Quelimane
Chinde
Chemba
Inyanga
Salisbury
Shamva
Sinoia
Hartley
Gatooma
Macequece
Rusapi
Umtali
Vila Fontes
Vila Pery
Melsetter
Beira
Nova Sofala
G. of Sofala
Chingune
Mambone
I. Bazaruto
C. São Sebastião
Gwelo
Gwaai
Dett
Selukwe
Fort Victoria
Bulawayo
Matopos
Gwanda
West Nicholson
Francistown
Okavango Swamp
Maun
Ngami L.
Makarikari (Salt)
Lundi
Sabi
Save
Jofane
Massangena
Limpopo
Messina
Louis Trichardt
Pafuri
Chigubo
Manhica
Inhambane
Inharrime
Guijá
Vila de João Belo
Vila Luiza
Lourenço Marques
Delagoa Bay
Goba
Mbabane
Pietersburg
Potgietersrust
Nylstroom
Lydenburg
Pretoria
Johannesburg
Germiston
Middelburg
Benoni
Mafeking (Capital of Bechuanaland Prot.)
Potchefstroom
Vryburg
Taungs
Upington
Kimberley
Warrenton
Kroonstad
Bethlehem
Newcastle
Ladysmith
Pietermaritzburg
Durban
Port Shepstone
Bloemfontein
Maseru
Kakamas
Griquatown
Prieska
Hopetown
De Aar
Britstown
Carnarvon
Hutchinson
Middelburg
Aliwal North
Barkly East
Maclear
Umtata
Queenstown
East London
Kingwilliamstown
Grahamstown
Cradock
Graaff Reinet
Willowmore
Beaufort West
Prince Albert
Touws River
Oudtshoorn
Knysna
Mossel Bay
Riversdale
Heidelberg
Swellendam
Algoa Bay
Port Elizabeth
Uitenhage
Clanwilliam
Okwa
Serowe
Palapye
Palla Road
Molepolole
Ramoutsa
Kanye
Nossob
Molopo
Kuruman
Kwito
Kwando
Livingstone
Mavinga
Sioma
Kavango
Aldabra Is. (Br.)
Cosmoledo Is. (Br.)
Astove I.
Providence I.
St. Pierre
Farquhar Is.
Grande Comore
Moroni
Mohéli
Anjouan
Dzaoudzi
Mayotte
Isles Glorieuses
C. d'Ambre
Diego Suarez
Antsirane
Nossi-Bé (Hellville)
Vohémar
Ananalava
Antalaha
Maroantsetra
B. d'Antongil
Mananara
I. Ste. Marie
Ambodofototra
Fenerive
Ambatondrazaka
Tamatave
Moramanga
Vatomandry
Tananarive
Ankaratra 8,550
Antsirabe
Ambositra
Fianarantsoa
Mananjary
Manakara
Vohipeno
Farafangana
Vangaindrano
Manantenina
Fort-Dauphin
Tsihombe
C. Ste. Marie
Tuléar
Onilahy
Manombo
Ihosi
Ambalavao
Ankazoabo
Morombe
Mangoky
Morondava
Tsiribihina
Miandrivazo
Miarinarivo
Antsalova
Maintirano
Morafenobe
Maevatanana
Marovoay
Majunga
Soalala
Sofia
C. St. André
Chesterfield
Juan da Nova
Bassas da India
I. Europa (Fr.)
SCALE OF MILES
0 25 50 100
I. aux Serpents
Flat I.
Round I.
Coin de Mire
Poudre d'Or
Poste de Flacq
Port Louis
Rose Hill
Curepipe
Black R. Mt. 2,711
Morne Brabant
Mahébourg
Souillac
MAURITIUS (Br.)
St. Denis
Ste. Suzanne
Le Port
St. Paul
St. Benoit
Piton des Neiges 10,069
Le Volcan 8,612
RÉUNION (Fr.)
St. Louis
St. Pierre
St. Joseph
St. Philippe
INDIAN OCEAN
Longitude 56° East of Greenwich 57°
55° 56° 57° 58°
20° 21°
20° L 25° M 30° N 35° O 40° P 45° R 50° S 55° T 60° U
11 0° 12 5° 13 10° 14 15° 15 20° 16 25° 17 30° 18 35° 19 40° 20

AUSTRALIA
and
NEW ZEALAND
BONNE PROJECTION
SCALE OF MILES
0 50 100 200 300 400 500
SCALE OF KILOMETRES
0 50 100 200 300 400 500
Capital of Country
State and Territorial Capitals
I N D O N E S I A
A R A F U R A
T I M O R
SEA
Wetar
Alor
Dili
Flores
Solor
OE-CUSSE
SAWU SEA
Kupang
Sawu Is.
Roti
Babar Is.
Selaru
Frederik Hendrik
Melville I.
Bathurst I.
C. Van Diemen
Cobourg Pen.
Dundas Str.
Croker I.
Goulburn Is.
Boucaut Bay
C. Stewart
Castlereagh B.
Elcho I.
Clarence Str.
Van Diemen Gulf
Darwin
Southport
Adelaide River
Burrundie
Pine Creek
Katherine
Mataranka
Roper R.
Urapunga
Limmen Bight
Pt. Blaze
Peron Is.
Anson B.
C. Ford
Joseph Bonaparte Gulf
C. Rulhieres
C. Londonderry
C. Talbot
Daly R.
A R N H E M
L A N D
Cartier I.
C. Bougainville
Long Reef
Admiralty Gulf
Montague Sound
Browse I.
York Sound
Brunswick B.
Adele I.
Collier B.
Yampi Sd.
Buccaneer Arch.
C. Lévêque
King Sd.
Lacepede Is.
C. Boileau
Dampier Land
Derby
Broome
Roebuck B.
Fitzroy R.
C. Latouche Treville
La Grange Bay
Eighty Mile Beach
King Leopold Ra.
Drysdale R.
Wyndham
Ord R.
Turkey Creek
Fitzroy Crossing
Hall's Creek
St. George Range
Victoria R.
Auvergne
Birdum
Daly Waters
Limmen B. R.
Borroloola
N O R T H E R N
Newcastle Waters
L. Woods
Powell Creek
Barkly Tableland
Alexandria Sta.
Tennant Creek
Murchison Ra.
The Granites
The Lander
Barrow Creek
T E R R I T O R Y
L. Mackay
Alice Springs (Stuart)
Arltunga
Macdonnell Ranges
Hermannsburg Mission Sta.
Ewaninga
James Ra.
Rodinga
L. Amadeus
Bundooma
The Palmer
Rumbalara
Charlotte Waters
ABORIGINAL RESERVE
Musgrave Ranges
The Alberga
Alberga
The Macumba
S O U T H
Oodnadatta
Algebuckina
Warrina
Stuarts Range
Coober Pedy (Stuarts Range)
William Creek
L. Maurice
A U S T R A L I A
Wynbring
Mt. Eba
Lake Torrens
Kingoonya
Woomera
L. Harris
L. Everard
Hughes
Fisher
Ooldea
Nullarbor Plain
Fowler's Bay
Penong
C. Nuyts
Streaky B.
Streaky Bay
L. Gairdner
Gawler Ra.
Buckleboo
Investigator's Group
Eyre's Pen.
Port Augusta
Whyalla
Port Pirie
Mount Hope
Port Lincoln
Spencer's Gulf
Edithburgh
Yorke Pen.
C. Spencer
Investigator Str.
Kangaroo I.
Kingscote
Port Hedland
C. Thouin
Dampier Arch.
Shellborough
De Grey R.
Balla Balla
Roebourne
Yule R.
Bamboo Creek
Marble Bar
Great Sandy Desert
Monte Bello Is.
Barrow I.
Fortescue R.
Nullagine
Muiron Is.
Exmouth G.
North West C.
Onslow
Hamersley Ra.
Mt. Bruce 4,025
W E S T E R N
L. Disappointment
L. Macdonald
Gibson Desert
L. Hopkins
Pt. Cloates
Ashburton R.
C. Farquhar
C. Cuvier
Geographe Chan.
Salt L.
Lyons R.
Bernier I.
Carnarvon
Dorre I.
Gascoyne R.
Shark B.
Wooramel R.
Naturaliste Chan.
Dirk Hartog I.
Steep Pt.
Murchison R.
Mt. Murchison 1,843
Meekatharra
Nannine
Wiluna
L. Carnegie
L. Wells
A U S T R A L I A
Big Bell
Cue
L. Austin
Mt. Magnet
Sandstone
Geelvink Chan.
Ajana
Yuna
Yalgoo
Salt L.
Morgans
Laverton
L. Carey
Great Victoria Desert
Salt Lakes
Northampton
Pindar
Mullewa
Youanmi
Leonora
L. Barlee
Geraldton
Morawa
Mingenew
Houtman Rocks (Abrolhos)
Dongarra
Menzies
Deakin
Darling Range
L. Moore
Broad Arrow
Kanowna
Haig
Forrest
Kalannie
Kalgoorlie
Boulder
Miling
Bonnie Rock
Moora
Coolgardie
L. Lefroy
Zanthus
Eucla
Merredin
Southern Cross
Northam
York
L. Cowan
Norseman
Perth
Fremantle
Rockingham
Corrigin
Narembeen
Hyden
Eyre
Pt. Dover
G R E A T
A U S T R A L I A N
B I G H T
Pt. Culver
Salmon Gums
Narrogin
Wagin
Newdegate
Pingrup
Ravensthorpe
Collie
Katanning
Bunbury
Geographe B.
Esperance
C. Arid
C. Naturaliste
Busselton
Ongerup
Hopetoun
Cape Le Grand
Archipelago of the Recherche
Nannup
Augusta
Northcliffe
C. Leeuwin
Flinders B.
Albany
Pt. D'Entrecasteaux
Torbay Head
I N D I A N
O C E A N
Moore R.
MILES
0 10 20 30 40
Darling Ra.
Goomalling
Gin Gin
Swan R.
Northam
Claremont
Guildford
Midland Jct.
York
Avon R.
Rottnest I.
Cottesloe
Perth
Fremantle
Karragullen
Beverley
Garden I.
Armadale-Kelmscott
Rockingham
Brookton
Peels Inlet
Mandurah
Mt. Cooke 1,909
C. Bouvard
Pinjarra
Hotham R.
Murray R.
L. Preston
Mt. William
Williams
Williams R.
Josbury
Two Wells
Gawler
Gawler R.
MILES
0 5 10 15
Williamstown
S. Para R.
Outer Harbour
Salisbury
Mt. Gawler
Kersbrook
Mt. Pleasant
Port Adelaide
Torrens R.
Hindmarsh
Adelaide
Gumeracha
Henley & Grange
Kensington and Norwood
Mt. Torrens
Glenelg
Mt. Lofty 2,332
Oakbank
Unley
Brighton
Mt.Lofty
Balhannah
Nairne
Reynella
Onkaparinga R.
Mt. Barker 1,679
Petwood
Callington
Noarlunga
Bugle Ranges
Strathalbyn
R. Bremer
Gulf of St. Vincent
A 115 B 120 C 125 D 130 E 135
105 110 A 115 B 120 C 125 D 130 E 135
1 10 2 15 3 20 4 25 5 30 6 35 7 40 8

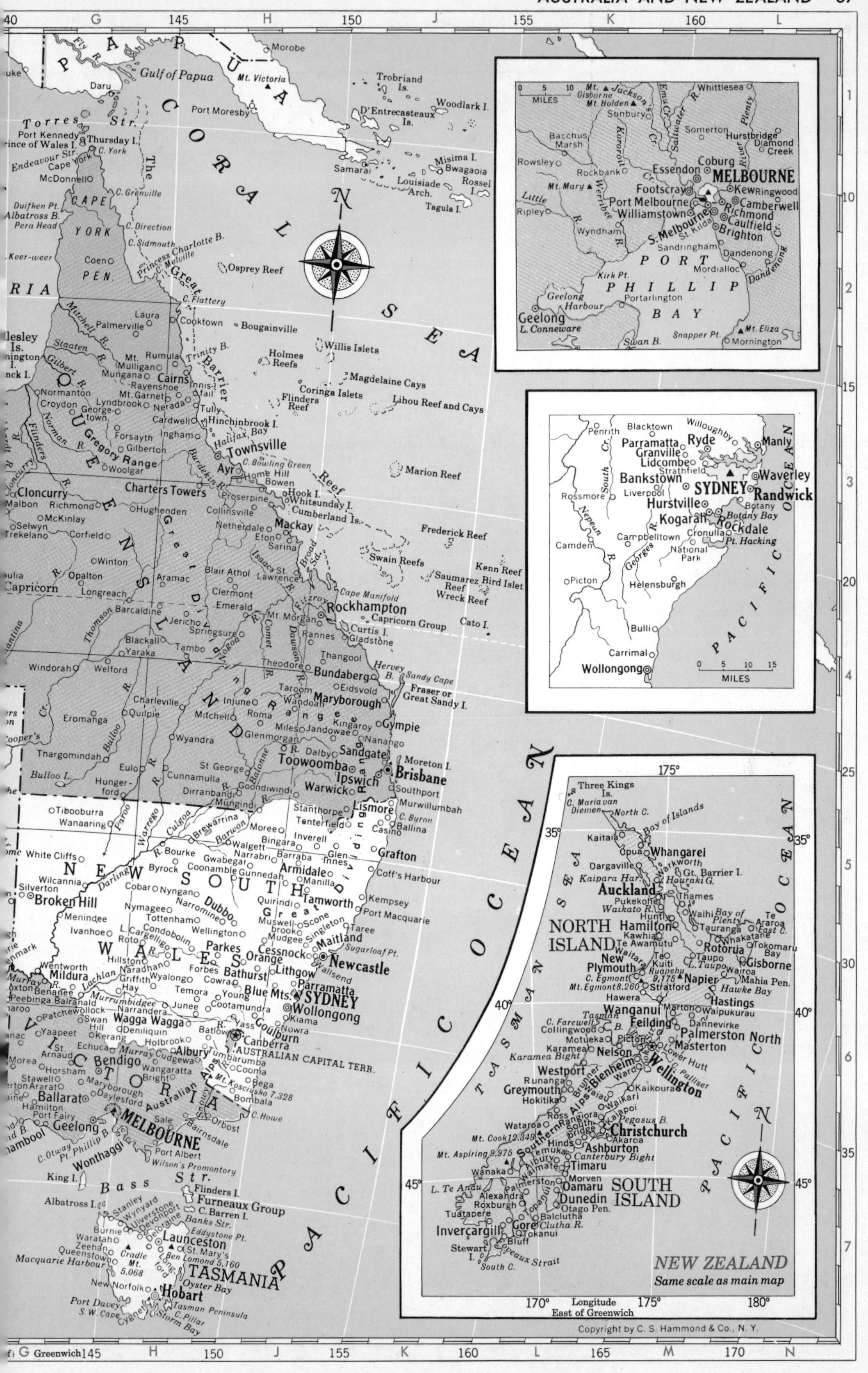
PAPUA
Gulf of Papua
Fly R.
Daru
Morobe
Mt. Victoria
Port Moresby
Trobriand Is.
Woodlark I.
D'Entrecasteaux Is.
Misima I.
Bwagaoia
Samarai
Louisiade Arch.
Rossel I.
Tagula I.
Torres Str.
Port Kennedy
Thursday I.
Prince of Wales I.
C. York
Endeavour Str.
Cape York
McDonnell
The
C. Grenville
Duifken Pt.
Albatross B.
Pera Head
CAPE YORK PEN.
C. Direction
C. Sidmouth
Princess Charlotte B.
C. Melville
Keer-weer
Coen
CORAL SEA
Osprey Reef
Great Barrier Reef
C. Flattery
Laura
Palmerville
Mitchell R.
Cooktown
Bougainville
Willis Islets
Holmes Reefs
Staaten R.
Trinity B.
Mt. Mulligan
Rumula
Mungana
Cairns
Innisfail
Ravenshoe
Mt. Garnet
Normanton
Croydon
Lyndbrook
Nerada
Georgetown
Tully
Magdelaine Cays
Coringa Islets
Flinders Reef
Lihou Reef and Cays
Gilbert R.
Norman R.
Flinders R.
Cardwell
Hinchinbrook I.
Forsayth
Ingham
Halifax Bay
Gregory Range
Gilberton
Townsville
Woolgar
C. Bowling Green
Burdekin R.
Ayr
Home Hill
Bowen
Marion Reef
QUEENSLAND
Cloncurry
Charters Towers
Proserpine
Hook I.
Whitsunday I.
Cumberland Is.
Malbon
Richmond
Hughenden
Collinsville
McKinlay
Selwyn
Trekelano
Corfield
Nethedale
Mackay
Eton
Sarina
Frederick Reef
Swain Reefs
Kenn Reef
Saumarez Reef
Bird Islet
Wreck Reef
Winton
Great Dividing Range
Isaacs R.
St. Lawrence
Broad Sd.
Opalton
Capricorn
Longreach
Aramac
Blair Athol
Clermont
Cape Manifold
Barcaldine
Emerald
Fitzroy R.
Thomson R.
Jericho
Mt. Morgan
Rockhampton
Capricorn Group
Cato I.
Springsure
Curtis I.
Gladstone
Blackall
Yaraka
Tambo
Comet R.
Dawson R.
Rannes
Thangool
Windorah
Welford
Theodore
Bundaberg
Hervey B.
Sandy Cape
Taroom
Eidsvold
Fraser or Great Sandy I.
Maryborough
Charleville
Quilpie
Injune
Wandoan
Eromanga
Mitchell
Roma
Kingaroy
Gympie
Miles
Jandowae
Nanango
Glenmorgan
Cooper's Cr.
Bulloo R.
Wyandra
Dalby
Sandgate
Thargomindah
Eulo
Balonne R.
Toowoomba
Moreton I.
Bulloo L.
St. George
Ipswich
Brisbane
Hungerford
Cunnamulla
Warwick
Southport
Dirranbandi
Goondiwindi
Mungindi
Stanthorpe
Lismore
Murwillumbah
Tibooburra
Wanaaring
Paroo
Warrego
Culgoa
Brewarrina
Barwon R.
Moree
Tenterfield
C. Byron
Ballina
Casino
Inverell
Bourke
Walgett
Bingara
Glen Innes
Grafton
White Cliffs
Byrock
Gwabegar
Narrabri
Barraba
Coonamble
Armidale
Coff's Harbour
Gunnedah
NEW SOUTH WALES
Wilcannia
Darling R.
Cobar
Nyngan
Manilla
Silverton
Broken Hill
Quirindi
Tamworth
Kempsey
Dubbo
Nymagee
Narromine
Port Macquarie
Menindee
Tottenham
Muswellbrook
Scone
Ivanhoe
Wellington
Taree
Condobolin
Mudgee
Singleton
L. Cargelligo
Roto
Parkes
Orange
Cessnock
Maitland
Sugarloaf Pt.
Newcastle
Wentworth
Hillston
Forbes
Bathurst
Lithgow
Mildura
Narrandera
Naradhan
Griffith
Wyalong
Cowra
Blue Mts.
Parramatta
SYDNEY
Lachlan R.
Murray R.
Hay
Temora
Young
Wollongong
Balranald
Murrumbidgee R.
Junee
Cootamundra
Kiama
Patchewollock
Swan Hill
Wagga Wagga
Yass
Goulburn
Nowra
Deniliquin
Batlow
Canberra
AUSTRALIAN CAPITAL TERR.
Kerang
Echuca
Holbrook
Albury
Tumbarumba
Cooma
VICTORIA
Bendigo
Wangaratta
Mt. Kosciusko 7,328
Bega
Horsham
Stawell
Ararat
Bright
Maryborough
Daylesford
Australian Alps
Bombala
Ballarat
Hamilton
Port Fairy
Geelong
MELBOURNE
Sale
Orbost
C. Howe
Bairnsdale
Warrnambool
C. Otway
Pt. Phillip B.
Wonthaggi
Port Albert
Wilson's Promontory
King I.
Bass Str.
Flinders I.
Furneaux Group
Albatross I.
C. Barren I.
Stanley
Wynyard
Ulverstone
Devonport
Banks Str.
Eddystone Pt.
Burnie
Waratah
Launceston
Zeehan
St. Mary's
Queenstown
Cradle Mt. 5,068
Ben Lomond 5,160
Macquarie Harbour
TASMANIA
New Norfolk
Oyster Bay
Hobart
Port Davey
S. W. Cape
Tasman Peninsula
C. Pillar
Storm Bay
PACIFIC OCEAN
MELBOURNE
MILES
Mt. Jackson
Gisborne
Mt. Holden
Sunbury
Emu Cr.
Saltwater R.
Whittlesea
Plenty River
Bacchus Marsh
Kororoit Cr.
Somerton
Hurstbridge
Diamond Creek
Rowsley
Rockbank
Essendon
Coburg
Mt. Mary
Werribee R.
Footscray
Kew
Ringwood
Little R.
Port Melbourne
Camberwell
Ripley
Williamstown
Richmond
Caulfield
Wyndham
S. Melbourne
St. Kilda
Brighton
Sandringham
Dandenong
PORT PHILLIP BAY
Mordialloc
Kirk Pt.
Geelong Harbour
Portarlington
Geelong
L. Connewarre
Swan B.
Snapper Pt.
Mt. Eliza
Mornington
SYDNEY
Penrith
Blacktown
Willoughby
Manly
South Cr.
Parramatta
Ryde
Granville
Lidcombe
Strathfield
Bankstown
Waverley
Rossmore
Liverpool
Randwick
Hurstville
Botany
Nepean R.
Kogarah
Botany Bay
Rockdale
Camden
Campbelltown
Cronulla
Georges R.
National Park
Pt. Hacking
Picton
Helensburgh
Bulli
Carrimal
Wollongong
MILES
NEW ZEALAND
Same scale as main map
Three Kings Is.
C. Maria van Diemen
North C.
Bay of Islands
Kaitaia
Whangarei
Opua
Dargaville
Warkworth
Gt. Barrier I.
Kaipara Har.
Hauraki G.
Auckland
Thames
Pukekohe
Waikato R.
Waihi
Bay of Plenty
Te Araroa
East C.
NORTH ISLAND
Hamilton
Huntly
Tauranga
Whakatane
Kawhia
Te Awamutu
Rotorua
Tokomaru Bay
Waitara
Te Kuiti
Taupo
L. Taupo
Gisborne
New Plymouth
Ruapehu 9,175
Wairoa
C. Egmont
Mt. Egmont 8,260
Stratford
Napier
Mahia Pen.
Hawke Bay
Hawera
Hastings
Wanganui
Marton
Waipukurau
Tasman B.
Feilding
Dannevirke
C. Farewell
Collingwood
Palmerston North
Motueka
Picton
Masterton
Karamea
Nelson
Karamea Bight
Blenheim
Lower Hutt
Wellington
Westport
C. Palliser
Runanga
Ward
Greymouth
Kaikoura
Hokitika
Waiau
Waikari
Ross
Rangiora
Kaiapoi
Wataroa
Pegasus B.
Christchurch
Mt. Cook 12,349
Southern Alps
Akaroa
Ashburton
Mt. Aspiring 9,975
Temuka
Hinds
Canterbury Bight
Waimate
Timaru
Wanaka
Morven
Palmerston
Oamaru
SOUTH ISLAND
L. Te Anau
Alexandra
Dunedin
Roxburgh
Otago Pen.
Tuatapere
Balclutha
Invercargill
Gore
Clutha R.
Tokanui
Bluff
Stewart I.
Foveaux Strait
South C.
TASMAN SEA
PACIFIC OCEAN
Longitude East of Greenwich
Greenwich

A 110° B 120° C 130° D 140° E 150° F 160° G 170° H
100° A 110° B Longitude C East 130° of D Greenwich E 150° F 160° G 170° H
Sian
Hwang Ho
Tsinan
Kaifeng
Chefoo
Inch'on
Seoul
YELLOW
Tsingtao
SEA
Mokp'o
Pusan
KOREA
Cheju I.
Korea Str.
SEA OF JAPAN
Akita
Aomori
Morioka
Tsuruoka
Sendai
Kanazawa
Niigata
Kyoto
Kobe
Tokyo
Yokohama
Nagoya
Osaka
Hiroshima
Shikoku
Nagasaki
Fukuoka
Kumamoto
Kyushu
Kagoshima
Izu-shichito
JAPAN
Süchow
Wanhsien
Yangtze
Nanking
Hankow
Kiang
Chungking
Soochow
Hangchow
Shanghai
Ningpo
EAST
CHINA
SEA
ASIA
CHINA
Siangtan
Changsha
Kanchow
Kian
Kweilin
Foochow
Wenchow
Wuchow
Canton
Chaoan
Amoy
Formosa Str.
Taipei
RYUKYU IS. (U.S. Adm.)
Amami-gunto
Naha
Okinawa
DAITO ISLANDS (U.S. Adm.)
Sakishima-gunto
Macao (Port.)
HONG KONG (Brit.)
Victoria
Tainan
Taiwan (Formosa)
Chichi-jima
Haha-jima
Kita-iwo-jima
Iwo-jima
Minami-iwo-jima
BONIN ISLANDS (U.S. Adm.)
VOLCANO ISLANDS (U.S. Adm.)
Marcus I. (U.S. Adm.)
Tropic of Can
Luzon Strait
Batan Is.
Babuyan Is.
C. Engaño
SOUTH CHINA SEA
PHILIPPINE SEA
Parece Vela (U.S. Adm.)
Farallon de Pajaros
Asuncion
MARIANA ISLANDS
Agrihan
Alamagan
Anatahan
Garapan
Saipan
Tinian
Rota
Guam (U.S.)
Agaña
Wake I. (U.S.)
Laoag
Baguio
Lingayen
Luzon
REPUBLIC OF THE PHILIPPINES
Quezon City
Manila
Corregidor I.
Batangas
Naga
Legaspi
Mindoro
San Bernardino Str.
Samar
Panay
Iloilo
Pto. Princesa
Palawan
Negros
Leyte
Cebu
SULU SEA
Cagayan
Mindanao
Davao
Balabac Str.
Zamboanga
Jesselton
Sandakan
N. BORNEO
Sulu Arch.
CELEBES SEA
Talaud Is.
Morotai
Tarakan
Manado
BORNEO (KALIMANTAN)
Makassar Strait
Ternate
Halmahera
Gulf of Tomini
Molucca Sea
CELEBES (SULAWESI)
Sula Is.
Buru
Ceram
Amboina
BANDA SEA
Makassar
Butung
Gulf of Bone
INDONESIA
FLORES SEA
Wetar
Alor
Dili
Bali
Lombok
Flores
Sumbawa
OE-CUSSE (Port.)
(Port.)
Timor
Sumba
Sawu Is.
Roti
Kupang
TIMOR SEA
Kai Is.
Aru Is.
Tanimbar Is.
Frederik Hendrik I.
Merauke
ARAFURA SEA
Waigeo
Sorong
Manokwari
Schouten Is.
Geelvink Bay
Hollandia
Fakfak
NETH. NEW GUINEA (IRIAN)
New Guinea
Fly
Daru
Gulf of Papua
Torres Str.
C. York
Port Moresby
Samarai
PAPUA
M I C R O N E S I A
Mariana Trench 35,640 ft. below sea level
Ulithi
Fais
Yap
Ngulu
Sorol
Gaferut
Faraulep
Woleai
Ifalik
Eauripik
Elato
PALAU IS.
Babelthuap
Koror
Angaur
Peleliu
Sonsorol
Pulo Anna
Merir
Tobi
Namonuito
Pulap
Puluwat
Lamotrek
Satawal
Hall Is.
Moen I.
Truk Is.
Pulusuk
Nomoi Is.
Oroluk
Senyavin Is.
Ponape
Mokil
Pingelap
Ngatik
Nukuoro
Kusaie
CAROLINE ISLANDS
TERRITORY OF THE PACIFIC ISLANDS (U. S. Trust Terr.)
Kapingamarangi
MARSHALL ISLANDS
Taongi Atoll
Bikini
Bikar
Eniwetok
Rongelap
Ailuk
Ralik Chain
Ratak Chain
Ujelang
Kwajalein
Wotje
Maloelap
Ailinglapalap
Majuro
Arno
Mili
Jaluit
Namorik
Kili
Ebon Atoll
Makin (Buta
Abaiang
Bairiki
Tarawa
Abemama
Nonouti
Beru
Onot
Tabiteuea
GILBERT ISLANDS
Nauru
Ocean I.
Nukumanu
(Austr.-N.Z.-Br.Trust)
M E L A N E S I A
TERR. OF NEW GUINEA (Austr. Trust Terr.)
Ninigo Gr.
Admiralty Is.
Manus
Lavongai
New Ireland
Kavieng
Aitape
Wewak
BISMARCK ARCH.
Rabaul
Namatanai
N.E. NEW GUINEA
Madang
Lae
Huon Gulf
Wau
New Britain
Gasmata
Sohano
Bougainville
Kieta
Choiseul
SOLOMON
SOLOMON SEA
Morobe
Trobriand Is.
D'Entrecasteaux Is.
New Georgia
Santa Ysabel
Auki
Malaita
Honiara
Guadalcanal
San Cristobal
SOLOMON ISLANDS PROT. (Br.)
Ontong Java (Lord Howe I.)
SANTA CRUZ IS.
Ndeni
Peu
Vanikoro
Tikopia
Rennell
ISLANDS
Louisiade Arch.
Nanumea
Niutao
Nui
Funa
Fonga
Nuk
ELLICE
Ahau
Ro
Torres Is.
Banks Is.
Espiritu Santo
Luganville
Malekula
NEW HEBRIDES
Ambrym
Efate
Vila
Erromanga
Tanna
Aneityum
(Br.-Fr. Condominium)
Vanua
Levu
Viti Levu
Nandi
Kanda
FIJI ISL
Huon Is.
Belep Is.
Uvea
Lifu
Maré
Loyalty Is.
New Caledonia
Bourail
Nouméa
I. of Pines
(French)
Chesterfield Is.
Bellona Reefs
(Briti
(New Zealand)
CORAL SEA
Willis Islets
Coringa Is.
Cato I.
Melville I.
Bathurst I.
Wessel Is.
C. Arnhem
Darwin
ARNHEM LAND
Groote Eylandt
Gulf of Carpentaria
Wellesley Is.
Cape York Pen.
Great Barrier Reef
Cooktown
Cairns
Jos. Bonaparte Gulf
Katherine
Daly Waters
C. Leveque
Wyndham
Derby
Broome
Fitzroy
Hall's Cr.
NORTHERN TERRITORY
Tennant Cr.
Barkly Tableland
Normanton
Flinders
Charters Towers
Townsville
Bowen
Mackay
Rockhampton
La Grange Bay
Port Hedland
Monte Bello Is.
Barrow I.
North West Cape
Onslow
Ashburton
Marble Bar
Great Sandy Desert
L. Mackay
Alice Sprs.
Macdonnell Ranges
L. Disappointment
Gibson Desert
Mt. Bruce
WESTERN AUSTRALIA
AUSTRALIA
Cloncurry
Hughenden
QUEENSLAND
Longreach
Blackall
Bundaberg
Fraser I.
Maryborough
Gympie
Charleville
Roma
Ipswich
Brisbane
Toowoomba
Lismore
Grafton
Cunnamulla
Cooper's Cr.
Simpson Desert
Oodnadatta
L. Amadeus
Musgrave Ranges
SOUTH AUSTRALIA
L. Eyre
Great Victoria Desert
Carnarvon
Gascoyne
Wiluna
Meekatharra
Dirk Hartogs I.
Laverton
Geraldton
L. Barlee
Kalgoorlie
Boulder
Nullarbor Plain
Great Australian Bight
Perth
Fremantle
Bunbury
Collie
Esperance
Arch. of the Recherche
C. Leeuwin
Albany
L. Frome
L. Torrens
L. Gairdner
Woomera
Port Augusta
Whyalla
Port Pirie
Port Lincoln
Spencer G.
Adelaide
Kangaroo I.
Mt. Gambier
Warrnambool
Ballarat
Geelong
King I.
Broken Hill
NEW SOUTH WALES
Darling
Murray
Tamworth
Armidale
Maitland
Newcastle
Sydney
Lithgow
Orange
Blue Mts.
Wollongong
Wagga Wagga
Canberra (Austr.Cap.Terr.)
Mt. Kosciusko
Albury
Bendigo
VICTORIA
Melbourne
Wonthaggi
C. Howe
Bass Str.
Furneaux Group
Launceston
Devonport
Hobart
TASMANIA
South East Cape
Norfolk I. (Austr.)
Kingston
Lord Howe I. (N.S.Wales)
TASMAN SEA
INDIAN OCEAN
North Cape
Whang
Auckland
Hamilton
Napi
Wanganui
NEW ZEALAND
Nelson
Cook Str.
We
Greymouth
South Island
Mt. Cook
Christch
Timaru
Dunedin
Foveaux Str.
Invercargill
Stewart I.
Boun

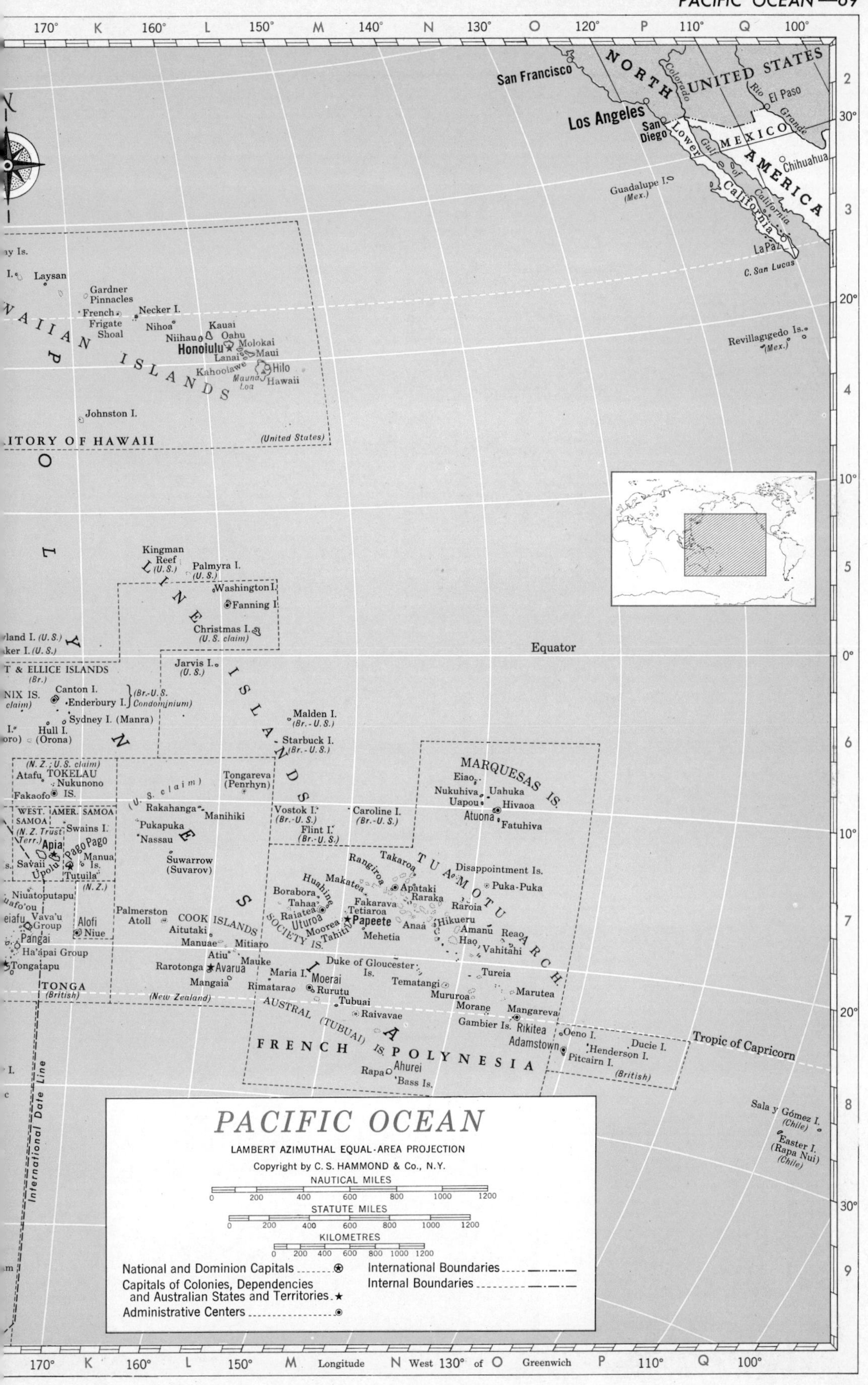

PACIFIC OCEAN
LAMBERT AZIMUTHAL EQUAL-AREA PROJECTION
Copyright by C. S. HAMMOND & Co., N.Y.
NAUTICAL MILES
STATUTE MILES
KILOMETRES
National and Dominion Capitals
Capitals of Colonies, Dependencies and Australian States and Territories
Administrative Centers
International Boundaries
Internal Boundaries
NORTH AMERICA
UNITED STATES
MEXICO
San Francisco
Los Angeles
San Diego
El Paso
Chihuahua
Lower California
Gulf of California
La Paz
C. San Lucas
Guadalupe I. (Mex.)
Revillagigedo Is. (Mex.)
HAWAIIAN ISLANDS
TERRITORY OF HAWAII (United States)
Laysan
Gardner Pinnacles
French Frigate Shoal
Necker I.
Nihoa
Niihau
Kauai
Oahu
Honolulu
Molokai
Lanai
Maui
Kahoolawe
Hilo
Mauna Loa
Hawaii
Johnston I.
LINE ISLANDS
Kingman Reef (U.S.)
Palmyra I. (U.S.)
Washington I.
Fanning I.
Christmas I. (U.S. claim)
Jarvis I. (U.S.)
Malden I. (Br.-U.S.)
Starbuck I. (Br.-U.S.)
Equator
Canton I.
Enderbury I.
(Br.-U.S. Condominium)
Sydney I. (Manra)
Hull I. (Orona)
TOKELAU IS.
(N.Z.; U.S. claim)
Atafu
Nukunono
Fakaofo
WEST. SAMOA (N.Z. Trust Terr.)
AMER. SAMOA
Swains I.
Apia
Pago Pago
Manua Is.
Savaii
Upolu
Tutuila
Niuatoputapu
Vava'u Group
Pangai
Ha'apai Group
Tongatapu
TONGA (British)
Alofi
Niue (N.Z.)
Tongareva (Penrhyn)
Rakahanga
Manihiki
Pukapuka
Nassau
Suwarrow (Suvarov)
Palmerston Atoll
COOK ISLANDS
Aitutaki
Manuae
Mitiaro
Atiu
Mauke
Rarotonga
Avarua
Mangaia
(New Zealand)
Vostok I. (Br.-U.S.)
Caroline I. (Br.-U.S.)
Flint I. (Br.-U.S.)
MARQUESAS IS.
Eiao
Nukuhiva
Uahuka
Uapou
Hivaoa
Atuona
Fatuhiva
TUAMOTU ARCH.
Takaroa
Rangiroa
Makatea
Apataki
Raraka
Fakarava
Tetiaroa
Papeete
Tahiti
Moorea
Uturoa
Raiatea
Tahaa
Borabora
Huahine
SOCIETY IS.
Mehetia
Anaa
Hikueru
Raroia
Amanu
Hao
Reao
Vahitahi
Disappointment Is.
Puka-Puka
Duke of Gloucester Is.
Tureia
Tematangi
Mururoa
Morane
Marutea
Mangareva
Gambier Is.
Rikitea
Maria I.
Rimatara
Moerai
Rurutu
Tubuai
Raivavae
AUSTRAL (TUBUAI) IS.
FRENCH POLYNESIA
Rapa
Ahurei
Bass Is.
Oeno I.
Ducie I.
Henderson I.
Pitcairn I.
Adamstown
(British)
Tropic of Capricorn
Sala y Gómez I. (Chile)
Easter I. (Rapa Nui) (Chile)
International Date Line
Longitude West of Greenwich

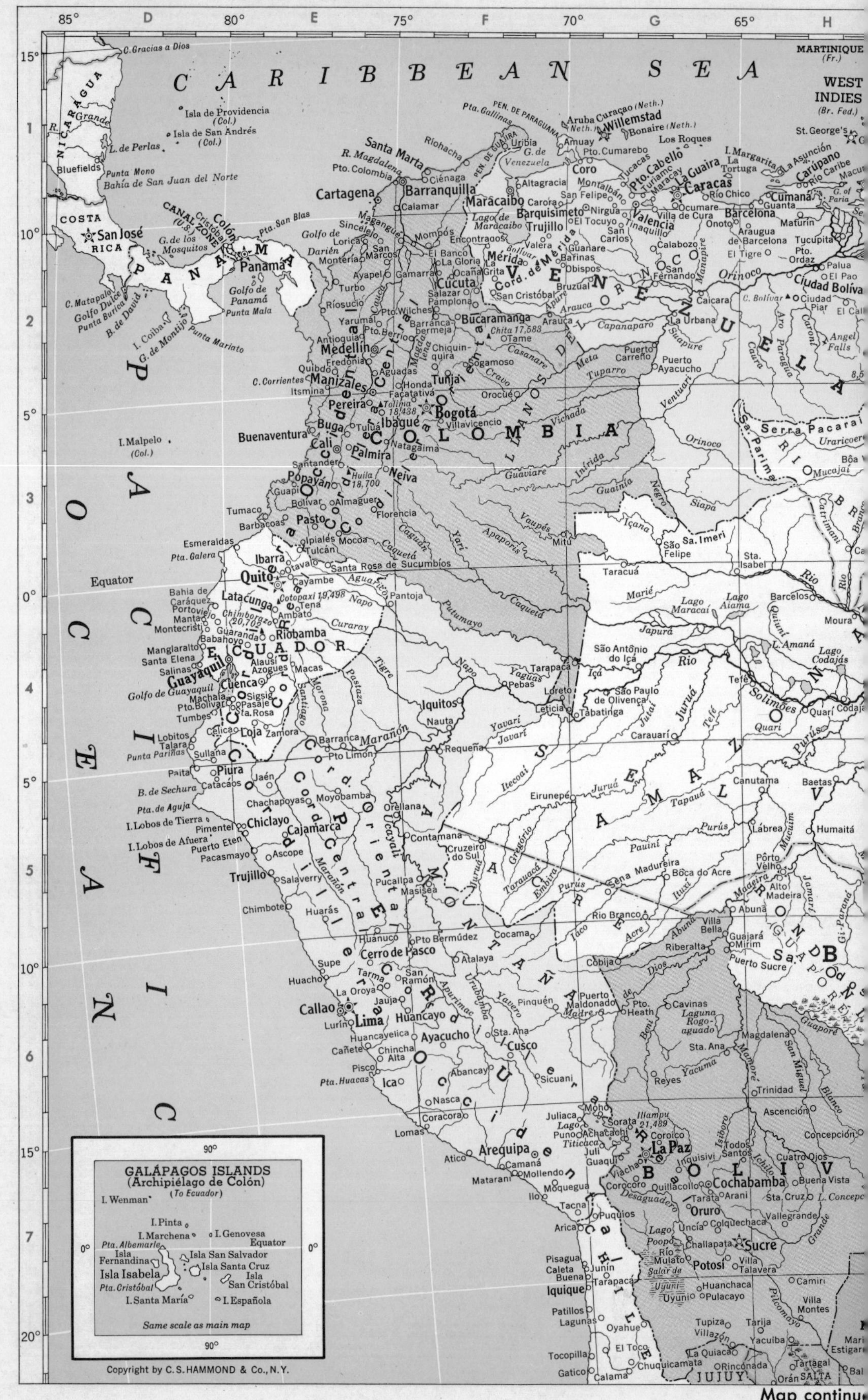
85°
D
80°
E
75°
F
70°
G
65°
H
CARIBBEAN SEA
MARTINIQUE (Fr.)
WEST INDIES (Br. Fed.)
C. Gracias a Dios
NICARAGUA
R. Grande
L. de Perlas
Bluefields
Punta Mono
Bahía de San Juan del Norte
Isla de Providencia (Col.)
Isla de San Andrés (Col.)
COSTA RICA
San José
CANAL ZONE (U.S.)
Cristóbal
Colón
Pta. San Blas
G. de los Mosquitos
PANAMA
Panamá
Golfo de Panamá
Punta Mala
C. Matapalo
Golfo Dulce
Punta Burica
B. de David
I. Coiba
G. de Montijo
Punta Mariato
Santa Marta
R. Magdalena
Pto. Colombia
Riohacha
Pta. Gallinas
PEN. DE PARAGUANA
PEN. DE GUAJIRA
Uribia
G. de Venezuela
Aruba
Curaçao (Neth.)
Willemstad
Bonaire (Neth.)
Amuay
Pto. Cumarebo
Los Roques
Coro
Cartagena
Barranquilla
Ciénaga
Calamar
Maracaibo
Lago de Maracaibo
Altagracia
Carora
Barquisimeto
Trujillo
San Felipe
Pto. Cabello
La Guaira
Caracas
Valencia
Maracay
Río Chico
I. Margarita
La Tortuga
La Asunción
Carúpano
Cumaná
Barcelona
Maturín
Golfo de Darién
Sincelejo
Magangué
Mompós
Lorica
Montería
San Marcos
El Banco
La Gloria
Encontrados
Mérida
Valera
Guanare
Barinas
Calabozo
San Fernando
Ciudad Bolívar
Orinoco
VENEZUELA
Cúcuta
Ocaña
San Cristóbal
Pamplona
Bucaramanga
Turbo
Riosucio
Yarumal
Pto. Wilches
Barrancabermeja
Chita 17,583
Tame
Arauca
Capanaparo
Puerto Carreño
Puerto Ayacucho
Antioquia
Medellín
Fredonia
Aguadas
Chiquinquirá
Sogamoso
Tunja
Quibdó
C. Corrientes
Manizales
Itsmina
Honda
Facatativá
Pereira
Tolima 18,438
Bogotá
Villavicencio
Orocué
Buenaventura
Buga
Tuluá
Ibagué
Cali
Palmira
Natagaima
COLOMBIA
LLANOS
I. Malpelo (Col.)
Santander
Popayán
Huila 18,700
Neiva
Guapi
Bolívar
Almaguer
Florencia
Tumaco
Barbacoas
Pasto
Ipiales
Mocoa
Tulcán
Esmeraldas
Pta. Galera
Ibarra
Otavalo
Santa Rosa de Sucumbíos
Equator
Quito
Cayambe
Aguarico
Pantoja
Latacunga
Cotopaxi 19,498
Tena
Napo
Bahía de Caráquez
Portoviejo
Manta
Montecristi
Chimborazo 20,702
Ambato
Riobamba
Guaranda
Babahoyo
Manglaralto
Santa Elena
Salinas
Guayaquil
ECUADOR
Alausí
Azogues
Macas
Golfo de Guayaquil
Cuenca
Machala
Sigsig
Pasaje
Pto. Bolívar
Sta. Rosa
Tumbes
Loja
Zamora
Lobitos
Talara
Punta Pariñas
Sullana
Paita
Piura
B. de Sechura
Catacaos
Pta. de Aguja
Jaén
Chachapoyas
Moyobamba
I. Lobos de Tierra
I. Lobos de Afuera
Pimentel
Chiclayo
Puerto Eten
Cajamarca
Pacasmayo
Ascope
Trujillo
Salaverry
Chimbote
Huarás
Iquitos
Nauta
Requeña
Barranca
Marañón
Pto. Limón
Orellana
Contamana
Pucallpa
Masisea
Ucayali
MONTAÑA
Huánuco
Pto. Bermúdez
Cerro de Pasco
Atalaya
Supe
Huacho
Tarma
San Ramón
La Oroya
Jauja
Callao
Lima
Lurín
Huancayo
Huancavelica
Ayacucho
Cañete
Chincha Alta
Pisco
Pta. Huacas
Ica
Nasca
Abancay
Cusco
Sicuani
Coracora
Lomas
Atico
Arequipa
Camaná
Mollendo
Matarani
Moquegua
Ilo
Tacna
Arica
Pisagua
Caleta Buena
Iquique
Patillos
Lagunas
Tocopilla
Gatico
Calama
Chuquicamata
El Toco
Oyahue
Tarapacá
Junín
PACIFIC OCEAN
Caquetá
Putumayo
Curaray
Tigre
Pastaza
Morona
Santiago
Tarapacá
Yaguas
Pebas
Loreto
Leticia
Tabatinga
Yavarí
Javarí
Mitú
Vaupés
Apaporis
Guaviare
Inírida
Guainía
Negro
Içana
São Felipe
Sa. Imeri
Taracuá
Sta. Isabel
Barcelos
Marié
Lago Maracaí
Lago Aiama
Japurá
Moura
L. Amaná
Lago Codajás
São Antônio do Içá
Içá
Rio
Tefé
Solimões
Quari
Codajás
São Paulo de Olivença
Jutaí
Juruá
Carauarí
Itecoaí
Eirunepé
Tapauá
Purús
Pauiní
Canutama
Lábrea
Baetas
Humaitá
AMAZONAS
ACRE
Cruzeiro do Sul
Gregório
Tarauacá
Embira
Sena Madureira
Bôca do Acre
Ituxi
Pôrto Velho
Alto Madeira
Madeira
Jamari
Abunã
Rio Branco
Xapuri
Acre
Villa Bella
Guajará Mirim
Riberalta
Cobija
Puerto Sucre
Cocama
Pinquén
Puerto Maldonado
Madre de Dios
Pto. Heath
Cavinas
Laguna Rogoaguado
Sta. Ana
Magdalena
Reyes
Yacuma
Trinidad
San Miguel
Ascención
Concepción
Mamoré
Guaporé
Beni
Illampu 21,489
Juliaca
Lago Titicaca
Puno
Achacachi
Sorata
Coroico
Juli
Guaqui
La Paz
Viacha
Inquisivi
Todos Santos
Corocoro
Quillacollo
Cochabamba
Cuatro Ojos
Buena Vista
Sta. Cruz
L. Concepción
Desaguadero
Tarata
Arani
Oruro
Puquios
Colquechaca
Vallegrande
Lago Poopó
Uncía
Challapata
Sucre
Río Mulato
Potosí
Villa Talavera
Salar de Uyuni
Uyuni
Huanchaca
Pulacayo
Camiri
Villa Montes
Pilcomayo
Tupiza
Tarija
Villazón
Yacuiba
La Quiaca
Rinconada
Tartagal
Orán
SALTA
JUJUY
BOLIVIA
Caroní
Angel Falls
Caura
Serra Pacaraima
Uraricoera
Sa. Parima
Mucajaí
Catrimani
Branco
Ventuari
Suapure
Meta
Tuparro
Vichada
Casanare
Cravo
Apure
Ciudad Piar
El Pao
Palua
El Callao
Caicara
La Urbana
Tucupita
Pto. Ordaz
El Tigre
Aragua de Barcelona
Onoto
Cumanacoa
Guanta
Ocumare
Villa de Cura
Nirgua
El Tocuyo
San Carlos
Tinaquillo
Turiamo
Tucacas
Obispos
Bruzual
Gamarra
Salazar
Ayapel
Atrato
GALÁPAGOS ISLANDS (Archipiélago de Colón) (To Ecuador)
90°
I. Wenman
I. Pinta
I. Marchena
I. Genovesa
Equator
0°
Pta. Albemarle
Isla Fernandina
Isla San Salvador
Isla Santa Cruz
Isla Isabela
Isla San Cristóbal
Pta. Cristóbal
I. Santa María
I. Española
Same scale as main map

Map continu

SOUTH AMERICA
Northern Part
LAMBERT AZIMUTHAL EQUAL-AREA PROJECTION
SCALE OF MILES
0 100 200 300 400 500
SCALE OF KILOMETRES
0 100 0 300 400 500
Capitals of Countries
Other Capitals
International Boundaries
Other Boundaries
J
55°
K
50°
L
45°
M
40°
N
35°
1
10°
2
5°
3
0°
4
5°
5
10°
6
15°
7
20°
ATLANTIC OCEAN
Equator
Georgetown
Paramaribo
Cayenne
SURINAM
(Neth.)
FRENCH
GUIANA
AMAPÁ
Macapá
Marajó
Belém
São Luís
Fortaleza
(Ceará)
Teresina
Natal
João Pessoa
(Paraíba)
Recife
(Pernambuco)
Maceió
Aracaju
Salvador (Bahia)
Vitória
Belo Horizonte
Brasília
FUTURE FEDERAL DISTRICT
Cuiabá
Goiás
RIO AMAZONAS
PARÁ
MARANHÃO
PIAUÍ
CEARÁ
RIO GRANDE DO NORTE
PARAÍBA
PERNAMBUCO
ALAGOAS
SERGIPE
BAHIA
GOIÁS
MATO GROSSO
MINAS GERAIS
ESPÍRITO SANTO
SÃO PAULO
ZONE IN DISPUTE
RIO DE JANEIRO
Campos
Juiz de Fora
Ilhéus
Santarém
Óbidos
Marabá
Carolina
Serra do Roncador
Serra do Estrondo
Serra da Desordem
Sa. dos Carajás
Sa. dos Gradaús
Planalto de Mato Grosso
Ilha do Bananal
Tocantins
Araguaia
Xingu
Tapajós
São Francisco
Paranaíba
Rio Grande
Corumbá
Campo Grande
Uberaba
Uberlândia
Ribeirão Prêto
Montes Claros
Feira de Sant' Ana
Campina Grande
Juàzeiro do Norte

es 72 and 73

Map continued

RIO DE JANEIRO
SÃO PAULO
Curitiba
Florianópolis
Pôrto Alegre
Montevideo
URUGUAY
RIO GRANDE DO SUL
SANTA CATARINA
ATLANTIC OCEAN
Tropic of Capricorn
Valparaiso
Santiago
Viña del Mar
PACIFIC OCEAN
ARGENTINA
BUENOS AIRES
La Plata
Avellaneda
Río de la Plata
Baía de Guanabara
Niterói
DISTRITO FEDERAL
Ilha do Governador
Copacabana
SCALE OF MILES
SOUTH ORKNEY IS.
Elephant I.
Clarence I.
Coronation I.
Laurie I.

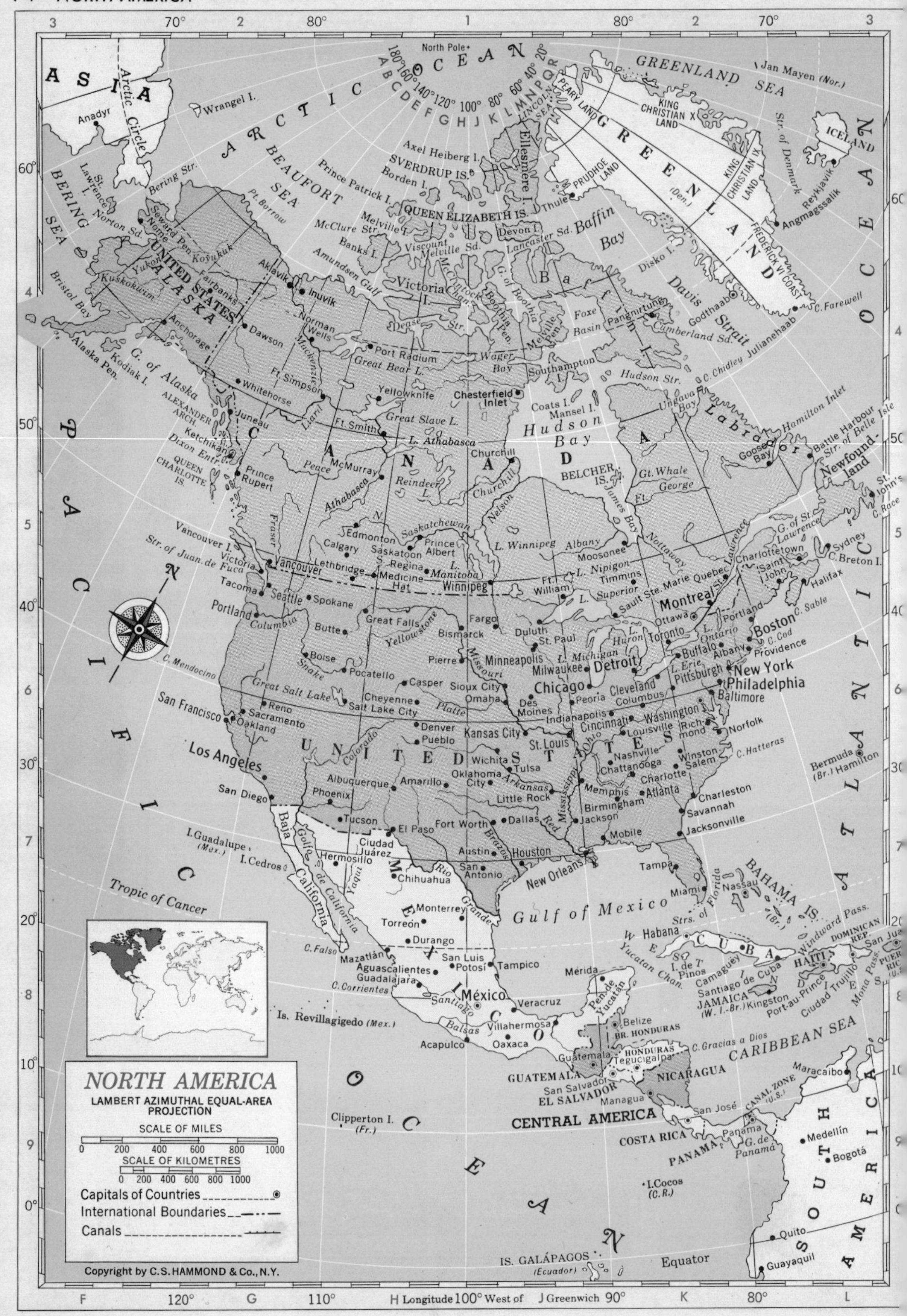
NORTH AMERICA
LAMBERT AZIMUTHAL EQUAL-AREA PROJECTION
SCALE OF MILES
0 200 400 600 800 1000
SCALE OF KILOMETRES
0 200 400 600 800 1000
Capitals of Countries
International Boundaries
Canals
Copyright by C.S. HAMMOND & Co., N.Y.
Longitude 100° West of Greenwich 90°
ARCTIC OCEAN
PACIFIC OCEAN
ATLANTIC OCEAN
North Pole
ASIA
Arctic Circle
Anadyr
Wrangel I.
BERING SEA
Bering Str.
BEAUFORT SEA
GREENLAND SEA
Jan Mayen (Nor.)
GREENLAND (Den.)
ICELAND
Reykjavik
PEARY LAND
KING CHRISTIAN X LAND
PRUDHOE LAND
KING CHRISTIAN IX LAND
FREDERICK VI COAST
Angmagssalik
Str. of Denmark
Thule
Axel Heiberg I.
SVERDRUP IS.
Ellesmere I.
Borden I.
Prince Patrick I.
QUEEN ELIZABETH IS.
Devon I.
Melville I.
McClure Str.
Banks I.
Viscount Melville Sd.
Lancaster Sd.
Baffin Bay
Disko I.
Davis Strait
Godthaab
Julianehaab
C. Farewell
Victoria I.
Amundsen Gulf
Baffin I.
Foxe Basin
Pangnirtung
Cumberland Sd.
Hudson Str.
C. Chidley
Ungava Bay
Labrador
Hamilton Inlet
Goose Bay
Battle Harbour
Str. of Belle Isle
Newfoundland
St. John's
C. Race
UNITED STATES
ALASKA
Nome
Seward Pen.
Norton Sd.
St. Lawrence I.
Yukon
Koyukuk
Kuskokwim
Fairbanks
Anchorage
Bristol Bay
Alaska Pen.
Kodiak I.
G. of Alaska
Aklavik
Inuvik
Dawson
Norman Wells
Whitehorse
Ft. Simpson
Juneau
ALEXANDER ARCH.
Ketchikan
Dixon Entr.
QUEEN CHARLOTTE IS.
Prince Rupert
CANADA
Port Radium
Great Bear L.
Yellowknife
Great Slave L.
Ft. Smith
L. Athabasca
Chesterfield Inlet
Wager Bay
Southampton I.
Coats I.
Mansel I.
Hudson Bay
Churchill
BELCHER IS.
James Bay
Gt. Whale
Ft. George
McMurray
Reindeer L.
Edmonton
Calgary
Saskatoon
Prince Albert
Regina
Medicine Hat
Lethbridge
Winnipeg
L. Winnipeg
Moosonee
Albany
L. Nipigon
Ft. William
Timmins
L. Superior
Sault Ste. Marie
Quebec
Montreal
Ottawa
Toronto
Charlottetown
Saint John
Halifax
Sydney
C. Breton I.
G. of St. Lawrence
Vancouver I.
Victoria
Vancouver
Str. of Juan de Fuca
Tacoma
Seattle
Spokane
Portland
Great Falls
Butte
Boise
Pocatello
Great Salt Lake
Salt Lake City
Cheyenne
Casper
Denver
Pueblo
Reno
Sacramento
San Francisco
Oakland
Los Angeles
San Diego
Phoenix
Tucson
Albuquerque
Amarillo
El Paso
C. Mendocino
Fargo
Bismarck
Pierre
Minneapolis
St. Paul
Duluth
Sioux City
Omaha
Des Moines
Kansas City
Wichita
Tulsa
Oklahoma City
Dallas
Fort Worth
Austin
San Antonio
Houston
New Orleans
Little Rock
Memphis
St. Louis
Milwaukee
Chicago
Detroit
Peoria
Indianapolis
Cincinnati
Louisville
Nashville
Chattanooga
Birmingham
Atlanta
Jackson
Mobile
Cleveland
Columbus
Pittsburgh
Buffalo
Albany
Boston
C. Cod
Providence
New York
Philadelphia
Baltimore
Washington
Richmond
Norfolk
Winston-Salem
Charlotte
C. Hatteras
Charleston
Savannah
Jacksonville
Tampa
Miami
Bermuda (Br.) Hamilton
BAHAMA IS. (Br.)
Nassau
Strs. of Florida
Gulf of Mexico
Tropic of Cancer
I. Guadalupe (Mex.)
I. Cedros
Hermosillo
Ciudad Juárez
Chihuahua
Monterrey
Torreón
Durango
Mazatlán
San Luis Potosí
Tampico
Aguascalientes
Guadalajara
C. Corrientes
C. Falso
México
Veracruz
Villahermosa
Oaxaca
Acapulco
Mérida
Pen. de Yucatán
Yucatan Chan.
Is. Revillagigedo (Mex.)
MEXICO
Belize
BR. HONDURAS
GUATEMALA
Guatemala
EL SALVADOR
San Salvador
HONDURAS
Tegucigalpa
C. Gracias a Dios
NICARAGUA
Managua
COSTA RICA
San José
PANAMA
Panama
G. de Panamá
CANAL ZONE (U.S.)
CENTRAL AMERICA
CARIBBEAN SEA
Habana
CUBA
I. de Pinos
Camagüey
Santiago de Cuba
JAMAICA (W. I.-Br.)
Kingston
HAITI
Port-au-Prince
DOMINICAN REP.
Ciudad Trujillo
Windward Pass.
Mona Pass.
Maracaibo
Medellín
Bogotá
SOUTH AMERICA
Quito
Guayaquil
Clipperton I. (Fr.)
I. Cocos (C.R.)
IS. GALÁPAGOS (Ecuador)
Equator

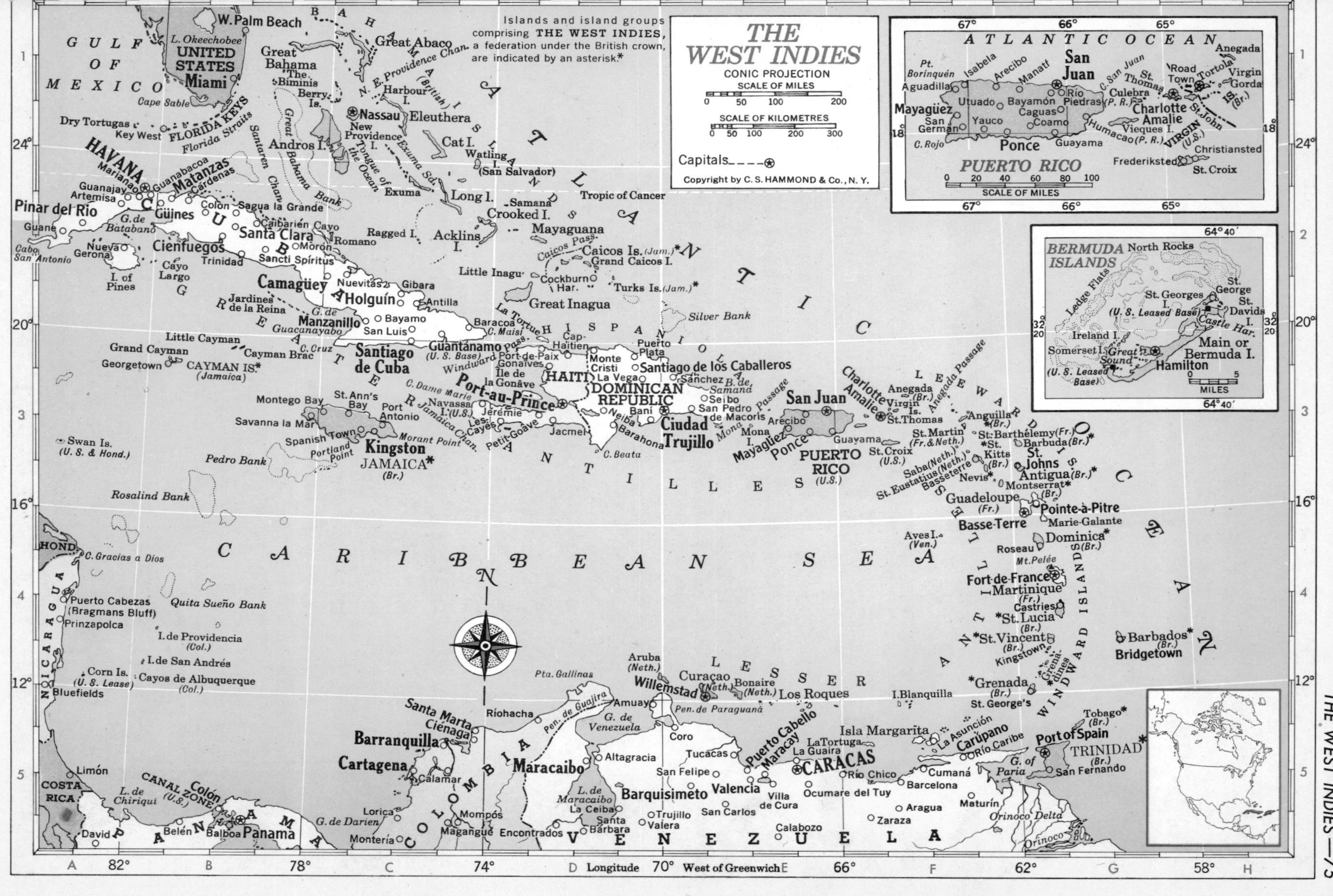
THE WEST INDIES
CONIC PROJECTION
SCALE OF MILES
0 50 100 200
SCALE OF KILOMETRES
0 50 100 200 300
Capitals
Copyright by C. S. HAMMOND & Co., N. Y.
Islands and island groups comprising THE WEST INDIES, a federation under the British crown, are indicated by an asterisk.*
PUERTO RICO
SCALE OF MILES
BERMUDA ISLANDS
ATLANTIC OCEAN
GULF OF MEXICO
CARIBBEAN SEA
LESSER ANTILLES
LEEWARD ISLANDS
WINDWARD ISLANDS
Tropic of Cancer
UNITED STATES
HAVANA
Kingston
JAMAICA*
Port-au-Prince
HAITI
DOMINICAN REPUBLIC
Ciudad Trujillo
San Juan
PUERTO RICO
CARACAS
VENEZUELA
COLOMBIA
PANAMA
Longitude
West of Greenwich

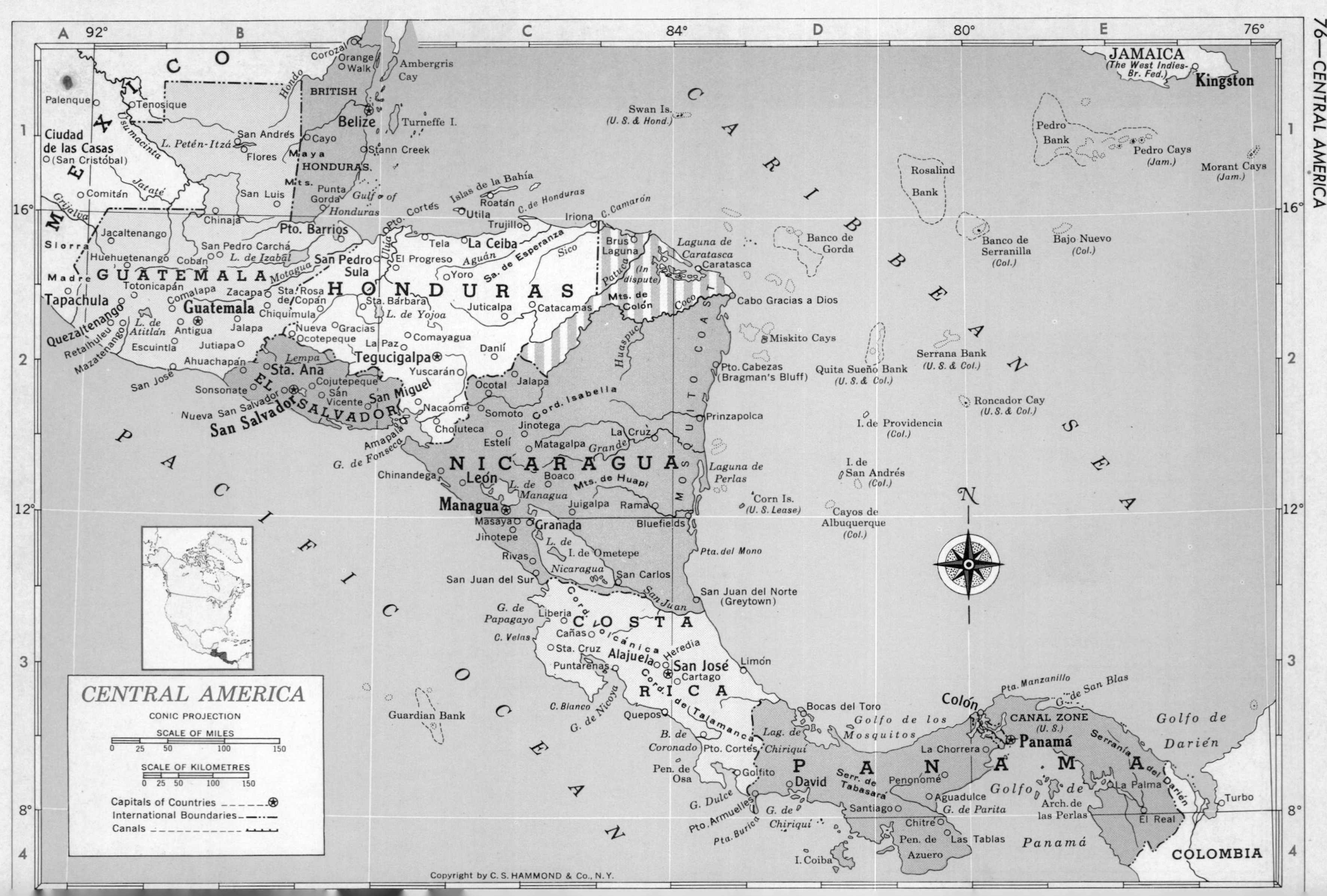
CENTRAL AMERICA
CONIC PROJECTION
SCALE OF MILES
0 25 50 100 150
SCALE OF KILOMETRES
0 25 50 100 150
Capitals of Countries
International Boundaries
Canals
Copyright by C. S. HAMMOND & Co., N. Y.
CARIBBEAN SEA
PACIFIC OCEAN
MEXICO
BRITISH HONDURAS
GUATEMALA
HONDURAS
EL SALVADOR
NICARAGUA
COSTA RICA
PANAMA
COLOMBIA
JAMAICA (The West Indies-Br. Fed.)
Kingston
CANAL ZONE (U. S.)
Guatemala
Belize
Tegucigalpa
San Salvador
Managua
San José
Panamá
Colón
Gulf of Honduras
Golfo de los Mosquitos
Golfo de Panamá
Golfo de Darién
Swan Is. (U. S. & Hond.)
Rosalind Bank
Pedro Bank
Serrana Bank (U. S. & Col.)
Quita Sueño Bank (U. S. & Col.)
I. de Providencia (Col.)
I. de San Andrés (Col.)
Corn Is. (U. S. Lease)

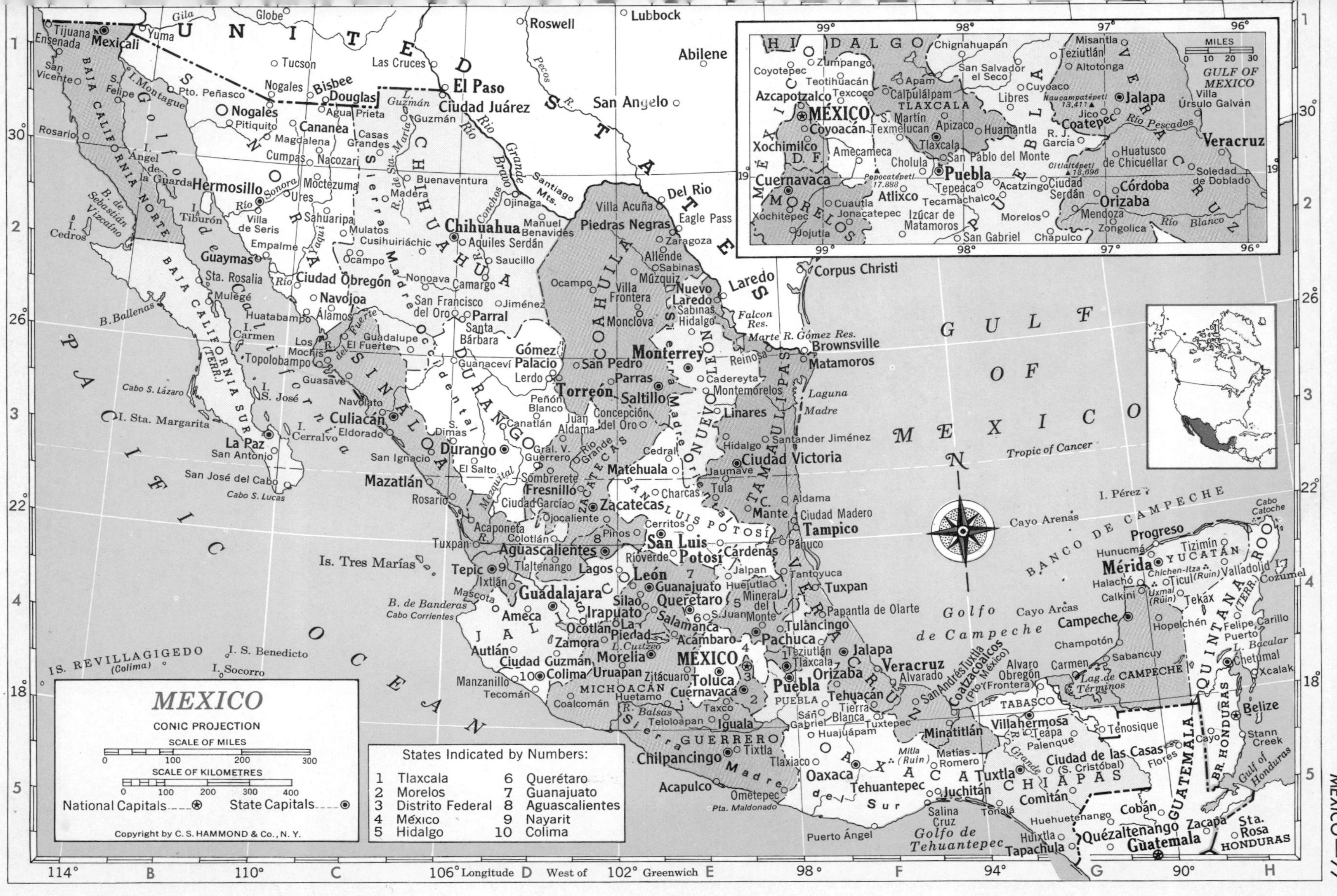
MEXICO
CONIC PROJECTION
SCALE OF MILES
0 100 200 300
SCALE OF KILOMETRES
0 100 200 300 400
National Capitals ⊛ State Capitals ◉
Copyright by C. S. HAMMOND & Co., N. Y.
States Indicated by Numbers:
1 Tlaxcala
2 Morelos
3 Distrito Federal
4 México
5 Hidalgo
6 Querétaro
7 Guanajuato
8 Aguascalientes
9 Nayarit
10 Colima
UNITED STATES
GULF OF MEXICO
PACIFIC OCEAN
Tropic of Cancer
MÉXICO
Guadalajara
Monterrey
Veracruz
Puebla
Mérida
Chihuahua
Durango
Mazatlán
Acapulco
Tampico
Golfo de California
Golfo de Tehuantepec
Golfo de Campeche
BAJA CALIFORNIA NORTE
BAJA CALIFORNIA SUR (TERR.)
GUATEMALA
BR. HONDURAS
106° Longitude West of 102° Greenwich

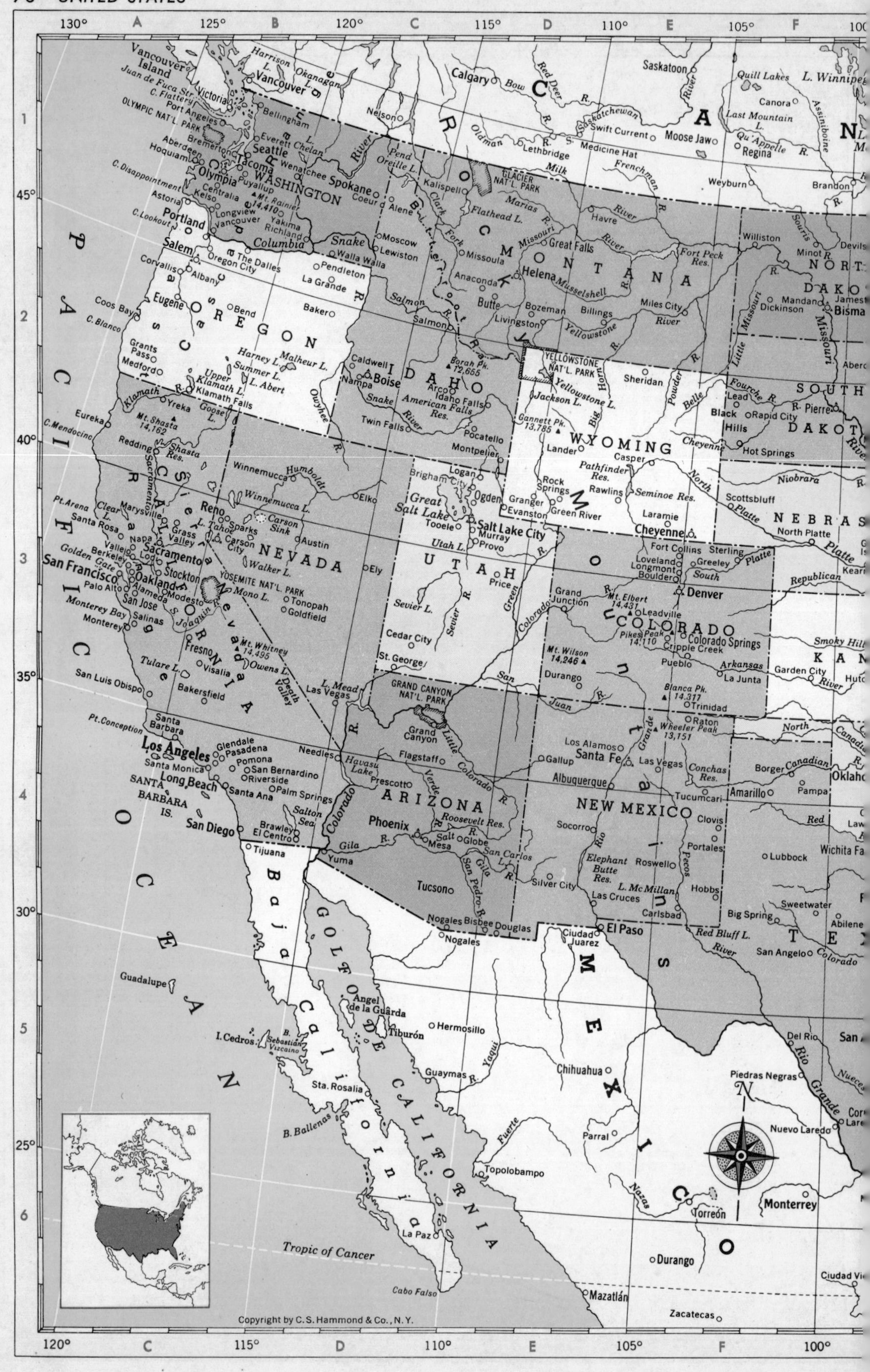

130° A 125° B 120° C 115° D 110° E 105° F
1
2
3
4
5
6
45°
40°
35°
30°
25°
PACIFIC OCEAN
Vancouver Island
Juan de Fuca Str.
C. Flattery
Victoria
Vancouver
Port Angeles
OLYMPIC NAT'L. PARK
Bellingham
Everett
Bremerton
Seattle
Aberdeen
Hoquiam
Tacoma
Olympia
Puyallup
WASHINGTON
C. Disappointment
Centralia
Mt. Rainier 14,410
Kelso
Astoria
Longview
Vancouver
Yakima
Richland
Wenatchee
Spokane
Coeur d'Alene
L. Chelan
Okanagan L.
Harrison L.
Columbia
Snake
Walla Walla
Moscow
Lewiston
Pendleton
La Grande
Baker
C. Lookout
Portland
Salem
Oregon City
The Dalles
Corvallis
Albany
Eugene
Bend
OREGON
Coos Bay
C. Blanco
Grants Pass
Medford
Harney L.
Malheur L.
Summer L.
L. Abert
Upper Klamath L.
Klamath Falls
Owyhee
Klamath
Yreka
Goose L.
Eureka
C. Mendocino
Mt. Shasta 14,162
Redding
Shasta Res.
Sacramento
Sierra Nevada
Pt. Arena
Clear L.
Santa Rosa
Marysville
Napa
Vallejo
Berkeley
Golden Gate
San Francisco
Oakland
Alameda
Palo Alto
San Jose
Sacramento
Lodi
Stockton
Modesto
Monterey Bay
Monterey
Salinas
San Joaquin
Fresno
CALIFORNIA
Tulare L.
Visalia
Bakersfield
San Luis Obispo
Pt. Conception
Santa Barbara
Los Angeles
Glendale
Pasadena
Santa Monica
Pomona
San Bernardino
Riverside
Long Beach
Santa Ana
Palm Springs
SANTA BARBARA IS.
Salton Sea
San Diego
Brawley
El Centro
Tijuana
Reno
Sparks
L. Tahoe
Carson City
Grass Valley
Carson Sink
Winnemucca
Winnemucca L.
Humboldt
Elko
Austin
NEVADA
Walker L.
Ely
YOSEMITE NAT'L. PARK
Mono L.
Tonopah
Goldfield
Mt. Whitney 14,495
Owens L.
Death Valley
L. Mead
Las Vegas
Needles
Havasu Lake
Colorado
Yuma
Gila
ROCKY MOUNTAINS
CANADA
Calgary
Bow
Red Deer R.
Saskatoon
Saskatchewan
Swift Current
Moose Jaw
Medicine Hat
Lethbridge
Oldman
Nelson
Quill Lakes
L. Winnipeg
Canora
Last Mountain L.
Assiniboine
Qu'Appelle R.
Regina
Weyburn
Brandon
Souris
Frenchman
Milk
GLACIER NAT'L. PARK
Kalispell
Pend Oreille L.
Flathead L.
Clark Fork
Marias R.
Missoula
Missouri
Great Falls
Havre
MONTANA
Helena
Anaconda
Butte
Musselshell
Bozeman
Billings
Livingston
Yellowstone
Miles City
Fort Peck Res.
Williston
Minot
Devils
Mandan
Dickinson
Bismarck
Little Missouri
Salmon
Salmon R.
IDAHO
Caldwell
Boise
Nampa
Borah Pk. 12,655
Arco
Idaho Falls
American Falls Res.
Snake River
Twin Falls
Pocatello
Montpelier
YELLOWSTONE NAT'L. PARK
Yellowstone L.
Jackson L.
Gannett Pk. 13,785
Sheridan
Powder
Big Horn
Belle Fourche R.
Lead
Rapid City
Black Hills
Pierre
Hot Springs
SOUTH DAKOTA
WYOMING
Lander
Casper
Pathfinder Res.
Rawlins
Seminoe Res.
Rock Springs
Granger
Evanston
Green River
Laramie
Cheyenne
North Platte
Scottsbluff
Niobrara
NEBRASKA
North Platte
Logan
Brigham City
Ogden
Great Salt Lake
Tooele
Salt Lake City
Murray
Provo
Utah L.
UTAH
Price
Green
Sevier L.
Sevier R.
Cedar City
St. George
GRAND CANYON NAT'L. PARK
Grand Canyon
Little Colorado
Flagstaff
Prescott
Verde
ARIZONA
Phoenix
Mesa
Salt R.
Globe
Roosevelt Res.
San Carlos L.
San Pedro R.
Tucson
Nogales
Bisbee
Douglas
Fort Collins
Loveland
Longmont
Boulder
Greeley
Sterling
South Platte
Denver
Grand Junction
Mt. Elbert 14,431
Leadville
COLORADO
Pikes Peak 14,110
Colorado Springs
Cripple Creek
Pueblo
Arkansas
La Junta
Mt. Wilson 14,246
Durango
San Juan R.
Blanca Pk. 14,317
Trinidad
Raton
Wheeler Peak 13,151
Los Alamos
Santa Fe
Gallup
Las Vegas
Conchas Res.
Albuquerque
NEW MEXICO
Tucumcari
Socorro
Rio Grande
Clovis
Portales
Elephant Butte Res.
Roswell
Pecos
L. McMillan
Silver City
Las Cruces
Hobbs
Carlsbad
El Paso
Ciudad Juarez
Red Bluff L.
Republican
Smoky Hill
KANSAS
Garden City
Hutchinson
Kearney
Borger
Canadian
Amarillo
Pampa
Oklahoma
Red
Lawton
Wichita Falls
Lubbock
Big Spring
Sweetwater
Abilene
San Angelo
Colorado
TEXAS
Del Rio
San Antonio
Nueces
Piedras Negras
Nuevo Laredo
Laredo
Monterrey
MEXICO
Baja California
GOLFO DE CALIFORNIA
Guadalupe
Angel de la Guarda
Tiburón
Hermosillo
I. Cedros
B. Sebastian Vizcaino
Yaqui
Guaymas
Chihuahua
Sta. Rosalia
B. Ballenas
Fuerte
Parral
Topolobampo
Nazas
Torreón
La Paz
Tropic of Cancer
Durango
Cabo Falso
Mazatlán
Zacatecas
Ciudad Victoria
N
Copyright by C.S. Hammond & Co., N.Y.
120° C 115° D 110° E 105° F 100°

UNITED STATES
excluding Alaska
POLYCONIC PROJECTION
SCALE OF MILES
0 50 100 200 300 400
SCALE OF KILOMETRES
0 100 200 300 400
Capitals of Countries
State Capitals
International Boundaries
95° H 90° J 85° K 80° L 75° M 70° N 65°
1
2
3
4
5
6
45°
40°
35°
30°
25°
West of Greenwich
C A N A D A
James Bay
Moosonee
L. Evans
Albany R.
Lake Nipigon
Lac Seul
Sioux Lookout
Kenora
Rainy Lake
Port Arthur
Fort William
Isle Royale
Lake Superior
Long L.
Ogoki R.
Kenogami R.
Missinaibi R.
Mattagami R.
Abitibi R.
Harricanaw R.
L. Abitibi
Cochrane
Timmins
L. Timiskaming
Cobalt
L. Timagami
Sault Ste. Marie
Sudbury
L. Nipissing
North Bay
Ottawa R.
Ottawa
Hull
Montreal
Trois Rivières
Quebec
Kempt L.
St. Maurice R.
Roberval
L. St. John
Chicoutimi
Saguenay
Rimouski
Rivière du Loup
St. Lawrence
Mistassini R.
Peribonka R.
Caribou
Houlton
Fredericton
Sherbrooke
Georgian Bay
Manitoulin I.
L. Simcoe
Peterborough
Kingston
Toronto
Hamilton
London
Niagara Falls
Lake Ontario
Lake Huron
Lake Michigan
Lake Erie
L. St. Clair
Windsor
MINNESOTA
Minneapolis
St. Paul
Duluth
Hibbing
Virginia
Brainerd
St. Cloud
Mille Lacs L.
Red Lake
Leech L.
Rainy International Falls
Vermilion L.
Faribault
Winona
Mankato
Rochester
Austin
WISCONSIN
Superior
Eau Claire
Wausau
Green Bay
Appleton
Oshkosh
Fond du Lac
La Crosse
Sheboygan
Milwaukee
Racine
Madison
Janesville
Beloit
MICHIGAN
Marquette
Houghton
Calumet
Cheboygan
Traverse City
Manistee
Muskegon
Grand Rapids
Bay City
Saginaw
Flint
Port Huron
Pontiac
Lansing
Battle Creek
Kalamazoo
Jackson
Ann Arbor
Detroit
IOWA
Mason City
Fort Dodge
Sioux City
Waterloo
Cedar Rapids
Dubuque
Davenport
Marshalltown
Newton
Iowa City
Muscatine
Des Moines
Council Bluffs
Oskaloosa
Ottumwa
Burlington
Fort Madison
Keokuk
ILLINOIS
Freeport
Rockford
Elgin
Chicago
Clinton
Moline
Rock Island
Joliet
Kankakee
Galesburg
Peoria
Bloomington
Champaign
Danville
Quincy
Springfield
Decatur
Alton
East St. Louis
Belleville
Cairo
INDIANA
Gary
South Bend
Elkhart
Fort Wayne
Kokomo
Marion
Muncie
Lafayette
Anderson
Indianapolis
Terre Haute
Evansville
New Albany
OHIO
Toledo
Sandusky
Cleveland
Akron
Youngstown
Canton
Lima
Mansfield
Steubenville
Wheeling
Springfield
Columbus
Zanesville
Dayton
Hamilton
Cincinnati
Portsmouth
Covington
Newport
Parkersburg
WEST VIRGINIA
Clarksburg
Fairmont
Charleston
Huntington
Bluefield
KENTUCKY
Ashland
Frankfort
Lexington
Louisville
Owensboro
Bowling Green
Paducah
Middlesboro
PENNSYLVANIA
Erie
Meadville
Oil City
New Castle
Pittsburgh
McKeesport
Altoona
Johnstown
Harrisburg
Lancaster
York
Williamsport
Wilkes-Barre
Scranton
Allentown
Reading
Philadelphia
Chester
NEW YORK
Buffalo
Jamestown
Rochester
Auburn
Syracuse
Oswego
Rome
Utica
Schenectady
Albany
Troy
Elmira
Binghamton
Watertown
Ogdensburg
Newburgh
New York
Long I.
NEW JERSEY
Paterson
Newark
Trenton
Camden
Atlantic City
C. May
Delaware Bay
DEL.
Dover
Wilmington
MD.
Baltimore
Cumberland
Hagerstown
Annapolis
Washington
Alexandria
Potomac R.
VIRGINIA
Charlottesville
Richmond
Petersburg
Lynchburg
Roanoke
Danville
Newport News
Portsmouth
Norfolk
C. Charles
Chesapeake Bay
VT.
Burlington
Lake Champlain
Montpelier
Rutland
N.H.
Berlin
Concord
Manchester
Nashua
Portsmouth
MAINE
Rumford
Waterville
Bangor
Augusta
Lewiston
Auburn
Portland
Biddeford
Calais
Eastport
MASS
Pittsfield
Springfield
Worcester
Lowell
Lawrence
Boston
Fall River
New Bedford
C. Cod
Nantucket I.
Martha's Vineyard
CONN
Hartford
Waterbury
New Haven
Bridgeport
New London
R.I.
Providence
Newport
Connecticut R.
NORTH CAROLINA
Winston-Salem
Greensboro
Durham
Raleigh
High Point
Charlotte
Gastonia
Asheville
Mt. Mitchell 6,684
Fayetteville
Goldsboro
New Bern
Wilmington
Rocky Mount
Albemarle Sd.
Pamlico Sd.
C. Hatteras
C. Lookout
C. Fear
SOUTH CAROLINA
Greenville
Spartanburg
Rock Hill
Anderson
Greenwood
Columbia
Florence
Georgetown
Charleston
L. Murray
L. Marion
L. Moultrie
Santee R.
TENNESSEE
Knoxville
Oak Ridge
Clarksville
Nashville
Columbia
Chattanooga
Chickamauga L.
Norris L.
Jackson
Memphis
Bristol
Cumberland R.
ARKANSAS
Fayetteville
Fort Smith
Jonesboro
Blytheville
Little Rock
Hot Springs Nat'l. Park
Pine Bluff
Texarkana
El Dorado
Arkansas River
White R.
Ouachita R.
MISSOURI
St. Joseph
Kansas City
Sedalia
Jefferson City
Columbia
Hannibal
Moberly
St. Louis
University City
Joplin
Springfield
Ozark Mts.
Cape Girardeau
Missouri R.
Osage R.
MISSISSIPPI
Clarksdale
Greenville
Columbus
Jackson
Vicksburg
Meridian
Laurel
Natchez
Hattiesburg
Biloxi
Gulfport
Sardis Res.
Yazoo R.
Pearl R.
ALABAMA
Huntsville
Florence
Gadsden
Birmingham
Bessemer
Anniston
Tuscaloosa
Selma
Montgomery
Phenix City
Dothan
Mobile
Mobile Bay
Tombigbee R.
Alabama R.
Wheeler L.
Mitchell L.
GEORGIA
Rome
Atlanta
La Grange
Lloyd Res.
Augusta
Macon
Columbus
Savannah
Brunswick
Waycross
Thomasville
Valdosta
Altamaha R.
Chattahoochee R.
Flint R.
Savannah R.
FLORIDA
Tallahassee
Pensacola
Panama City
Apalachee Bay
Gainesville
Jacksonville
St. Augustine
Daytona Beach
C. Canaveral
Sanford
Orlando
Lakeland
Tampa
St. Petersburg
Tampa Bay
L. Okeechobee
Palm Beach
W. Palm Beach
Fort Myers
Charlotte Har.
The Everglades
Miami
Miami Beach
Ten Thousand Is.
C. Sable
Florida Bay
Key West
FLORIDA KEYS
Florida Strait
LOUISIANA
Shreveport
Monroe
Alexandria
Baton Rouge
Bogalusa
Lake Charles
New Orleans
L. Pontchartrain
Grand L.
Mississippi Delta
Red R.
Sabine R.
Mississippi River
TEXAS
Marshall
Longview
Tyler
Palestine
Paris
Beaumont
Port Arthur
Galveston
Galveston Bay
Matagorda Bay
Oklahoma
Muskogee
McAlester
Kansas
Fort Scott
GULF OF MEXICO
ATLANTIC OCEAN
BAHAMA ISLANDS
Gt. Abaco I.
Gt. Bahama I.
Eleuthera
Nassau
Andros I.
Cat I.
Exuma Sound
Exuma
Long I.
Santaren Channel
CUBA
Habana

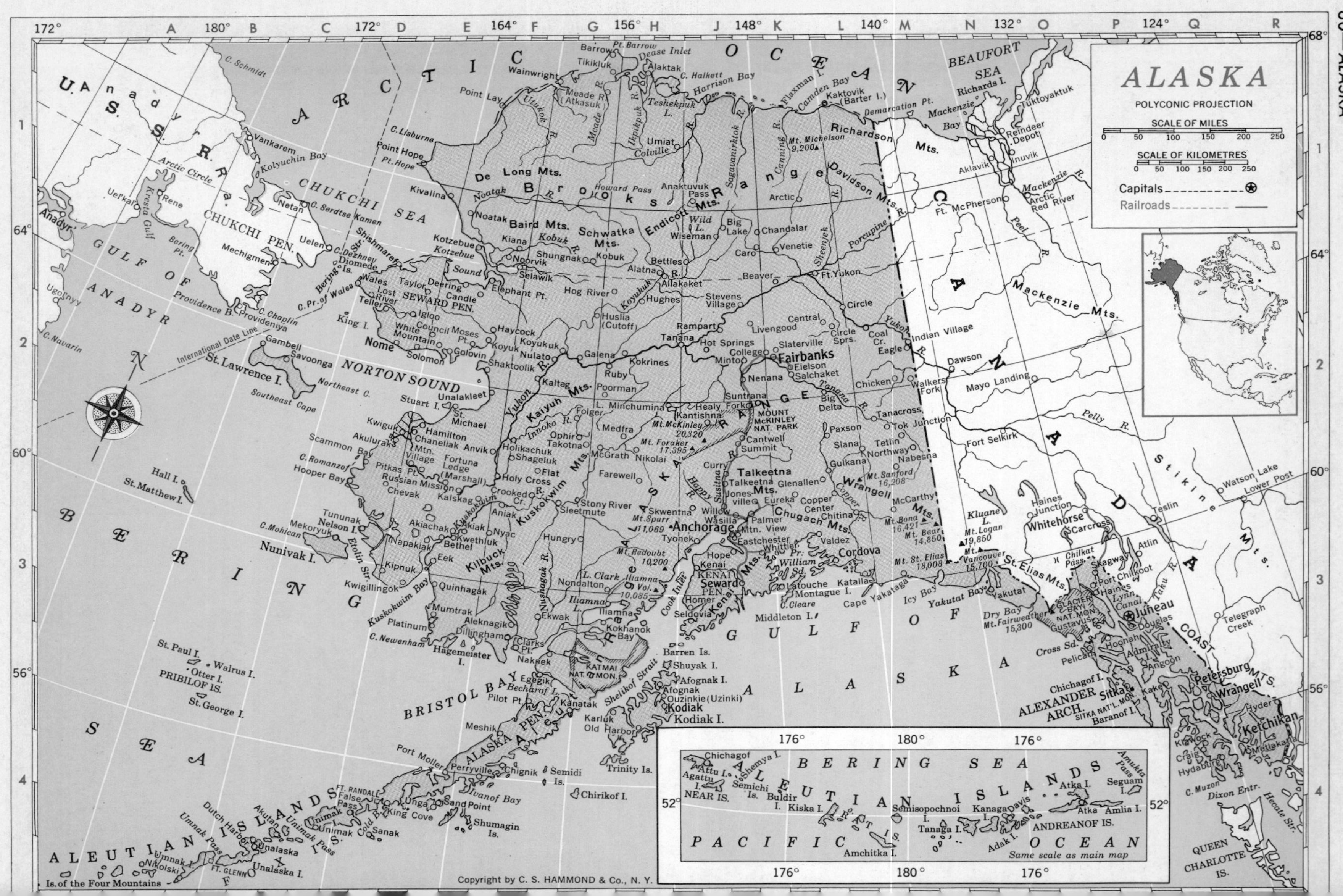

ALASKA
POLYCONIC PROJECTION
SCALE OF MILES
0 50 100 150 200 250
SCALE OF KILOMETRES
0 50 100 150 200 250
Capitals
Railroads
ARCTIC OCEAN
BEAUFORT SEA
CHUKCHI SEA
BERING SEA
GULF OF ALASKA
GULF OF ANADYR
NORTON SOUND
BRISTOL BAY
PACIFIC OCEAN
ALEUTIAN ISLANDS
CANADA
U.S.S.R.
CHUKCHI PEN.
SEWARD PEN.
ALASKA PEN.
KENAI PEN.
Brooks Range
Endicott Mts.
Baird Mts.
Schwatka Mts.
De Long Mts.
Richardson Mts.
Davidson Mts.
Mackenzie Mts.
Stikine Mts.
COAST MTS.
St. Elias Mts.
Wrangell Mts.
Chugach Mts.
Kenai Mts.
Alaska Range
Kuskokwim Mts.
Kaiyuh Mts.
Kilbuck Mts.
Mt. McKinley 20,320
Mt. Foraker 17,395
Mt. Logan 19,850
Mt. St. Elias 18,008
Mt. Sanford 16,208
Mt. Michelson 9,200
MOUNT McKINLEY NAT. PARK
KATMAI NAT. MON.
GLACIER BAY NAT. MON.
Yukon R.
Tanana R.
Kuskokwim R.
Koyukuk R.
Porcupine R.
Copper R.
Susitna R.
Nushagak R.
Noatak R.
Kobuk R.
Colville R.
Peel R.
Pelly R.
Mackenzie R.
Juneau
Fairbanks
Anchorage
Nome
Kodiak
Sitka
Ketchikan
Seward
Valdez
Cordova
Whitehorse
Dawson
Barrow
Kotzebue
Bethel
Talkeetna
Wrangell
Petersburg
Skagway
Haines
Kodiak I.
Nunivak I.
St. Lawrence I.
St. Matthew I.
Hall I.
PRIBILOF IS.
St. Paul I.
St. George I.
Unimak I.
Unalaska I.
Umnak I.
Shumagin Is.
Trinity Is.
Chirikof I.
Semidi Is.
Barren Is.
Afognak I.
Middleton I.
Montague I.
ALEXANDER ARCH.
QUEEN CHARLOTTE IS.
Dixon Entr.
Hecate Str.
Cook Inlet
Shelikof Strait
Iliamna L.
Kluane L.
Yakutat Bay
Icy Bay
Kotzebue Sound
Bering Str.
International Date Line
Arctic Circle
B E R I N G S E A
A L E U T I A N I S L A N D S
NEAR IS.
RAT IS.
ANDREANOF IS.
Attu I.
Agattu I.
Kiska I.
Amchitka I.
Adak I.
Atka I.
Amlia I.
Seguam I.
Amukta Pass
P A C I F I C O C E A N
Same scale as main map
Is. of the Four Mountains
Copyright by C. S. HAMMOND & Co., N. Y.

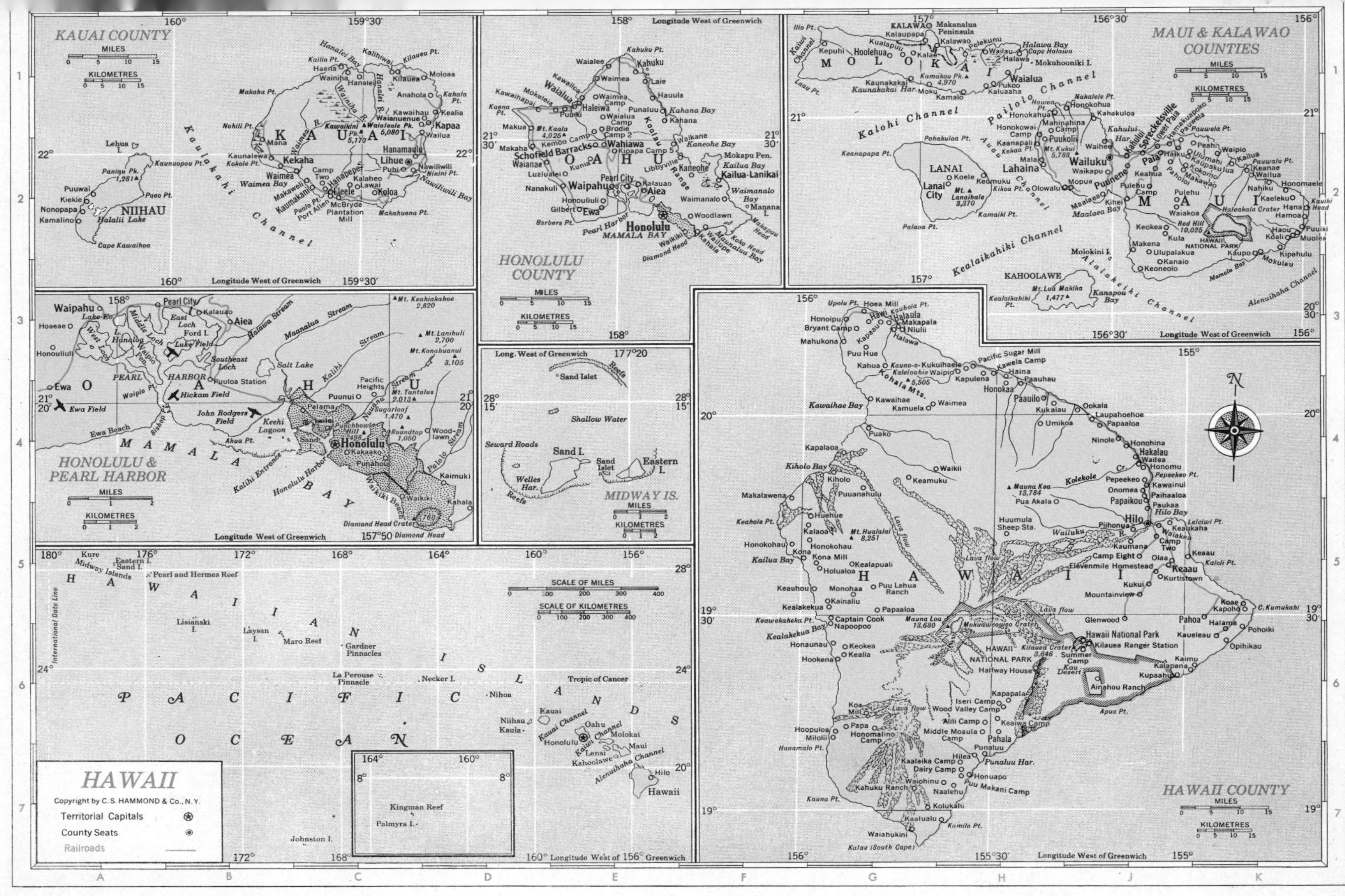

KAUAI COUNTY
HONOLULU COUNTY
MAUI & KALAWAO COUNTIES
HONOLULU & PEARL HARBOR
MIDWAY IS.
HAWAII COUNTY
HAWAIIAN ISLANDS
PACIFIC OCEAN
HAWAII
Copyright by C. S. HAMMOND & Co., N.Y.
Territorial Capitals
County Seats
Railroads

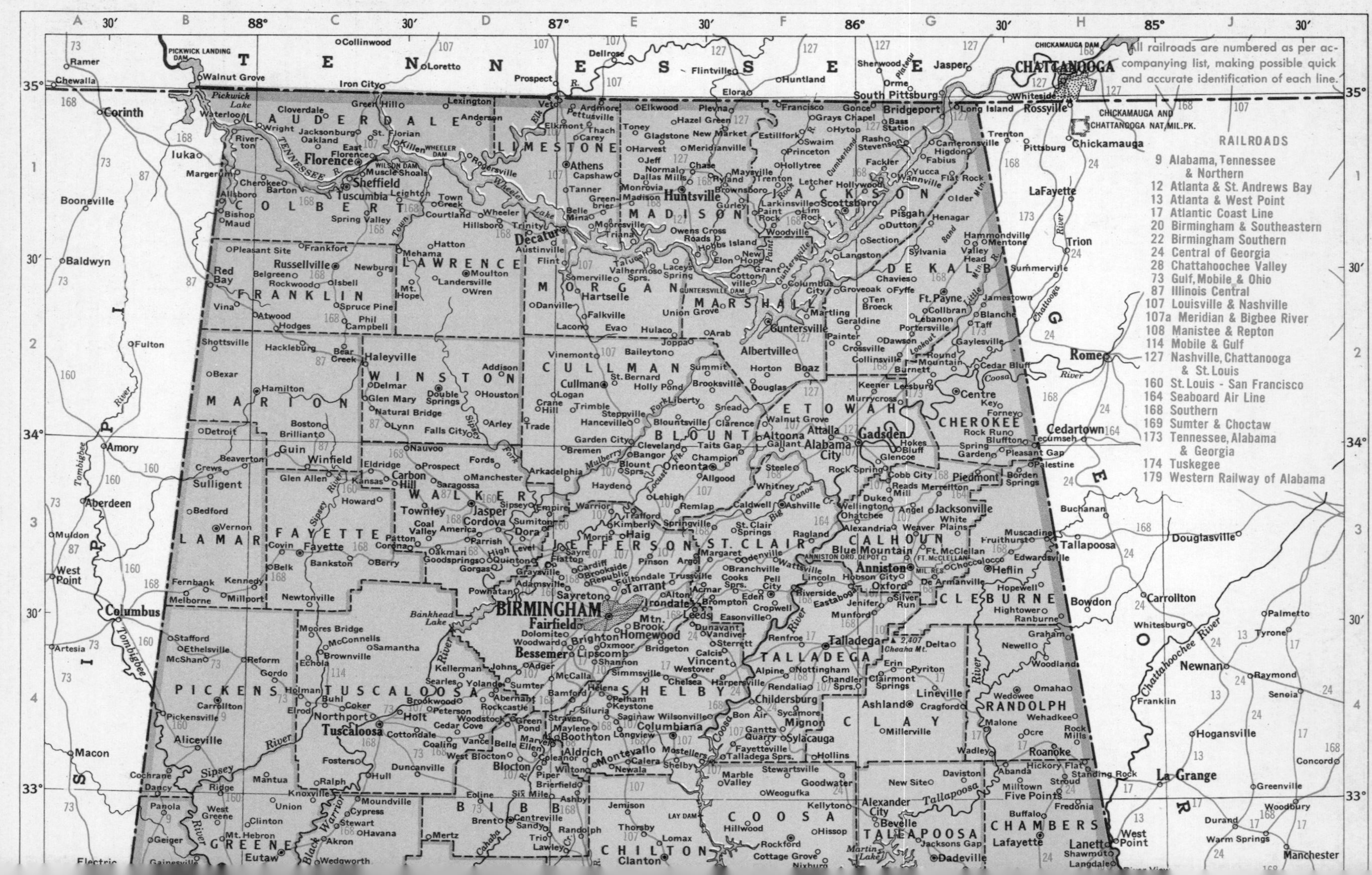
All railroads are numbered as per accompanying list, making possible quick and accurate identification of each line.
RAILROADS
9 Alabama, Tennessee & Northern
12 Atlanta & St. Andrews Bay
13 Atlanta & West Point
17 Atlantic Coast Line
20 Birmingham & Southeastern
22 Birmingham Southern
24 Central of Georgia
28 Chattahoochee Valley
73 Gulf, Mobile & Ohio
87 Illinois Central
107 Louisville & Nashville
107a Meridian & Bigbee River
108 Manistee & Repton
114 Mobile & Gulf
127 Nashville, Chattanooga & St. Louis
160 St. Louis - San Francisco
164 Seaboard Air Line
168 Southern
169 Sumter & Choctaw
173 Tennessee, Alabama & Georgia
174 Tuskegee
179 Western Railway of Alabama

ALABAMA
SCALE OF MILES
0 5 10 20 30 40
State Capitals
County Seats
Railroads
164
F L O R I D A
G U L F O F M E X I C O
MONTGOMERY
MOBILE
PENSACOLA
Longitude West of Greenwich
Copyright by C. S. Hammond & Co., N. Y.

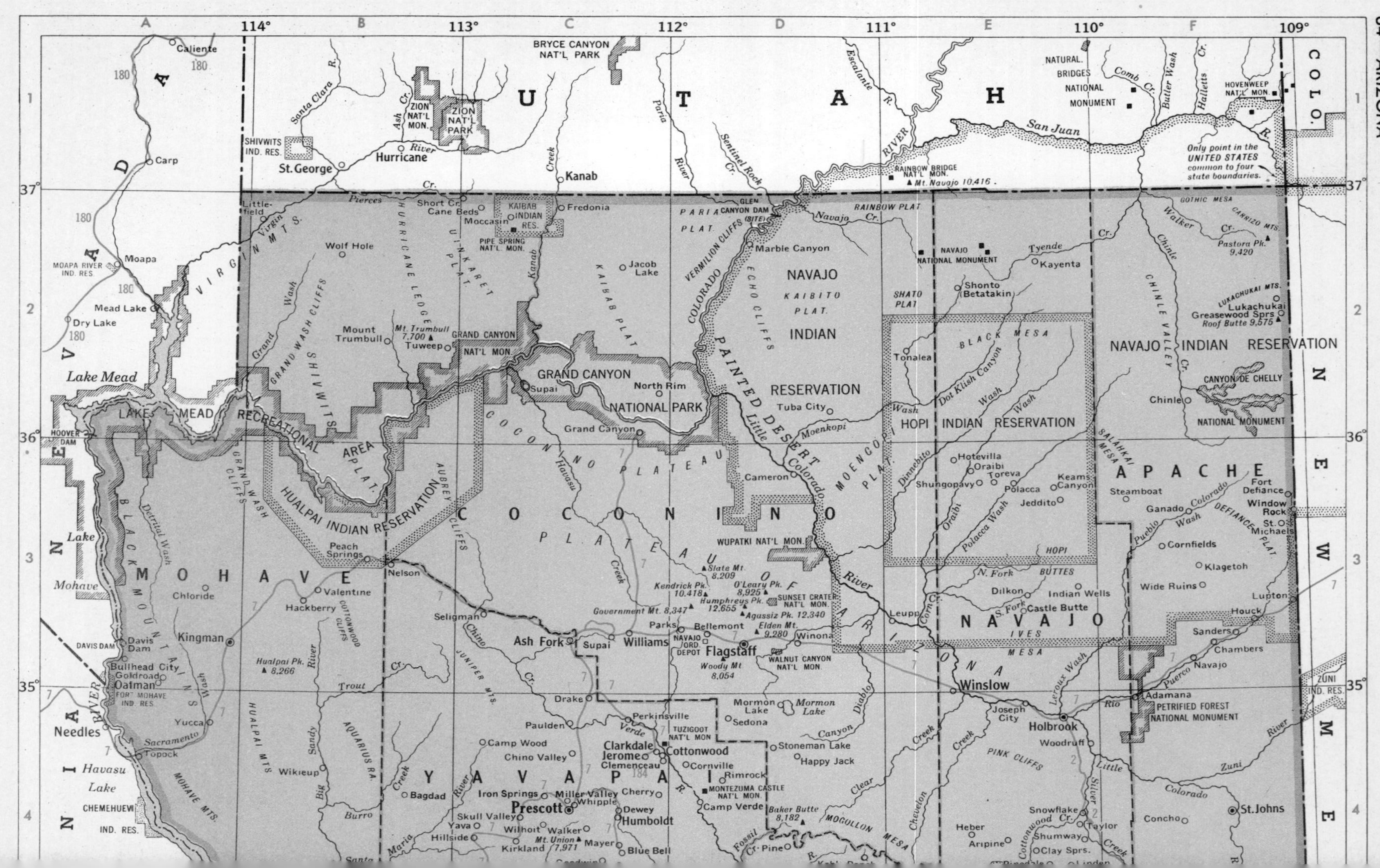

UTAH
COLO.
NEW MEXICO
NEVADA
ARIZONA
COCONINO
MOHAVE
YAVAPAI
NAVAJO
APACHE
NAVAJO INDIAN RESERVATION
HOPI INDIAN RESERVATION
HUALPAI INDIAN RESERVATION
GRAND CANYON NATIONAL PARK
GRAND CANYON NAT'L MON.
LAKE MEAD RECREATIONAL AREA
Lake Mead
HOOVER DAM
DAVIS DAM
Lake Mohave
Only point in the UNITED STATES common to four state boundaries.
PAINTED DESERT
PETRIFIED FOREST NATIONAL MONUMENT
CANYON DE CHELLY NATIONAL MONUMENT
NAVAJO NATIONAL MONUMENT
RAINBOW BRIDGE NAT'L MON.
Mt. Navajo 10,416
NATURAL BRIDGES NATIONAL MONUMENT
HOVENWEEP NAT'L MON.
BRYCE CANYON NAT'L PARK
ZION NAT'L PARK
ZION NAT'L MON.
PIPE SPRING NAT'L MON.
KAIBAB INDIAN RES.
SHIVWITS IND. RES.
MOAPA RIVER IND. RES.
FORT MOHAVE IND. RES.
CHEMEHUEVI IND. RES.
ZUNI IND. RES.
WUPATKI NAT'L MON.
SUNSET CRATER NAT'L MON.
WALNUT CANYON NAT'L MON.
TUZIGOOT NAT'L MON
MONTEZUMA CASTLE NAT'L MON.
Humphreys Pk. 12,655
Agassiz Pk. 12,340
Kendrick Pk. 10,418
Hualpai Pk. 8,266
KAIBAB PLAT.
COCONINO PLATEAU
CHINLE VALLEY
ECHO CLIFFS
VERMILION CLIFFS
GRAND WASH CLIFFS
AUBREY CLIFFS
HURRICANE LEDGE
BLACK MOUNTAINS
HUALPAI MTS
MOHAVE MTS.
AQUARIUS RA.
MOGOLLON MESA
PINK CLIFFS
COLORADO RIVER
Little Colorado
San Juan
Flagstaff
Williams
Ash Fork
Kingman
Prescott
Winslow
Holbrook
St. Johns
Needles
Oatman
Tuba City
Kayenta
Chinle
Ganado
Window Rock
Fort Defiance
Cameron
Jerome
Clarkdale
Cottonwood
Sedona
Seligman
Peach Springs
Fredonia
Kanab
St. George
Hurricane
Jacob Lake
Marble Canyon
Supai
Grand Canyon
North Rim
Tonalea
Keams Canyon
Leupp
Joseph City
Snowflake
Camp Verde
Humboldt
Bagdad
Chloride
Bullhead City
Topock
Yucca
Wikieup
Hackberry
Valentine

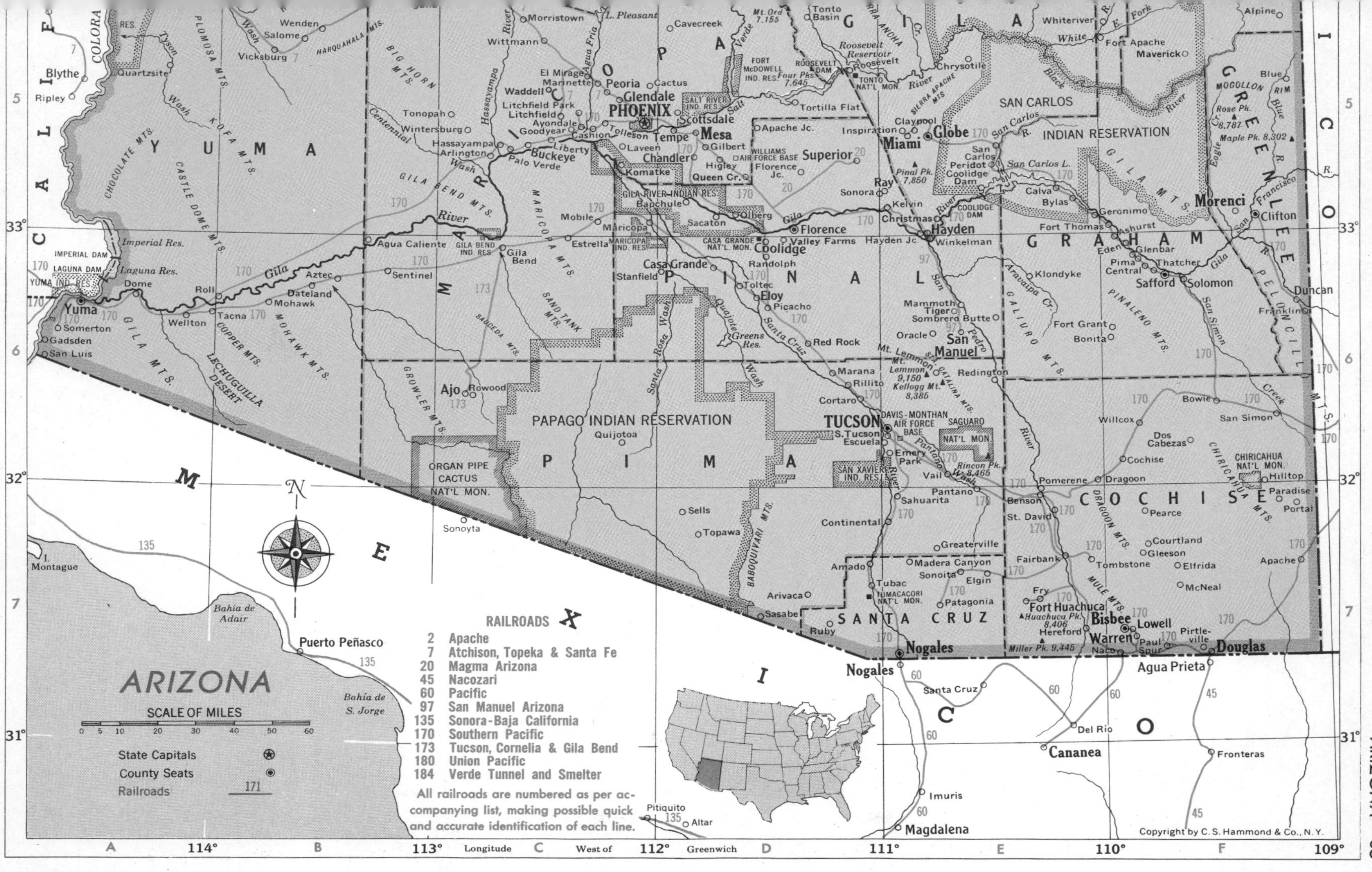
ARIZONA
SCALE OF MILES
0 5 10 20 30 40 50 60
State Capitals
County Seats
Railroads
171
RAILROADS
2 Apache
7 Atchison, Topeka & Santa Fe
20 Magma Arizona
45 Nacozari
60 Pacific
97 San Manuel Arizona
135 Sonora-Baja California
170 Southern Pacific
173 Tucson, Cornelia & Gila Bend
180 Union Pacific
184 Verde Tunnel and Smelter
All railroads are numbered as per accompanying list, making possible quick and accurate identification of each line.
YUMA
MARICOPA
PINAL
GILA
GRAHAM
GREENLEE
PIMA
SANTA CRUZ
COCHISE
CALIF.
MEXICO
PHOENIX
TUCSON
Yuma
Nogales
Douglas
Bisbee
Globe
Florence
Safford
Clifton
PAPAGO INDIAN RESERVATION
SAN CARLOS INDIAN RESERVATION
ORGAN PIPE CACTUS NAT'L MON.
Puerto Peñasco
Bahía de Adair
Bahía de S. Jorge
Cananea
Magdalena
Agua Prieta
A 114° B 113° Longitude C West of 112° Greenwich D 111° E 110° F 109°
Copyright by C. S. Hammond & Co., N. Y.

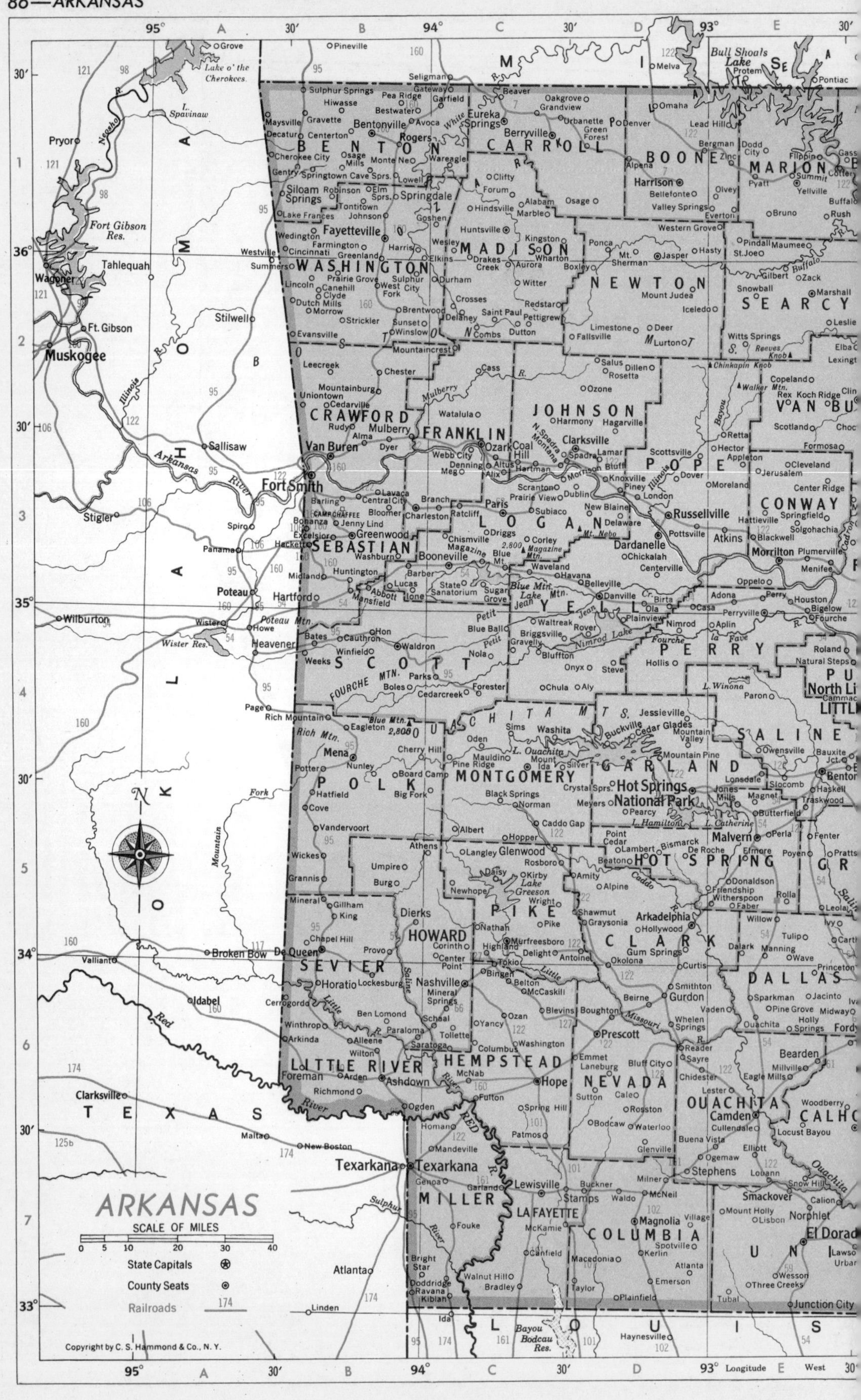
ARKANSAS
SCALE OF MILES
0 5 10 20 30 40
State Capitals
County Seats
Railroads 174
Copyright by C. S. Hammond & Co., N. Y.
BENTON
CARROLL
BOONE
MARION
WASHINGTON
MADISON
NEWTON
SEARCY
CRAWFORD
FRANKLIN
JOHNSON
POPE
VAN BU
CONWAY
SEBASTIAN
LOGAN
YELL
PERRY
SCOTT
POLK
MONTGOMERY
GARLAND
SALINE
HOT SPRING
PIKE
CLARK
HOWARD
SEVIER
LITTLE RIVER
HEMPSTEAD
NEVADA
DALLAS
OUACHITA
MILLER
LA FAYETTE
COLUMBIA
TEXAS
OKLAHOMA
Fort Smith
Hot Springs National Park
Texarkana
95° 30′ 94° 30′ 93° Longitude West

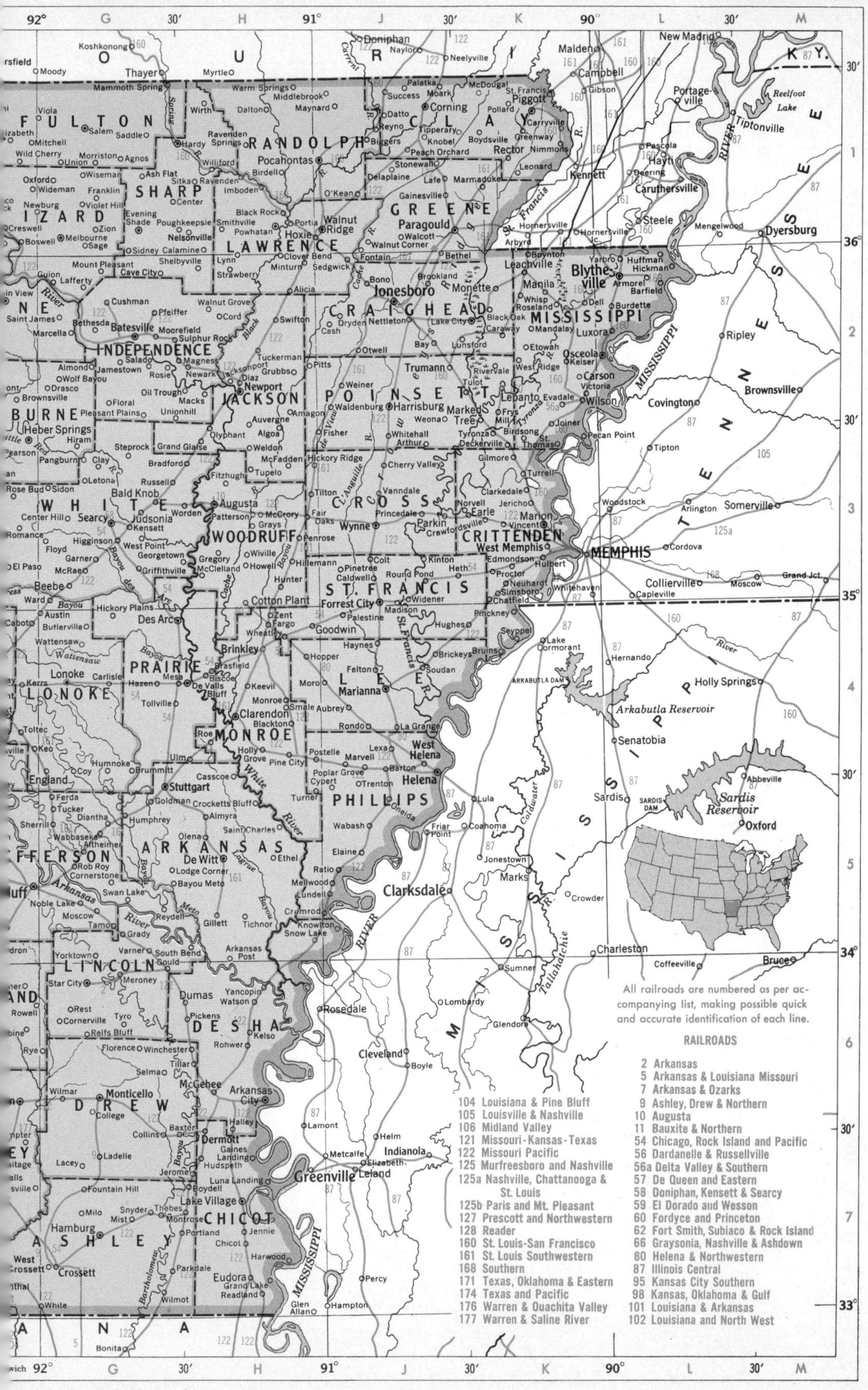
All railroads are numbered as per accompanying list, making possible quick and accurate identification of each line.
RAILROADS
2 Arkansas
5 Arkansas & Louisiana Missouri
7 Arkansas & Ozarks
9 Ashley, Drew & Northern
10 Augusta
11 Bauxite & Northern
54 Chicago, Rock Island and Pacific
56 Dardanelle & Russellville
56a Delta Valley & Southern
57 De Queen and Eastern
58 Doniphan, Kensett & Searcy
59 El Dorado and Wesson
60 Fordyce and Princeton
62 Fort Smith, Subiaco & Rock Island
66 Graysonia, Nashville & Ashdown
80 Helena & Northwestern
87 Illinois Central
95 Kansas City Southern
98 Kansas, Oklahoma & Gulf
101 Louisiana & Arkansas
102 Louisiana and North West
104 Louisiana & Pine Bluff
105 Louisville & Nashville
106 Midland Valley
121 Missouri-Kansas-Texas
122 Missouri Pacific
125 Murfreesboro and Nashville
125a Nashville, Chattanooga & St. Louis
125b Paris and Mt. Pleasant
127 Prescott and Northwestern
128 Reader
160 St. Louis-San Francisco
161 St. Louis Southwestern
168 Southern
171 Texas, Oklahoma & Eastern
174 Texas and Pacific
176 Warren & Ouachita Valley
177 Warren & Saline River

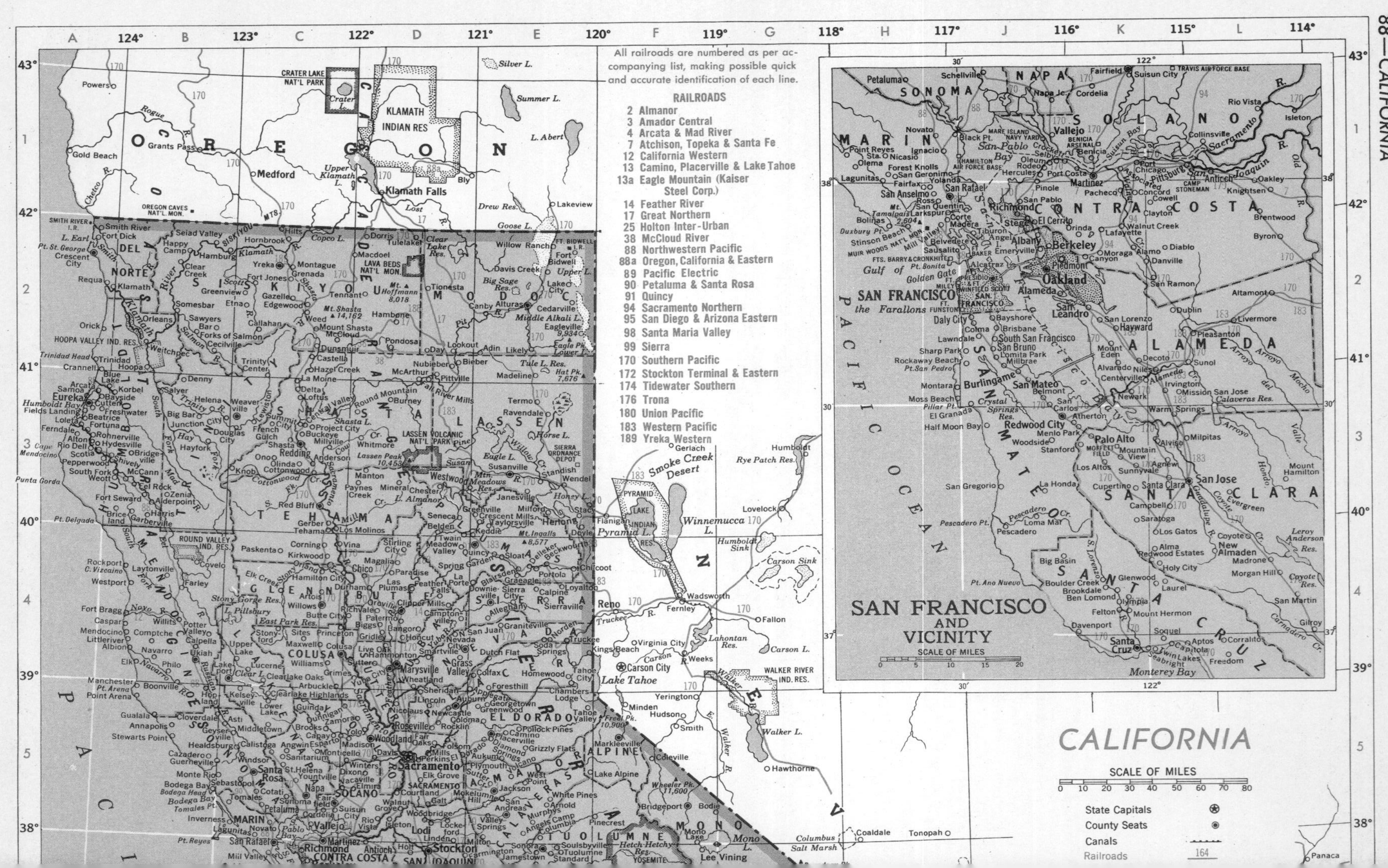
All railroads are numbered as per accompanying list, making possible quick and accurate identification of each line.
RAILROADS
2 Almanor
3 Amador Central
4 Arcata & Mad River
7 Atchison, Topeka & Santa Fe
12 California Western
13 Camino, Placerville & Lake Tahoe
13a Eagle Mountain (Kaiser Steel Corp.)
14 Feather River
17 Great Northern
25 Holton Inter-Urban
38 McCloud River
88 Northwestern Pacific
88a Oregon, California & Eastern
89 Pacific Electric
90 Petaluma & Santa Rosa
91 Quincy
94 Sacramento Northern
95 San Diego & Arizona Eastern
98 Santa Maria Valley
99 Sierra
170 Southern Pacific
172 Stockton Terminal & Eastern
174 Tidewater Southern
176 Trona
180 Union Pacific
183 Western Pacific
189 Yreka Western
SAN FRANCISCO AND VICINITY
SCALE OF MILES
CALIFORNIA
SCALE OF MILES
State Capitals
County Seats
Canals
Railroads
OREGON
PACIFIC OCEAN

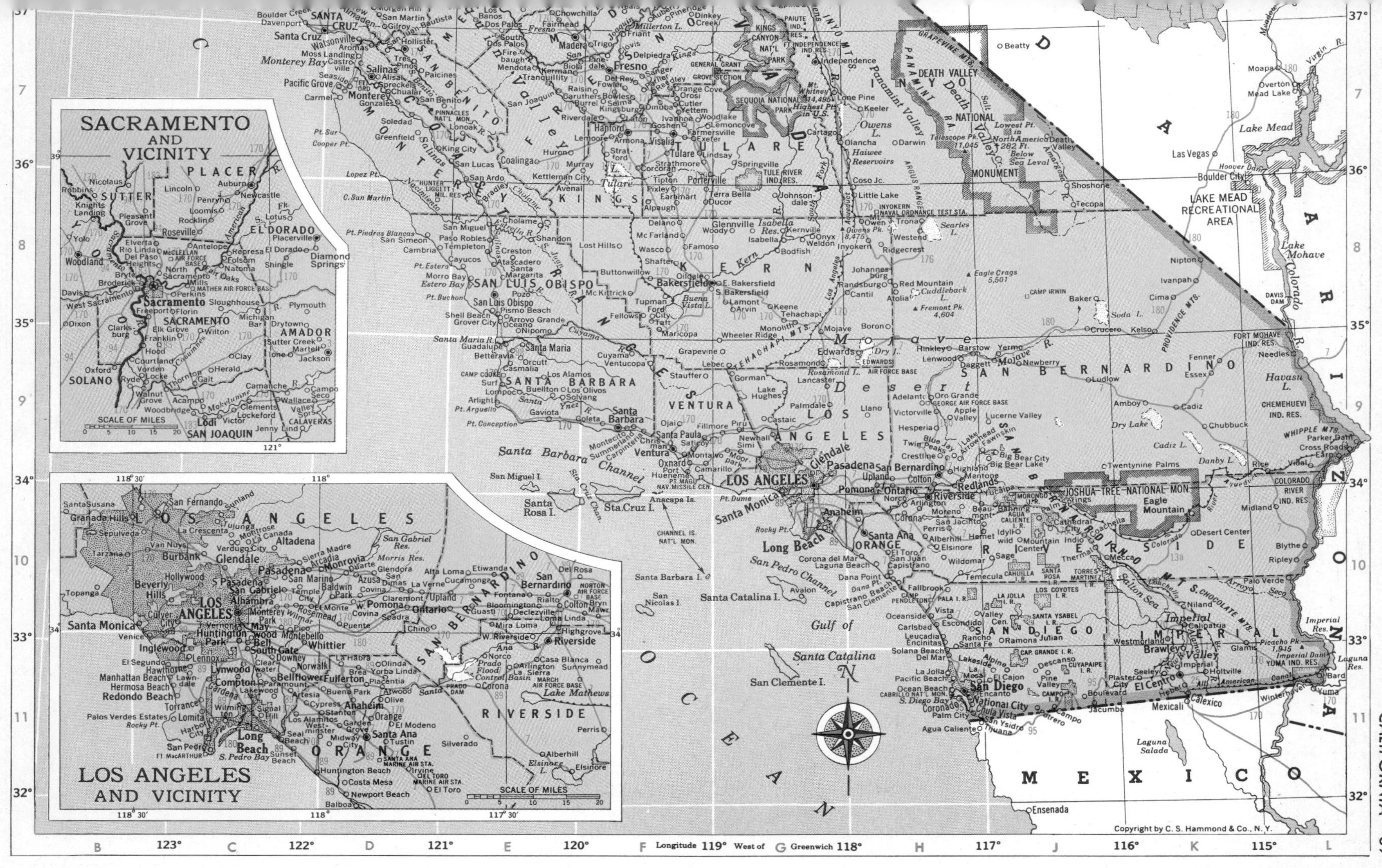
SACRAMENTO AND VICINITY
LOS ANGELES AND VICINITY
SCALE OF MILES
SAN BERNARDINO
LOS ANGELES
RIVERSIDE
IMPERIAL
SAN DIEGO
ORANGE
KERN
VENTURA
SANTA BARBARA
SAN LUIS OBISPO
MONTEREY
KINGS
TULARE
INYO
MEXICO
ARIZONA
NEVADA
OCEAN
DEATH VALLEY NATIONAL MONUMENT
JOSHUA TREE NATIONAL MON.
LAKE MEAD RECREATIONAL AREA
SEQUOIA NATIONAL PARK
Mojave Desert
Salton Sea
Lake Mead
Lake Mohave
Colorado R.
Santa Catalina I.
San Clemente I.
Santa Barbara Channel
San Pedro Channel
Gulf of Santa Catalina
Longitude 119° West of Greenwich 118°
Copyright by C. S. Hammond & Co., N. Y.

RAILROADS
7 Atchison, Topeka & Santa Fe
45 Chicago, Burlington & Quincy
54 Chicago, Rock Island & Pacific
54a Colorado
55 Colorado & South-Eastern
56 Colorado & Southern
57 Colorado & Wyoming

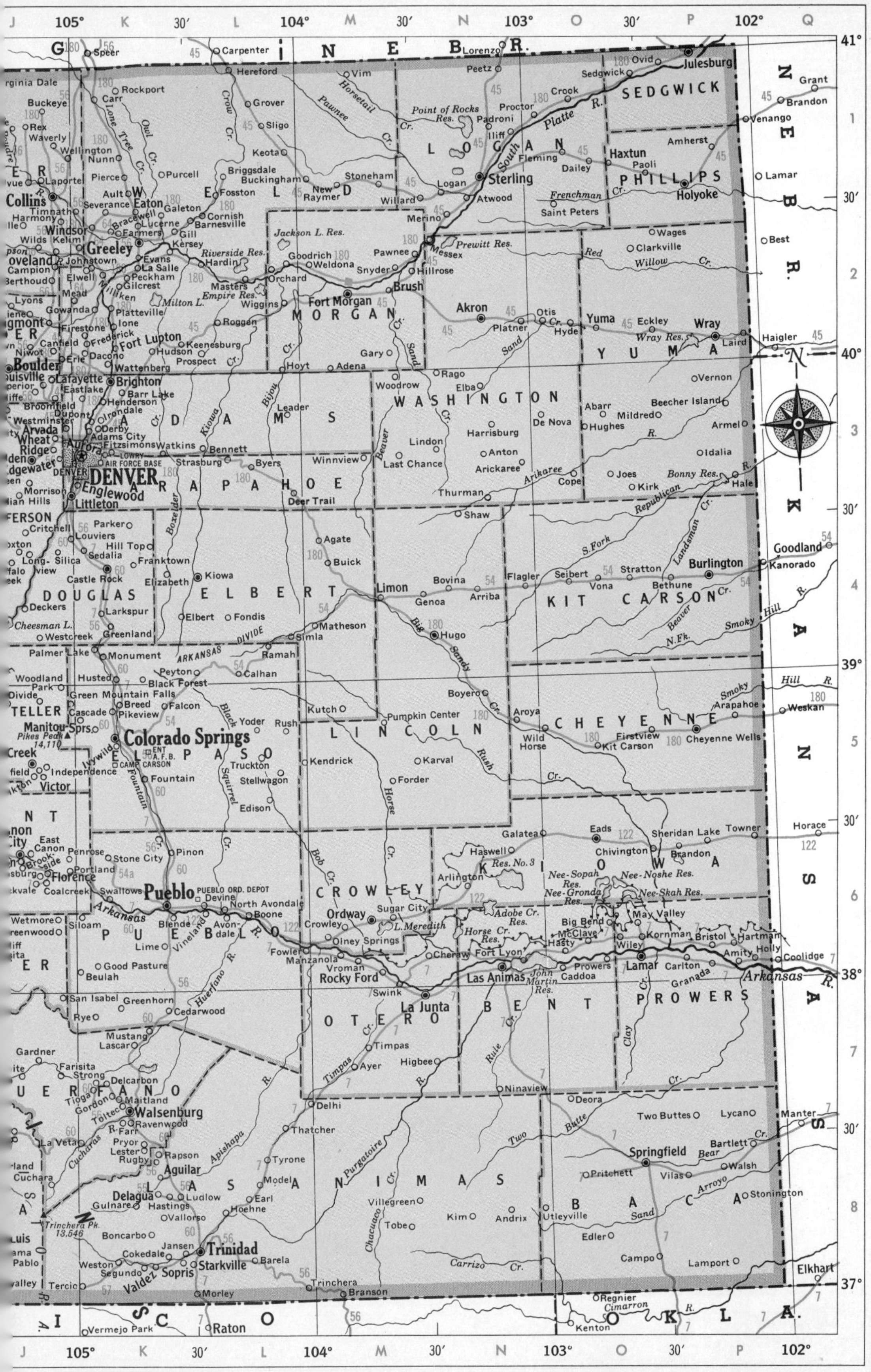

60 Denver & Rio Grande Western
64 Great Western
122 Missouri Pacific
125 Rio Grande Southern
126 San Luis Central
127 San Luis Valley Southern
180 Union Pacific

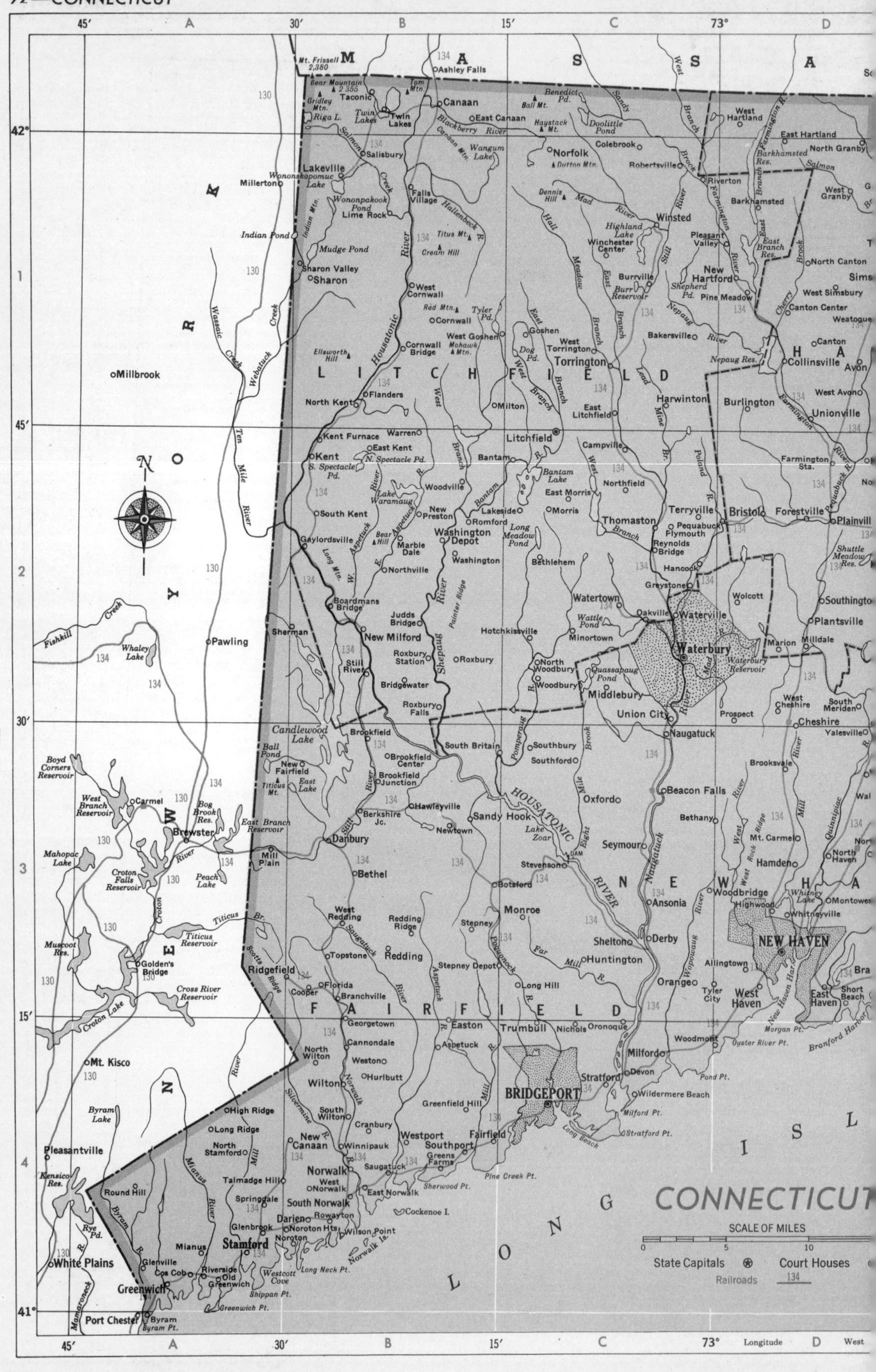
CONNECTICUT
SCALE OF MILES
0
5
10
State Capitals
Court Houses
Railroads
134
Longitude
West
MASSACHUSETTS
NEW YORK
LITCHFIELD
FAIRFIELD
NEW HAVEN
LONG ISLAND
HOUSATONIC RIVER
Mt. Frissell 2,380
Bear Mountain 2,355
Ashley Falls
Taconic
Gridley Mtn.
Riga L.
Twin Lakes
Tom Mtn.
Canaan
East Canaan
Blackberry River
Benedict Pd.
Ball Mt.
Haystack Mt.
Doolittle Pond
Sandy Brook
West Branch
West Hartland
East Hartland
North Granby
Barkhamsted Res.
Salmon
Salisbury
Lakeville
Wononskopomuc Lake
Millerton
Wangum Lake
Norfolk
Dutton Mtn.
Colebrook
Robertsville
Riverton
Barkhamsted
West Granby
Falls Village
Wononpakook Pond
Lime Rock
Indian Pond
Indian Mtn.
Mudge Pond
Sharon Valley
Sharon
Hallenbeck R.
Titus Mt.
Cream Hill
Dennis Hill
Mad River
Highland Lake
Winsted
Winchester Center
Pleasant Valley
East Branch Res.
North Canton
Burrville
Burr Reservoir
New Hartford
Shepherd Pd.
Pine Meadow
West Simsbury
Canton Center
Weatogue
West Cornwall
Red Mtn.
Cornwall
Tyler Pd.
Goshen
West Goshen
Cornwall Bridge
Mohawk Mtn.
Ellsworth Hill
Dog Pd.
West Torrington
Torrington
Bakersville
Nepaug River
Nepaug Res.
Canton
Collinsville
Avon
Wassaic Creek
Webatuck Creek
Millbrook
Flanders
North Kent
Milton
East Litchfield
Harwinton
Burlington
West Avon
Unionville
Ten Mile River
Kent Furnace
Warren
Litchfield
Campville
East Kent
N. Spectacle Pd.
Kent
S. Spectacle Pd.
Bantam
Bantam Lake
Farmington Sta.
Woodville
Lake Waramaug
East Morris
Northfield
South Kent
New Preston
Lakeside
Morris
Terryville
Bristol
Forestville
Plainville
Thomaston
Pequabuck
Plymouth
Romford
Gaylordsville
Bear Hill
Marble Dale
Washington Depot
Long Meadow Pond
Reynolds Bridge
Washington
Bethlehem
Hancock
Shuttle Meadow Res.
Northville
Long Mtn.
Greystone
Wolcott
Southington
Boardmans Bridge
Judds Bridge
Watertown
Oakville
Waterville
Plantsville
Sherman
New Milford
Painter Ridge
Hotchkissville
Wattle Pond
Minortown
Waterbury
Marion
Milldale
Fishkill Creek
Pawling
Whaley Lake
Still River
Roxbury Station
Shepaug River
Roxbury
North Woodbury
Quassapaug Pond
Waterbury Reservoir
Woodbury
Bridgewater
Middlebury
West Cheshire
South Meriden
Roxbury Falls
Union City
Prospect
Cheshire
Candlewood Lake
Brookfield
South Britain
Southbury
Naugatuck
Yalesville
Ball Pond
Boyd Corners Reservoir
New Fairfield
Brookfield Center
Southford
Brookfield Junction
Brooksvale
Titicus Mt.
East Lake
West Branch Reservoir
Carmel
Bog Brook Res.
Hawleyville
Oxford
Beacon Falls
Berkshire Jc.
Sandy Hook
Brewster
East Branch Reservoir
Newtown
Lake Zoar
Bethany
Mahopac Lake
Danbury
Mill Plain
Seymour
Mt. Carmel
Croton River
Stevenson
Croton Falls Reservoir
Peach Lake
Bethel
Botsford
Hamden
North Haven
Naugatuck
Ansonia
Woodbridge
Highwood
Whitney Lake
Montowese
Whitneyville
Titicus Br.
West Redding
Monroe
Redding Ridge
Stepney
Muscoot Res.
Titicus Reservoir
Saugatuck
Topstone
Redding
Shelton
Derby
Golden's Bridge
Ridgefield
Stepney Depot
Huntington
Far Mill R.
Allingtown
Wepawaug River
Cross River Reservoir
Florida
Cooper
Branchville
Long Hill
Orange
Tyler City
West Haven
East Haven
Short Beach
Croton Lake
Georgetown
Easton
Trumbull
Nichols
Oronoque
Cannondale
Aspetuck
Woodmont
Oyster River Pt.
Morgan Pt.
Branford Harbor
Mt. Kisco
North Wilton
Weston
Milford
Devon
Wilton
Hurlbutt
Stratford
Pond Pt.
Byram Lake
High Ridge
Silvermine
South Wilton
Greenfield Hill
BRIDGEPORT
Wildermere Beach
Milford Pt.
Long Ridge
Cranbury
Westport
Fairfield
Stratford Pt.
Long Beach
North Stamford
New Canaan
Winnipauk
Southport
Pleasantville
Norwalk
Saugatuck
Greens Farms
Pine Creek Pt.
Kensico Res.
Talmadge Hill
West Norwalk
Sherwood Pt.
Round Hill
Springdale
South Norwalk
East Norwalk
Cockenoe I.
Byram R.
Mianus River
Darien
Rowayton
Rye Pd.
Glenbrook
Noroton Hts.
Wilson Point
Mianus
Stamford
Noroton
Norwalk Is.
White Plains
Glenville
Cos Cob
Riverside
Old Greenwich
Westcott Cove
Long Neck Pt.
Shippan Pt.
Greenwich
Mamaroneck
Greenwich Pt.
Port Chester
Byram
Byram Pt.

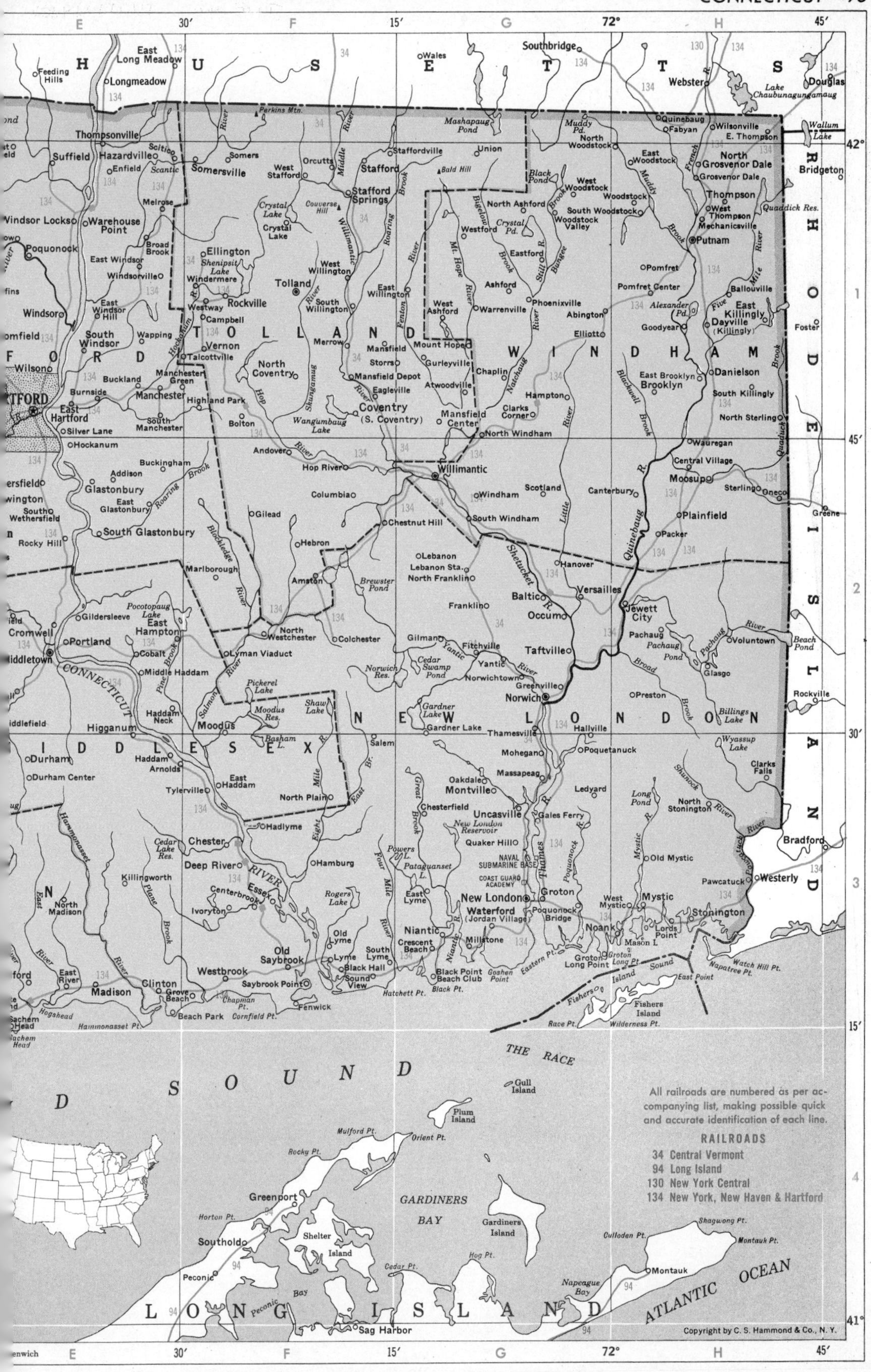
All railroads are numbered as per accompanying list, making possible quick and accurate identification of each line.
RAILROADS
34 Central Vermont
94 Long Island
130 New York Central
134 New York, New Haven & Hartford
Copyright by C. S. Hammond & Co., N. Y.

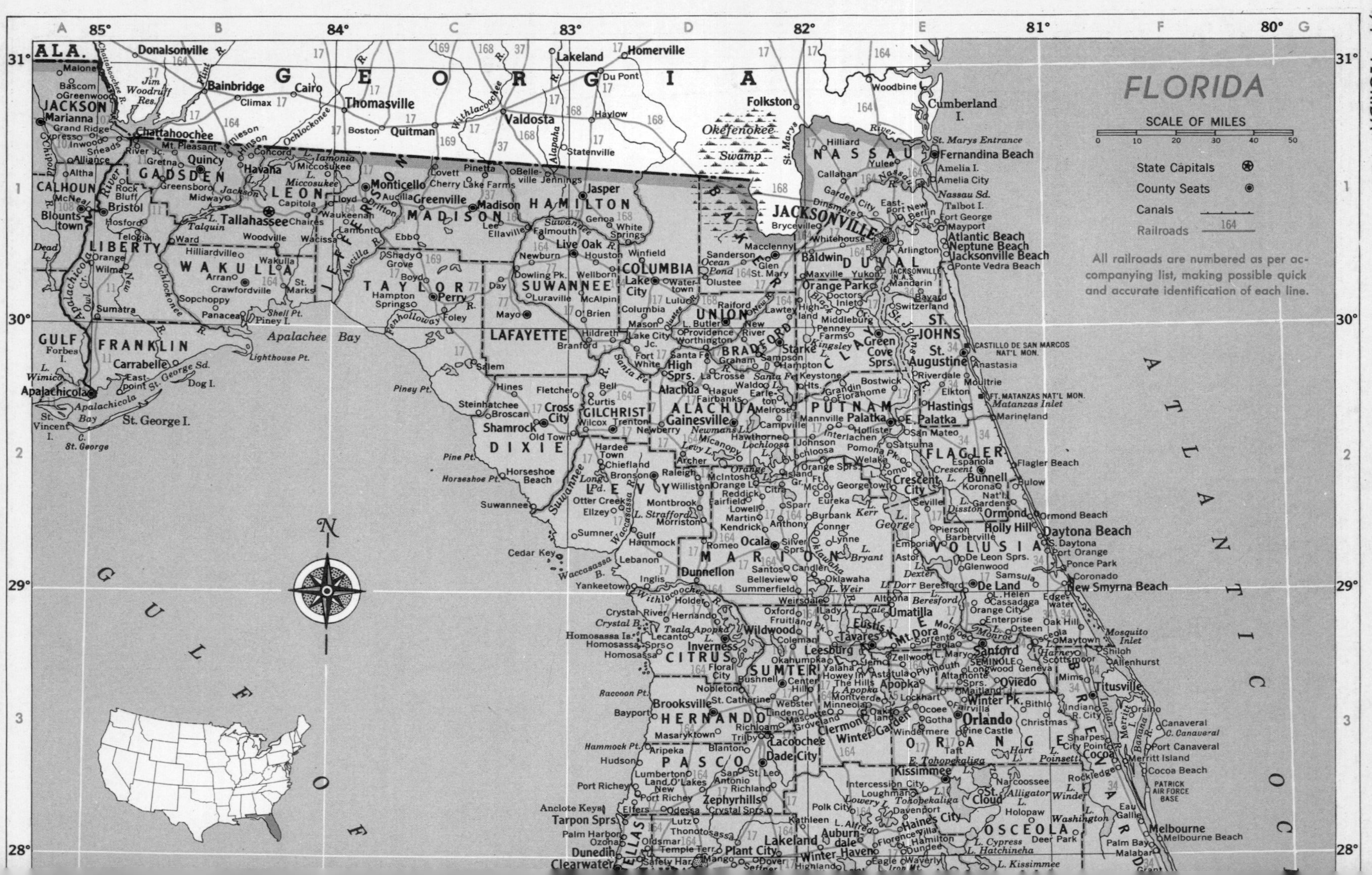
FLORIDA
SCALE OF MILES
0 10 20 30 40 50
State Capitals
County Seats
Canals
Railroads 164
All railroads are numbered as per accompanying list, making possible quick and accurate identification of each line.
ATLANTIC OC
GULF OF
GEORGIA
ALA.
Apalachee Bay
Okefenokee Swamp
CASTILLO DE SAN MARCOS NAT'L MON.
FT. MATANZAS NAT'L MON.
PATRICK AIR FORCE BASE

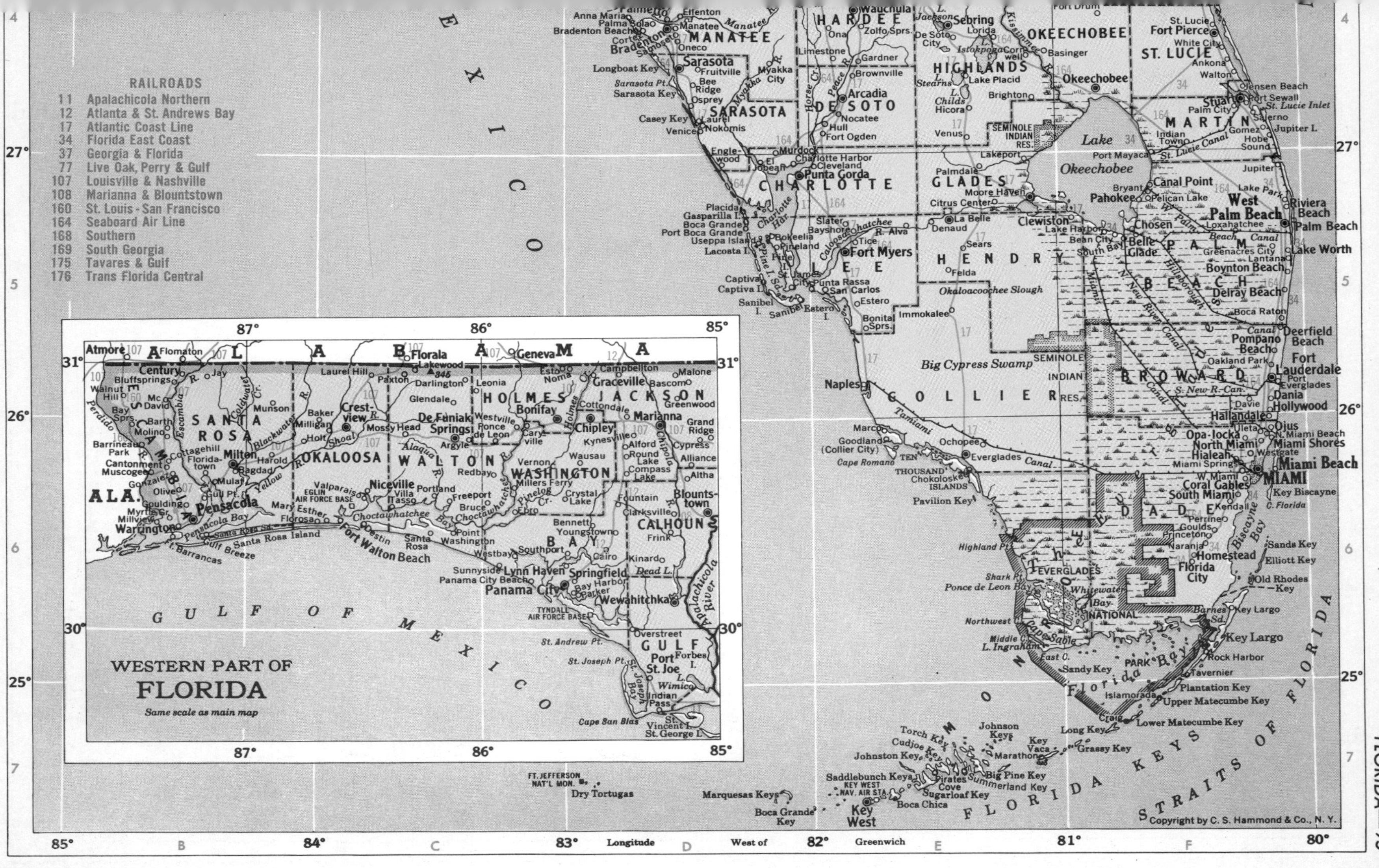
RAILROADS
11 Apalachicola Northern
12 Atlanta & St. Andrews Bay
17 Atlantic Coast Line
34 Florida East Coast
37 Georgia & Florida
77 Live Oak, Perry & Gulf
107 Louisville & Nashville
108 Marianna & Blountstown
160 St. Louis - San Francisco
164 Seaboard Air Line
168 Southern
169 South Georgia
175 Tavares & Gulf
176 Trans Florida Central
WESTERN PART OF
FLORIDA
Same scale as main map
GULF OF MEXICO
FLORIDA KEYS
STRAITS OF FLORIDA
Longitude West of Greenwich
Copyright by C. S. Hammond & Co., N. Y.

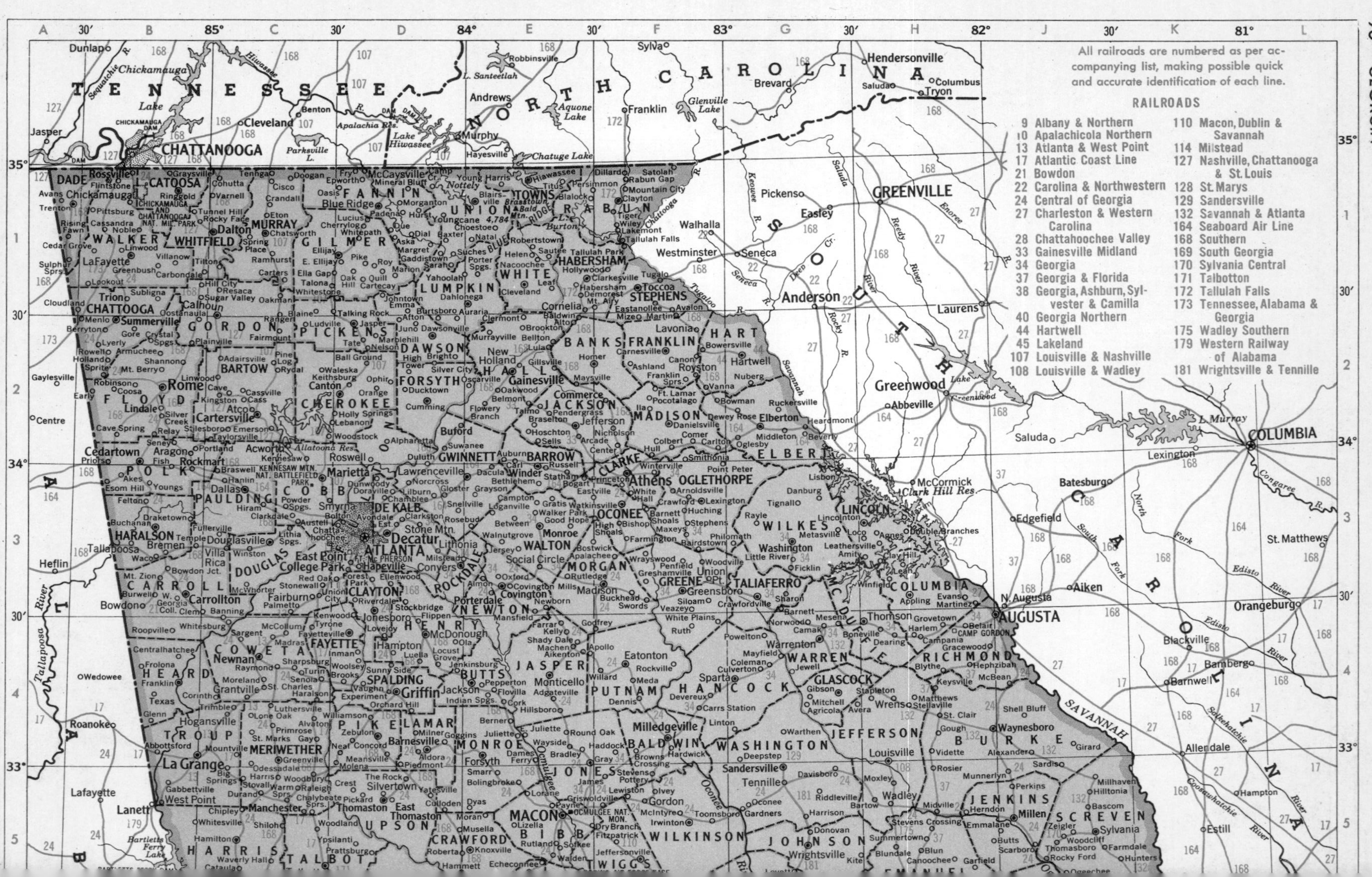

All railroads are numbered as per accompanying list, making possible quick and accurate identification of each line.
RAILROADS
9 Albany & Northern
10 Apalachicola Northern
13 Atlanta & West Point
17 Atlantic Coast Line
21 Bowdon
22 Carolina & Northwestern
24 Central of Georgia
27 Charleston & Western Carolina
28 Chattahoochee Valley
33 Gainesville Midland
34 Georgia
37 Georgia & Florida
38 Georgia, Ashburn, Sylvester & Camilla
40 Georgia Northern
44 Hartwell
45 Lakeland
107 Louisville & Nashville
108 Louisville & Wadley
110 Macon, Dublin & Savannah
114 Milstead
127 Nashville, Chattanooga & St. Louis
128 St. Marys
129 Sandersville
132 Savannah & Atlanta
164 Seaboard Air Line
168 Southern
169 South Georgia
170 Sylvania Central
171 Talbotton
172 Tallulah Falls
173 Tennessee, Alabama & Georgia
175 Wadley Southern
179 Western Railway of Alabama
181 Wrightsville & Tennille
TENNESSEE
NORTH CAROLINA
SOUTH CAROLINA
ALABAMA
CHATTANOOGA
ATLANTA
AUGUSTA
COLUMBIA
GREENVILLE
MACON

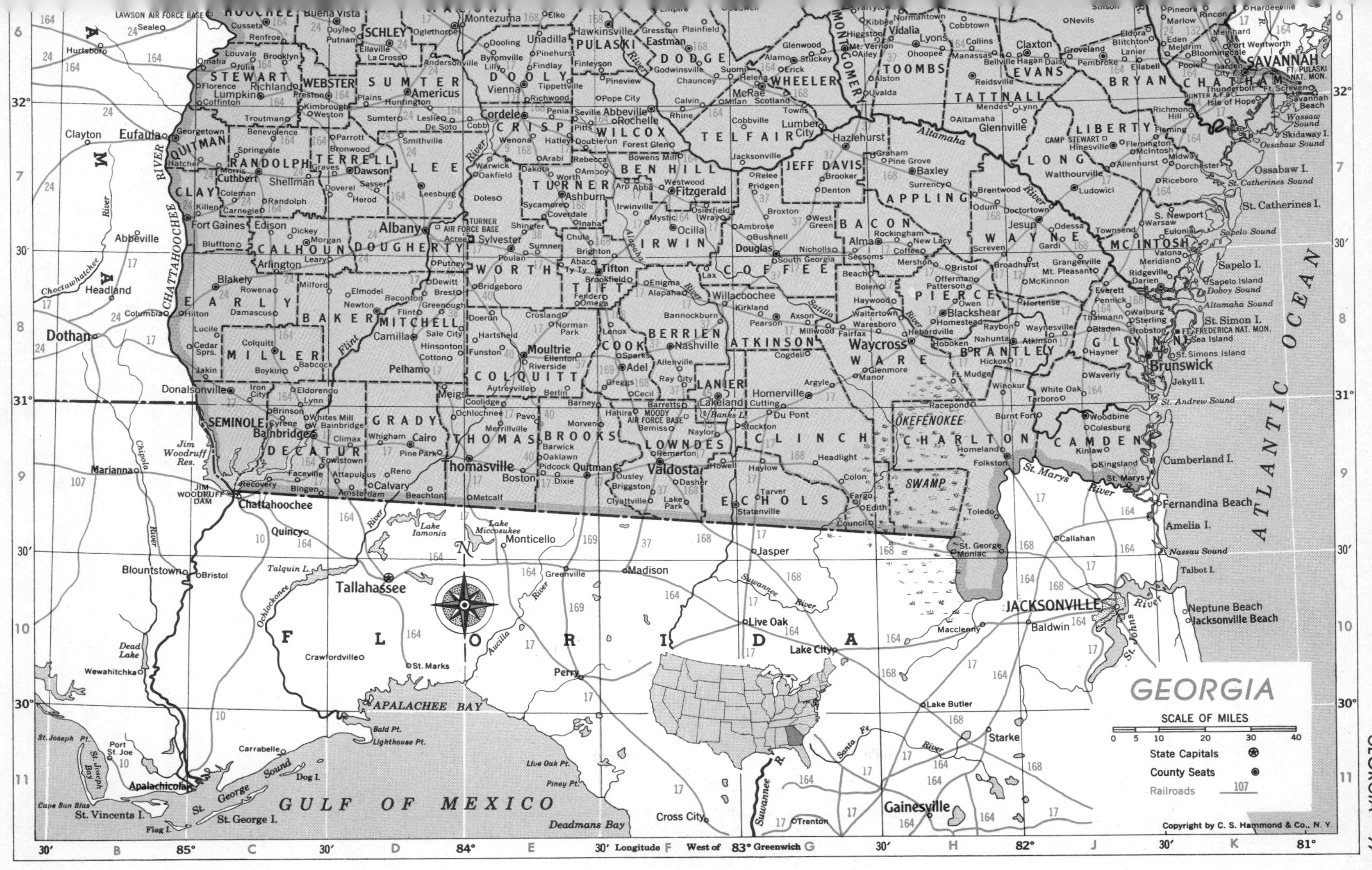
GEORGIA
SCALE OF MILES
0 5 10 20 30 40
State Capitals
County Seats
Railroads
107
Copyright by C. S. Hammond & Co., N. Y.
ATLANTIC OCEAN
GULF OF MEXICO
APALACHEE BAY
FLORIDA
ALABAMA
OKEFENOKEE SWAMP
SAVANNAH
JACKSONVILLE
Tallahassee
Brunswick
Waycross
Valdosta
Thomasville
Albany
Gainesville
Dothan
Longitude West of 83° Greenwich
CHATTAHOOCHEE RIVER

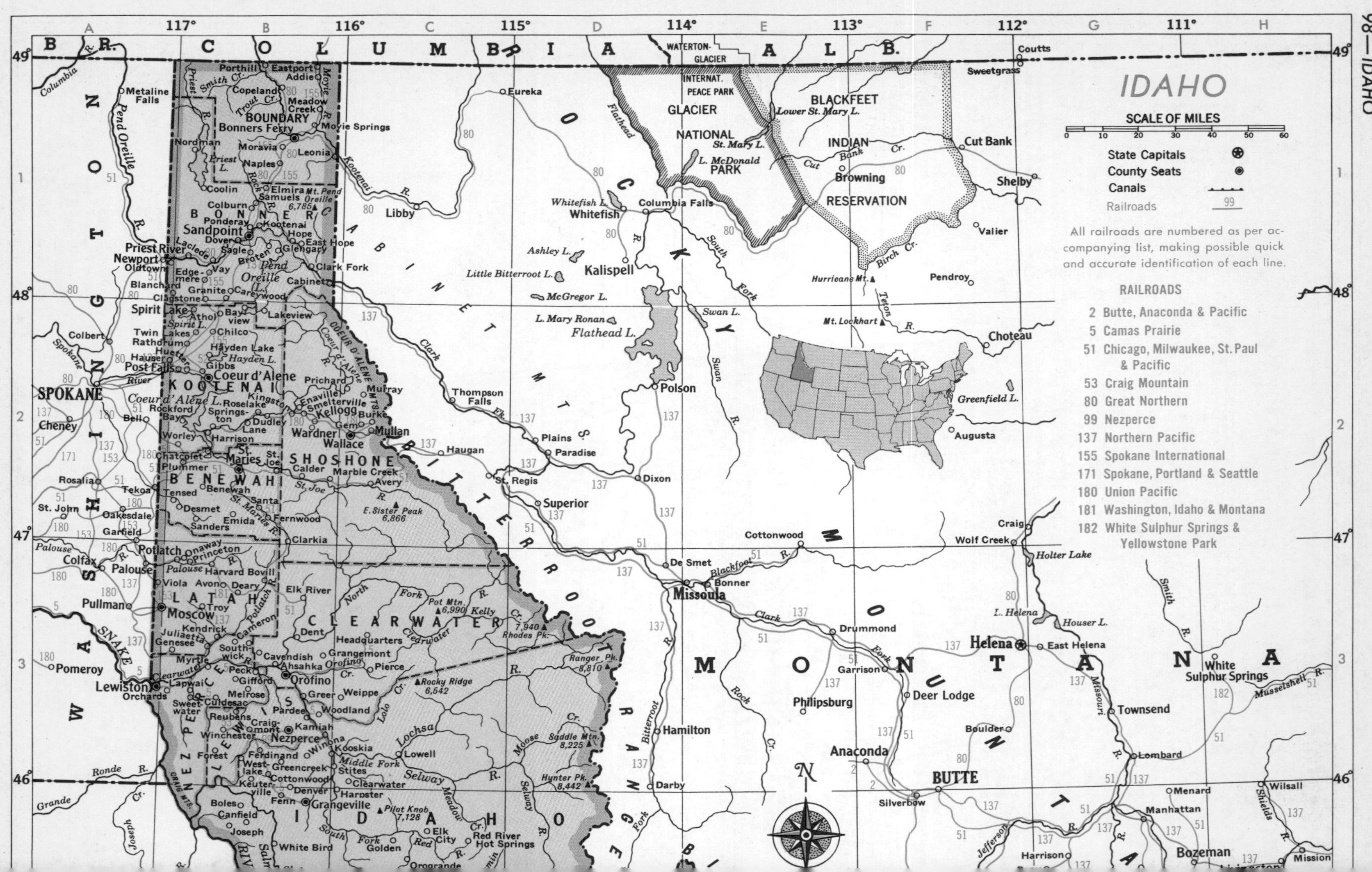
IDAHO
SCALE OF MILES
0 10 20 30 40 50 60
State Capitals
County Seats
Canals
Railroads 99
All railroads are numbered as per accompanying list, making possible quick and accurate identification of each line.
RAILROADS
2 Butte, Anaconda & Pacific
5 Camas Prairie
51 Chicago, Milwaukee, St. Paul & Pacific
53 Craig Mountain
80 Great Northern
99 Nezperce
137 Northern Pacific
155 Spokane International
171 Spokane, Portland & Seattle
180 Union Pacific
181 Washington, Idaho & Montana
182 White Sulphur Springs & Yellowstone Park

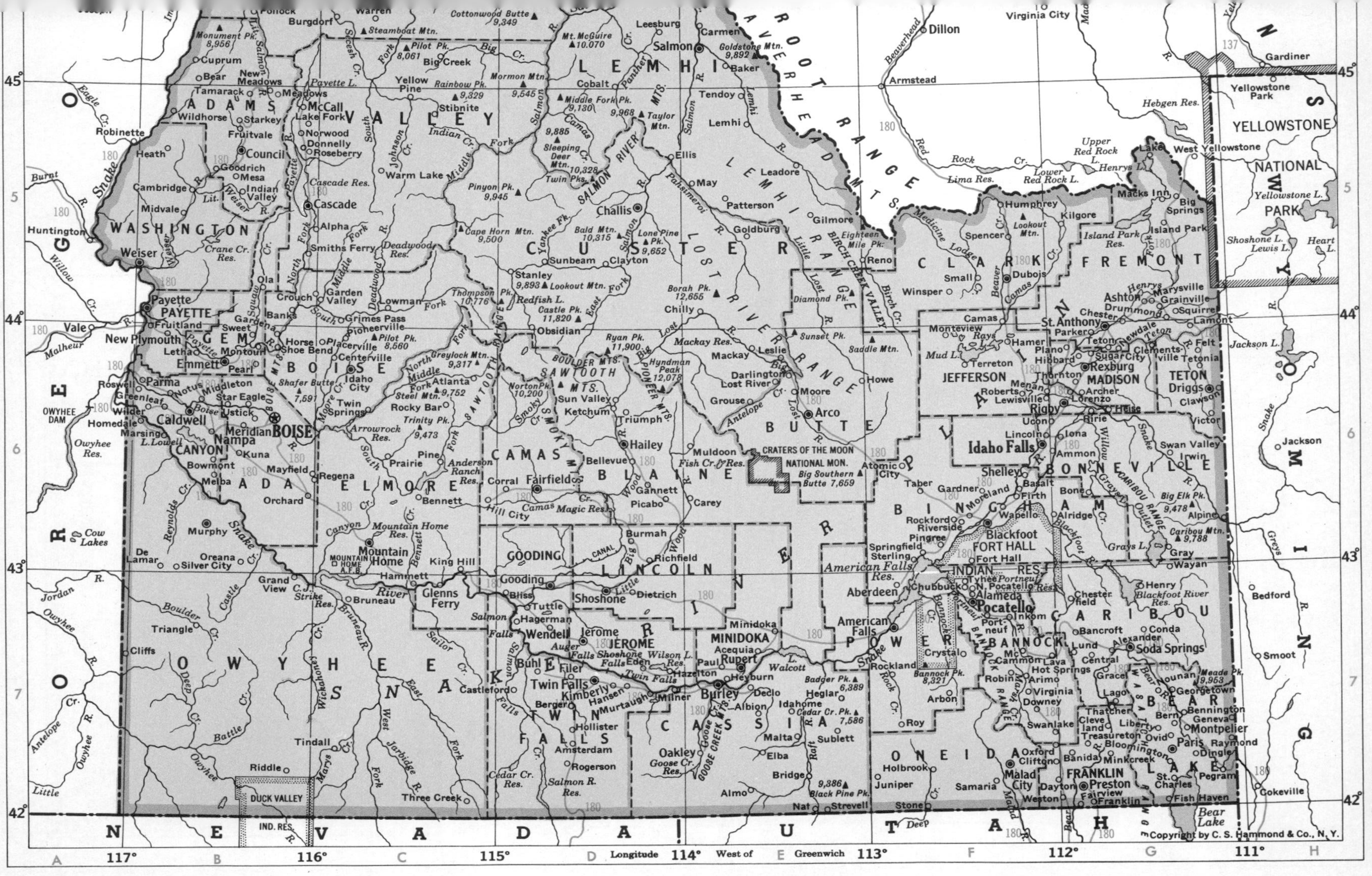
O R E G O N
W Y O M I N G
M O N T A N A
N E V A D A
U T A H
LEMHI
CUSTER
BUTTE
CLARK
FREMONT
JEFFERSON
MADISON
TETON
BONNEVILLE
BINGHAM
BANNOCK
CARIBOU
BEAR LAKE
FRANKLIN
ONEIDA
POWER
CASSIA
MINIDOKA
JEROME
LINCOLN
GOODING
TWIN FALLS
CAMAS
BLAINE
ELMORE
OWYHEE
ADA
CANYON
BOISE
GEM
PAYETTE
WASHINGTON
ADAMS
VALLEY
YELLOWSTONE NATIONAL PARK
CRATERS OF THE MOON NATIONAL MON.
FORT HALL INDIAN RES.
DUCK VALLEY IND. RES.
ROOT RANGE
AVERHEAD MTS.
LEMHI RANGE
LOST RIVER RANGE
BIRCH CREEK VALLEY
SALMON RIVER MTS.
SAWTOOTH MTS.
SAWTOOTH RANGE
BOULDER MTS.
SMOKY MTS.
PIONEER MTS.
BOISE MTS.
CARIBOU RANGE
BANNOCK RANGE
GOOSE CREEK MTS.
WASATCH RANGE
Boise
Idaho Falls
Pocatello
Twin Falls
Nampa
Caldwell
Salmon
Challis
Arco
Rexburg
St. Anthony
Blackfoot
American Falls
Burley
Rupert
Jerome
Shoshone
Gooding
Hailey
Fairfield
Mountain Home
Weiser
Payette
Emmett
Council
Cascade
McCall
Soda Springs
Preston
Malad City
Montpelier
Paris
Driggs
Dubois
Rigby
Murphy
Idaho City
Dillon
Virginia City
Jackson
Vale
Copyright by C. S. Hammond & Co., N. Y.
Longitude 114° West of Greenwich
117° 116° 115° 114° 113° 112° 111°
45° 44° 43° 42°

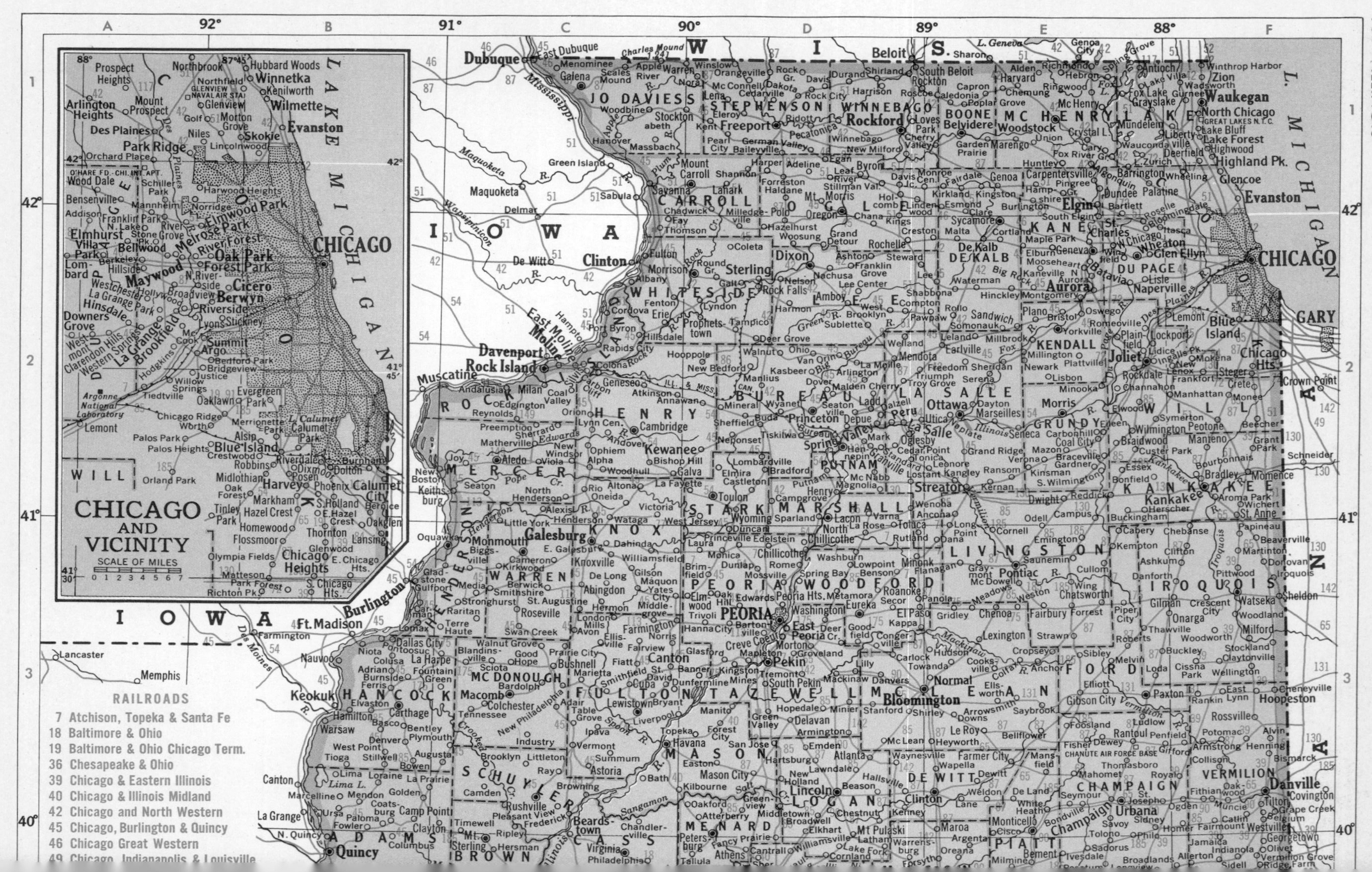
CHICAGO AND VICINITY
SCALE OF MILES
RAILROADS
7 Atchison, Topeka & Santa Fe
18 Baltimore & Ohio
19 Baltimore & Ohio Chicago Term.
36 Chesapeake & Ohio
39 Chicago & Eastern Illinois
40 Chicago & Illinois Midland
42 Chicago and North Western
45 Chicago, Burlington & Quincy
46 Chicago Great Western

72 Elgin, Joliet & Eastern
76 Erie
77 Galesburg & Great Eastern
84 Grand Trunk
85 Gulf, Mobile & Ohio
86 Hoopple, Yorktown & Tampico
87 Illinois Central
90 Illinois Terminal
91 Indiana Harbor Belt
97 La Salle & Bureau County
98 Litchfield & Madison
107 Louisville & Nashville
113 Minneapolis & St. Louis
117 Minneapolis, St. Paul & Sault Ste. Marie
120 Missouri - Illinois
121 Missouri - Kansas - Texas
122 Missouri Pacific
130 New York Central
131 New York, Chicago & St. Louis
138 Paducah & Illinois
142 Pennsylvania
143 Peoria and Pekin Union
149 Rock Island Southern
160 St. Louis - San Francisco
161 St. Louis Southwestern
168 Southern
175 Toledo, Peoria & Western
185 Wabash
ILLINOIS
SCALE OF MILES
0 5 10 20 30 40
State Capitals
County Seats
Canals
Railroads
Longitude West 90° of Greenwich
Copyright by C. S. Hammond & Co., N. Y.

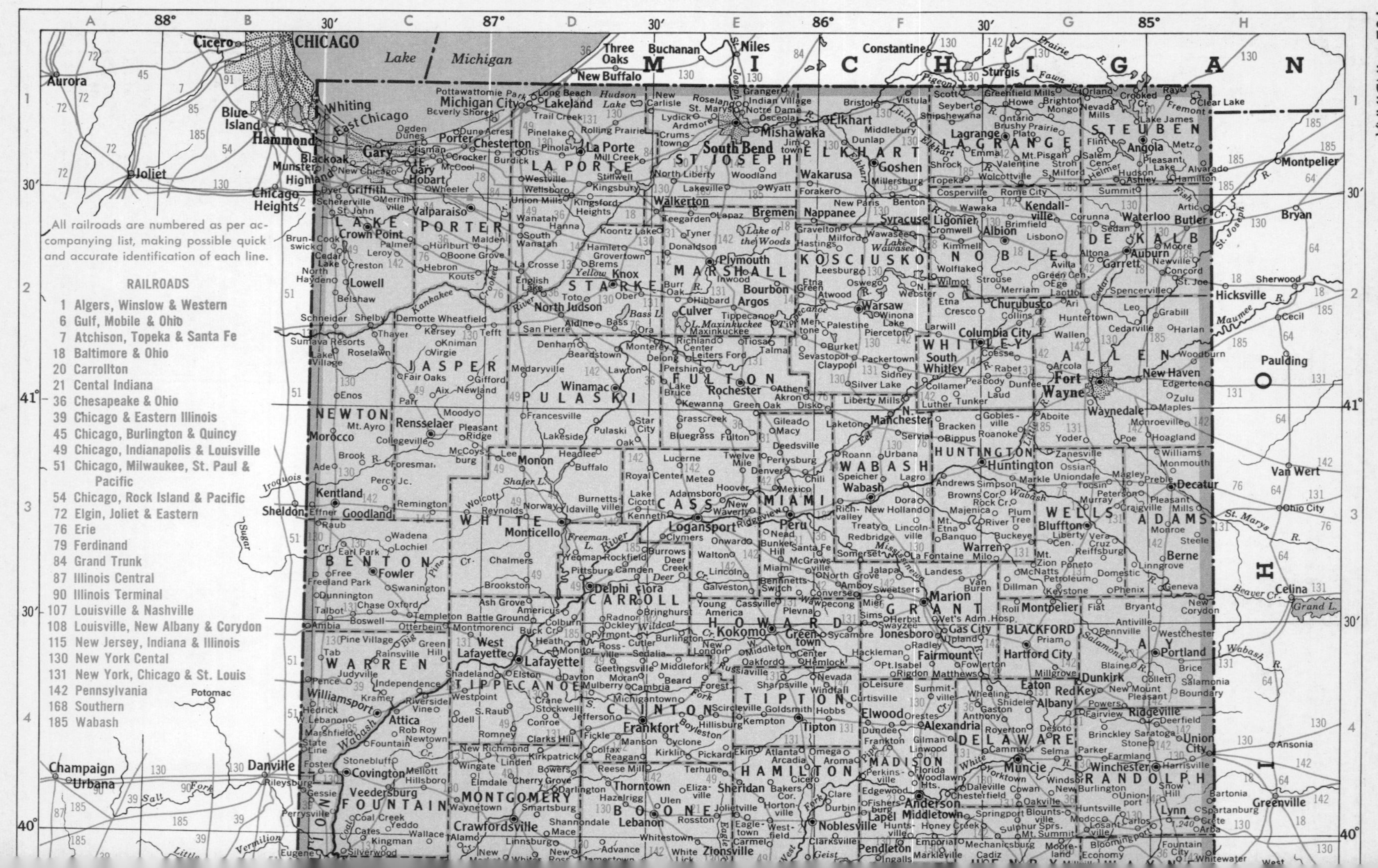
M I C H I G A N
O H I O
I L L I N O I S
Lake Michigan
CHICAGO
South Bend
Fort Wayne
Lafayette
Kokomo
Muncie
Anderson
Logansport
Elkhart
Goshen
Gary
Hammond
Michigan City
La Porte
Valparaiso
Huntington
Marion
Frankfort
Crawfordsville
Lebanon
Noblesville
Warsaw
Peru
Wabash
Plymouth
Rochester
LAKE
PORTER
LA PORTE
ST JOSEPH
ELKHART
LAGRANGE
STEUBEN
NOBLE
DE KALB
ALLEN
WHITLEY
KOSCIUSKO
MARSHALL
STARKE
JASPER
NEWTON
PULASKI
FULTON
WABASH
HUNTINGTON
WELLS
ADAMS
MIAMI
CASS
WHITE
BENTON
CARROLL
HOWARD
GRANT
BLACKFORD
JAY
RANDOLPH
DELAWARE
MADISON
HAMILTON
TIPTON
CLINTON
BOONE
TIPPECANOE
WARREN
FOUNTAIN
MONTGOMERY
All railroads are numbered as per accompanying list, making possible quick and accurate identification of each line.
RAILROADS
1 Algers, Winslow & Western
6 Gulf, Mobile & Ohio
7 Atchison, Topeka & Santa Fe
18 Baltimore & Ohio
20 Carrollton
21 Cental Indiana
36 Chesapeake & Ohio
39 Chicago & Eastern Illinois
45 Chicago, Burlington & Quincy
49 Chicago, Indianapolis & Louisville
51 Chicago, Milwaukee, St. Paul & Pacific
54 Chicago, Rock Island & Pacific
72 Elgin, Joliet & Eastern
76 Erie
79 Ferdinand
84 Grand Trunk
87 Illinois Central
90 Illinois Terminal
107 Louisville & Nashville
108 Louisville, New Albany & Corydon
115 New Jersey, Indiana & Illinois
130 New York Cental
131 New York, Chicago & St. Louis
142 Pennsylvania
168 Southern
185 Wabash

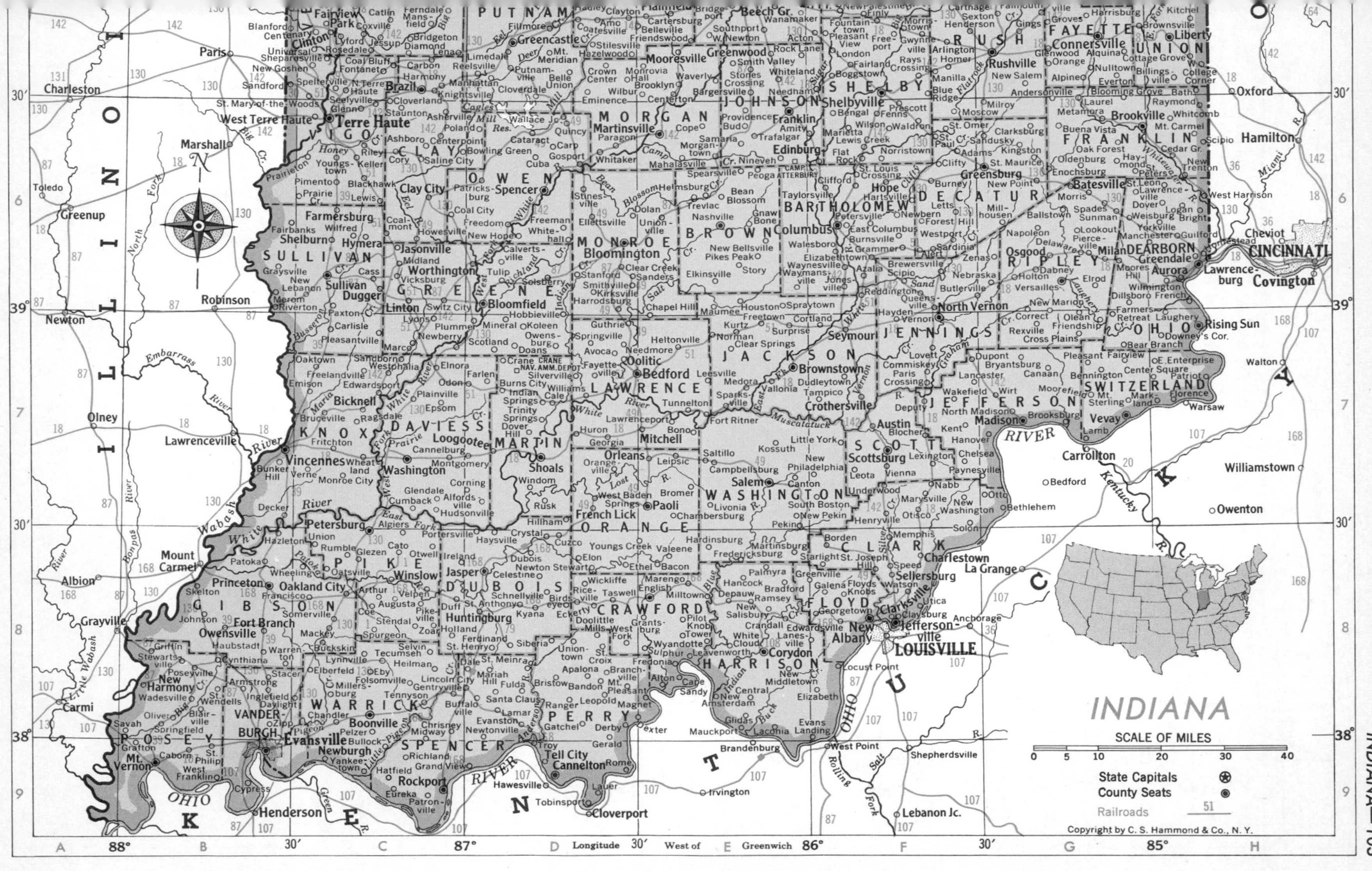
INDIANA
SCALE OF MILES
0 5 10 20 30 40
State Capitals
County Seats
Railroads
Copyright by C. S. Hammond & Co., N. Y.
Longitude West of Greenwich
LOUISVILLE
CINCINNATI
Evansville
Terre Haute
Bloomington
Columbus
Vincennes
OHIO RIVER
KENTUCKY
ILLINOIS
OHIO

M I N N E
S. DAK.
NEBRASKA
MISSOURI
M I S S
LYON
OSCEOLA
DICKINSON
EMMET
KOSSUTH
WINNEBAGO
SIOUX
O'BRIEN
CLAY
PALO ALTO
HANCOCK
PLYMOUTH
CHEROKEE
BUENA VISTA
POCAHONTAS
HUMBOLDT
WRIGHT
WOODBURY
IDA
SAC
CALHOUN
WEBSTER
HAMILTON
MONONA
CRAWFORD
CARROLL
GREENE
BOONE
HARRISON
SHELBY
AUDUBON
GUTHRIE
DALLAS
POTTAWATTAMIE
CASS
ADAIR
MADISON
MILLS
MONTGOMERY
ADAMS
UNION
CLARKE
FREMONT
PAGE
TAYLOR
RINGGOLD
DECATUR
SIOUX CITY
OMAHA
Council Bluffs
Fort Dodge
Le Mars
Storm Lake
Spencer
Sheldon
Cherokee
Denison
Carroll
Boone
Jefferson
Atlantic
Creston
Red Oak
Shenandoah
Clarinda
Glenwood
Harlan
Logan
Onawa
Sac City
Emmetsburg
Estherville
Algona
Clarion
Webster City
West Des Moines
Winterset
Osceola
Fremont
Nebraska City
Plattsmouth
Blair
Worthington
Fairmont
Blue Earth
Maryville
MISSOURI
Copyright by C. S. HAMMOND & Co., N. Y.
Longitude West of

IOWA
SCALE OF MILES
0 5 10 20 30 40
State Capitals
County Seats
Railroads 87
MITCHELL
HOWARD
WINNESHIEK
ALLAMAKEE
FLOYD
CHICKASAW
FAYETTE
CLAYTON
BUTLER
BREMER
BLACK HAWK
BUCHANAN
DELAWARE
DUBUQUE
GRUNDY
TAMA
BENTON
LINN
JONES
JACKSON
CLINTON
CEDAR
SCOTT
MARSHALL
POWESHIEK
IOWA
JOHNSON
MUSCATINE
JASPER
MAHASKA
KEOKUK
WASHINGTON
LOUISA
MONROE
WAPELLO
JEFFERSON
HENRY
DES MOINES
APPANOOSE
DAVIS
VAN BUREN
LEE
WIS.
ILL.
MISSISSIPPI
RAILROADS
7 Atchison, Topeka & Santa Fe
35 Charles City Western
42 Chicago & North Western
45 Chicago, Burlington & Quincy
46 Chicago Great Western
51 Chicago, Milwaukee, St. Paul & Pacific
54 Chicago, Rock Island & Pacific
55 Chicago, St. Paul, Minneapolis & Omaha
66 Davenport, Rock Island & North Western
67 Fort Dodge, Des Moines & Southern (Electric)
80 Great Northern
87 Illinois Central
113 Minneapolis & St. Louis
122 Missouri Pacific
175 Toledo, Peoria & Western
180 Union Pacific
185 Wabash
190 Waterloo, Cedar Falls & Northern

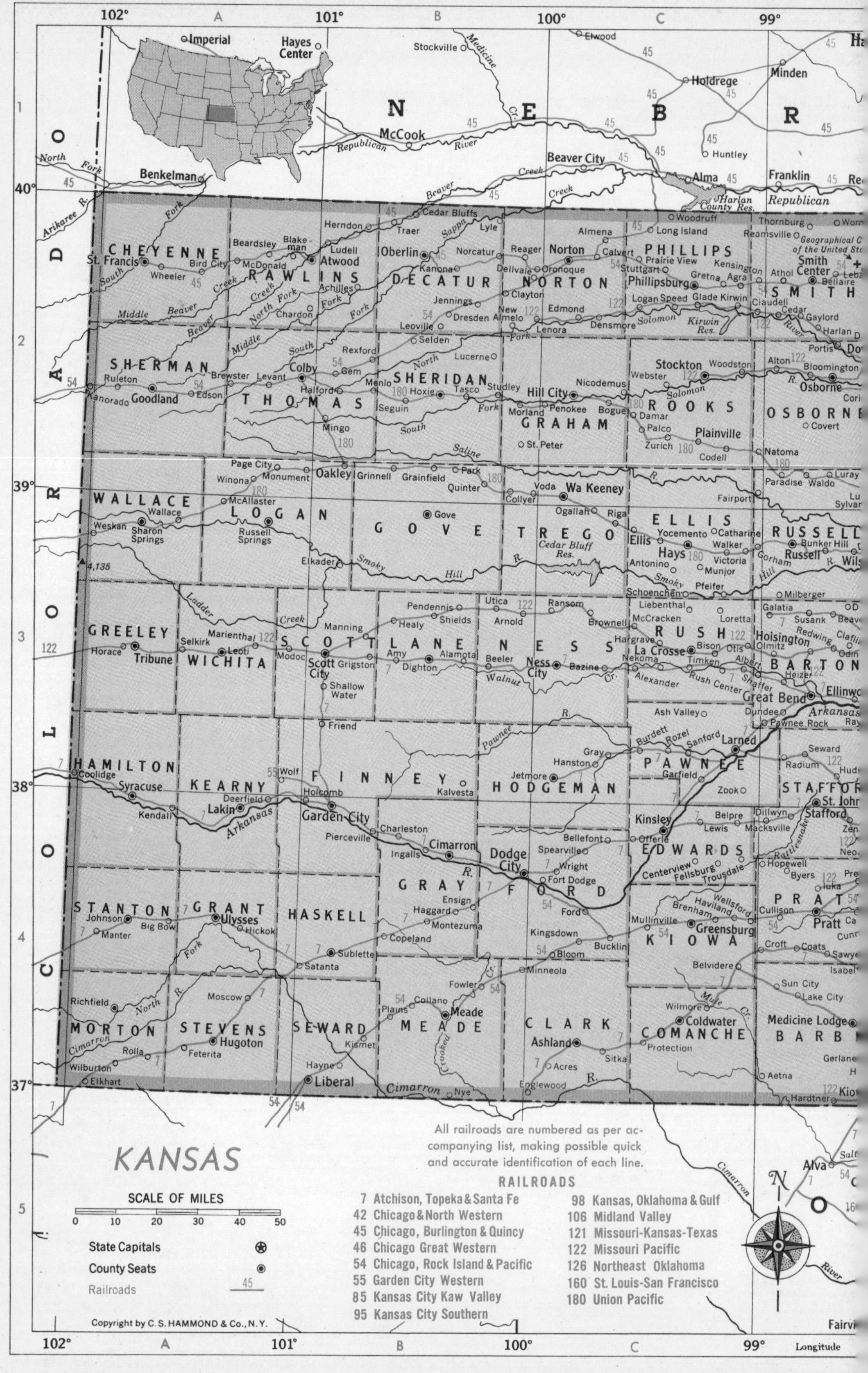
KANSAS
SCALE OF MILES
0 10 20 30 40 50
State Capitals
County Seats
Railroads
All railroads are numbered as per accompanying list, making possible quick and accurate identification of each line.
RAILROADS
7 Atchison, Topeka & Santa Fe
42 Chicago & North Western
45 Chicago, Burlington & Quincy
46 Chicago Great Western
54 Chicago, Rock Island & Pacific
55 Garden City Western
85 Kansas City Kaw Valley
95 Kansas City Southern
98 Kansas, Oklahoma & Gulf
106 Midland Valley
121 Missouri-Kansas-Texas
122 Missouri Pacific
126 Northeast Oklahoma
160 St. Louis-San Francisco
180 Union Pacific
Copyright by C. S. HAMMOND & Co., N. Y.
NEBR
COLORADO
CHEYENNE
RAWLINS
DECATUR
NORTON
PHILLIPS
SMITH
SHERMAN
THOMAS
SHERIDAN
GRAHAM
ROOKS
OSBORNE
WALLACE
LOGAN
GOVE
TREGO
ELLIS
RUSSELL
GREELEY
WICHITA
SCOTT
LANE
NESS
RUSH
BARTON
HAMILTON
KEARNY
FINNEY
HODGEMAN
PAWNEE
STAFFORD
GRAY
FORD
EDWARDS
PRATT
STANTON
GRANT
HASKELL
KIOWA
MORTON
STEVENS
SEWARD
MEADE
CLARK
COMANCHE
BARBER
102°
101°
100°
99°
40°
39°
38°
37°
A
B
C
1
2
3
4
5
Longitude

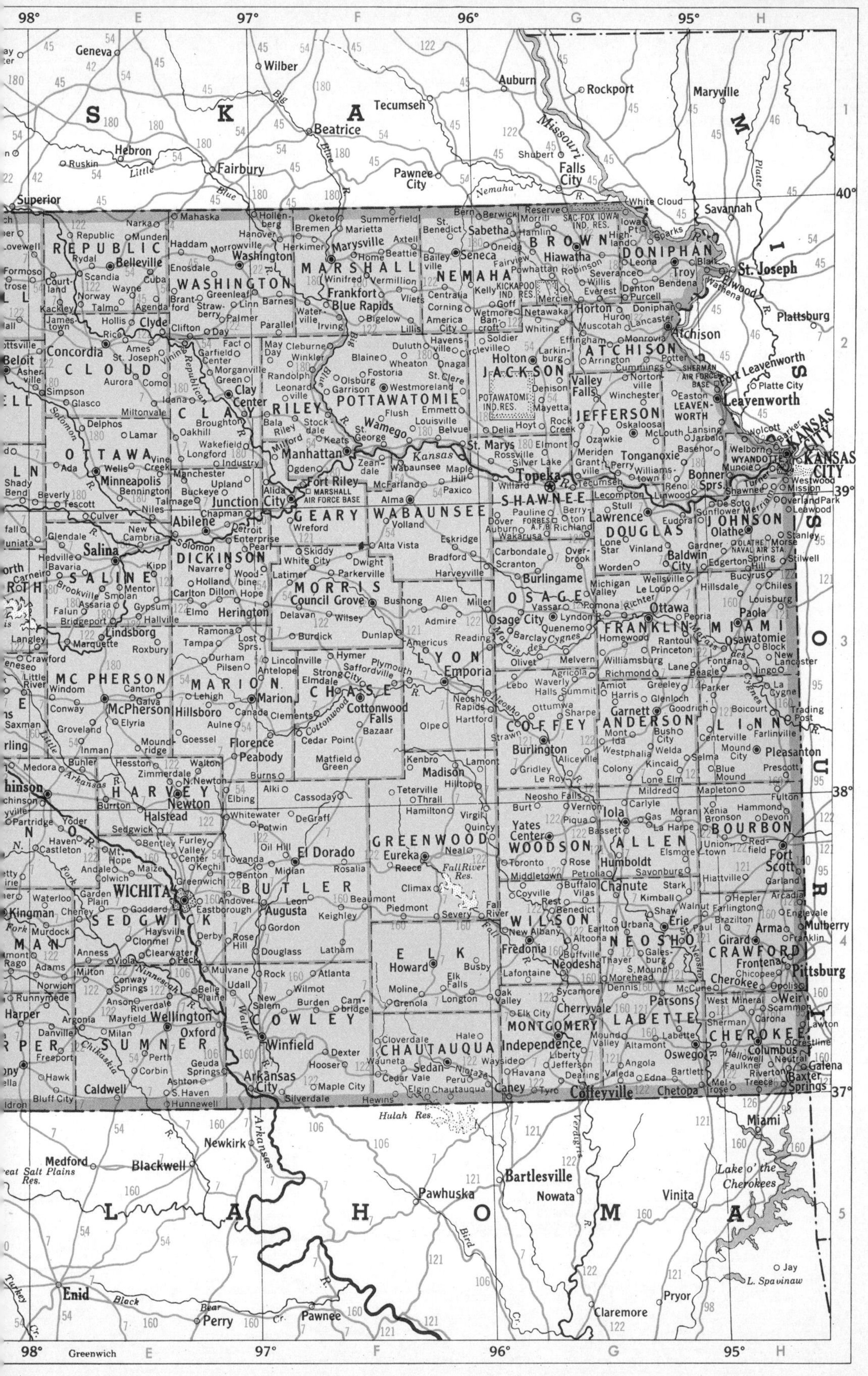
98°
E
97°
F
96°
G
95°
H
1
2
3
4
5
40°
39°
38°
37°
Greenwich
S K A
M I S S O U R I
L A H O M A
REPUBLIC
WASHINGTON
MARSHALL
NEMAHA
BROWN
DONIPHAN
CLOUD
CLAY
RILEY
POTTAWATOMIE
JACKSON
ATCHISON
JEFFERSON
LEAVENWORTH
WYANDOTTE
OTTAWA
GEARY
WABAUNSEE
SHAWNEE
DOUGLAS
JOHNSON
SALINE
DICKINSON
MORRIS
OSAGE
FRANKLIN
MIAMI
MC PHERSON
MARION
CHASE
LYON
COFFEY
ANDERSON
LINN
HARVEY
BUTLER
GREENWOOD
WOODSON
ALLEN
BOURBON
SEDGWICK
ELK
WILSON
NEOSHO
CRAWFORD
SUMNER
COWLEY
CHAUTAUQUA
MONTGOMERY
LABETTE
CHEROKEE
Geneva
Wilber
Auburn
Rockport
Maryville
Tecumseh
Beatrice
Hebron
Fairbury
Pawnee City
Falls City
Superior
Savannah
St. Joseph
Plattsburg
Belleville
Washington
Marysville
Seneca
Sabetha
Hiawatha
Troy
Atchison
Concordia
Clay Center
Holton
Leavenworth
Fort Leavenworth
Manhattan
Wamego
Topeka
Lawrence
KANSAS CITY
Olathe
Junction City
Fort Riley
Abilene
Salina
Council Grove
Ottawa
Paola
McPherson
Marion
Emporia
Burlington
Garnett
Newton
El Dorado
Eureka
Iola
Fort Scott
WICHITA
Augusta
Chanute
Girard
Pittsburg
Wellington
Winfield
Arkansas City
Independence
Coffeyville
Parsons
Oswego
Columbus
Fredonia
Miami
Medford
Blackwell
Newkirk
Bartlesville
Pawhuska
Nowata
Vinita
Enid
Perry
Pawnee
Claremore
Pryor
Lake o' the Cherokees
L. Spavinaw
Missouri
Kansas R.
Arkansas
Neosho
Verdigris

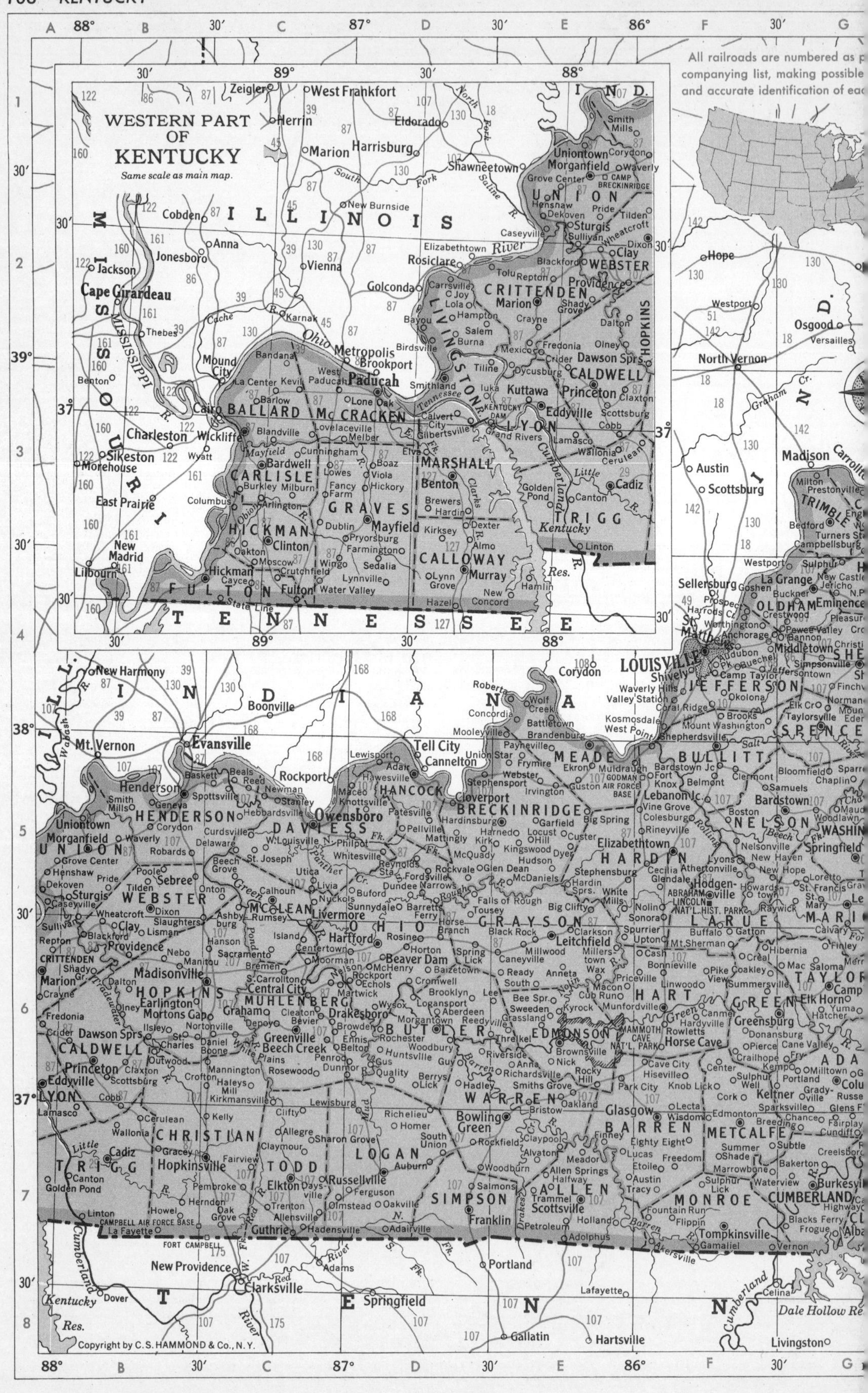
WESTERN PART OF KENTUCKY
Same scale as main map.
All railroads are numbered as p
companying list, making possible
and accurate identification of eac
ILLINOIS
MISSOURI
IND.
TENNESSEE
INDIANA
ILL.
BALLARD
McCRACKEN
CARLISLE
GRAVES
HICKMAN
FULTON
CALLOWAY
MARSHALL
LIVINGSTON
CRITTENDEN
UNION
WEBSTER
HOPKINS
CALDWELL
LYON
TRIGG
HENDERSON
DAVIESS
HANCOCK
BRECKINRIDGE
MEADE
McLEAN
OHIO
GRAYSON
HARDIN
BULLITT
JEFFERSON
OLDHAM
TRIMBLE
SPENCER
NELSON
LARUE
HART
EDMONSON
BUTLER
MUHLENBERG
CHRISTIAN
TODD
LOGAN
SIMPSON
WARREN
ALLEN
BARREN
METCALFE
MONROE
CUMBERLAND
GREEN
TAYLOR
LOUISVILLE
Paducah
Owensboro
Evansville
Bowling Green
Hopkinsville
Clarksville
Copyright by C. S. HAMMOND & Co., N. Y.

KENTUCKY
SCALE OF MILES
0 5 10 20 30 40
State Capitals
County Seats
Railroads 107
RAILROADS
2 Artemus - Jellico
18 Baltimore & Ohio
29 Cadiz
32 Carrollton
36 Chesapeake & Ohio
39 Chicago & Eastern Illinois
45 Chicago, Burlington & Quincy
49 Chicago, Indianapolis & Louisville
66 Clinchfield
72 East Tennessee and Western North Carolina
75 Detroit, Toledo & Ironton
78 Flemingsburg & Northern
82 Frankfort & Cincinnati
86 Gulf, Mobile & Ohio
87 Illinois Central
90 Interstate
97 Kentucky & Tennessee
107 Louisville & Nashville
122 Missouri Pacific
125 Morehead & North Fork
127 Nashville, Chattanooga & St. Louis
130 New York Central
133 Norfolk & Western
134 Oneida & Western
138 Paducah & Illinois
142 Pennsylvania
160 St. Louis - San Francisco
161 St. Louis Southwestern
168 Southern
175 Tennessee Central
OHIO
CINCINNATI
BOONE
KENTON
CAMPBELL
Covington
Newport
Ft.Thomas
Bellevue
Dayton
Ludlow
Erlanger
Elsmere
Florence
Burlington
Hebron
Constance
Addyston
Monterey
Francisville
Taylorsport
Park Hills
Southgate
Highland Hts.
Cold Spring
Melbourne
Silver Grove
Fruit Hill
Newtown
MILES
0 1 2 3 4 5
Hamilton
Oxford
Eaton
Harrison
Blanchester
Hillsboro
Batavia
Sardinia
Georgetown
West Union
Portsmouth
South Portsmouth
Ironton
Ashland
Greenup
Russell
Catlettsburg
Maysville
Augusta
Vanceburg
Lexington
Frankfort
Paris
Winchester
Mount Sterling
Richmond
Berea
Nicholasville
Cynthiana
Georgetown
Carlisle
Flemingsburg
Morehead
Grayson
Olive Hill
Louisa
Paintsville
Prestonsburg
Salyersville
Jackson
Hazard
Hyden
Whitesburg
Harlan
Pineville
Middlesboro
Barbourville
Williamsburg
London
Manchester
Somerset
Stanford
Lancaster
Mount Vernon
Pikeville
Jenkins
Inez
Beattyville
Booneville
McKee
Stanton
Frenchburg
West Liberty
Sandy Hook
Hindman
Irvine
Campton
Whitley City
Stearns
Cumberland Gap
Pennington Gap
Big Stone Gap
Norton
Wise
Appalachia
Kingsport
Bristol
Jellico
La Follette
Rogersville
Elizabethton
Williamson
Logan
Holden
Grundy
WEST VA.
VIRGINIA
TENNESSEE
BOURBON
FAYETTE
CLARK
MADISON
JACKSON
ROCKCASTLE
LAUREL
KNOX
WHITLEY
BELL
HARLAN
LETCHER
PERRY
LESLIE
CLAY
OWSLEY
BREATHITT
KNOTT
FLOYD
PIKE
MARTIN
JOHNSON
MAGOFFIN
WOLFE
LEE
ESTILL
POWELL
MENIFEE
MORGAN
LAWRENCE
ELLIOTT
ROWAN
BATH
MONTGOMERY
FLEMING
NICHOLAS
HARRISON
SCOTT
ROBERTSON
MASON
BRACKEN
PENDLETON
GRANT
LEWIS
GREENUP
CARTER
BOYD
JESSAMINE
GARRARD
LINCOLN
PULASKI
McCREARY
Ohio River
Licking R.
Kentucky R.
Big Sandy R.
Cumberland R.
Clinch R.
Holston R.
Powell R.
Norris Lake
Big Black Mountain 4,150
Greenwich

LOUISIANA
SCALE OF MILES
State Capitals
Parish Seats
Canals
Railroads
ARKANSAS
TEXAS
GULF OF MEXICO
SHREVEPORT
Alexandria
MONROE
Lake Charles
Lafayette
CADDO
BOSSIER
WEBSTER
CLAIBORNE
UNION
MOREHOUSE
WEST CARROLL
LINCOLN
OUACHITA
RICHLAND
BIENVILLE
JACKSON
CALDWELL
FRANKLIN
DE SOTO
RED RIVER
WINN
TENSAS
NATCHITOCHES
LA SALLE
CATAHOULA
SABINE
GRANT
RAPIDES
AVOYELLES
VERNON
CONCORDIA
BEAUREGARD
ALLEN
EVANGELINE
ST. LANDRY
POINTE COUPEE
WEST FELICIANA
WEST BATON ROUGE
CALCASIEU
JEFFERSON DAVIS
ACADIA
LAFAYETTE
ST. MARTIN
IBERIA
CAMERON
VERMILION
ST. MARY
IBERVILLE
MADISON

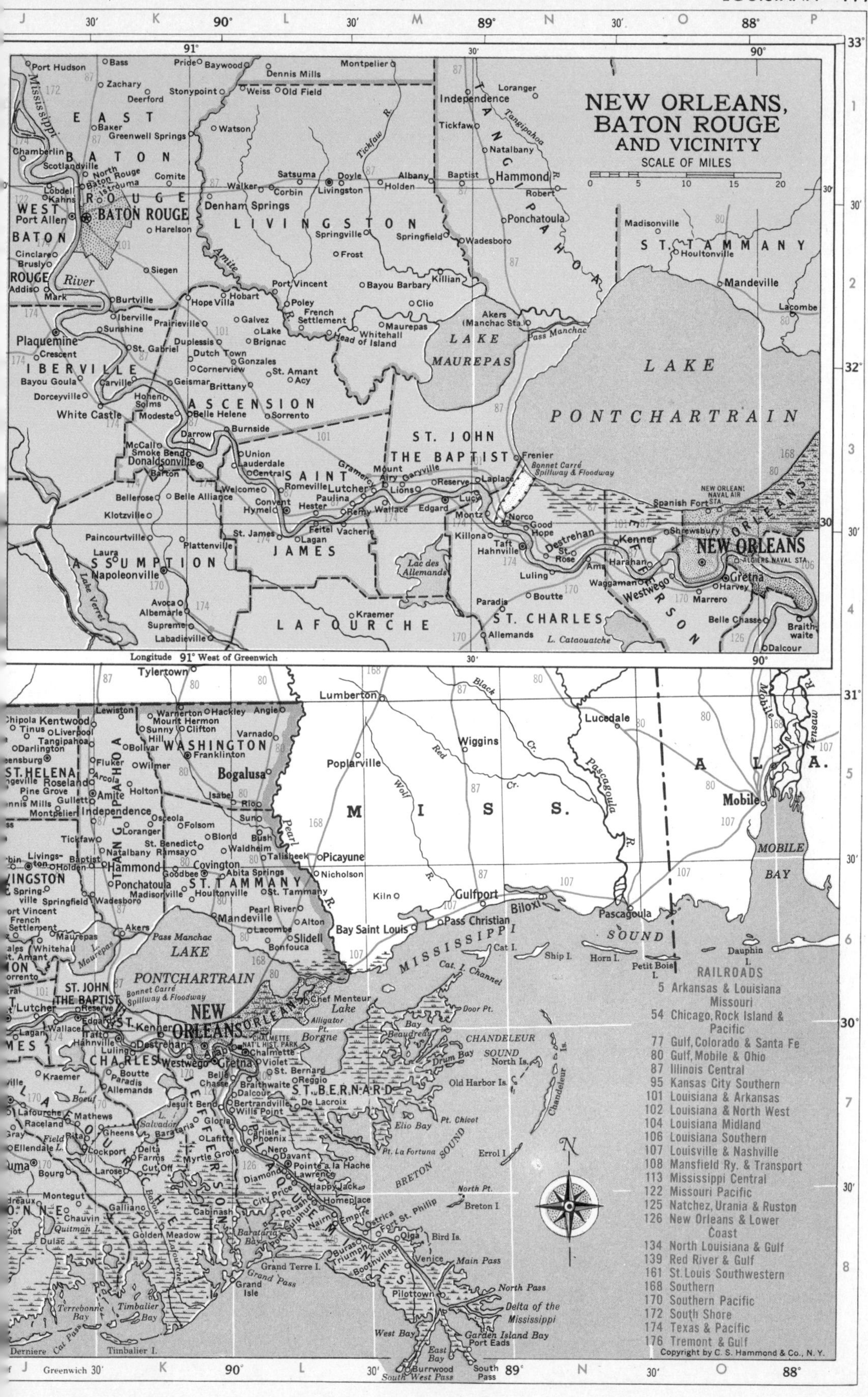
NEW ORLEANS, BATON ROUGE AND VICINITY
SCALE OF MILES
0 5 10 15 20
EAST BATON ROUGE
WEST BATON ROUGE
BATON ROUGE
LIVINGSTON
TANGIPAHOA
ST. TAMMANY
IBERVILLE
ASCENSION
ST. JOHN THE BAPTIST
SAINT JAMES
ASSUMPTION
LAFOURCHE
ST. CHARLES
JEFFERSON
ORLEANS
NEW ORLEANS
LAKE MAUREPAS
LAKE PONTCHARTRAIN
Lac des Allemands
L. Cataouatche
Bonnet Carré Spillway & Floodway
Longitude 91° West of Greenwich
WASHINGTON
ST. HELENA
Bogalusa
MISS.
ALA.
Mobile
MOBILE BAY
MISSISSIPPI SOUND
Gulfport
Biloxi
Pascagoula
Bay Saint Louis
Pass Christian
Picayune
Lucedale
Wiggins
Poplarville
Lumberton
Ship I.
Horn I.
Petit Bois I.
Dauphin I.
Cat I.
Lake Borgne
CHANDELEUR SOUND
Chandeleur Is.
BRETON SOUND
ST. BERNARD
PLAQUEMINES
TERREBONNE
Delta of the Mississippi
Main Pass
North Pass
South Pass
South West Pass
N
RAILROADS
5 Arkansas & Louisiana Missouri
54 Chicago, Rock Island & Pacific
77 Gulf, Colorado & Santa Fe
80 Gulf, Mobile & Ohio
87 Illinois Central
95 Kansas City Southern
101 Louisiana & Arkansas
102 Louisiana & North West
104 Louisiana Midland
106 Louisiana Southern
107 Louisville & Nashville
108 Mansfield Ry. & Transport
113 Mississippi Central
122 Missouri Pacific
125 Natchez, Urania & Ruston
126 New Orleans & Lower Coast
134 North Louisiana & Gulf
139 Red River & Gulf
161 St. Louis Southwestern
168 Southern
170 Southern Pacific
172 South Shore
174 Texas & Pacific
176 Tremont & Gulf
Copyright by C. S. Hammond & Co., N. Y.

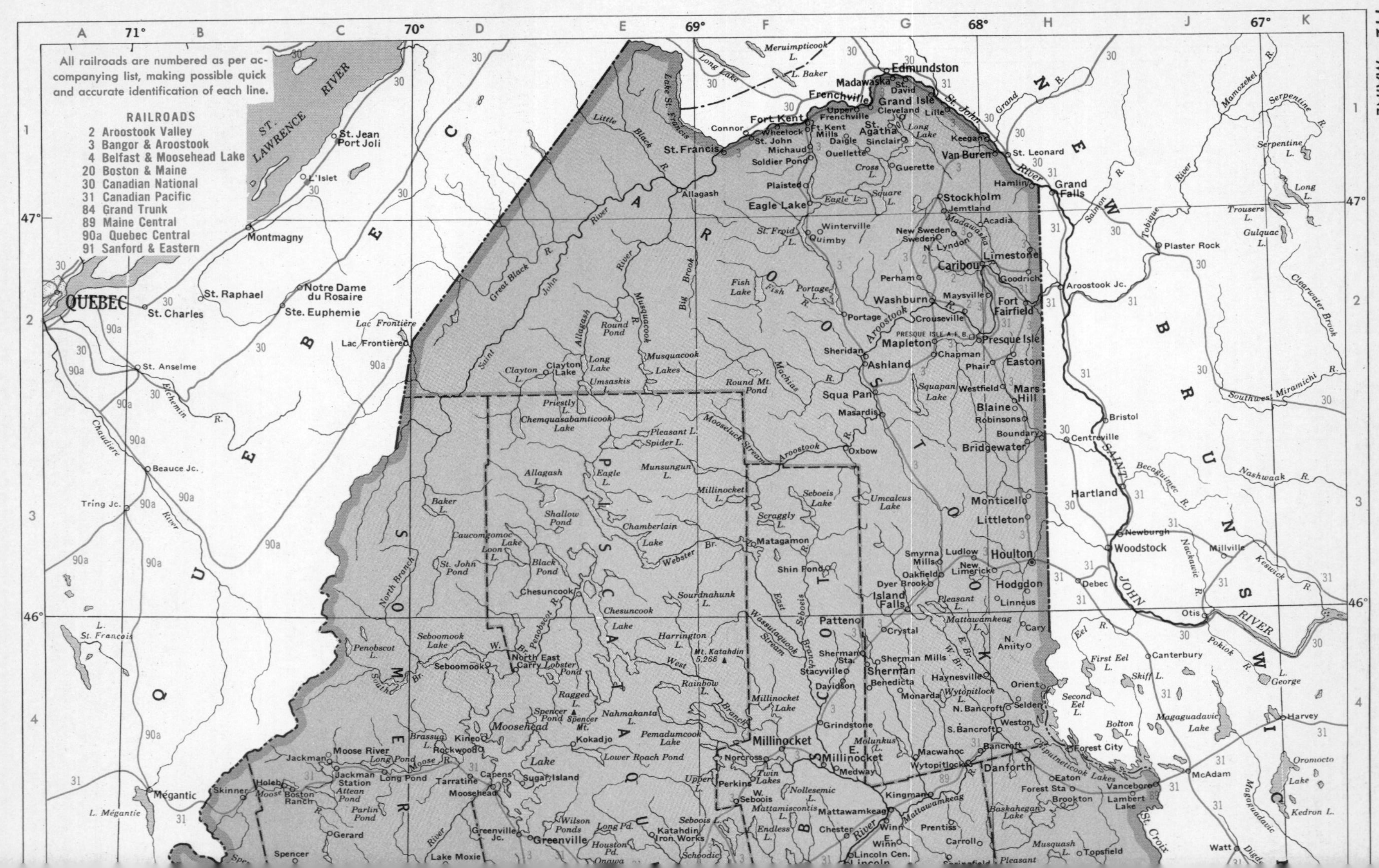
All railroads are numbered as per accompanying list, making possible quick and accurate identification of each line.
RAILROADS
2 Aroostook Valley
3 Bangor & Aroostook
4 Belfast & Moosehead Lake
20 Boston & Maine
30 Canadian National
31 Canadian Pacific
84 Grand Trunk
89 Maine Central
90a Quebec Central
91 Sanford & Eastern
ST. LAWRENCE RIVER
QUEBEC
NEW BRUNSWICK
AROOSTOOK
PISCATAQUIS
PENOBSCOT
SOMERSET
SAINT JOHN RIVER
47°
46°
67°
68°
69°
70°
71°
Edmundston
Madawaska
Grand Isle
Frenchville
Fort Kent
St. Francis
Van Buren
Grand Falls
St. Leonard
Stockholm
Eagle Lake
Caribou
Limestone
Washburn
Fort Fairfield
Presque Isle
Mapleton
Ashland
Easton
Mars Hill
Squa Pan
Oxbow
Bridgewater
Monticello
Littleton
Houlton
Hodgdon
Island Falls
Patten
Sherman
Millinocket
E. Millinocket
Danforth
Allagash
Plaster Rock
Aroostook Jc.
Bristol
Hartland
Woodstock
McAdam
Vanceboro
Forest City
Montmagny
St. Charles
St. Raphael
Notre Dame du Rosaire
Ste. Euphemie
Lac Frontière
St. Anselme
Beauce Jc.
Tring Jc.
Mégantic
Jackman
Moose River
Rockwood
Kineo
Moosehead Lake
Kokadjo
Greenville
Mt. Katahdin 5,268
Chamberlain Lake
Chesuncook Lake
Mattawamkeag

MAINE
SCALE OF MILES
0 5 10 20 30 40
State Capitals
County Seats
Railroads
84
ATLANTIC OCEAN
NEW HAMPSHIRE
WASHINGTON
HANCOCK
WALDO
KENNEBEC
LINCOLN
KNOX
SAGADAHOC
CUMBERLAND
ANDROSCOGGIN
OXFORD
FRANKLIN
PENOBSCOT
YORK
BANGOR
Augusta
PORTLAND
LEWISTON
Mt. Desert Island
Mt. Desert Rock
Machias Seal I. (Sovereignty undetermined)
Grand Manan Channel
Longitude West of Greenwich
A 71° B C 70° D E 69° F G 68° H J 67°
Copyright by C. S. Hammond & Co., N. Y.

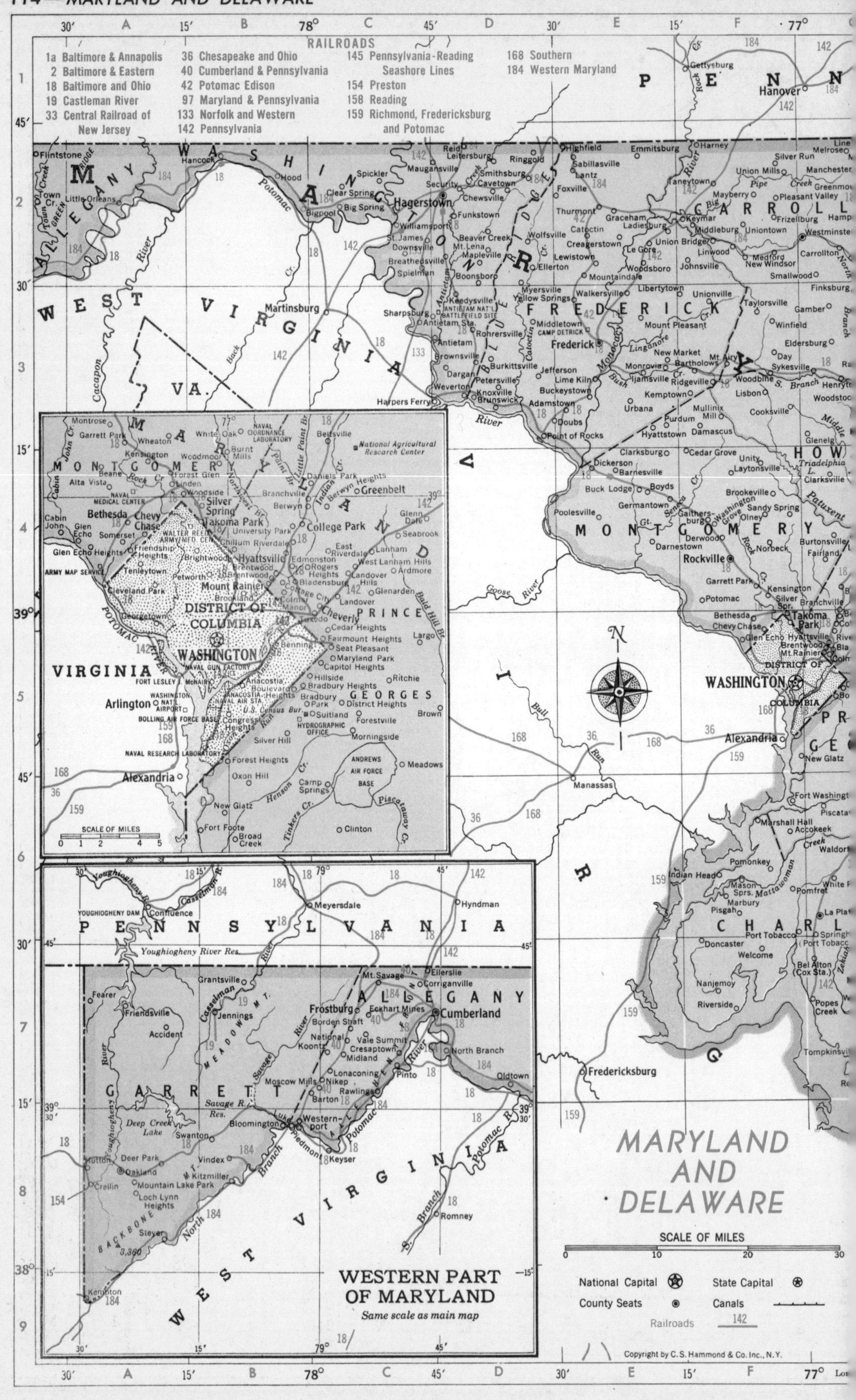
RAILROADS
1a Baltimore & Annapolis
2 Baltimore & Eastern
18 Baltimore and Ohio
19 Castleman River
33 Central Railroad of New Jersey
36 Chesapeake and Ohio
40 Cumberland & Pennsylvania
42 Potomac Edison
97 Maryland & Pennsylvania
133 Norfolk and Western
142 Pennsylvania
145 Pennsylvania-Reading Seashore Lines
154 Preston
158 Reading
159 Richmond, Fredericksburg and Potomac
168 Southern
184 Western Maryland
MARYLAND AND DELAWARE
SCALE OF MILES
0 10 20 30
National Capital
State Capital
County Seats
Canals
Railroads 142
Copyright by C. S. Hammond & Co. Inc., N.Y.
WESTERN PART OF MARYLAND
Same scale as main map
SCALE OF MILES
0 1 2 4 5
DISTRICT OF COLUMBIA
WASHINGTON
VIRGINIA
WEST VIRGINIA
PENNSYLVANIA
ALLEGANY
WASHINGTON
FREDERICK
MONTGOMERY
CARROLL
GARRETT
PRINCE GEORGES
CHARLES
Hagerstown
Frederick
Rockville
Cumberland
Oakland
Martinsburg
Harpers Ferry
Alexandria
Arlington
Manassas
Fredericksburg
Gettysburg
Hanover
Westminster
Frostburg
Westernport
Keyser
Romney
Hyndman
Meyersdale
Bethesda
Silver Spring
Takoma Park
College Park
Greenbelt
Hyattsville
Mount Rainier
Cheverly
Chevy Chase
Kensington
Wheaton
La Plata
Indian Head
Port Tobacco
Emmitsburg
Thurmont
Brunswick
Middletown
New Market
Mount Airy
Damascus
Gaithersburg
Poolesville
Germantown
Potomac
Monocacy
BLUE RIDGE
BACKBONE MT.
Deep Creek Lake
Youghiogheny River Res.
Savage R. Res.
3,360

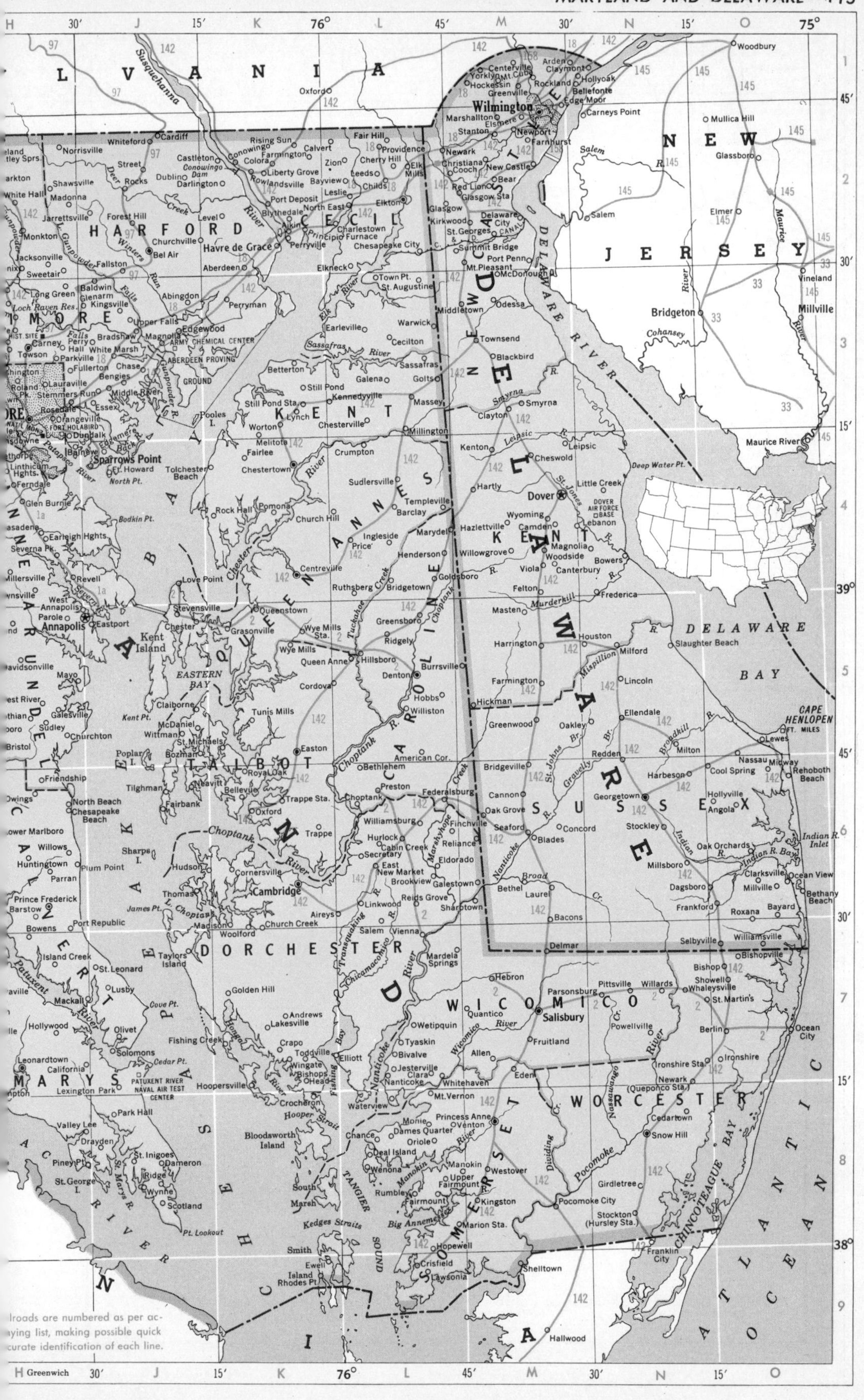

lroads are numbered as per ac-
ying list, making possible quick
curate identification of each line.

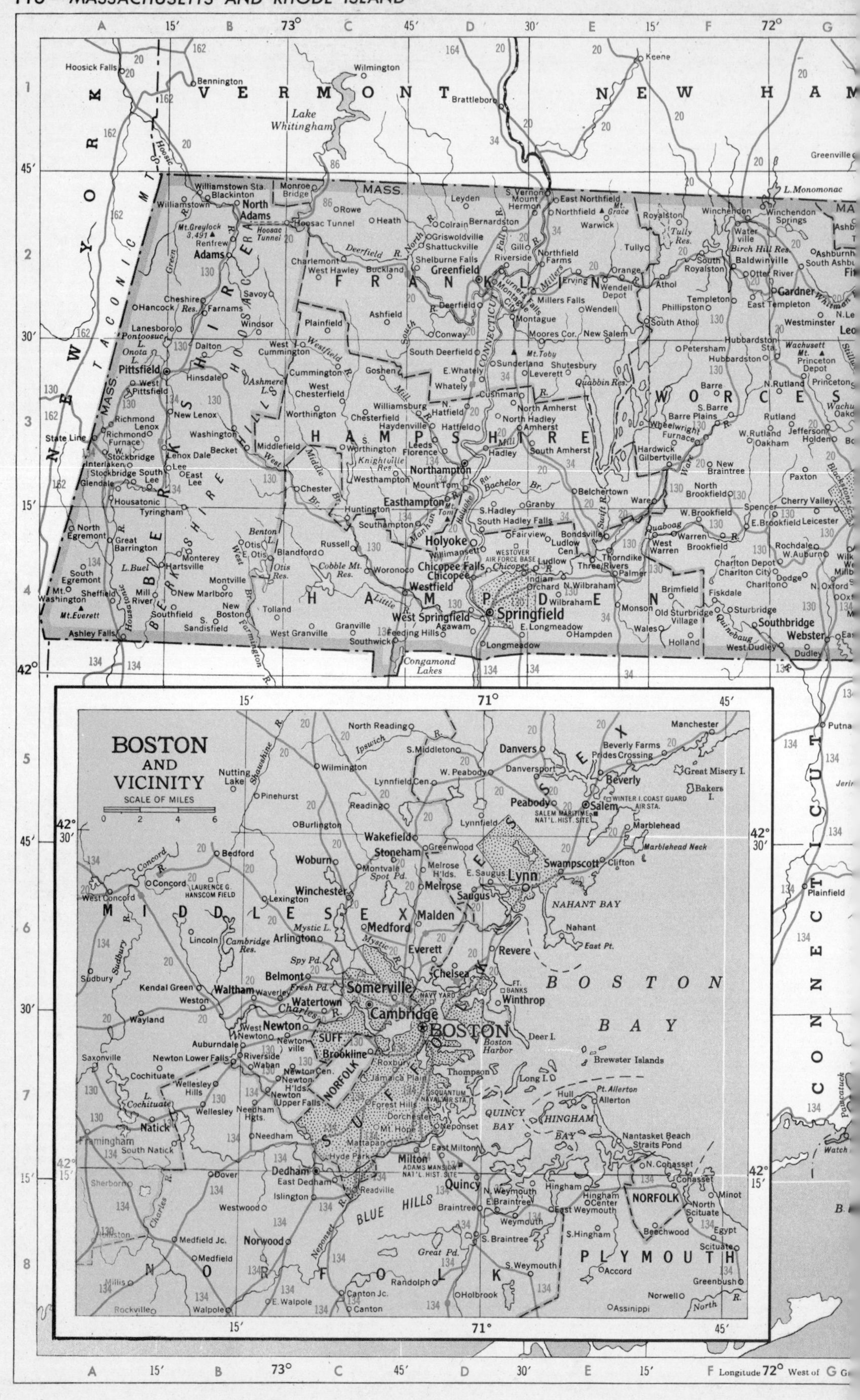

VERMONT
NEW HAMPSHIRE
NEW YORK
CONNECTICUT
MASS.
FRANKLIN
HAMPSHIRE
HAMPDEN
BERKSHIRE
WORCESTER
TACONIC MTS.
HOOSAC RANGE
BERKSHIRE HILLS
Lake Whitingham
Hoosick Falls
Bennington
Wilmington
Brattleboro
Keene
Williamstown
North Adams
Adams
Mt. Greylock 3,491
Hoosac Tunnel
Pittsfield
Dalton
Lenox
Stockbridge
Great Barrington
Sheffield
Mt. Everett
Greenfield
Deerfield
Northampton
Easthampton
Holyoke
Chicopee
Chicopee Falls
Westfield
West Springfield
Springfield
Longmeadow
Amherst
Ware
Palmer
Athol
Orange
Gardner
Winchendon
Southbridge
Webster
Quabbin Res.
WESTOVER AIR FORCE BASE
Congamond Lakes
Putnam
Plainfield
BOSTON AND VICINITY
SCALE OF MILES
0 2 4 6
North Reading
Wilmington
Danvers
Beverly
Salem
Peabody
Marblehead
Lynn
Swampscott
NAHANT BAY
Nahant
Concord
Lexington
Woburn
Winchester
Wakefield
Stoneham
Melrose
Malden
Medford
Arlington
Everett
Chelsea
Revere
Winthrop
Somerville
Cambridge
BOSTON
Belmont
Waltham
Watertown
Newton
Brookline
Wellesley
Natick
Framingham
Needham
Dedham
Milton
Quincy
Braintree
Weymouth
Hingham
Hull
Norwood
Walpole
Canton
Randolph
Holbrook
BOSTON BAY
Boston Harbor
QUINCY BAY
HINGHAM BAY
Brewster Islands
BLUE HILLS
MIDDLESEX
ESSEX
SUFFOLK
NORFOLK
PLYMOUTH
Scituate
Cohasset
Longitude 72° West of G

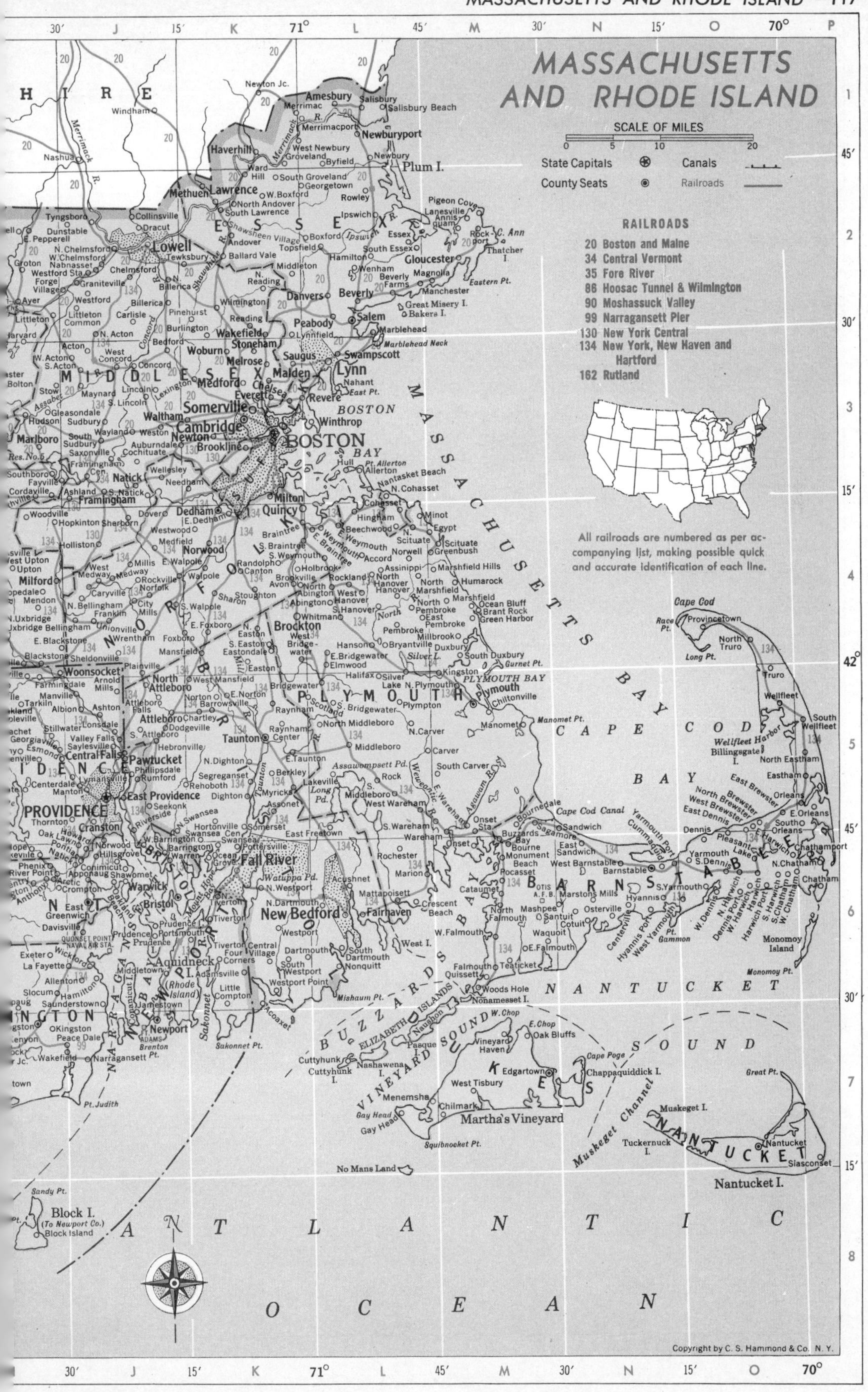
MASSACHUSETTS AND RHODE ISLAND
SCALE OF MILES
0 5 10 20
State Capitals
County Seats
Canals
Railroads
RAILROADS
20 Boston and Maine
34 Central Vermont
35 Fore River
86 Hoosac Tunnel & Wilmington
90 Moshassuck Valley
99 Narragansett Pier
130 New York Central
134 New York, New Haven and Hartford
162 Rutland
All railroads are numbered as per accompanying list, making possible quick and accurate identification of each line.
MASSACHUSETTS BAY
CAPE COD BAY
NANTUCKET SOUND
BUZZARDS BAY
ATLANTIC OCEAN
BOSTON
PROVIDENCE
Martha's Vineyard
Nantucket I.
Block I.
Copyright by C. S. Hammond & Co. N. Y.

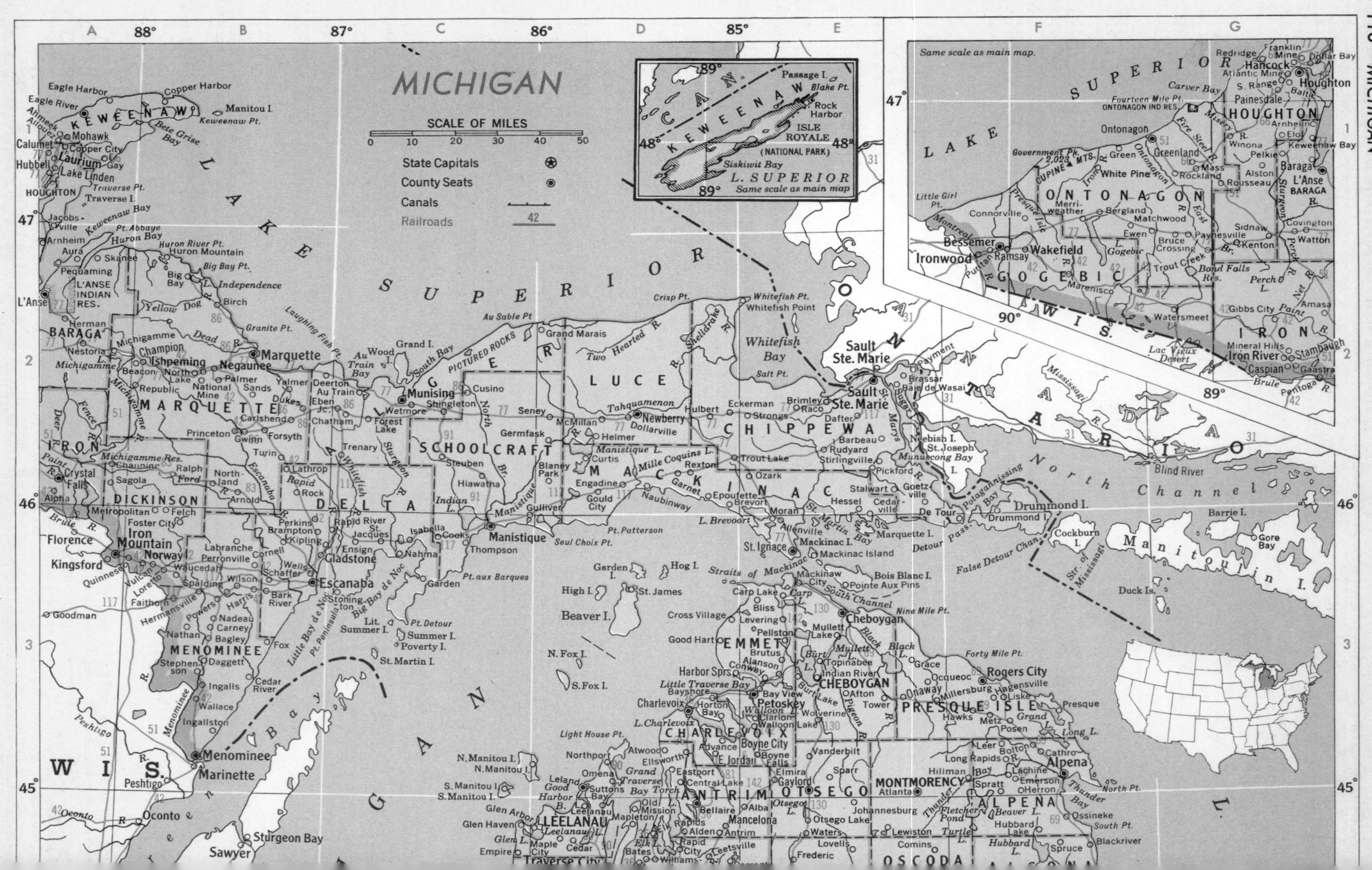
MICHIGAN
SCALE OF MILES
0 10 20 30 40 50
State Capitals
County Seats
Canals
Railroads
Same scale as main map.
ISLE ROYALE (NATIONAL PARK)
L. SUPERIOR
Same scale as main map
LAKE SUPERIOR
WIS.
ONTARIO
Manitoulin I.
North Channel
Whitefish Bay
Straits of Mackinac
Green Bay

panying list, making possible quick and
accurate identification of each line.
RAILROADS
4 Ann Arbor
6 Boyne City
18 Baltimore & Ohio
25 Canadian National
31 Canadian Pacific
36 Chesapeake & Ohio
42 Chicago & North Western
51 Chicago, Milwaukee, St. Paul & Pacific
66 Copper Range
69 Detroit & Mackinac
72 Detroit & Toledo Shore Line
73 Detroit, Caro & Sandusky
74 Detroit Terminal
75 Detroit, Toledo & Ironton
77 Duluth, South Shore and Atlantic
81 East Jordan & Southern
83 Escanaba & Lake Superior
84 Grand Trunk
85 Green Bay & Western
86 Lake Superior & Ishpeming
89 Ludington & Northern
90 Manistee & Northeastern
91 Manistique & Lake Superior
117 Minneapolis, St. Paul & Sault Ste. Marie
130 New York Central
131 New York, Chicago & St. Louis
142 Pennsylvania
147 Port Huron & Detroit
185 Wabash
LAKE MICHIGAN
LAKE HURON
Saginaw Bay
LAKE ST. CLAIR
LAKE ERIE
ONT.
CANADA
ILL.
INDIANA
OHIO
MASON
LAKE
OSCEOLA
CLARE
GLADWIN
ARENAC
WEXFORD
MISSAUKEE
ROSCOMMON
OGEMAW
IOSCO
OCEANA
NEWAYGO
MECOSTA
ISABELLA
MIDLAND
BAY
HURON
TUSCOLA
SANILAC
MUSKEGON
MONTCALM
GRATIOT
SAGINAW
OTTAWA
KENT
IONIA
CLINTON
SHIAWASSEE
GENESEE
LAPEER
ST. CLAIR
ALLEGAN
BARRY
EATON
INGHAM
LIVINGSTON
OAKLAND
MACOMB
VAN BUREN
KALAMAZOO
CALHOUN
JACKSON
WASHTENAW
WAYNE
CASS
ST. JOSEPH
BRANCH
HILLSDALE
LENAWEE
MONROE
Ludington
Manistee
Cadillac
Muskegon
Muskegon Heights
Grand Haven
Holland
GRAND RAPIDS
Big Rapids
Mt. Pleasant
Midland
Bay City
Saginaw
Flint
Owosso
Lansing
Pontiac
DETROIT
WINDSOR
Port Huron
Sarnia
Kalamazoo
Battle Creek
Jackson
Ann Arbor
Ypsilanti
Adrian
Monroe
TOLEDO
SOUTH BEND
Benton Harbor
St. Joseph
Kenosha
Birmingham
Royal Oak
Hamtramck
Highland Park
Dearborn
Grosse Pointe
Wyandotte
Trenton
MILES
0 5 10
88° 87° 86° 85° 84° 83°
Longitude West of Greenwich
44° 43° 42°
B C D E F G
5 6 7
Copyright by C. S. Hammond & Co., N. Y.

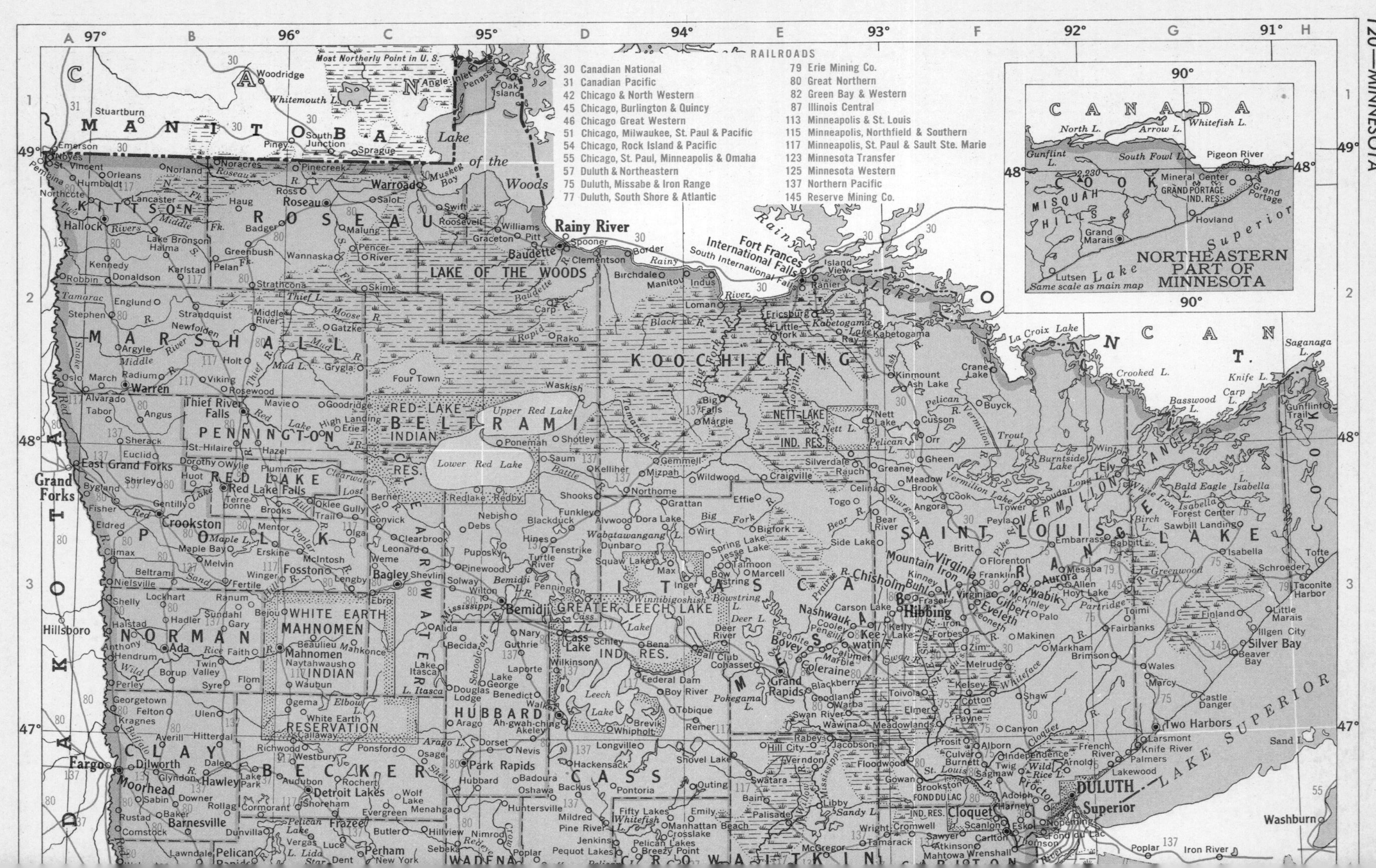
RAILROADS
30 Canadian National
31 Canadian Pacific
42 Chicago & North Western
45 Chicago, Burlington & Quincy
46 Chicago Great Western
51 Chicago, Milwaukee, St. Paul & Pacific
54 Chicago, Rock Island & Pacific
55 Chicago, St. Paul, Minneapolis & Omaha
57 Duluth & Northeastern
75 Duluth, Missabe & Iron Range
77 Duluth, South Shore & Atlantic
79 Erie Mining Co.
80 Great Northern
82 Green Bay & Western
87 Illinois Central
113 Minneapolis & St. Louis
115 Minneapolis, Northfield & Southern
117 Minneapolis, St. Paul & Sault Ste. Marie
123 Minnesota Transfer
125 Minnesota Western
137 Northern Pacific
145 Reserve Mining Co.
NORTHEASTERN PART OF MINNESOTA
Same scale as main map
Most Northerly Point in U. S.

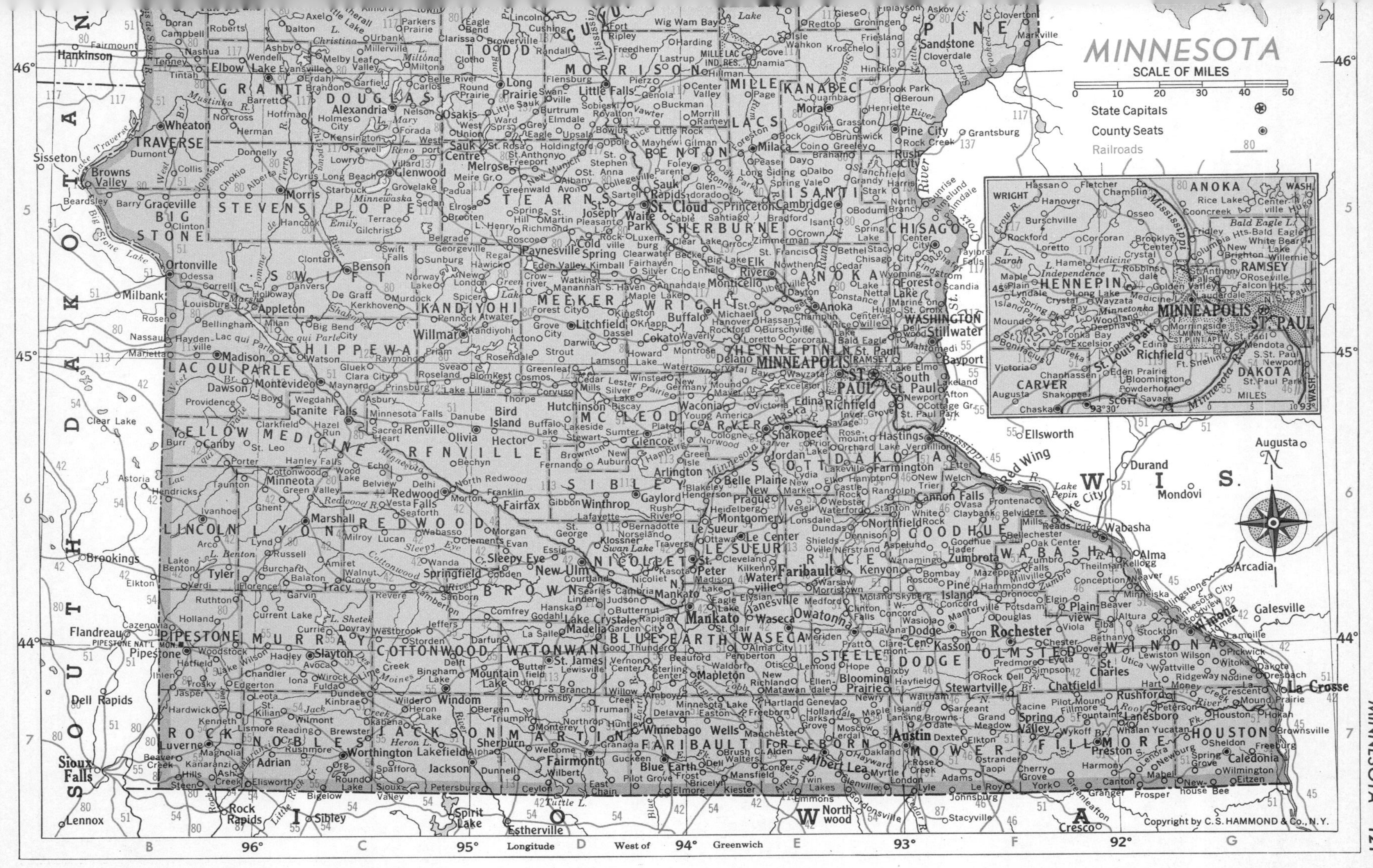
MINNESOTA
SCALE OF MILES
0 10 20 30 40 50
State Capitals
County Seats
Railroads
Longitude West of Greenwich
Copyright by C. S. HAMMOND & Co., N. Y.

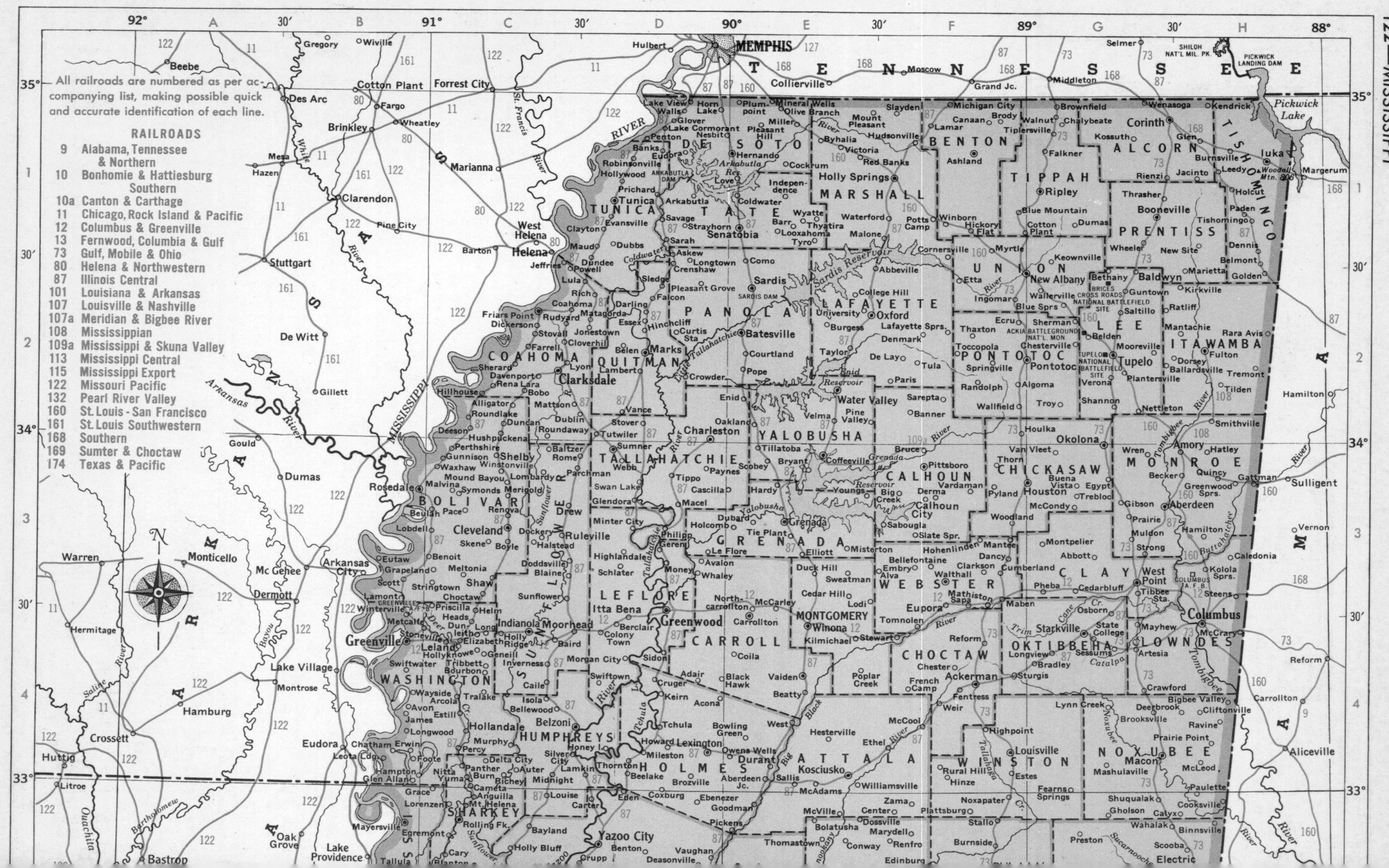
All railroads are numbered as per accompanying list, making possible quick and accurate identification of each line.
RAILROADS
9 Alabama, Tennessee & Northern
10 Bonhomie & Hattiesburg Southern
10a Canton & Carthage
11 Chicago, Rock Island & Pacific
12 Columbus & Greenville
13 Fernwood, Columbia & Gulf
73 Gulf, Mobile & Ohio
80 Helena & Northwestern
87 Illinois Central
101 Louisiana & Arkansas
107 Louisville & Nashville
107a Meridian & Bigbee River
108 Mississippian
109a Mississippi & Skuna Valley
113 Mississippi Central
115 Mississippi Export
122 Missouri Pacific
132 Pearl River Valley
160 St. Louis - San Francisco
161 St. Louis Southwestern
168 Southern
169 Sumter & Choctaw
174 Texas & Pacific

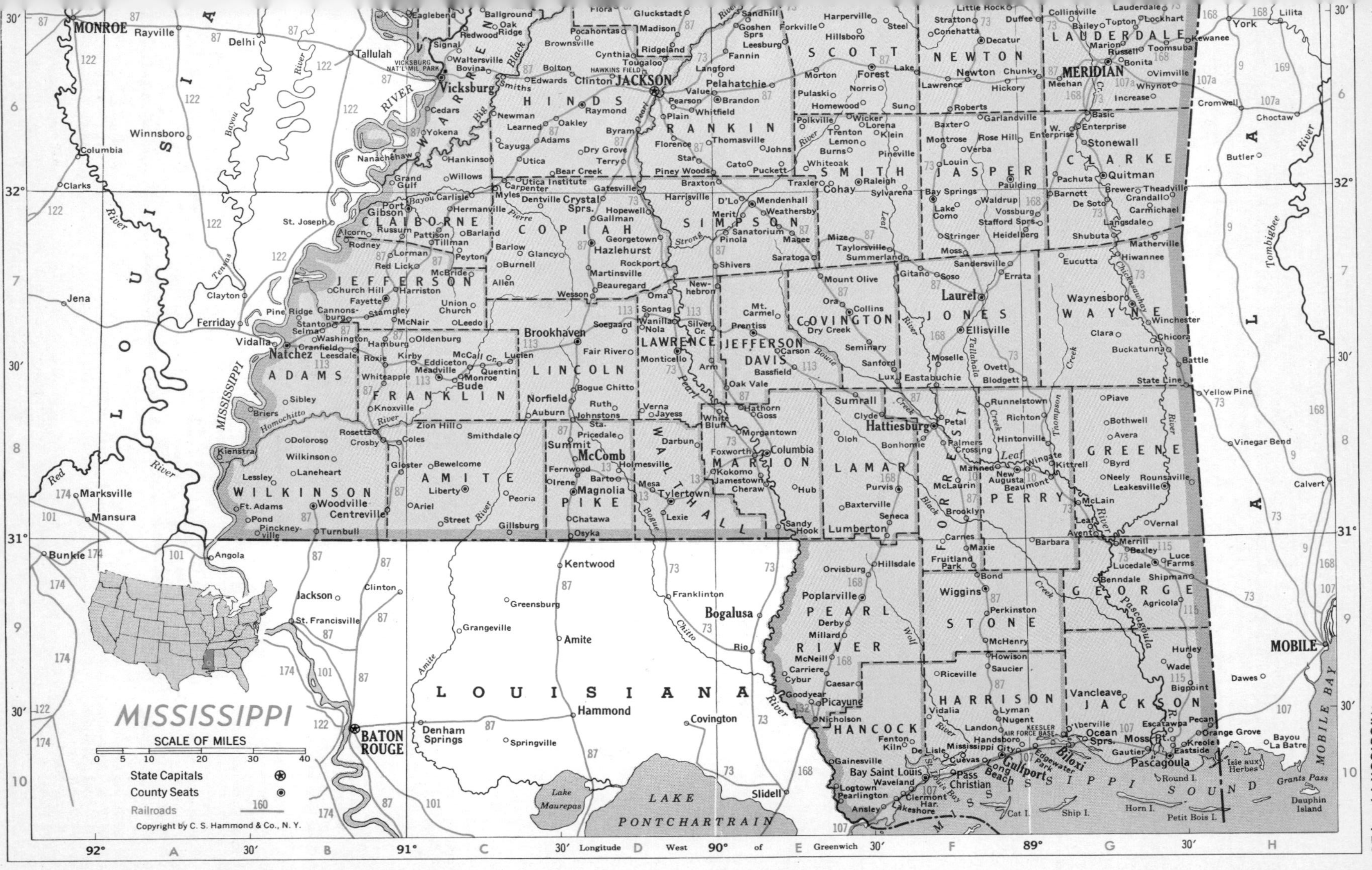
MISSISSIPPI
SCALE OF MILES
0 5 10 20 30 40
State Capitals
County Seats
Railroads
Copyright by C. S. Hammond & Co., N. Y.
LOUISIANA
ALABAMA
MOBILE BAY
MISSISSIPPI SOUND
LAKE PONTCHARTRAIN
Lake Maurepas
MOBILE
BATON ROUGE
JACKSON
MERIDIAN
Longitude West 90° of Greenwich

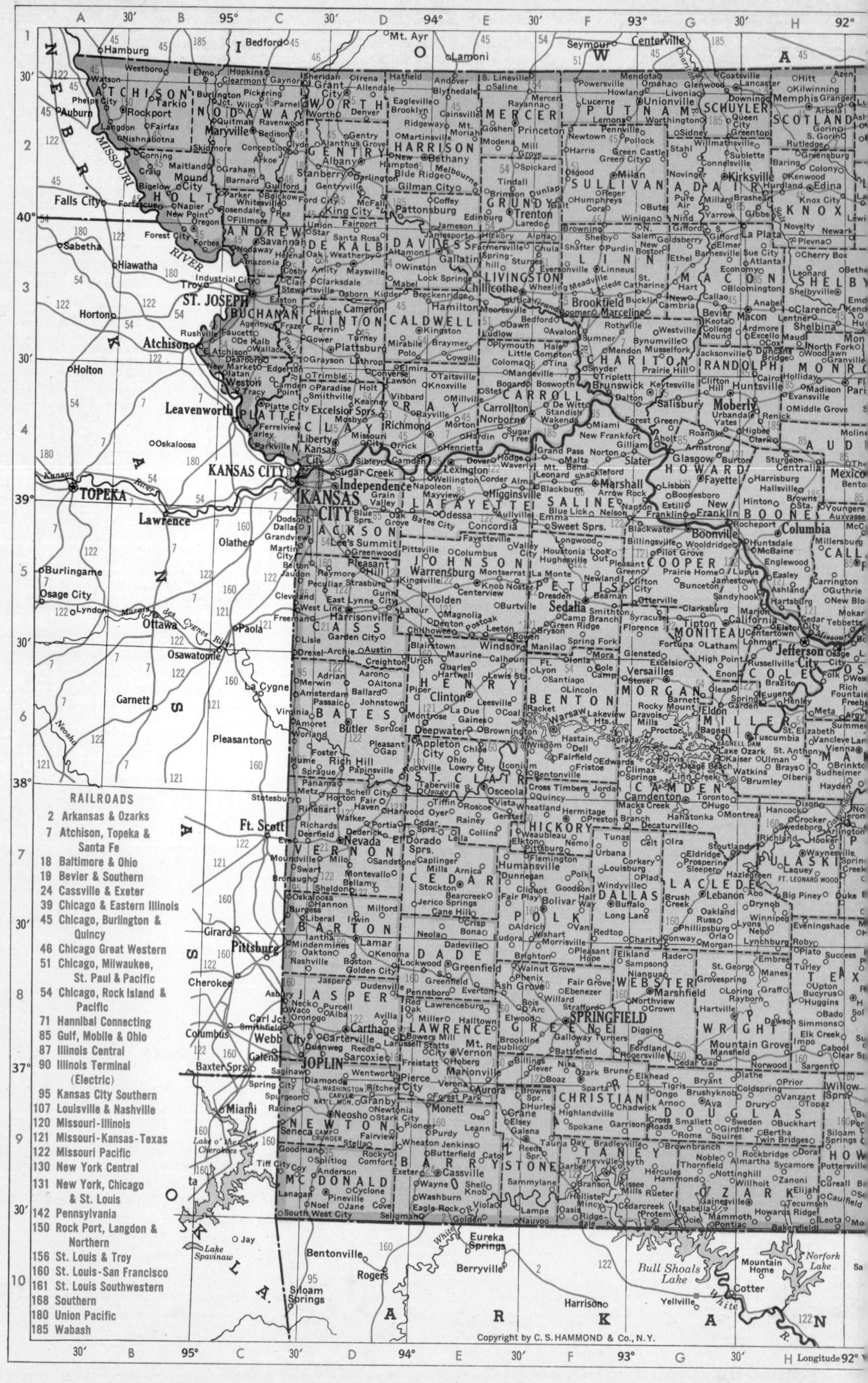

RAILROADS
2 Arkansas & Ozarks
7 Atchison, Topeka & Santa Fe
18 Baltimore & Ohio
19 Bevier & Southern
24 Cassville & Exeter
39 Chicago & Eastern Illinois
45 Chicago, Burlington & Quincy
46 Chicago Great Western
51 Chicago, Milwaukee, St. Paul & Pacific
54 Chicago, Rock Island & Pacific
71 Hannibal Connecting
85 Gulf, Mobile & Ohio
87 Illinois Central
90 Illinois Terminal (Electric)
95 Kansas City Southern
107 Louisville & Nashville
120 Missouri-Illinois
121 Missouri-Kansas-Texas
122 Missouri Pacific
130 New York Central
131 New York, Chicago & St. Louis
142 Pennsylvania
150 Rock Port, Langdon & Northern
156 St. Louis & Troy
160 St. Louis-San Francisco
161 St. Louis Southwestern
168 Southern
180 Union Pacific
185 Wabash
ATCHISON
NODAWAY
WORTH
HARRISON
MERCER
PUTNAM
SCHUYLER
SCOTLAND
HOLT
GENTRY
GRUNDY
SULLIVAN
ADAIR
KNOX
ANDREW
DE KALB
DAVIESS
LIVINGSTON
LINN
MACON
SHELBY
BUCHANAN
CLINTON
CALDWELL
CHARITON
RANDOLPH
PLATTE
CLAY
RAY
CARROLL
HOWARD
BOONE
LAFAYETTE
SALINE
JACKSON
JOHNSON
PETTIS
COOPER
CASS
HENRY
BENTON
MORGAN
MONITEAU
COLE
BATES
ST. CLAIR
HICKORY
CAMDEN
MILLER
VERNON
CEDAR
POLK
DALLAS
LACLEDE
PULASKI
BARTON
DADE
GREENE
WEBSTER
WRIGHT
JASPER
LAWRENCE
CHRISTIAN
DOUGLAS
NEWTON
BARRY
STONE
TANEY
OZARK
McDONALD
ST. JOSEPH
KANSAS CITY
Independence
Sedalia
Jefferson City
Columbia
SPRINGFIELD
JOPLIN
TOPEKA
Leavenworth
Atchison
Lawrence
Ottawa
Ft. Scott
Pittsburg
Bull Shoals Lake
Norfork Lake
Lake o' the Cherokees
Lake Spavinaw
MISSOURI RIVER
Copyright by C. S. HAMMOND & Co., N.Y.

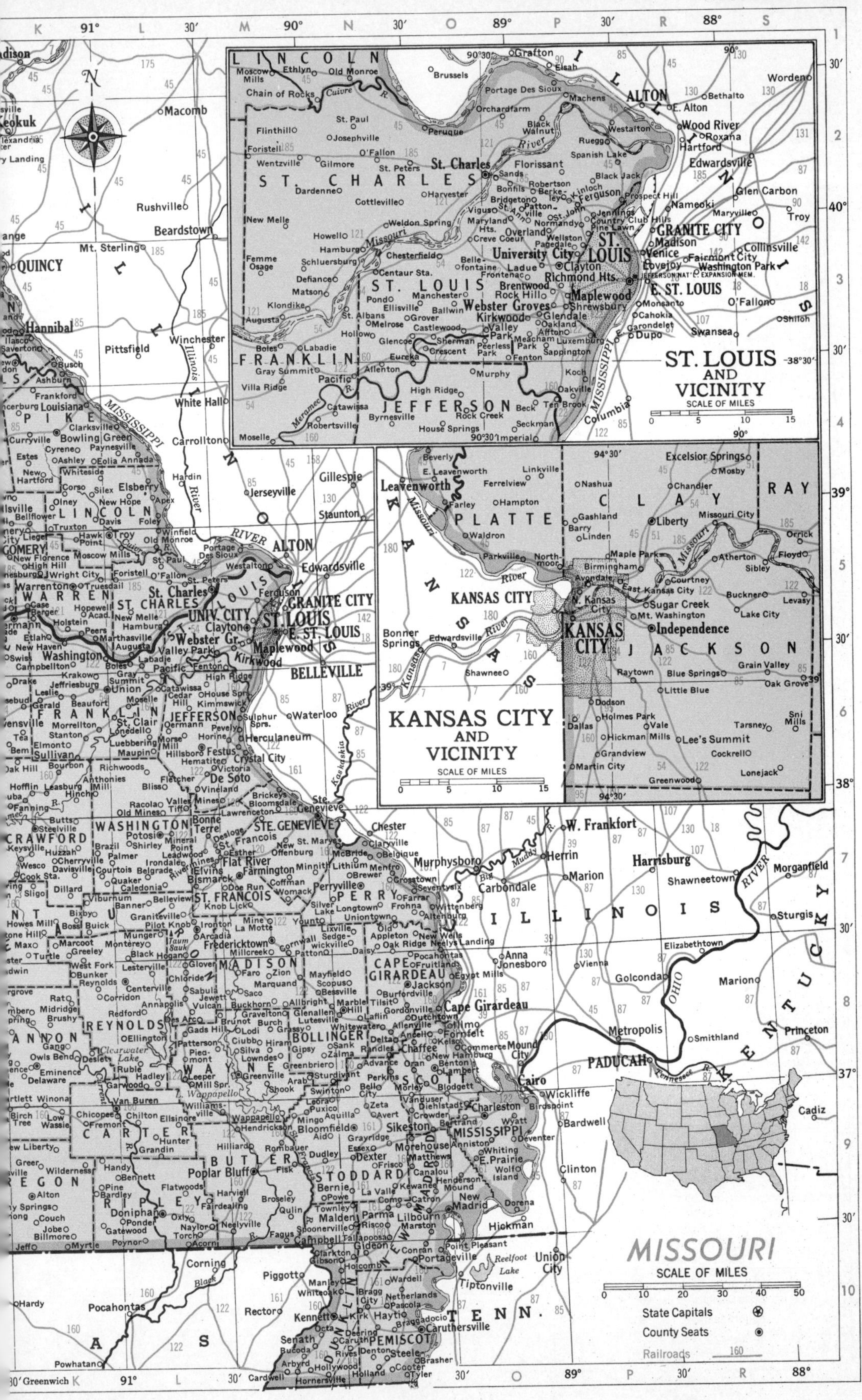
ST. LOUIS AND VICINITY
SCALE OF MILES
KANSAS CITY AND VICINITY
SCALE OF MILES
MISSOURI
SCALE OF MILES
State Capitals
County Seats
Railroads
ILLINOIS
KENTUCKY
TENN.
KANSAS

MONTANA
SCALE OF MILES
0 10 20 40 60 80
State Capitals
County Seats
Railroads 137
Copyright by C.S. Hammond & Co., N.Y.
All railroads are numbered as per accompanying list, making possible quick and accurate identification of each line.
BRITISH COLUMBIA
ALBERTA
CANADA
IDAHO
LINCOLN
FLATHEAD
SANDERS
LAKE
MINERAL
MISSOULA
RAVALLI
GRANITE
POWELL
LEWIS AND CLARK
DEER LODGE
SILVER BOW
BEAVERHEAD
MADISON
JEFFERSON
BROADWATER
GALLATIN
MEAGHER
CASCADE
TETON
PONDERA
TOOLE
LIBERTY
GLACIER
PARK
GLACIER NATIONAL PARK
BLACKFEET INDIAN RESERVATION
FLATHEAD INDIAN RESERVATION
YELLOWSTONE NATIONAL PARK
BITTERROOT RANGE
CONTINENTAL DIVIDE
BIG HOLE BATTLEFIELD NAT'L MON.
Helena
Missoula
GREAT FALLS
BUTTE
Anaconda
Bozeman
Kalispell
Dillon
Lethbridge
Medicine Hat

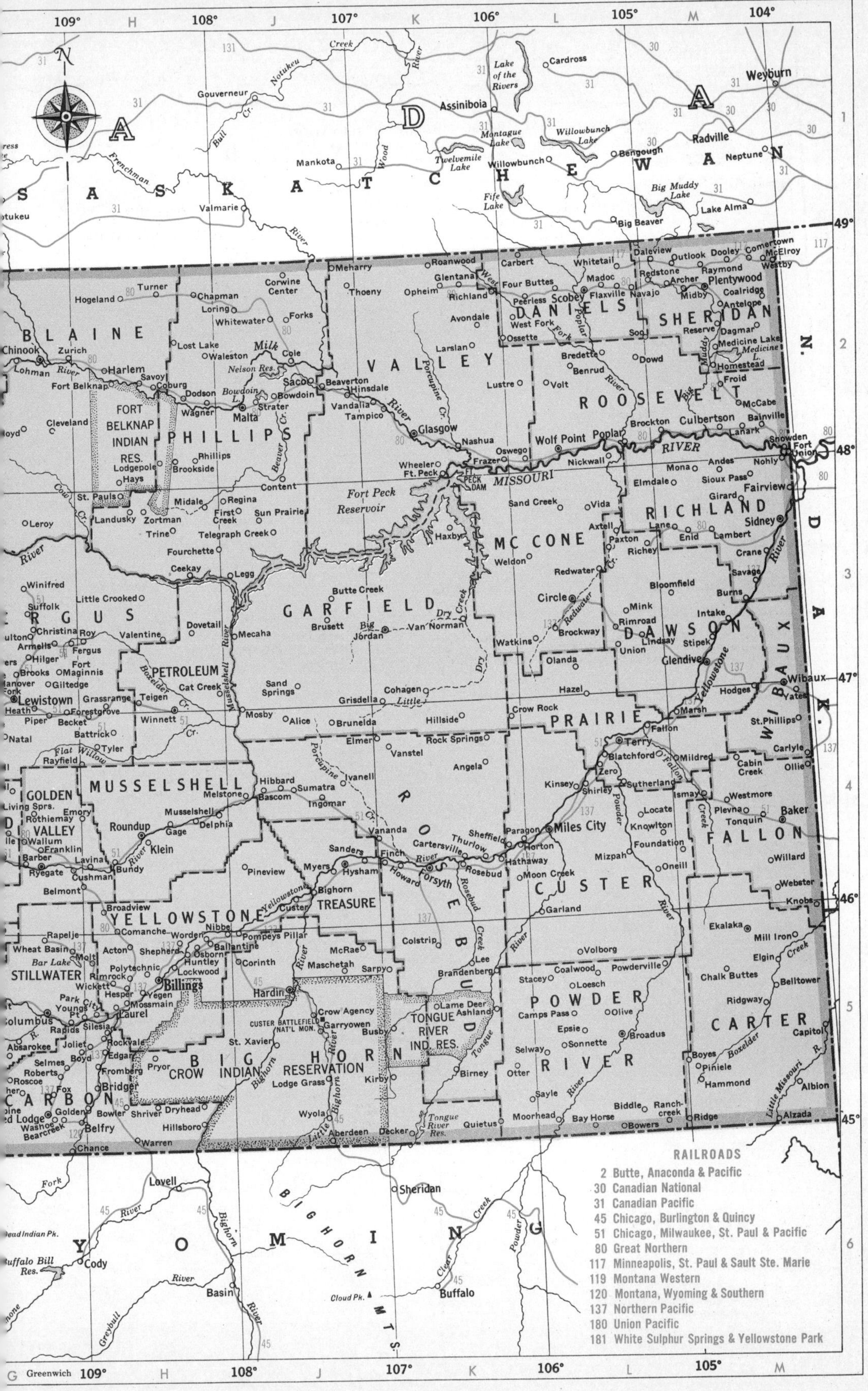

109°
H
108°
J
107°
K
106°
L
105°
M
104°
SASKATCHEWAN
N. DAK.
WYOMING
49°
48°
47°
46°
45°
1
2
3
4
5
6
Gouverneur
Notukeu
Creek
Lake of the Rivers
Cardross
Weyburn
Assiniboia
Mankota
Wood
Montague Lake
Willowbunch Lake
Twelvemile Lake
Willowbunch
Bengough
Radville
Neptune
Frenchman
Valmarie
Fife Lake
Big Muddy Lake
Lake Alma
Big Beaver
Bull Cr.
BLAINE
PHILLIPS
VALLEY
DANIELS
SHERIDAN
ROOSEVELT
RICHLAND
MC CONE
GARFIELD
DAWSON
PRAIRIE
WIBAUX
FERGUS
PETROLEUM
GOLDEN VALLEY
MUSSELSHELL
ROSEBUD
CUSTER
FALLON
TREASURE
YELLOWSTONE
STILLWATER
CARBON
BIG HORN
POWDER RIVER
CARTER
FORT BELKNAP INDIAN RES.
CROW INDIAN RESERVATION
TONGUE RIVER IND. RES.
CUSTER BATTLEFIELD NAT'L MON.
Fort Peck Reservoir
PECK DAM
MISSOURI RIVER
Milk River
Yellowstone
Chinook
Zurich
Harlem
Fort Belknap
Savoy
Coburg
Dodson
Malta
Saco
Hinsdale
Glasgow
Nashua
Wolf Point
Poplar
Culbertson
Bainville
Snowden
Fort Union
Plentywood
Scobey
Sidney
Fairview
Circle
Glendive
Wibaux
Terry
Miles City
Forsyth
Hysham
Roundup
Lewistown
Winnett
Jordan
Billings
Laurel
Hardin
Columbus
Red Lodge
Bridger
Broadus
Ekalaka
Baker
Sheridan
Lovell
Cody
Basin
Buffalo
Cloud Pk.
BIGHORN MTS.
RAILROADS
2 Butte, Anaconda & Pacific
30 Canadian National
31 Canadian Pacific
45 Chicago, Burlington & Quincy
51 Chicago, Milwaukee, St. Paul & Pacific
80 Great Northern
117 Minneapolis, St. Paul & Sault Ste. Marie
119 Montana Western
120 Montana, Wyoming & Southern
137 Northern Pacific
180 Union Pacific
181 White Sulphur Springs & Yellowstone Park
G
Greenwich 109°
H
108°
J
107°
K
106°
L
105°
M

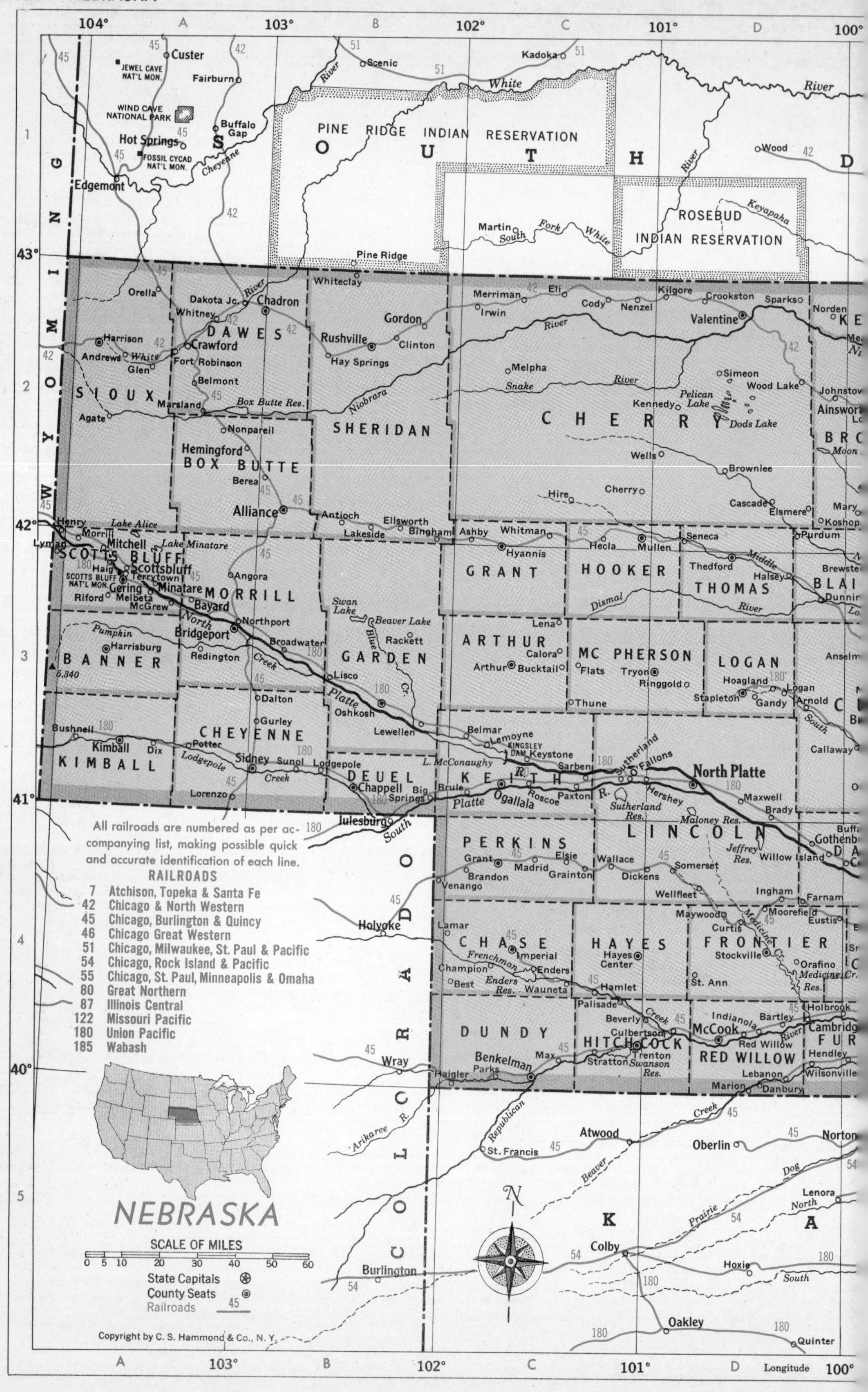
104°
103°
102°
101°
100°
A
B
C
D
43°
42°
41°
40°
1
2
3
4
5
PINE RIDGE INDIAN RESERVATION
ROSEBUD INDIAN RESERVATION
S O U T H D
W Y O M I N G
C O L O R A D O
K A
JEWEL CAVE NAT'L MON.
WIND CAVE NATIONAL PARK
FOSSIL CYCAD NAT'L MON.
SCOTTS BLUFF NAT'L MON.
Custer
Fairburn
Buffalo Gap
Hot Springs
Edgemont
Scenic
Kadoka
Martin
Pine Ridge
Wood
White River
Cheyenne
Keyapaha
South Fork White
SIOUX
DAWES
SHERIDAN
CHERRY
BOX BUTTE
SCOTTS BLUFF
MORRILL
GARDEN
GRANT
HOOKER
THOMAS
ARTHUR
MC PHERSON
LOGAN
BANNER
KIMBALL
CHEYENNE
DEUEL
KEITH
LINCOLN
PERKINS
CHASE
HAYES
FRONTIER
DUNDY
HITCHCOCK
RED WILLOW
Harrison
Andrews
Glen
Agate
Orella
Whitney
Dakota Jc.
Chadron
Crawford
Fort Robinson
Belmont
Marsland
Box Butte Res.
Whiteclay
Rushville
Hay Springs
Gordon
Clinton
Niobrara
Merriman
Irwin
Eli
Cody
Nenzel
Kilgore
Crookston
Sparks
Valentine
Norden
Melpha
Snake
Simeon
Wood Lake
Kennedy
Pelican Lake
Dods Lake
Wells
Brownlee
Hire
Cherry
Cascade
Elsmere
Johnstown
Ainsworth
Mary
Koshop
Nonpareil
Hemingford
Berea
Alliance
Antioch
Lakeside
Ellsworth
Bingham
Ashby
Whitman
Hyannis
Hecla
Mullen
Seneca
Thedford
Halsey
Middle
Dismal
Purdum
Brewster
Dunning
Henry
Lyman
Morrill
Lake Alice
Mitchell
Lake Minatare
Haig
Scottsbluff
Terrytown
Gering
Minatare
Melbeta
McGrew
Riford
Bayard
Angora
Northport
Bridgeport
North Platte
Pumpkin
Harrisburg
Redington
Broadwater
Swan Lake
Beaver Lake
Rackett
Blue Cr.
Lena
Calora
Arthur
Bucktail
Flats
Tryon
Ringgold
Hoagland
Stapleton
Logan
Gandy
Arnold
Anselmo
Callaway
5,340
Lisco
Oshkosh
Lewellen
Dalton
Gurley
Thune
Belmar
Lemoyne
KINGSLEY DAM
Keystone
L. McConaughy
Sarben
Sutherland
Fallons
North Platte
Maxwell
Brady
Gothenburg
Bushnell
Kimball
Dix
Potter
Sidney
Sunol
Lodgepole
Lodgepole Creek
Lorenzo
Chappell
Big Springs
Brule
Ogallala
Roscoe
Paxton
Hershey
Sutherland Res.
Maloney Res.
Jeffrey Res.
Willow Island
Julesburg
South Platte R.
Grant
Brandon
Madrid
Elsie
Grainton
Venango
Wallace
Dickens
Somerset
Wellfleet
Ingham
Farnam
Maywood
Moorefield
Eustis
Curtis
Medicine Cr.
Holyoke
Lamar
Imperial
Frenchman
Champion
Enders
Enders Res.
Best
Wauneta
Hayes Center
Hamlet
Stockville
Orafino
St. Ann
Palisade
Beverly
Culbertson
McCook
Indianola
Bartley
Holbrook
Cambridge
Red Willow
Trenton
Stratton
Swanson Res.
Max
Benkelman
Parks
Haigler
Wray
Hendley
Lebanon
Wilsonville
Marion
Danbury
Republican
Arikaree R.
St. Francis
Atwood
Beaver
Oberlin
Norton
Lenora
Dog
North
Prairie
Colby
Hoxie
South
Burlington
Oakley
Quinter
All railroads are numbered as per accompanying list, making possible quick and accurate identification of each line.
RAILROADS
7 Atchison, Topeka & Santa Fe
42 Chicago & North Western
45 Chicago, Burlington & Quincy
46 Chicago Great Western
51 Chicago, Milwaukee, St. Paul & Pacific
54 Chicago, Rock Island & Pacific
55 Chicago, St. Paul, Minneapolis & Omaha
80 Great Northern
87 Illinois Central
122 Missouri Pacific
180 Union Pacific
185 Wabash
NEBRASKA
SCALE OF MILES
0 5 10 20 30 40 50 60
State Capitals
County Seats
Railroads 45
N
Longitude

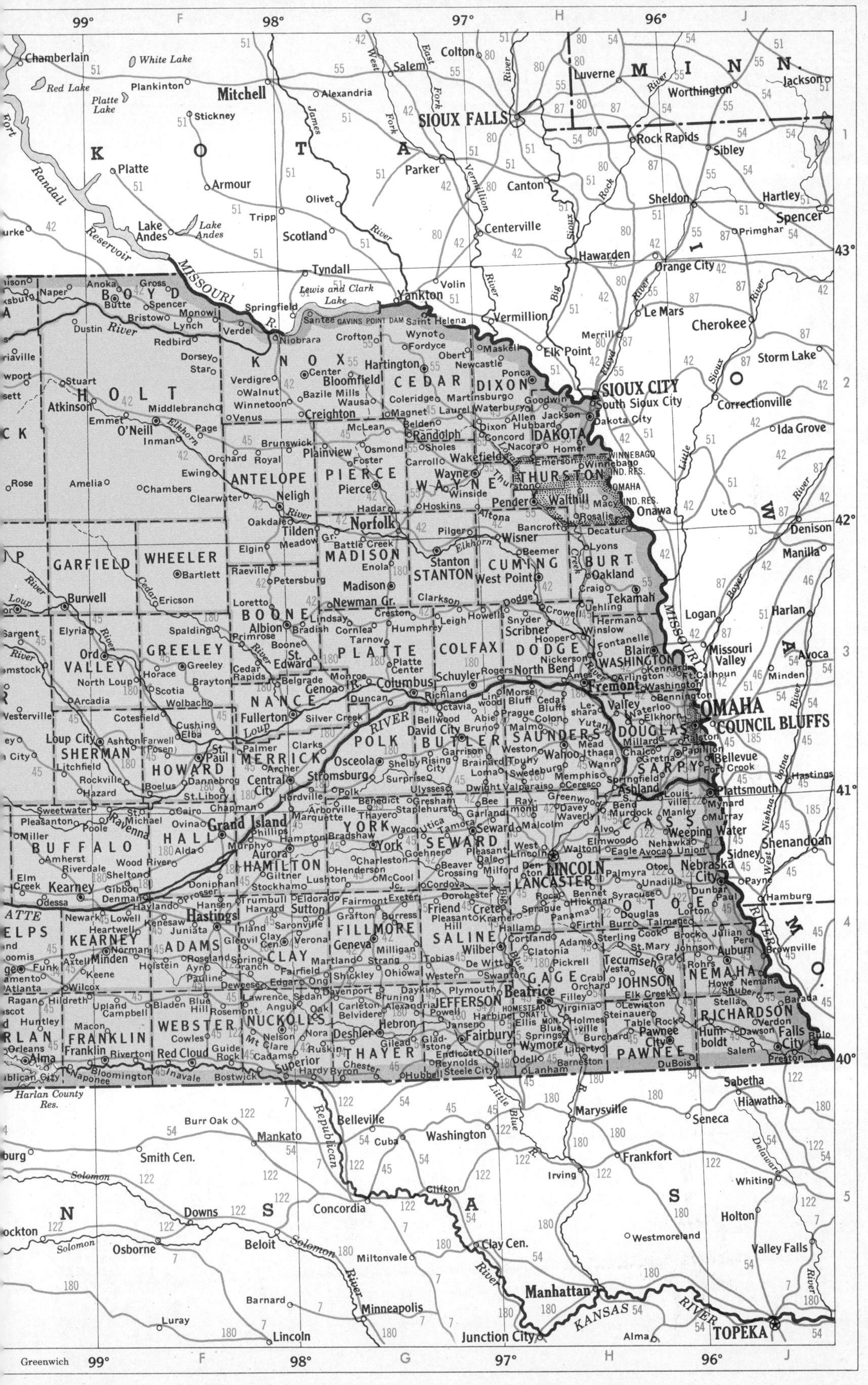

99°
F
98°
G
97°
H
96°
J
43°
42°
41°
40°
1
2
3
4
5
Greenwich
K O T A
M I N N.
I O W A
MO.
N S A S
SIOUX FALLS
Mitchell
Chamberlain
White Lake
Plankinton
Alexandria
Salem
Colton
Luverne
Worthington
Jackson
Stickney
Platte
Armour
Parker
Canton
Rock Rapids
Sibley
Sheldon
Hartley
Spencer
Primghar
Olivet
Tripp
Lake Andes
Scotland
Centerville
Hawarden
Orange City
Tyndall
Lewis and Clark Lake
Yankton
Volin
Vermillion
Le Mars
Cherokee
Storm Lake
Springfield
GAVINS POINT DAM
Elk Point
SIOUX CITY
South Sioux City
Dakota City
Correctionville
Ida Grove
Randall Reservoir
MISSOURI
BOYD
KNOX
CEDAR
DIXON
HOLT
DAKOTA
ANTELOPE
PIERCE
WAYNE
THURSTON
WINNEBAGO IND. RES.
OMAHA IND. RES.
Onawa
Denison
GARFIELD
WHEELER
MADISON
STANTON
CUMING
BURT
BOONE
PLATTE
COLFAX
DODGE
WASHINGTON
GREELEY
VALLEY
NANCE
SHERMAN
HOWARD
MERRICK
POLK
BUTLER
SAUNDERS
DOUGLAS
SARPY
OMAHA
COUNCIL BLUFFS
BUFFALO
HALL
HAMILTON
YORK
SEWARD
LANCASTER
CASS
OTOE
KEARNEY
ADAMS
CLAY
FILLMORE
SALINE
GAGE
JOHNSON
NEMAHA
FRANKLIN
WEBSTER
NUCKOLLS
THAYER
JEFFERSON
PAWNEE
RICHARDSON
LINCOLN
Grand Island
Hastings
Kearney
Norfolk
Columbus
Fremont
Beatrice
Nebraska City
Plattsmouth
Falls City
O'Neill
Atkinson
Neligh
Madison
Wayne
Tekamah
Blair
Wahoo
Seward
York
Aurora
Central City
Fullerton
Albion
St. Paul
Ord
Burwell
Bartlett
Minden
Red Cloud
Superior
Hebron
Fairbury
Crete
Wilber
Tecumseh
Auburn
Pawnee City
Harlan County Res.
Republican
Belleville
Marysville
Sabetha
Hiawatha
Seneca
Washington
Mankato
Burr Oak
Smith Cen.
Concordia
Clifton
Frankfort
Holton
Clay Cen.
Osborne
Downs
Beloit
Minneapolis
Manhattan
Junction City
Lincoln
TOPEKA
KANSAS RIVER
Valley Falls
Westmoreland
Solomon River

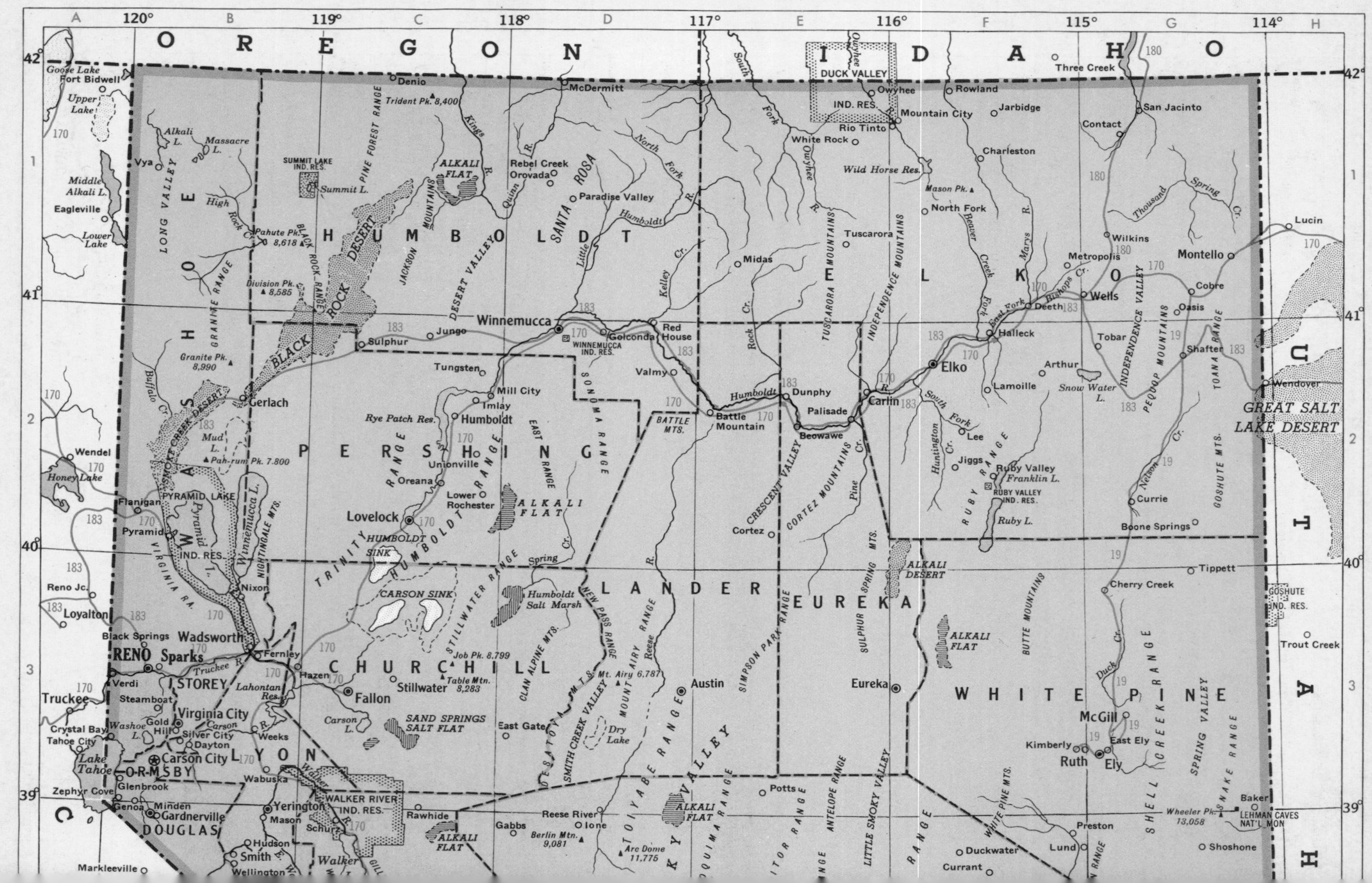
OREGON
IDAHO
UTAH
HUMBOLDT
ELKO
WHITE PINE
EUREKA
LANDER
PERSHING
WASHOE
CHURCHILL
LYON
STOREY
ORMSBY
DOUGLAS
Winnemucca
Elko
Wells
Ely
Eureka
Austin
Lovelock
Fallon
RENO
Sparks
Carson City
Virginia City
Yerington
Gerlach
McDermitt
Battle Mountain
Carlin
Ruth
McGill
GREAT SALT LAKE DESERT
BLACK ROCK DESERT
SMOKE CREEK DESERT
CARSON SINK
HUMBOLDT SINK
Pyramid L.
Winnemucca L.
Lake Tahoe
Wheeler Pk. 13,058
LEHMAN CAVES NAT'L MON.
DUCK VALLEY IND. RES.
PYRAMID LAKE IND. RES.
WALKER RIVER IND. RES.
GOSHUTE IND. RES.

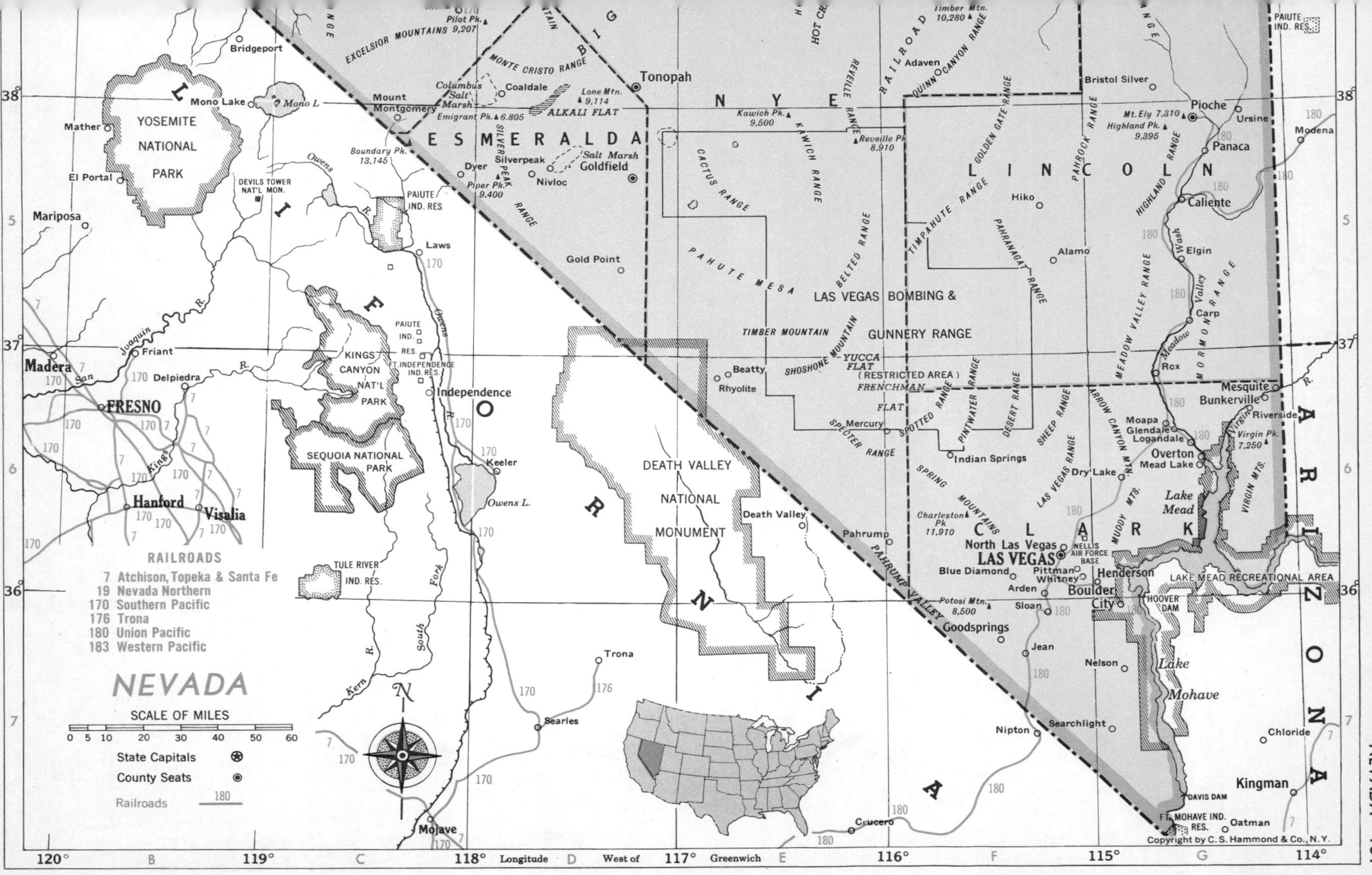
NEVADA
SCALE OF MILES
0 5 10 20 30 40 50 60
State Capitals
County Seats
Railroads
RAILROADS
7 Atchison, Topeka & Santa Fe
19 Nevada Northern
170 Southern Pacific
176 Trona
180 Union Pacific
183 Western Pacific
A R I Z O N A
C A L I F O R N I A
L I N C O L N
C L A R K
N Y E
E S M E R A L D A
LAS VEGAS BOMBING & GUNNERY RANGE
DEATH VALLEY NATIONAL MONUMENT
YOSEMITE NATIONAL PARK
KINGS CANYON NAT'L PARK
SEQUOIA NATIONAL PARK
LAKE MEAD RECREATIONAL AREA
HOOVER DAM
DAVIS DAM
Lake Mead
Lake Mohave
LAS VEGAS
North Las Vegas
Henderson
Boulder City
Tonopah
Goldfield
Pioche
Caliente
Panaca
Beatty
Rhyolite
Mesquite
Bunkerville
Overton
Kingman
FRESNO
Madera
Hanford
Visalia
Independence
Mojave
Searles
Trona
Pahrump
PAHRUMP VALLEY
SPRING MOUNTAINS
Charleston Pk. 11,910
Potosi Mtn. 8,500
Mt. Ely 7,310
Highland Pk. 9,395
Kawich Pk. 9,500
Boundary Pk. 13,145
Reveille Pk. 8,910
Lone Mtn. 9,114
Piper Pk. 9,400
Virgin Pk. 7,250
YUCCA FLAT (RESTRICTED AREA)
FRENCHMAN FLAT
TIMBER MOUNTAIN
SHOSHONE MOUNTAIN
KAWICH RANGE
CACTUS RANGE
PAHUTE MESA
BELTED RANGE
TIMPAHUTE RANGE
PAHRANAGAT RANGE
GOLDEN GATE RANGE
PAHROCK RANGE
DESERT RANGE
SHEEP RANGE
LAS VEGAS RANGE
ARROW CANYON MTN.
MUDDY MTS.
VIRGIN MTS.
MORMON RANGE
MEADOW VALLEY RANGE
HIGHLAND RANGE
SILVER PEAK RANGE
MONTE CRISTO RANGE
EXCELSIOR MOUNTAINS
ALKALI FLAT
TULE RIVER IND. RES.
PAIUTE IND. RES.
FT. MOHAVE IND. RES.
DEVILS TOWER NAT'L MON.
NELLIS AIR FORCE BASE
38° 37° 36°
120° 119° 118° 117° 116° 115° 114°
Longitude West of Greenwich
Copyright by C. S. Hammond & Co., N.Y.

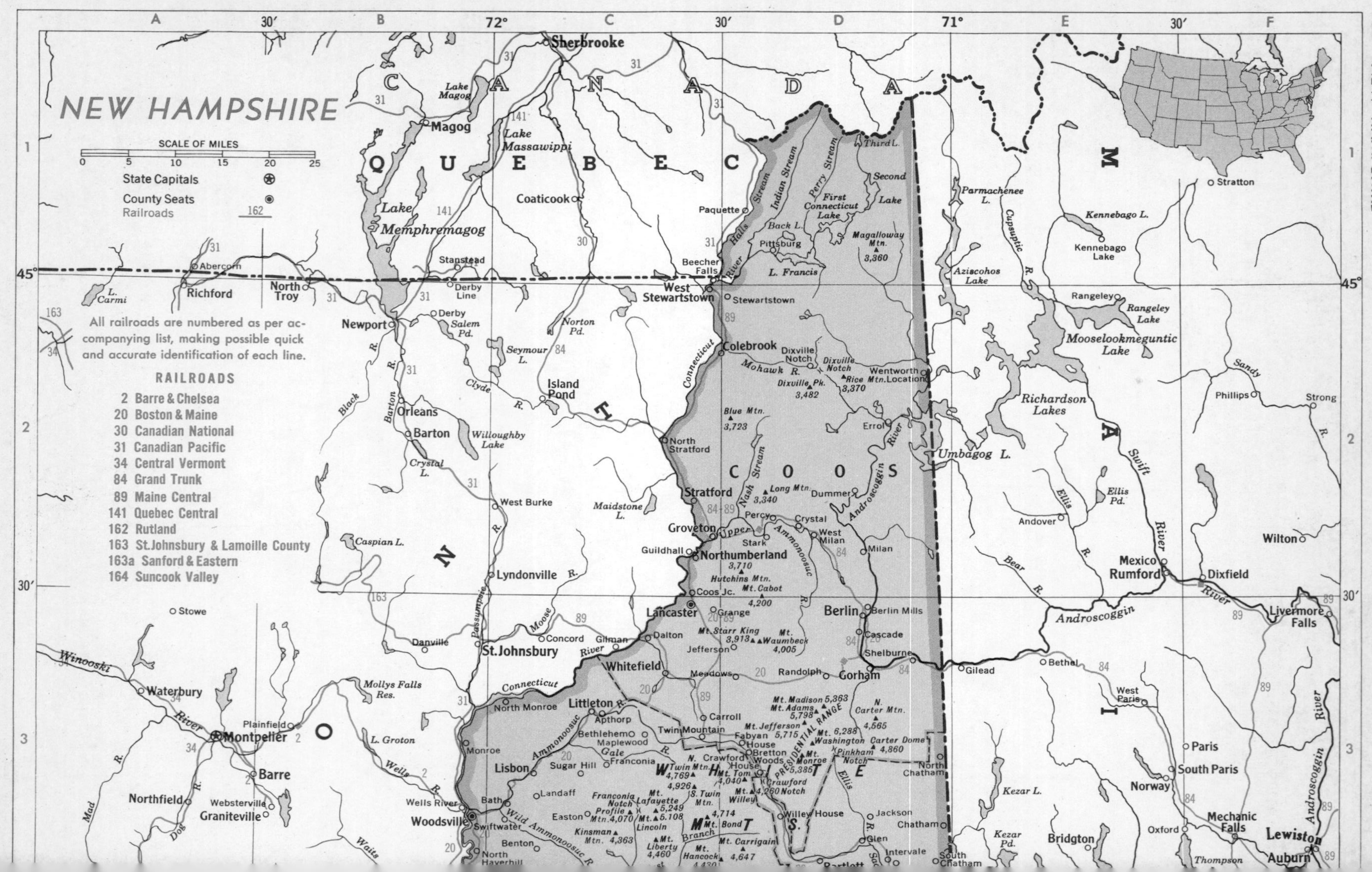
NEW HAMPSHIRE
SCALE OF MILES
0 5 10 15 20 25
State Capitals
County Seats
Railroads
162
All railroads are numbered as per accompanying list, making possible quick and accurate identification of each line.
RAILROADS
2 Barre & Chelsea
20 Boston & Maine
30 Canadian National
31 Canadian Pacific
34 Central Vermont
84 Grand Trunk
89 Maine Central
141 Quebec Central
162 Rutland
163 St.Johnsbury & Lamoille County
163a Sanford & Eastern
164 Suncook Valley
QUEBEC
CANADA
MAINE
VERMONT
COOS
WHITE MTS.

ATLANTIC OCEAN
CARROLL
BELKNAP
MERRIMACK
STRAFFORD
ROCKINGHAM
SULLIVAN
CHESHIRE
HILLSBORO
MAINE
VERMONT
MASSACHUSETTS
PORTLAND
West-brook
Yarmouth
Gorham
South Windham
Sebago Lake
Saco
Biddeford
Old Orchard Beach
Kennebunkport
Kennebunk
Sanford
Springvale
Limerick
Somersworth
Rochester
East Rochester
Dover
Portsmouth
Rye
Hampton
Exeter
Seabrook
Amesbury
Newbury-port
Haverhill
Ipswich
Gloucester
Rockport
Plum I.
ISLES OF SHOALS
Newmarket
Kingston
Derry
Londonderry
MANCHESTER
Nashua
Hudson
LAWRENCE
LOWELL
Methuen
N. Andover
Andover
Salem
Concord
Penacook
Hopkinton
Suncook
Hooksett
Pittsfield
Laconia
Lakeport
Belmont
Tilton
Franklin
Bristol
Meredith
Ashland
Plymouth
Campton
Tamworth
Ossipee
Wakefield
Wolfeboro
Alton
Farmington
Lake Winnipesaukee
Hanover
Lebanon
Canaan
Enfield
New London
Andover
Warner
Boscawen
Henniker
Hillsboro
Weare
Goffstown
Bedford
Amherst
Milford
Merrimack
Wilton
Greenville
Peterborough
Jaffrey
East Jaffrey
Keene
Marlboro
Swanzey
Hinsdale
Walpole
Charlestown
Claremont
Newport
Sunapee
White River Jc.
West Lebanon
Woodstock
Windsor
Springfield
Bellows Falls
Brattleboro
Ludlow
Chester
Winchendon
Athol
Greenfield
Shelburne Falls
Connecticut River
Copyright by C. S. Hammond & Co., N. Y.

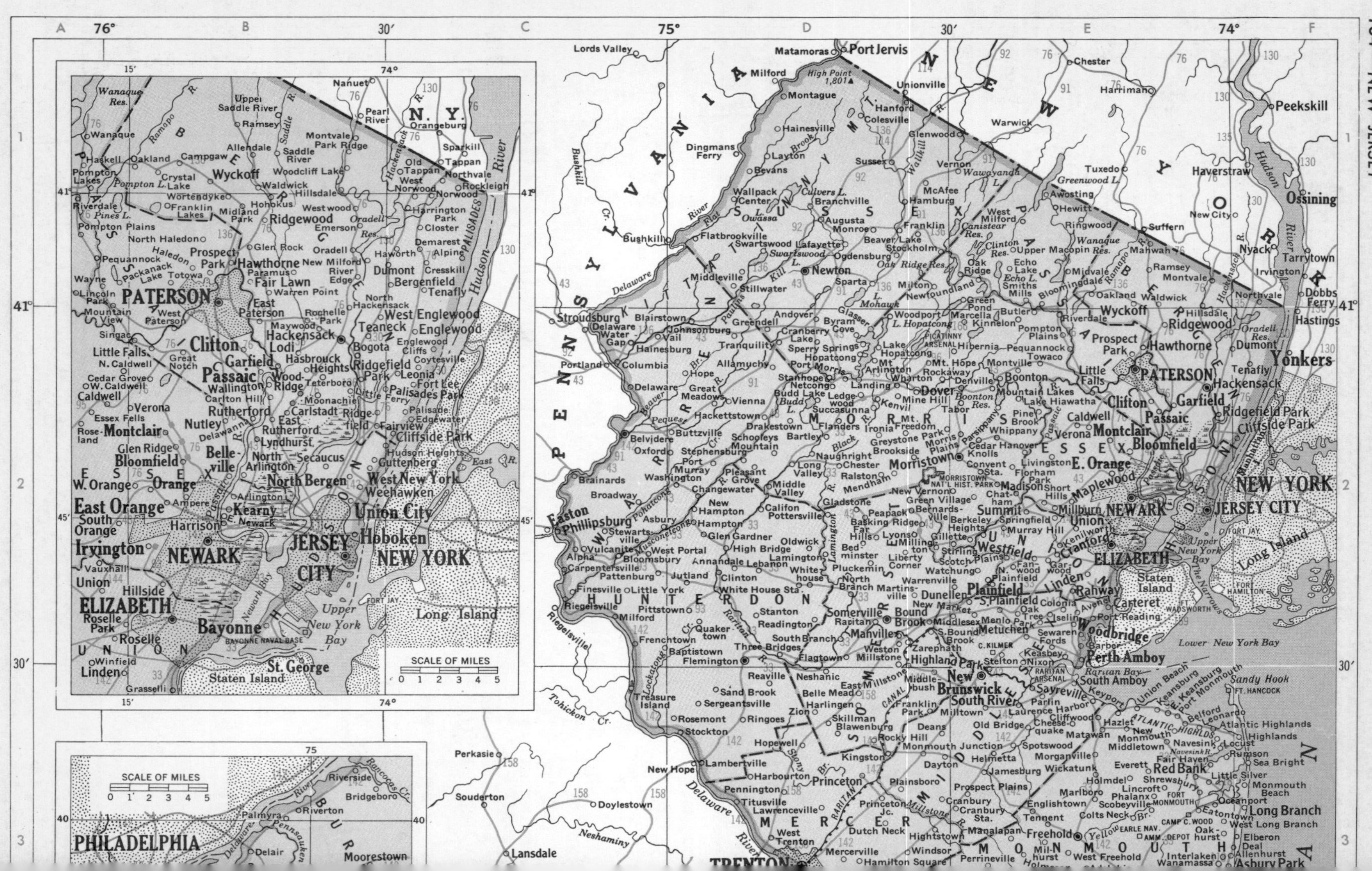

SCALE OF MILES
NEW YORK
JERSEY CITY
NEWARK
PATERSON
ELIZABETH
TRENTON
PHILADELPHIA
Yonkers
Hoboken
Bayonne
Perth Amboy
New Brunswick
Morristown
Newton
Port Jervis
Long Branch
Asbury Park
Staten Island
Long Island
Hudson River
Lower New York Bay

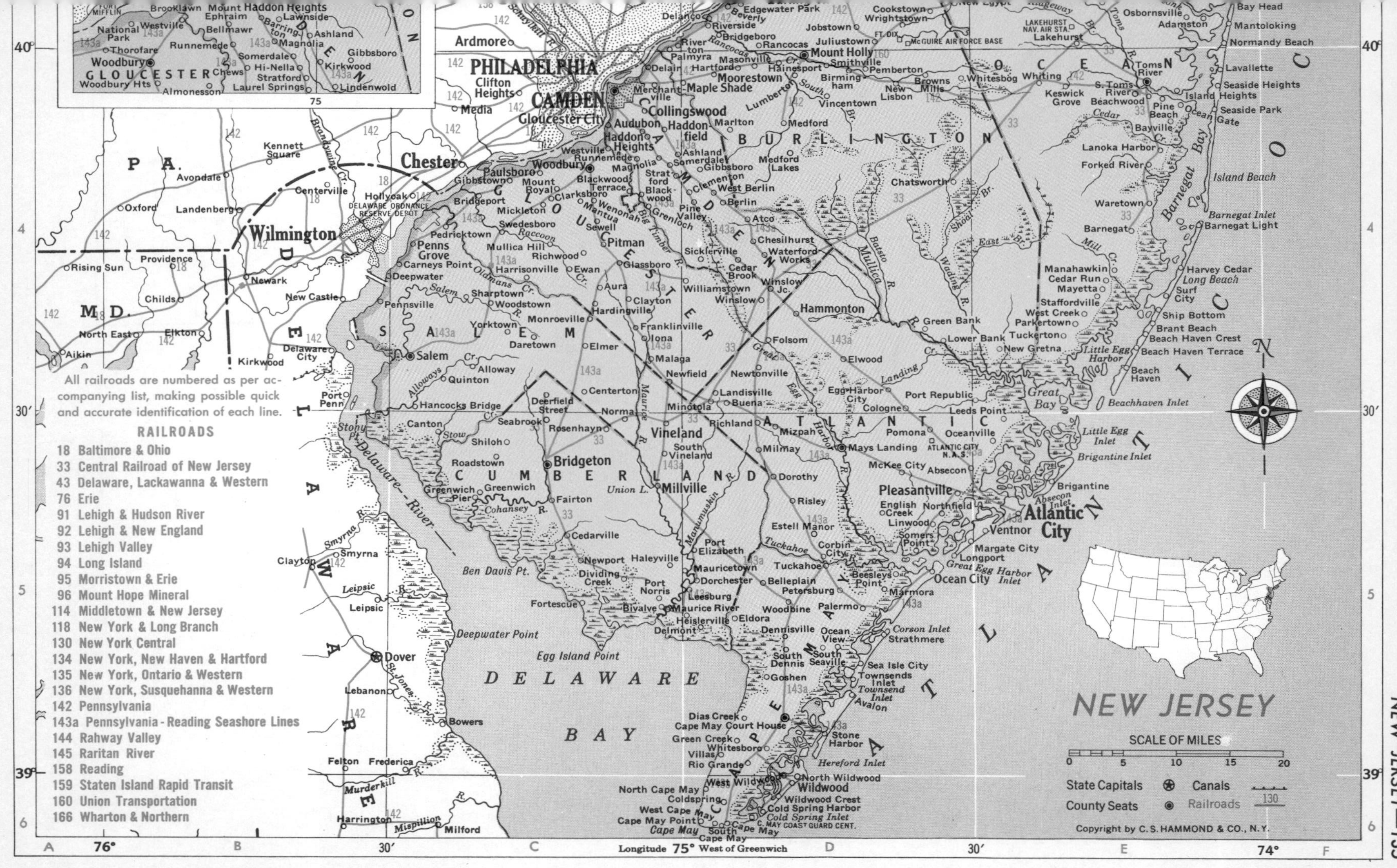

NEW JERSEY—135

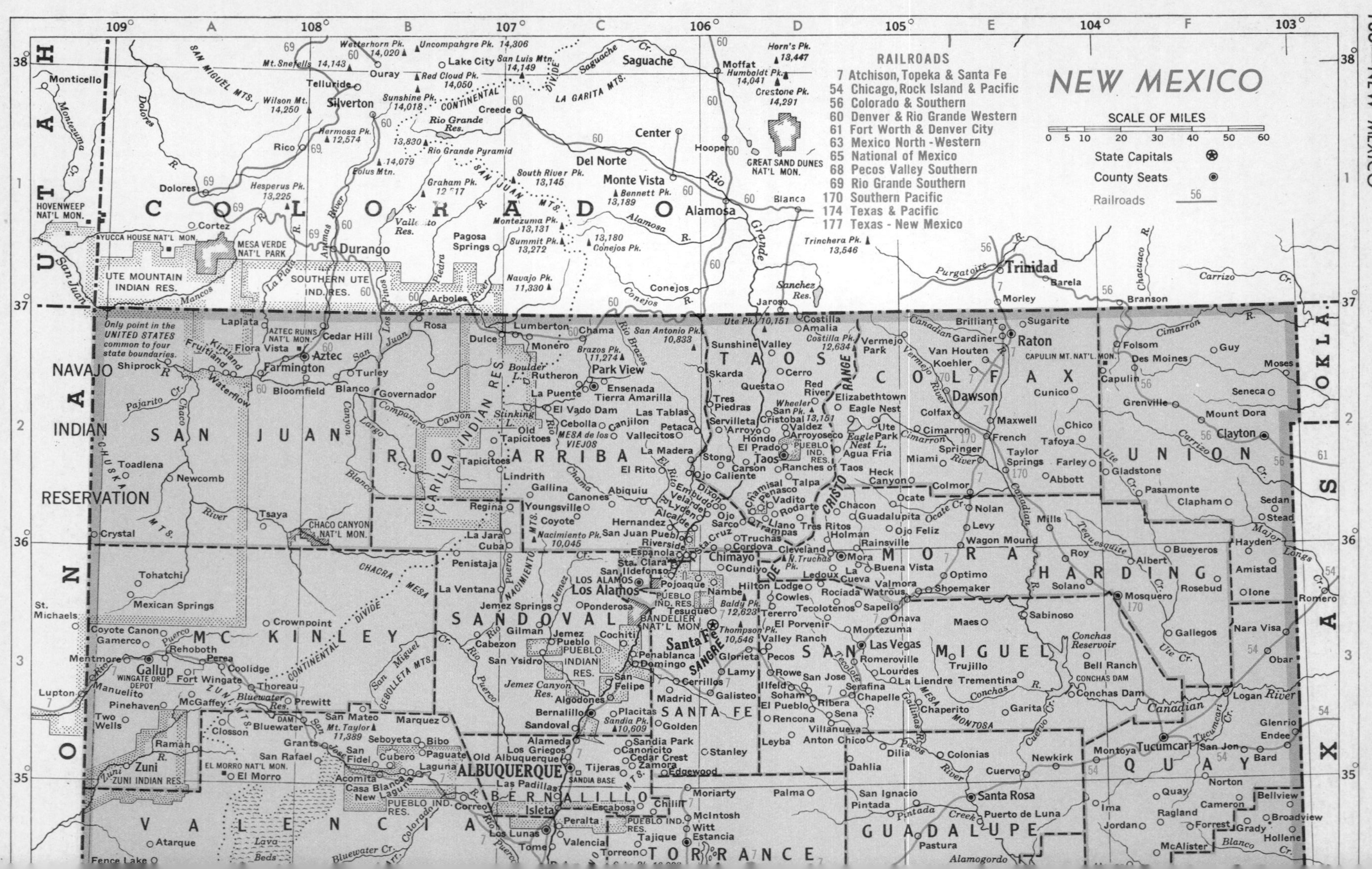
NEW MEXICO
SCALE OF MILES
0 5 10 20 30 40 50 60
State Capitals
County Seats
Railroads 56
RAILROADS
7 Atchison, Topeka & Santa Fe
54 Chicago, Rock Island & Pacific
56 Colorado & Southern
60 Denver & Rio Grande Western
61 Fort Worth & Denver City
63 Mexico North - Western
65 National of Mexico
68 Pecos Valley Southern
69 Rio Grande Southern
170 Southern Pacific
174 Texas & Pacific
177 Texas - New Mexico

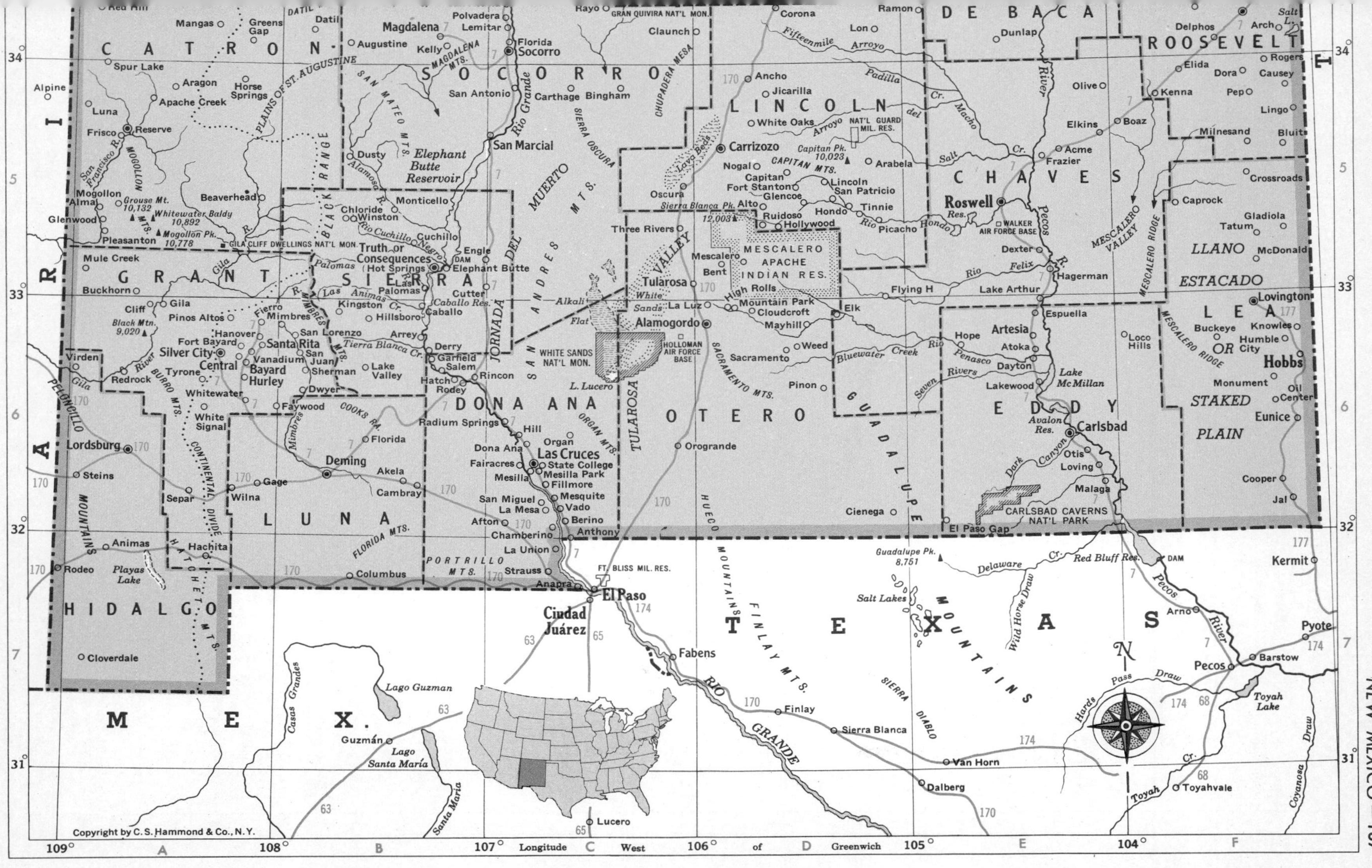
CATRON
SOCORRO
LINCOLN
CHAVES
DE BACA
ROOSEVELT
GRANT
SIERRA
DONA ANA
OTERO
EDDY
LEA
LUNA
HIDALGO
ARIZ.
TEXAS
MEX.
LLANO ESTACADO
STAKED PLAIN
GUADALUPE MOUNTAINS
SACRAMENTO MTS.
SAN ANDRES MTS.
JORNADA DEL MUERTO
TULAROSA VALLEY
WHITE SANDS NAT'L MON.
HOLLOMAN AIR FORCE BASE
MESCALERO APACHE INDIAN RES.
CARLSBAD CAVERNS NAT'L PARK
WALKER AIR FORCE BASE
FT. BLISS MIL. RES.
CONTINENTAL DIVIDE
PLAINS OF ST. AUGUSTINE
RIO GRANDE
Pecos River
Elephant Butte Reservoir
Socorro
Magdalena
Reserve
Carrizozo
Roswell
Carlsbad
Artesia
Hobbs
Lovington
Alamogordo
Tularosa
Las Cruces
Deming
Lordsburg
Silver City
Truth or Consequences
El Paso
Ciudad Juárez
Fabens
Van Horn
Pecos
Kermit
Copyright by C.S. Hammond & Co., N.Y.
Longitude West of Greenwich

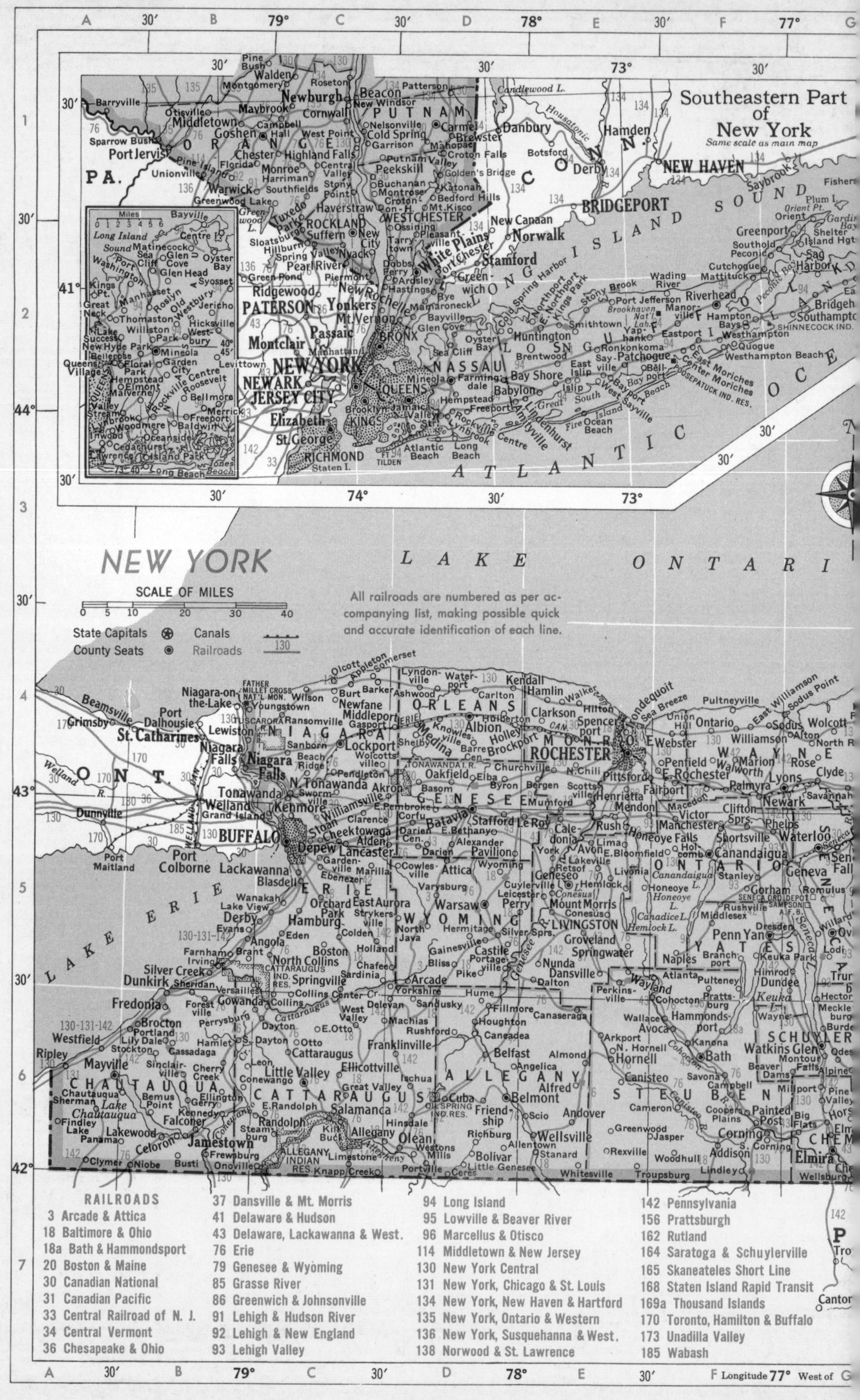
Southeastern Part of New York
Same scale as main map
NEW YORK
SCALE OF MILES
0 5 10 20 30 40
State Capitals
County Seats
Canals
Railroads
All railroads are numbered as per accompanying list, making possible quick and accurate identification of each line.
LAKE ONTARIO
LAKE ERIE
ATLANTIC OCEAN
LONG ISLAND SOUND
RAILROADS
3 Arcade & Attica
18 Baltimore & Ohio
18a Bath & Hammondsport
20 Boston & Maine
30 Canadian National
31 Canadian Pacific
33 Central Railroad of N. J.
34 Central Vermont
36 Chesapeake & Ohio
37 Dansville & Mt. Morris
41 Delaware & Hudson
43 Delaware, Lackawanna & West.
76 Erie
79 Genesee & Wyoming
85 Grasse River
86 Greenwich & Johnsonville
91 Lehigh & Hudson River
92 Lehigh & New England
93 Lehigh Valley
94 Long Island
95 Lowville & Beaver River
96 Marcellus & Otisco
114 Middletown & New Jersey
130 New York Central
131 New York, Chicago & St. Louis
134 New York, New Haven & Hartford
135 New York, Ontario & Western
136 New York, Susquehanna & West.
138 Norwood & St. Lawrence
142 Pennsylvania
156 Prattsburgh
162 Rutland
164 Saratoga & Schuylerville
165 Skaneateles Short Line
168 Staten Island Rapid Transit
169a Thousand Islands
170 Toronto, Hamilton & Buffalo
173 Unadilla Valley
185 Wabash
Longitude 77° West of G

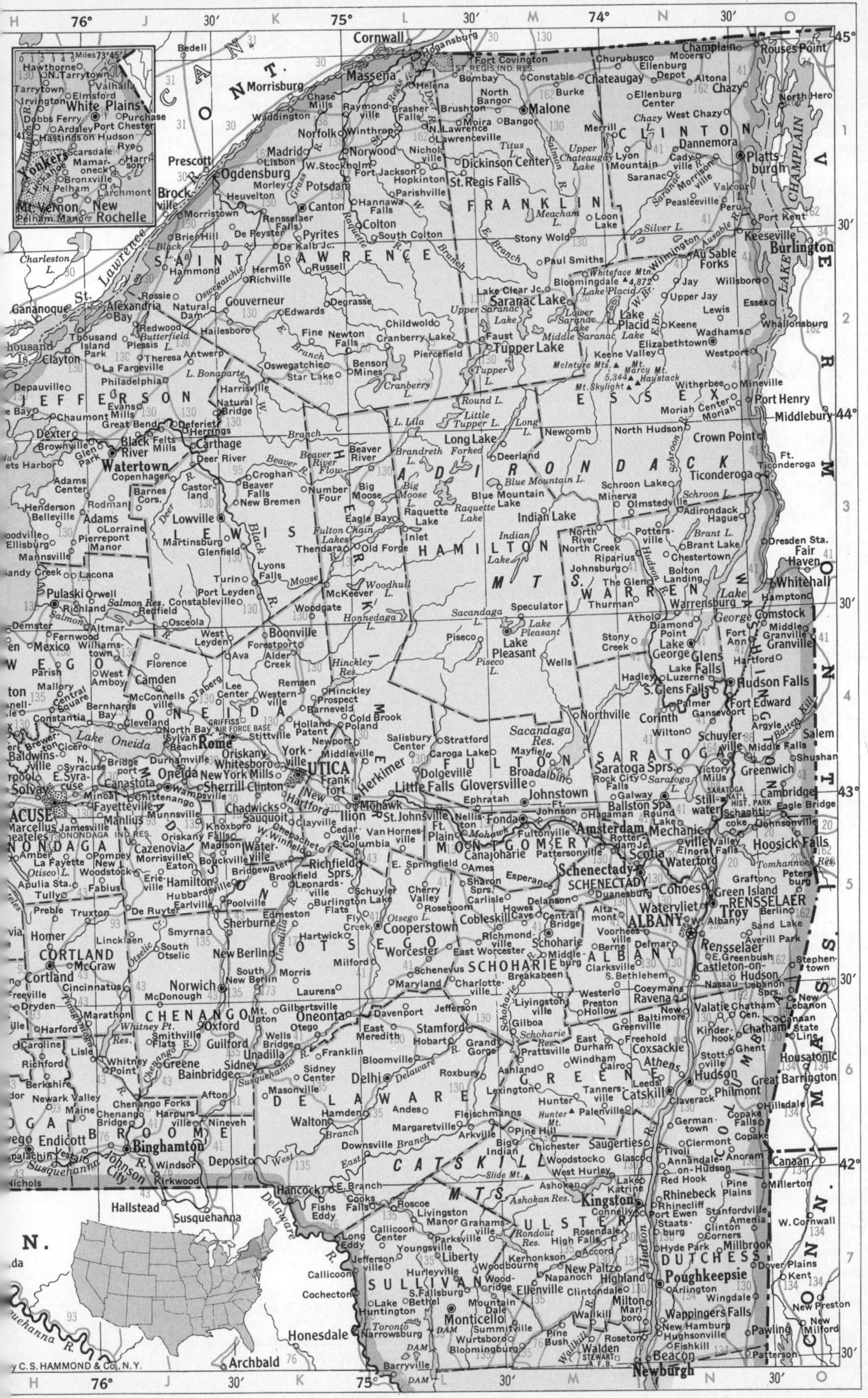

CANADA
ONT.
SAINT LAWRENCE
FRANKLIN
CLINTON
ESSEX
JEFFERSON
LEWIS
HAMILTON
HERKIMER
WARREN
ADIRONDACK MTS.
ONEIDA
MADISON
ONONDAGA
CORTLAND
CHENANGO
BROOME
OTSEGO
DELAWARE
SCHOHARIE
MONTGOMERY
FULTON
SARATOGA
SCHENECTADY
ALBANY
RENSSELAER
GREENE
COLUMBIA
ULSTER
SULLIVAN
DUTCHESS
CATSKILL MTS.
WASHINGTON
VERMONT
MASSACHUSETTS
CONN.
LAKE CHAMPLAIN
Lake Oneida
St. Lawrence
Cornwall
Massena
Ogdensburg
Malone
Plattsburgh
Burlington
Watertown
Saranac Lake
Tupper Lake
Lake Placid
Rome
UTICA
Oneida
Herkimer
Little Falls
Gloversville
Johnstown
Amsterdam
Schenectady
ALBANY
Troy
Rensselaer
Cohoes
Glens Falls
Saratoga Sprs.
Cooperstown
Oneonta
Norwich
Cortland
Binghamton
Endicott
Johnson City
Kingston
Poughkeepsie
Newburgh
Beacon
Hudson
Catskill
Monticello
Yonkers
White Plains
New Rochelle
Mt. Vernon
Whiteface Mtn. 4,872
Mt. Marcy 5,344
Slide Mt.
Hunter Mt.
76°
75°
74°
45°
44°
43°
42°
30′
H J K L M N O
1 2 3 4 5 6 7
C.S. HAMMOND & Co., N.Y.

VIRGINIA
TENN.
SOUTH CAROLINA
ALLEGHANY
ASHE
SURRY
STOKES
ROCKINGHAM
CASWELL
WATAUGA
WILKES
YADKIN
FORSYTH
GUILFORD
ALAMANCE
ORANGE
MITCHELL
AVERY
CALDWELL
ALEXANDER
IREDELL
DAVIE
DAVIDSON
RANDOLPH
CHATHAM
BURKE
MC DOWELL
CATAWBA
ROWAN
LINCOLN
CABARRUS
RUTHERFORD
CLEVELAND
GASTON
POLK
MECKLENBURG
STANLY
MONTGOMERY
MOORE
LEE
UNION
ANSON
RICHMOND
SCOTLAND
HOKE
WINSTON-SALEM
High Point
Greensboro
Charlotte
Gastonia
Spartanburg
Rock Hill
APPALACHIAN MTS.
STONE MTS.
UNAKA MTS.
BLUE RIDGE
SCALE OF MILES
0 5 10 15 20 25
GREAT SMOKY MTS.
MADISON
YANCEY
HAYWOOD
BUNCOMBE
Asheville
SWAIN
GRAHAM
CHEROKEE
CLAY
MACON
JACKSON
TRANSYLVANIA
HENDERSON
GEORGIA
WESTERN PART OF
NORTH CAROLINA
Same scale as main map.
Longitude We

NORTH CAROLINA
ATLANTIC
OCEAN
ALBEMARLE SOUND
PAMLICO SOUND
ONSLOW BAY
RALEIGH BAY
All railroads are numbered as per accompanying list, making possible quick and accurate identification of each line.
..ROADS
..en & Rockfish
..der
.. & Danville
..ic & East Carolina
.. & Western
.. Coast Line
..rt Morehead
..ountain
..ear
.. & Northwestern
.. Southern
27 Charleston & Western Carolina
28 Cliffside
66 Clinchfield
69 Durham & Southern
71 East Carolina
72 East Tennessee & Western North Carolina
75 Graham County
78 High Point, Thomasville & Denton
81 Laurinburg & Southern
82 Lawndale Ry. & Industrial Co.
107 Louisville & Nashville
133 Norfolk & Western
135 Norfolk Southern
150 Piedmont & Northern
163 Rockingham
164 Seaboard Air Line
168 Southern
172 Tallulah Falls
177 Virginia & Carolina Southern
178 Warrenton
182 Winston-Salem Southbound
SCALE OF MILES
0 10 20 30 40 50
State Capitals
County Seats
Canals
Railroads
Copyright by C. S. Hammond & Co., N. Y.

SASKATCHEWAN
MANITOBA
MONTANA
SOUTH DAKOTA
DIVIDE
BURKE
RENVILLE
BOTTINEAU
WILLIAMS
MOUNTRAIL
WARD
MCHENRY
MC KENZIE
MC LEAN
SHERIDAN
DUNN
MERCER
OLIVER
GOLDEN VALLEY
BILLINGS
STARK
MORTON
BURLEIGH
SLOPE
HETTINGER
GRANT
SIOUX
BOWMAN
ADAMS
FORT BERTHOLD INDIAN RESERVATION
STANDING ROCK INDIAN RESERVATION
Garrison Reservoir
GARRISON DAM
THEODORE ROOSEVELT NAT'L MEM. PARK (NORTH UNIT)
THEODORE ROOSEVELT NAT'L MEM. PARK (ELKHORN RANCH SITE)
THEODORE ROOSEVELT NAT'L MEM. PARK (SOUTH UNIT)
Missouri River
Bismarck
Minot
Williston
Dickinson
Mandan
Estevan
Black Butte 3,468
104°
103°
102°
101°
49°
48°
47°
46°

NORTH DAKOTA
SCALE OF MILES
0 10 20 30
State Capitals
County Seats
Railroads 117
All railroads are numbered as per accompanying list, making possible quick and accurate identification of each line.
RAILROADS
30 Canadian National
31 Canadian Pacific
42 Chicago and North Western
51 Chicago, Milwaukee, St. Paul and Pacific
80 Great Northern
81 Midland Continental
113 Minneapolis & St. Louis
117 Minneapolis, St. Paul & Sault Ste. Marie
137 Northern Pacific
MANITOBA
MINNESOTA
SOUTH DAKOTA
CAVALIER
PEMBINA
TOWNER
ROLETTE
RAMSEY
WALSH
BENSON
NELSON
GRAND FORKS
EDDY
WELLS
FOSTER
GRIGGS
STEELE
TRAILL
STUTSMAN
BARNES
CASS
KIDDER
LOGAN
LA MOURE
RANSOM
RICHLAND
McINTOSH
DICKEY
SARGENT
Langdon
Cando
Devils Lake
Grafton
Grand Forks
New Rockford
Carrington
Cooperstown
Finley
Hillsboro
Jamestown
Valley City
Fargo
Moorhead
Napoleon
La Moure
Lisbon
Wahpeton
Ashley
Ellendale
Forman
Rugby
Bisbee
Lakota
Red River
Sheyenne River
James River
Copyright by C. S. Hammond & Co., N. Y.
100° of Greenwich 99° 98° 97°

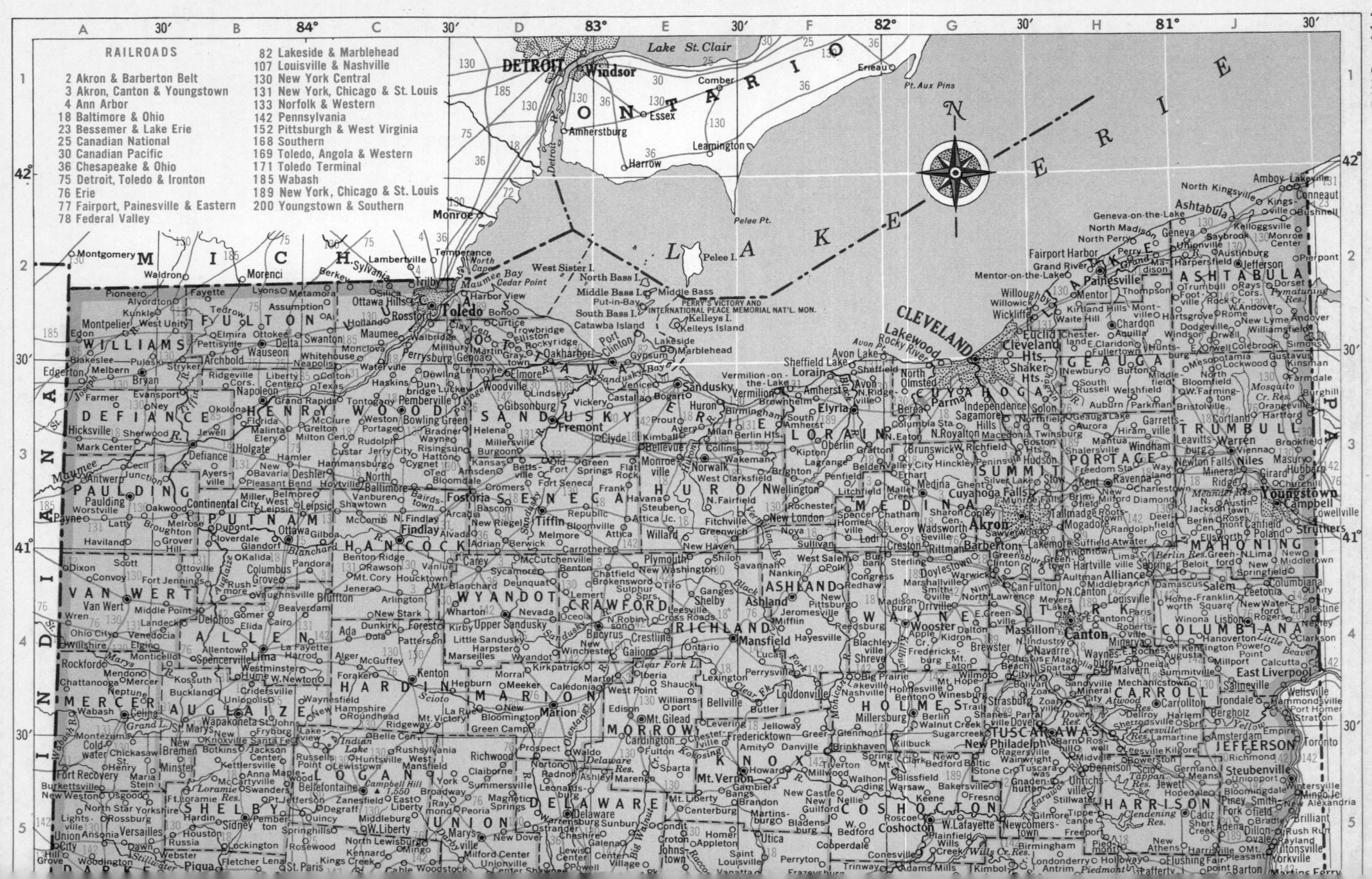
RAILROADS
2 Akron & Barberton Belt
3 Akron, Canton & Youngstown
4 Ann Arbor
18 Baltimore & Ohio
23 Bessemer & Lake Erie
25 Canadian National
30 Canadian Pacific
36 Chesapeake & Ohio
75 Detroit, Toledo & Ironton
76 Erie
77 Fairport, Painesville & Eastern
78 Federal Valley
82 Lakeside & Marblehead
107 Louisville & Nashville
130 New York Central
131 New York, Chicago & St. Louis
133 Norfolk & Western
142 Pennsylvania
152 Pittsburgh & West Virginia
168 Southern
169 Toledo, Angola & Western
171 Toledo Terminal
185 Wabash
189 New York, Chicago & St. Louis
200 Youngstown & Southern
LAKE ERIE
ONTARIO
MICHIGAN
INDIANA
PA
Lake St. Clair
DETROIT
Windsor
CLEVELAND
Toledo
Akron
Canton
Youngstown
Sandusky
Mansfield
PERRY'S VICTORY AND INTERNATIONAL PEACE MEMORIAL NAT'L. MON.

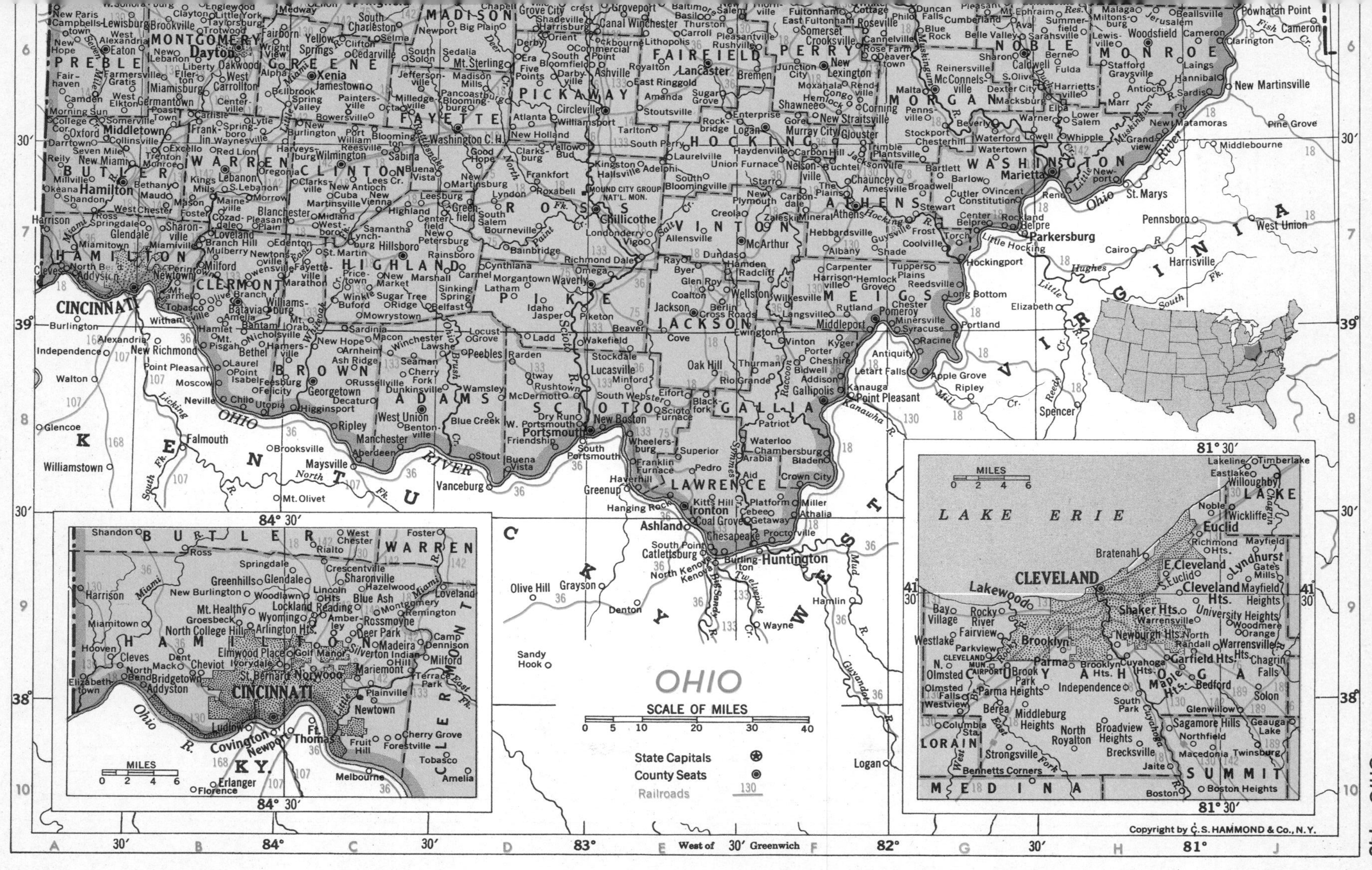
OHIO
SCALE OF MILES
0 5 10 20 30 40
State Capitals
County Seats
Railroads
LAKE ERIE
CLEVELAND
CINCINNATI
MILES
0 2 4 6
West of 30′ Greenwich
KENTUCKY
WEST VIRGINIA
Copyright by C. S. HAMMOND & Co., N.Y.

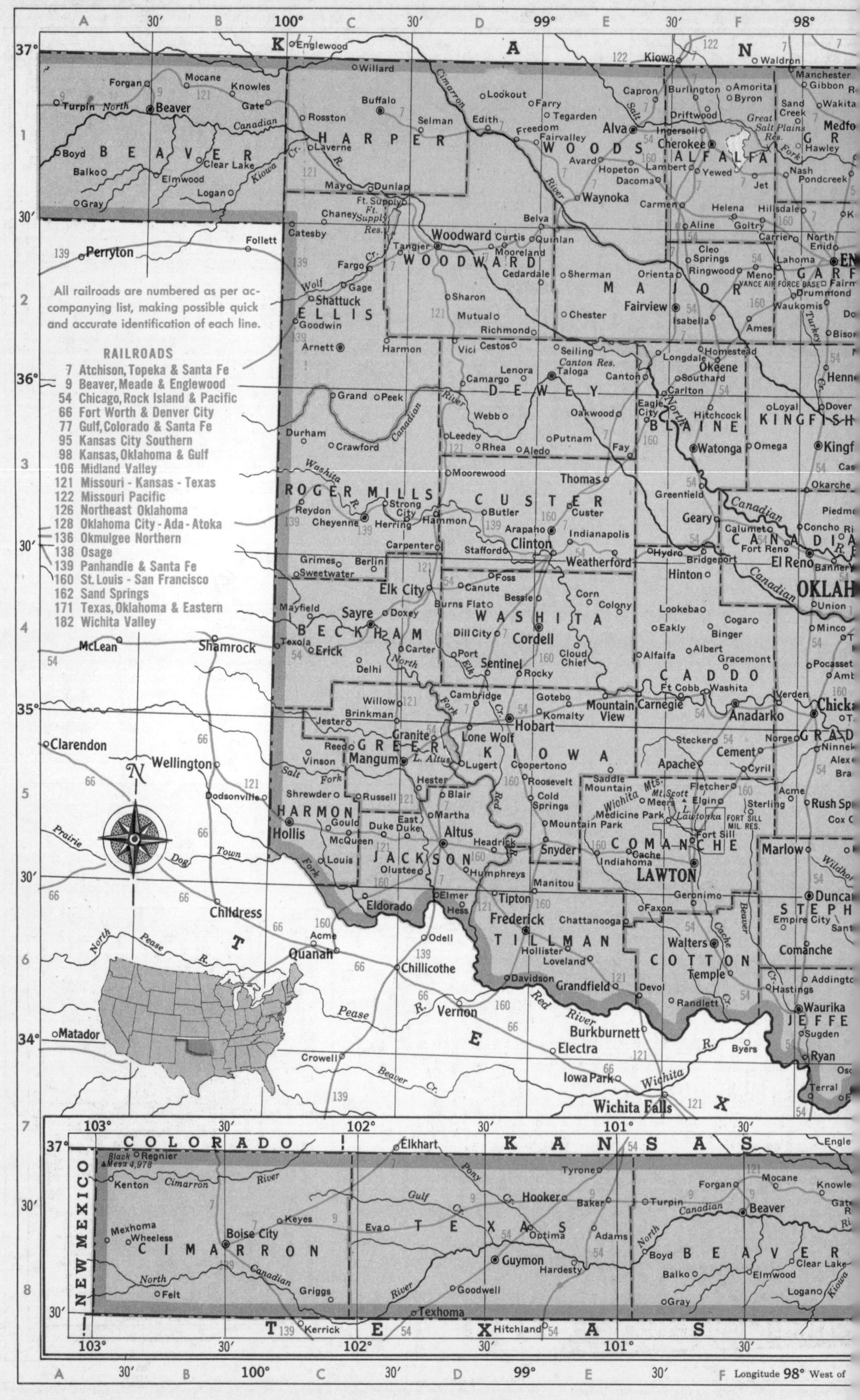
All railroads are numbered as per accompanying list, making possible quick and accurate identification of each line.
RAILROADS
7 Atchison, Topeka & Santa Fe
9 Beaver, Meade & Englewood
54 Chicago, Rock Island & Pacific
66 Fort Worth & Denver City
77 Gulf, Colorado & Santa Fe
95 Kansas City Southern
98 Kansas, Oklahoma & Gulf
106 Midland Valley
121 Missouri - Kansas - Texas
122 Missouri Pacific
126 Northeast Oklahoma
128 Oklahoma City - Ada - Atoka
136 Okmulgee Northern
138 Osage
139 Panhandle & Santa Fe
160 St. Louis - San Francisco
162 Sand Springs
171 Texas, Oklahoma & Eastern
182 Wichita Valley
K A N S A S
T E X A S
BEAVER
HARPER
WOODS
ALFALFA
WOODWARD
MAJOR
ELLIS
DEWEY
BLAINE
ROGER MILLS
CUSTER
CANADIAN
BECKHAM
WASHITA
CADDO
GREER
KIOWA
HARMON
JACKSON
COMANCHE
TILLMAN
COTTON
JEFFERSON
CIMARRON
TEXAS
COLORADO
NEW MEXICO
Beaver
Woodward
Alva
Cherokee
Fairview
Watonga
Taloga
Arnett
Cheyenne
Arapaho
Clinton
Weatherford
Sayre
Elk City
Cordell
Hobart
Mangum
Hollis
Altus
Frederick
LAWTON
Anadarko
Chickasha
El Reno
Duncan
Waurika
Walters
Boise City
Guymon
Perryton
Shamrock
Childress
Quanah
Vernon
Wichita Falls
Longitude 98° West of

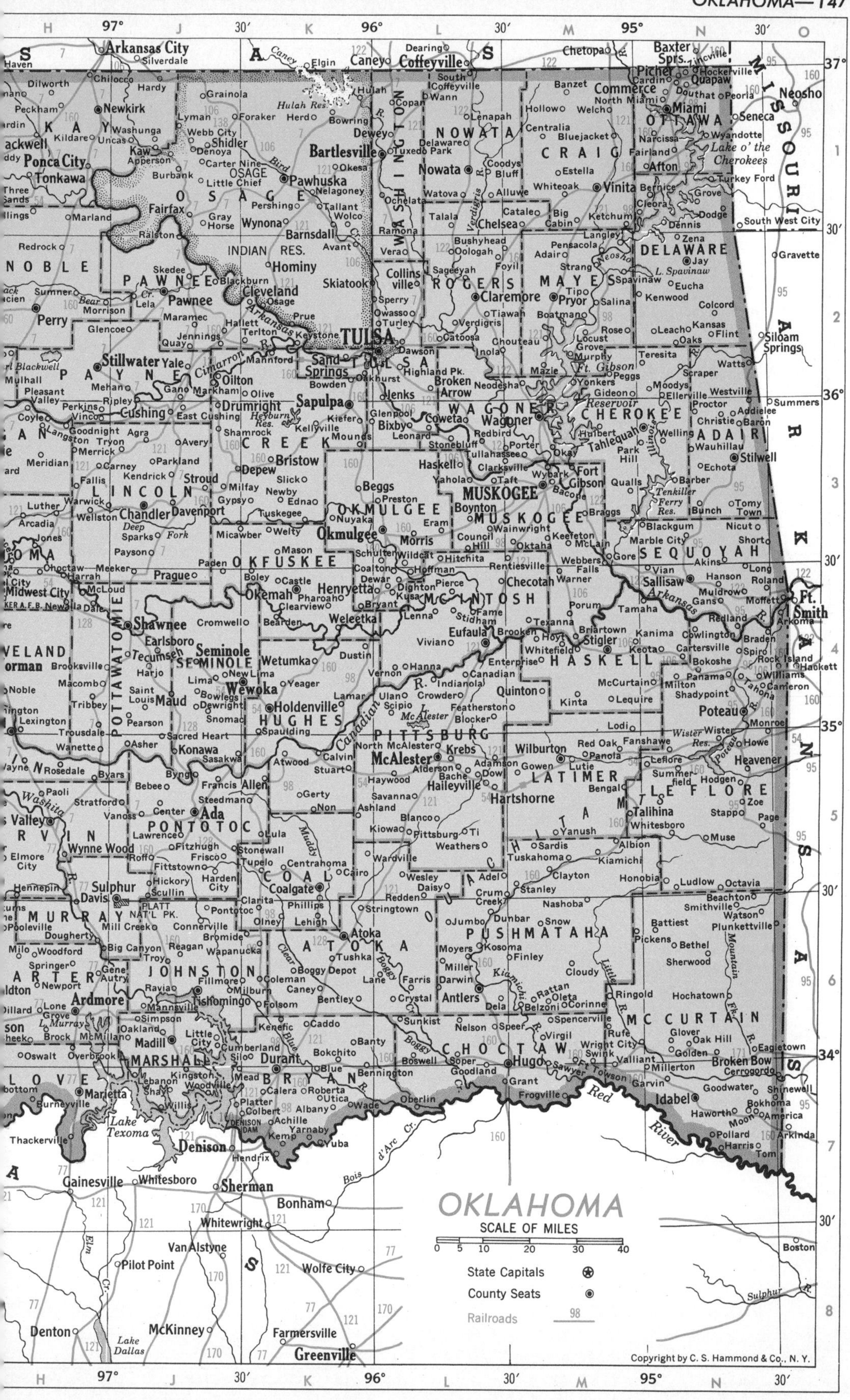
OKLAHOMA
SCALE OF MILES
0 5 10 20 30 40
State Capitals
County Seats
Railroads
Copyright by C. S. Hammond & Co., N. Y.
H
97°
J
30′
K
96°
L
M
95°
N
O
37°
36°
35°
34°
1
2
3
4
5
6
7
8
KAY
OSAGE
NOBLE
PAWNEE
PAYNE
CREEK
LINCOLN
OKFUSKEE
OKMULGEE
TULSA
WASHINGTON
NOWATA
CRAIG
OTTAWA
DELAWARE
ROGERS
MAYES
WAGONER
CHEROKEE
ADAIR
MUSKOGEE
SEQUOYAH
McINTOSH
HASKELL
LE FLORE
LATIMER
PITTSBURG
HUGHES
SEMINOLE
POTTAWATOMIE
PONTOTOC
COAL
ATOKA
PUSHMATAHA
McCURTAIN
CHOCTAW
BRYAN
JOHNSTON
MARSHALL
MURRAY
LOVE
OSAGE INDIAN RES.
MISSOURI
ARKANSAS
Arkansas City
Silverdale
Caney
Coffeyville
Dearing
Elgin
Chetopa
Baxter Sprs.
Picher
Cardin
Quapaw
Hockerville
Zincville
Commerce
North Miami
Miami
Peoria
Douthat
Neosho
Seneca
Wyandotte
Narcissa
Fairland
Afton
Lake o' the Cherokees
Turkey Ford
Grove
Bernice
Cleora
Dodge
Dennis
South West City
Gravette
Jay
L. Spavinaw
Eucha
Kenwood
Colcord
Kansas
Flint
Siloam Springs
Zena
Newkirk
Chilocco
Hardy
Dilworth
Peckham
Kildare
Uncas
Washunga
Kaw
Ponca City
Apperson
Tonkawa
Three Sands
Marland
Burbank
Fairfax
Ralston
Grainola
Foraker
Lyman
Webb City
Shidler
Denoya
Carter Nine
Little Chief
Pawhuska
Hulah Res.
Hulah
Herd
Bowring
Dewey
Bartlesville
Okesa
Nelagoney
Pershing
Tallant
Wolco
Gray Horse
Wynona
Barnsdall
Avant
Hominy
Skiatook
Bird
Copan
Wann
South Coffeyville
Lenapah
Delaware
Tuxedo Park
Nowata
Coodys Bluff
Alluwe
Watova
Ochelata
Ramona
Vera
Talala
Chelsea
Cataleo
Big Cabin
Ketchum
Vinita
Bluejacket
Welch
Hollow
Banzet
Centralia
Estella
Whiteoak
Langley
Pensacola
Adair
Strang
Spavinaw
Salina
Tipo
Pryor
Bushyhead
Oologah
Foyil
Sageeyah
Collinsville
Claremore
Sperry
Owasso
Turley
Tiawah
Verdigris
Catoosa
Chouteau
Inola
Boatman
Rose
Locust Grove
Murphy
Leach
Oaks
Teresita
Watts
Mazie
Ft. Gibson
Peggs
Yonkers
Gideon
Moodys
Ellerville
Westville
Proctor
Summers
Addielee
Baron
Christie
Scraper
Reservoir
Redrock
Perry
Sumner
Bear Cr.
Morrison
Glencoe
Lela
Skedee
Blackburn
Pawnee
Cleveland
Osage
Maramec
Hallett
Terlton
Prue
Jennings
Quay
Keystone
Arkansas
TULSA
Dawson
Sand Springs
Highland Pk.
Oakhurst
Bowden
Jenks
Broken Arrow
Neodesha
Stillwater
Yale
Cimarron
Mannford
Oilton
Blackwell
Mulhall
Mehan
Gano
Markham
Olive
Pleasant Valley
Ripley
Perkins
Vinco
Cushing
East Cushing
Drumright
Sapulpa
Heyburn Res.
Kellyville
Kiefer
Glenpool
Bixby
Leonard
Mounds
Coweta
Wagoner
Redbird
Stonebluff
Porter
Tullahassee
Okay
Clarksville
Hulbert
Tahlequah
Welling
Park Hill
Wauhillau
Stilwell
Echota
Coyle
Langston
Goodnight
Agra
Tryon
Merrick
Avery
Meridian
Carney
Parkland
Fallis
Kendrick
Stroud
Shamrock
Bristow
Depew
Slick
Milfay
Newby
Edna
Gypsy
Warwick
Wellston
Chandler
Davenport
Luther
Arcadia
Jones
Deep Fork
Sparks
Payson
Tuskegee
Micawber
Welty
Nuyaka
Okmulgee
Beggs
Preston
Eram
Morris
Haskell
Yahola
Taft
Wybark
Fort Gibson
Bacone
MUSKOGEE
Boynton
Council Hill
Wainwright
Oktaha
Keefeton
McLain
Braggs
Qualls
Barber
Tenkiller Ferry Res.
Bunch
Tomy Town
Blackgum
Marble City
Nicut
Short
Gore
Webbers Falls
Akins
Long
Hanson
Roland
Vian
Sallisaw
Muldrow
Gans
Moffett
Ft. Smith
Arkoma
Redland
Mason
Paden
Prague
Meeker
Choctaw
Harrah
Midwest City
McLoud
Dale
Boley
Castle
Okemah
Henryetta
Pharoah
Clearview
Dewar
Schulter
Wildcat
Hitchita
Coalton
Hoffman
Dighton
Kusa
Pierce
Rentiesville
Checotah
Warner
Porum
Tamaha
Bryant
Lenna
Fame
Stidham
Texanna
Eufaula
Brooken
Briartown
Kanima
Cowlington
Braden
Spiro
Shawnee
Cromwell
Earlsboro
Tecumseh
Seminole
Bearden
Weleetka
Vivian
Hoyt
Whitefield
Stigler
Keota
Cartersville
Bokoshe
Rock Island
Hackett
Brooksville
Harjo
Wetumka
New Lima
Lima
Dustin
Hanna
Enterprise
Indianola
Canadian
Panama
Williams
Cameron
Macomb
Saint Louis
Maud
Bowlegs
Wewoka
Yeager
Vernon
Lamar
Ulan
Crowder
Quinton
McCurtain
Milton
Shadypoint
Poteau
Tribbey
Dewright
Holdenville
Scipio
McAlester L.
Featherston
Kinta
Lequire
Pearson
Snomac
Spaulding
Blocker
Lodi
Lexington
Trousdale
Sacred Heart
Konawa
Asher
Wanette
Canadian R.
North McAlester
Krebs
Wilburton
Red Oak
Fanshawe
Panola
Wister
Wister Res.
Monroe
Howe
Heavener
Rosedale
Byars
Sasakwa
Byng
Atwood
Calvin
Stuart
McAlester
Alderson
Adamson
Gowen
Lutie
Dow
Bache
Haileyville
Hartshorne
Bengal
Leflore
Summerfield
Hodgen
Zoe
Stapp
Page
Paoli
Stratford
Francis
Allen
Steedman
Bebee
Gerty
Haywood
Savanna
Non
Ashland
Vanoss
Center
Ada
Lula
Blanco
Kiowa
Pittsburg
Ti
Weathers
Yanush
Talihina
Whitesboro
Muse
Lawrence
Wynne Wood
Roff
Fitzhugh
Frisco
Stonewall
Tupelo
Centrahoma
Muddy Boggy
Wardville
Sardis
Tuskahoma
Albion
Kiamichi
Honobia
Elmore City
Fittstown
Hickory
Scullin
Harden City
Coalgate
Cairo
Wesley
Daisy
Adel
Clayton
Stanley
Ludlow
Octavia
Sulphur
Davis
Hennepin
PLATT NAT'L PK.
Pontotoc
Clarita
Phillips
Redden
Stringtown
Crum Creek
Nashoba
Beachton
Smithville
Watson
Plunkettville
Pooleville
Mill Creek
Connerville
Olney
Lehigh
Jumbo
Dunbar
Snow
Battiest
Pickens
Bethel
Sherwood
Mountain Fk.
Milo
Woodford
Dougherty
Big Canyon
Reagan
Bromide
Wapanucka
Atoka
Tushka
Moyers
Kosoma
Finley
Cloudy
Springer
Troy
Gene Autry
Newport
Fillmore
Boggy Depot
Miller
Darwin
Lane
Farris
Kiamichi R.
Ardmore
Ravia
Milburn
Coleman
Caney
Tishomingo
Mannsville
Folsom
Bentley
Crystal
Antlers
Rattan
Oleta
Dela
Belzoni
Corinne
Ringold
Hochatown
Lone Grove
L. Murray
Brock
McMillan
Simpson
Oakland
Madill
Little City
Cumberland
Kenefic
Caddo
Sunkist
Nelson
Speer
Spencerville
Virgil
Rufe
Glover
Oak Hill
Eagletown
Oswalt
Overbrook
Silo
Durant
Bokchito
Banty
Boswell
Soper
Goodland
Hugo
Sawyer
Wright City
Swink
Golden
Valliant
Millerton
Broken Bow
Cerrogordo
Ft. Towson
Garvin
Kingston
Woodville
Mead
Blue
Bennington
Marietta
Lebanon
Shay
Willis
Calera
Roberta
Utica
Platter
Colbert
Albany
Wade
Oberlin
Grant
Frogville
Red River
Idabel
Goodwater
Shinewell
Bokhoma
America
Haworth
Moon
Arkinda
Pollard
Harris
Tom
Burneyville
Thackerville
Lake Texoma
Denison Dam
Achille
Kemp
Yarnaby
Yuba
Bois d'Arc Cr.
Denison
Hendrix
Gainesville
Whitesboro
Sherman
Bonham
Whitewright
Van Alstyne
Pilot Point
Wolfe City
Elm Cr.
McKinney
Farmersville
Greenville
Denton
Lake Dallas
Boston
Sulphur R.

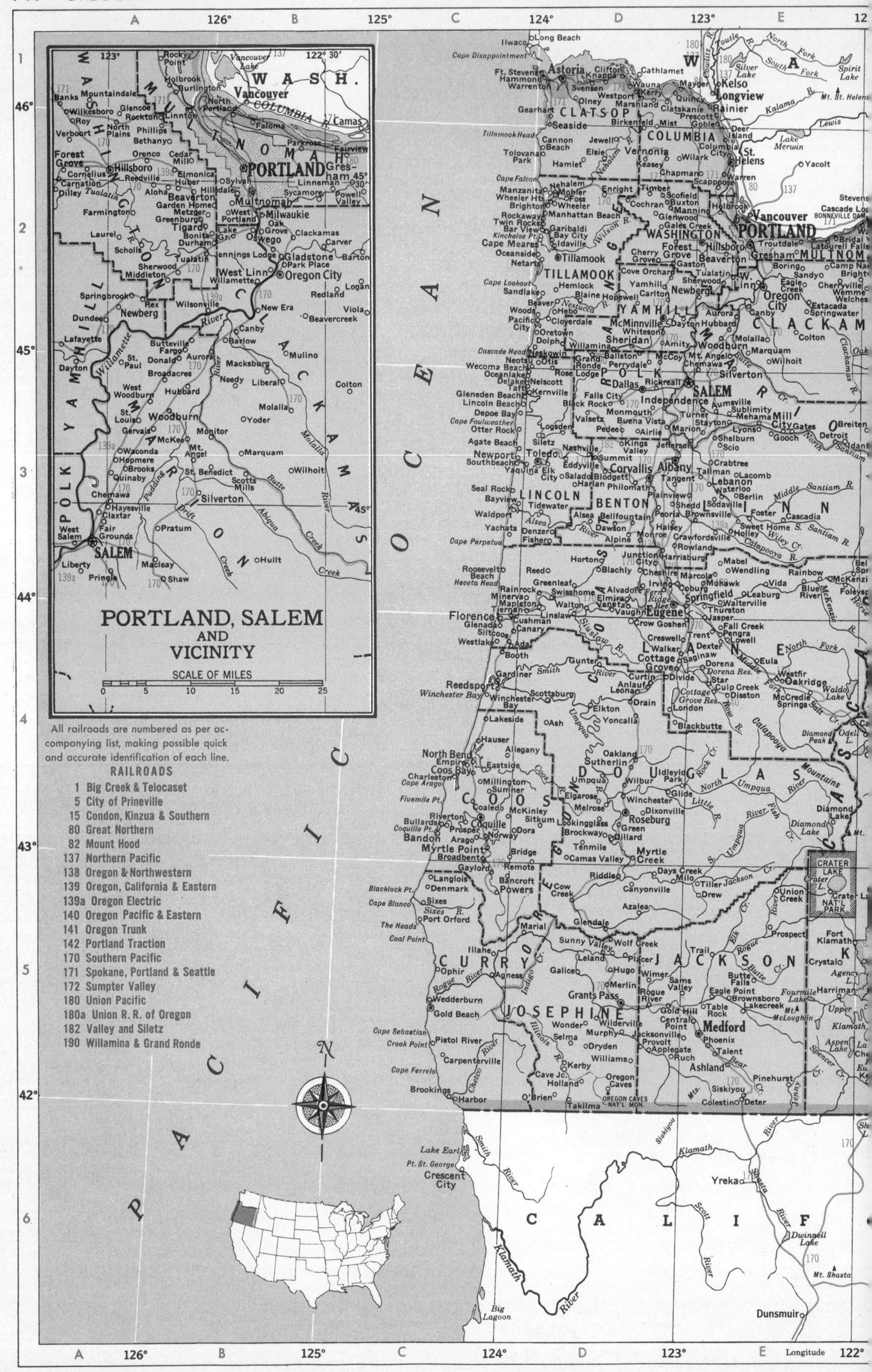
PORTLAND, SALEM AND VICINITY
SCALE OF MILES
0 5 10 15 20 25
All railroads are numbered as per accompanying list, making possible quick and accurate identification of each line.
RAILROADS
1 Big Creek & Telocaset
5 City of Prineville
15 Condon, Kinzua & Southern
80 Great Northern
82 Mount Hood
137 Northern Pacific
138 Oregon & Northwestern
139 Oregon, California & Eastern
139a Oregon Electric
140 Oregon Pacific & Eastern
141 Oregon Trunk
142 Portland Traction
170 Southern Pacific
171 Spokane, Portland & Seattle
172 Sumpter Valley
180 Union Pacific
180a Union R. R. of Oregon
182 Valley and Siletz
190 Willamina & Grand Ronde
PACIFIC OCEAN
CALIF
Longitude

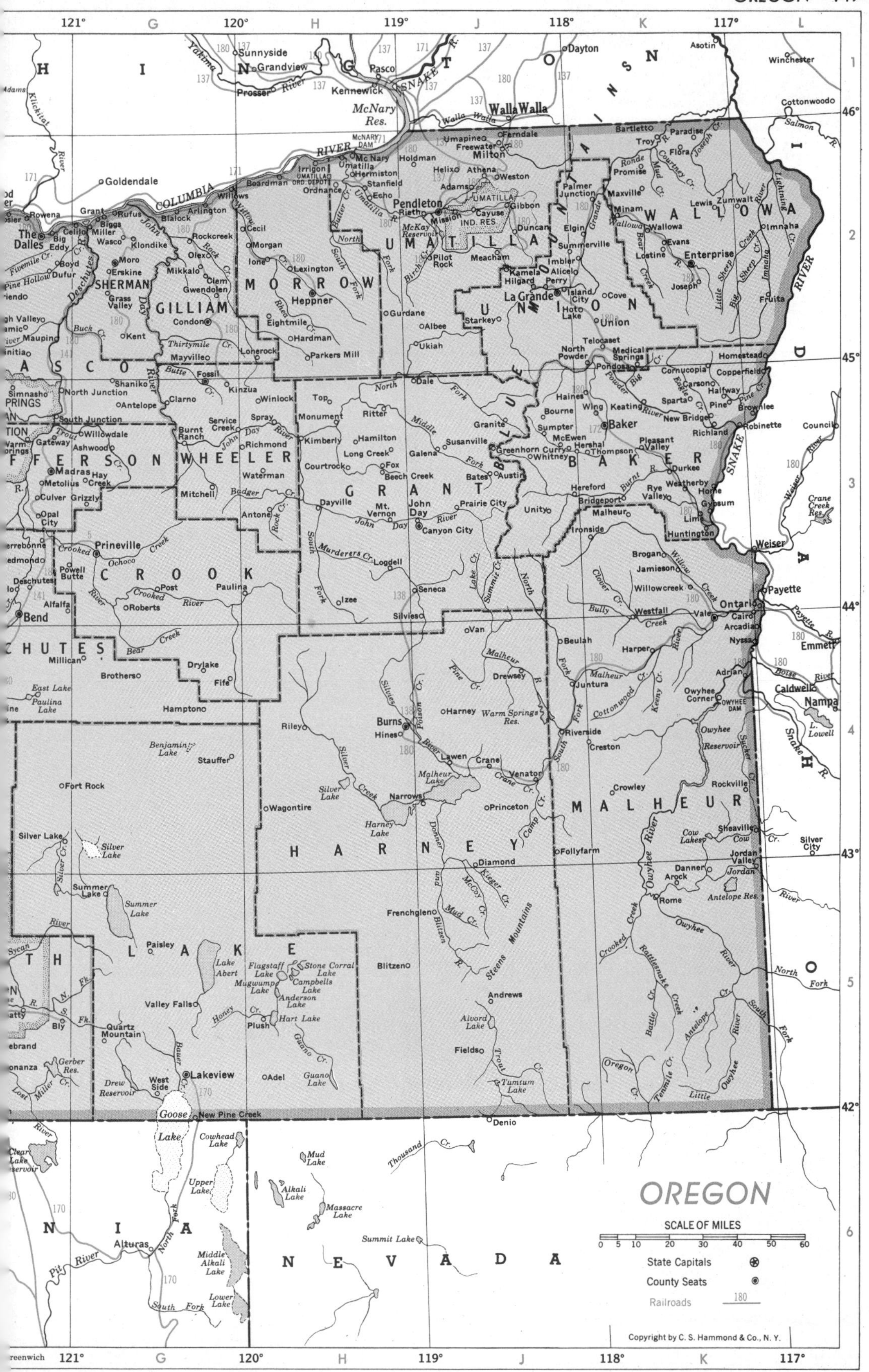
OREGON
SCALE OF MILES
0 5 10 20 30 40 50 60
State Capitals
County Seats
Railroads 180
Copyright by C. S. Hammond & Co., N. Y.
121° G 120° H 119° J 118° K 117° L
Greenwich
46°
45°
44°
43°
42°
1
2
3
4
5
6
UMATILLA
MORROW
GILLIAM
SHERMAN
WASCO
WHEELER
JEFFERSON
CROOK
GRANT
UNION
WALLOWA
BAKER
MALHEUR
HARNEY
LAKE
DESCHUTES
NEVADA
IDAHO
WASHINGTON
CALIFORNIA
BLUE MOUNTAINS
Steens Mountains
COLUMBIA RIVER
SNAKE RIVER
John Day River
Deschutes R.
Malheur R.
Owyhee River
Silvies R.
Powder River
Burnt R.
Grande Ronde R.
Imnaha R.
Umatilla R.
McNary Res.
McNary Dam
Umatilla Ind. Res.
Malheur Lake
Harney Lake
Summer Lake
Lake Abert
Goose Lake
Silver Lake
Alvord Lake
Owyhee Reservoir
Antelope Res.
Warm Springs Res.
Pendleton
Heppner
Condon
Moro
The Dalles
Fossil
Madras
Prineville
Bend
Canyon City
John Day
La Grande
Enterprise
Baker
Vale
Ontario
Burns
Hines
Lakeview
Walla Walla
Dayton
Asotin
Pasco
Kennewick
Sunnyside
Grandview
Prosser
Goldendale
Weiser
Payette
Nampa
Caldwell
Emmett
Alturas
Denio
Milton
Freewater
Athena
Hermiston
Umatilla
Boardman
Arlington
Lexington
Ione
Echo
Pilot Rock
Elgin
Union
Cove
Imbler
Joseph
Wallowa
Lostine
Halfway
Huntington
Haines
Sumpter
Unity
Jordan Valley
Nyssa
Adrian
Juntura
Drewsey
Crane
Lawen
Frenchglen
Fields
Andrews
Diamond
Paisley
Plush
Adel
Valley Falls
Fort Rock
Silver Lake
Hampton
Brothers
Millican
Paulina
Post
Powell Butte
Culver
Metolius
Shaniko
Antelope
Maupin
Spray
Kimberly
Monument
Long Creek
Dayville
Mt. Vernon
Prairie City
Seneca
Izee
Ukiah
Riley
Wagontire
Rome
Arock
Danner
Crowley
Riverside
Beulah
Westfall
Harper
Rockville
Sheaville
Follyfarm
Thompson
Richland
Copperfield
Homestead
Durkee
Rye Valley
Ironside
Brogan
Jamieson
Willowcreek
New Pine Creek
Quartz Mountain
Bly
West Side
Drew Reservoir
Gerber Res.
Hart Lake
Crump Lake
Mugwump Lake
Flagstaff Lake
Campbells Lake
Anderson Lake
Guano Lake
Tumtum Lake
Cowhead Lake
Upper Lake
Middle Alkali Lake
Lower Lake
Mud Lake
Alkali Lake
Massacre Lake
Summit Lake
Thousand Cr.
Pit River
North Fork
South Fork

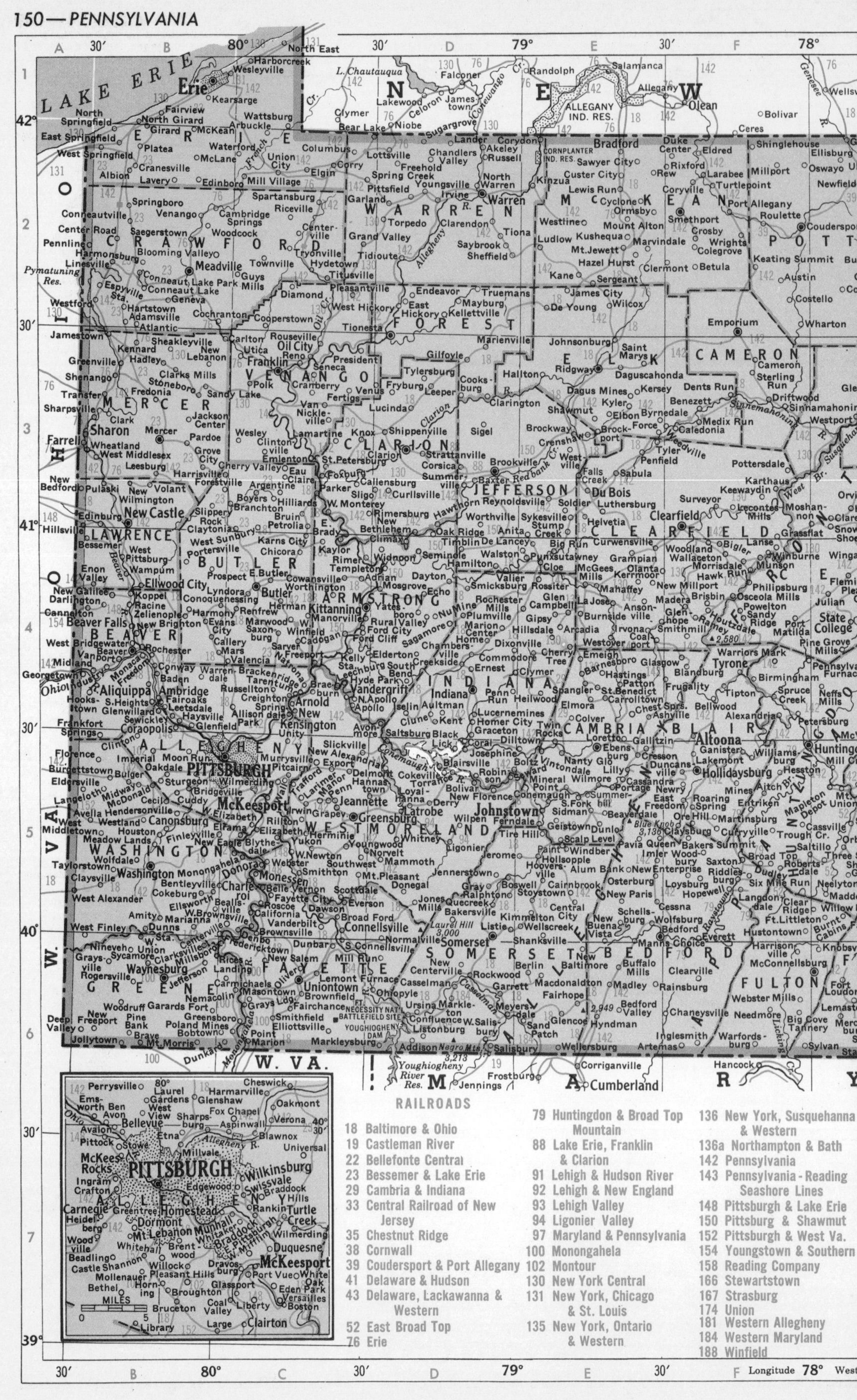
LAKE ERIE
N E W Y O R K
O H I O
W. VA.
M A R Y L A N D
ERIE
CRAWFORD
WARREN
McKEAN
POTTER
MERCER
VENANGO
FOREST
ELK
CAMERON
LAWRENCE
BUTLER
CLARION
JEFFERSON
CLEARFIELD
BEAVER
ARMSTRONG
INDIANA
CAMBRIA
BLAIR
ALLEGHENY
WESTMORELAND
WASHINGTON
GREENE
FAYETTE
SOMERSET
BEDFORD
FULTON
PITTSBURGH
Erie
Meadville
Warren
Franklin
Oil City
Sharon
New Castle
Butler
Kittanning
Indiana
Johnstown
Altoona
Hollidaysburg
Greensburg
Washington
Uniontown
Somerset
Bedford
McKeesport
Clearfield
Bradford
Olean
Cumberland
MILES
RAILROADS
18 Baltimore & Ohio
19 Castleman River
22 Bellefonte Central
23 Bessemer & Lake Erie
29 Cambria & Indiana
33 Central Railroad of New Jersey
35 Chestnut Ridge
38 Cornwall
39 Coudersport & Port Allegany
41 Delaware & Hudson
43 Delaware, Lackawanna & Western
52 East Broad Top
76 Erie
79 Huntingdon & Broad Top Mountain
88 Lake Erie, Franklin & Clarion
91 Lehigh & Hudson River
92 Lehigh & New England
93 Lehigh Valley
94 Ligonier Valley
97 Maryland & Pennsylvania
100 Monongahela
102 Montour
130 New York Central
131 New York, Chicago & St. Louis
135 New York, Ontario & Western
136 New York, Susquehanna & Western
136a Northampton & Bath
142 Pennsylvania
143 Pennsylvania-Reading Seashore Lines
148 Pittsburgh & Lake Erie
150 Pittsburg & Shawmut
152 Pittsburgh & West Va.
154 Youngstown & Southern
158 Reading Company
166 Stewartstown
167 Strasburg
174 Union
181 Western Allegheny
184 Western Maryland
188 Winfield
Longitude 78° West

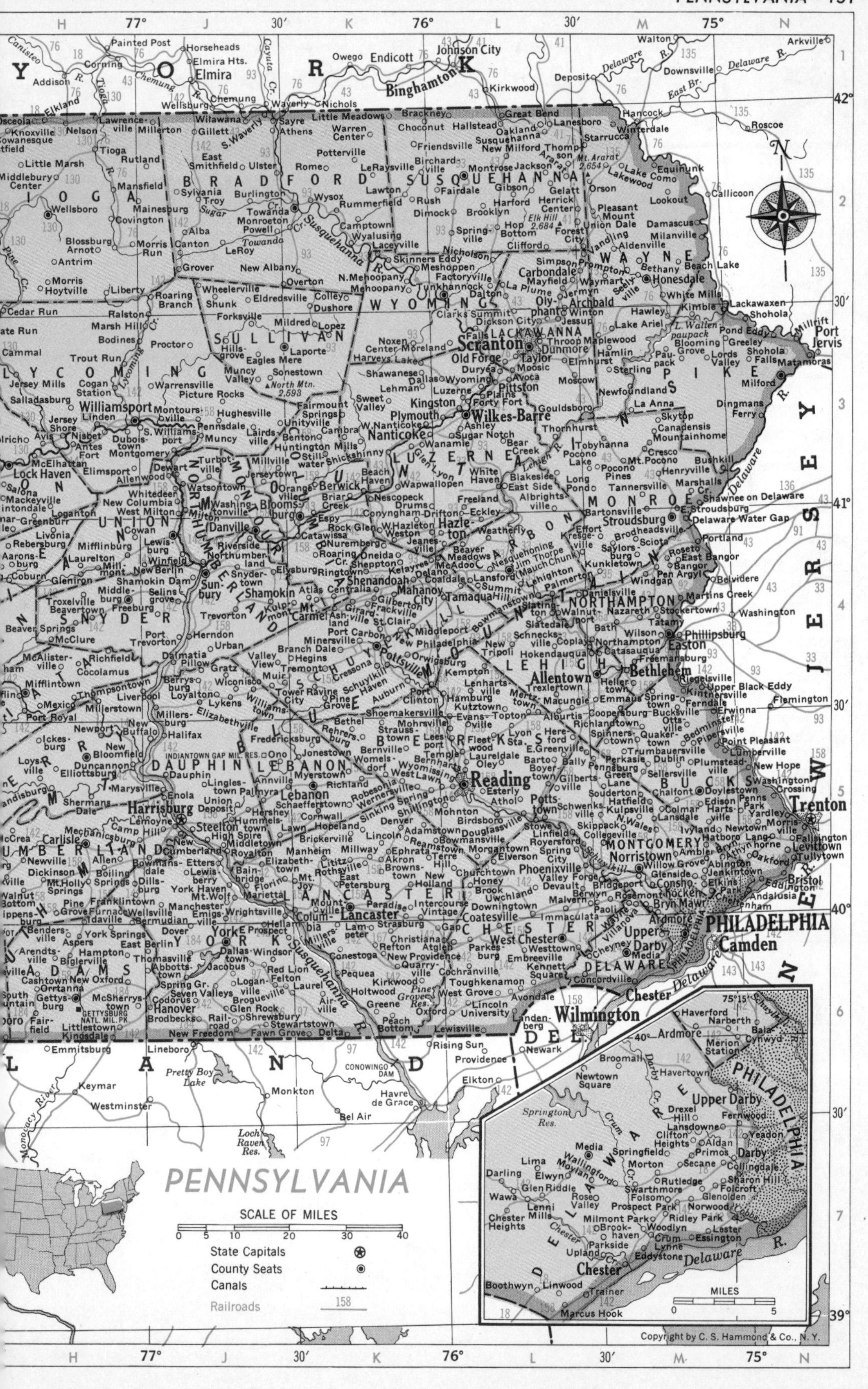
PENNSYLVANIA
SCALE OF MILES
0 5 10 20 30 40
State Capitals
County Seats
Canals
Railroads
158
PHILADELPHIA
Camden
Trenton
Harrisburg
Scranton
Wilkes-Barre
Reading
Allentown
Bethlehem
Lancaster
Wilmington
Chester
MILES
0 5
Copyright by C. S. Hammond & Co., N. Y.

SOUTH CAROLINA
SCALE OF MILES
0 5 10 20 30 40
State Capitals
County Seats
Canals
Railroads
17
Longitude
AUGUSTA
Greenville
GREENVILLE
Spartanburg
SPARTANBURG
PICKENS
OCONEE
ANDERSON
ABBEVILLE
GREENWOOD
LAURENS
NEWBERRY
SALUDA
EDGEFIELD
MC CORMICK
AIKEN
BARNWELL
ALLENDALE
CHEROKEE
UNION
LEXINGTON
Clark Hill Res.
Savannah River
BLUE RIDGE
NORTH
GEORGIA
SAVANNAH RIVER ATOMIC ENERGY RESERVATION

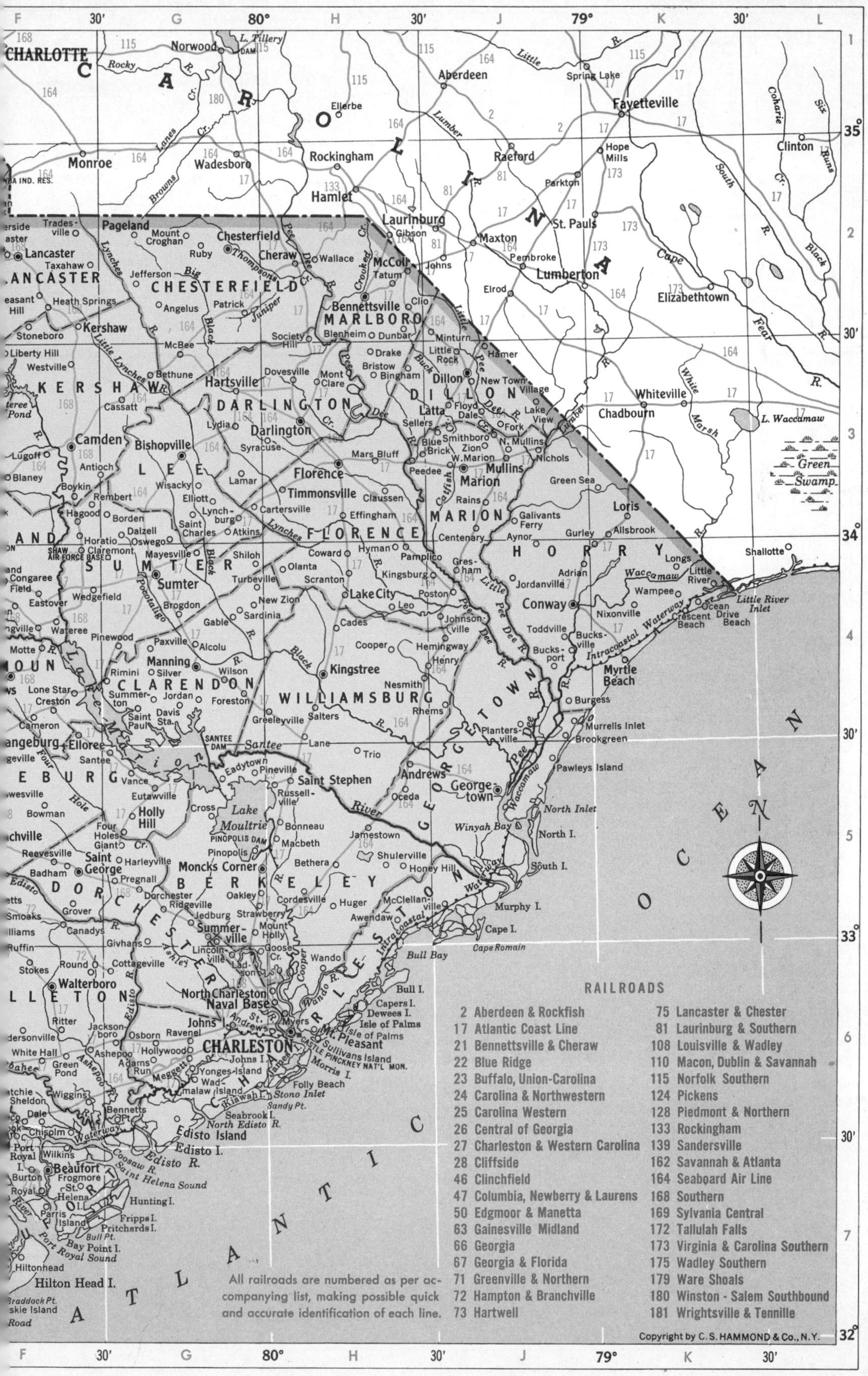
RAILROADS
2 Aberdeen & Rockfish
17 Atlantic Coast Line
21 Bennettsville & Cheraw
22 Blue Ridge
23 Buffalo, Union-Carolina
24 Carolina & Northwestern
25 Carolina Western
26 Central of Georgia
27 Charleston & Western Carolina
28 Cliffside
46 Clinchfield
47 Columbia, Newberry & Laurens
50 Edgmoor & Manetta
63 Gainesville Midland
66 Georgia
67 Georgia & Florida
71 Greenville & Northern
72 Hampton & Branchville
73 Hartwell
75 Lancaster & Chester
81 Laurinburg & Southern
108 Louisville & Wadley
110 Macon, Dublin & Savannah
115 Norfolk Southern
124 Pickens
128 Piedmont & Northern
133 Rockingham
139 Sandersville
162 Savannah & Atlanta
164 Seaboard Air Line
168 Southern
169 Sylvania Central
172 Tallulah Falls
173 Virginia & Carolina Southern
175 Wadley Southern
179 Ware Shoals
180 Winston - Salem Southbound
181 Wrightsville & Tennille
All railroads are numbered as per accompanying list, making possible quick and accurate identification of each line.
ATLANTIC OCEAN
Copyright by C. S. HAMMOND & Co., N.Y.

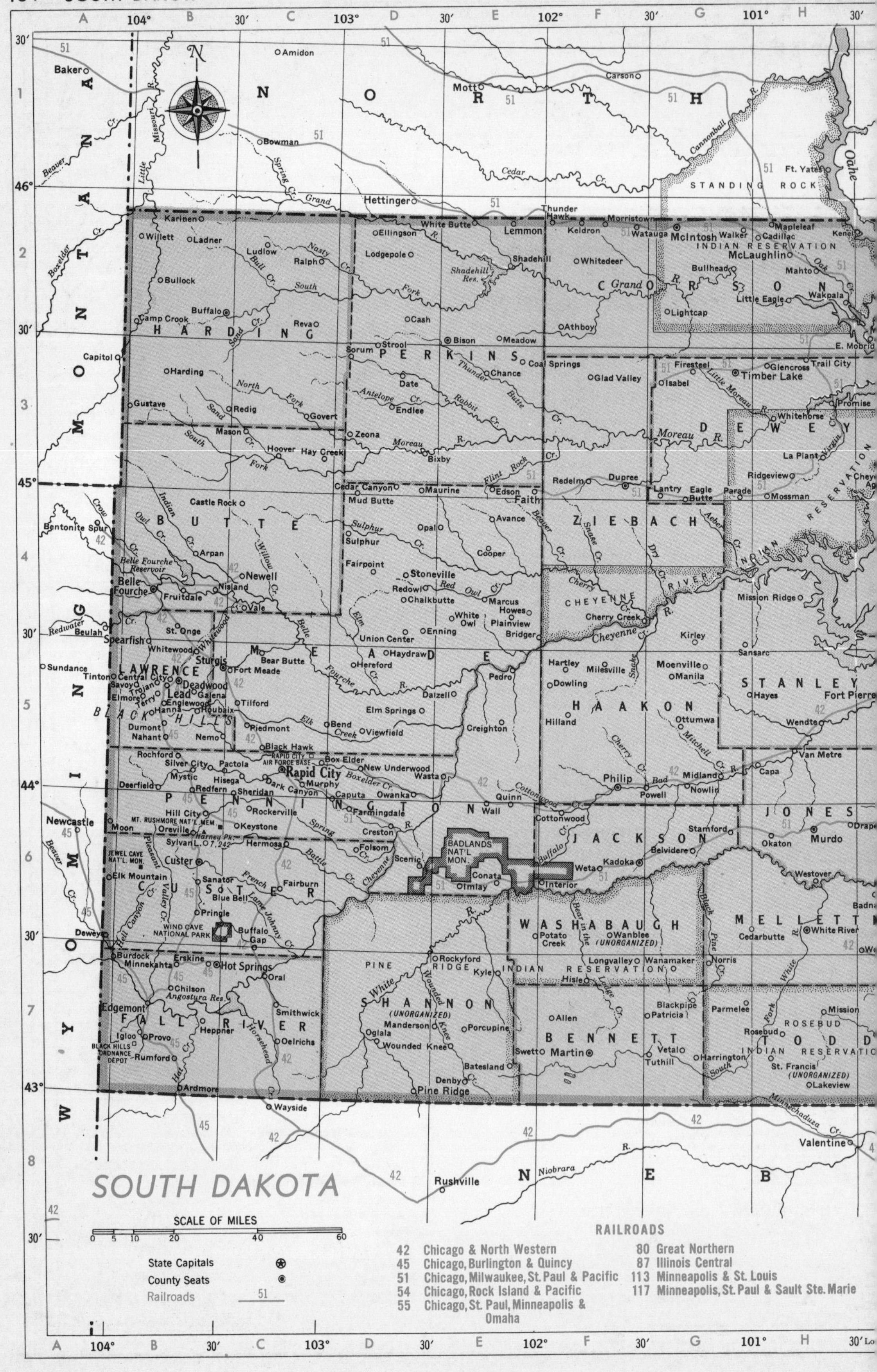
SOUTH DAKOTA
SCALE OF MILES
0 5 10 20 40 60
State Capitals
County Seats
Railroads
RAILROADS
42 Chicago & North Western
45 Chicago, Burlington & Quincy
51 Chicago, Milwaukee, St. Paul & Pacific
54 Chicago, Rock Island & Pacific
55 Chicago, St. Paul, Minneapolis & Omaha
80 Great Northern
87 Illinois Central
113 Minneapolis & St. Louis
117 Minneapolis, St. Paul & Sault Ste. Marie
A B C D E F G H
104° 30′ 103° 30′ 102° 30′ 101° 30′
46° 45° 44° 43°
N O R T H
M O N T A N A
W Y O M I N G
N E B
HARDING
PERKINS
BUTTE
MEADE
LAWRENCE
PENNINGTON
CUSTER
FALL RIVER
SHANNON (UNORGANIZED)
WASHABAUGH (UNORGANIZED)
BENNETT
JACKSON
HAAKON
ZIEBACH
DEWEY
CORSON
STANLEY
JONES
MELLETTE
TODD (UNORGANIZED)
CHEYENNE
STANDING ROCK INDIAN RESERVATION
CHEYENNE RIVER INDIAN RESERVATION
PINE RIDGE INDIAN RESERVATION
ROSEBUD INDIAN RESERVATION
BADLANDS NAT'L MON.
WIND CAVE NATIONAL PARK
JEWEL CAVE NAT'L MON.
MT. RUSHMORE NAT'L MEM.
BLACK HILLS
RAPID CITY AIR FORCE BASE
BLACK HILLS ORDNANCE DEPOT
Harney Pk. 7,242
Rapid City
Pierre
Lemmon
Sturgis
Deadwood
Lead
Spearfish
Belle Fourche
Philip
Murdo
Kadoka
Martin
Hot Springs
Custer
Buffalo
Bison
Faith
Timber Lake
McIntosh
McLaughlin
Fort Pierre
White River
Pine Ridge
Valentine
Rushville
Hettinger
Bowman
Amidon
Mott
Carson
Baker
Newcastle
Sundance
Beulah
Cheyenne R.
White R.
Moreau R.
Grand R.
Belle Fourche R.
Bad R.
Angostura Res.
Shadehill Res.
Belle Fourche Reservoir
Oahe
Niobrara R.

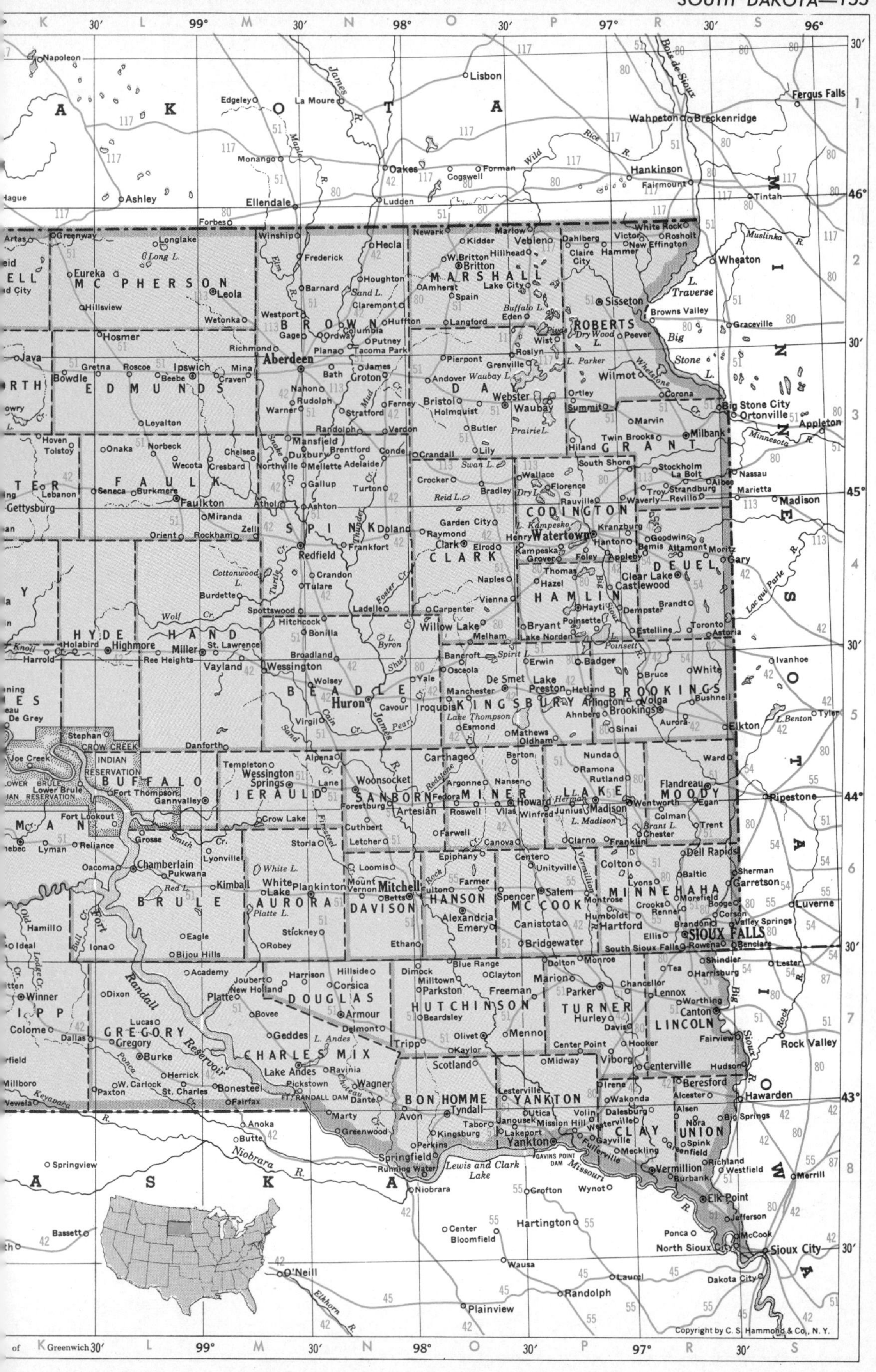

MC PHERSON
BROWN
MARSHALL
ROBERTS
EDMUNDS
DAY
GRANT
FAULK
SPINK
CLARK
CODINGTON
DEUEL
HAMLIN
HYDE
HAND
BEADLE
KINGSBURY
BROOKINGS
BUFFALO
JERAULD
SANBORN
MINER
LAKE
MOODY
BRULE
AURORA
DAVISON
HANSON
MC COOK
MINNEHAHA
GREGORY
DOUGLAS
HUTCHINSON
TURNER
LINCOLN
CHARLES MIX
BON HOMME
YANKTON
CLAY
UNION
CROW CREEK INDIAN RESERVATION
LOWER BRULE INDIAN RESERVATION
Aberdeen
Watertown
Huron
Mitchell
Sioux Falls
Yankton
Redfield
Brookings
Lewis and Clark Lake
Randall Reservoir
Missouri R.
Niobrara R.
Big Stone L.
L. Traverse
Sioux City
Fergus Falls
Copyright by C. S. Hammond & Co., N. Y.

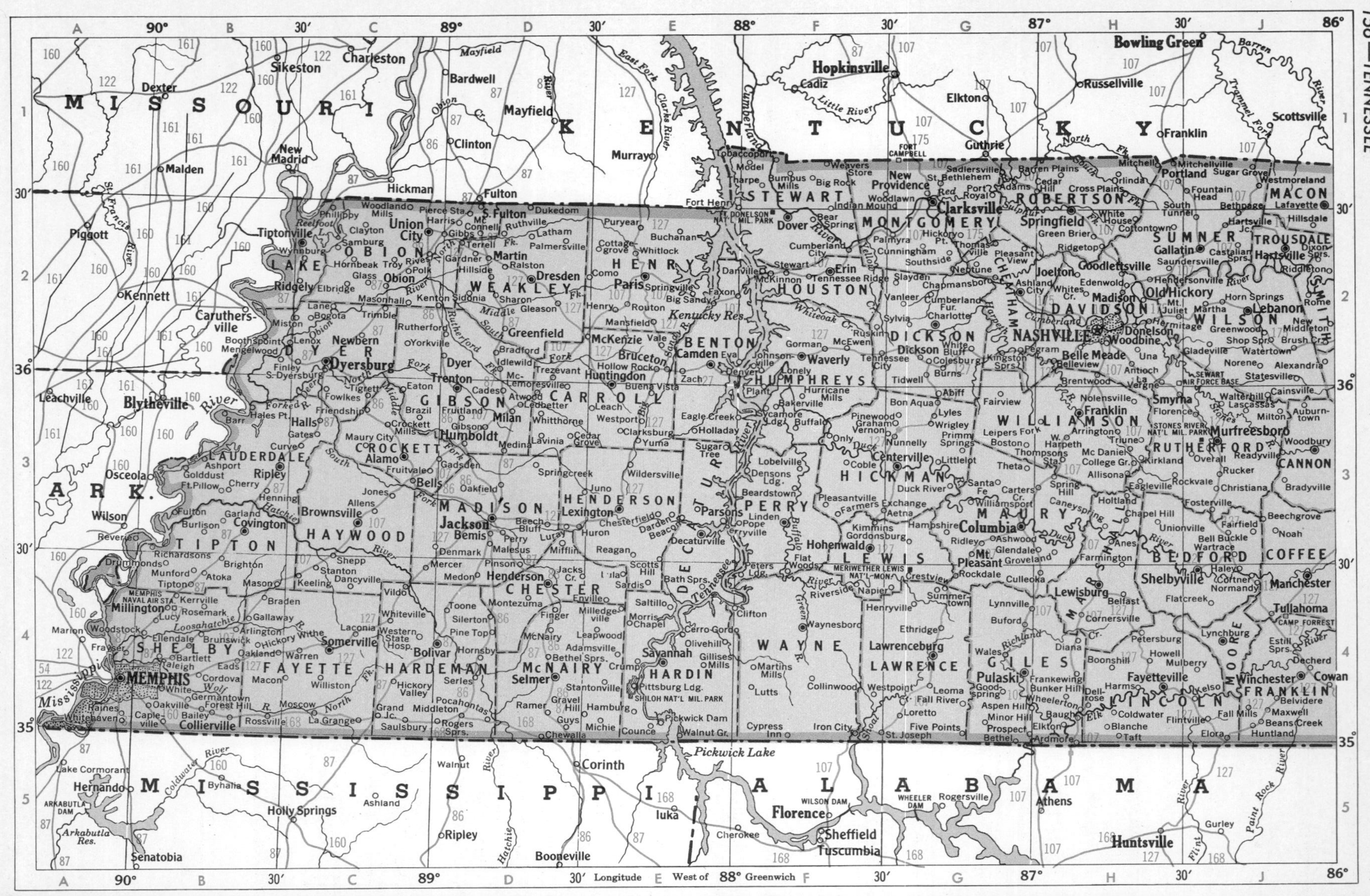

MISSOURI
KENTUCKY
ARK.
MISSISSIPPI
ALABAMA
LAKE
OBION
WEAKLEY
HENRY
STEWART
MONTGOMERY
ROBERTSON
SUMNER
MACON
TROUSDALE
SMITH
WILSON
DAVIDSON
CHEATHAM
DICKSON
HOUSTON
HUMPHREYS
BENTON
CARROLL
GIBSON
DYER
LAUDERDALE
CROCKETT
HAYWOOD
TIPTON
SHELBY
FAYETTE
HARDEMAN
MADISON
HENDERSON
DECATUR
PERRY
HICKMAN
WILLIAMSON
RUTHERFORD
CANNON
BEDFORD
COFFEE
FRANKLIN
LINCOLN
MOORE
GILES
MAURY
MARSHALL
LEWIS
LAWRENCE
WAYNE
HARDIN
McNAIRY
CHESTER
MEMPHIS
NASHVILLE
Jackson
Clarksville
Murfreesboro
Columbia
Dyersburg
Paris
Union City
Kentucky Res.
Pickwick Lake
Cumberland
Tennessee
Mississippi
Longitude West of 88° Greenwich

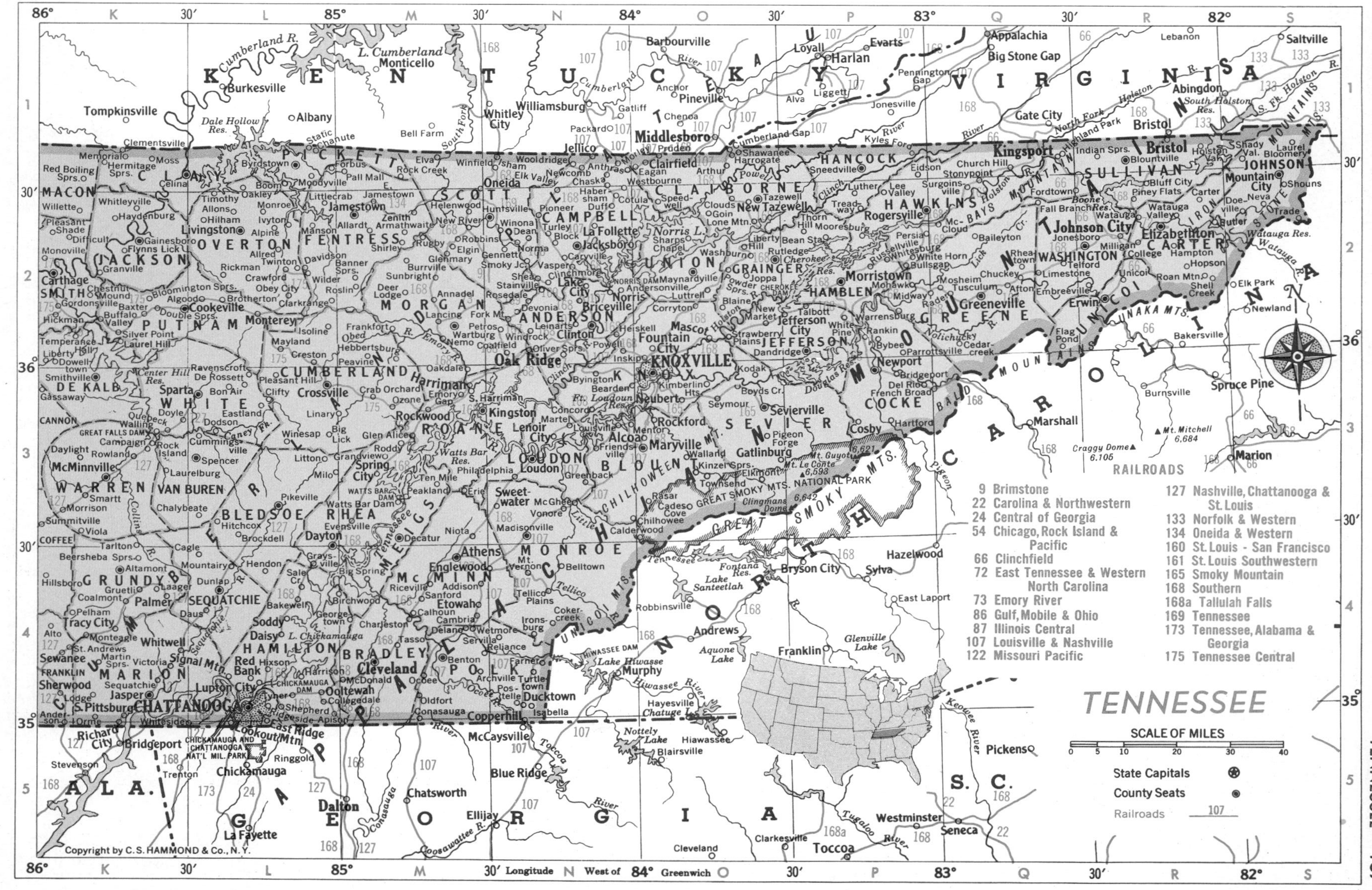
TENNESSEE
SCALE OF MILES
0 5 10 20 30 40
State Capitals
County Seats
Railroads 107
RAILROADS
9 Brimstone
22 Carolina & Northwestern
24 Central of Georgia
54 Chicago, Rock Island & Pacific
66 Clinchfield
72 East Tennessee & Western North Carolina
73 Emory River
86 Gulf, Mobile & Ohio
87 Illinois Central
107 Louisville & Nashville
122 Missouri Pacific
127 Nashville, Chattanooga & St. Louis
133 Norfolk & Western
134 Oneida & Western
160 St. Louis - San Francisco
161 St. Louis Southwestern
165 Smoky Mountain
168 Southern
168a Tallulah Falls
169 Tennessee
173 Tennessee, Alabama & Georgia
175 Tennessee Central
KENTUCKY
VIRGINIA
NORTH CAROLINA
GEORGIA
S. C.
ALA.
GREAT SMOKY MTS. NATIONAL PARK
KNOXVILLE
CHATTANOOGA
Oak Ridge
Bristol
Kingsport
Johnson City
30′ Longitude N West of 84° Greenwich
Copyright by C.S. HAMMOND & Co., N.Y.

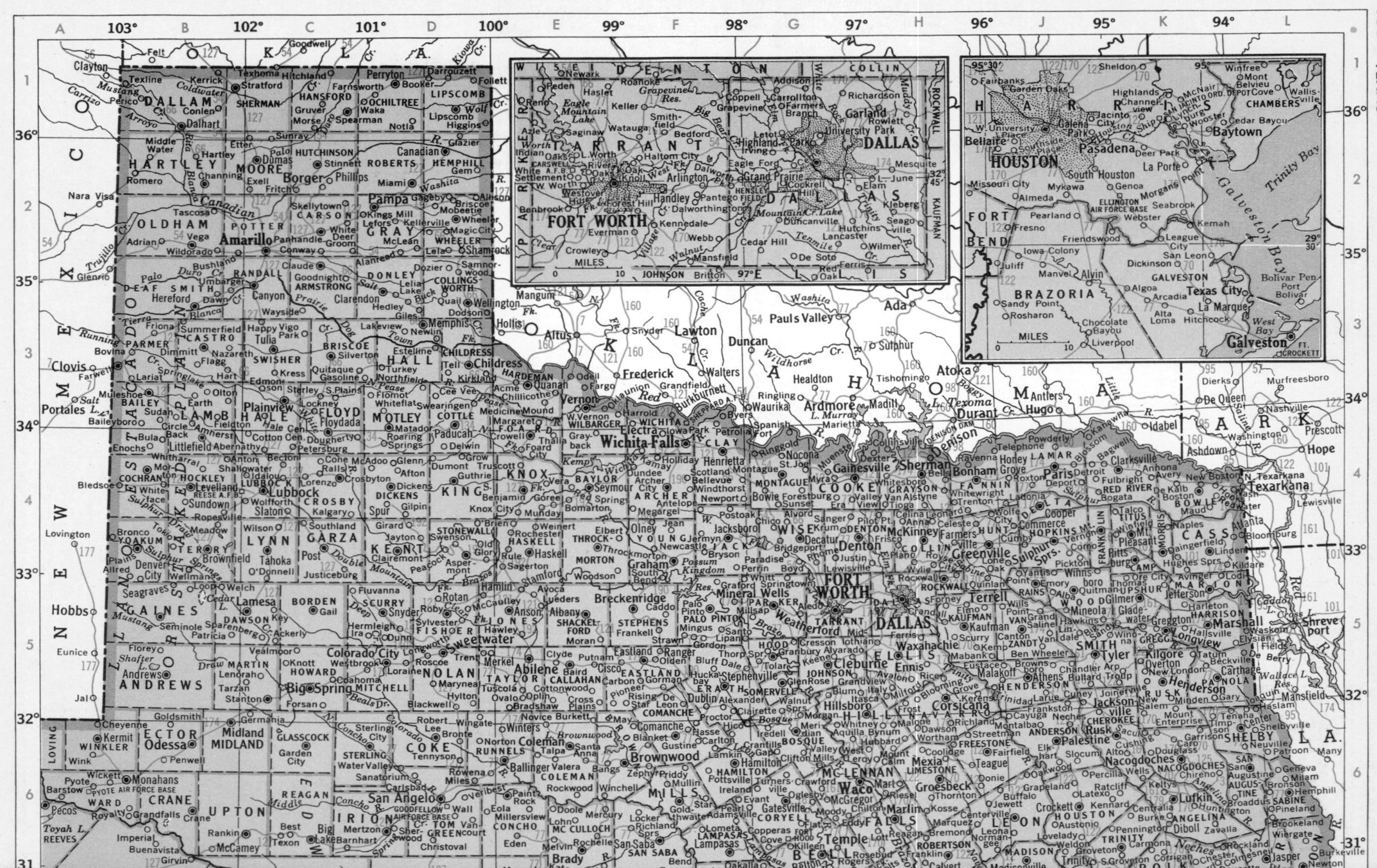

G U L F
O F
M E X I C O
All railroads are numbered as per accompanying list, making possible quick and accurate identification of each line.
3 Angelina & Neches River
7 Atchison, Topeka & Santa Fe
12 Burlington-Rock Island
54 Chicago, Rock Island & Pacific
56 Colorado & Southern
57 De Queen & Eastern
66 Fort Worth & Denver City
70 Galveston, Houston & Henderson
77 Gulf, Colorado & Santa Fe
94 Kansas City, Mexico & Orient
95 Kansas City Southern
98 Kansas, Oklahoma & Gulf
101 Louisiana & Arkansas
109 Mexico North-Western
121 Missouri-Kansas-Texas
122 Missouri Pacific
123 Moscow, Camden & San Augustine
125 Nacogdoches & Southeastern
126 National of Mexico
127 Panhandle & Santa Fe
128 Paris & Mt. Pleasant
129 Pecos Valley Southern
134 Quanah, Acme & Pacific
139 Rockdale, Sandow & Southern
140 Roscoe, Snyder & Pacific
160 St. Louis-San Francisco
161 St. Louis Southwestern
170 Southern Pacific
174 Texas & Pacific
176 Texas Mexican
177 Texas-New Mexico
179 Texas South-Eastern
188 Waco, Beaumont, Trinity & Sabine
190 Wichita Falls & Southern
192 Wichita Valley
TEXAS
SCALE OF MILES
0 20 40 60 80 100
State Capitals
County Seats
Railroads 170
Copyright by C. S. HAMMOND & Co., N. Y.
Longitude 98° West of Greenwich 97°
WESTERN PART OF TEXAS
Same scale as main map
M E X I C O

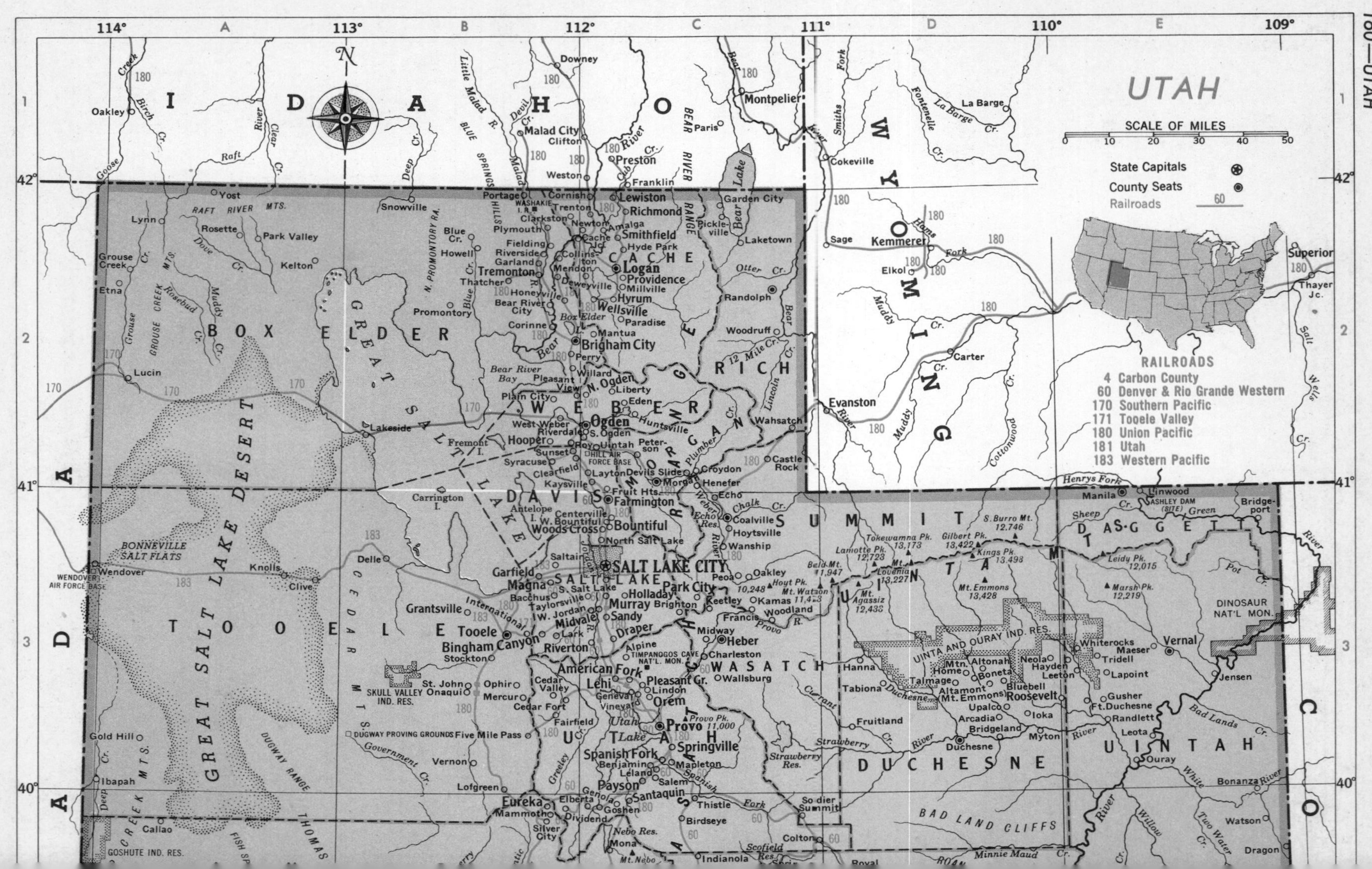
UTAH
SCALE OF MILES
0 10 20 30 40 50
State Capitals
County Seats
Railroads
RAILROADS
4 Carbon County
60 Denver & Rio Grande Western
170 Southern Pacific
171 Tooele Valley
180 Union Pacific
181 Utah
183 Western Pacific
I D A H O
W Y O M I N G
C O
GREAT SALT LAKE
GREAT SALT LAKE DESERT
BONNEVILLE SALT FLATS
BOX ELDER
CACHE
RICH
WEBER
DAVIS
MORGAN
SUMMIT
DAGGETT
UINTAH
DUCHESNE
WASATCH
SALT LAKE
TOOELE
UTAH
SALT LAKE CITY
Ogden
Logan
Provo
Brigham City
DINOSAUR NAT'L MON.
UINTA AND OURAY IND. RES.
SKULL VALLEY IND. RES.
GOSHUTE IND. RES.
DUGWAY PROVING GROUNDS
TIMPANOGOS CAVE NAT'L MON.
WENDOVER AIR FORCE BASE
HILL AIR FORCE BASE
BEAR RIVER RANGE
RAFT RIVER MTS.
GROUSE CREEK MTS.
N. PROMONTORY RA.
CEDAR MTS.
DUGWAY RANGE
BAD LAND CLIFFS
114° 113° 112° 111° 110° 109°
42° 41° 40°

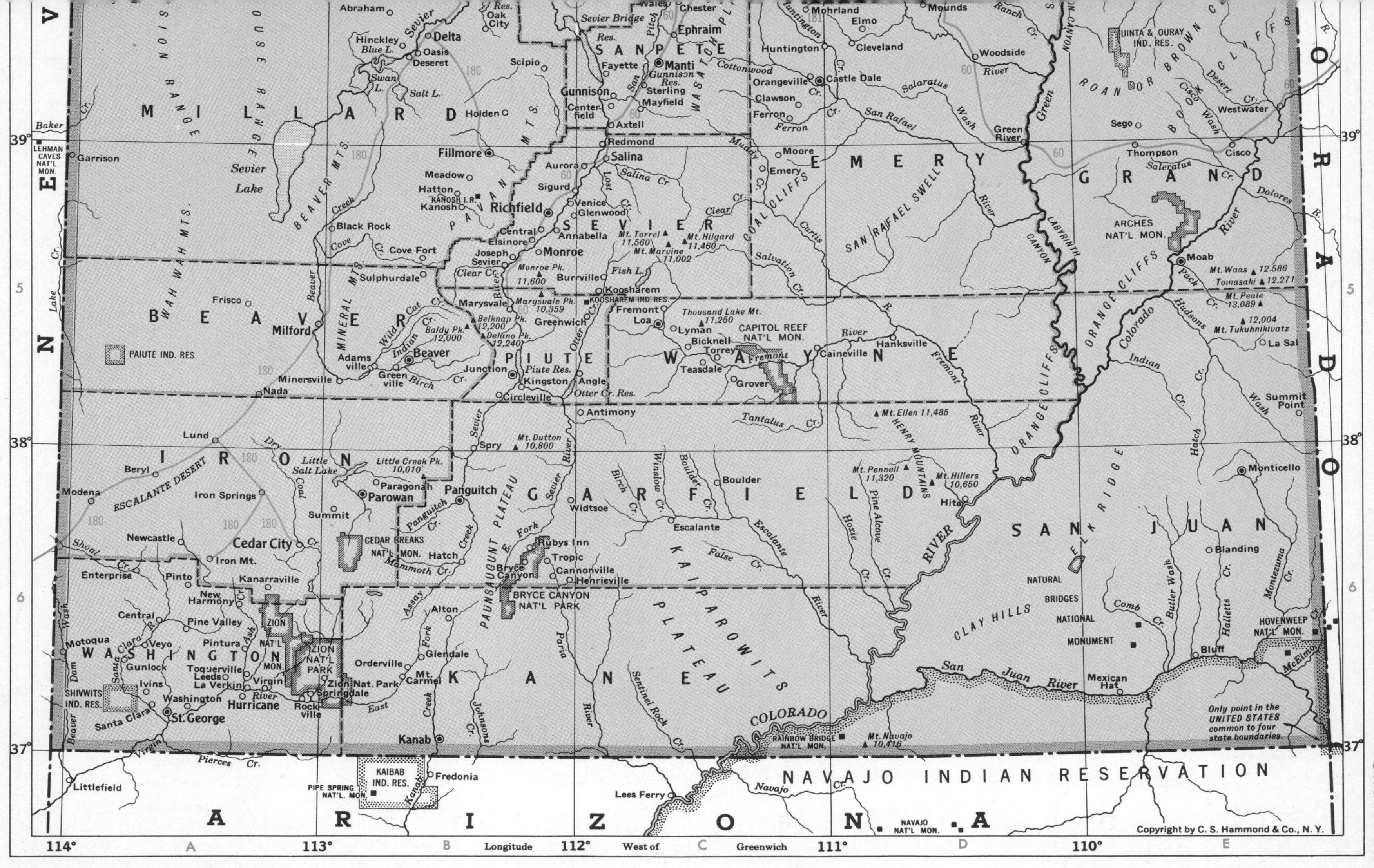
C O L O R A D O
A R I Z O N A
N E V A D A
M I L L A R D
S A N P E T E
S E V I E R
E M E R Y
G R A N D
B E A V E R
P I U T E
W A Y N E
I R O N
G A R F I E L D
S A N J U A N
W A S H I N G T O N
K A N E
NAVAJO INDIAN RESERVATION
UINTA & OURAY IND. RES.
ARCHES NAT'L MON.
CAPITOL REEF NAT'L MON.
NATURAL BRIDGES NATIONAL MONUMENT
HOVENWEEP NAT'L MON.
RAINBOW BRIDGE NAT'L MON.
NAVAJO NAT'L MON.
BRYCE CANYON NAT'L PARK
CEDAR BREAKS NAT'L MON.
ZION NAT'L PARK
ZION NAT'L MON.
PIPE SPRING NAT'L MON.
KAIBAB IND. RES.
SHIVWITS IND. RES.
PAIUTE IND. RES.
KOOSHAREM IND. RES.
KANOSH I.R.
LEHMAN CAVES NAT'L MON.
ORANGE CLIFFS
COAL CLIFFS
SAN RAFAEL SWELL
HENRY MOUNTAINS
KAIPAROWITS PLATEAU
PAUNSAUGUNT PLATEAU
CLAY HILLS
ELK RIDGE
LABYRINTH CANYON
ESCALANTE DESERT
MINERAL MTS.
BEAVER MTS.
WAH WAH MTS.
PAVANT MTS.
WASATCH PLATEAU
ROAN OR BROWN CLIFFS
BOOK CLIFFS
Sevier Lake
Moab
Monticello
Blanding
Bluff
Mexican Hat
Green River
Hanksville
Richfield
Salina
Manti
Ephraim
Fillmore
Delta
Beaver
Milford
Panguitch
Parowan
Cedar City
Kanab
St. George
Hurricane
Escalante
Loa
Junction
Marysvale
Castle Dale
Huntington
Mt. Waas 12,586
Tomasaki 12,271
Mt. Peale 13,089
Mt. Tukuhnikivatz 12,004
Mt. Ellen 11,485
Mt. Pennell 11,320
Mt. Hillers 10,650
Mt. Navajo 10,416
Only point in the UNITED STATES common to four state boundaries.
Longitude West of Greenwich
114°
113°
112°
111°
110°
39°
38°
37°
Copyright by C. S. Hammond & Co., N. Y.

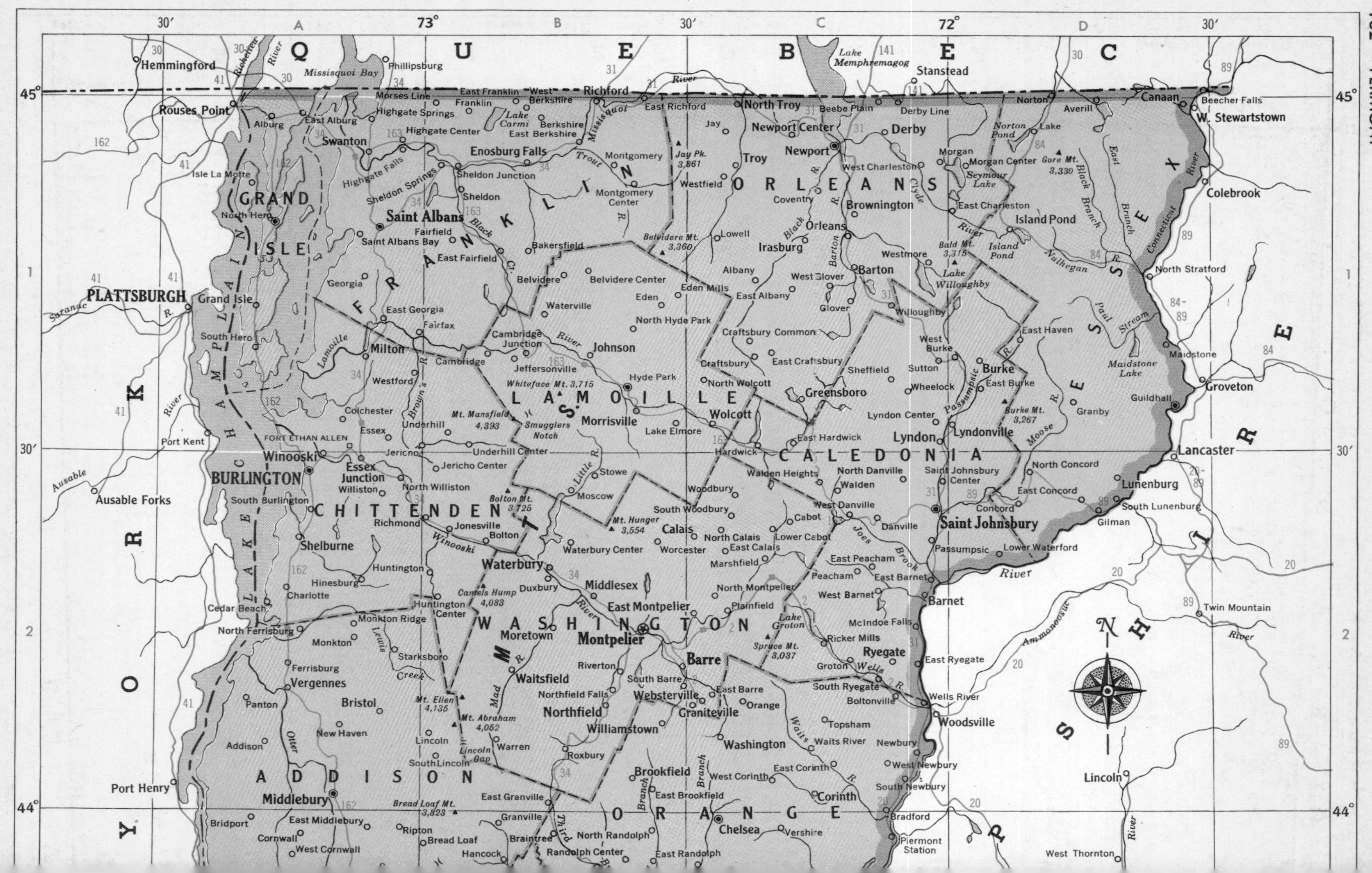
QUEBEC
NEW YORK
NEW HAMPSHIRE
GRAND ISLE
FRANKLIN
ORLEANS
ESSEX
LAMOILLE
CALEDONIA
CHITTENDEN
WASHINGTON
ADDISON
ORANGE
LAKE CHAMPLAIN
Lake Memphremagog
Missisquoi Bay
Connecticut River
Winooski River
Lamoille River
Saint Albans
Swanton
Enosburg Falls
Richford
Newport
Derby
Barton
Orleans
Island Pond
Lyndonville
Saint Johnsbury
Barnet
Hardwick
Morrisville
Johnson
Stowe
Montpelier
Barre
Waterbury
Northfield
Burlington
Winooski
Essex Junction
Shelburne
Vergennes
Bristol
Middlebury
Chelsea
Randolph
Alburg
North Hero
Grand Isle
Plattsburgh
Rouses Point
Hemmingford
Stanstead
Canaan
Colebrook
Groveton
Lancaster
Lunenburg
Woodsville
Port Henry
Jay Pk. 3,861
Mt. Mansfield 4,393
Camels Hump 4,083
Mt. Ellen 4,135
Mt. Abraham 4,052
Spruce Mt. 3,037
Burke Mt. 3,267
Gore Mt. 3,330
Belvidere Mt. 3,360
Whiteface Mt. 3,715
Bolton Mt. 3,725
Mt. Hunger 3,554
Bread Loaf Mt. 3,823
Smugglers Notch
45°
44°
73°
72°
30'

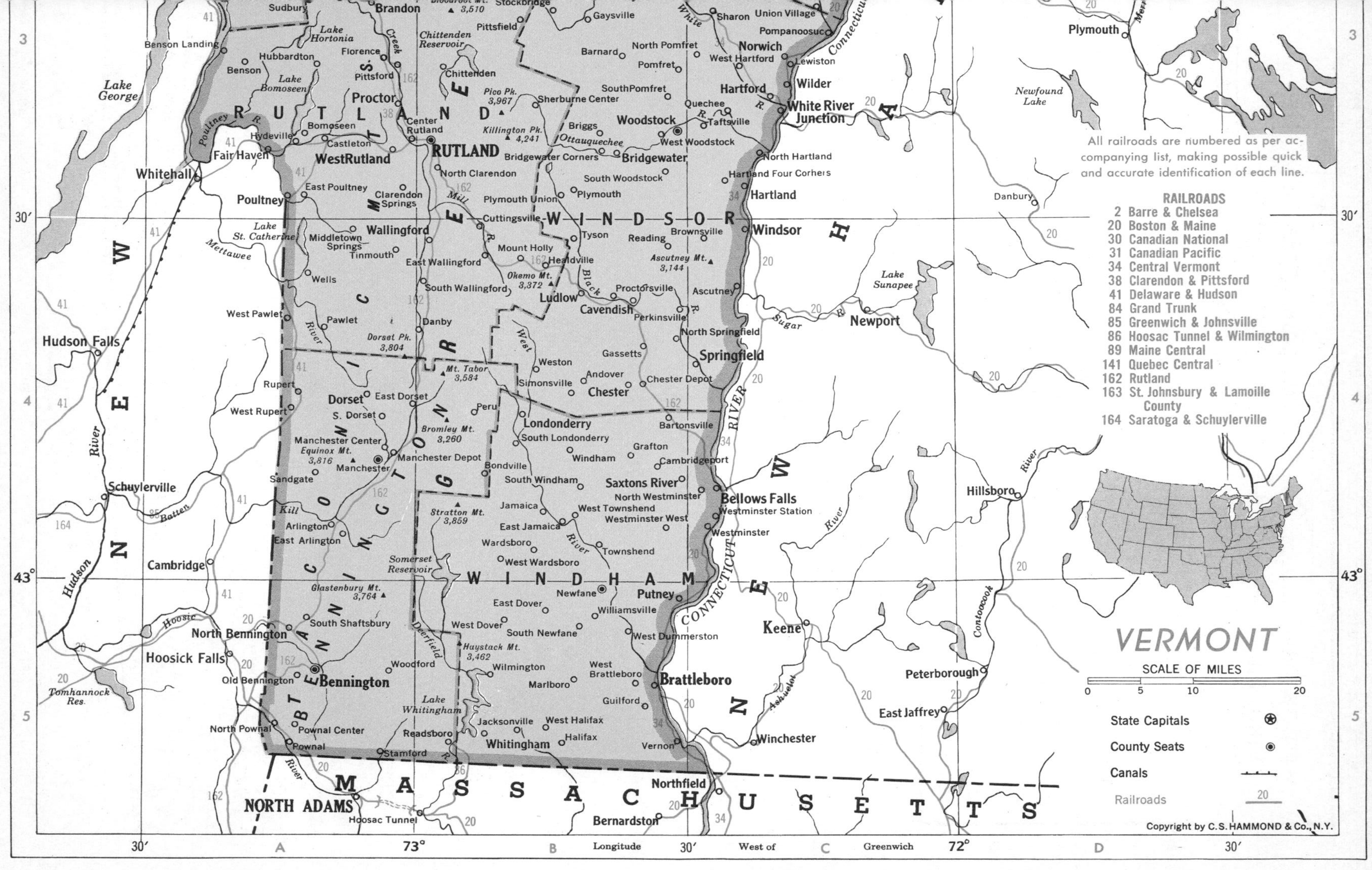
VERMONT
SCALE OF MILES
0 5 10 20
State Capitals
County Seats
Canals
Railroads
All railroads are numbered as per accompanying list, making possible quick and accurate identification of each line.
RAILROADS
2 Barre & Chelsea
20 Boston & Maine
30 Canadian National
31 Canadian Pacific
34 Central Vermont
38 Clarendon & Pittsford
41 Delaware & Hudson
84 Grand Trunk
85 Greenwich & Johnsville
86 Hoosac Tunnel & Wilmington
89 Maine Central
141 Quebec Central
162 Rutland
163 St. Johnsbury & Lamoille County
164 Saratoga & Schuylerville
Copyright by C.S. HAMMOND & Co., N.Y.
RUTLAND
WINDSOR
WINDHAM
BENNINGTON
NEW YORK
NEW HAMPSHIRE
MASSACHUSETTS
CONNECTICUT RIVER
RUTLAND
Rutland
Bennington
Manchester
Woodstock
Windsor
Springfield
Ludlow
Chester
Bellows Falls
Brattleboro
Putney
Newfane
Keene
NORTH ADAMS
Longitude West of Greenwich
73°
72°
43°
30′

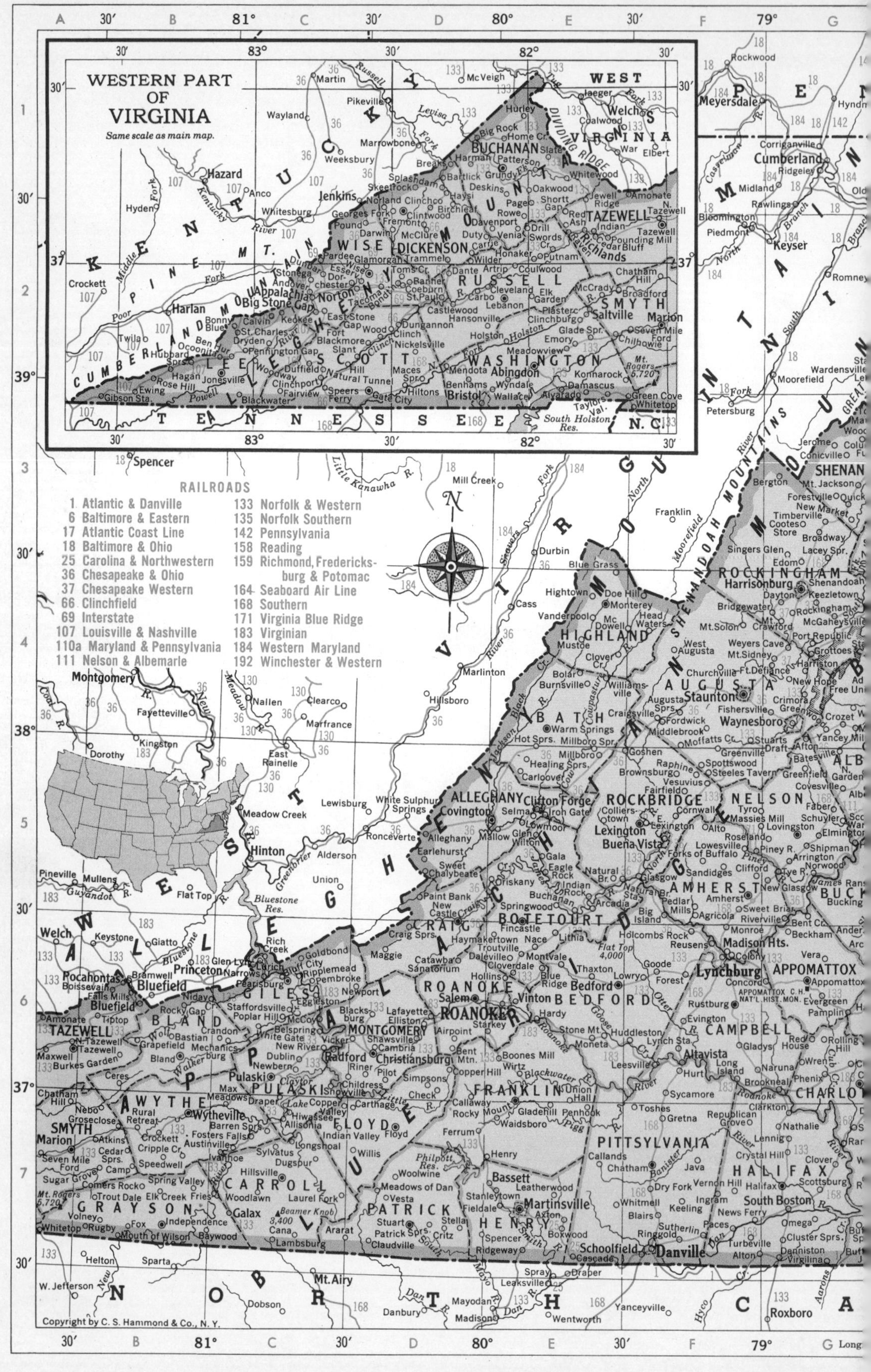

WESTERN PART OF VIRGINIA
Same scale as main map.
RAILROADS
1 Atlantic & Danville
6 Baltimore & Eastern
17 Atlantic Coast Line
18 Baltimore & Ohio
25 Carolina & Northwestern
36 Chesapeake & Ohio
37 Chesapeake Western
66 Clinchfield
69 Interstate
107 Louisville & Nashville
110a Maryland & Pennsylvania
111 Nelson & Albemarle
133 Norfolk & Western
135 Norfolk Southern
142 Pennsylvania
158 Reading
159 Richmond, Fredericksburg & Potomac
164 Seaboard Air Line
168 Southern
171 Virginia Blue Ridge
183 Virginian
184 Western Maryland
192 Winchester & Western
KENTUCKY
WEST VIRGINIA
TENNESSEE
N.C.
BUCHANAN
TAZEWELL
WISE
DICKENSON
RUSSELL
SMYTH
LEE
SCOTT
WASHINGTON
CUMBERLAND MOUNTAIN
PINE MT.
ALLEGHENY MOUNTAINS
SHENANDOAH MOUNTAINS
HIGHLAND
AUGUSTA
BATH
ROCKINGHAM
ALLEGHANY
ROCKBRIDGE
NELSON
AMHERST
BOTETOURT
CRAIG
GILES
BLAND
ROANOKE
BEDFORD
CAMPBELL
APPOMATTOX
MONTGOMERY
PULASKI
WYTHE
FLOYD
FRANKLIN
CARROLL
GRAYSON
PATRICK
HENRY
PITTSYLVANIA
HALIFAX
BLUE RIDGE
NORTH CAROLINA
Roanoke
Lynchburg
Danville
Bristol
Staunton
Harrisonburg
Lexington
Martinsville
Copyright by C. S. Hammond & Co., N. Y.

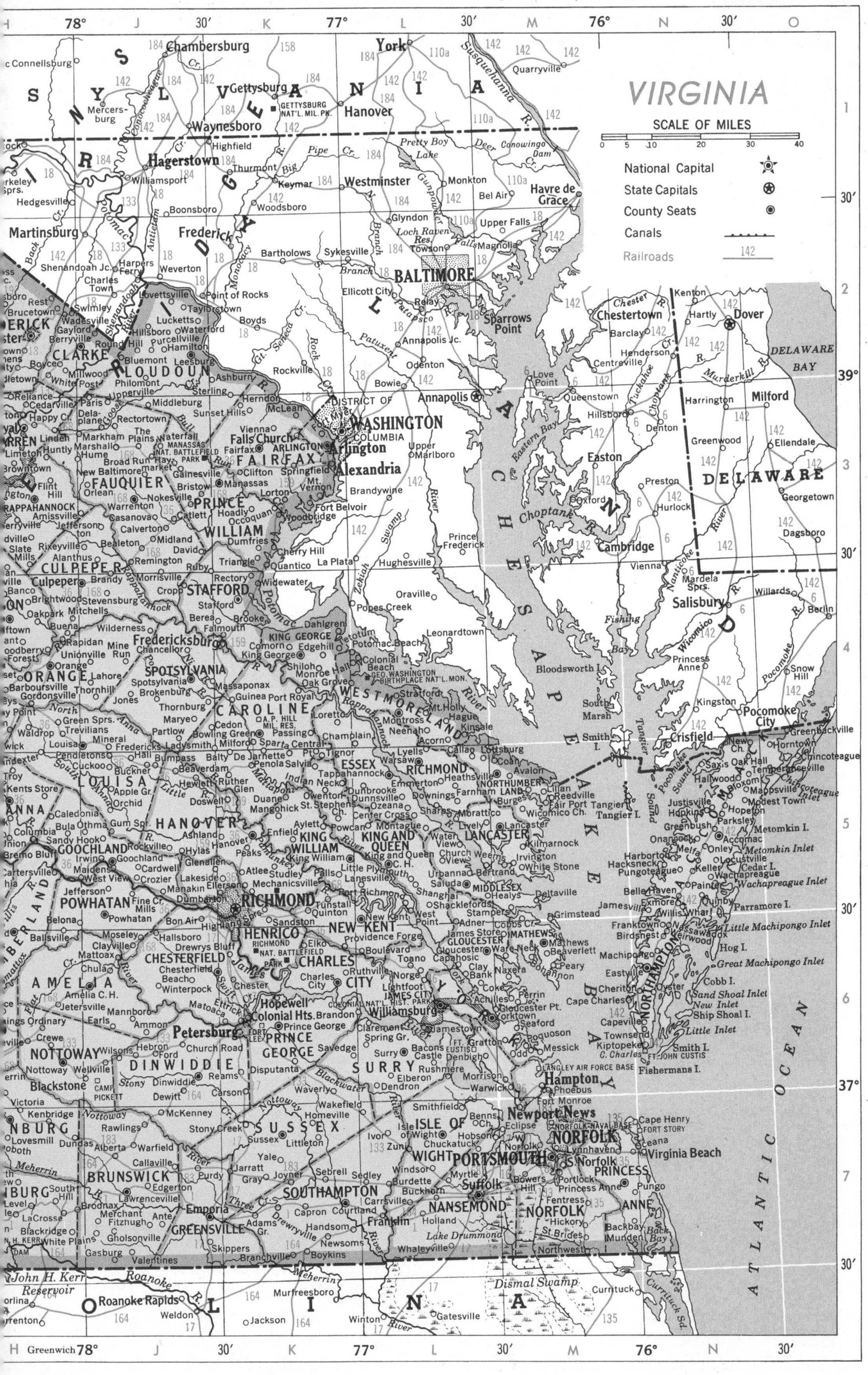
VIRGINIA
SCALE OF MILES
0 5 10 20 30 40
National Capital
State Capitals
County Seats
Canals
Railroads
142
DELAWARE BAY
ATLANTIC OCEAN
CHESAPEAKE BAY
PENNSYLVANIA
DELAWARE
WASHINGTON
DISTRICT OF COLUMBIA
BALTIMORE
RICHMOND
NORFOLK
PORTSMOUTH
Greenwich 78°

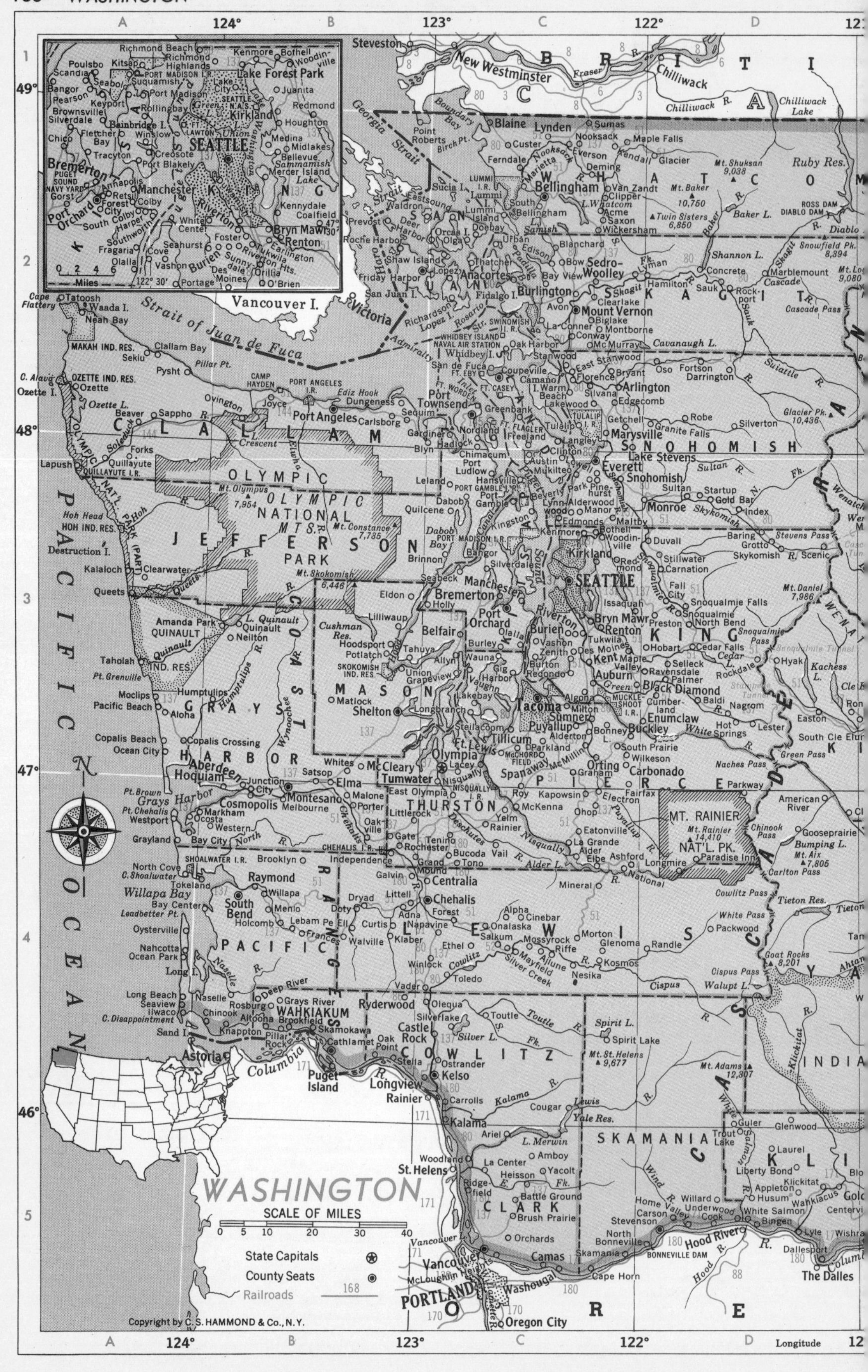
WASHINGTON
SCALE OF MILES
0 5 10 20 30 40
State Capitals
County Seats
Railroads
SEATTLE
Tacoma
Olympia
Bellingham
Everett
Bremerton
Vancouver
PORTLAND
Oregon City
Victoria
Vancouver I.
Strait of Juan de Fuca
PACIFIC OCEAN
CLALLAM
JEFFERSON
GRAYS HARBOR
PACIFIC
WAHKIAKUM
COWLITZ
CLARK
SKAMANIA
LEWIS
THURSTON
MASON
KITSAP
KING
PIERCE
SNOHOMISH
SKAGIT
WHATCOM
SAN JUAN
ISLAND
OLYMPIC NATIONAL PARK
MT. RAINIER NAT'L. PK.
COAST RANGE
CASCADE
BRITISH
Columbia R.
Mt. Olympus 7,954
Mt. Rainier 14,410
Mt. St. Helens 9,677
Mt. Adams 12,307
Mt. Baker 10,750
Longitude
124°
123°
122°
49°
48°
47°
46°

OKANOGAN
FERRY
STEVENS
PEND OREILLE
COLVILLE INDIAN RESERVATION
DOUGLAS
LINCOLN
SPOKANE
GRANT
ADAMS
WHITMAN
FRANKLIN
GARFIELD
COLUMBIA
ASOTIN
WALLA WALLA
BENTON
All railroads are numbered as per accompanying list, making possible quick and accurate identification of each line.
RAILROADS
3 British Columbia Electric
5 Camas Prairie
6 Canadian National
8 Canadian Pacific
51 Chicago, Milwaukee, St. Paul & Pacific
52 Cowlitz, Chehalis & Cascade
80 Great Northern
86 Longview, Portland & Northern
88 Mount Hood
137 Northern Pacific
139a Oregon Electric
141 Oregon Trunk
143 Pacific Coast
144 Port Angeles Western
145 Port Townsend
155 Spokane, International
170 Southern Pacific
171 Spokane, Portland & Seattle
180 Union Pacific
181 Walla Walla Valley
182 Washington, Idaho & Montana
183 Waterville

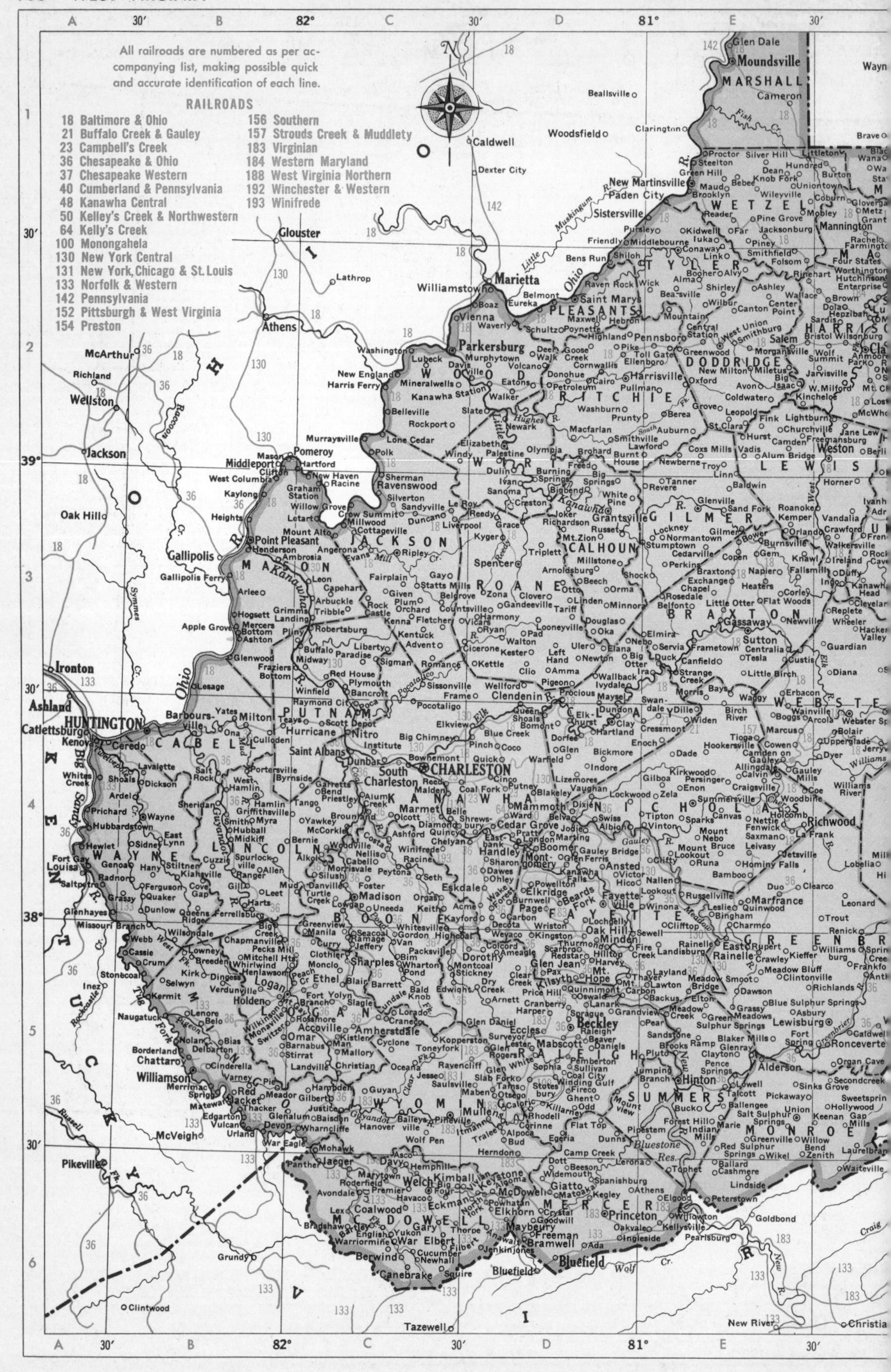
All railroads are numbered as per accompanying list, making possible quick and accurate identification of each line.
RAILROADS
18 Baltimore & Ohio
21 Buffalo Creek & Gauley
23 Campbell's Creek
36 Chesapeake & Ohio
37 Chesapeake Western
40 Cumberland & Pennsylvania
48 Kanawha Central
50 Kelley's Creek & Northwestern
64 Kelly's Creek
100 Monongahela
130 New York Central
131 New York, Chicago & St. Louis
133 Norfolk & Western
142 Pennsylvania
152 Pittsburgh & West Virginia
154 Preston
156 Southern
157 Strouds Creek & Muddlety
183 Virginian
184 Western Maryland
188 West Virginia Northern
192 Winchester & Western
193 Winifrede
OHIO
KENTUCKY
V I
MARSHALL
WETZEL
TYLER
PLEASANTS
WOOD
RITCHIE
DODDRIDGE
WIRT
JACKSON
MASON
CALHOUN
GILMER
LEWIS
ROANE
BRAXTON
PUTNAM
CABELL
KANAWHA
CLAY
NICHOLAS
WEBSTER
WAYNE
LINCOLN
BOONE
FAYETTE
LOGAN
MINGO
RALEIGH
WYOMING
SUMMERS
MONROE
MERCER
McDOWELL
GREENBRIER
CHARLESTON
HUNTINGTON
Parkersburg
Wheeling
Moundsville
Beckley
Bluefield
Williamson
Point Pleasant
Princeton
Logan
Welch
Hinton
Marietta
Ironton
Ashland
Gallipolis

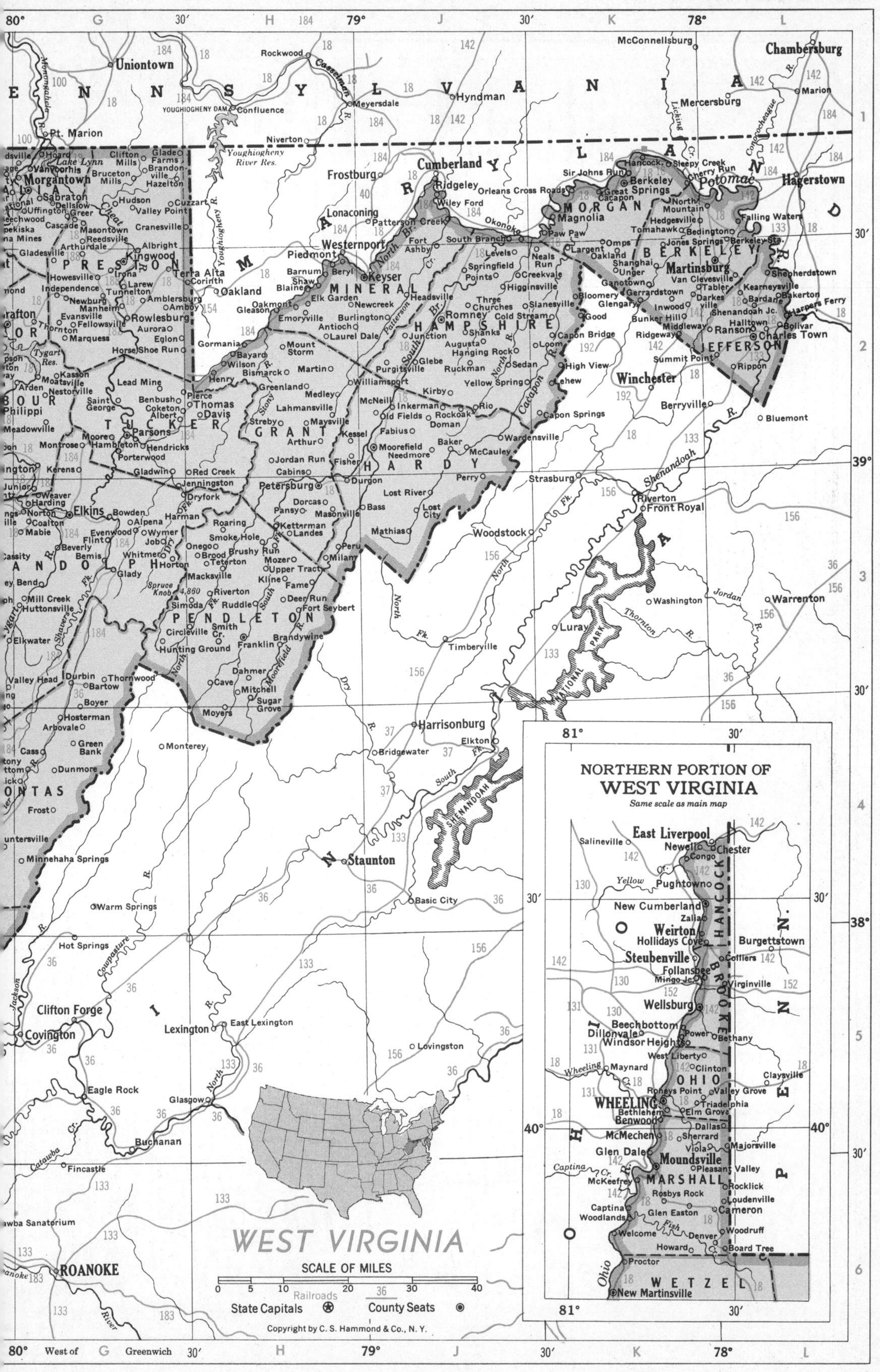
WEST VIRGINIA
SCALE OF MILES
0 5 10 20 30 40
Railroads
36
State Capitals
County Seats
Copyright by C. S. Hammond & Co., N. Y.
80° West of Greenwich
NORTHERN PORTION OF
WEST VIRGINIA
Same scale as main map
PENNSYLVANIA
MARYLAND
VIRGINIA
OHIO
PRESTON
MINERAL
HAMPSHIRE
MORGAN
BERKELEY
JEFFERSON
TUCKER
GRANT
HARDY
RANDOLPH
PENDLETON
HANCOCK
BROOKE
OHIO
MARSHALL
WETZEL
Uniontown
Pt. Marion
Morgantown
Kingwood
Rowlesburg
Terra Alta
Oakland
Cumberland
Frostburg
Westernport
Piedmont
Keyser
Romney
Moorefield
Petersburg
Parsons
Thomas
Davis
Elkins
Franklin
Berkeley Springs
Martinsburg
Charles Town
Harpers Ferry
Hagerstown
Chambersburg
Winchester
Front Royal
Woodstock
Luray
Harrisonburg
Staunton
Lexington
Clifton Forge
Covington
ROANOKE
Warrenton
Monterey
East Liverpool
Chester
Newell
Weirton
Steubenville
Follansbee
Wellsburg
WHEELING
Benwood
McMechen
Glen Dale
Moundsville
New Martinsville
Potomac
Shenandoah
Cheat
Ohio

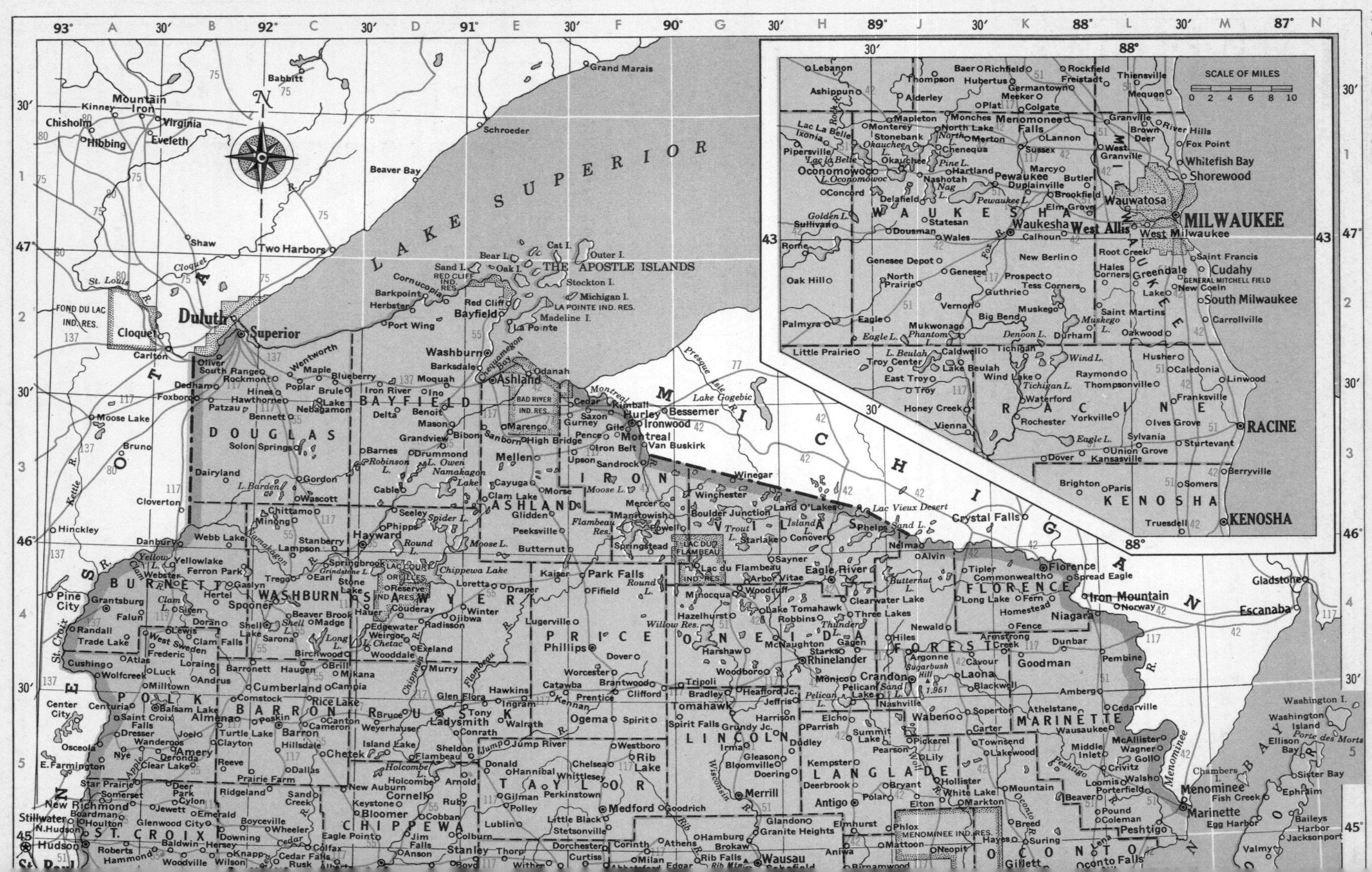
LAKE SUPERIOR
THE APOSTLE ISLANDS
MICHIGAN
SCALE OF MILES
MILWAUKEE
RACINE
KENOSHA
WAUKESHA
Wauwatosa
West Allis
Shorewood
South Milwaukee
Cudahy
Duluth
Superior
Ashland
Bayfield
Washburn
Ironwood
Hurley
Bessemer
Iron Mountain
Escanaba
Menominee
Marinette
Rhinelander
Antigo
Merrill
Wausau
Phillips
Medford
Hayward
Spooner
DOUGLAS
BAYFIELD
ASHLAND
IRON
VILAS
ONEIDA
FOREST
FLORENCE
MARINETTE
LANGLADE
LINCOLN
PRICE
TAYLOR
SAWYER
WASHBURN
BURNETT
POLK
BARRON
RUSK
CHIPPEWA
ST. CROIX

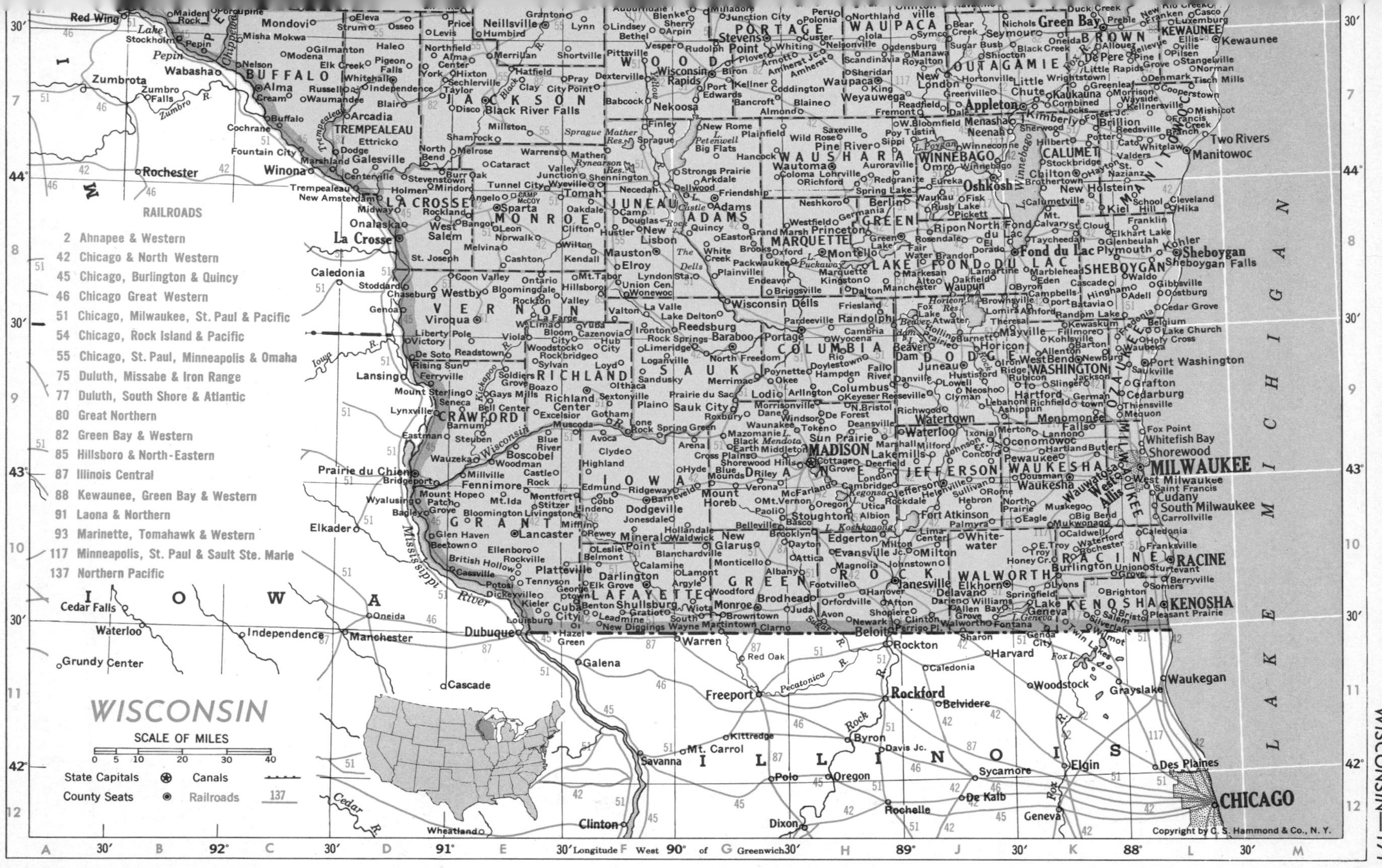
RAILROADS
2 Ahnapee & Western
42 Chicago & North Western
45 Chicago, Burlington & Quincy
46 Chicago Great Western
51 Chicago, Milwaukee, St. Paul & Pacific
54 Chicago, Rock Island & Pacific
55 Chicago, St. Paul, Minneapolis & Omaha
75 Duluth, Missabe & Iron Range
77 Duluth, South Shore & Atlantic
80 Great Northern
82 Green Bay & Western
85 Hillsboro & North-Eastern
87 Illinois Central
88 Kewaunee, Green Bay & Western
91 Laona & Northern
93 Marinette, Tomahawk & Western
117 Minneapolis, St. Paul & Sault Ste. Marie
137 Northern Pacific
WISCONSIN
SCALE OF MILES
0 5 10 20 30 40
State Capitals
County Seats
Canals
Railroads 137
LAKE MICHIGAN
IOWA
ILLINOIS
MILWAUKEE
MADISON
CHICAGO
30′ Longitude West 90° of Greenwich 30′
Copyright by C. S. Hammond & Co., N. Y.

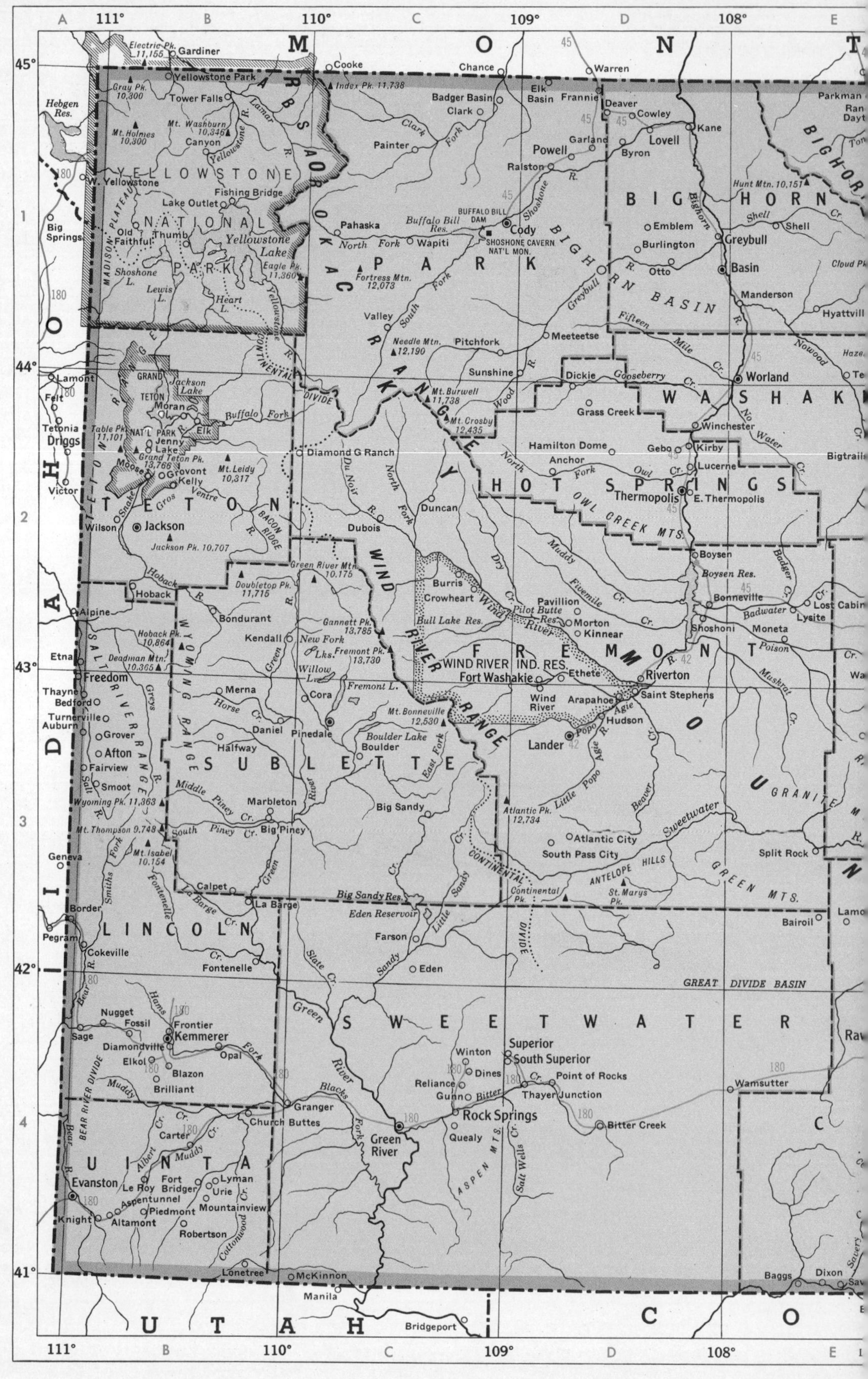

A
B
C
D
E
111°
110°
109°
108°
45°
44°
43°
42°
41°
1
2
3
4
M O N T
I D A H O
U T A H
C O
Electric Pk. 11,155
Gardiner
Cooke
Chance
Warren
Yellowstone Park
Index Pk. 11,738
Gray Pk. 10,300
Tower Falls
Hebgen Res.
Mt. Holmes 10,300
Mt. Washburn 10,346
Canyon
Lamar R.
Yellowstone R.
ABSAROKA RANGE
YELLOWSTONE NATIONAL PARK
W. Yellowstone
Lake Outlet
Fishing Bridge
Big Springs
Old Faithful
Thumb
Yellowstone Lake
MADISON PLATEAU
Shoshone L.
Lewis L.
Heart L.
Eagle Pk. 11,360
Badger Basin
Clark
Elk Basin
Frannie
Deaver
Cowley
Kane
Clark Fork
Painter
Powell
Garland
Lovell
Byron
Ralston
Shoshone R.
BUFFALO BILL DAM
Buffalo Bill Res.
Cody
SHOSHONE CAVERN NAT'L MON.
Pahaska
North Fork
Wapiti
PARK
Fortress Mtn. 12,073
Valley
South Fork
Needle Mtn. 12,190
Pitchfork
Meeteetse
Sunshine
Mt. Burwell 11,738
Mt. Crosby 12,435
Wood R.
BIG HORN
Hunt Mtn. 10,151
Shell Cr.
Shell
Emblem
Burlington
Greybull
Otto
Basin
Cloud Pk
Manderson
Hyattvill
BIG HORN BASIN
Greybull R.
Bighorn R.
Fifteen Mile Cr.
Nowood
Parkman
Dayt
BIGHORN
Worland
Dickie
Gooseberry Cr.
WASHAKIE
Grass Creek
Winchester
No Water Cr.
Hamilton Dome
Gebo
Kirby
Anchor
Owl Cr.
Lucerne
Bigtrails
North Fork
HOT SPRINGS
Thermopolis
E. Thermopolis
OWL CREEK MTS.
Lamont
Felt
Tetonia
Driggs
Victor
GRAND TETON
Jackson Lake
Moran
NAT'L PARK
Elk
Buffalo Fork
Table Pk. 11,101
Jenny Lake
Grand Teton Pk. 13,766
Moose
Grovont
Kelly
Mt. Leidy 10,317
Gros Ventre R.
TETON
TETON RANGE
Wilson
Jackson
Jackson Pk. 10,707
BACON RIDGE
CONTINENTAL DIVIDE
Diamond G Ranch
Du Noir R.
North Fork
Duncan
Dubois
Green River Mtn. 10,175
WIND RIVER
Dry Cr.
Muddy Cr.
Boysen
Boysen Res.
Badger Cr.
Hoback
Doubletop Pk. 11,715
Burris
Crowheart
Wind River
Fivemile Cr.
Bonneville
Lost Cabin
Lysite
Badwater Cr.
Alpine
Bondurant
Bull Lake Res.
Pilot Butte Res.
Pavillion
Morton
Kinnear
Shoshoni
Moneta
Poison Cr.
Hoback Pk. 10,864
WYOMING RANGE
Gannett Pk. 13,785
Kendall
New Fork Lks.
Fremont Pk. 13,730
FREMONT
Etna
Deadman Mtn. 10,365
Willow L.
WIND RIVER IND. RES.
Fort Washakie
Ethete
Riverton
Muskrat Cr.
Freedom
Thayne
Bedford
Merna
Cora
Fremont L.
Wind River
Arapahoe
Saint Stephens
SALT RIVER RANGE
Greys R.
Horse Cr.
Mt. Bonneville 12,530
WIND RIVER RANGE
Popo Agie R.
Hudson
Turnerville
Auburn
Grover
Daniel
Pinedale
Boulder Lake
Boulder
Lander
Afton
Halfway
SUBLETTE
East Fork
Fairview
Smoot
Salt R.
Middle Piney Cr.
Marbleton
Little Popo Agie
Beaver Cr.
GRANITE
Wyoming Pk. 11,363
Big Sandy
Atlantic Pk. 12,734
Sweetwater
Mt. Thompson 9,748
South Piney Cr.
Big Piney
Atlantic City
Split Rock
Geneva
Mt. Isabel 10,154
South Pass City
ANTELOPE HILLS
GREEN MTS.
Smiths Fork
Fontenelle
Calpet
Green R.
Little Sandy Cr.
St. Marys Pk.
Continental Pk.
La Barge Cr.
Big Sandy Res.
La Barge
Border
Eden Reservoir
Bairoil
Lamo
Pegram
LINCOLN
Farson
Cokeville
Fontenelle Cr.
Slate Cr.
Sandy Cr.
Eden
Bear R.
GREAT DIVIDE BASIN
Hams Fork
Nugget
Fossil
Frontier
Green R.
SWEETWATER
Sage
Kemmerer
Superior
South Superior
Ra
Diamondville
Opal
Winton
Elkol
Blazon
Dines
Point of Rocks
Reliance
Bitter Cr.
Wamsutter
Muddy Cr.
Brilliant
Gunn
Thayer Junction
BEAR RIVER DIVIDE
Blacks Fork
Granger
Rock Springs
Church Buttes
Bitter Creek
Carter
Quealy
Green River
ASPEN MTS.
Salt Wells Cr.
UINTA
Albert Cr.
Muddy Cr.
Evanston
Fort Bridger
Lyman
Le Roy
Urie
Aspentunnel
Piedmont
Mountainview
Knight
Altamont
Robertson
Cottonwood Cr.
Lonetree
McKinnon
Manila
Bridgeport
Baggs
Dixon
Savery
45
42
80
180

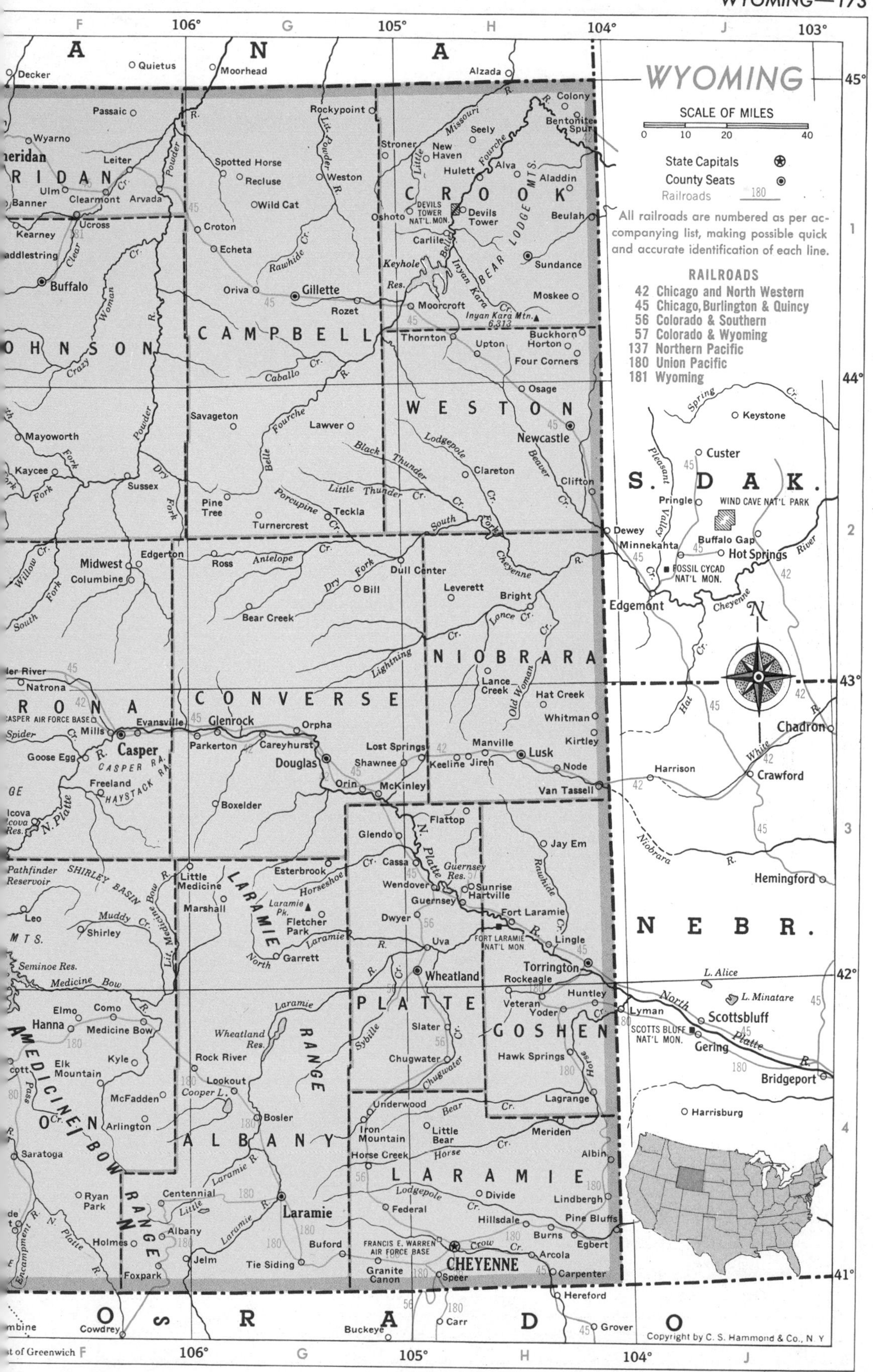
WYOMING
SCALE OF MILES
0 10 20 40
State Capitals
County Seats
Railroads 180
All railroads are numbered as per accompanying list, making possible quick and accurate identification of each line.
RAILROADS
42 Chicago and North Western
45 Chicago, Burlington & Quincy
56 Colorado & Southern
57 Colorado & Wyoming
137 Northern Pacific
180 Union Pacific
181 Wyoming
F 106° G 105° H 104° J 103°
45° 44° 43° 42° 41°
1 2 3 4
C A N A D A
S. DAK.
NEBR.
C O L O R A D O
CROOK
CAMPBELL
WESTON
JOHNSON
SHERIDAN
CONVERSE
NIOBRARA
NATRONA
PLATTE
GOSHEN
LARAMIE
ALBANY
LARAMIE RANGE
MEDICINE BOW RANGE
BEAR LODGE MTS.
Decker
Quietus
Moorhead
Alzada
Colony
Bentonite Spur
Passaic
Rockypoint
Wyarno
Sheridan
Leiter
Spotted Horse
Recluse
Weston
Stoner
New Haven
Seely
Hulett
Alva
Aladdin
Ulm
Clearmont
Arvada
Banner
Wild Cat
Oshoto
DEVILS TOWER NAT'L. MON.
Devils Tower
Beulah
Ucross
Kearney
Saddlestring
Croton
Echeta
Carlile
Keyhole Res.
Sundance
Buffalo
Oriva
Gillette
Rozet
Moorcroft
Moskee
Inyan Kara Mtn. 6,313
Thornton
Upton
Buckhorn
Horton
Four Corners
Osage
Savageton
Lawver
Mayoworth
Newcastle
Clareton
Kaycee
Sussex
Clifton
Pine Tree
Turnercrest
Teckla
Dewey
Minnekahta
Edgerton
Midwest
Columbine
Ross
Dull Center
Bill
Leverett
Bright
Bear Creek
Edgemont
Natrona
CASPER AIR FORCE BASE
Mills
Casper
Evansville
Glenrock
Orpha
Parkerton
Careyhurst
Douglas
Lost Springs
Shawnee
Orin
McKinley
Keeline
Jireh
Manville
Lusk
Node
Van Tassell
Lance Creek
Hat Creek
Whitman
Kirtley
Goose Egg
CASPER RA.
HAYSTACK RA.
Freeland
Boxelder
Flattop
Glendo
Jay Em
Esterbrook
Little Medicine
Cassa
Guernsey Res.
Wendover
Sunrise
Hartville
Guernsey
Fort Laramie
FORT LARAMIE NAT'L MON.
Lingle
Marshall
Laramie Pk.
Fletcher Park
Garrett
Dwyer
Uva
Leo
Shirley
SHIRLEY BASIN
Pathfinder Reservoir
Seminoe Res.
Wheatland
Torrington
Rockeagle
Huntley
Veteran
Yoder
Elmo
Como
Hanna
Medicine Bow
Wheatland Res.
Rock River
Slater
Chugwater
Hawk Springs
Elk Mountain
Kyle
Lookout
Cooper L.
McFadden
Arlington
Bosler
Lagrange
Underwood
Iron Mountain
Little Bear
Meriden
Saratoga
Horse Creek
Albin
Ryan Park
Centennial
Divide
Lindbergh
Federal
Pine Bluffs
Laramie
Hillsdale
Albany
Burns
Egbert
Holmes
Buford
FRANCIS E. WARREN AIR FORCE BASE
Cheyenne
Arcola
Jelm
Tie Siding
Granite Canon
Speer
Carpenter
Foxpark
Hereford
Cowdrey
Buckeye
Carr
Grover
Keystone
Custer
Pringle
WIND CAVE NAT'L PARK
Buffalo Gap
Hot Springs
FOSSIL CYCAD NAT'L MON.
Chadron
Harrison
Crawford
Hemingford
L. Alice
L. Minatare
Lyman
Scottsbluff
SCOTTS BLUFF NAT'L MON.
Gering
Bridgeport
Harrisburg
Copyright by C. S. Hammond & Co., N. Y.
Meridian West of Greenwich

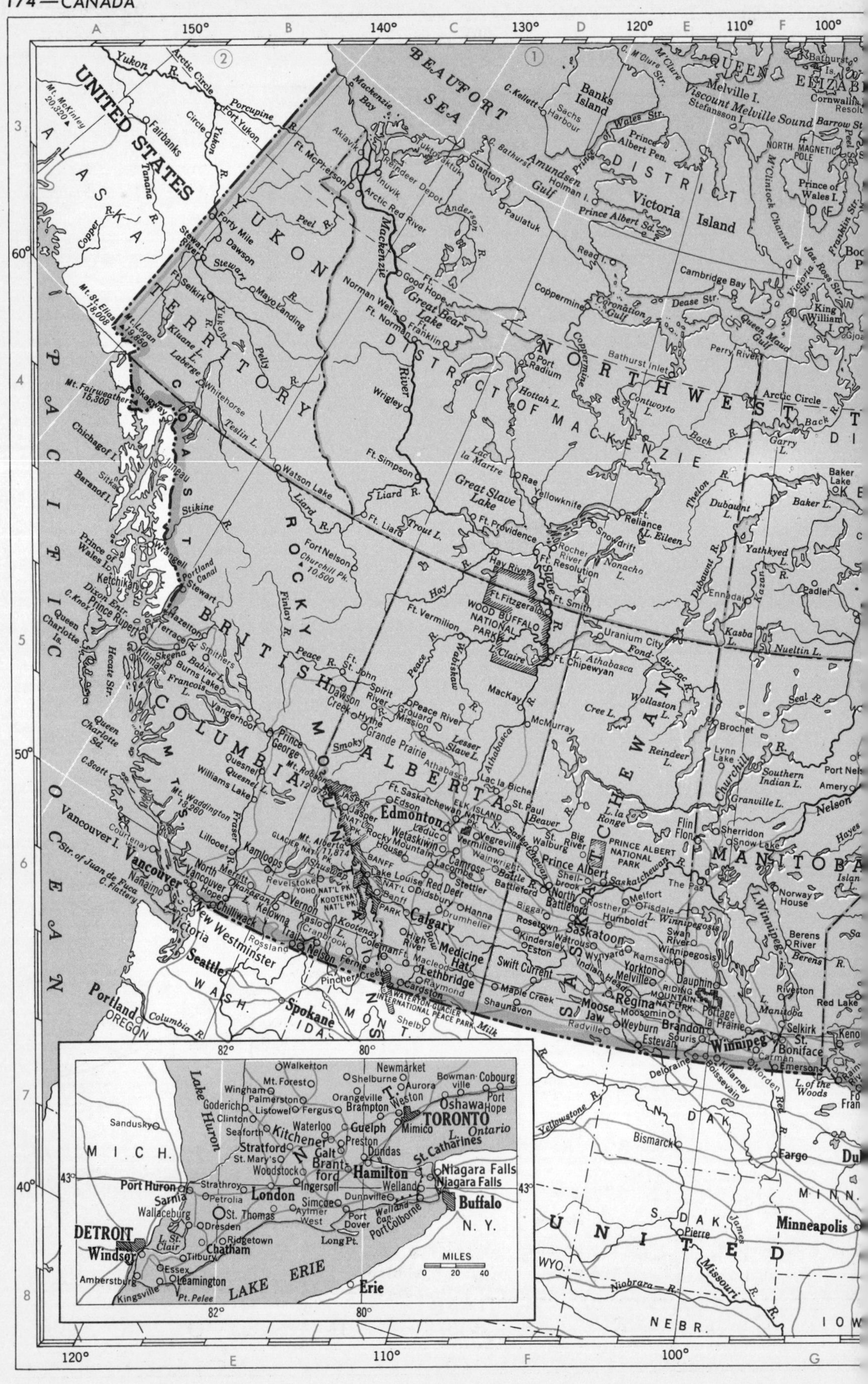
BEAUFORT SEA
PACIFIC OCEAN
UNITED STATES
ALASKA
YUKON TERRITORY
DISTRICT OF MACKENZIE
NORTHWEST
BRITISH COLUMBIA
ALBERTA
SASKATCHEWAN
MANITOBA
ROCKY MTS.
COAST MTS.
Victoria Island
Banks Island
Great Bear Lake
Great Slave Lake
Edmonton
Calgary
Vancouver
Victoria
Regina
Saskatoon
Winnipeg
Seattle
Spokane
Portland
WOOD BUFFALO NATIONAL PARK
PRINCE ALBERT NATIONAL PARK
Lake Huron
L. Ontario
LAKE ERIE
TORONTO
Hamilton
London
Kitchener
DETROIT
Windsor
Buffalo
Erie
MILES

CANADA
CONIC PROJECTION
SCALE OF MILES
0 50 100 200 300
SCALE OF KILOMETRES
0 50 100 200 300 400 500
Capitals of Countries
Provincial Capitals
International Boundaries
Provincial Boundaries
Canals
Railroads
Copyright by C. S. Hammond & Co., N.Y.
GREENLAND
BAFFIN BAY
DAVIS STRAIT
BAFFIN ISLAND
FOXE BASIN
Hudson Str.
Ungava Peninsula
Ungava Bay
ATLANTIC OCEAN
HUDSON BAY
James Bay
LABRADOR
NEWFOUNDLAND
QUEBEC
ONTARIO
NEW BRUNSWICK
NOVA SCOTIA
PRINCE EDWARD I.
Gulf of St. Lawrence
MAINE
VT.
N.H.
MASS.
CONN.
R.I.
N.Y.
PA.
MICH.
ILLINOIS
UNITED STATES
Lake Superior
Lake Huron
L. Ontario
L. Erie
L. Michigan
Georgian Bay
MONTRÉAL
Québec
Ottawa
TORONTO
Halifax
St. John's
Fredericton
Charlottetown
BOSTON
NEW YORK
DETROIT
Buffalo
Cleveland
Albany
Hamilton
London
Windsor
Kingston
Sherbrooke
Trois-Rivières
Saint John
Moncton
Sydney
Sault Ste. Marie
Sudbury
North Bay
Timmins
Chicoutimi
Rimouski
Gaspé
Corner Brook
Gander
Grand Falls
Goose Airport
Schefferville
Ft. Chimo
Port Harrison
Great Whale River
Moosonee
Fort Albany
Pond Inlet
Clyde
Frobisher Bay
Lake Harbour
Cape Dorset
Resolution I.
Akpatok I.
C. Chidley
Hebron
Nain
Hopedale
Cartwright
Belle Isle
Anticosti I.
Sable I.
C. Race
ST. PIERRE & MIQUELON (Fr.)
West of Greenwich
74° 73° 72°
46°
MILES 0 10 20
Berthierville
Sorel
Victoriaville
Joliette
Drummondville
St.-Jérôme
Lachute
MONTRÉAL
Richmond
St. Hyacinthe
Lachine
Longueuil
St. Lambert
Sherbrooke
Verdun
Granby
Beauharnois
St. Jean
Farnham
Valleyfield
Bedford
Magog

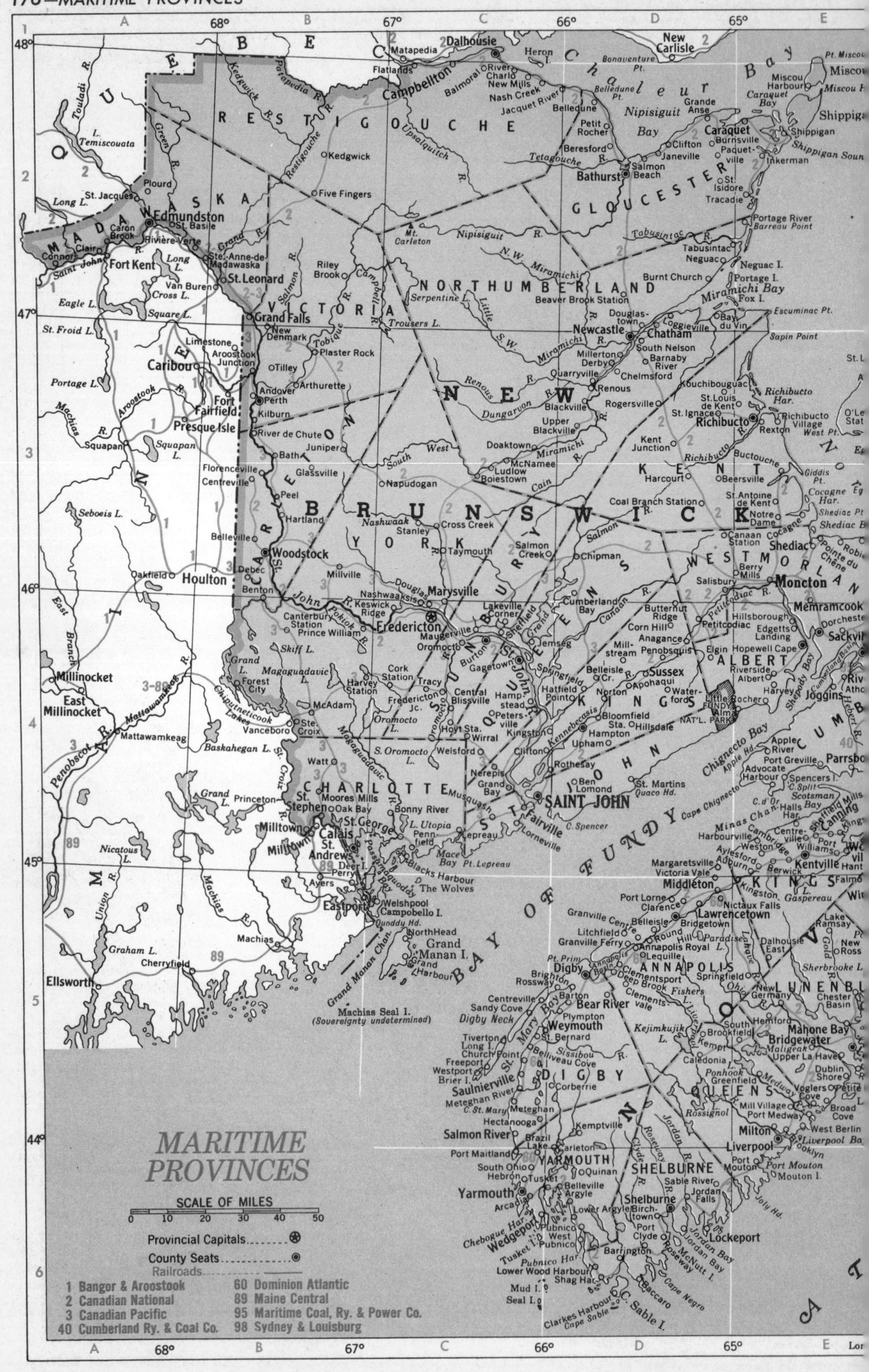
MARITIME PROVINCES
SCALE OF MILES
0 10 20 30 40 50
Provincial Capitals
County Seats
Railroads
1 Bangor & Aroostook
2 Canadian National
3 Canadian Pacific
40 Cumberland Ry. & Coal Co.
60 Dominion Atlantic
89 Maine Central
95 Maritime Coal, Ry. & Power Co.
98 Sydney & Louisburg
QUEBEC
MAINE
NEW BRUNSWICK
RESTIGOUCHE
MADAWASKA
VICTORIA
GLOUCESTER
NORTHUMBERLAND
CARLETON
YORK
SUNBURY
QUEENS
KENT
WESTMORLAND
ALBERT
KINGS
SAINT JOHN
CHARLOTTE
ANNAPOLIS
DIGBY
YARMOUTH
SHELBURNE
LUNENBURG
BAY OF FUNDY
Chaleur Bay
Miramichi Bay
Chignecto Bay
Minas Chan.
Passamaquoddy Bay
Grand Manan I.
Machias Seal I.
(Sovereignty undetermined)
Dalhousie
Campbellton
Bathurst
Edmundston
Grand Falls
Woodstock
Houlton
Caribou
Presque Isle
Fredericton
Marysville
Newcastle
Chatham
Richibucto
Moncton
Sackville
Sussex
SAINT JOHN
Fairville
St. Stephen
Calais
St. Andrews
Eastport
Millinocket
Ellsworth
Digby
Yarmouth
Shelburne
Lockeport
Liverpool
Bridgewater
Kentville
Middleton
Lawrencetown
Annapolis Royal
Weymouth
Bear River
48°
47°
46°
45°
44°
68°
67°
66°
65°

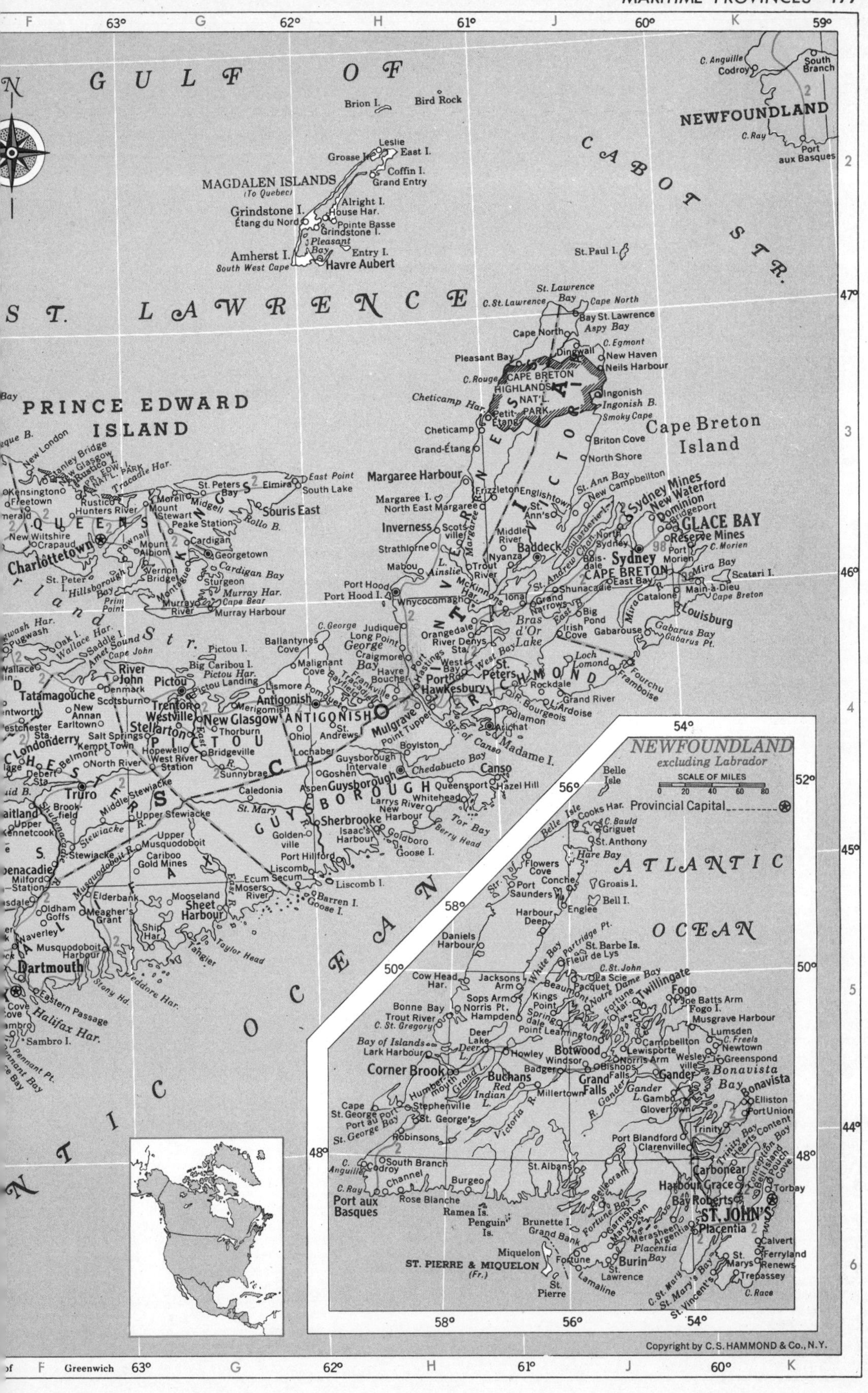
GULF OF ST. LAWRENCE
CABOT STR.
MAGDALEN ISLANDS
(To Quebec)
Brion I.
Bird Rock
Grindstone I.
Amherst I.
Havre Aubert
St. Paul I.
NEWFOUNDLAND
C. Ray
Port aux Basques
PRINCE EDWARD ISLAND
QUEENS
KINGS
Charlottetown
Souris East
Georgetown
Northumberland Str.
Cape Breton Island
CAPE BRETON HIGHLANDS NAT'L. PARK
VICTORIA
INVERNESS
RICHMOND
CAPE BRETON
Sydney
Sydney Mines
New Waterford
Glace Bay
Louisburg
Baddeck
Bras d'Or Lake
Port Hawkesbury
Mulgrave
Str. of Canso
Antigonish
ANTIGONISH
New Glasgow
PICTOU
Pictou
Truro
COLCHESTER
HALIFAX
GUYSBOROUGH
Guysborough
Canso
Sherbrooke
Sheet Harbour
Dartmouth
Halifax Har.
ATLANTIC OCEAN
NEWFOUNDLAND
excluding Labrador
SCALE OF MILES
0 20 40 60 80
Provincial Capital
Belle Isle
Str. of Belle Isle
Corner Brook
Grand Falls
Gander
Botwood
Twillingate
Fogo
Bonavista Bay
Bonavista
Trinity Bay
Carbonear
Harbour Grace
Bay Roberts
ST. JOHN'S
Placentia
Burin
Fortune Bay
Placentia Bay
St. Mary's Bay
C. Race
ST. PIERRE & MIQUELON (Fr.)
Copyright by C.S. HAMMOND & Co., N.Y.
Greenwich 63° 62° 61° 60° 59°
47° 46° 45° 44°

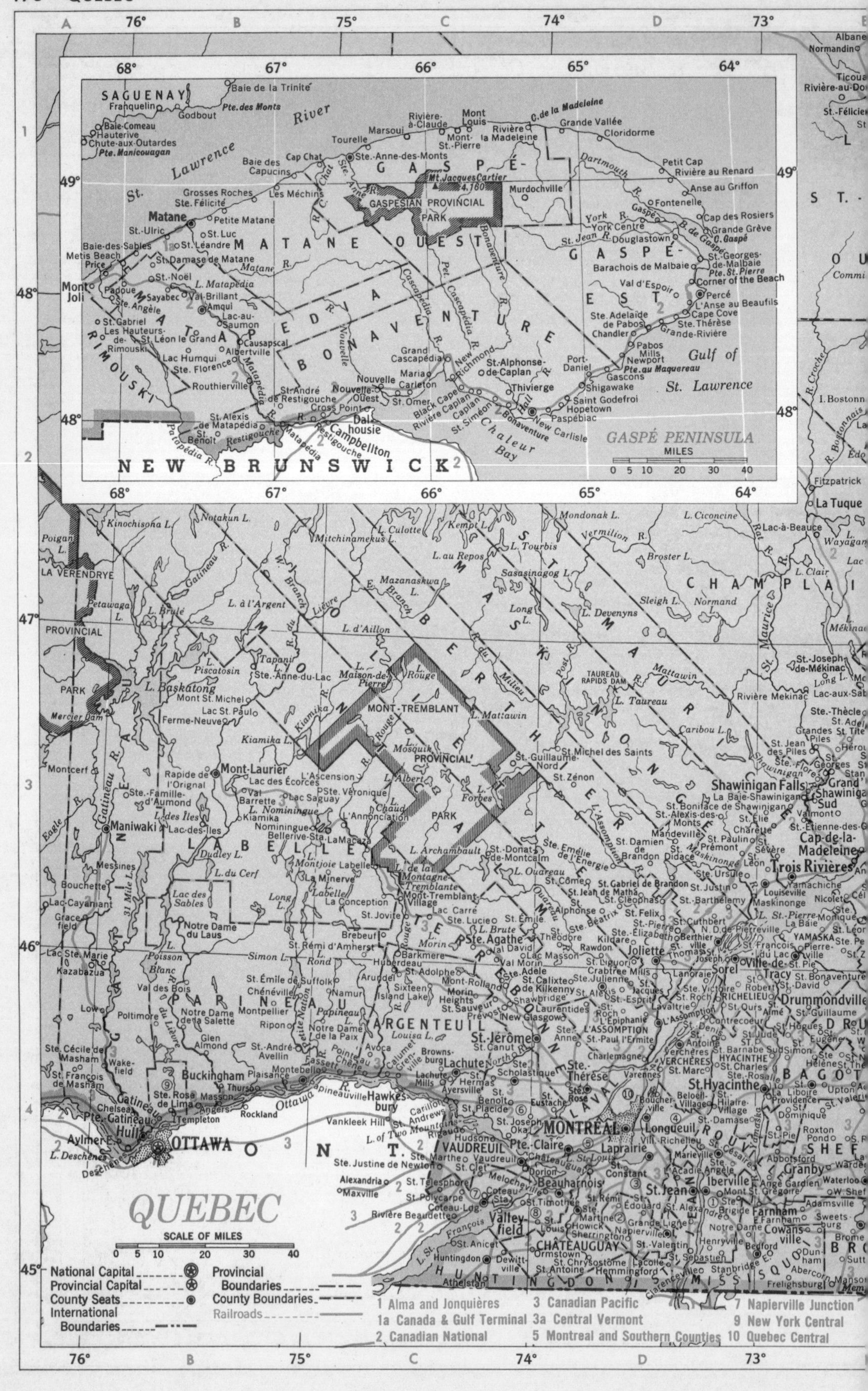
QUEBEC
SCALE OF MILES
0 5 10 20 30 40
National Capital
Provincial Capital
County Seats
International Boundaries
Provincial Boundaries
County Boundaries
Railroads
1 Alma and Jonquières
1a Canada & Gulf Terminal
2 Canadian National
3 Canadian Pacific
3a Central Vermont
5 Montreal and Southern Counties
7 Napierville Junction
9 New York Central
10 Quebec Central
GASPÉ PENINSULA
MILES
0 5 10 20 30 40
NEW BRUNSWICK
Gulf of St. Lawrence
St. Lawrence River
Chaleur Bay
SAGUENAY
MATANE
MATAPEDIA
RIMOUSKI
BONAVENTURE
GASPÉ-OUEST
GASPÉ-EST
GASPESIAN PROVINCIAL PARK
Mt. Jacques Cartier 4,160
Matane
Campbellton
Dalhousie
Percé
Gaspé
Murdochville
Ste.-Anne-des-Monts
Amqui
New Carlisle
Chandler
MONT-TREMBLANT PROVINCIAL PARK
LA VERENDRYE PROVINCIAL PARK
PONTIAC
LABELLE
PAPINEAU
ARGENTEUIL
TERREBONNE
BERTHIER
MASKINONGÉ
ST. MAURICE
CHAMPLAIN
JOLIETTE
MONTCALM
L'ASSOMPTION
VERCHÈRES
RICHELIEU
ST. HYACINTHE
BAGOT
SHEFFORD
ROUVILLE
ST. JEAN
IBERVILLE
MISSISQUOI
HUNTINGDON
CHATEAUGUAY
BEAUHARNOIS
VAUDREUIL
SOULANGES
LAVAL
YAMASKA
DRUMMOND
ONT.
OTTAWA
MONTREAL
Hull
Trois Rivières
Shawinigan Falls
Mont-Laurier
Maniwaki
Buckingham
Lachute
Joliette
Sorel
St. Hyacinthe
Granby
Drummondville
St.-Jérôme
Valleyfield
Ste. Agathe
Longueuil
St. Jean
La Tuque
Cap-de-la-Madeleine
L. Baskatong
Ottawa R.
Gatineau R.
L. of Two Mountains
St. Maurice R.
St. François R.
Richelieu R.
L. St.-Pierre

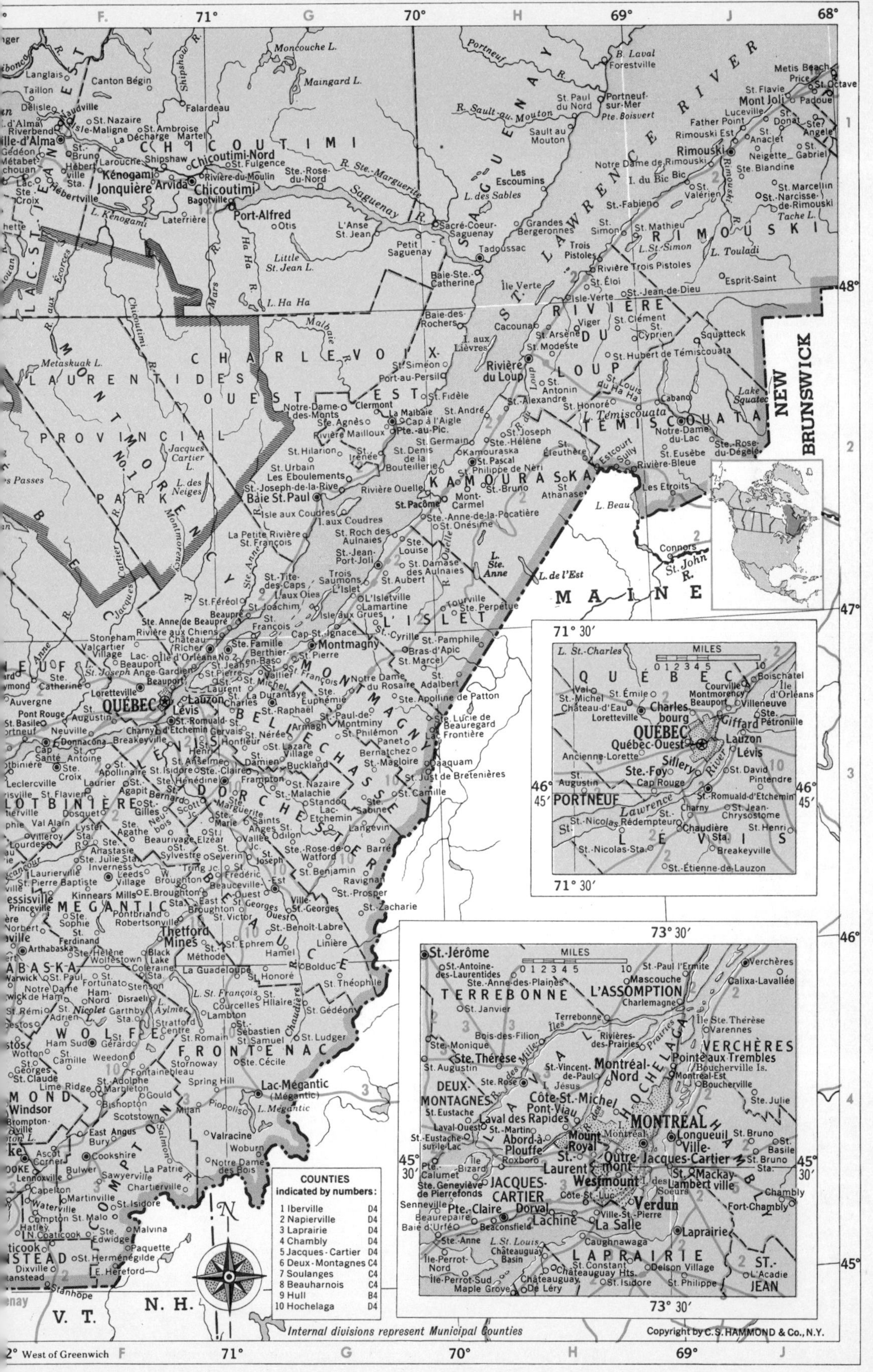
COUNTIES
indicated by numbers:
1 Iberville D4
2 Napierville D4
3 Laprairie D4
4 Chambly D4
5 Jacques-Cartier D4
6 Deux-Montagnes C4
7 Soulanges C4
8 Beauharnois C4
9 Hull B4
10 Hochelaga D4
Internal divisions represent Municipal Counties
Copyright by C.S. HAMMOND & Co., N.Y.
West of Greenwich
CHICOUTIMI
CHARLEVOIX
LAURENTIDES
PROVINCIAL PARK
MONTMORENCY
KAMOURASKA
TEMISCOUATA
RIVIÈRE DU LOUP
RIMOUSKI
SAGUENAY
MONTMAGNY
L'ISLET
BELLECHASSE
DORCHESTER
LÉVIS
LOTBINIÈRE
MEGANTIC
BEAUCE
FRONTENAC
WOLFE
COMPTON
NEW BRUNSWICK
MAINE
N. H.
V. T.
QUÉBEC
Lauzon
Lévis
Chicoutimi
Rimouski
Rivière du Loup
Thetford Mines
Lac-Mégantic
ST. LAWRENCE RIVER
TERREBONNE
L'ASSOMPTION
VERCHÈRES
DEUX-MONTAGNES
JACQUES-CARTIER
LAPRAIRIE
MONTREAL
Verdun
Westmount
Lachine
ST.-JEAN

Sudbury
Copper Cliff
North Bay
Lake Nipissing
Sturgeon Falls
ALGOMA
SUDBURY
Elliot Lake
Blind River
Espanola
North Channel
MANITOULIN
Manitoulin Island
GEORGIAN BAY
PARRY SOUND
Parry Sound
LAKE HURON
MICHIGAN
Alpena
Thunder Bay
Harrisville
Oscoda
Port Austin
Harbor Beach
Port Huron
Sarnia
Owen Sound
Meaford
Nottawasaga Bay
Collingwood
Midland
Penetanguishene
Orillia
Barrie
SIMCOE
GREY
BRUCE
DUFFERIN
WELLINGTON
HURON
PERTH
WATERLOO
HALTON
PEEL
YORK
Goderich
Stratford
Kitchener
Guelph
Galt
Brantford
HAMILTON
Toronto
Oakville
Burlington
OXFORD
Woodstock
MIDDLESEX
LONDON
LAMBTON
St. Thomas
ELGIN
NORFOLK
Simcoe
HALDIMAND
LINCOLN
KENT
Chatham
ESSEX
WINDSOR
DETROIT
Leamington
Lake St. Clair
LAKE ERIE
ERIE
PA.
N.Y.
Long Point Bay
POINT PELÉE NAT'L PARK
RONDEAU PROVINCIAL PARK
GEORGIAN BAY IS. NAT'L PARK
IPPERWASH PROV. PARK
Copyright by C. S. HAMMOND & CO., N. Y.
Longitude 80° West of Greenwi

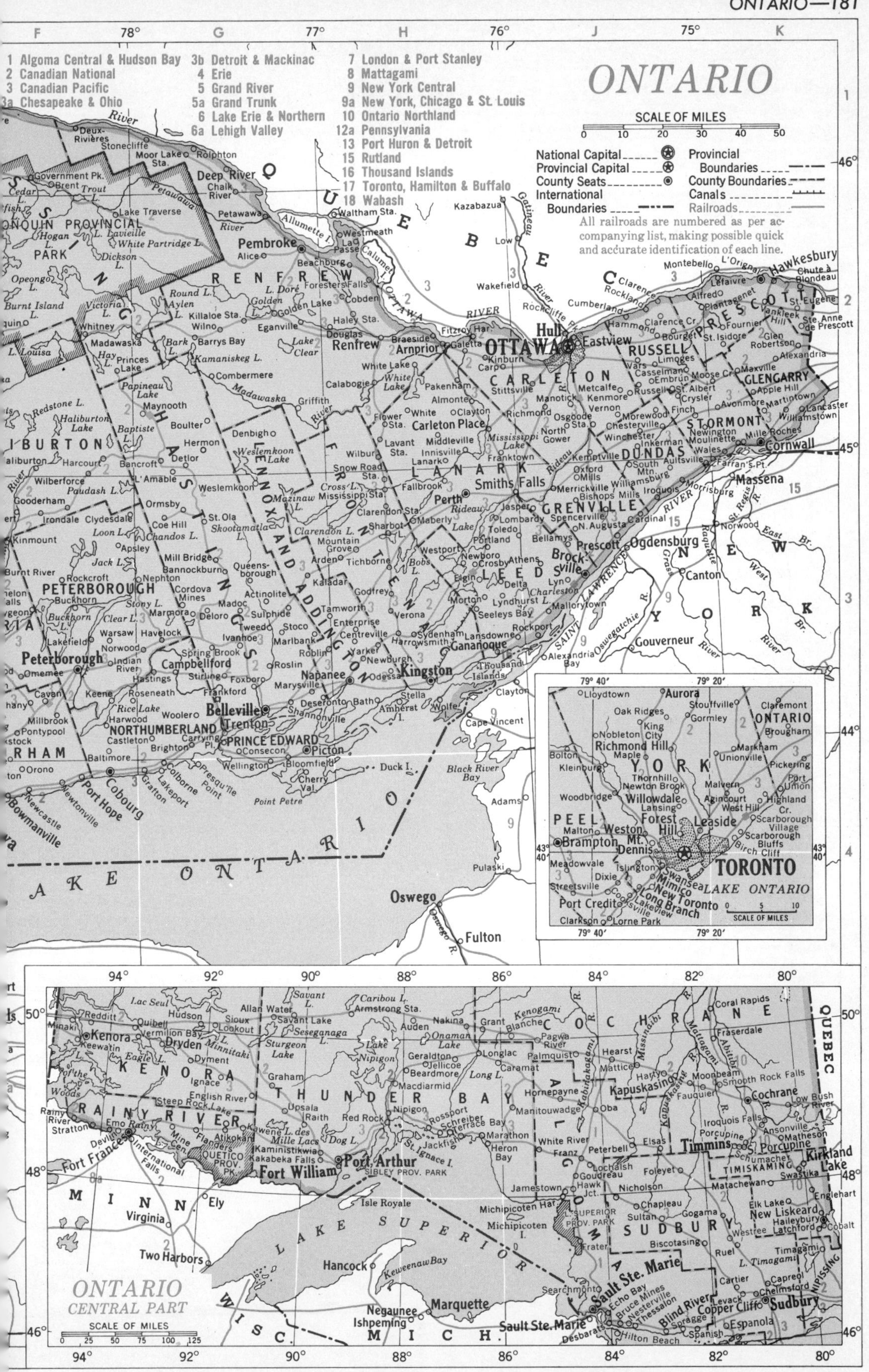
ONTARIO
SCALE OF MILES
0 10 20 30 40 50
National Capital
Provincial Capital
County Seats
International Boundaries
Provincial Boundaries
County Boundaries
Canals
Railroads
All railroads are numbered as per accompanying list, making possible quick and accurate identification of each line.
1 Algoma Central & Hudson Bay
2 Canadian National
3 Canadian Pacific
3a Chesapeake & Ohio
3b Detroit & Mackinac
4 Erie
5 Grand River
5a Grand Trunk
6 Lake Erie & Northern
6a Lehigh Valley
7 London & Port Stanley
8 Mattagami
9 New York Central
9a New York, Chicago & St. Louis
10 Ontario Northland
12a Pennsylvania
13 Port Huron & Detroit
15 Rutland
16 Thousand Islands
17 Toronto, Hamilton & Buffalo
18 Wabash
78°
77°
76°
75°
46°
45°
44°
43°
F
G
H
J
K
QUEBEC
OTTAWA
Hull
Eastview
Pembroke
Renfrew
Arnprior
Carleton Place
Smiths Falls
Perth
Brockville
Prescott
Ogdensburg
Cornwall
Massena
Hawkesbury
Kingston
Gananoque
Napanee
Belleville
Trenton
Picton
Peterborough
Campbellford
Cobourg
Port Hope
Bowmanville
Oswego
Fulton
Gouverneur
Canton
Deep River
Chalk River
Petawawa
RENFREW
CARLETON
RUSSELL
PRESCOTT
GLENGARRY
STORMONT
DUNDAS
GRENVILLE
LEEDS
LANARK
FRONTENAC
LENNOX AND ADDINGTON
HASTINGS
PETERBOROUGH
NORTHUMBERLAND
PRINCE EDWARD
ALGONQUIN PROVINCIAL PARK
LAKE ONTARIO
OTTAWA RIVER
SAINT LAWRENCE RIVER
NEW YORK
79° 40′
79° 20′
TORONTO
LAKE ONTARIO
YORK
PEEL
ONTARIO
Aurora
Richmond Hill
Willowdale
Leaside
Weston
Brampton
Mimico
New Toronto
Long Branch
Port Credit
Scarborough Village
Scarborough Bluffs
SCALE OF MILES
0 5 10
94°
92°
90°
88°
86°
84°
82°
80°
50°
48°
46°
ONTARIO
CENTRAL PART
SCALE OF MILES
0 25 50 75 100 125
Kenora
Dryden
Fort Frances
Port Arthur
Fort William
Kapuskasing
Cochrane
Timmins
Kirkland Lake
New Liskeard
Haileybury
Cobalt
Sudbury
Copper Cliff
Blind River
Sault Ste. Marie
Marquette
Hancock
Ely
Virginia
Two Harbors
KENORA
RAINY RIVER
THUNDER BAY
COCHRANE
ALGOMA
SUDBURY
TIMISKAMING
NIPISSING
LAKE SUPERIOR
MINN.
WISC.
MICH.
QUEBEC
QUETICO PROV. PK.
SIBLEY PROV. PARK
Isle Royale

102°
A
101°
B
100°
C
99°
D
98°
E
53°
52°
51°
50°
49°
Longitude
Overflowing River
Dawson Bay
Red Deer L.
Red Deer R.
Westgate
Barrows
National Mills
Rice Creek
Mafeking
Bellsite
Armit L.
Novra
Birch River
Bowsman
Lenswood
Big Woody
Crestview
Harlington
Swan River
Minitonas
Renwer
Cowan
Kenville
Durban
Benito
Camperville
Sclater
Duck River
Wellman L.
Pine River
Pulp River
Zalicia
DUCK MT. PROV. PK.
DUCK MOUNTAIN
Childs L.
Laurie L.
Walkerburn
Boggy Creek
San Clara
Zelena
Makaroff
Merridale
Deepdale
Roblin
Shortdale
Shevlin
Bield
Tummel
Bluewing
Shell Valley
Petlura
Grand View
Gilbert Plains
Dauphin
Dropmore
Lennard
Riding Park
Birch-view
Inglis
Shellmouth
Endcliffe
Russell
Harrowby
Silverton Sta.
Millwood
Ste. Madeleine
St. Lazare
Victor
McAuley
Moosomin
Elkhorn
Maryfield
Garland
Kulish
Ethelbert
Ward
Fork River
Bodham
Ukraina
Baldy Mtn. 2,727
Mink Creek
Drifting River
Grifton
Venlaw
Halicz
Sifton
Ashville
Winnipegosis
Cedar Lake
Spruce I.
Channel I.
Dawson Bay
Pelican Bay
Pelican Rapids
Shoal R.
Swan Lake
Pelican L.
LAKE WINNIPEGOSIS
Birch I.
Duck Bay
Sagemace Bay
Salt Pt.
Mossy R.
Fishing River
Valley River
Dauphin Lake
Volga
Meadowlands
Oak Brae
Cross Lake
Grand Rapids
Selkirk I.
Morrison Lake
Katimik Lake
Kawinaw L.
Soul L.
McKay L.
Pickerel L.
Sisib L.
Atim L.
Chitek L.
Inland L.
Waterhen Lake
Skownan
Waterhen
Meadow Portage
Crane River
Toutes-Aides
Rorketon
Guynemer
Moose Bay
Million
Magnet
Moore Dale
East Bay
Methley
Lonely L.
Valpoy
Ste.-Rose-du-Lac
Ochre River
Makinak
Kergwenan
Laurier
Ste. Amelie
Turtle R.
Eddystone
Shergrove
Ebb and Flow Lake
Reedy Cr.
Kinosota
Wapah
The Narrows
Basket L.
Gypsumville
Homebrook
Davis Point
Portage Bay
Peonan Pt.
Steep Rock
LAKE MANITOBA
Cayer
Reykjavik
Lonely Lake
Long Point
LAKE WINNIPEG
Sandy Is.
Wicked Pt.
Dancing Pt.
Reindeer I.
Poplar Pt.
Negginan
George I.
Big Stone Pt.
Berens I.
Commissioner I.
Kinwow Bay
Anderson L.
Sturgeon Bay
Anama Bay
Dauphin R.
Gypsum L.
Ridley
St. Martin Sta.
Lake St. Martin
Fairford
Hilbre
Birch Bay
Faulkner
Grahamdale
Spearhill
Bayton
Moosehorn
Silver Bay
Ashern
Zant
Oakview
Dog L.
Hayland
Vogar
Overton
Siglunes
Macross
Camper
Pebble Beach
Oatfield
Mulvihill
Eriksdale
Scotch Bay
Pine View
Lily Bay
Long Pt.
Minnewakan
Lundar
Clarkleigh
Marius
Oak Point
Mantagao R.
N. Birch L.
Fisher R.
Harwill
Hodgson
Lit. Birch L.
Fisherton
Sleeve L.
Fisher Branch
Broad Valley
Sylvan
Vidir
Jackhead Har.
L. St. Patrick
L. St. George
L. St. Andrew
Red Rose
Fisher Bay
Koostatak
Dallas
Egg
Zbaraz
Hamrlik
Skylake
Poplar-field
Sharpewood
Vannes
Deer Horn
Suffren
Stony Hill
Lillesve
Rembrandt
Chatfield
Otto
Neveton
Narcisse
Markland
Vestfold
Clematis
Sandridge
Inwood
Komarno
N. Shoal L.
Ideal
Pleasant Home
St. Laurent
Harperville
Loch Monar
W. Shoal L.
E. Shoal L.
Erinview
Lake Francis
Gunton
St. Ambroise
St. Marks
Balmoral
Woodlands
Argyle
Bonnie Doon
Delta Station
Lakeland
Warrenton
Marquette
Stony Mt.
Grosse Isle
RIDING MOUNTAIN NATIONAL PARK
Clear L.
Wasagaming
Onanole
Bethel
Scandinavia
Crawford Park
Horodo
Rackham
Elphinstone
Rogers
Sandy Lake
Erickson
Hilltop
Mountain Road
Elk Ranch
Birnie
Crocus
Polonia
Ozerna
Cracknell
Ruthenia
Glen Elmo
Mears
Birdtail
Marco
Seech
Olha
Angusville
Rossburn
Binscarth
Vista
Oakburn
Foxwarren
Solsgirth
Menzie
Birtle
Kelloe
Shoal Lake
Strathclair
Minnedosa R.
Newdale
Clanwilliam
Beulah
Isabella
Decker
Lavinia
Mc Connell
Basswood
Minnedosa
Uno
Cardale
Willen
Miniota
Crandall
Hamiota
Moline
Manson
Arrow River
Oak River
Rapid City
Reeder
Pope
Pettapiece
Kirkella
Two Creeks
Oakner
Harmsworth
Wheatland
Rivers
Lenore
Kenton
Harding
Bradwardine
Carnegie
Hargrave
Virden
Butler
Routledge
Cromer
Scarth
Ebor
Woodnorth
Oak Lake
Griswold
Alexander
Kemnay
Brandon
Terence
Beresford
Glen Souris
Rounthwaite
Oak L.
Plum L.
Plum Cr.
Hayfield
Souris
Ewart
Belleview
Pipestone
Sinclair
Reston
Findlay
Deleau
Carroll
Nesbitt
Marshy L.
Bunclody
Methven
Grande-Clairière
Hartney
Fairfax
Heaslip Sta.
Hilton
Bede
Underhill
Elgin
Minto
Tilston
Broomhill
Lauder
Regent
Margaret
Napinka
Dand
Croll
Dunrea
Melita
Medora
Whitewater Lake
Elva
Pierson
Deloraine
Whitewater
Boissevain
Waskada
Goodlands
Mountainside
Horton
Desford
Coulter
Lyleton
Wakopa
Bannerman
INTERNATIONAL PEACE GARDEN
TURTLE MT.
Ninga
Pelican Lake
Killarney
Holmfield
Lena
Smith Hill
Cartwright
Rock L.
Pembina
Neelin
Glenora
Crystal City
Mather
Pilot Mound
Clearwater
Snowflake
Fallison
Franklin
Neepawa
Keyes
Cordova
Hallboro
Mekiwin
Helston
Mentmore
Moorepark
Brookdale
Oberon
Justice
Harte
Wellwood
Forrest Sta.
Ingelow
Petrel
Douglas Sta.
Chater
Carberry
Shilo
Castle Point
Pratt
Lavenham
Assiniboine
Treherne
Rathwell
St. Claude
Holland
Stockton
Landseer
Wawanesa
Glenboro
Cypress River
Notre Dame de Lourdes
Roseisle
Bruxelles
Cardinal
St. Lupicin
Belmont
St. Alphonse
Mariapolis
Swan Lake
Somerset
Baldur
Greenway
Dry River
Swan L.
Indian Sprs.
Altamont
St. Leon
Wood Bay
La Rivière
Manitou
Darlingford
Kaleida
Purves
Mowbray
Thornhill
Morden
North Star
Windygates
Winkler
Haskett
Reinland
Gretna
Altona
Plum Coulee
St. Joseph
Letellier
Halbstadt
Horndean
St. Jean-Baptiste
Rosenfeld
Roland
Myrtle
Kane
Morris
Lowe Farm
Sewell
Rosebank
Miami
Deerwood
Learys
Stephenfield
Carman
Graysville
Home-wood
Brunkild
Sperling
McTavish
Rosenort
Silver Plains
Domain
Ste.-Agathe
Osborne
Union Pt.
Starbuck
Sanford
La Salle
Glenlea
Fannystelle
Culross
Elm Creek
Haywood
Layland
Springstein
St. Charles
St. François Xavier
Bénard
Elie
Newton Siding
Oakville
Fortier
Eustache
St. Eustache
Meadows
Rosser
Mid. Church
WINNIPEG
St. James
Ft. Garry
Whyte
Portage la Prairie
High Bluff
Poplar Pt.
Oakland
Reaburn
Macdonald
Westbourne
Beaver
Edrans
Muir
Katrime
Golden St.
Woodside
Gladstone
Ogilvie
Arden
Rossburn Jc.
Eden
Bethany
Langruth
Plumas
Tenby
Grass River
Amaranth
Waldersee
Kelwood
Glenella
Riding Mt.
Glencairn
Norgate
Reeve
McCreary
Bellhampton
Harcus
Glenhope
Alonsa
Bluff Creek
Portia
Gregg
Firdale
Sidney
Austin
Macgregor
Bagot
Edwin
Melbourne
Rossendale
SASKATCHEWAN
NORTH DAKOTA
Ledwyn
Geyser
Silver
Meleb
Fraserw
Malon
Teu
Dun
Pete
Cland
Ridg
Stonew
St. An
Mukuto

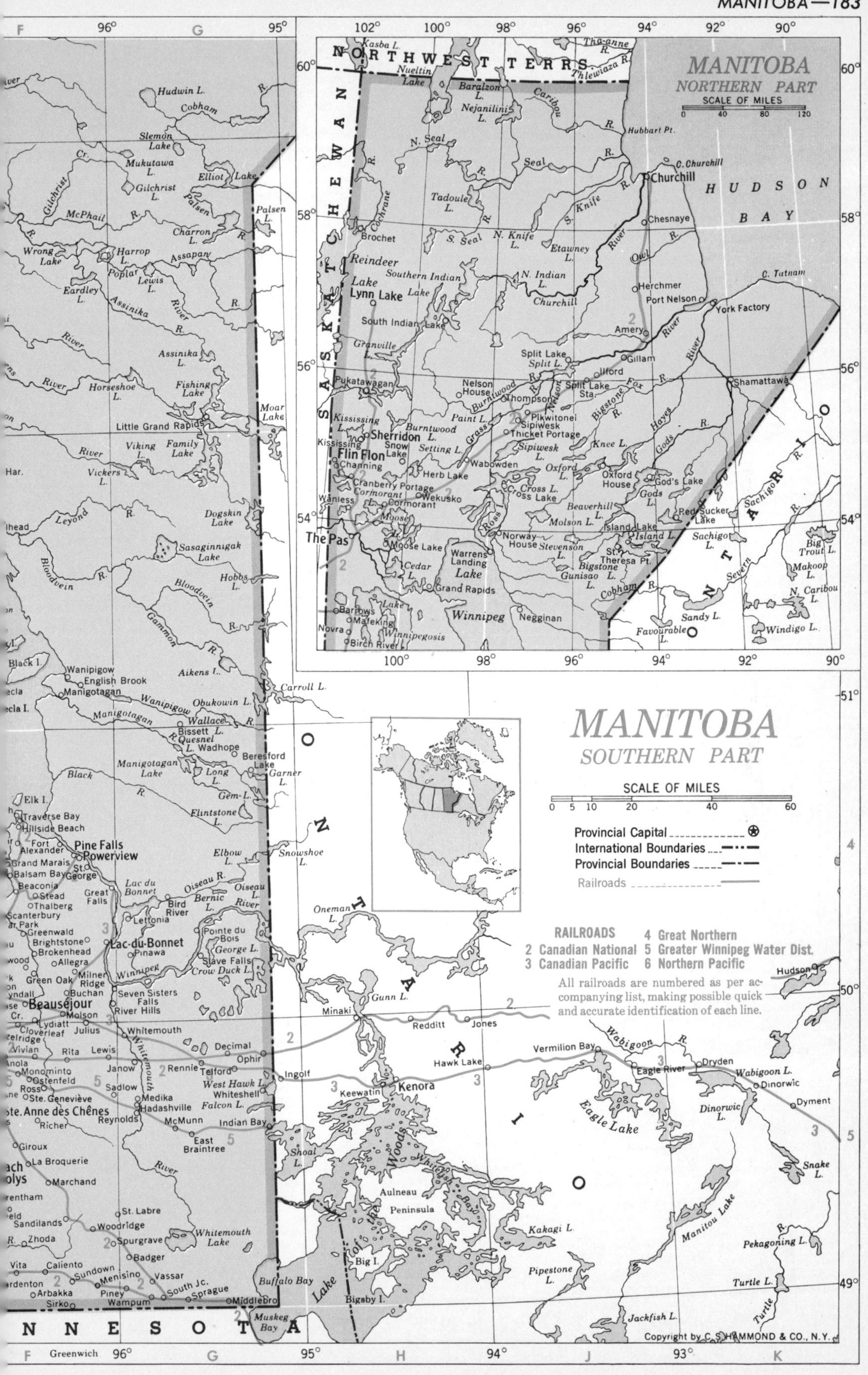
MANITOBA
NORTHERN PART
SCALE OF MILES
0 40 80 120
NORTHWEST TERRS.
SASKATCHEWAN
HUDSON BAY
ONTARIO
Churchill
Flin Flon
The Pas
Lynn Lake
Sherridon
Winnipeg
MANITOBA
SOUTHERN PART
SCALE OF MILES
0 5 10 20 40 60
Provincial Capital
International Boundaries
Provincial Boundaries
Railroads
RAILROADS
2 Canadian National
3 Canadian Pacific
4 Great Northern
5 Greater Winnipeg Water Dist.
6 Northern Pacific
All railroads are numbered as per accompanying list, making possible quick and accurate identification of each line.
ONTARIO
MINNESOTA
Pine Falls
Powerview
Lac-du-Bonnet
Beauséjour
Ste. Anne des Chênes
Kenora
Lake of the Woods
Eagle Lake
Copyright by C. S. HAMMOND & CO., N. Y.

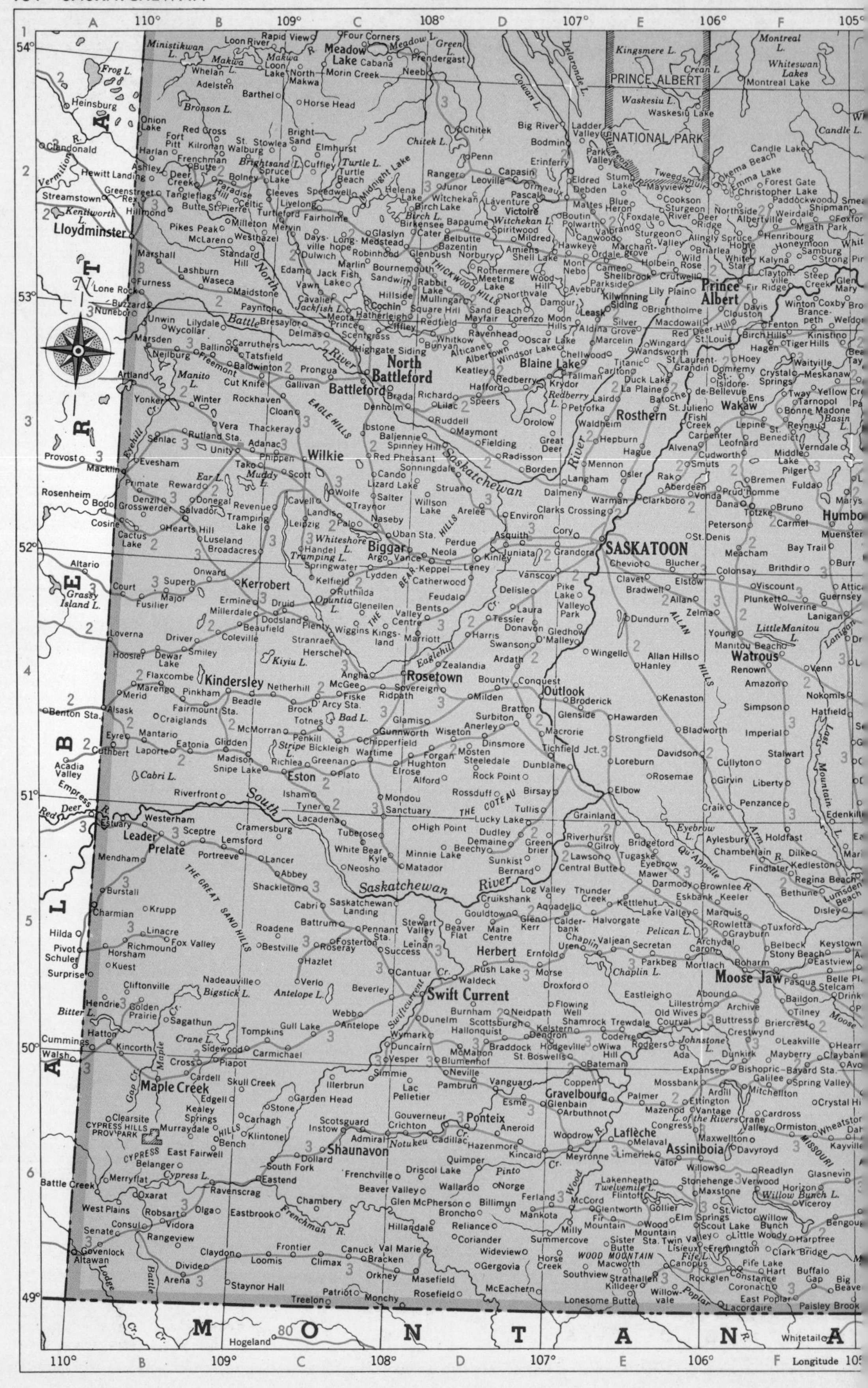
110°
109°
108°
107°
106°
105°
54°
53°
52°
51°
50°
49°
A
B
C
D
E
F
1
2
3
4
5
6
Ministikwan L.
Loon River
Rapid View
Makwa L.
Makwa
Loon Lake
Whelan
Adelsten
North Makwa
Four Corners
Meadow Lake
Cabana
Morin Creek
Meadow L.
Green L.
Prendergast
Neeb
Barthel
Horse Head
Bronson L.
Frog L.
Heinsburg
Onion Lake
Fort Pitt
Red Cross
Kilronan
Frenchman Butte
St. Walburg
Stowlea
Bright Sand
Elmhurst
Brightsand L.
Cuffley
Turtle L.
Turtle Beach
Chitek
Chitek L.
Penn
Clandonald
Vermilion R.
Harlan
Ashley
Hewitt Landing
Deer Creek
Bolney
Spruce Lake
Paradise Hill
Greenstreet
Rex
Tangleflags
Celtic
Cleeves
Speedwell
Midnight Lake
Helena Lake
Streamstown
Butte St. Pierre
Turtleford
Livelong
Fairholme
Birch Lake
Birch L.
Ranger
Junor
Witchekan
Leoville
Capasin
Laventure
Witchekan L.
Spiritwood
Kenilworth L.
Hillmond
Milleton
Mervin
Pikes Peak
Westhazel
McLaren
Lloydminster
Days-ville
Long-hope
Glaslyn
Medstead
Birkensee
Cater
Bapaume
Belbutte
Bazentin
Norbury
Mildred
Marshall
Standard Hill
Dulwich
Robinhood
Glenbush
Marlin
Bournemouth
Lashburn
Waseca
Edam
Jack Fish Lake
Vawn
Sandwith
Rabbit Lake
Thickwood Hills
Rothermere
Meeting Lake
Lone Rock
Furness
Maidstone
Cavalier
Jackfish L.
Hillside
Mullingar
Buzzard
Nunebor
Paynton
Cochin
Square Hill
Sand Beach
Mayfair
Northvale
Unwin
Wycollar
Lilydale
Battle R.
Bresaylor
Meota
Prince
Hatherleigh
Iffley
Redfield
Delmas
Scentgrass
Whitkow
Bunyan
Marsden
Ballinora
Carruthers
Highgate Siding
Neilburg
Freemont
Tatsfield
Baldwinton
North Battleford
Prongua
Artland
Manito L.
Cut Knife
Gallivan
Battleford
Brada
Richard
Denholm
Lilac
Yonker
Winter
Rockhaven
Cloan
Eagle Hills
Vera
Rutland Sta.
Thackeray
Ibstone
Baljennie
Ruddell
Maymont
Senlac
Unity
Adanac
Spinney Hill
Fielding
Provost
Macklin
Evesham
Phippen
Wilkie
Red Pheasant
Sonningdale
Radisson
Tako
Muddy L.
Scott
Cando
Borden
Ear L.
Primate
Reward
Wolfe
Lizard Lake
Salter
Struan
Saskatchewan
Rosenheim
Bodo
Denzil
Grosswerder
Donegal
Salvador
Revenue
Cavell
Traynor
Willson Lake
Arelee
Cosine
Tramping Lake
Landis
Leipzig
Palo
Naseby
Hearts Hill
Luseland
Whiteshore L.
Uban Sta.
Perdue
Cactus Lake
Broadacres
Biggar
Handel
Tramping L.
Argo
Vance
Neola
Altario
Onward
Springwater
Keppel
Kelfield
Lydden
Catherwood
Court
Superb
Kerrobert
Major
Fusilier
Grassy Island L.
Ruthilda
Ermine
Druid
Opuntia L.
Glenellen
Bents
Feudal
Millerdale
Dodsland
Valley Centre
Beaufield
Plenty
Wiggins
Kingsland
Loverna
Driver
Coleville
Stranraer
Marriott
Smiley
Hoosier
Dewar Lake
Herschel
Kiyiu L.
Eaglehill Cr.
Zealandia
Flaxcombe
Kindersley
Anglia
Rosetown
Marengo
Merid
Pinkham
Netherhill
McGee
Fiske
Sovereign
Ridpath
Beadle
Brock
D'Arcy Sta.
Benton Sta.
Alsask
Fairmount Sta.
Craiglands
Bad L.
Totnes
Glamis
Eyre
Mantario
McMorran
Penkill
Gunnworth
Wiseton
Eatonia
Glidden
Stripe L.
Bickleigh
Chipperfield
Cuthbert
Laporte
Madison
Richlea
Wartime
Forgan
Greenan
Hughton
Acadia Valley
Snipe Lake
Eston
Plato
Elrose
Alford
Cabri L.
Empress
Riverfront
Isham
Mondou
Red Deer R.
South
Tyner
Sanctuary
Westerham
Lacadena
Estuary
Cramersburg
Tuberose
High Point
Sceptre
Leader
Lemsford
Prelate
White Bear
Kyle
Minnie Lake
Mendham
Portreeve
Lancer
Neosho
Matador
Abbey
The Great Sand Hills
Shackleton
Burstall
Saskatchewan River
Cabri
Saskatchewan Landing
Charmian
Krupp
Hilda
Battrum
Roadene
Stewart Valley
Pennant Sta.
Linacre
Fosterton
Pivot
Richmound
Fox Valley
Bestville
Roseray
Leinan
Success
Schuler
Horsham
Hazlet
Kuest
Surprise
Cantuar Cr.
Nadeauville
Verlo
Antelope L.
Beverley
Cliftonville
Bigstick L.
Swift Current
Hendrie
Golden Prairie
Bitter L.
Sagathun
Webb
Antelope
Gull Lake
Tompkins
Swiftcurrent Cr.
Dunelm
Wymark
Hatton
Crane L.
Cummings
Kincorth
Maple Cr.
Sidewood
Carmichael
Duncairn
Walsh
Cross
Piapot
Vesper
Gap Cr.
Cardell
Skull Creek
Simmie
Maple Creek
Edgell
Illerbrun
Lac Pelletier
Garden Head
Kealey Springs
Stone
Clearsite
Cypress Hills Prov. Park
Murraydale
Carnagh
Hills
Klintonel
Bench
Scotsguard
Instow
Gouverneur
Crichton
Admiral
Shaunavon
East Fairwell
Cypress
Belanger
Dollard
South Fork
Battle Creek
Merryflat
Cypress L.
Eastend
Ravenscrag
Frenchville
Beaver Valley
Chambery
Oxarat
West Plains
Robsart
Olga
Eastbrook
Frenchman R.
Glen McPherson
Consul
Vidora
Senate
Rangeview
Hillandale
Govenlock
Altawan
Claydon
Loomis
Frontier
Climax
Canuck
Val Marie
Bracken
Divide
Arena
Lodge Cr.
Battle Cr.
Staynor Hall
Orkney
Masefield
Patriot
Monchy
Rosefield
Treelon
Hogeland
80
Big River
Ladder Valley
Bodmin
Erinferry
Park Valley
Rangers
Victoire
Pascal
Ormeaux
Eldred
Debden
Mattes
Boutin
Polwarth
Canwood
Hawkeye
Amiens
Shell Lake
Mont Nebo
Wood Hill
Avebury
Damour
Leask
Aldina
Moon Hills
Lorenzo
Ravenhead
Oscar Lake
Alticane
Albertown
Windsor Lake
Blaine Lake
Chellwood
Keatley
Redberry
Tallman
Hafford
Krydor
Redberry L.
Speers
Orolow
Great Deer
Petrofka
Laird
Cowan L.
Delaronde L.
Kingsmere L.
Prince Albert
Crean L.
Waskesiu L.
Waskesiu Lake
National Park
Tweedsmuir
Mayview
Stump Lake
Blue Heron
Foxdale
Valbrand
Cookson
Sturgeon River
Deer Ridge
Sturgeon Valley
Marchant-Grove
Ordale
Cameo
Holbein
Wild Rose
Briarlea
Shellbrook
Parkside
Crutwell
Lily Plain
Prince Albert
Kilwinning Siding
Brightholme
Silver Grove
Marcelin
Macdowall
Red Deer Hill
Wingard
St. Louis
Wandsworth
St. Laurent-Grandin
Domremy
Titanic
Carlton
Duck Lake
St. Isidore-de-Bellevue
La Plaine
Batoche
St. Julien
Fish Creek
Rosthern
Waldheim
Hepburn
Hague
Carpenter
Alvena
Cudworth
Smuts
Mennon
Osler
Rak
Aberdeen
Vonda
Langham
Dalmeny
Warman
Clarkboro
Clarks Crossing
Environ
Asquith
Cory
Juniata
Kinley
Grandora
Saskatoon
St. Denis
Cheviot
Blucher
Clavet
Bradwell
Elstow
Allan
Zelma
Dundurn
Allan Hills
Hanley
Wingello
Vanscoy
Delisle
Pike Lake
Valley Park
Laura
Tessier
Donavon
Gledhow
O'Malley
Harris
Swanson
Ardath
Bounty
Conquest
Outlook
Broderick
Milden
Glenside
Hawarden
Kenaston
Bladworth
Bratton
Surbiton
Anerley
Macrorie
Strongfield
Dinsmore
Mosten
Steeledale
Tichfield Jct.
Loreburn
Davidson
Dunblane
Rosemae
Rock Point
Rossduff
Birsay
Elbow
The Coteau
Tullis
Lucky Lake
Grainland
Dudley
Demaine
Beechy
Green-brier
Riverhurst
Gilroy
Sunkist
Bernard
Lawson
Central Butte
Tugaske
Eyebrow
Mawer
Darmody
Bridgeford
Long Valley
Thunder Creek
Kettlehut
Cruikshank
Aquadell
Gouldtown
Glen Kerr
Main Centre
Beaver Flat
Calder-bank
Halvorgate
Lake Valley
Herbert
Ernfold
Uren
Chaplin
Valjean
Secretan
Parkbeg
Chaplin L.
Rush Lake
Waldeck
Morse
Droxford
Eastleigh
Burnham
Neidpath
Flowing Well
Scottsburgh
Hallonquist
Kelstern
Shamrock
Trewdale
Old Wives
Courval
Lillestrom
Abound
Coderre
Rodgers
Johnstone L.
Braddock
McMahon
Blumenhof
Hodgeville
Wiwa Hill
St. Boswells
Bateman
Neville
Pambrun
Vanguard
Coppen
Gravelbourg
Glenbain
Arbuthnot
Esme
Palmer
Ponteix
Aneroid
Notukeu Cr.
Cadillac
Hazenmore
Kincaid
Woodrow
Meyronne
Lafleche
Melaval
Assiniboia
Quimper
Pinto
Driscol Lake
Wallard
Norge
Billimun
Ferland
Mankota
Wood R.
McCord
Glentworth
Fir Mountain
Wood Mountain
Sister Butte
Summercove
Reliance
Broncho
Coriander
Wideview
Gergovia
Horse Creek
Wood Mountain
Southview
Macworth
Strathallen
Killdeer
Willow-vale
McEachern
Lonesome Butte
Poplar R.
Montreal L.
Whiteswan Lakes
Montreal Lake
Candle L.
Candle Lake
Okema Beach
Emma Lake
Forest Gate
Christopher Lake
Paddockwood
Northside
Weirdale
Albertville
Shipman
Henribourg
Meath Park
Honeymoon
Spruce Home
White Star
Samburg
Kalyna
Strong Pine
Clayton-ville
Steep Creek
Glen Mary
Fir Ridge
Davis
Clouston
Winton
Coxby
Brance-peth
Fenton
Birch Hills
Kinistino
Hagen
Tiger Hills
Hoey
Waityville
Crystal Springs
Meskanaw
Tway
Yellow Creek
Tarnopol
Wakaw
Ens
Bonne Madone
Lepine
St. Benedict
Reynaud
Basin L.
Leofnard
Verndale
Middle Lake
Pilger
Bremen
Fulda
Prud'homme
Dana
Totzke
Bruno
Peterson
Carmel
Humboldt
Muenster
Meacham
Bay Trail
Colonsay
Brithdir
Burr
Viscount
Plunkett
Wolverine
Guernsey
Lanigan
LittleManitou L.
Young
Manitou Beach
Watrous
Renown
Venn
Amazon
Nokomis
Simpson
Hatfield
Imperial
Last Mountain L.
Stalwart
Cullyton
Girvin
Liberty
Craik
Penzance
Eyebrow L.
Aylesbury
Holdfast
Edenkillie
Chamberlain
Dilke
Arm R.
Findlater
Kedleston
Regina Beach
Brownlee
Eskbank
Keeler
Bethune
Lumsden Beach
Disley
Marquis
Rowletta
Grayburn
Tuxford
Pelican L.
Archydal
Caron
Mortlach
Belbeck
Stony Beach
Keystown
Boharm
Eastview
Moose Jaw
Pasqua
Belle Plaine
Stelcam
Baildon
Archive
Tilney
Buttress
Briercrest
Crestwynd
Leakville
Dunkirk
Mayberry
Claybank
Bishopric
Bayard Sta.
Avonlea
Mossbank
Galilee
Spring Valley
Ardill
Mitchellton
Crystal Hill
Ettington
Mazenod
Vantage
Cardross
Congress
L. of the Rivers
Crane Valley
Ormiston
Wheatston
Maxwellton
Davyroyd
Kayville
Limerick
Vator
Willows
Readlyn
Glasnevin
Lakenheath
Twelvemile L.
Stonehenge
Verwood
Horizon
Flintoft
Maxstone
Willow Bunch L.
Viceroy
Gollier
Elm Springs
St. Victor
Willow Bunch
Scout Lake
Bengough
Twin Valley
Little Woody
Harptree
Lisieux
Fife L.
Fremington
Clark Bridge
Canopus
Fife Lake
Hart
Buffalo Gap
Rockglen
Constance
Coronach
Big Beaver
East Poplar
Lacordaire
Paisley Brook
Whitetail
Alberta
Montana
Longitude

SASKATCHEWAN
SASKATCHEWAN NORTHERN PART
N. W. TERR'S.
ALBERTA
MANITOBA
NORTH DAKOTA
SCALE OF MILES
0 5 10 20 40 60
Provincial Capital
International Boundaries
Provincial Boundaries
Railroads
RAILROADS
2 Canadian National
3 Canadian Pacific
80 Great Northern
117 Minneapolis, St. Paul & Sault Ste. Marie
All railroads are numbered as per accompanying list, making possible quick and accurate identification of each line.
PRINCE ALBERT NAT'L PK.
Flin Flon
Yorkton
Melville
Weyburn
Estevan
Moosomin
Kamsack
Canora
Tisdale
Nipawin
Wadena
Wynyard
Indian Head
Fort Qu'Appelle
Oxbow
Arcola
Kelvington
Copyright by C. S. HAMMOND & CO., N.Y.

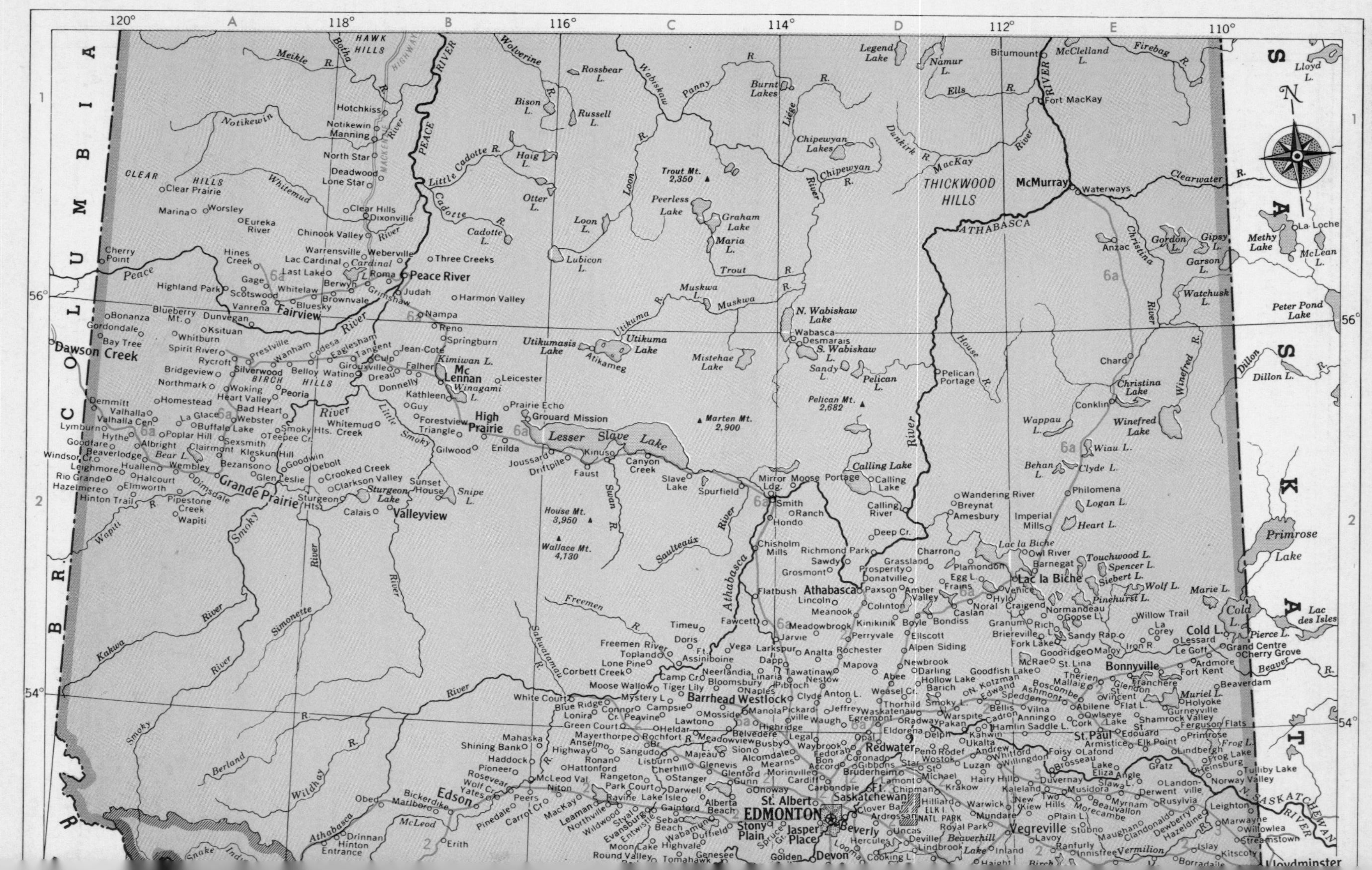

S A S K A T
C O L U M B I A
B R
120°
118°
116°
114°
112°
110°
56°
54°
A
B
C
D
E
1
2
THICKWOOD HILLS
CLEAR HILLS
HAWK HILLS
BIRCH HILLS
ATHABASCA
PEACE RIVER
McMurray
Fort MacKay
Waterways
Peace River
Fairview
Grande Prairie
Dawson Creek
Valleyview
High Prairie
Mc Lennan
Slave Lake
Lesser Slave Lake
Athabasca
Westlock
Barrhead
Lac la Biche
Bonnyville
St. Paul
Vegreville
Redwater
EDMONTON
St. Albert
Jasper Place
Stony Plain
Edson
Devon
Cold L.
Primrose Lake
Lac des Isles
Peter Pond Lake
Methy Lake
Christina Lake
Winefred Lake
Calling Lake
Utikuma Lake
N. Wabiskaw Lake
S. Wabiskaw L.
Peerless Lake
Graham Lake
Pelican Mt. 2,682
Marten Mt. 2,900
Trout Mt. 2,350
House Mt. 3,950
Wallace Mt. 4,130
N. SASKATCHEWAN RIVER
Lloydminster
Smoky
Wapiti
Athabasca

ALBERTA
SOUTHERN PART
SCALE OF MILES
0 20 40 60 80 100
Provincial Capital
International Boundaries
Provincial Boundaries
Railroads
Highways
RAILROADS
2 Canadian National
3 Canadian Pacific
4 Great Northern
6a Northern Alberta
ALBERTA
NORTHERN PART
Copyright by C. S. HAMMOND & CO., N.Y.
West of Greenwich
Longitude

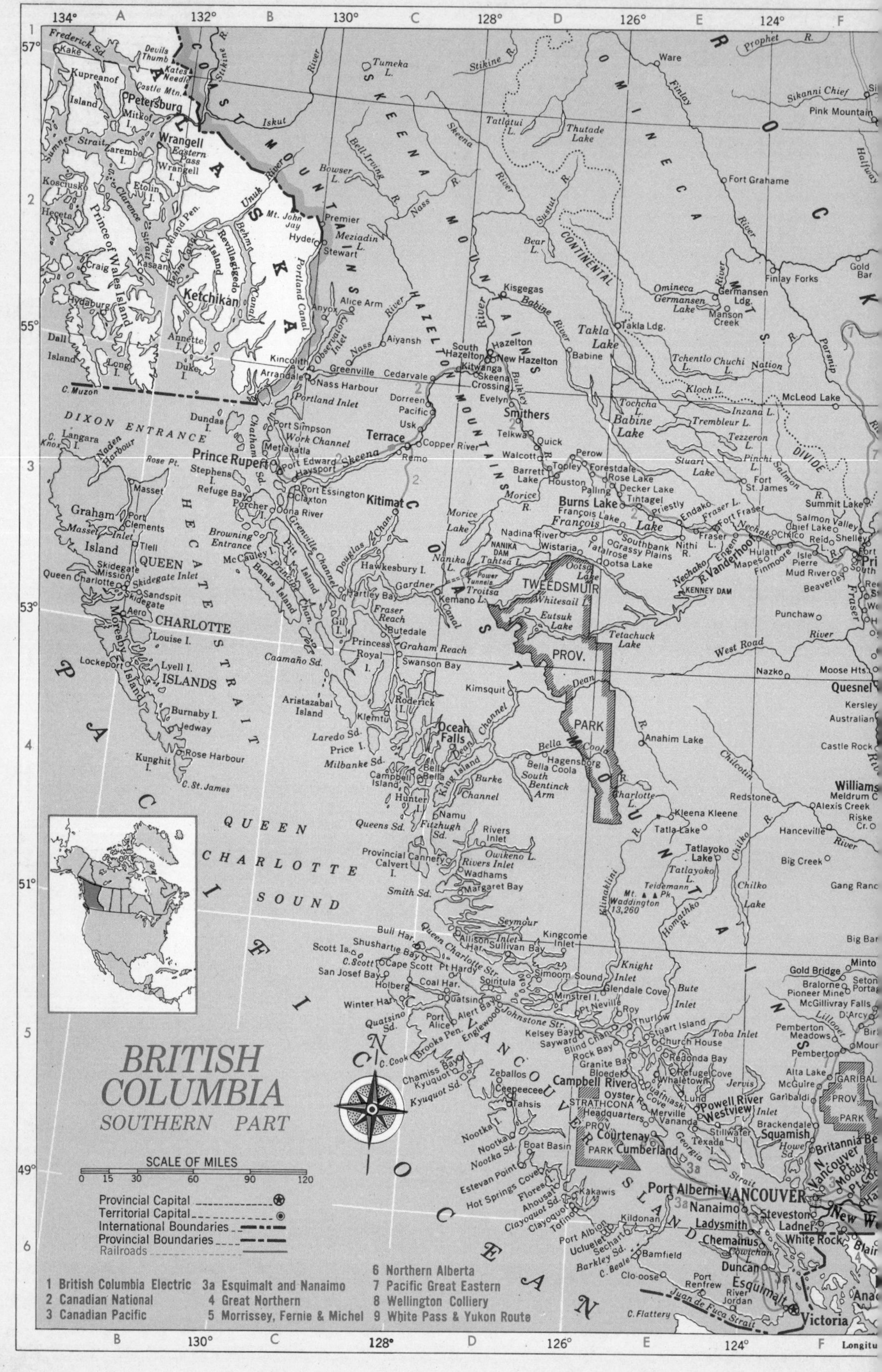
BRITISH
COLUMBIA
SOUTHERN PART
SCALE OF MILES
0 15 30 60 90 120
Provincial Capital
Territorial Capital
International Boundaries
Provincial Boundaries
Railroads
1 British Columbia Electric
2 Canadian National
3 Canadian Pacific
3a Esquimalt and Nanaimo
4 Great Northern
5 Morrissey, Fernie & Michel
6 Northern Alberta
7 Pacific Great Eastern
8 Wellington Colliery
9 White Pass & Yukon Route
134° A 132° B 130° C 128° D 126° E 124° F
B 130° C 128° D 126° E 124° F Longitu
57° 55° 53° 51° 49°
1 2 3 4 5 6
ALASKA
COAST MOUNTAINS
SKEENA MOUNTAINS
HAZELTON MOUNTAINS
OMINECA MOUNTAINS
COAST MOUNTAINS
CONTINENTAL DIVIDE
DIXON ENTRANCE
HECATE STRAIT
QUEEN CHARLOTTE ISLANDS
QUEEN CHARLOTTE SOUND
PACIFIC OCEAN
VANCOUVER ISLAND
TWEEDSMUIR PROV. PARK
STRATHCONA PROV. PARK
GARIBALDI PROV. PARK
Petersburg
Wrangell
Ketchikan
Prince of Wales Island
Prince Rupert
Terrace
Kitimat
Smithers
Hazelton
New Hazelton
Burns Lake
Ocean Falls
Bella Coola
Quesnel
Williams
Campbell River
Powell River
Westview
Courtenay
Cumberland
Port Alberni
VANCOUVER
Nanaimo
Ladysmith
Chemainus
Duncan
Esquimalt
Victoria
Squamish
Steveston
Ladner
White Rock
Mt. Waddington 13,260
Teidemann Pk.
Juan de Fuca Strait
Strait of Georgia
Takla Lake
Babine Lake
Kenney Dam

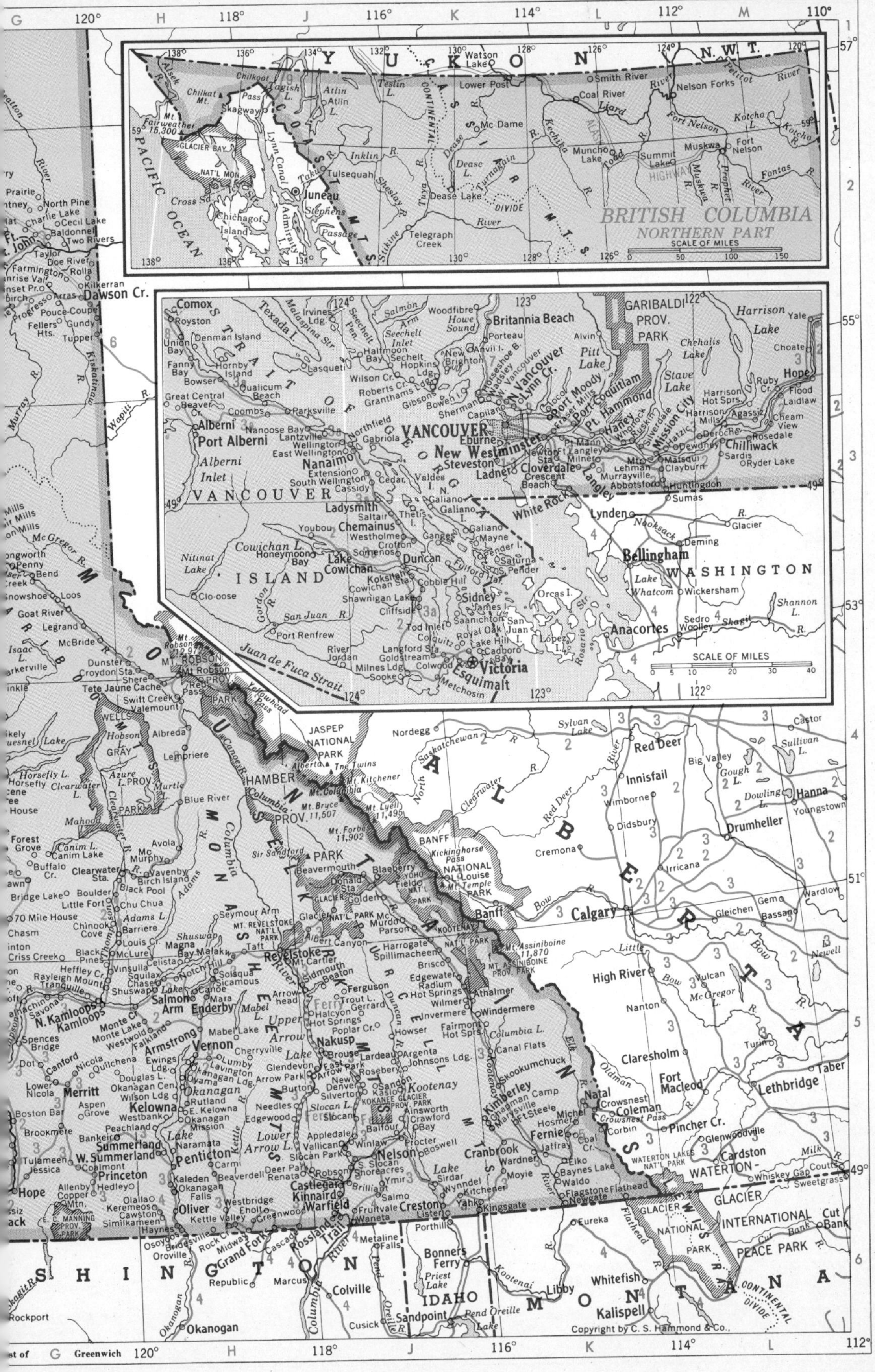
BRITISH COLUMBIA
NORTHERN PART
SCALE OF MILES
YUKON
N.W.T.
PACIFIC OCEAN
VANCOUVER
New Westminster
Victoria
Nanaimo
VANCOUVER ISLAND
WASHINGTON
Bellingham
ALBERTA
Calgary
Red Deer
Lethbridge
Banff
MONTANA
IDAHO
Kamloops
Nelson
Penticton
Kelowna
Vernon
Revelstoke
Dawson Cr.
Cranbrook
Trail
Copyright by C. S. Hammond & Co.
Greenwich

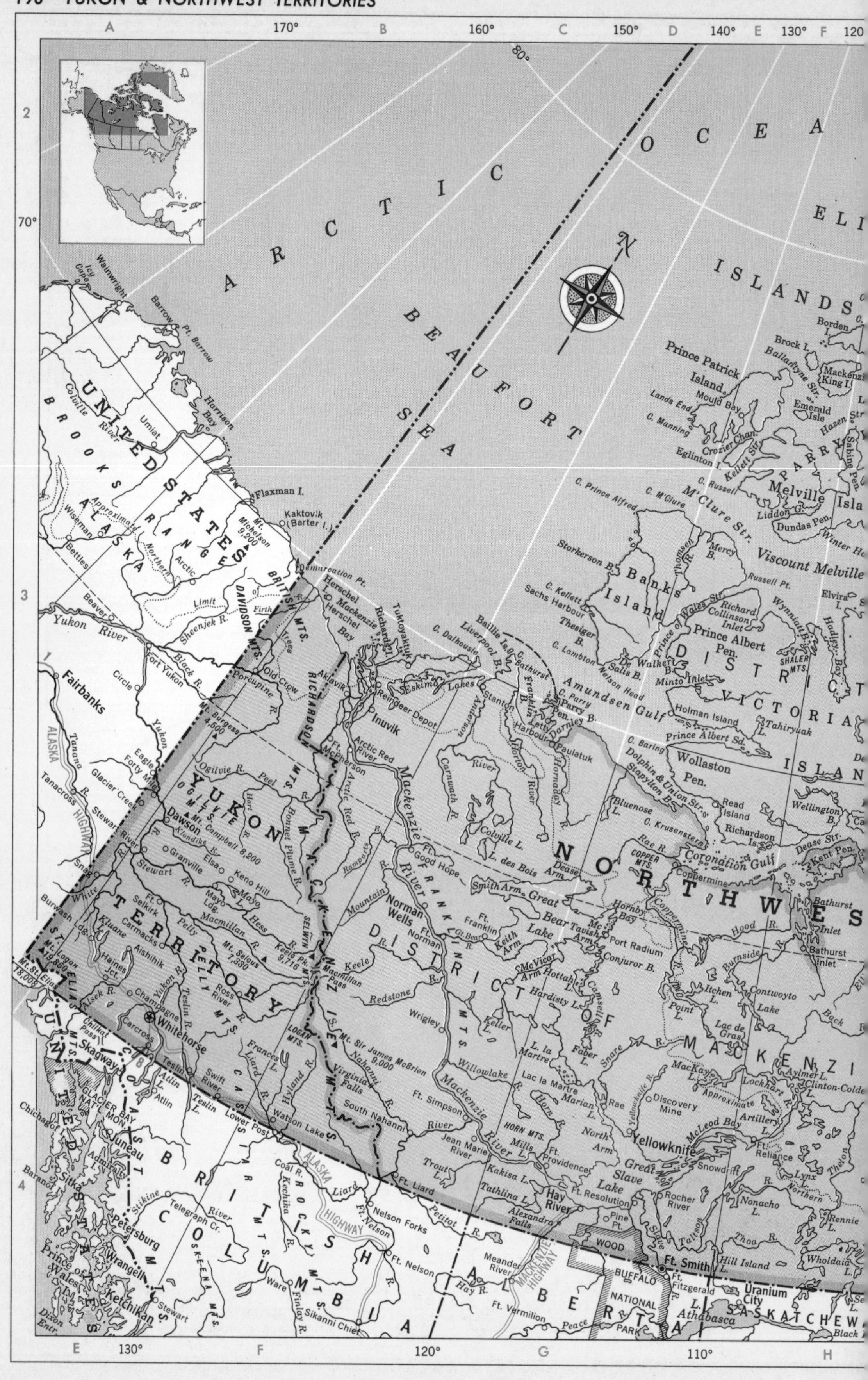
ARCTIC OCEAN
BEAUFORT SEA
ISLANDS
Prince Patrick Island
Mould Bay
Banks Island
Sachs Harbour
Melville Isla
Viscount Melville
M'Clure Str.
Amundsen Gulf
VICTORIA ISLAN
Prince Albert Pen.
Wollaston Pen.
Coronation Gulf
Coppermine
NORTHWES
DISTRICT OF MACKENZI
DISTRICT OF FRANKLIN
YUKON TERRITORY
Whitehorse
Dawson
Mayo
Keno Hill
Inuvik
Aklavik
Tuktoyaktuk
Norman Wells
Great Bear Lake
Port Radium
Great Slave Lake
Yellowknife
Hay River
Ft. Smith
Ft. Simpson
Ft. Resolution
Ft. Providence
Ft. Liard
Ft. Nelson
Watson Lake
Mackenzie River
UNITED STATES
ALASKA
BROOKS RANGE
Fairbanks
Barrow
Pt. Barrow
Yukon River
Fort Yukon
BRITISH COLUMBIA
ALBERTA
SASKATCHEW
Uranium City
Lake Athabasca
WOOD BUFFALO NATIONAL PARK
ALASKA HIGHWAY
MACKENZIE HIGHWAY
RICHARDSON MTS.
MACKENZIE MTS.
OGILVIE MTS.
ST. ELIAS MTS.
Mt. Logan 19,850
Mt. St. Elias 18,008
Juneau
Skagway
Ketchikan
Wrangell
Petersburg
Sitka
A B C D E F
E F G H
170° 160° 150° 140° 130° 120
130° 120° 110°
2 3 4
70°

YUKON AND NORTHWEST TERRITORIES
SCALE OF MILES
0 50 100 200 300
Territorial Capitals
Administrative Center (N. W. Terr.)
International Boundaries
Provincial & Territorial Boundaries
District Boundaries
Railroads
Highways
1 Alaska 8 White Pass & Yukon
All railroads are numbered as per accompanying list, making possible quick and accurate identification of each line.
GREENLAND (Denmark)
Baffin Bay
Davis Strait
Hudson Strait
Hudson Bay
Foxe Basin
Foxe Channel
Ungava Bay
Ungava Peninsula
QUEBEC
FRANKLIN
BAFFIN ISLAND
DISTRICT OF KEEWATIN
TERRITORIES
ELLESMERE ISLAND
Devon Island
Southampton I.
MANITOBA
All islands in Hudson and James Bays lie within the District of Keewatin.
Arctic Circle
Longitude West of Greenwich
Copyright by C.S. HAMMOND & Co., N.Y.

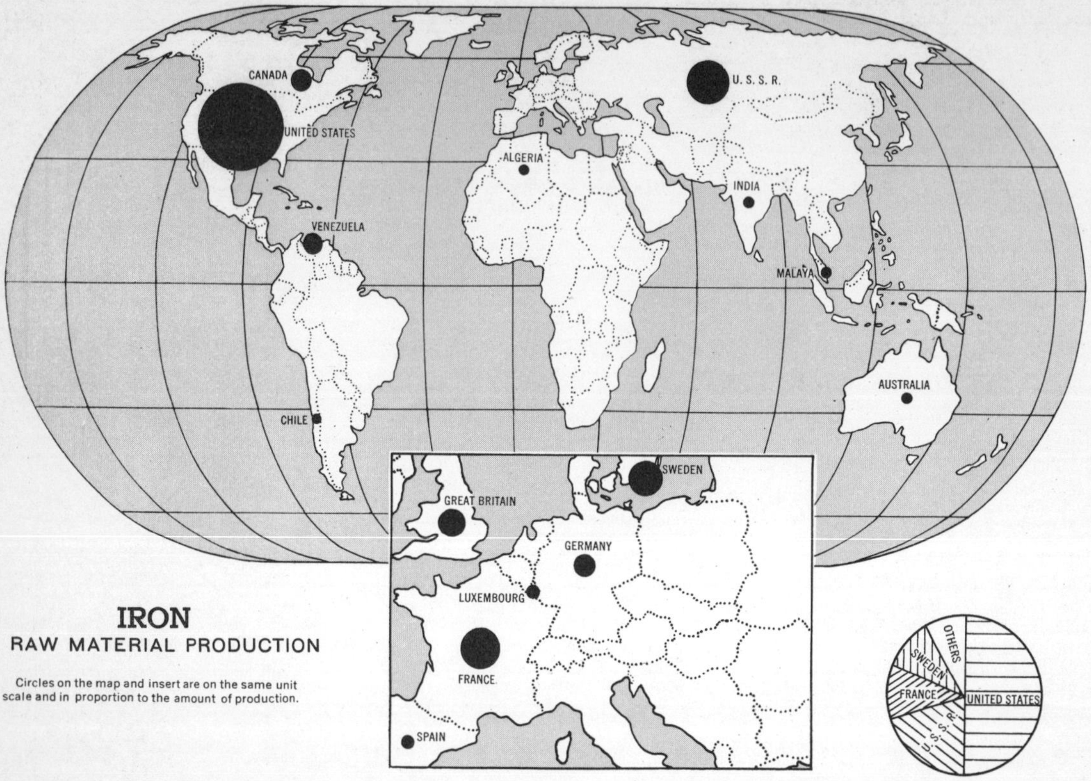

IRON
RAW MATERIAL PRODUCTION

Circles on the map and insert are on the same unit scale and in proportion to the amount of production.

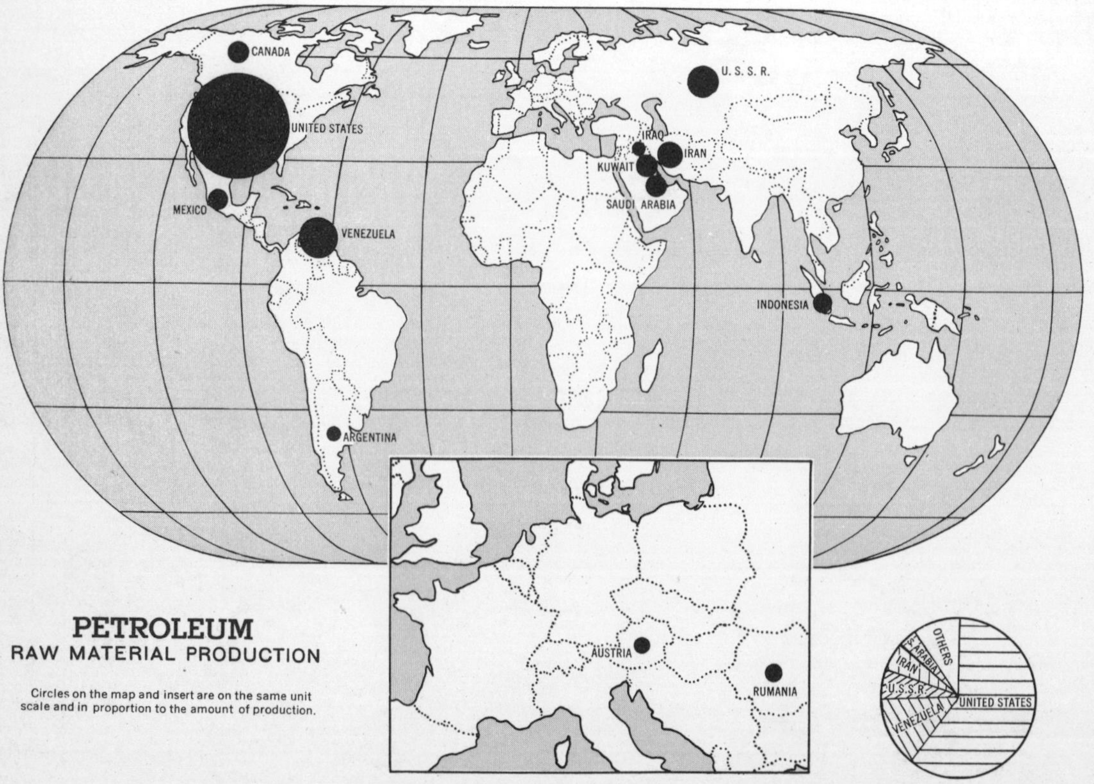

PETROLEUM
RAW MATERIAL PRODUCTION

Circles on the map and insert are on the same unit scale and in proportion to the amount of production.

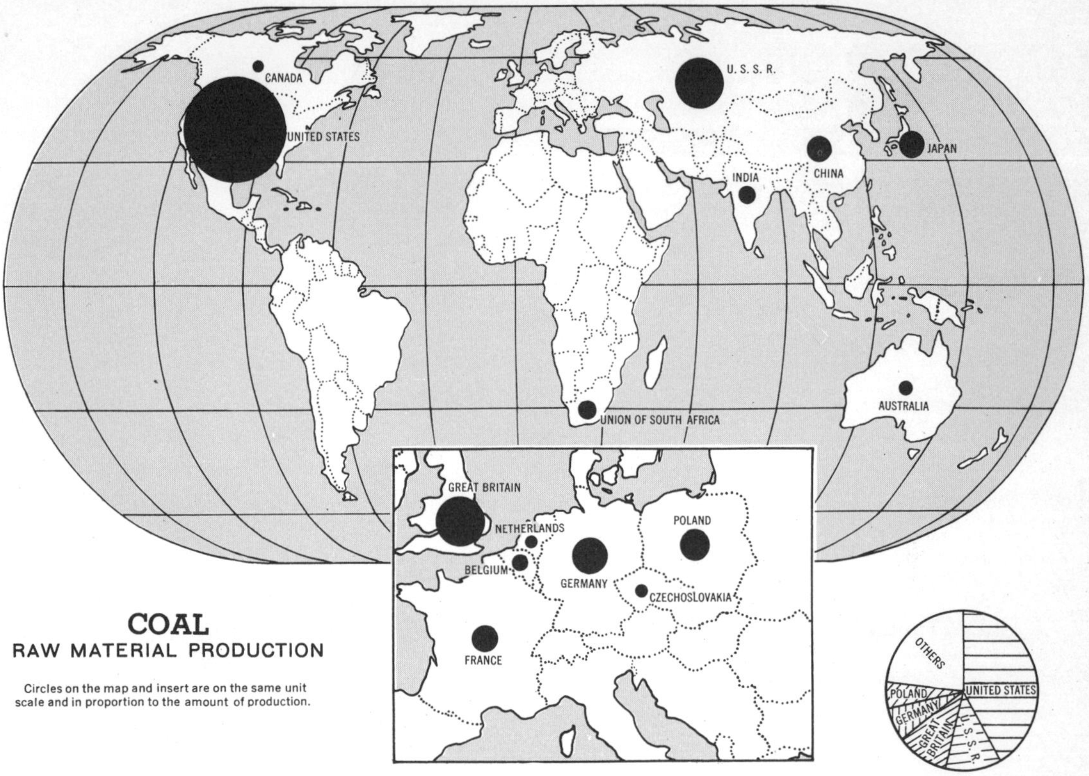

COAL
RAW MATERIAL PRODUCTION

Circles on the map and insert are on the same unit scale and in proportion to the amount of production.

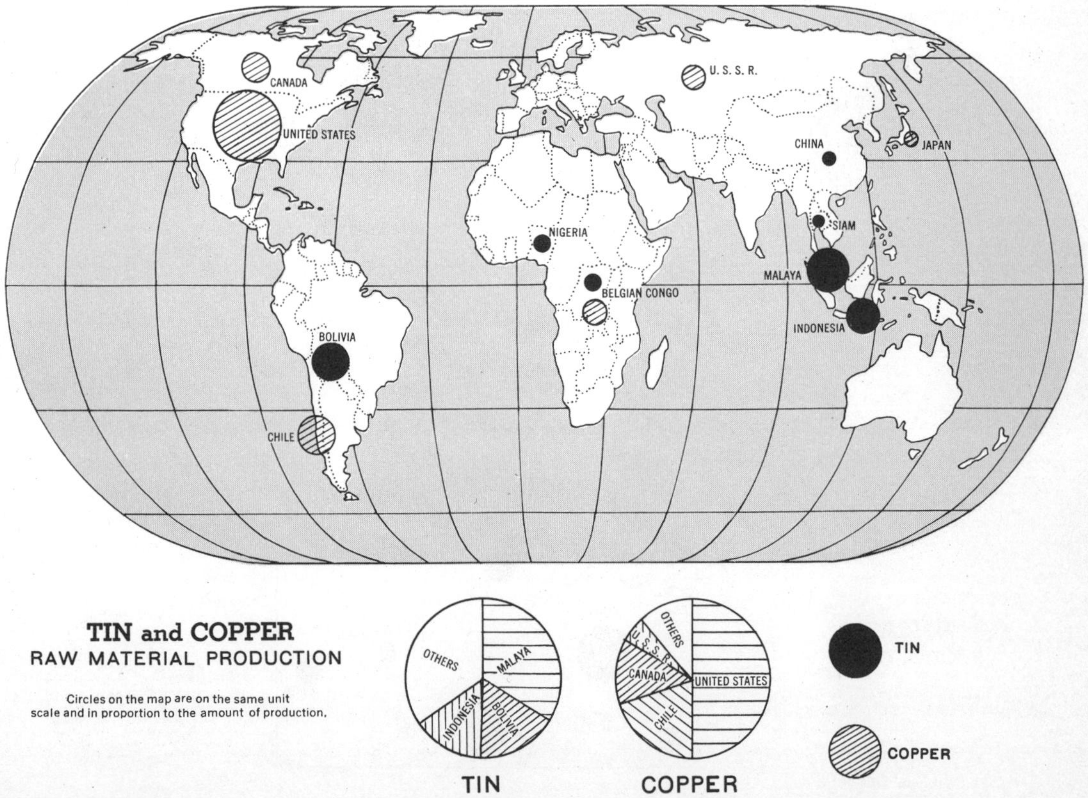

TIN and COPPER
RAW MATERIAL PRODUCTION

Circles on the map are on the same unit scale and in proportion to the amount of production.

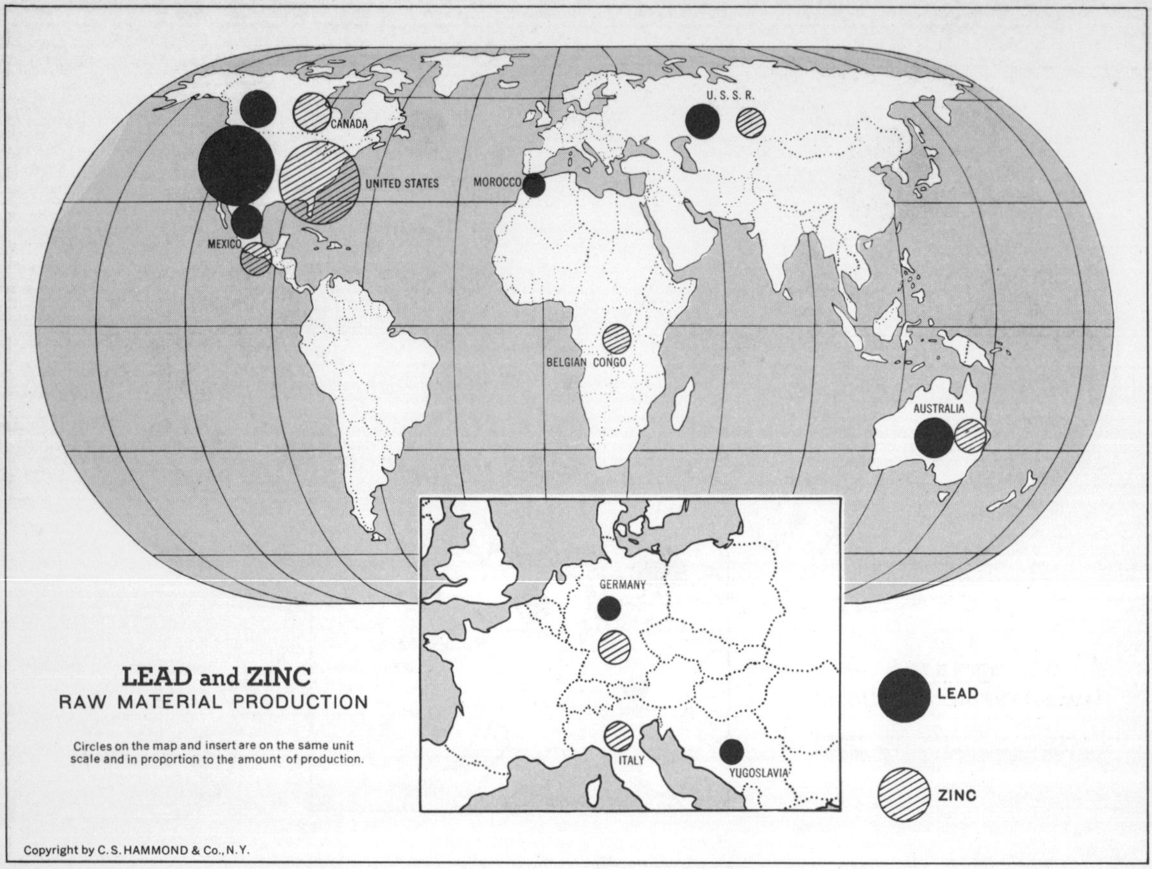

LEAD and ZINC
RAW MATERIAL PRODUCTION

Circles on the map and insert are on the same unit scale and in proportion to the amount of production.

CANADA
UNITED STATES
MEXICO
MOROCCO
U. S. S. R.
BELGIAN CONGO
AUSTRALIA
GERMANY
ITALY
YUGOSLAVIA

LEAD
ZINC

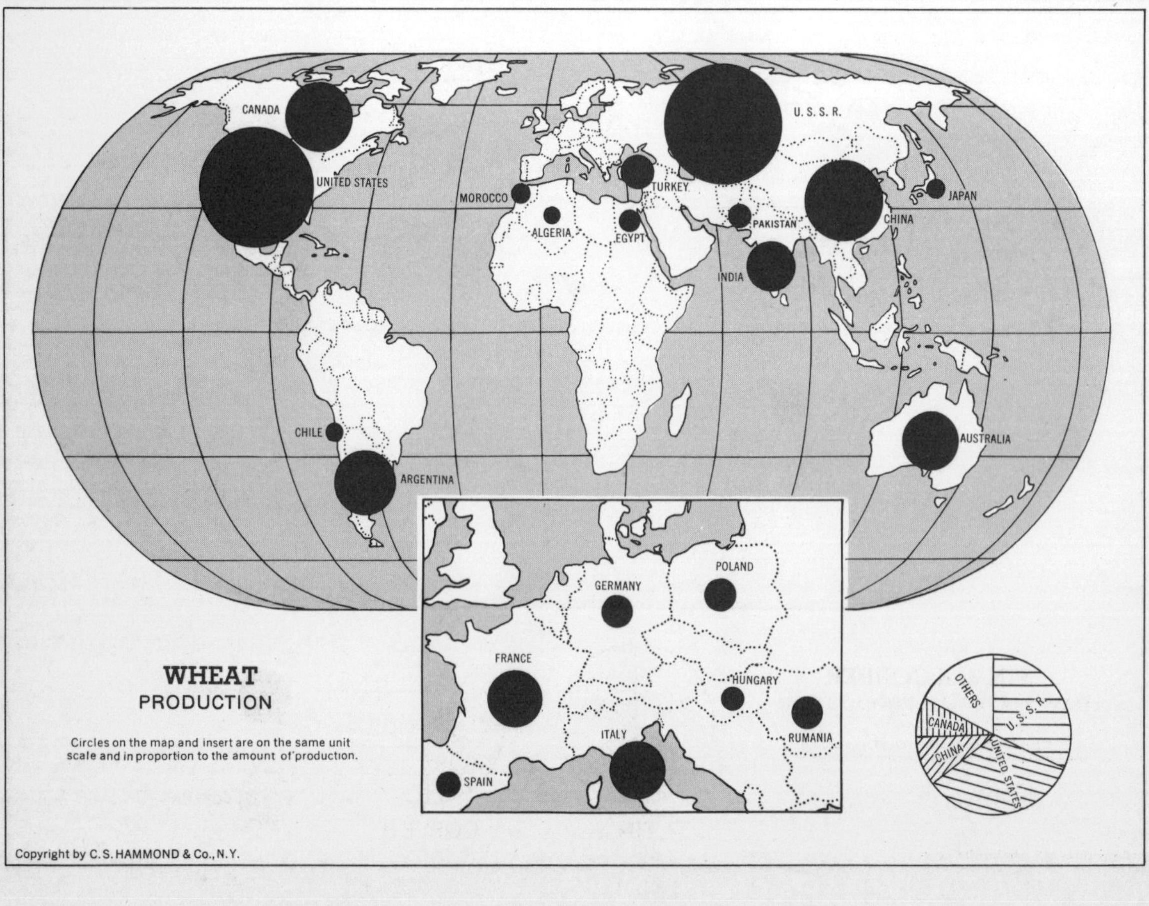

WHEAT
PRODUCTION

Circles on the map and insert are on the same unit scale and in proportion to the amount of production.

CANADA
UNITED STATES
MOROCCO
ALGERIA
EGYPT
TURKEY
U. S. S. R.
PAKISTAN
INDIA
CHINA
JAPAN
CHILE
ARGENTINA
AUSTRALIA
POLAND
GERMANY
FRANCE
HUNGARY
RUMANIA
ITALY
SPAIN

OTHERS
U. S. S. R.
CANADA
CHINA
UNITED STATES

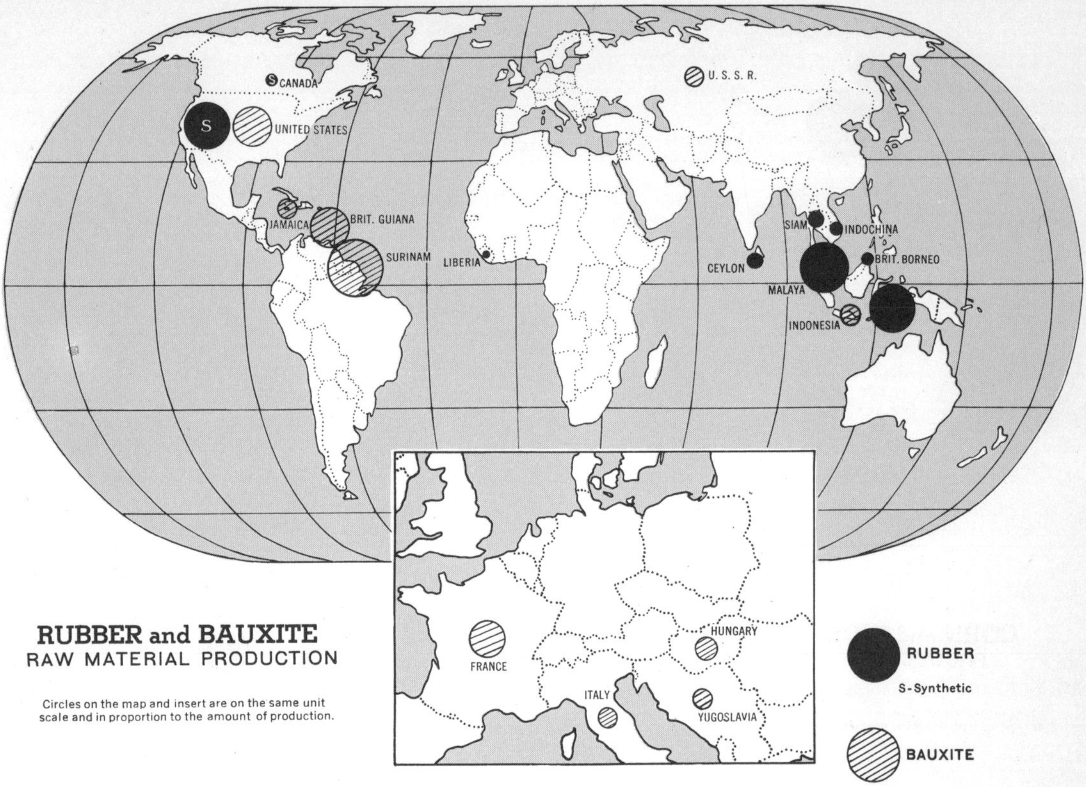

RUBBER and BAUXITE
RAW MATERIAL PRODUCTION

Circles on the map and insert are on the same unit scale and in proportion to the amount of production.

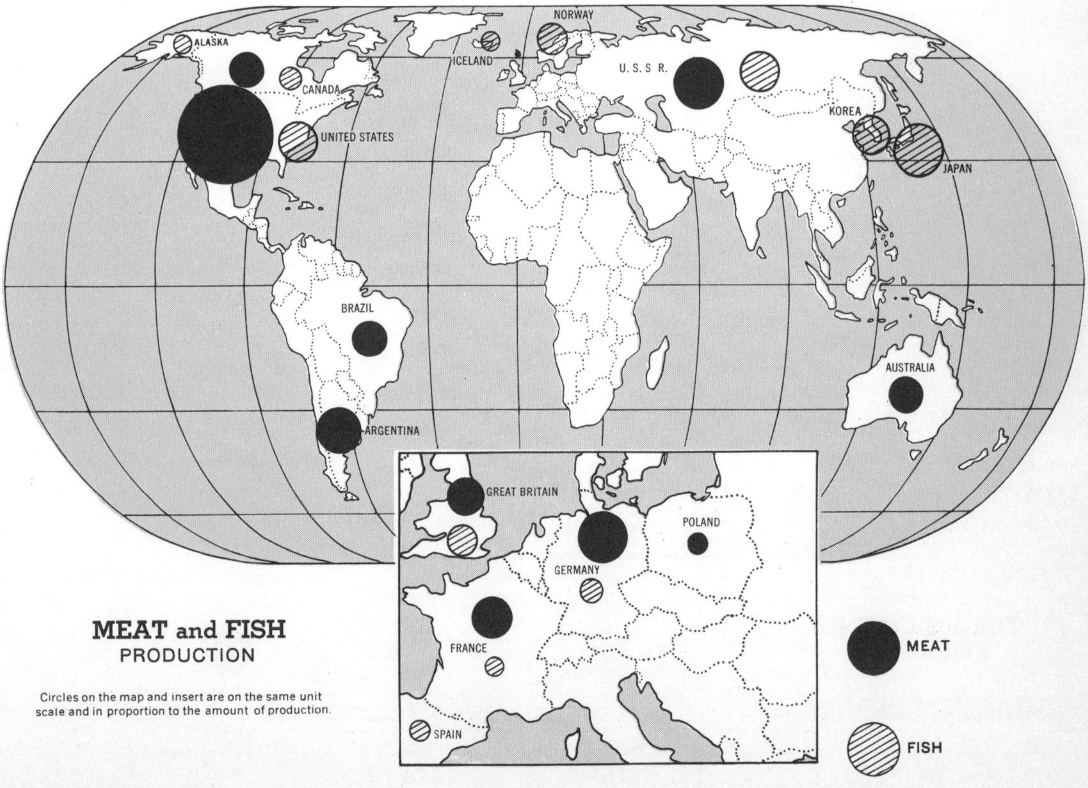

MEAT and FISH
PRODUCTION

Circles on the map and insert are on the same unit scale and in proportion to the amount of production.

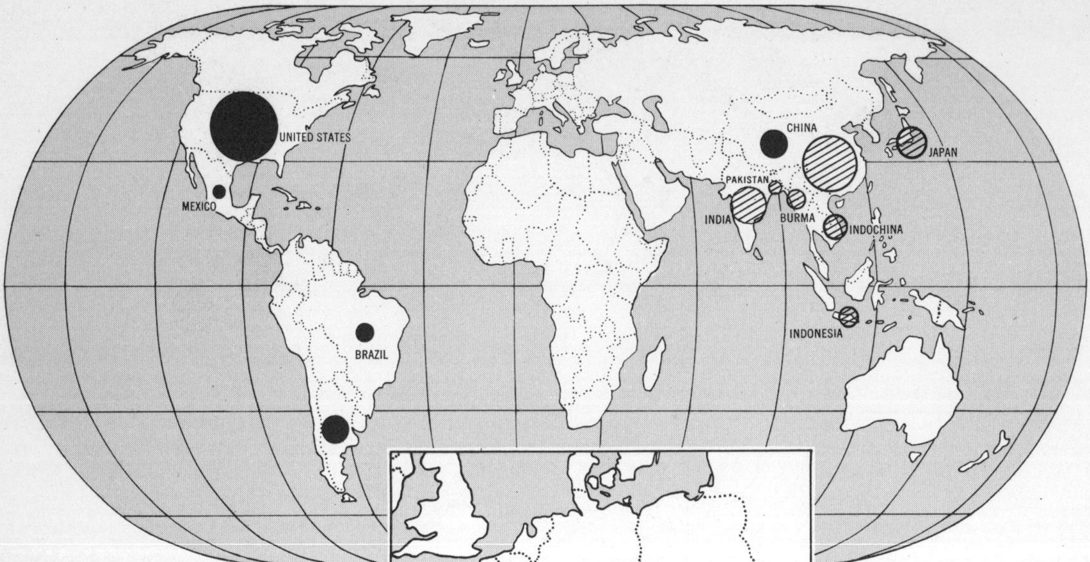

UNITED STATES
MEXICO
BRAZIL
CHINA
JAPAN
PAKISTAN
INDIA
BURMA
INDOCHINA
INDONESIA
RUMANIA
YUGOSLAVIA

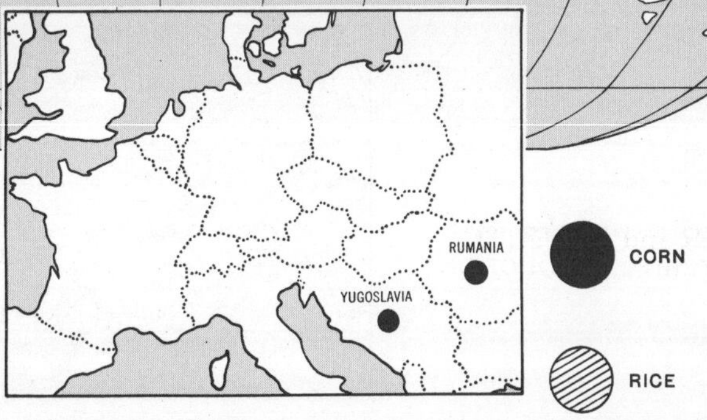

CORN and RICE PRODUCTION

Circles on the map and insert are on the same unit scale and in proportion to the amount of production.

CORN

RICE

U. S. S. R.
CHINA
JAPAN
CUBA
MEXICO
GUATEMALA
EL SALVADOR
COLOMBIA
INDIA
CEYLON
INDONESIA
BRAZIL
MADAGASCAR

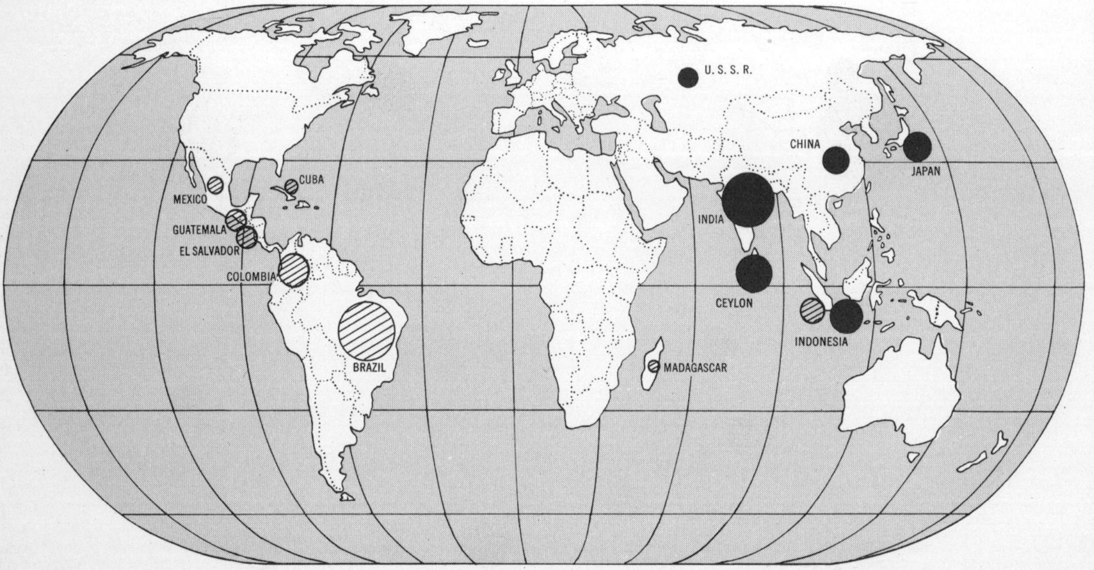

TEA and COFFEE PRODUCTION

Circles on the map are on the same unit scale and in proportion to the amount of production.

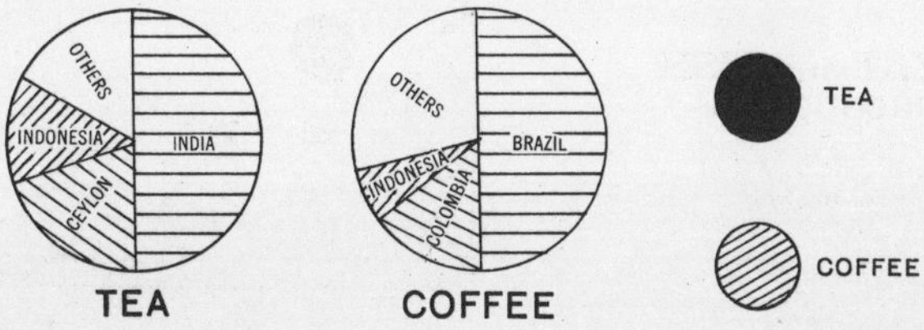

OTHERS
INDONESIA
INDIA
CEYLON

TEA

OTHERS
BRAZIL
INDONESIA
COLOMBIA

COFFEE

TEA

COFFEE

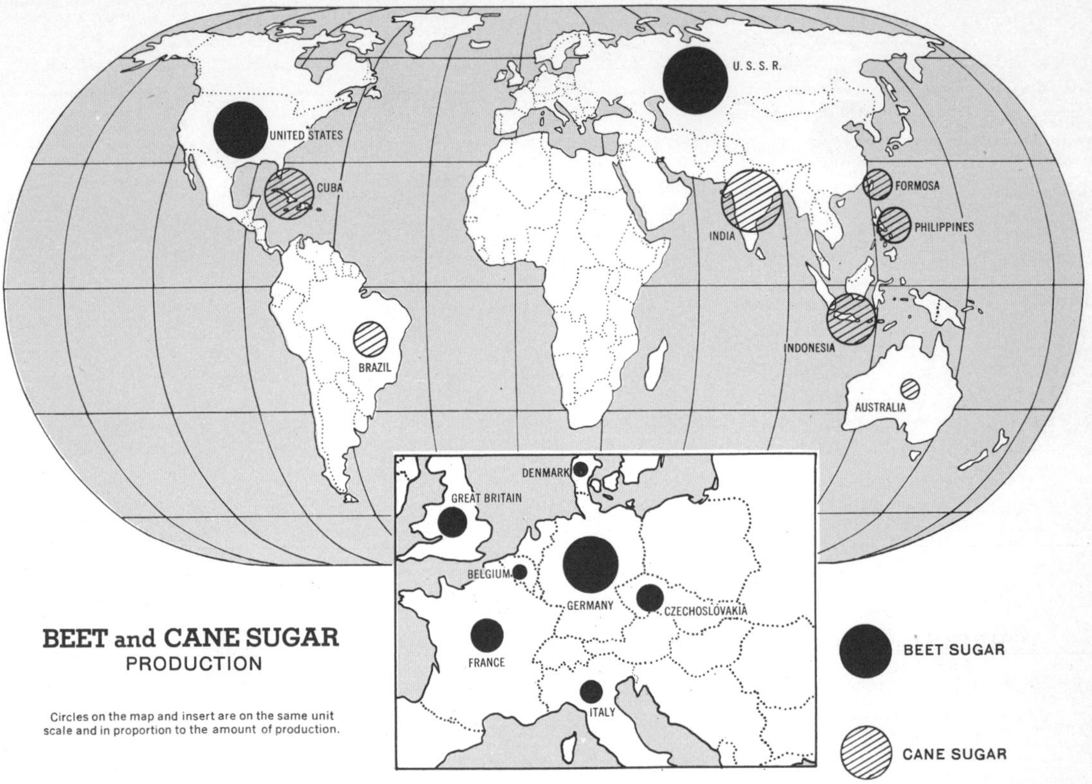

BEET and CANE SUGAR
PRODUCTION

Circles on the map and insert are on the same unit scale and in proportion to the amount of production.

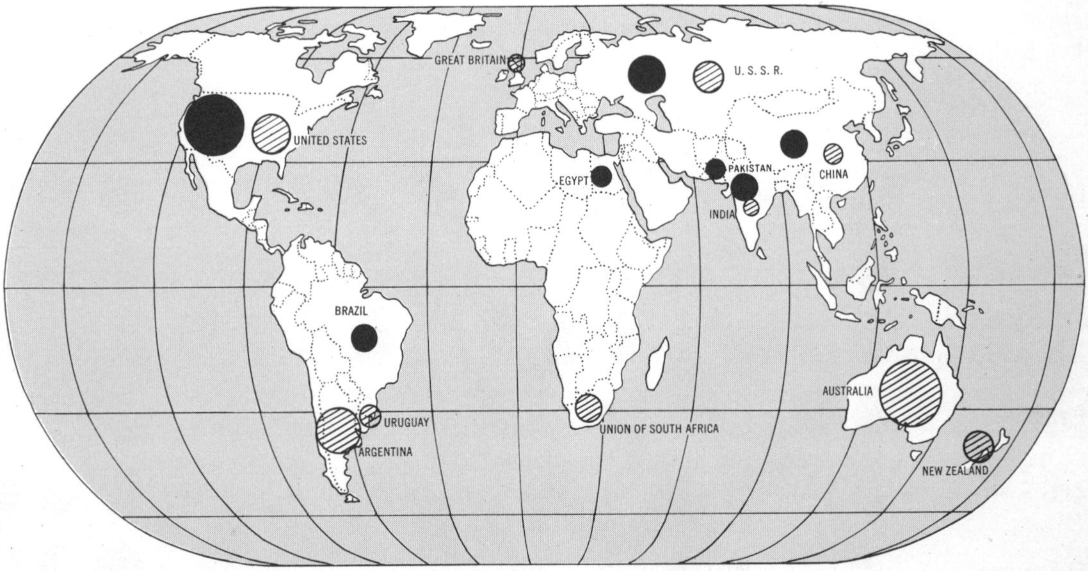

COTTON and WOOL
PRODUCTION

Circles on the map are on the same unit scale and in proportion to the amount of production.

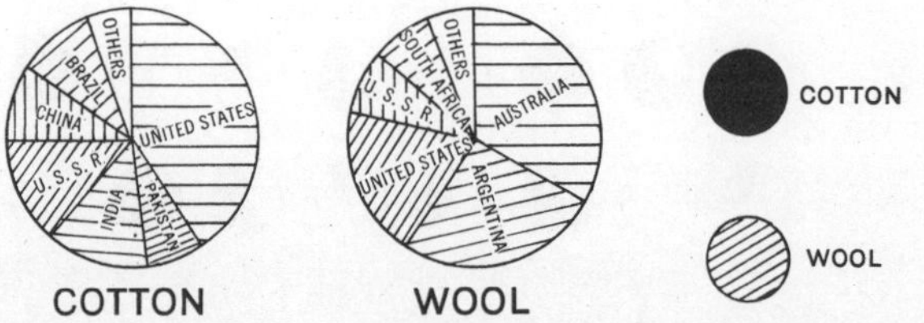

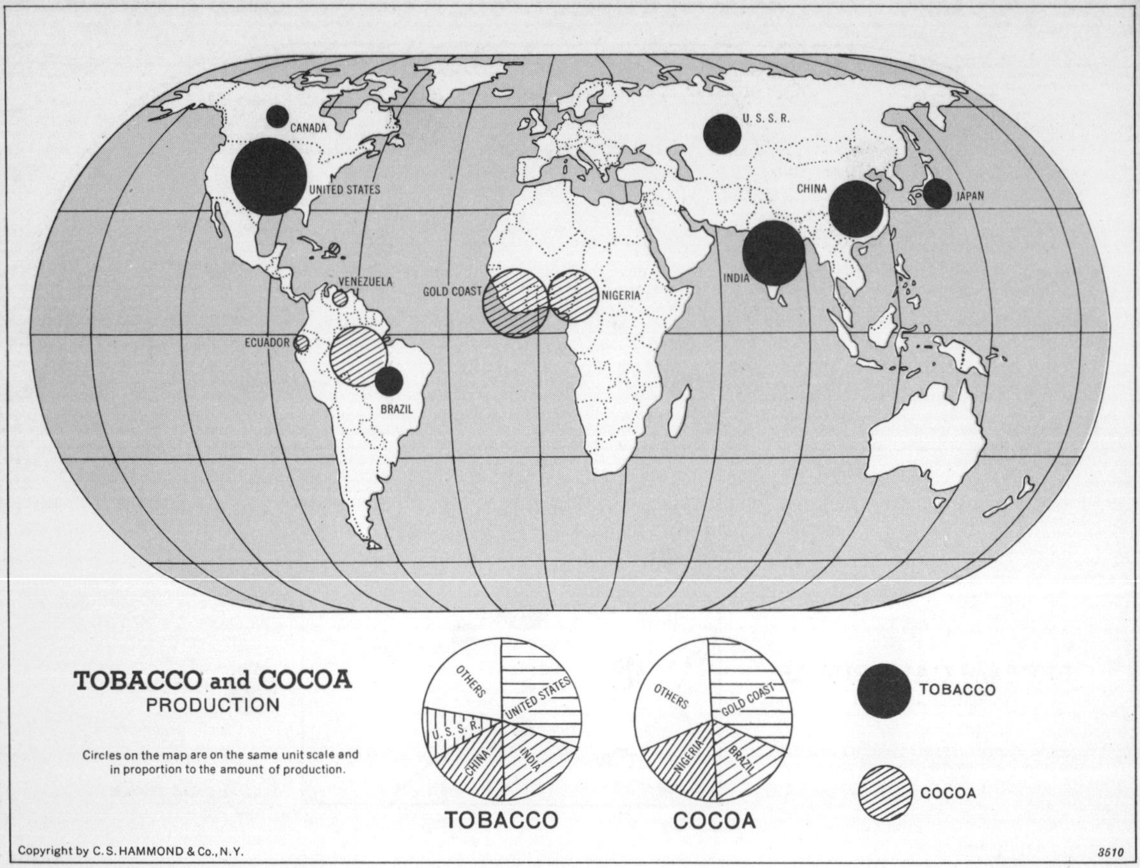
CANADA
UNITED STATES
VENEZUELA
ECUADOR
BRAZIL
GOLD COAST
NIGERIA
U. S. S. R.
CHINA
JAPAN
INDIA
TOBACCO and COCOA
PRODUCTION
Circles on the map are on the same unit scale and in proportion to the amount of production.
OTHERS
UNITED STATES
U. S. S. R.
CHINA
INDIA
TOBACCO
OTHERS
GOLD COAST
NIGERIA
BRAZIL
COCOA
TOBACCO
COCOA
Copyright by C. S. HAMMOND & Co., N.Y.
3510

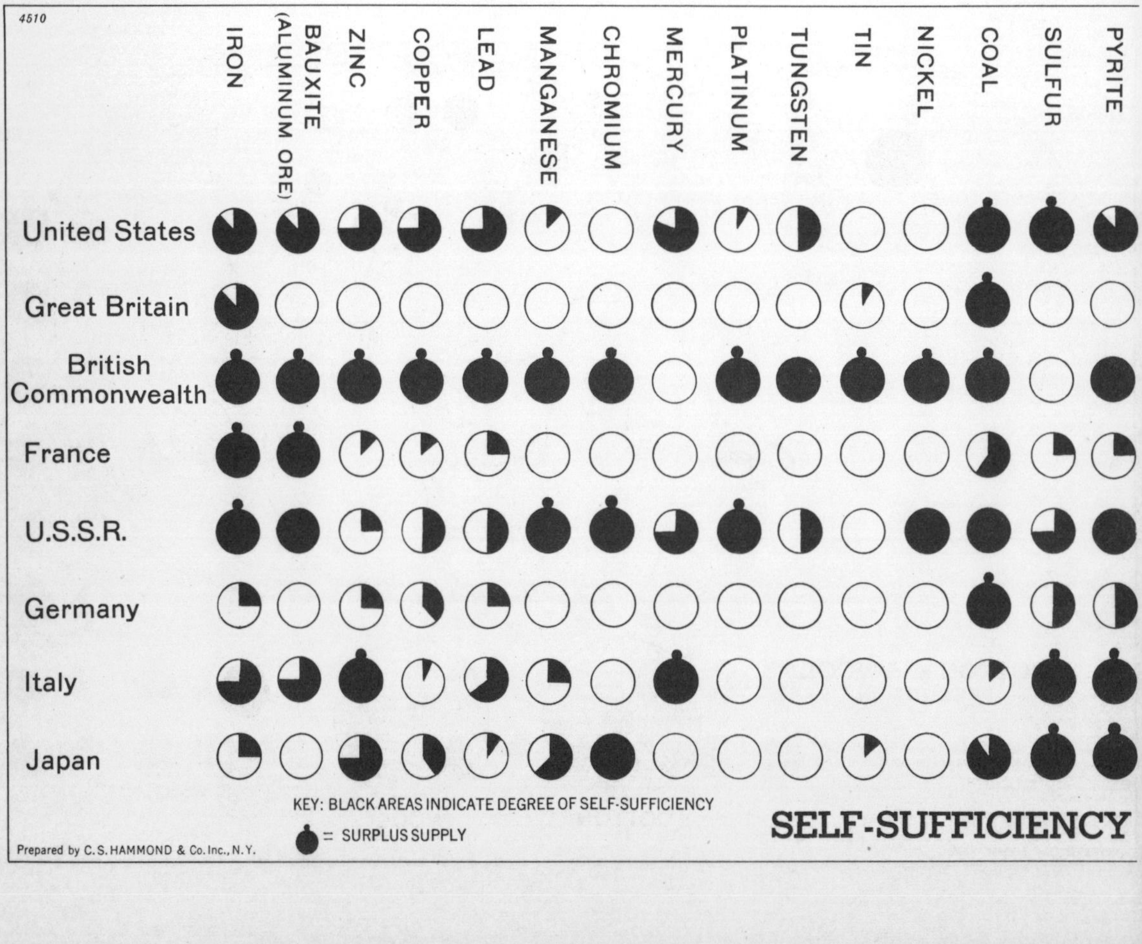
4510
IRON
BAUXITE (ALUMINUM ORE)
ZINC
COPPER
LEAD
MANGANESE
CHROMIUM
MERCURY
PLATINUM
TUNGSTEN
TIN
NICKEL
COAL
SULFUR
PYRITE
United States
Great Britain
British Commonwealth
France
U.S.S.R.
Germany
Italy
Japan
KEY: BLACK AREAS INDICATE DEGREE OF SELF-SUFFICIENCY
= SURPLUS SUPPLY
SELF-SUFFICIENCY
Prepared by C. S. HAMMOND & Co. Inc., N.Y.

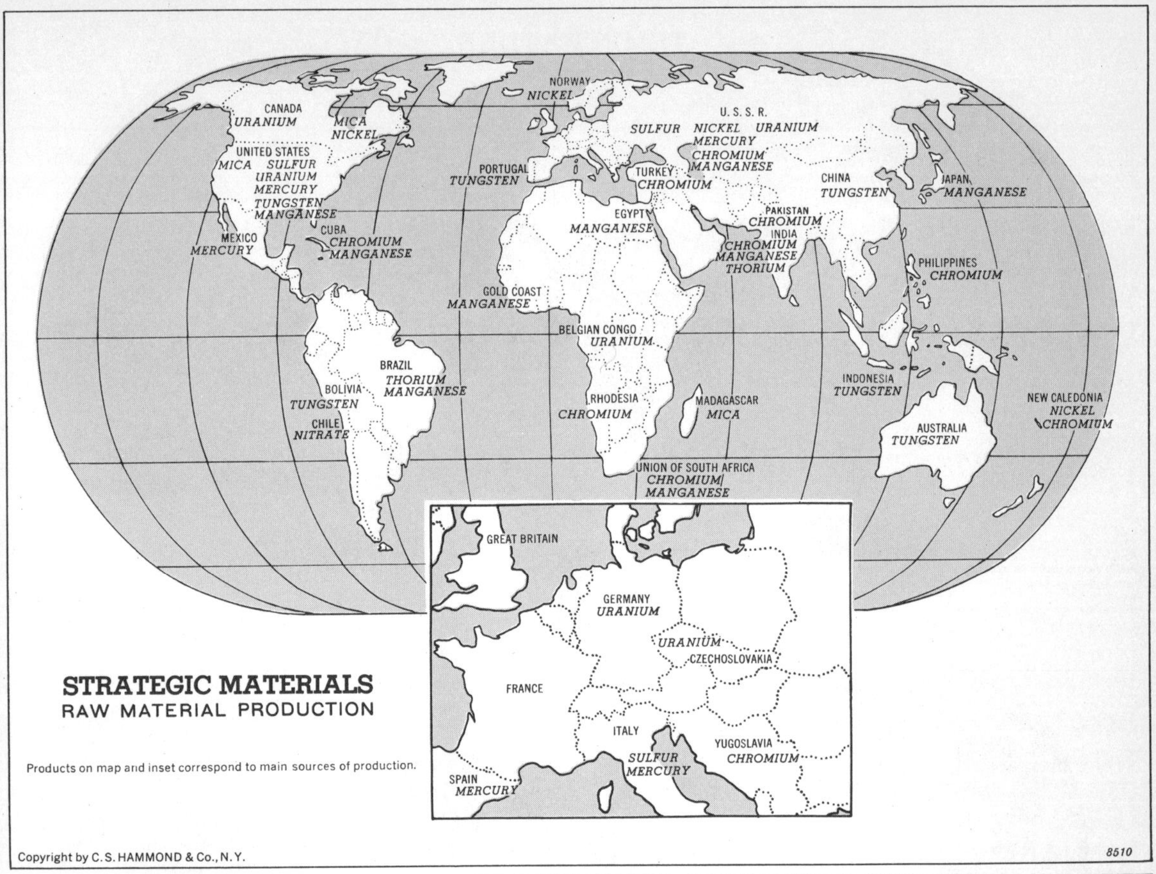

CANADA *URANIUM*
MICA NICKEL
UNITED STATES *MICA SULFUR URANIUM MERCURY TUNGSTEN MANGANESE*
MEXICO *MERCURY*
CUBA *CHROMIUM MANGANESE*
NORWAY *NICKEL*
PORTUGAL *TUNGSTEN*
U. S. S. R. *SULFUR NICKEL URANIUM MERCURY CHROMIUM MANGANESE*
TURKEY *CHROMIUM*
CHINA *TUNGSTEN*
JAPAN *MANGANESE*
EGYPT *MANGANESE*
PAKISTAN *CHROMIUM*
INDIA *CHROMIUM MANGANESE THORIUM*
PHILIPPINES *CHROMIUM*
GOLD COAST *MANGANESE*
BELGIAN CONGO *URANIUM*
BRAZIL *THORIUM MANGANESE*
BOLIVIA *TUNGSTEN*
CHILE *NITRATE*
RHODESIA *CHROMIUM*
MADAGASCAR *MICA*
INDONESIA *TUNGSTEN*
NEW CALEDONIA *NICKEL CHROMIUM*
AUSTRALIA *TUNGSTEN*
UNION OF SOUTH AFRICA *CHROMIUM MANGANESE*

GREAT BRITAIN
GERMANY *URANIUM*
URANIUM CZECHOSLOVAKIA
FRANCE
ITALY *SULFUR MERCURY*
YUGOSLAVIA *CHROMIUM*
SPAIN *MERCURY*

STRATEGIC MATERIALS
RAW MATERIAL PRODUCTION

Products on map and inset correspond to main sources of production.

8510

POTASH | MAGNESITE | PHOSPHATES | PETROLEUM | MICA | FOOD | WHEAT | SUGAR | BEEF | PORK | DAIRY PROD. | RUBBER | WOOL | COTTON | RAYON | SILK | HIDES | CHEMICALS

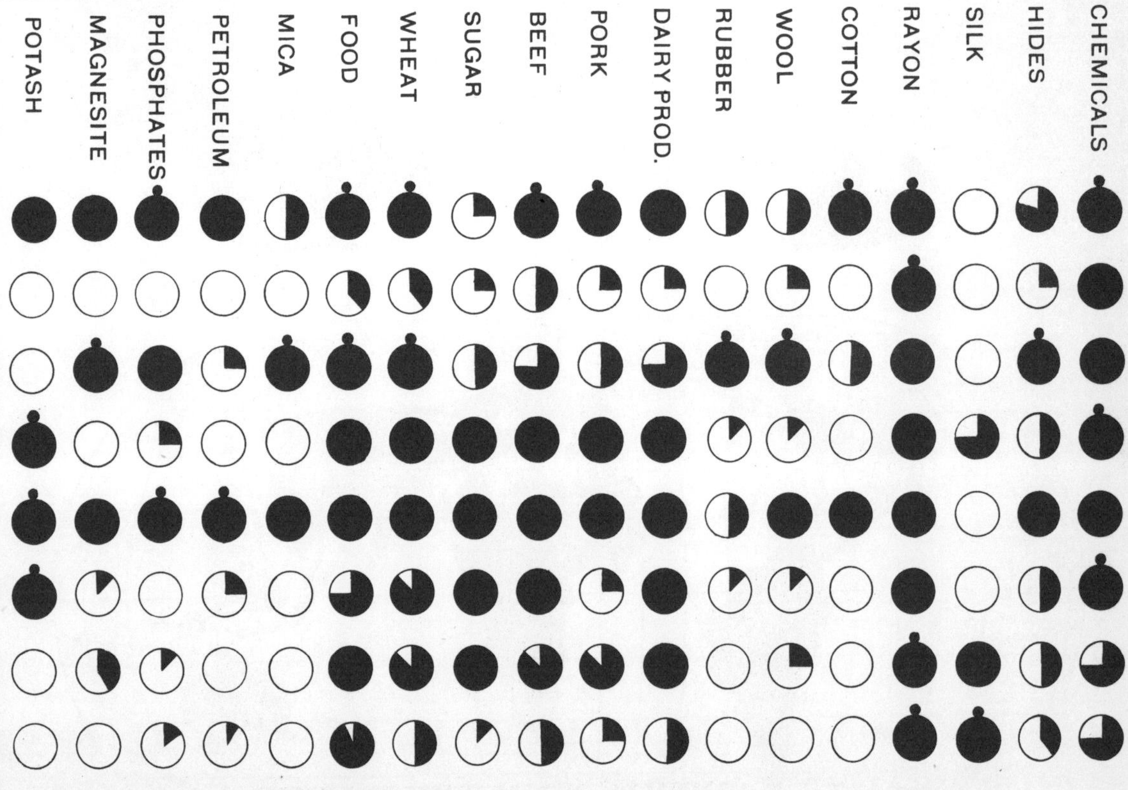

IN RAW MATERIALS

COURTESY HEADQUARTERS ARMY SERVICE FORCES

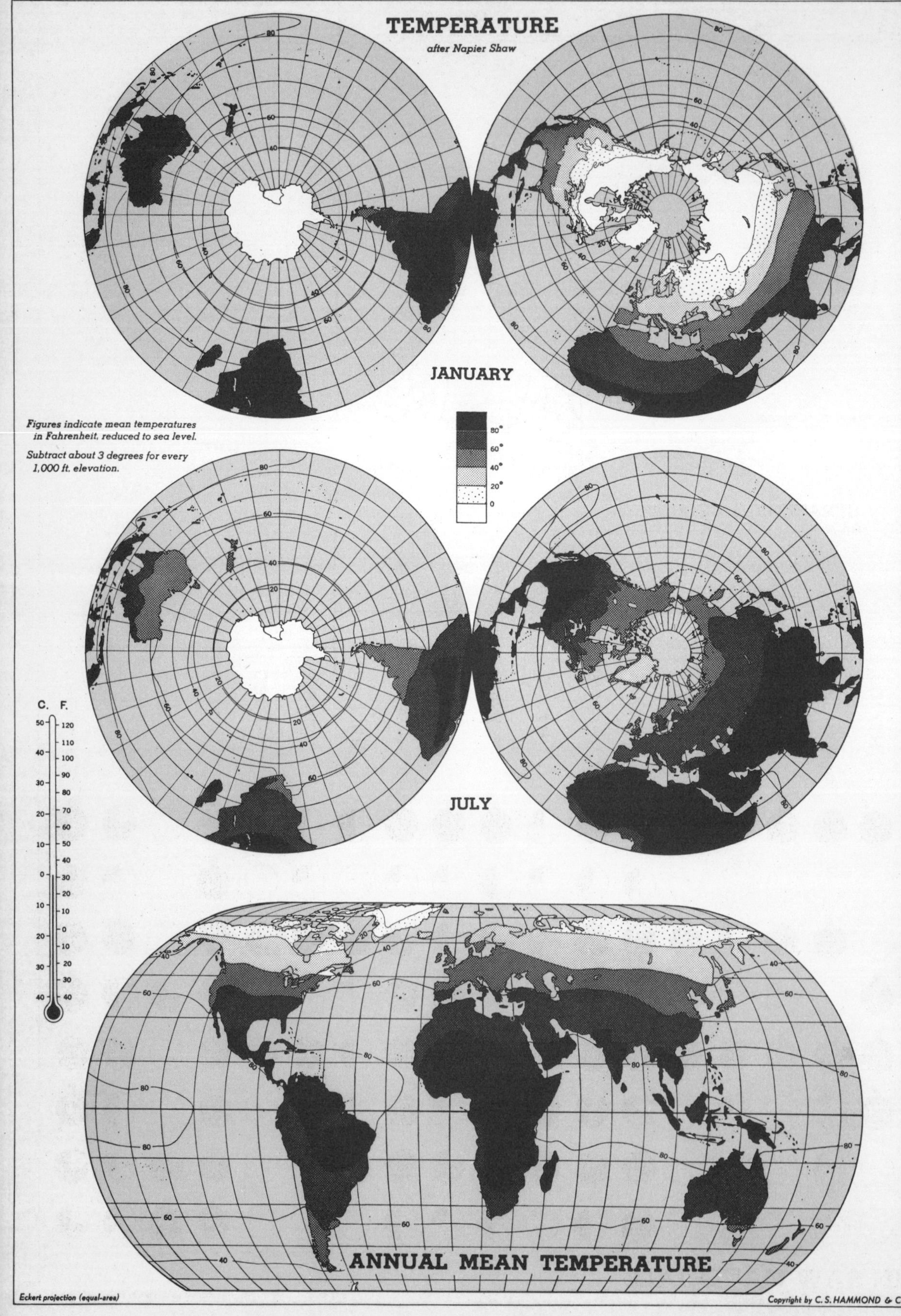
TEMPERATURE
after Napier Shaw
JANUARY
Figures indicate mean temperatures in Fahrenheit, reduced to sea level.
Subtract about 3 degrees for every 1,000 ft. elevation.
80°
60°
40°
20°
0
JULY
C. F.
ANNUAL MEAN TEMPERATURE
Eckert projection (equal-area)

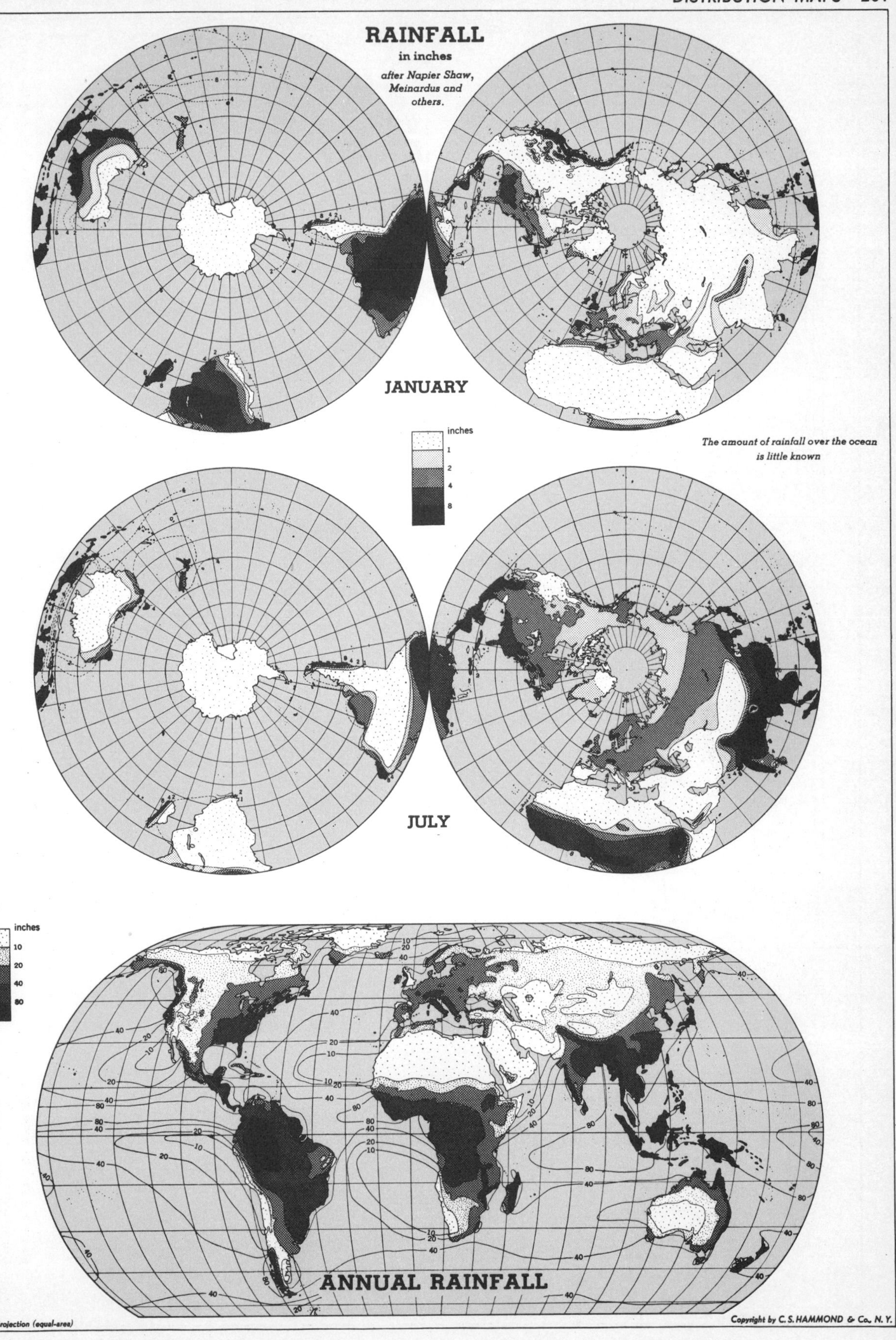
RAINFALL
in inches
after Napier Shaw, Meinardus and others.
JANUARY
inches
1
2
4
8
The amount of rainfall over the ocean is little known
JULY
inches
10
20
40
80
ANNUAL RAINFALL
...ert projection (equal-area)
Copyright by C. S. HAMMOND & Co., N. Y.

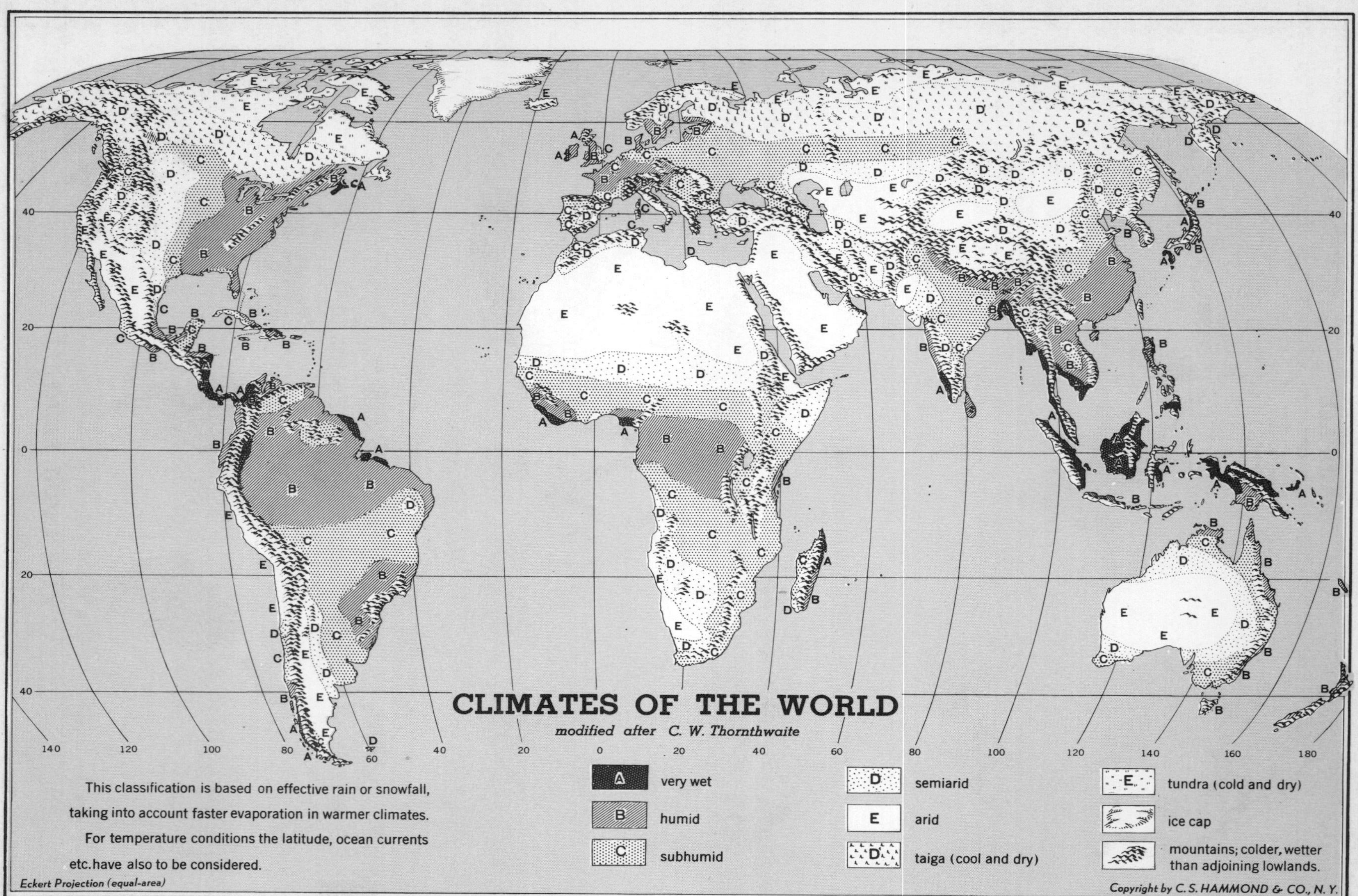
CLIMATES OF THE WORLD
modified after C. W. Thornthwaite
A very wet
B humid
C subhumid
D semiarid
E arid
D taiga (cool and dry)
E tundra (cold and dry)
ice cap
mountains; colder, wetter than adjoining lowlands.
This classification is based on effective rain or snowfall, taking into account faster evaporation in warmer climates.
For temperature conditions the latitude, ocean currents etc. have also to be considered.
Eckert Projection (equal-area)
Copyright by C. S. HAMMOND & CO., N. Y.

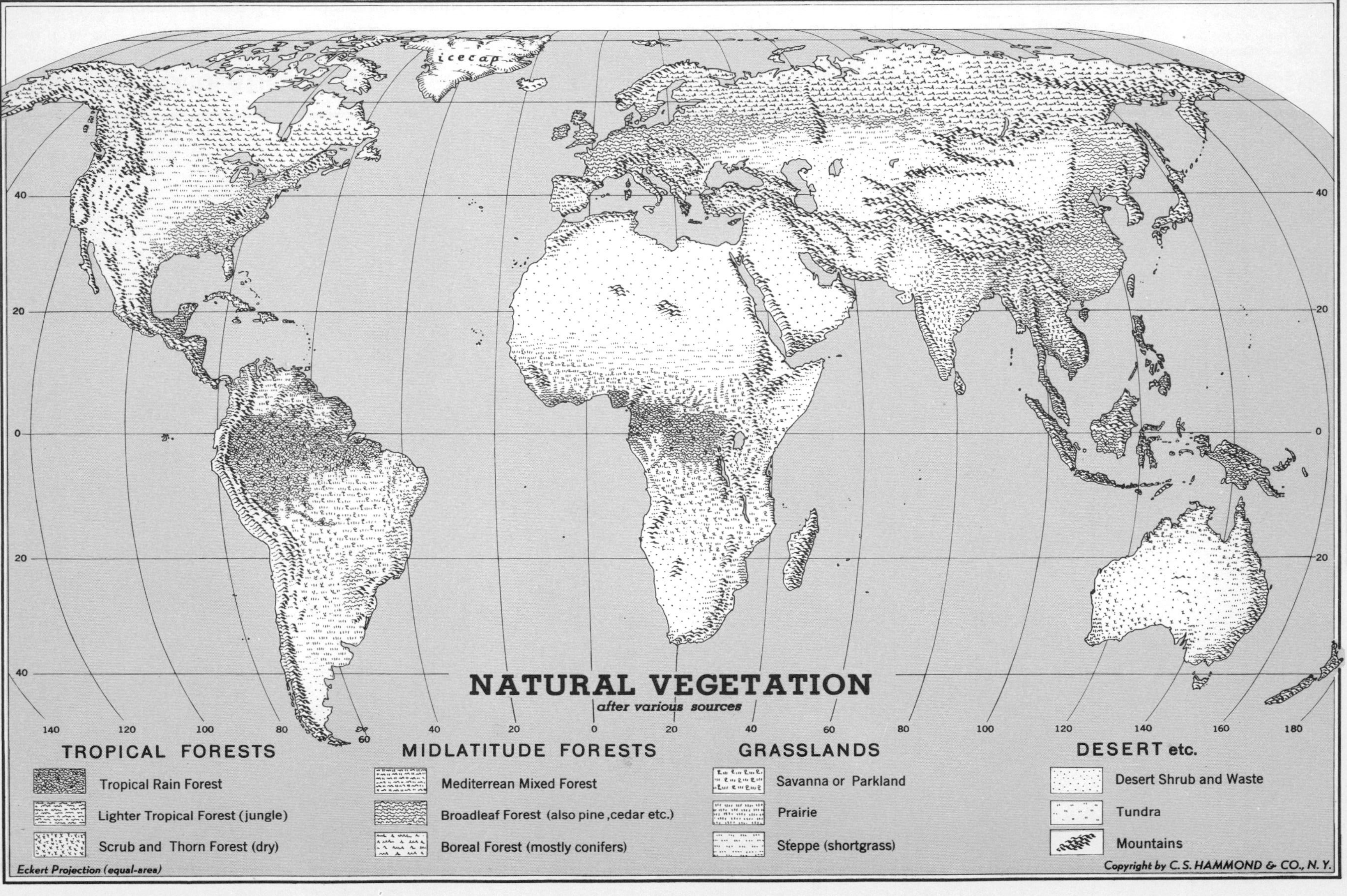
NATURAL VEGETATION
after various sources
icecap
TROPICAL FORESTS
Tropical Rain Forest
Lighter Tropical Forest (jungle)
Scrub and Thorn Forest (dry)
MIDLATITUDE FORESTS
Mediterrean Mixed Forest
Broadleaf Forest (also pine, cedar etc.)
Boreal Forest (mostly conifers)
GRASSLANDS
Savanna or Parkland
Prairie
Steppe (shortgrass)
DESERT etc.
Desert Shrub and Waste
Tundra
Mountains
Eckert Projection (equal-area)
Copyright by C. S. HAMMOND & CO., N. Y.

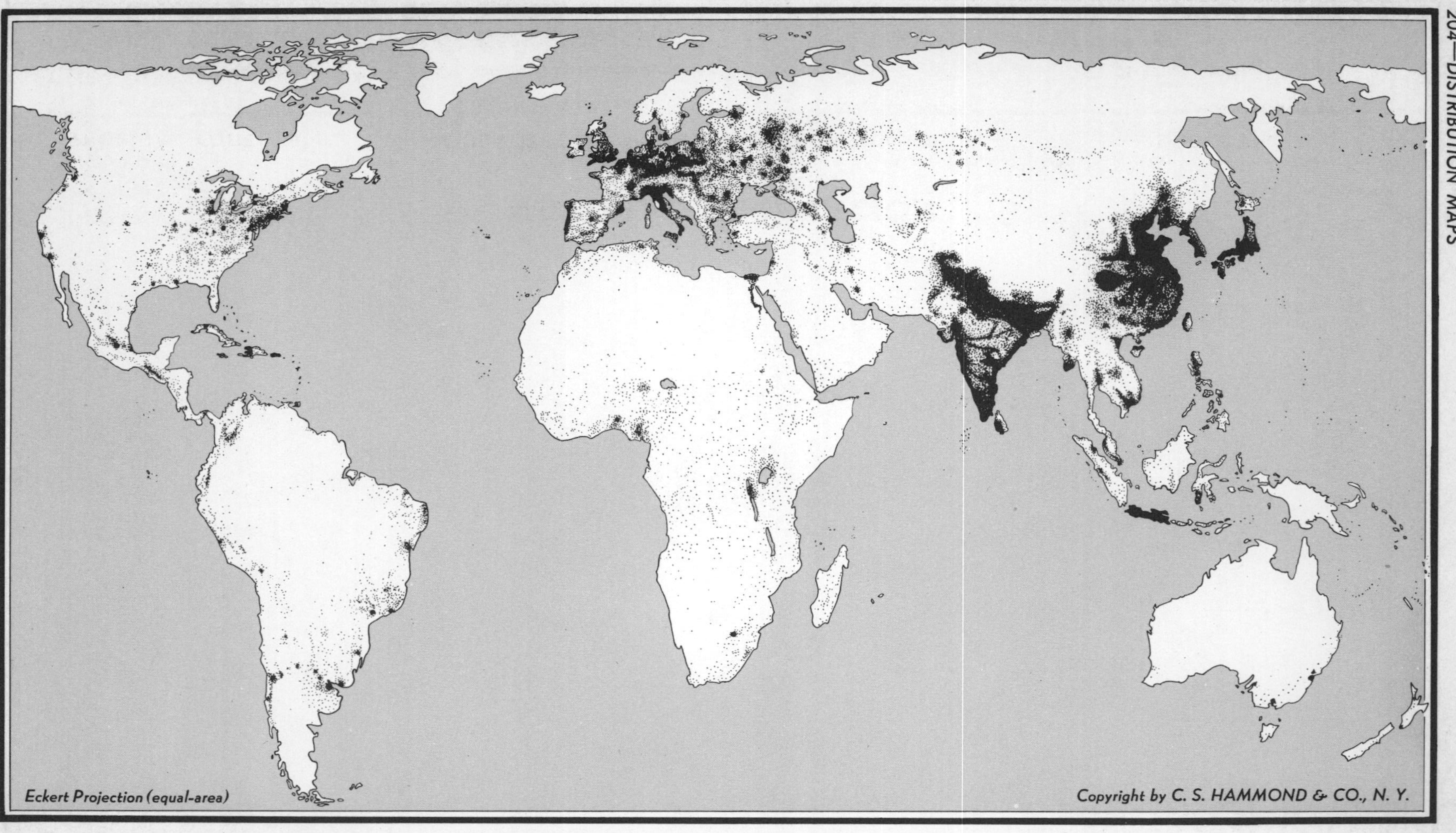

DENSITY OF POPULATION. *One of the most outstanding facts of human geography is the extremely uneven distribution of people over the Earth. One-half of the Earth's surface has less than 3 people per square mile, while in the lowlands of India, China, Java and Japan rural density reaches the incredible congestion of 2000-3000 per square mile. Three-fourths of the Earth's population live in four relatively small areas; Northeastern United States, North-Central Europe, India and the Far East.*

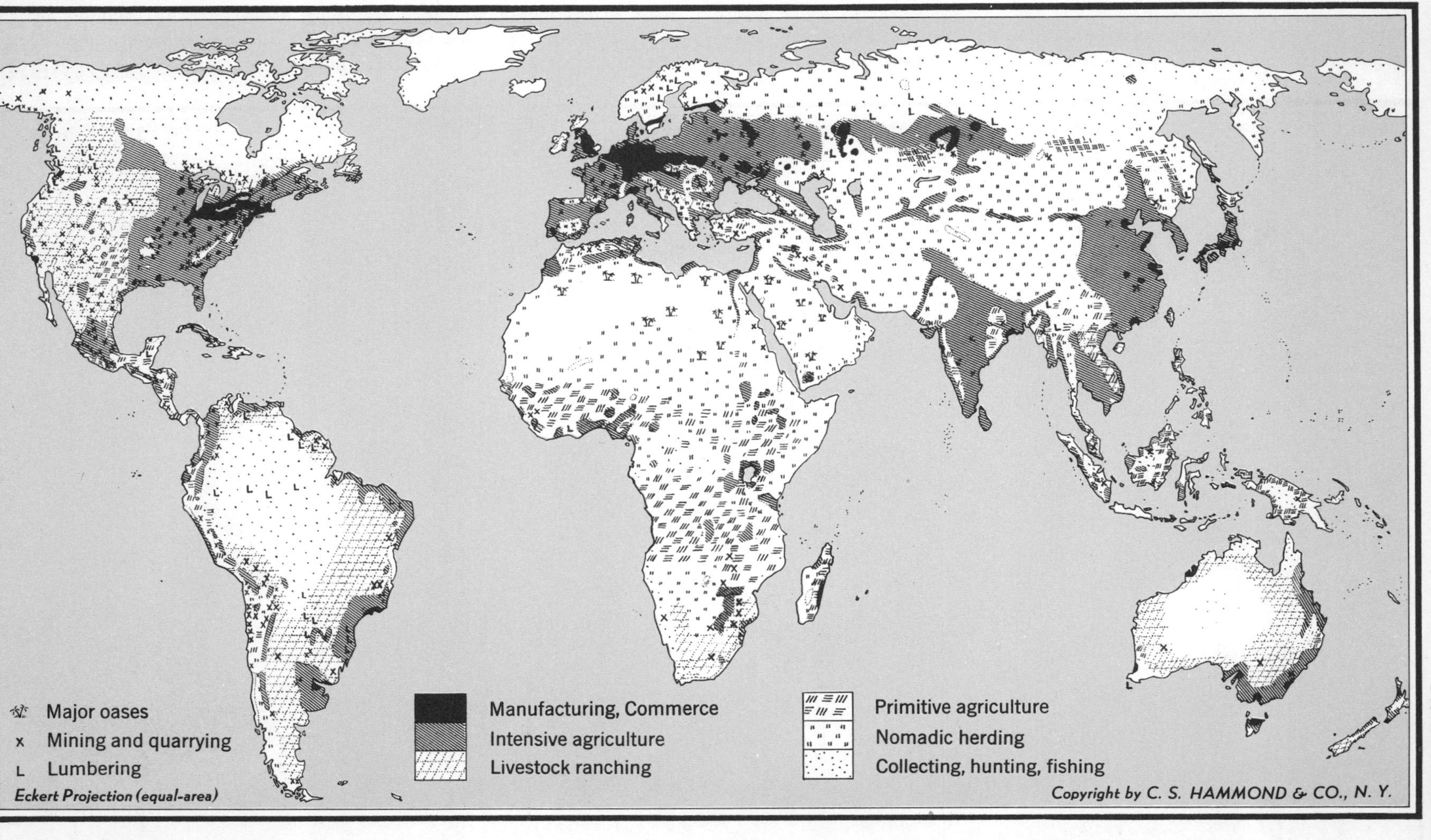

OCCUPATIONS. *Correlation with the density of population shows that the most densely populated areas fall into the regions of manufacturing and intensive farming. All other economies require considerable space. The most sparsely inhabited areas are those of collecting, hunting and fishing. Areas with practically no habitation are left blank.*

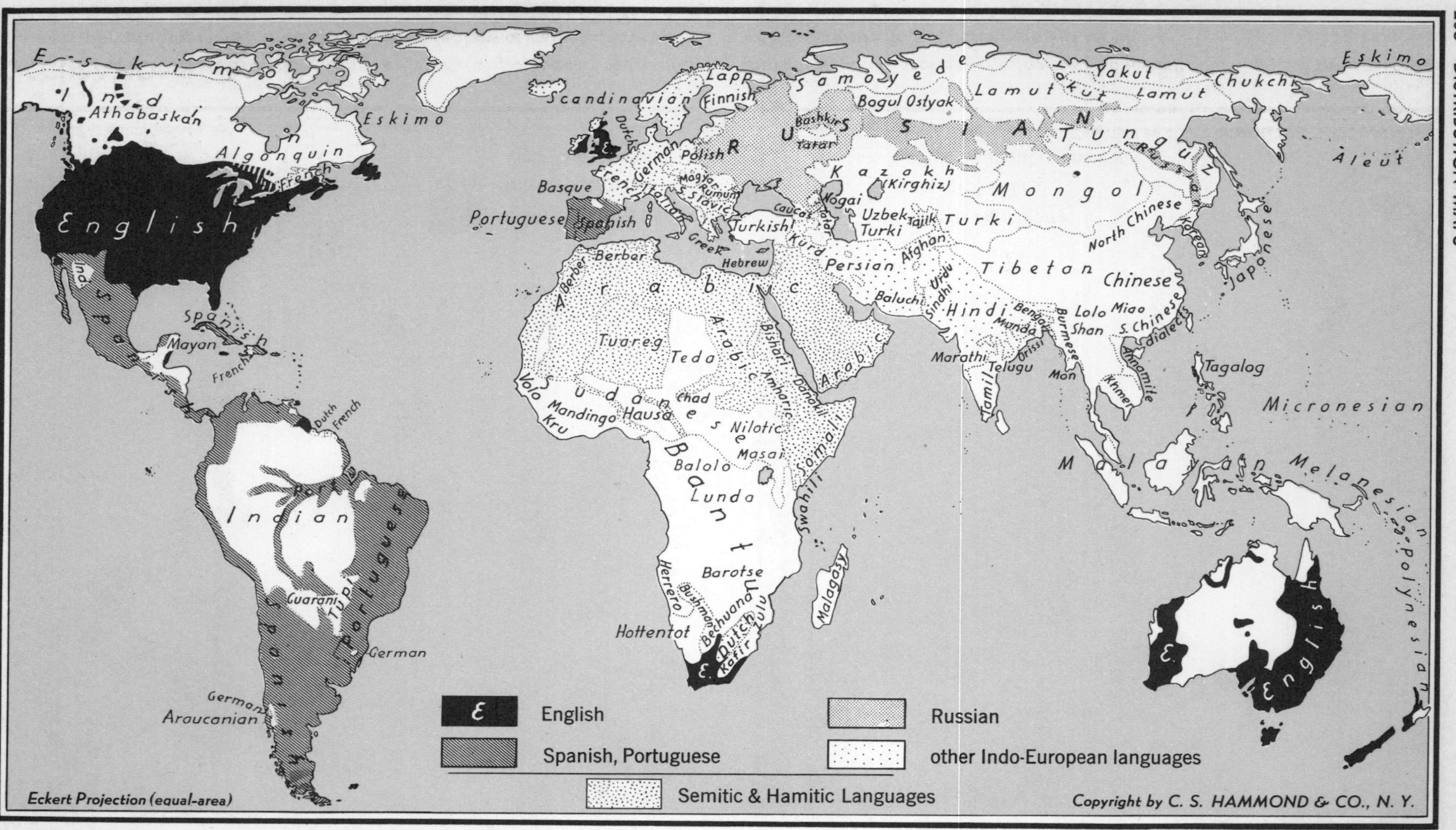

LANGUAGES. *Several hundred different languages are spoken in the World, and in many places two or more languages are spoken, sometimes by the same people. The map above shows the dominant languages in each locality. English, French, Spanish, Russian, Arabic and Swahili are spoken by many people as a second language for commerce or travel.*

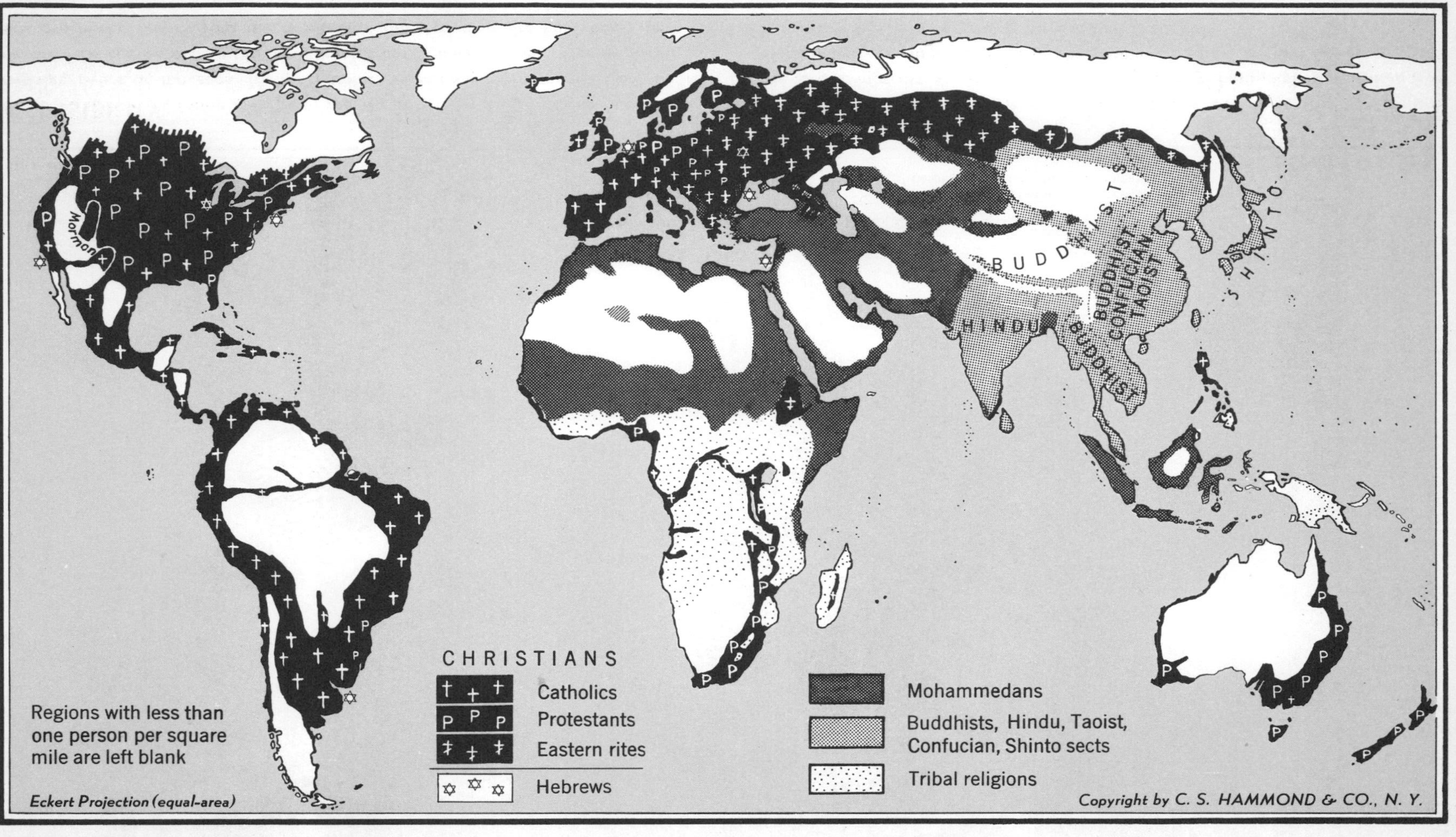

RELIGIONS. *Most people of the Earth belong to four major religions: Christians, Mohammedans, Brahmans, Buddhists and derivatives. The Eastern rites of the Christians include the Greek Orthodox, Greek Catholic, Armenian, Syrian, Coptic and more minor churches. The lamaism of Tibet and Mongolia differs a great deal from Buddhism in Burma and Thailand. In the religion of China the teachings of Buddha, Confucius and Tao are mixed, while in Shinto a great deal of ancestor and emperor worship is added. About 11 million Hebrews live scattered over the globe, chiefly in cities and in the state of Israel.*

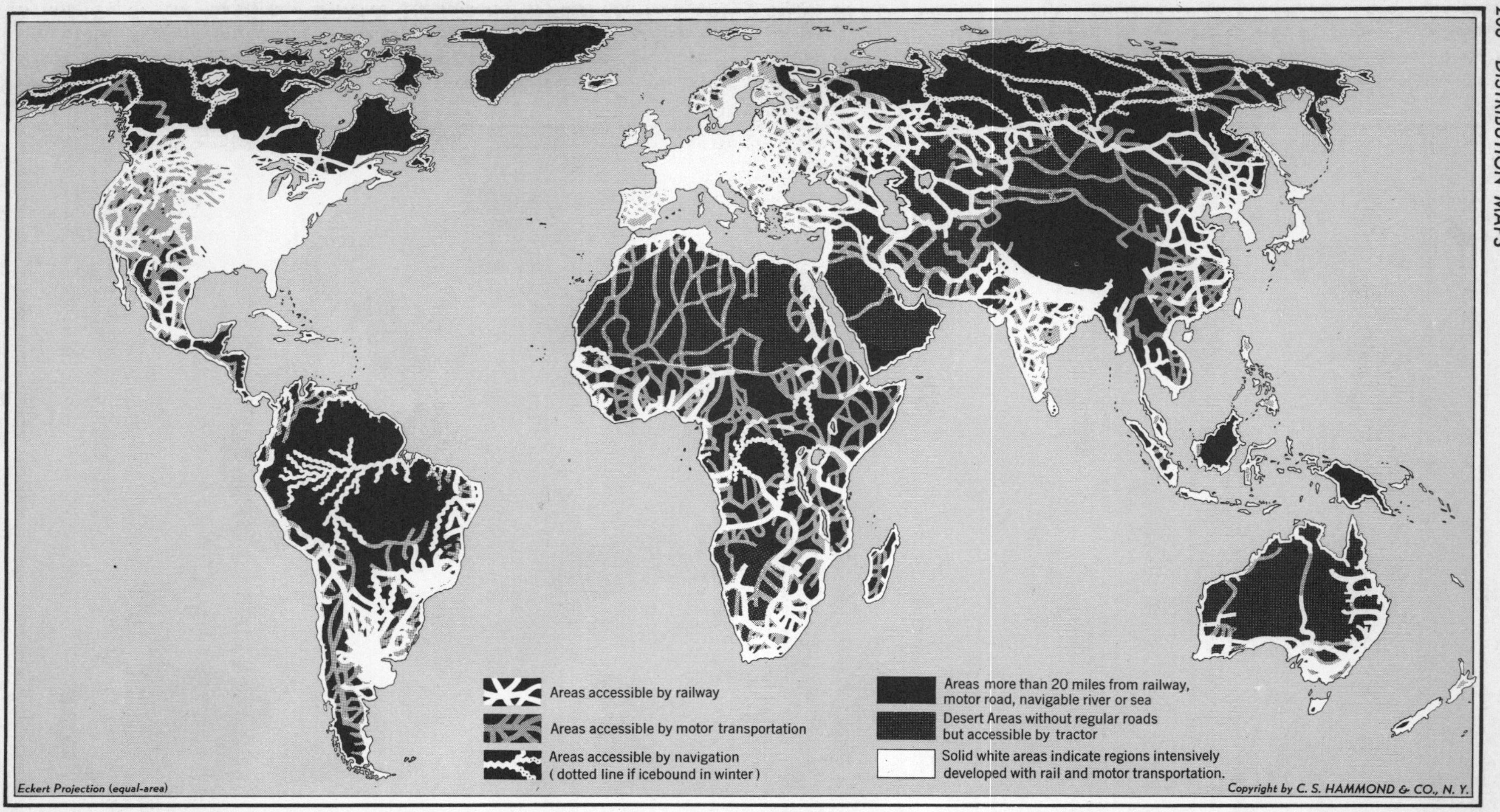

ACCESSIBILITY. *Many regions in the world are far from railways, roads, navigable rivers or the seas. Their economic development is retarded because their products can be brought to the world's markets only at great expense. Such areas are in the tundra (alpine), the boreal forest and in the equatorial rain forest regions. Desert areas, if not too mountainous, can be crossed by tractors. The largest inaccessible area is in Tibet, on account of high mountains, the alpine climate and isolationist attitude of the people. Airplane transportation will help to bring inaccessible areas into the orbit of civilization.*

ILLUSTRATED GEOGRAPHY OF THE WORLD

Introduction

The headline events of the last half-century have made the average American acutely curious of the vast world beyond the national borders of the American homeland. Constant repetition has tended to make this thought a cliche, yet it is one of the most significant truths of our time. This new national concern for the external world and its problems is one of the hopeful signs pointing to a better future for mankind.

One of the main roads to a better knowledge of this fascinating planet is a thorough indoctrination in the golden lore of geography. This science is not a narrow and limited scholarly discipline but a universal department of knowledge drawing on the sum total of man's explorations in the field of thought. The very pervasiveness of earth science makes it intriguing reading for the average non-specialist. At the same time that it entertains, it also builds a permanent edifice of information for the general reader. As more individuals discover this golden key to understanding the tumultuous happenings of the day, our collective actions in the field of enlightened citizenship will gain immeasurably in effectiveness.

CONTENTS

Canadian National Railroads

Ragged peaks and stoney crags form the watercourse for Emperor Falls in British Columbia.

NORTH AMERICA – Lying across the wide expanse of the Atlantic Ocean, was a new World waiting discovery and recognition. Europe was completely unaware of its existence for many centuries. Its discovery was destined to change the whole course of history and affect the fortunes of men and nations the world over. More than that, its discovery ushered in a whole new era of civilization, and marked the first faltering step towards the exploration and charting of all lands and waters of the world.

No discovery, before or since, has added more to man's opportunities and the wealth of the world; or played a more important part in shaping a world's destiny. Yet, its discoverer died in ignorance of his epoch-making contribution to the world. It remained for those who followed to prove the existence of a New World.

Landing on one of the Bahamas, how was Columbus to know that his quest for a new route to the East Indies had led him to an island outpost of two fabulous empires ? . . . now but a bare few hours by air travel from the sister continents of North and South America. In his wildest dreams Columbus could not have conceived of a land extending virtually from the North Pole to the South Pole, for a distance of some nine thousand miles.

We can imagine Balboa's thrill twenty-one years later, when he fought his way across the rocky Ithmus of Panama to gaze upon the Pacific. But, how was he to know that this narrow ribbon of tapering land joined two vast domains ? That, from where he stood, an unbroken expanse of land reached northward for forty-five hundred miles, and actually spread out into a gigantic fan three thousand miles wide ? Also, that, to the south a similar, though lesser triangle of land, reached thousands of miles below the equator to the icy waters of the Antarctic ?

Today these are historical incidents of common knowledge, thanks to the intrepid discoverers, explorers and map-makers. We take their hard won glories for granted, and even forget the adventure and romance that has gone into the making of our geographical maps.

We must be constantly reminded that, of all the continents of the world, North America is the most favored for natural wealth, climate and position on the earth. Being situated between the two largest oceans has protected the people of North America from enemy invasion, and also enabled them to develop an extensive commerce. The millions of square miles of fertile soil and untold mineral wealth has provided a standard of living unknown elsewhere in the world. Hence, composed of peoples from all over the world, its inhabitants have enjoyed peace and plenty, without fear of their independent ways of life being encroached upon, or destroyed by jealous and covetous neighbors. We can be assured that such a fortunate people will not easily relinquish what they have come to hold so dear.

The principal geographical features of North America are its two mountain ranges and the intervening central plains. The high and rugged mountains to the westward extend from the tip of Alaska to the base of the Isthmus of Panama, or from the northern to the southern extremity of the continent. These mountain ranges include the Coastal system that hugs the Pacific Coast, and the Rocky Mountains that branch out eastward and southward across the United States to become, in Mexico and Central America, the Sierra Madres. The Cascade Mountains, which farther south become the Sierra Nevada, are separate ranges that work inland from the coastal mountains. These diverging mountain chains in the east and west, form the bulwark for a number of high plateaus that lie between. The land adjoining the Cascade Mountains is the Columbia Plateau, while farther south lies the Colorado Plateau. In between is the arid region of the Great Basin. The Great Salt Lake is all that remains to reveal that this vast area was once a geologic lake.

In the east, extending from the Gulf of Saint Lawrence to the Gulf of Mexico is the Appalachian Range. These mountains are older and less rugged than the Rockies. Time has worn them down and rounded their peaks. On the side toward the Atlantic Ocean, they merge with the Piedmont Plateau, which slopes off into a coastal plain.

The great central plains that slope towards the center, and lie between the Rocky Mountain and Appalachian Highlands describe a giant "V" which extends from the Arctic Ocean to the Gulf of Mexico.

More varieties of climate prevail in North America than in any other land in the world. The greater part of the continent, however, enjoys a temperate and invigorating climate. The inhabitants of the far north must adjust themselves to the rigors of Arctic weather, Mexico endures sub-tropical temperatures, and Central America a tropical heat. Even from the east to west there is a wide variety of climate due to difference in altitude, and other conditions not affected by latitude.

To an airman soaring above the shifting panorama of North America, the realization must come that this is indeed a rich land of fertile soils, spreading forests, rolling plains, inland lakes, and mighty rivers. There is hardly an area of any size on the entire continent but contains, on the surface or beneath it, a species of natural wealth. On the western coast, the great Pacific Ocean, generally a protective barrier, separating most of North America from the shores of Asia, offers little promise of isolation at its far northwest corner. While eight thousand miles separate the peoples of China from the United States, Russia and Alaska almost meet at the Bering Strait, which is only fifty-seven miles wide.

North Carolina News Bureau

The American South contains unusually picturesque mountain scenery.

ALASKA—Purchased from Russia in 1867 for a pittance proved to be the most valued of U.S. possessions and was to be the 49th state. The Senate voted June 30, 1958 for Alaskan statehood. Although partially in the Arctic Circle, it is by no means the frozen and inhospitable land its latitude would suggest. Alaska has a wide area of equable climate. Along its mountainous and island-fringed coast, the warm Japanese Current keeps the temperature at all times above zero. This rises in the summer to a seasonal heat of 80°. These sections endure drenching rain, caused by the condensation of warm winds striking the snow-capped peaks of the mountains. In the center of Alaska is a broad upland where grasses, flowers and mosses grow.

The Yukon River, rising in Canada, swings across Alaska for fifteen hundred miles, twelve hundred of which are navigable. Although frozen for two-thirds of the year, this river is a main artery of travel. Dog sled teams replace the large steamers during the months when it is ice-bound. A half million acres of land is cultivated in the Yukon Valley, and even though the growing season is short, the Arctic days provide long hours of sunshine.

First known as "Seward's Folly," Alaska justified its purchase within a few short years and has proved a veritable storehouse of treasure. Each year it produces more than twice its purchase price, in minerals alone.

The popular conception of the Arctic does, however, exist in the northern regions. Here the ground thaws only a few inches at the surface during the summer. Except for a few Eskimo and reindeer, there is comparatively no life or vegetation able to survive the rigors of the frigid climate.

While at one time Alaska was a remote and unexplored country, today with ever increasing population and extensive building and improvement of roads, development is steadily expanding.

The Aleutian islands are strung out in a broad arc off the tip of Alaska for a thousand miles and separate the Bering Sea from the North Pacific. Numbering about one hundred and fifty islands, they are the tops of submerged mountains. Included in the purchase of Alaska, they have great strategic value as air bases and weather observing stations for the United States.

CANADA—The three thousand mile boundary between the United States and Canada is convincing proof that two great nations may live side by side in peace and harmony. For over a hundred years this boundary line —the longest in the world—has been free from fortification of any kind by either nation. In a world that has been repeatedly torn by war during the past century here is lasting evidence that national progress, pride and ambition can exist without adjoining countries being tempted to encroach on the other's domain.

Canada is the largest domain of the British Commonwealth. It extends from the icy waters of the Arctic to the borders of the United States, and from east to west its greatest distance is 3,700 miles. Its area is greater than that of the United States and nearly as large as the continent of Europe.

Canada is a vast diversified land of fertile plains, of mountains and rivers, and countless lakes. Over 6 per cent of the total is water area, affording ready power for her ever increasing industrial development. Like the United States it can be roughly divided into three sections; the eastern highlands, a great level central plain, and mountain ranges extending from the Rockies to the Pacific.

In the east the Appalachian region is a beautiful land of hilly or mountainous terrain with very heavily forested sections and fertile farm lands. Just west of the highlands lies the St. Lawrence Valley including the Ontario peninsula, the hub of Canada's industry. In this area, rich in minerals, forests, water power and fertile land, is the highest concentration of population. Moderate climate combined with valuable accessible resources have made this section of the greatest economic importance. Northwest of the Valley is the Canadian Shield, an area characterized by low hills, countless lakes connected by streams and rapids. Here is Canada's greatest store of resources, minerals, forests, furs and water power. In the interior Plains is the great wheat belt. In the west, parallel to the Pacific, is the magnificent mountain country formed by the Cordilleran Mountain System. In addition to minerals and valuable forests, this area, in the fertile valleys, produces much of Canada's fruit and vegetable crops.

Although primarily an agricultural country, Canada has developed rapidly in recent years as an industrial country. Lumbering is of great importance, which is to be expected, for the forests of Canada are among the largest in the world. Furs have been an important source of wealth since the early days of the Hudson's Bay Company, and the fishing grounds of Canada are the largest and most productive on earth. Wheat is the principal crop of the prairie provinces, and Canada is one of the biggest producers and exporters of this grain.

The provinces in the southern sections of Canada enjoy much the same climate as exists in the Great Lakes regions of the United States. The southern parts of Ontario and Quebec have less severe winters, but the northern sections of these provinces have very severe winters, with short, hot summers. The prairies experience great extremes in temperature, while moderate rainfall in this region favors wheat production.

About half of the population is of British origin and one quarter is French. The remaining fourth is principally Russian, German, Austrian and Scandinavian. Some hundred thousand Indians live mostly on reservations.

UNITED STATES—In a little over one hundred and fifty years the United States of America has written an amazing chapter in history. In that brief period a wilderness has been tamed, and a powerful nation has arisen to take its place among the foremost countries of the world. A land populated by every race, creed and color, and a haven of refuge for the oppressed, its phenomenal growth has never been equalled. Far removed from the traditions and hampering fetters of the Old World, it has charted a new course in government. Its freedom loving people have devoted their energies to developing the riches that Nature has so lavishly supplied.

The United States has reached its present position of greatness because of a number of reasons. It is blessed with a climate that cannot be surpassed elsewhere in the world, and is rich in mineral wealth beyond that of any other country. With a coastline on three sides well supplied with harbors, it is ideally situated for trade with the rest of the world. Its rivers and lakes are navigable and give easy access into the interior of the country. The variety of climate and the fertility of the soil make a great diversity of crops possible.

Climate has made the people of the United States energetic, and Nature has endowed the land with more than enough to meet their needs. This country's way of life has provided the incentive for continually bettering the standards of living of its people. All this has brought continued economic, cultural and scientific progress.

The United States is the greatest manufacturing nation in the world, with half the

Gendreau

An attraction for all visitors to Mexico is Xochimilco's floating gardens.

population depending upon industry for a living. It has the finest systems of transportation and communication, including the great majority of the automobiles in the world. More than half the coal, and a quarter of the iron in the world, as well as large deposits of almost all important minerals are found here.

The three principal geographical features are a continuation of those in Canada. They are the eastern highlands, comprising the Appalachian Range, the broad central plains, and the Rockies and Coastal ranges in the Far West.

A closer study of the geography of the United States does much to explain the growth of the nation. For example, the stony soil of New England discouraged farming and caused the early settlers to turn to manufacturing and commerce. The swift streams furnished water power and the jagged coastline provided bays for harboring the ships from Europe. Farther south, the coastal plains widen out into broad stretches of fertile land, and the rivers are short and deep. This led to the development of the large plantations in the deep South, where the climate is favorable to crops that require long hot summers. Here the coastal plain includes half of Georgia, all of Florida, and extends along the Gulf of Mexico. It reaches into the interior as far north as southern Illinois.

The lake and prairie region of the upper Mississippi Valley is one of the most fertile in the world, and is linked by waterways with the East and South through the Great Lakes and the Mississippi River system. The Great Plains region, depending upon the nature of the topsoil and the amount of rainfall, is either grain or grazing country, with valuable deposits of oil in Texas and Oklahoma.

The great size of the country and the seemingly endless store of natural wealth, both above and below the surface of the earth, have been responsible for great waste in the past. Fortunately, strict conservation measures are now in force to protect the resources of the earth for future generations and to assure them an equal place in this "Land of Opportunity".

MEXICO—Beyond the southern border of the United States and across the Rio Grande, where North America begins to taper sharply to a point, lies Latin America. It is difficult to conceive of the contrast to be found beyond this man-made boundary with the rest of the continent. It is another world, with a totally different culture, another language, and traditions and customs which set it apart from its northern neighbors.

About one-fourth the area of the United States, Mexico swings south for about eleven hundred miles, ending in the narrow hook of the peninsula of Yucatan.

While half of Mexico lies in the torrid zone, its climate is determined more by elevation than latitude. Along the coast the weather is hot and humid, with luxuriant tropical vegetation. As the land rises the climate changes to temperate and the mountain peaks are snow-clad. Two mountain chains, that are a continuation of those in the United States, converge and meet at the southern tip, leaving a flat tableland between. The average altitude of this plateau is about 6,500 feet. Mexico's highest concentration of population is here where the fertile land, ideal climate and favorable rainfall afford excellent conditions for agricultural crops. Although industrial development has increased rapidly in recent years and most of Mexico's wealth is derived from her mines and petroleum, the great majority of the people are still employed in agricultural pursuits. Except for the coastal plain bordering the Gulf of Mexico, mountains and plateaus occupy the greater part of Mexico. Lying in both the temperate and torrid zones allows the country to produce a greater variety of crops than is possible in most other countries.

Mexico is a beautiful and picturesque country with ancient ruins of pyramids and temples still standing as mute evidence of a flourishing civilization that existed before the coming of the Spanish invaders in the early fifteenth century.

CENTRAL AMERICA—As North America decreases in size from a land of magnificent distance to a slender neck of land where the Isthmus of Panama joins South America, the sizes of its nations shrink to even greater extent. In Central America a string of six small countries, Guatemala, Honduras, El Salvador, Nicaragua, Costa Rica and Panama, is confined to an area less than that of the State of Texas. Their total population does not equal that of New York City.

The Cordilleras, a continuation of the mountain chains starting far north in Alaska, extend the entire length of the land. Many of the peaks are volcanic and frequent eruptions occur. These mountains have formed many high and fertile plateaus which provide fine pasturage for livestock and rich soil for a diversity of crops. As in Mexico, the tropical climate of the lower regions is tempered by the elevation of the high plateaus. There are a number of harbors on both coasts, with the principal seaports on the Caribbean Sea. Most of the rivers that flow into the Caribbean are navigable.

These agricultural nations have become increasingly important in the past few years. With the organizing of the Pan-American Union, the growth of air travel, and the fostering of a new spirit of co-operation between the republics of North and South America, Central America's future became one of promise. When global war shut off supplies of many important crops to the Western world from the East, it was found that here in the Americas could be grown many necessities that formerly had been imported from afar. Great variation in soils, rainfall, and terrain afford an enormous variety of tropical, semi-tropical and temperate crops. Experiments have successfully produced important quantities of spices, fibres, and essential oils for medicinal and industrial purposes that were introduced from the East. Among the important crops exported almost exclusively to the United States are bananas, natural rubber, coffee, rope fibres, cacao and sugar.

Although there is potential mineral wealth in most of the countries of Central America this resource, for the most part, has been unexploited. Much of the land is heavily forested and some of the world's most valuable woods such as mahogany, rosewood, teak and ebony are found here. However, only a very small part of the forests have been as yet cut for commercial purposes.

Pan-American-Grace Airways

Peru's cultural past is evident to all who visit her attractive cities.

ISLANDS OF THE CARIBBEAN—The Caribbean Sea is a vital water link between the Americas and the West Indies. With the opening of the Panama Canal it took on added importance as a trade route for the ships of the world.

The island republics and colonies lying in the Caribbean have likewise become increasingly important with the passing years, both for their economic and strategic value.

The West Indies, numbering hundreds of islands, extend in a sweeping arc beginning near southern Florida and ending off the coast of Venezuela. Columbus named the islands, in the belief that he had reached India. Most of the islands, forming two main groups, the Greater and the Lesser Antilles, are mountainous. However, there is sufficient fertile land to afford a variety of tropical products. In general the climate is hot but is tempered by the sea breezes. All the islands are subject to tropical hurricanes and in many regions there are occasional volcanic eruptions.

With the greater part of the West Indies under the control of the United States and Great Britain, the islands enjoy advantages not usually possessed by small independent countries. Nearness to markets and the great manufacturing centers, and cheap ocean transportation are added advantages. As with the Central American republics, the West Indies have enjoyed increased production and trade with the importation of new crops from the East that are now grown throughout Middle America.

SOUTH AMERICA—It is a common error to think of South America as being directly south of the United States. A glance at the globe will show that this is far from the truth. Except for the bulge to the west and the southern tip, all of South America is east of the Atlantic coast boundary of the United States. This places South America much closer to Africa than North America is to Europe. A theory has been advanced, though never proved, that at one time Africa and South America were joined.

Smaller than North America by nearly two million square miles, and representing one-seventh of the world's total land area,

South America is the fourth largest continent.

With the equator crossing South America on a line with the Amazon River, two-thirds of this southern neighbor is in the tropics and the balance in the temperate zone. In common with other lands situated in the Southern Hemisphere, it has the further disadvantage of being far removed from the principal world markets. These factors, together with the history of the continent, explain why it has not developed as rapidly as the United States, although discovered at the same time. But in spite of the handicaps of climate, position and history, South America has an extensive trade with the United States and Europe. And, although for centuries the Spaniards robbed it of its buried treasures, South America still possesses great mineral wealth.

South of the Isthmus of Panama, the great line of mountains which extends the entire length of North America becomes the mighty Andes. Second only to the Himalayas, they follow the western coast to Cape Horn, rising steeply from the Pacific in long ranges of snow-capped peaks and wide plateaus. Mount Aconcagua is the highest peak in the Americas and rises to a height of twenty-three thousand feet. Several lesser peaks are active volcanos. To the south the range begins to narrow and the coast is bordered by a tattered fringe of islands clothed with pines and swept by fierce northwesterly winds.

On the east are two broad plateaus, the Guiana and Brazilian highlands, which might be compared with the Laurentian highlands and the Appalachian chain of North America. Between the eastern slope of the Andes and these plateaus lie broad lowlands. The grassy, tree dotted plains, or *llanos,* of the Orinoco Basin in Venezuela and Colombia, provide fine pasturage between the dry and rainy seasons. In the dry season they practically revert to desert. To the south are the dry plains, or *pampas,* of Northern Argentina, which is the great cattle country of the continent.

The Amazon—largest river system in the world—drains over one-third of the continent. This area is equal to two-thirds that of the United States. This mighty river is thirty-five hundred miles long and in places is over fifty miles wide. It flows through the densest tropical forest in the world and much of it is unexplored.

The La Plata River is actually the estuary for three rivers, the Parana, with a drainage area almost as large as that of the Mississippi, the Uruguay and the Paraguay. Buenos Aires, metropolis of the Southern Hemisphere is situated on the south bank of the La Plata 175 miles from the Atlantic. Buenos Aires is one of the world's most beautiful cities and important seaports. The above mentioned rivers drain Northern Argentina, Uruguay and Paraguay.

Other rivers of less importance are the São Francisco of Brazil, the Magdalena of Colombia, the Orinoco of Venezuela, and the Río Colorado of Argentina.

Lying in the Andes at an altitude of over twelve thousand feet is Lake Titicaca. With an area over half that of Lake Erie, it is the highest navigable lake in the world.

Much of Argentina and Chile are in southern latitudes that compare with the northern latitudes of the United States, but there are only sections where the climate is similar. Parts of Chile have a climate that compares with the Pacific coast states, and sections of Argentina and Uruguay are comparable to the east coast of the United States.

The heat is insufferable and the rainfall extremely heavy in the low Orinoco and Amazon Valleys. In the northern countries, while hot, the climate is tempered by the highlands. At the extreme southern tip the seasons are exactly the opposite of those in North America, but there is not the variation in temperature. This is due to the influence of oceans and mountains.

The only important indentations on the Pacific are found along the rugged coast of southern Chile and the Gulf of Guayaquil in Ecuador.

The high temperature and humidity of the tropical regions, together with many insects and diseases, discourage the activity of white people and even sap the strength of the natives. Large areas of swamp and rugged mountains have made the development of transportation difficult and expensive. Only with the growth of air travel has it been possible for the Andean countries to contact one another with relative ease.

In the main, South America is sparsely settled, with the greatest density of population along the coasts. The original inhabitants were Indians, but, due to the early colonization by the Spanish and Portuguese, many of the present inhabitants are *mestizos,* a mixture of Indian and Spanish or Portuguese blood. The remainder is largely composed of Italian and German immigrants. Except in Brazil, where the official language is Portuguese, Spanish is spoken in all the other independent countries.

The three countries of Chile, Argentina and Uruguay, where there has been the largest European immigration, are making rapid industrial progress. The rest of South America is still largely agricultural. Most of the countries produce only one or two major products and there is little diversity of crops. Practically all exports are raw materials, while imports are manufactured goods.

With the exception of the three colonies of British, French and Dutch Guiana, all of South America is composed of independent republics. In spite of a common language and form of government there is little interchange between countries. In general they are more concerned with world trade than dealing with each other.

Since the early coming of the Spaniards, South America has continued to yield great stores of precious metals. The Andes are rich in minerals, and the eastern highlands contain iron, gold, and diamonds. Some coal is found in Brazil, Chile and Colombia, but not in great quantity. Water-power and oil are being utilized to make up for this lack.

Ecuador, Peru and Chile are all west coast countries, which, until the opening of the Panama Canal, were practically isolated from the rest of the world. Bolivia, having no outlet to the sea, moves nearly all of her exports through the seaports of Chile and Peru.

Brazilian Government Trade Bureau

Although in the torrid zone, Brazil's climate is tempered by rainfall, favorable winds and altitude.

CHILE—Sometimes called the "Shoestring Republic," Chile stretches along the west coast for twenty-six hundred miles, from the borders of Peru to Cape Horn. It has a variety of climate ranging from frigid to torrid. This long, narrow and mountainous country is one of the most progressvie in South America. It is one of the three republics where there are more white people than natives. The other two are Argentina and Uruguay.

From north to south Chile is divided into three regions: the desert, a dry sub-tropical region which includes the coast, and a section that is forested. The greatest mineral region lies between Santiago and the Peruvian border. In the northern half of this area are the nitrate fields which have produced almost the entire world's supply of this important fertilizer. The nitrate beds located in the Pacific coastal desert (Atacama) were wrested from Peru during the War of the Pacific (1879-83) from which Chile emerged victorious. Chile's fame as a nitrate region has waned with the introduction of synthetic nitrate into world industry. The country is now seeking to stimulate the

1. The Alcazar, Segovia, Spain.
2. Bridge and Cathedral, Dinant, Belgium.
3. Plaza del Congreso, Buenos Aires, Argentina.
4. Castle of Neuschwanstein, Bavaria, Germany.
5. Lindbergh Theatre from across the lagoon, Mexico City.
6. Looking into the crater of Vesuvius, Naples, Italy.
7. View of the Capitol, Havana, Cuba.
8. The Sphinx at Gizah, Egypt.
9. The famous St. Sophia Mosque, Constantinople, Turkey.
10. Scene in Devonshire, England.
11. A typical canti-lever bridge over a canal in Holland.
12. Camp at Wapta, Canadian Rockies.
13. The Harbor front at Algiers.
14. Morro Castle, Havana, Cuba.
15. A typical farm house in Czechoslovakia.

export of wine, honey and livestock. In the southern half there are deposits of copper, iron, gold and silver. Chile ranks next to the United States in the mining of copper and supplies about 20 per cent of the world's output.

PERU—This country is an extension of the narrow and arid coastal plain in northern Chile, with the Andes occupying fully half of the land. A densely wooded tropical region drops down in the east to meet the low plains of Brazil.

About a fourth of the population is white, most of whom are Spanish. The balance are *mestizos* (mixed) or Indians. Descendants of the ancient Incas, the Indians of Peru, are found principally living on the high mountain slopes of the Andes, and sailing their strange fiber craft on Lake Titicaca. These Indians have domesticated the llama and the alpaca, two animals which are native to this region, and which have never been raised successfully elsewhere. The llama is a sure-footed animal upon which the Indians depend for food, clothing and transportation. Used as a beast of burden in this lofty arid country, the llama, like the camel, can go several days without water. The alpaca is too small to carry loads and is raised for its very long wool.

ECUADOR—Peru and Ecuador have a similar climate and topography except for the northern part of the coastal plain of Ecuador. This plain is as fertile as any area in South America and is the principal agricultural section of Ecuador. The principal crops are cacao and coffee, the former heading the articles of export. Ecuador's coffee has been increasing in importance since its cacao, blighted by witches'-broom, has suffered an appreciable decrease in export. Tagua, a substitute for ivory, is produced in limited quantities. Ecuador is world-famous for its amazing variety of wild birds. The country contains one-fourth of all recorded species in South America.

BOLIVIA—Shut off from the sea by Chile and Peru, Bolivia is one of the most sparsely populated countries in the world. It consists of a high plateau in the southwest that is cold and dry, and wet tropical lowlands in the north and east. Though Bolivia's surface is three-fifths lowlands, the country includes one of the highest inhabitable regions in the world. The Andes spread out into two great chains of mountains which enclose a plateau nearly as high as the peaks themselves. Lake Titicaca, one of the highest of the larger lakes in the world, is situated on this plateau.

Bolivia ranks next to the Malay Peninsula and the Indonesian islands in its tin deposits, and is well supplied with nearly all the known metals. Strangely enough, although having local supplies of coal, necessary in smelting, it is usually cheaper to import coal.

Lack of capital, the high cost of transportation, and the scarcity of labor, have retarded mining in all the countries of the Andes. Only the natives can do manual labor in the high altitudes and the people are not inclined toward mining. However, mining is the chief industry. Aside from tin, there is abundant amounts of gold, copper, bismuth, antimony, lead, zinc, wolfram and oil. Tobacco, wine and vanilla, together with quinine and rubber, are exported.

BRAZIL—Covering nearly half the continent and with half the population, Brazil lies almost entirely in the tropics. This republic is 10 per cent larger than the United States, and has three times the area of Argentina.

The Amazon and its tributaries have a total length of over nineteen thousand miles, of which thirteen thousand are navigable. This huge system extends through more than half the country's area.

The great plateau country, known as the Brazilian Highlands, lies in the south and east. It is composed of numerous mountain ranges and river valleys. Rio de Janeiro, the second largest city on the continent, is located in this region. Hemmed in by mountains and a wide bay, it has one of the finest and most beautiful harbors in the world.

Brazil at one time was the greatest rubber-producing country. Brazil has embarked on a program of intensified manufacturing. Silk, cotton and woolen mills have sprung up all over the eastern seaboard. Shoes and hats are becoming major products. Many paper mills are being built to utilize some of the billion acres of forests that cover half the land area. Its greatest mineral wealth has yet to be exploited, though one of the largest estimated deposits of iron ore in the world is now being developed. The country produces nearly fifty percent of the world's coffee. Efforts to do away with the one-crop system are gaining success and coffee is no longer the economic tyrant that it was. A growing cacao industry now ranks second in the world, while tobacco, rice, cotton and sugar are attaining commercial significance.

URUGUAY—This is the smallest republic in South America. It has a fine climate with the winds of the ocean modifying the temperature.

Since the Spanish brought sheep and cattle to the grassy plains of Uruguay in the 17th century, it has been a stock raising country. Today it is one of the leading meat producers of the world. Only a small percentage of the arable land is devoted to the raising of crops and it is limited in both minerals and manufacturing.

PARAGUAY—One of the two republics of South Amercia that is completely surrounded by other nations. Little has been done to develop its natural resources.

Most of the surface of western Paraguay is a low, swampy and unhealthy plain. The climate in the north is hot and unsuited to the white man. Most of the people live in the southern area east of the Paraguay River. It is a country of small villages, grazing, and farm lands, which depends upon the rivers for means of transportation.

Extending from Bolivia, across the western third of Paraguay, and south into Argentina, is the Gran Chaco, a great plain.

THE ARGENTINE REPUBLIC—The early colonists' anticipation of finding silver and gold in Argentina prompted them to name the country for the Latin word meaning silver. Although the colonists' search for great mineral wealth was in vain, the fertile soil and temperate climate have fostered the country's great economic progress. The Republic is the second largest of the South American countries.

Pan-American-Grace Airways

The most cosmopolitan city of South America, Buenos Aires has been strongly influenced by Europe.

The Gran Chaco, in the northern part, is a land of forests, lakes and swamps, which is largely unexplored. The grassy plains of the *Pampas* occupy a large area of Argentina. This cattle country and farm land extends from the Atlantic coast to the Andes in the west, and northwest to the highlands which reach into Brazil. The rich grazing lands, which have led to Argentina becoming a large exporter of meat and wool are in the center of the *Pampas;* the largest meat refrigerating plant in the world is at Buenos Aires.

Only about 10 per cent of the land is under cultivation, although it has been said that 80 per cent is capable of producing crops, grass or forests. An idea may be gained from this of the great possibilities for future development that lie ahead.

Argentina is an agricultural and commercial, rather than an industrial country. It has been hindered in the development of manufacture by a shortage of coal, the lack of water power, and an inadequate supply of minerals.

Descendants of the Spanish settlers are

the leaders of the country, with most of the farm population consisting of Italians. Immigrants from the British Isles have taken to sheep raising, and many Germans have migrated to Argentina. Today half of the population is foreign-born or are descendants of immigrants.

NORTH COAST COUNTRIES—Colombia, Venezuela, and the British, French and Dutch Guianas, are all on the north coast.

COLOMBIA—The only South American country having a coastline along both the Atlantic and Pacific oceans. Half the country is high in the rugged Andes; the other half lies in unhealthy tropical plains. Three cordilleras of the Andes traverse in a parallel line from north and south which forms a barrier between the seacoast and the rich inland valleys. The chief source of wealth is coffee. Colombian coffee is the finest in the world and the bean is jealously guarded. Ninety percent of the exported coffee is shipped to the United States. A type from the area around Medellin commands the highest price per pound in the world. Surpassed by Brazil in quantity, Colombia's coffee yields to none in quality. Next to coffee in export value is oil. The fields are to a large extent a continuation of those in Venezuela. Production has been over twenty million barrels since World War II. Other resources include platinum, emeralds and coal.

VENEZUELA—One of the most productive oil regions in the world, is on the coast of the Caribbean. Easy access to this coast from the interior affords great possibilities for commercial and industrial development. Venezuela's land area is distinguished by its llanos or wide lowlands along the Orinoco River. The river is navigable for a course of 700 miles and is connected to the Amazon system by a canal. Coffee, chiefly from the basin of the Maracaibo, is second only to that of Colombia. A ranking producer of petroleum, Venezuela's exploitation of oil is fraught with difficulties which have never been successfully surmounted. Virgin forests cover the country and include about 600 species of wood. At Margarita is located a profitable pearl industry. Salt, asphalt, coal and gold figure as the main mineral resources.

THE GUIANAS—On the north coast of South America are the only European possessions on the continent. Their combined area is 178,000 square miles. The surface is composed of an alluvial plain at sea-level and another plain farther south which is distinguished by hills and forested mountains. The climate is tolerable except in the south where the northeast trade winds do not prevail. Though their topography is similar their economic importance varies greatly from east to west. British Guiana, about the size of Great Britain, is the most highly developed. Dutch Guiana (Surinam) has no important industries except the mining of bauxite. French Guiana, the easternmost colony, is of little importance economically. Its sparse population and the excessive emphasis placed on the mining of gold has led to the neglect of its fertile soil. Mineral resources in the form of gold and diamonds are equally divided among the Guianas.

EUROPE—Eurasia is the world's largest land mass and includes both Europe and Asia. Europe occupies about a third of the western end of Eurasia, and, with the exception of Australia, is the smallest continent. It is the most densely populated for its size and no other continent has so many separate nations. Nearly all of these countries have distinctive customs and speak different languages. This does much to explain Europe's turbulent history.

Actually Europe is a huge peninsula, subdivided into a number of lesser peninsulas, caused by the oceans and inland seas which encroach upon it. Its irregular form, together with the mountain barriers, and the presence of important islands near the continent, have contributed to the growth of individual nations. Differences in language and customs have a natural tendency to arouse a strong nationalistic spirit. This keeps people apart and makes them suspicious of those with different customs, and who speak alien tongues. Among mountain people an independent spirit and love of freedom is even more pronounced.

In the northwest, two peninsulas are

formed by the Baltic Sea. The countries of Norway and Sweden occupy the Scandinavian Peninsula. Denmark is on the Jutland Peninsula between the Baltic and North Seas. To the south, Portugal and Spain comprise the Iberian Peninsula. The peninsular boot of Italy thrusts out into the Mediterranean, and the Balkan Peninsula is surrounded by the Black Sea and the Adriatic, Ionian and Aegean Seas of the Mediterranean.

Great Britain is prevented from being a peninsula only by the narrow English Channel, and was once a part of the mainland. The entire course of history has been changed by this strip of water which made England an island. The same may be said for the Straits of Gibraltar separating Europe from Africa. But for this nine-mile passage, the Mediterranean would have had no outlet to the Atlantic.

Europe may be divided into five natural regions: (1) the Northwest Highlands, (2) the Central Plains, (3) the Central Highlands, (4) the Southern Mountains and Plateaus, and (5) the Southern Lowlands.

Most of the British Isles, a section of France, and a good part of the Scandinavian Peninsula are included in the Northwest Highlands. This is the coastal region with excellent harbors where men have mcde their living by the sea, and commerce has become most important. In those places where coal and iron are found it has led to an industrial life. This highland region enjoys a cool, temperate climate and people are energetic.

The great Central Plains extend from the British Isles to the Ural Mountains that separate Europe from Asia. These plains range from the tundra regions of the Far North to the Caspian Sea, the Caucasus Mountains, and the Black Sea of the Southeast. In the Southwest they reach into southern France. Within such an extensive area there are naturally great differences in climate. There is also great diversity of vegetation and the occupations of the people.

South of the Arctic tundra belt are extensive evergreen forests that reach westward to the Scandinavian Peninsula. In the grasslands to the south of the forests are large areas used for the growing of grain,

British Travel Association

England's rolling countryside is specked with tiny cottages which augment the natural beauty of the landscape.

and stock grazing is the chiet occupation in the drier southeastern sections. This is the region of the dry and treeless steppes.

The Central Highlands include the plateau in central France and take in parts of Belgium, southern Germany, Austria, and the Czecho-Slovakian area. It is the region of forest, water-power, and varied mineral resources. The industrial districts of Central Europe are the outgrowth of the great deposits of coal and iron found here.

The impressive peaks of the Alps rise south of the Central Highlands, forming one of the many ranges of Southern Europe. The Apennines extend the length of Italy, and other ranges follow the eastern coast of the Adriatic through Yugoslavia and Albania to the southern tip of Greece. Spreading out to the east they include most of the Balkan Peninsula. To the north the Carpathian Mountains swing east and north around the valley of the Danube and then run northeast to almost circle the Plain of Hungary. Farther to the east, the Caucasus Mountains reach from the Black to the Caspian Sea. Separating France and Spain are the Pyrenees, and the Sierra Nevadas are in southern Spain bordering the Mediterranean.

The Alps are particularly famous for their scenic grandeur. The Sierra Nevadas and Carpathian Mountains are rich in mineral resources, and some of the world's greatest oil fields are in the Caucasus. The mountains of Italy lack valuable ores and have been largely stripped of their forests.

The Southern Lowlands of the Danube Valley and the Plain of Hungary represent some of the finest farming and grazing land in the world.

The extreme irregularity of the European coastline has been of great importance to the life of the people. With the North and Baltic Seas, the Mediterranean and Black Seas, penetrating far into the interior, only Central Europe and Eastern Russia are very far from the coast. Although the combined areas of South America and Africa are nearly five times that of Europe, the coastline of Europe is longer.

A majority of the great seaports of the world are in Western Europe. Its people have led the world in sea-faring.

Europe has a generally mild, temperate climate, particularly in the western areas, which are warmed by ocean currents and the winds blowing over these waters. Even the British Isles have a mild climate in spite of being in the same latitude as Labrador. Greater extremes of temperature exist in eastern Europe where these winds lose their moderating effect.

Due to the Alps blocking the cold north winds, and the influence of the warm waters of the Mediterranean, the southern shores of Europe enjoy a mild year-round climate. Excepting in eastern Europe, where the rainfall is light, there is generally sufficient moisture for agriculture.

An abundance of mineral resources, fine forests, rich farmlands, water-power, and the seas plentifully supplied with fish, have encouraged Europe's growth. An invigorating climate, waterways, harbors and access to the oceans of the world, have contributed to its commercial importance.

The climate and natural resources of each country have largely determined their individual occupations and prosperity.

GREAT BRITAIN AND NORTHERN IRELAND—The British Isles and the British Commonwealth of Nations owe much of their commercial and industrial growth to the daring and initiative of their early mariners. Although we usually think of the British Isles as comprising Great Britain and Ireland, it actually consists of nearly five thousand islands. Within the small compass of the islands there is a considerable variety of topography.

In Northern Ireland there are many lakes, including the largest one of the island, Lough Neagh, as well as a range known as the Mourne Mountains. A large portion of the country consists of the basalt plateau of Antrim.

Northern Ireland, or Ulster, as the six counties are sometimes called, is the seat of a very extensive lace and linen industry. In County Down and County Antrim there are highgrade deposits of granite and bauxite which are being exploited. Shipbuilding is a major industry centered in the capital, Belfast.

In Scotland the three well-marked divisions stand out, the highlands, the southern uplands, and between these two, the central lowlands, into which four-fifths of the population is crowded. The lowlands contain the richest agricultural land, as well as the coal fields. They are penetrated by three great estuaries, the Firths of Tay and Forth on the east, and of Clyde on the west, so that communication coastwise or overseas is everywhere easy.

Scotland has some of the largest shipbuilding yards in the world on the Firth of Clyde. Sheep and cattle are raised in large numbers since the land is not well suited to agriculture.

The Welsh cliffy upland is flanked to the north and east by small coal fields, but the greatest field lies to the south. A belt of limestone running from Bill of Portland to Tees Bay, and bearing at many points valuable iron ores, serves as a rough boundary of industrial England, for to the south and east of it, apart from the metropolis, agricultural interests predominate. Lying to the west of the limestone band is the Devon-

Cornwall peninsula, where great bosses of granite and slate form the famous moors.

Wales, after 700 years as a part of the English kingdom, retains its individuality and is nationalistic in speech, dress and customs. The Welsh language is Celtic, akin to the Gaelic of Ireland. It is the only speech of nearly one-tenth of the people.

Channel Islands, lying across the English Channel off the coast of Normandy, and Scilly Islands, lying southwest of Land's End, enjoy an almost complete freedom from frost and severe weather.

Because of the density of population Great Britain is far from self-sustaining and must depend upon the raw materials and products of other countries. This has led to the development of her world-wide commerce, a large part of which is carried on with her far-flung and numerous colonies. Agriculture is intensive with much importance placed on livestock. Many of the world's most valuable breeds of farm animals have been developed on English farms. This is exemplified by such names as Guernsey, Shropshire, Jersey, Hereford, Hampshire and Plymouth.

IRELAND—Except for coastal hills and mountains, the country is largely an ill-drained plain dotted with lakes and peat-bogs, and crossed by the sluggish Shannon. In the southwest is the beautiful Killarney Lakes region which attracts many tourists each year. Although little of the land is suitable for large scale agriculture, grass and fodder crops are abundant and provide stockraising needs which is the major industry of the country. The Shannon River, Royal Canal, and the Grand Canal provide an excellent inland waterway system of transportation. Shannon airport, near Limerick, is a major international airway terminal. Horse-breeding is the most famous of Irish farm industries. A prosperous tourist trade is developing.

NORWAY AND SWEDEN—With its saw-toothed coast, great fiords, and neighboring islands, it is natural that Norway, occupying the western part of the Scandanavian peninsula, would be a maritime country. Norway's long coast line, facing the

Belgian Government Information Center

The European peasant has long been a factor in the economic development of the Old World.

Atlantic, is edged with lofty cliffs and seamed with deep fiords. Islands, countless in number, fringe the coast. Most of the country is a rocky, rugged and barren land, about 20 per cent of which is forested. The rivers are short and torrential, but provide the finest salmon fishing in Europe. The Kjolen Mountains which form the backbone of the peninsula separate Norway from Sweden. These mountains rise in many parts to over 6,000 feet, the highest peaks being over 8,000 feet.

Norway is the land of the "midnight sun". From Trondheim northward at least a part of the disk of the sun is visible from May through July. But the winter nights are 17 hours long and midday seems like twilight during the winter months. Another striking feature is that much of the area above the Arctic Circle is warmer than some regions further south. Northeast Norway is the warmest part of the country in the summer.

Sweden consists primarily of a tableland sloping from the Kjolen Range to the Baltic. No less than 8 per cent of the surface of Sweden is water, the immense number of lakes covering almost 15,000 square miles. The two largest, Vanern and Vattern, in the southern portion of the country, are connected by a system of canals. Besides the large number of small islands which fringe

Suomen-Matkat

The snow-encrusted northlands of Scandinavia force its northernmost inhabitants to lead nomadic existences.

the coast, Sweden includes the two large Baltic islands of Gotland and Oland. Most of the people live in the southern part of their country while the Norwegians have settled chiefly near the fiords. Hydro-electric development is in an advanced stage in both countries.

In Sweden, iron deposits are among the richest in the world. Swedish steel is universally famous for its fine qualities. The making of machinery for export is a major industry. Swedish agriculture is in a very high state of development, and exports wheat, bacon and butter in large quantities. In forestry and sawmilling the nation has evolved such advanced methods that foreign technicians in the industry often go to Sweden to study logging and forestry. Nearly half of her exports are in pulp and paper products.

DENMARK—Denmark occupies a peninsula and numerous islands lying at the entrance to the Baltic. It is a lowland country characterized by many lakes, ponds and short rivers. Its sandy shores are shallow, with lagoons shut in by shifting sand bars. Most of Denmark is farm land, about half of which is used for grazing. The Faeroe Islands produce fish, mutton and wool for the homeland.

Dairy farming is the country's chief industry, the products of which comprise nearly all her exports. Greenland, the largest island in the world, is Denmark's only possession.

ICELAND—The republic is an island in the north Atlantic consisting of a great tableland averaging 2,000 feet above sea level. Of its whole area barely a quarter is habitable. The surface is dotted by over 100 volcanic peaks. There are many boiling springs and the geysers are world-famous. It is too cold for agriculture but has rich grazing land for sheep and cattle.

FINLAND—Finland consists of a great plateau, ranging from 400 to 600 feet in elevation. The southern half of the plateau has about 25 per cent of its area occupied by thousands of shallow lakes, many of them linked by short natural or artificial channels, providing many miles of navigable waterways. Forests cover the greater part of the country which has led to lumbering, paper-making and the manufacture of woodenware. Over half the population is engaged in agricultural pursuits which are carried on under great difficulties.

THE NETHERLANDS—The tiny kingdom of the Netherlands, lacking natural resources has been largely a nation of seafarers for centuries. Along the canals, the meadows are often ten or twelve feet below the water line, and between the land and the sea at high tide there may be a difference of twenty-five feet or more. The land is protected by embankments and dikes, and it may be pictured as a great trough, the floor of which slopes down from east and southeast toward the North Sea. The rivers which flow across the country from the higher continent beyond, are at their mouths, frequently below the level of the sea, into which they have to be lifted by canals and locks across the dams or dikes. A large part of the land has been reclaimed from the sea and little by little it has become a fertile country.

BELGIUM—Smaller than Holland, Belgium is the most densely populated country in Europe. Situated between England, Holland, France and Germany, it is in the very center of industrial Europe. The country is well watered, and has two principal rivers, the Scheldt and the Maas. Four-fifths of the land is under cultivation, and although over half the people are engaged in either farming or stock raising the country still does not raise sufficient food to feed her people. Belgium's intensive industrialization has been at the expense of its agriculture, for the valley of the Sambre-Meuse, the chief industrial center, is also the richest farming land. Metals from the Katanga region of the Belgian Congo are intensifying industrial activities, and Belgium is regaining her prewar level of output. The textile industry is reviving also. The nation furnishes a great variety of farm products and is known for its world-famous breed of horses.

LUXEMBURG—The Grand Duchy of Luxemburg, smaller than the state of Rhode Island, is one of Europe's oldest states. An abundant store of iron ore has encouraged mining, smelting and some manufacturing. International trade of the duchy has been carried on through a customs union with Belgium.

LIECHTENSTEIN—Only 27 square miles larger than San Marino, Liechtenstein is separated from Switzerland by the Rhine river and is bounded by Austria in the east. The population is largely German but Switzerland administers its postal and telegraph facilities, and its currency is Swiss. It also belongs to the Swiss customs union. The tillable soil, a long strip along the Rhine river, yields grapes, grains and pasturage for a small cattle industry.

FRANCE—France is largely an agricultural country where the farmers, instead of living on their farms, usually live in nearby villages. Although rich in minerals, it has lagged behind both England and Germany as an industrial country. The surface is diversified, but much of it is lowland, with a few level plains. In the center is a triangular plateau called the Auvergne Mountains, with a height of something over 3,000 feet. The Cevennes form the eastern edge of this plateau, and from them to the Vosges, the tableland continues. There is a mountainous area in Brittany, but the greatest heights are on the

Austria State Tourist Dept.

Austria's small villages are nestled among the deep valleys of its mountainous countryside.

frontiers, the Jura, the Pyrenees, and the Alps separating it respectively from Switzerland, Spain and Italy. The Ardennes in the northeast are less lofty. The Seine drains the north, the Loire and the Garonne the west, and the Rhone the east and south. France enjoys a delightful climate. Only in the region of the Alps is real winter encountered. Protected by the mountains to the north, the balmy area along the Mediterranean is a magnet that has drawn countless vacationers. Many semi-tropical plants and fruits are grown in this section. Indeed, France's greatest resource is her soil. Grape culture is by far the leading agricultural pursuit, for France produces a billion gallons of wine in a vintage year. Yet, the country imports millions of gallons. Textile production, particularly the silk industry centered around Lyons, is a valuable undertaking in the country; cotton mills are the leading producers of goods.

MONACO—The Principality of Monaco is one of the smallest states in the world. It possesses the administrative organs and institutions of larger nations in miniature. It has no taxes for it is supported by the gambling casino of Monte Carlo from which its own citizens are barred. The most striking feature of this 370 acre state is the Monagasque Acropolis on a headland 200 feet above the water. The Prince's Palace, a magnificent structure, is located on it. On the Mediterranean coast, surrounded by the Riviera of France, Monaco offers to the tourist auto-racing, skiing, bathing, sailing, and of course, gambling. There is also an oceanographic museum.

SWITZERLAND—This rugged little country is a completely land-locked republic nestling among the beautiful Alps. It has succeeded in maintaining its neutrality and independence while the rest of Europe engaged in costly and devastating wars. Between Lake Constance on the Rhine and Lake Geneve on the Rhone are Lakes Neuchatel, Zurich, Lucerne, Brienz, Thun, all of which drain to the Aar. Lake Geneve and Lake Constance each exceed 200 square miles in area. Many of Switzerland's mountains are permanently covered with snow. Capitalizing upon its wonderful mountain and lake scenery, and making the most of its limited resources, Switzerland has become one of the most prosperous of the smaller nations. With its snow-capped peaks rising from ten to fifteen thousand feet, it has been the playground of Europe for many years.

GERMANY—There are two natural regions in Germany, the northern plain and southern highlands. The former is the most extensive agricultural region. The land which borders Denmark is favorable to the grazing of cattle, and, in the northeast, large numbers of sheep and goats are raised. The minerals found in the central highlands have had the greatest influence upon the development of Germany in the last fifty years.

Except for ample supplies of coal and potash, Germany is deficient in natural resources. During the glacial period, sand was deposited over the plains region and as a result the soil is not naturally fertile. Only by intensive cultivation and the heavy use of fertilizers, made from potash, is much of the soil made productive. Germany's great scientific development has been largely the result of solving agricultural problems, and of searching for new uses to utilize the coal reserves.

Germany's only access to the ocean, and world trade, is through the Baltic and North Seas. To make the most of this she has developed a remarkable system of waterways. The Rhine rises in the Alps and flows through the fertile lowlands of western Germany to the border of Holland, and thence to the sea. The Elbe, Weser, and the Oder flow north across the low plain of Germany. The Oder empties into the Baltic. The Elbe and Weser flow into the North Sea. All three are navigable far inland for ocean-going vessels. The rivers, together with fifteen hundred miles of canals, form a network of waterways which provide cheap transportation.

AUSTRIA AND HUNGARY—Austria is characterized by its beautiful mountain scenery, over 90 percent of the land is classified as mountainous, which has contributed to development of one of its largest industries—tourist and resort trade. However, over 80 per cent of the land is productive and half of this is under cultivation. In contrast, Hungary is largely comprised of a low fertile plain. The country is primarily agricultural and is a great grain and wine producer.

CZECHOSLOVAKIA—This land - locked country contains strategic routes between north and south Europe of economic and political value. The country has two large mountain ranges, the Carpathian in the east and the Sudeten in the west. Czechoslovakia is famous for its subterranean caverns and its spas and mineral springs. The people are energetic and progressive and there are valuable forest resources, fertile soil and varied mineral deposits.

THE BALKANS—They include Rumania, Yugoslavia, Bulgaria, Albania, Greece and European Turkey. Located at the gateway to Asia, and on a natural route connecting the two continents, this region has been a battleground for centuries. Repeated invasions from various directions have resulted in a number of racial groups and religious beliefs. The rugged nature of the country has isolated the people into many rival factions with intense racial and national spirit.

YUGOSLAVIA consists essentially of a mountainous core, which stretches from the Dinaric Alps in the northwest to the Balkan Mountains on the Bulgarian frontier. The only valley which cuts the mountains and forms a passageway is that of the Marava River, which with that of the Vardar, leads from Beograd to Thessalonike. Beyond the Sava-Danube, as far as the northern boundary, the land is low and swampy near the rivers, with a few minor elevations. The chief concentrations of people are around Zagreb and Beograd. Yugoslavia has recently experienced a crisis resulting from a boycott by the Cominform countries and the Soviet Union. Forced to turn to the West, the nation has signed trade agreements with several Western European states. Its greatest problem is the lack of communications between its regions. The more highly developed coastal areas have access to outside markets, but the distribution of economic aid further inland is hampered by the mountains which impose a rugged barrier between the provinces.

RUMANIA—In western Rumania the Carpathian Mountains from the northwest and the Transylvanian Alps from the southwest meet in the center to form a crescent. To the north and west of this crescent is the Transylvanian plateau; to the south and east are the plains of Moldavia and Walachia. The principal rivers are the Danube in the south which enters the Black Sea at Sulina, and the Prut in the northeast and the Siret in the southeast—both of which connect with the Danube.

BULGARIA—The country is hilly and well watered by numerous streams, of which the Isker, Struma and Maritza are the most important. Although nearly one-third of the country's area is in forests, only a small part of the wood is used commercially since about one-fourth of the forest area is completely unproductive. Many of the forests consist of scrub timber and a sizeable portion of the good forests are inaccessible. Eighty percent of Bulgaria's population is employed in agriculture, the chief crops being tobacco and cereals. Attar of rose and silk are important products.

TWA Transworld Airline

The coastal cities of Portugal draw heavily on the sea for their principal commodity.

ALBANIA—Albania is a mountainous country on the western side of the Peninsula. In the center, part of the plateau is cultivable, and in the south there is fertile alluvial soil with grazing land on the slopes.

GREECE—With a very long coast line on the Aegean and Ionian Seas, and a large number of islands, including Crete, Mitylene, Dodecanese and Chios, the area is generally mountainous. The mountains, though not very high, divide the country into a number of small districts, between which communication is difficult. It is the sea which links the different regions of Greece.

ITALY—Once the hub of the known world, Italy's importance declined as the age of exploration and discovery opened up the ocean routes of the world. Taking no part in this period of conquest and empire building, she did not acquire colonies. Lacking unity she was in no position to demand her share of the rich prizes of newly discovered land being acquired by other European nations.

With the opening of the Suez Canal and tunnels through the Alps, her trade somewhat improved, but the absence of the necessary minerals prevented her from keeping pace with industrial development elsewhere in Europe.

The south slope of the Alps belongs to Italy. At the point where the Alps reach the Mediterranean, the Apennines begin. These mountains follow the length of Italy and form a rugged backbone which extends through the island of Sicily. The southern and western parts of the peninsula have been subjected to volcanic eruptions, and Vesuvius, Etna, and Stromboli are still active volcanoes. The chief lowlands are in the Po Valley with narrow coastal plains east and west of the Apennines. The majority of the people, and most of the agriculture and manufacturing, are located in the Po Valley. Consequently Northern Italy does not experience the poverty to be found in Southern Italy. It is from the south that most of the immigrants to the United States have come.

Italy's colorful history, scenery and balmy climate have attracted many tourists which has in some measure offset an unfavorable balance of trade.

SAN MARINO—San Marino is one of the oldest republics in the world and is the smallest. It has always been on good terms with its big neighbor, Italy, by whom it is surrounded. The state was founded in the fourth century by Marinius of Dalmatia, a stonecutter. Except for a few invasions, its liberty has been respected, even by Napoleon. During World War II it declared war against Germany and was occupied by the Germans and subsequently liberated by the British. Much of its revenue is obtained through the sale of its postage stamps issued for the benefit of collectors.

SPAIN AND PORTUGAL—About three-fourths of the Iberian Peninsula is a granite plateau with a range of mountains dividing it in the center. The rivers that flow through this region through deep gorges block transportation and are unsuited for navigation, waterpower or irrigation. The dry climate, lack of water, a rugged land formation, poor soil and an absence of transportation have been great obstacles standing in the way of the economic development of both Spain and Portugal. A portion of the land in the valleys and plains has been made fertile through irrigation and farming is the main industry. Fishing is important along the Portugal coast, although a great part of the coast is too rugged for harbors. There are forests in most of the higher areas where half the world's supply of cork is produced.

ANDORRA—Tiny Andorra is in the Pyrenees Mountains between France and Spain. It is not a republic, as is often supposed, but a joint dependency of France and the Bishops of Urgel in Spain. Its mountains are high and arid, and its valleys contain poor soil so that the people are nearly all engaged in pastoral pursuits. The one product of the soil is tobacco. Sheep-herding is the main industry, and the need of hay for winter forage further limits the use of soil for any other crop.

POLAND—Poland was for many years a chiefly agricultural country but good supplies of coal, lead, iron and zinc have helped her industrial progress to such an extent that it is now almost equally industrial and agricultural. Most of the land is comprised of a plain, although there are low hills in the northeast in Pomerania. The lower regions of the Vistula have marshes, sand dunes and lakes. The central plain of Poland with an elevation of about 500 feet is traversed by great rivers, the most important being the Oder and the Vistula. Her strategic position near the Baltic Sea, and the lack of natural boundaries and barriers, have long made the people of this country, as well as those of the former Baltic States, the victims of stronger nations seeking an outlet to the sea.

U. S. S. R.—Almost three times the size of the United States and comprising more than one-seventh of the world's land surface, the Union of Soviet Socialist Republics sprawls across two continents. Most of Russia is a great plain reaching from the Pacific to its western boundaries. Its position in northern latitudes and the absence of protecting barriers result in an extreme climate with long, cold winters. Vladivostok, on the Pacific coast, and the ports on the Arctic Ocean and Baltic Sea are closed by ice during the long winter months. Vladivostok, however, is kept open the year round by ice-breakers. In no part of the land is the rainfall heavy, and there are frequent and widespread droughts, which bring hunger and starvation to its people.

From the Black Sea in the south to the Arctic Ocean, and from the Baltic Sea to the Ural Mountains, which divide Asiatic Russia from European Russia, is a vast lowland. To the east of the Urals is Siberia, two-thirds of which is a flat, unbroken plain. In the far north the ground has been found to be frozen to a depth of over six hundred feet. This presents peculiar problems, if the government is to succeed with plans to mine the ores found there and industrialize this Arctic region. Here in the tundra country the moss, upon which the reindeer of the nomadic tribes feed, is often five feet thick.

South of the tundra belt is a great evergreen forest covering billions of acres, where lumbering and fur-trapping are the chief occupations.

Russia's supply of minerals is so great and widely scattered that the extent of many of the deposits is still unknown. There are immense reserves of coal in both European and Asiatic Russia. Copper, platinum, iron, gold, manganese and other minerals are found in the Urals. Some of the richest petroleum deposits in the world are located in the Baku region of the Caspian Sea.

Great strides have been made in industrial development, with the manufacture of iron and steel, machinery, textiles and leather goods in the lead.

In spite of climate, high cost of manufacture and difficulties of transportation, the U. S. S. R. is a country that is largely self-sustaining, and has become increasingly important industrially.

AFRICA—The term "sleeping giant," which has often been used in referring to China, can best be applied to Africa. This second largest continent is three times the size of China, and is richer in natural resources, but it has only one-third the population. Although two of the world's oldest civilizations once flourished along its northern shores in Egypt and Carthage, the rest of Africa long remained shrouded in mystery.

TWA—Trans World Airline

Many natural phenomena, like these hot springs, are present in Africa's terrain.

Joined to Asia by a land bridge at the Isthmus of Suez, and only separated from Europe by the narrow Strait of Gibraltar, it was not until the nineteenth century that Europe finally set about the conquest of the "Dark Continent." For centuries an unfavorable climate and natural barriers combined to guard its secrets and hold back development.

Almost midway of its length Africa is crossed by the equator. Being triangular in shape, this places most of the continent in unhealthy torrid regions. Added to this its coastline is steep and regular, and offers few places for ships to anchor. The rivers as regards navigability cannot be considered in the same light as the great rivers of Europe, Asia and the Americas. None, except the Nile and the Congo, has unimpeded entrance to the sea.

The deltas of the Niger and the Zambesi are choked by silt and, on nearly all, navigation is impeded by shoal or cataract. Nevertheless the Congo and the Nile with their tributaries have many thousands of miles of navigable waterways, as have the Niger, the Benue and the Zambesi.

To the north, the Sahara Desert proved an effective barrier of sand and intense heat, which for hundreds of years prevented any important exchange of ideas or trade between the white man of the north and the black man in the south. Extending from the Atlantic to the River Nile, and reaching from the Mediterranean to the Sudan, the dry Sahara is a region of desolation. What trade existed between Asia, Europe and Africa followed caravan routes which led from oasis to oasis. The only life to be found there is at these scattered oases.

It was only following the explorations of Livingstone, Stanley and others in the last century, that Europe became aware of the possibilities existing in Africa. Then, suddenly awakened to the great wealth that had been overlooked, the European powers rushed in to carve out vast empires. When they had finished only two sections remained which were not possessions or dependencies of the white man. Only the Republic of Liberia and the Kingdom of Ethiopia remained, where the native African had a voice in the government of his affairs. Later Egypt became independent, and the Union of South Africa acquired a dominion status in the British Commonwealth. Following the second world war, Libya, Sudan, Morocco, Tunisia and Ghana (formerly Gold Coast) became independent.

Africa is a great plateau, over four thousand miles long from north to south. The average height of the entire continent is over two thousand feet above sea level. Its loftiest peak is nearly twenty thousand feet high, while the Qattara Depression in the Libyan Desert sinks to four hundred feet below sea level.

The Atlas Mountains parallel the north coast of Africa, with their southern slopes dropping down to the Sahara. The Sudan Belt, which extends south from the Sahara to the Gold Coast and the Gulf of Guinea, is a lower region of hills, valleys and plains. To the southwest are the low Cameroon Mountains; and another chain in the eastern part follows the Red Sea.

In Eastern Africa, a ridge of highlands reaches below the equator to form a series of mountain ranges. It is here that the great lakes region is found. Only in North America are there lakes which compare to these in size. Unlike the mountain ranges of other continents, those of Africa do not follow a regular pattern. This, together with their location, provides an unusual drainage system. A mountain ridge separates the lakes that drain into the three great rivers, the Nile, the Congo and the Zambesi. This ridge dictates the direction of their courses, with the Nile flowing north toward the Mediterranean, the Congo twisting and turning to finally reach the Atlantic to the west, and the Zambesi flowing east to empty into the Indian Ocean. Each river follows a devious course through the mountains before finding a way over the edge of the plateau to reach the sea. This results in many falls and rapids which interrupt transportation. The Victoria Falls on the Zambesi, the rapids of the Congo, and the cataracts of the Nile are typical.

The Congo, winding through the gloomy depths of the fever-infested forests, is three thousand miles long. It is second only to the Amazon of South America in the volume of water it empties into the sea. The Nile travels four thousand miles before reaching the Mediterranean, and today, as in ancient times, makes Egypt a habitable country. As the Nile winds slowly through the Sahara, the evaporation is so great that the river would dry up before reaching the sea were it not fed by rivers from the high Abyssinian Mountains. It is these waters of the Blue Nile which bring the great Nile floods and supply the water for irrigation to make of Egypt a fertile strip of land hemmed in by cliffs and burning sands. Africa's fourth large river, the Niger, while rising only one hundred and fifty miles from the ocean, flows twenty-five hundred miles before reaching the Atlantic.

Africa is a land of climatic contradictions. At the equator the temperature ranges from typical jungle weather at the lower levels, to a climate similar to that found well over a thousand miles to the north. This occurs in the high altitudes of the mountains. Along the Mediterranean, the weather compares with that of southern Europe. The weather in the Congo Basin is always hot and humid, although to the east, in the mountain and lake region, it is tempered by the higher altitudes. In the far south, around Capetown, the weather is mild and sunny like the climate of southern California. The same extremes exist in rainfall. At the equator it is excessive, with periods of torrential rains. Traveling north or south from this wet center there is less and less rain, with parts of the Sahara never getting a drop.

Plant life varies with the rainfall. The dense, matted tropical jungles, which are exceeded only in size by the forests of the Amazon, give way to grassy plains and open forests. The only vegetation in the Sahara is around the springs that nourish the oases. Because the hot winds of the south are blocked by the Atlas Mountains, the entire coastal area of North Africa from the Atlantic to the Nile River is agriculturally productive.

Africa is a strange mixture of white and black races. The four original races of Hamites and Semites, Negroes and Hottentots have become so intermingled that it is no longer possible to draw clear lines between racial groups. The Hamites and Semites of North Africa are white and Mohammedans. The Negroes and Hottentots are the black people of Central and South Africa. While probably members of the Negro race, the Hottentots have distinctive characteristics which put them in a class by themselves. These native tribes have a barbaric form of worship. The Sudanese, blackest of the Negroes, were sought by the early slave traders. For over three hundred years millions of these poor blacks were seized and transported to strange lands.

The slave trade was started by the son of a man who accompanied Columbus to America. Needing labor in her New World colonies to replace the Indian slaves, who preferred death to captivity, Spain granted each Spanish colonist the right to import twelve African Negroes. A year later the king of Spain bestowed a grant upon the Dutch allowing them to take four thousand slaves a year. Soon the "black ivory trade" had grown to huge proportions, and it has been estimated that as many as two million

TWA—Trans World Airline

Africa's varied topography lends itself to all sorts of livlihoods ranging from the industrial to the pastoral.

slaves were removed from Africa in a single year.

In recent years Africa has been undergoing tremendous changes. Railroads, motor roads and airlines continue to reach out and draw distant points closer together. Modern engineering genius is overcoming the obstacles imposed by climate and land formation, and Africa is rapidly taking its place among the more fortunate continents.

TUNISIA—Battleground of World War II, is the most productive land in North Africa. Its fertile valleys produce grain and tropical fruits. Seat of ancient Carthage, it was once the wealthiest city of its time until Rome destroyed it during the Punic Wars.

LIBYA— Is relatively unprotected from the scorching desert winds and, consequently, the least valuable of North African regions. However, the coastal areas are cultivated with the aid of shade and irrigation.

EGYPT—In the heart of the Nile valley, has been one of the most productive regions in the world since recorded time. Recent dam construction regulating the flow of the Nile has increased the productivity of the soil. Agricultural methods are the same today as they were 6,000 years ago.

SUDAN (former Anglo-Egyptian)—Embracing the upper Nile basin to the borders of Uganda and Ethiopia, produces gum arabic for the entire world. Cotton is raised in the fertile areas between the Blue and the White Niles. Dates, ivory and meat are also exported.

ETHIOPIA—The first country to be liberated by the Allies in World War II, has many undeveloped resources. Gold and platinum are mined. The Djimmah Province produces a fine, robust coffee. There is, as yet, only one railroad which leads out of the country. The Italians, true to the Roman tradition, built 4,340 miles of roads while they were occupying the country.

UGANDA—The Source of the Nile River. Much of the country is situated in the lofty mountains of East Africa. The climate is usually mild because of the altitude of the land.

KENYA—Eastern gateway to Central Africa abounds in big game. The lowlands bordering the Indian Ocean are fertile, the climate bearable. Western Kenya is a high plateau with isolated towering peaks, snow-capped the year 'round.

TANGANYIKA—Within its borders is Kilimanjaro, Africa's highest known peak located a few miles north of the equator. Tanganyika is famous as the gorilla country of Africa. Its jungle brims with wildlife, thereby making it a paradise for big-game hunters.

NYASALAND—A British protectorate, lies along the west shore of Lake Nyasa. Semi-autonomous and self-supporting, it has a good system of roads and railways.

UNION OF SOUTH AFRICA comprises the Transvaal, Orange Free State, Natal and the Cape of Good Hope. Its northern areas contain many valuable minerals, chief of which is gold and diamonds. Most of the world's diamonds and half the world's gold are exported from this country.

NORTHERN RHODESIA—Crown Colony on the borders of the jungles of Central Africa and the wide plains of South Africa. Copper, lead and cattle comprise its principal forms of wealth. Victoria Falls, the world's highest, are on the Zambesi River in Northern Rhodesia.

SOUTHERN RHODESIA—Border region, is well suited to agriculture and European settlement. It possesses vast amounts of gold, asbestos and chrome.

ANGOLA or Portuguese West Africa, on Africa's west coast, is a huge treeless plain, arid in many places. Diamonds are mined, and recently coffee has been cultivated for export.

The grazing lands of Ruanda-Urundi have been added to the Belgian Congo, and a ten-year plan to develop the Congo region has been inaugurated. The Belgian Congo has the richest terrain in Africa. Metals, both common and rare, are imbedded in its soil.

The most important product of the Gold Coast is cacao. Some diamonds and gold are mined to a limited extent.

LIBERIA—Long unimportant economically, is presently producing rubber and coffee for export.

French colonies are located in most of West Africa. The areas from Dakar southward yield rubber, mahogany, ebony, cacao and coffee. The interior of West Africa merges with the Sahara Desert. A narrow savanna region stretches across the French lands to the headwaters of the Nile. This area contains some of Africa's large lakes and is the best suited for grazing. The great forests on its southern edge lead into the jungles of the Congo and Cameroons. The region is a habitat for a diversity of animal life including the leopard, lion and rhinoceros as well as some of the larger animals of the country.

MADAGASCAR—One of the world's largest islands, is located off the east coast of Africa. Graphite, copper and precious stones form a part of its mineral resources.

AUSTRALIA—This island continent of the South Seas is the smallest, and last to be discovered of all the continents.

The United States and Australia are nations of about the same age and size, and in other respects have much in common. The loss of America as a British Colony directly led to the settling of Australia. It was first claimed for the British Crown in 1788 as a settlement for British convicts who had previously been sent to America. Landing in a virgin country, the early pioneers of the two countries had to conquer the wilderness before creating a nation. In the process of so doing the people of both lands developed similar characteristics. In later years Australia even patterned its constitution after that of the United States.

But, whereas the United States became a melting pot for all the races and creeds in the world, Australia has been peopled almost entirely by British stock. Today 97 per cent of the population are descendants of British colonists, and 86 per cent are Australian born. Strict laws have confined immigration to the white race. Few of the natives who originally inhabited Australia remain. These aborigines are similar to the African Negro but not so intelligent, and are believed to be a separate race.

Almost half of Australia lies within the tropics, but being surrounded by great oceans, the continent has a mild climate throughout the year. Snow normally falls only in the high mountains in the winter. Since the seasons are the reverse of those in the United States, this occurs in their winter months of June, July, and August.

Australia is said to be most level in surface and regular in outline of all the continents. There is an entire absence of towering mountains. The highest peak is only about seventy-three hundred feet above sea level. The mountains parallel the east coast, with, by far, the greater part of the continent a vast, irregular, and undulating plateau.

Australia can be regarded as falling into four well-defined regions: (1) The Great Plateau in the west extends over about half of the continent; (2) The Eastern Highlands follow along the whole of the eastern coastline, rarely exceeding a distance of a hundred miles inland; (3) The Central Basin is a lowland area much of which was once a sea-bed; and (4) the Coastal Plains, which form a rim surrounding most of the continent.

New Zealand Consulate

Modified by ocean currents, New Zealand's climate remains moderate.

Despite rich coastal lands and an immense grazing area in the interior, much of this interior is unsuited for agriculture. It is a great arid region of desert and semi-desert which is sparsely settled and will never support a dense population. The heaviest rainfall is in the tropical regions of the north, and there is adequate moisture along the south coast and southern part of the highlands. Elsewhere there is insufficient rain. But for the presence of innumerable artesian wells scattered over wide areas, much more of the country would be without water. It is these wells that make stock-raising possible, but because of its mineral content, the water is seldom used for agriculture or human use.

The major rivers of Australia are of two types—those which flow toward the coast and are similar to such rivers in other parts of the world; and the inland rivers which gradually lose their water as they flow away from the coastal regions. The headwaters of most of these inland rivers are in the Eastern Highlands.

The Murray River with its tributaries is the main river system and flows into the ocean on the south coast. The Gilbert, Norman and Flinders are the principal streams flowing into the Gulf of Carpentaria in the north. On the west the Murchison, Gascoyne, Ashburton and Fitzroy empty into the Indian Ocean.

The rivers which flow inland vary greatly in volume during the year. For long periods they are mere strings of waterholes, but during floods their waters spread out over the flat country for many miles. Most of their waters evaporate or soak into the ground before they flow very far. In the center of the continent the rivers flow into Lake Eyre when there is sufficient water in them, but generally they are merely beds of dry sand.

The lakes that appear to be scattered so liberally over the land are also a disappointment as they are little more than shallow basins that carry water only after rains.

Great Barrier Reef, the largest of all coral formations, follows the northeast coast for twelve hundred miles of Australia's twelve-thousand-mile coastline. Except in a few places this reef is impassable to ships, but it does provide an inner passage for coastal navigation. There are good harbors on the southeastern coast.

Wherever there is sufficient moisture for grass to grow, the land is especially adapted to grazing. This land has proved the most suitable in the world for raising sheep. Merino sheep, which produce a very fine quality of wool, comprise most of the flocks. The heavy fleece from these sheep exceeds that of breeds raised elsewhere, so, although Australia produces less than one-sixth of the world's sheep, the wool yield is more than a quarter of the world's requirement.

Lacking navigable rivers, most of the transportation is by railways. These have been of first importance in developing the country, but one great drawback of railroad transportation is that there are several gauges. During the last twenty-five years there has been a steady expansion of motor roads, and air routes are rapidly increasing.

In addition to the mainland and the island of Tasmania, Australia has extensive territorial interests. These comprise the Trust Territory of New Guinea, Papua, Nauru and Norfolk Island.

The Trust Territory of New Guinea includes the northeastern section of New Guinea, the Bismarck Archipelago, and the northern islands of the Solomon group. Scattered over a sea area of more than one million square miles, these islands are mountainous with limited coastal areas suitable for cultivation.

NEW ZEALAND—Two large islands and several small ones make up New Zealand. Situated about twelve hundred miles southeast of Australia, New Zealand is a lonely member of the British Commonwealth.

The two principal islands, North and South Island are separated by Cook Strait which is ninety miles wide. Close as they are to each other, these islands have little in common except that they are both mountainous. North Island is of volcanic origin and consists chiefly of forested hills and plateaus. South Island is more rugged with glaciers and snow-clad peaks that rival the Alps of Switzerland.

PACIFIC ISLANDS—The Pacific Islands fall into three major regions: Polynesia, Micronesia and Melanesia.

Polynesia, or "Many islands," consists of widely scattered groups and a few isolated islands forming a rough triangle. The Hawaiian Islands are at the northern point, twenty degrees north of the Equator. The Fiji Islands, at the western point of the triangle, are the meeting place of Polynesian and Melanesian cultures, the people being of mixed stock. The easternmost point lies in the Gambier group of the Tuamota Archipelago, although isolated Pitcairn Island, inhabited by Anglo-Tahitian descendants of the mutinous crew of the "Bounty," is generally included geographically. Within this area lies the most highly developed group of Pacific peoples, a mixture of white, black and yellow racial stocks, the Polynesians. Famous as navigators, they crossed the Pacific from Asia hundreds of years ago, and sailed their canoes eastward to their present homes. For the most part, the islands are mountainous, volcanic and covered with dense vegetation, often fringed by coral reefs. Along the equator and in the southeast, low coral atolls predominate, often only a few feet above sea level, and frequently torn by hurricanes.

The people, often easy-going to the point of idleness, are not always used in local production, some Chinese having been hired to do manual work. Famous for dancing and feasting, the generally happy Polynesians strive to maintain their early customs against the inroads of European traders, missionaries and government regulations.

In the western Pacific, for the most part north of the equator, lies Micronesia, or "little islands," confined to the Marianas, Carolines, Marshall Islands, and Gilbert and Ellice Islands. Except for the latter islands, they are mostly volcanic and coral-fringed, and are peopled by a light-skinned group—the latest arrivals in the Pacific. These inhabitants show more evidence of a recent black and yellow mixture.

The earliest inhabited area of the Pacific, New Guinea and the islands spreading to the southeast of it, is known as Melanesia, the "black islands." Of early Negroid stock, this area was generally by-passed by the later Polynesians and Micronesians, as settlement was already established. Melanesia is a rapidly developing area, rich in minerals as well as the usual coconuts. Today the people range from Europeanized workers in the plantations of New Caledonia and Fiji, and the missions of the New Guinea coast, to half-naked savages, often head-hunters and cannibals, in the higher regions of New Guinea.

ASIA—To say that this is the largest continent in the world gives no idea of its immensity. Covering one-third of the land area of the world, Asia is more than a million square miles larger than the combined areas of North and South America. It extends from the ice-bound regions of the Arctic Circle to the sun-burnt islands of the Tropics. It claims the highest and lowest elevations, as well as the wettest and driest areas in the world. Mount Everest is the highest and the Dead Sea the lowest. Assam is the wettest, and Northern Siberia the driest. Asia is the cradle of the earliest civilization and is now the home of over half the population of the world.

Gendreau

The vast expanse of the Pacific Ocean contains thousands of uninhabited coral isles.

Man has drawn a line separating Asia from Europe but the only natural division is the low Ural Mountains and a depression extending from the mountains to the Caspian Sea. Only a man-made canal at the Isthmus of Suez separates Asia from Africa.

Washed by three oceans and a number of seas, Asia has a coast line over thirty thousand miles in length. Deep indentations along the irregular coast form seas, such as the Bay of Bengal and the Arabian Sea. Twisting and pointed peninsulas reach far out into the oceans. The shores are dotted with archipelagos and island groups. Among the island groups are Japan, the Philippines, and Indonesia, all of which have become as important as mainland countries.

The mountain ranges that sweep across Europe from west to east continue in long parallel lines through Asia. These mountain chains rise in height, first curving away from one another, and then closing in abruptly in a knot of massed mountains which has been referred to as "the roof of the world." Eastward, the awe-inspiring Himalayas reach to the plateau of Tibet, turn suddenly south through Indochina in long lines of deep, forested ravines, and disappear in a string of islands, drowned by the waters of the Indian Ocean. The Himalayas, covered with eternal snows and scored by mighty glaciers, are the highest mountains in the world. From Mount Everest, their loftiest peak, they drop steeply down to the low river plains below.

To the north of the mountains lies the great plain of Northern Asia, a continuation of the North European plain. Broken only by the Urals it sinks slowly to the frozen Arctic shore. To the south, in India and Arabia, are two low plateaus with steep sides, and the river lowlands of Mesopotamia and the Ganges plain.

This enormous continent is drained by many large rivers. Flowing toward the Arctic Ocean are the Ob, Yenisei and Lena Rivers. They are often blocked with ice for months and flood the surrounding country in thaw. In the east the silt carried down by the rivers has built the wide alluvial plains of China. The Hwang-ho, or Yellow River, flows into the Yellow Sea. Yellow is a sacred color, for this is the color of the silt deposited by the great river on the fertile plain, where crowded millions of Chinese grow their crops and find their livelihood. The Yangtse Kiang, or Blue River, rises in Tibet and passes through deep walls before winding sluggishly across the lowlands of China. These rivers often overflow in disastrous floods and have changed their courses many times.

The Ganges, Indus and Brahmaputra have built up the fertile lowlands of North India and are slowly extending it in broad, swampy deltas, out to sea.

Covering so many degrees of latitude, the climate of Asia would naturally show great variation. There are great extremes of cold and heat in the Siberian lowlands and Northern China. Great areas in the center of the continent, far from the sea, are dry; with tropical conditions prevailing in the south. The heaviest rainfall anywhere in the world is in some localities of Southeastern Asia and everywhere in the eastern region there is sufficient moisture for agriculture. In Assam, India, the rainfall averages about thirty-five feet a year.

There is every type of vegetation, ranging from tundra mosses in the extreme north to tropical plant life in the south. There are great stores of mineral wealth, but much of this is still undeveloped. Asia has been slow to awaken to the possibilities of an industrialized civilization.

Southwestern Asia is that section of the continent lying between India and the Aegean Sea. It is a rugged, mountainous country which includes the two desert plateaus of Iran and Arabia, and the rich lowlands of the Tigris and Euphrates valley.

Great nations flourished in Southwestern Asia several thousand years before the birth of Christ. Composed almost entirely of the white race, their civilizations contributed much to the early nations along the Mediterranean. Mongolian hordes invaded these lands in the thirteenth century, almost destroying the civilizations which they found. Growing in power, a mighty nation which spread into Africa and Europe came into being. The Turks are descendants of these war-like people.

TURKEY—Surrounded by mountains on three sides is a high, dry plateau which slopes to the fertile shores of the Mediterranean. Among the chief mountains are the Taurus range, stretching from the southwestern shore of the Aegean to the north of Syria, their principal peaks rising from 7,000 to 10,000 feet; the Bulgar Mountains rising over 10,000 feet; and the Ala Mountains, north of Seyhan, rising 8,000 to 10,000 feet high. The highest peak in the country is Mt. Ararat, 17,915 feet. Flowing into the Black Sea are the Coruh, the Yesil Irmak, the Kizil Irmak and the Sakariya. Into the Mediterranean flow the Seyhan and Ceyhan. In the east of Asia Minor are the headwaters of both the Euphrates and the Tigris as well as of the Araks.

ISRAEL—After 2,000 years the Jewish people realized their dream of an independent homeland with the establishment of the new state of Israel in 1948. Lying between Egypt and Jordan on the eastern shores of the Mediterranean, the country is a hot and arid land. The new nation's economy is based on the cultivation of citrus fruit for export made possible by extensive irrigation of the lands of Zionist sponsored settlements. Oil refining, chemical production and light industry are also important to the economy.

SYRIA AND LEBANON—The occupations of the people of these countries have not changed since Biblical times, and are similar to those of Turkey. Mostly agricultural, there is little mineral wealth, and manufacturing is largely for local markets. Lebanon is mainly mountainous with a fertile valley lying in the center between the Lebanon Mountains on the west coast and the Anti-Lebanon Mountains which form the eastern border between Lebanon and Syria. Syria consists largely of desert surrounded by mountains. In the northeast, the Euphrates flows across the desert and irrigates a valuable strip of agricultural land. Other fertile areas are found near Homs and Hama, both in the northwest, and Damascus and the Jebel Druze district in the southwest.

TWA—Trans World Airline

Flocks of sheep and goats are the economic mainstay of the Arab's life.

IRAQ—Once the site of the Babylonian Empire, the region of the Tigris and Euphrates is the "Fertile Crescent" of ancient times. The country is a great alluvial plain, bounded on the north by Kurdistan, on the east by Iran, on the south by the Persian Gulf, and on the west by the Syrian and Arabian Deserts. Northern Iraq has a valuable supply of oil which is piped to Haifa and Tripoli.

IRAN (Persia)—Most of the country is plateau, surrounded by mountain chains, except in the east where huge salt deserts are found. An extension of the mountain ranges, locally known as the Khorasan Mountains of the Hindu Kush, enters on the northeast from Afghanistan and merges into the Elburz Range south of the Caspian, the highest peak being Mt. Demavend. Except for narrow fertile areas along the Caspian Sea and Persian Gulf the land is too dry to sustain many people.

ARABIA—The Arabian Peninsula is a land composed almost entirely of desert, mostly of a barren and stony type, with an abundance of sand in the southeast. Besides scattered oases there are only a few small areas in Arabia with enough rainfall to permit the growing of crops. Saudi Arabia, which occupies the central two-thirds of the peninsula, has experimented with modern, mechanized methods of irrigation to improve farming conditions, and a modern railroad now reaches the interior from the Persian Gulf. The finest Arabian horses and camels are raised in the central highlands. Discovery of valuable oil reserves in the desert near the Persian Gulf fostered new economic development, and many local sheikhs, or tribal rulers, have become suddenly rich. Pearling, once important in the Gulf, is now declining. In the mountain valleys of Yemen is the most fertile soil of the peninsula, and its Red Sea ports, such as Mocha and Hodeida handle its coffee and other exports, as well as pearls from nearby islands.

AFGHANISTAN—Barren tablelands, deep ravines and snow-covered mountains leave

TWA—Trans World Airline

Representative of the fine architecture of India is the luxurious structure of the Taj Mahal.

Afghanistan an unproductive land. Lying as a barrier between Siberia and India, it has been the scene of many invasions and conquests but the war-like Afghans have never been completely vanquished. Cereals, fruits and vegetables are grown only in small areas under irrigation, and the fat-tailed sheep—a native of the country—furnishes meat and a butter substitute.

PAKISTAN—Pakistan is divided into two widely separated sections. The larger part, West Pakistan on the Arabian Sea, consists of the fertile Indus valley, the extremely rugged Northwest frontier and arid Baluchistan. Cereal raising and cotton production are concentrated in the Indus Valley which possesses one of the oldest and most efficient canal irrigation systems in the world. East Pakistan, on the Bay of Bengal, occupies the lower Ganges-Brahmaputra delta and the Assam highland foothills. This nation, while almost wholly Mohammedan in religion, is influenced politically and culturally not only by the Islamic world to the west but also the neighboring Hindu civilization of India.

INDIA—For over four thousand years, India has been at the mercy of marauding and conquering races. Unlike many lesser countries, who have successfully thrown off the yoke of oppression, India, until recently, has always been subject to foreign rule. As a result it is a confusion of races, castes, and religions, with a civilization ranging from the highest type of culture to the most primitive. In 1947 India was granted independence and now takes her place among the important powers of the globe.

Except for the rocky slopes of the mountains, the soil is fertile and supports the largest agricultural population in the world. Like the farmers of France, a large majority of these people live in small villages surrounded by tilled fields. And, while primitive methods and equipment are used, surprisingly large crops are raised. Disastrous droughts, due to the vagaries of the weather, and the famines which followed, have been partially relieved by government sponsored irrigation works and the construction of railroads and motor roads.

SIKKIM, NEPAL AND BHUTAN—These three small independent states are shut off from the outside world by the Himalayas. Several of the world's highest mountains, including Mount Everest, are in southern Nepal. Their inhabitants are energetic people who raise cattle, wheat, rice, tobacco and spices which they export in exchange for necessary manufactured goods, sugar, oil, etc.

CEYLON—The island of Ceylon has been called the "Pearl of the Orient." Situated off the southern coast of India it is famous for its tea, precious stones and tropical beauty. The broad coastal strip which surrounds the central mountains is, for the most part, fertile and produces a luxuriant vegetation. Although the climate is tropical, sea breezes temper the heat.

INDOCHINA—Included on this southeastern peninsula of Asia are a part of Burma, Thailand, Indochina and the Malayan Federation. Most of the peninsula is characterized by heavily forested valleys and mountain ridges of the Himalayas running the length of the land. This is the great rice-producing region, and most of the world's rubber comes from this area. The rainfall is heavy in the entire area and the land is very productive. In the dense forests are valuable stands of prize woods, teak, ebony and other trees used for their wood or gum. Agriculture is the chief industry throughout the peninsula but there are many important deposits of valuable minerals. Modern methods of agriculture and mining have been introduced. Singapore, situated on an island at the extreme southern end of the peninsula, commands one of the most important sea routes in the world.

THE MALAY ARCHIPELAGO — The world's largest group of islands extends from Sumatra to the Philippine Islands off the coast of China, and includes many thousands of islands. With the exception of the Philippines, and parts of Timor, Borneo and New Guinea, the archipelago was ruled for hundreds of years by the Netherlands.

INDONESIA—Colonization and development begun by the Dutch in the XVIIth century has resulted in the richest and most important island group in the world.

Most of the islands are mountainous and of volcanic origin. At one time they were a part of the mainland connecting Asia with Australia. Java is the most productive and highly developed of the East Indies. It is one of the most densely populated regions in the world. Much of the land is divided into native farms and large plantations. The plantation crops are chiefly for export.

Next to Greenland, New Guinea and Borneo are the largest islands in the world. Sumatra and Celebes are next in size in the East Indies. Much of the mineral wealth of these islands is yet untouched. Borneo is crossed almost in the middle by the equator and few white people occupy the island because of the humidity and heat. Petroleum is an important resource of Borneo, Sumatra and Java, and two small islands adjoining Sumatra have valuable deposits of tin. Bali, while one of the lesser islands, has been one of the most publicized, and is favored by tourists as a tropical paradise.

PHILIPPINE ISLANDS—Numbering over seven thousand islands, Philippines, like other islands of the Malay Archipelago, are the tops of drowned mountains protruding from the sea. There are well watered fertile plains between the mountains. Being near the equator the temperature is never very low Although the days are warm, the nights are usually cool. Some of the many volcanoes in the Philippines are still active and the islands are subject to earthquakes.

Publishers' Photo Service

Japan's development as a leading industrial nation has not effaced her customs and traditions.

CHINA—Chinese civilization is of greater antiquity than any other existent world culture. It has shown great powers of survival and has possessed the ability to absorb all foreign influences without losing its own identity.

The Chinese people are patient, industrious, and have great physical endurance. They are among the world's best farmers, having grown more food for longer periods on the same land, without exhausting the soil, than any other people. They take naturally to mechanics and are fine traders and business men.

With the possible exception of Africa, China has the largest undeveloped natural resources in the world. There are rich de-

Indonesia Information Office

Asian art has been stimulated by many technical and cultural institutions.

posits of coal, with China ranking second to the United States in total reserves. Iron ore reserves are large enough to meet its needs for many years to come. It is believed that China has one of the most valuable deposits of copper, and tin has been a leading mineral export.

China is a land of garden farmers and the soil is cultivated intensively. Few animals are raised, which conserves acreage for food crops. Hence the Chinese diet consists almost entirely of vegetable products. In a relatively mild climate people can subsist on less food than in a colder region. Rice is the most important crop but almost every known crop is raised.

Inner Mongolia, Tibet and Sinkiang are outer provinces of China. Until the building of railroads and motor roads they were reached entirely by caravan routes. This region has extreme temperatures and is largely desert. The Great Wall was built to keep the Mongols out of China. Tibet, until recently opened up to British trade, excluded all foreigners. Sinkiang consists almost entirely of a desert basin.

MONGOLIAN REPUBLIC—This almost entirely pastoral country consists largely of an arid plateau composed mainly of the Gobi Desert. In the northwest are high mountains whose streams flow into numerous sizable lakes. The Mongolian people are almost entirely a nomadic race who wander from place to place seeking new pastures for their herds of cattle.

JAPAN—The chief feature of the country is its mountainous character, for each island has a mountainous backbone. Fujiyama, the highest mountain, reaches 12,395 feet. One of the most notable physical features is the Inland Sea or Japanese Mediterranean. It is almost entirely landlocked and surrounded by chains of volcanoes, of which few are now active. The climate is temperate and healthful, with abundant rainfall.

Only 20 per cent of the land can be cultivated and the balance is largely mountainous, with frequent destructive earthquakes and volcanic activity. While minerals have been a major factor in her industrial growth, Japan is not well supplied with them. The only large mineral deposits are coal and copper, with some gold, silver and lead. The petroleum produced falls far short of her needs.

The low standard of living and the small amount of land suitable for cultivation have made farming highly intensive. A large percentage of the farms are only an acre or two in size and most of the farmers are forced to carry on some other occupation to exist.

Manufacturing has risen rapidly in Japan with the production of textiles leading. Because of low wages and nearness to the Oriental market, Japan has been able to compete in cheaper goods to the disadvantage of other countries.

KOREA—Korea's strategic position between the Asiatic mainland and Japan has made it an historic pathway for invasion. Coveted at different times by China, Russia and Japan, she lost her independence early in the century to the Japanese Empire. During the second World War, Korea was promised her independence, but the end of the fighting brought her only division between the great powers and later renewed military conflict.

Physically and economically Korea is divided into two contrasting natural regions. The agricultural heart of the nation is south of the thirty-eighth parallel, producing chiefly rice and barley. North of the parallel, industry and mining of coal and iron predominate.

INDEX OF PRINCIPAL CITIES OF THE WORLD

This alphabetical list of cities and towns gives statistics of population based on the latest official census reports or most recent reliable estimates. Each line begins with the name of a place, followed by the name of the country or state, the population, the index reference and plate number. This index reference gives the location of the city or town name on the accompanying map plates. The name is found within the square formed by the two lines of latitude or longitude which enclose each of the co-ordinates—i.e. the marginal letters and numbers. In the case of maps consisting entirely of insets, the name is found near the intersection point of imaginary lines connecting the co-ordinates.

Where space on the map has not permitted giving the complete form of a name, the extended form is shown in the index. Where a place may be known under different names or by various spellings of the same name, the different forms have been included, to a large extent, in the index. Where an alternative spelling in parentheses is shown on the map itself, the first name gives the local official form, the conventional form following in parentheses.

* Capitals of countries, states and provinces. † Population figure includes suburbs.